Consciousness Studies

Consciousness Studies

Cross-Cultural Perspectives

by K. RAMAKRISHNA RAO

McFarland & Company, Inc., Publishers
Jefferson, North Carolina, and London

The present work is a reprint of the illustrated case bound edition of Consciousness Studies: Cross-Cultural Perspectives, *first published in 2002 by McFarland.*

LIBRARY OF CONGRESS CATALOGUING-IN-PUBLICATION DATA

Rao, K. Ramakrishna, 1932–
Consciousness studies : cross-cultural perspectives /
by K. Ramakrishna Rao.
p.   cm.
Includes bibliographical references and index.

ISBN 0-7864-2278-5 (softcover : 50# alkaline paper) ∞

1. Consciousness.   I. Title.
B808.9.R35   2005   126.21   2002006092

British Library cataloguing data are available

Cover photograph © 2005 PhotoSpin

Manufactured in the United States of America

*McFarland & Company, Inc., Publishers
Box 611, Jefferson, North Carolina 28640
www.mcfarlandpub.com*

Saluting his statesmanly vision and virtues,
commending his chastely charisma and leadership,
and remembering fondly the kindness and courtesies shown
and the many stimulating thoughts
and stirring and stoic hopes we shared

I dedicate this book to the memory of

Dr. Nandamuri Taraka Rama Rao
Former Chief-Minister of Andhra Pradesh

NTR was a friend to me and a mentor to many. He
touched lives by millions. Those he blessed became leaders
by the thousands. What he was able to accomplish during
a short political stint is outstanding, only hinting at what
he could have achieved if things were a bit different.

Contents

Preface

My interest in the cross-cultural studies of consciousness dates back to the early seventies. We at Andhra University had hoped that this would be one of the thrust areas in the newly established Department of Psychology and Parapsychology. Later I was instrumental as the head of Andhra University in the establishment of the Institute for Yoga and Consciousness. My presidential address at the 33rd annual convention of the Parapsychological Association in Washington, D.C., was on consciousness and psi (Rao 1991). I later edited a volume *Cultivating Consciousness* (Praeger, 1993).

The thought of writing a book on Eastern and Western perspectives on consciousness came about several years ago in a conversation with John Fetzer, the founder of the Fetzer Institute. I was at a meeting in Kalamazoo organized by the Fetzer Foundation. At the lunch table one afternoon, John and I discussed Yoga, Eastern philosophy and paranormal phenomena. John showed special interest in what I was saying about cross-cultural comparisons and the complementarity of the seemingly conflicting postulates of science and religion on questions concerning who we are and where we are headed. My point was that all traditions,

whether Eastern or Western, scientific or religious, contain certain aspects of truth. Truth, however, gets fragmented as each tradition attempts to find its identity by clinging to some aspects while ignoring or rejecting others. Therefore, the quest to discover the whole truth must begin with exploring the complementary contributions of different traditions and cultures. John liked the idea and said that I should write a book on Eastern and Western traditions in the area of consciousness.

It took me several years after my conversation with John Fetzer to gear up to write this book. As soon as the project got started and I made some headway, several changes in my personal life took place. I left the Foundation for Research on the Nature of Man in Durham, N.C., and joined the government of Andhra Pradesh as the head of the State Planning Board. This shift away from an academic and research environment and to a political and bureaucratic quagmire almost killed the book project. However, leaving the AP Government in 1996 and settled in Visakhapatnam in what I thought was semi-retirement, I found myself drawn back to the unfinished project. The first draft of the book was ready by 1997. I felt, however, that I should not rush into publishing it without further exchanges with colleagues in the field. So I decided to teach a course on this topic to get feedback from the inquiring young minds and present my ideas in departmental seminars. This led me first to the University of Tennessee at Chattanooga and more recently to the University of North Carolina at Chapel Hill. The class at UTC consisted mostly of graduate students. At UNC the students were largely undergraduate seniors in psychology. Teaching these courses, using the manuscript of this book as required reading, has been a very rewarding experience, enabling me to revise the manuscript suitably to make it readable and appropriate to interested students of the subject in the Western world.

The reader will find some repetitions in the book. Considering the nature of the subject that involves both the Eastern and Western concepts and keeping in view that the book will be read in English speaking countries in East and West, I felt that some core ideas need to be restated. My students invariably thought that it was helpful.

I was benefited by the comments of several colleagues who attended my seminars. Also, Stanley Krippner, John Palmer, Douglas Stokes and Jean Burns have read the manuscript in its various stages of prog-

ress. I thank them for their comments, which I found very useful. Part of the way I was helped by the Fetzer Institute. I was especially beholden to Rob Lehman, former president, for his encouragement and support.

There are many others, including the members of my family, who made it possible for me to write this book. First, my wife, Sarojini, allowed me to be away from her for many months at a time to teach at UTC and UNC. My eldest daughter, Rani Rao, and her husband, Sarath Gangavarapu, provided their hospitality in Chattanooga. So did my younger daughter, Vani Rao, and her husband, Murali Mohan Chilukuri, in Chapel Hill. My grandson, Vivek Ram, typed part of the manuscript. N. V. V. S. S. Markandeyulu offered the secretarial services in India. Cami Meador rechecked the references. Jhansi Rani prepared the index. To all the above and the scholars and scientists too numerous to name here on whose contributions this work rests I offer my appreciation and acknowledge my indebtedness.

K. Ramakrishna Rao
Institute for Human Science and Service
Visakhapatnam 530 003
India

Introduction

At the outset the most perplexing fact about consciousness is that it is too familiar and intimate to ignore and yet too complex and elusive to understand and explain. The variety of attempts to describe and explain consciousness reminds us of the legendary blind men seeking to describe the elephant. Although consciousness is something that is embedded in all our experience and is considered basic to all our knowing, no one seems to know what exactly it is. Conceptual confusions and failure to arrive at shared meanings vitiate philosophical discourse and psychological and neurophysiological discussions of consciousness. The contemporary multidisciplinary interest in the study of consciousness goes beyond philosophers, psychologists and neuroscientists to include physicists, cognitive theorists, information technologists and New Age people. The problem is further exasperating to someone like the author, who happens to live in two worlds, as it were, sharing two distinct and divergent traditions.

Consciousness is a widely used and much abused concept. Abandoned for its nebulous content, abhorred for its ambiguity, and discarded because of its nonphysical connotations, consciousness has languished for a better part of the twentieth century as an area unworthy of scholarly and scientific pursuit. Only in recent years have we seen its resurgence. Whether or not this newfound enthusiasm would make a difference and impact on our understanding of who we are and what the place of consciousness in the universe is depends to a large extent on how we go about studying it.

Historically consciousness studies have shown their strength and weakness. The weakness consists in the multiplicity and diversity of connotations of the core concept, the incoherent contexts of its emphasis and the debilitating cross-purposes of those interested in studying it. The strength lies in the vast ground it covers, which could be a valuable channel for communication between and across disciplines. The multicultural perspectives of consciousness could serve as bridges that link different traditions. The common place consciousness finds in both science and spiritual discourse could make it the long sought interface between science and religion. Thus consciousness studies, as a transdisciplinary endeavor, have the potential for transforming the past weaknesses into future strengths.

The tableaux of living intellectual traditions around the world is a matrix of four constituents, the Greek, the Jewish, the Chinese and the Indian. The Greek and the Jewish constitute what is now regarded as the Western, whereas the Chinese and the Indian together are often referred to as the Eastern. There are of course significant differences between them. For example, the Chinese tradition, as seen in Taoism as well as Confucianism, has been consistently humanistic with emphasis on man in society, whereas in India the emphasis has been on the inner spirit and on its relation to the universe. The Chinese thinkers were less concerned with metaphysical and epistemological issues than their Indian counterparts. Again, within each of these traditions, there are significant differences. For example, the Vedanta and the Mimamsa systems in Indian thought differ in their emphasis on contemplation and action. What characterizes a tradition are the dominant trends and the central ideas that place more emphasis on one aspect than another, an emphasis that leads to significant developments in some areas and not in others. In this sense, we will find major and distinctive contributions to knowledge by each of the traditions in certain spheres. Their contributions in some ways complement each other and together they provide a more comprehensive understanding of a subject.

Human beings as conscious subjects function at two levels. On the one hand, their awareness is directed outward towards objects and events, fellow beings, their appearances and actions. On the other hand, the awareness is sometimes focused inward, to one's own thoughts, feelings and being. The two-dimensional activities go undistinguished in the early stages of cognitive development, but they are differentiated as such with maturation. As we share our experiences, we learn that our awareness of the world of objects and events is essentially similar. Consequently, we ascribe objectivity to them and tend to regard them as entities independent of our perceptions of them. At the same time, we find that inward awareness is very much personal and that access to it is restricted almost entirely to one self, the experiencing subject. As we partake in both the processes, the outward and the inward, and use the outcomes as knowledge items, there arises the distinction between the subjective and the objective in our experience. The subjective here refers to the peculiarly personal and private aspects, whereas the objective relates to those presumed to be independent of the cognizing person and considered publicly verifiable.

The two knowledge domains necessarily raise relevant ontological questions regarding the primacy of the subjective and objective items of knowledge. No one would ordinarily dispute the existence of subjective awareness, even though the primacy of it as fundamental for understanding consciousness may be questioned, because it is not accessible for intersubject validation. Likewise, one may ascribe primacy to subjective awareness on the ground that it alone is authentic by being directly accessible, unlike the knowledge relating to the outward objects, which is mediated and available only indirectly.

Human experience is, however, a confluence of the two, the subjective and the objective. Though the two can be and are conceptually distinguished, they blend harmoniously in human experience. As we focus our awareness outward, the objects manifest in our personal experience. Our inner awareness itself becomes an object of awareness when the attention is directed inward. The "objective" component of experience, i.e., the awareness of the outward, insofar as it is known subjectively, requires shared subjective exercises that bestow objectivity on it. Rules of logic and rationality have evolved as guiding principles, and the development of the scientific method is a natural culmination of these efforts. Now, the question is whether the scientific method and logical discourse that appear to adequately reveal the outward can be applied to the inward experience as well. Attempts to apply the logic of objectivity in the realm of inner awareness have led to reductive exercises designed to translate inner experiences into outward phenomena. However, it is conceivable that there may be other strategies that can be effective in rendering what are ordinarily seen as fleeting, evanescent and subjective personal experiences into shared phenomena. In other words, it may be possible to transform inner experiences into "objectively," i.e., intersubjectively verifiable phenomena without reducing them into outward phenomena. Eastern and Western approaches to the study of consciousness appear to offer different perspectives on it. The dominant trends that characterize Eastern and Western traditions differ markedly (a) in the emphasis they place on the subjective and objective, i.e., the view from within and the view from outside, (b) on the presumed relations between the two, and (c) on the appropriateness of the methods to transform or translate subjective items of experience and knowledge into objective phenomena and vice versa.

The difference in the relative emphasis on the inward or the outward focus is the starting point of divergence between Eastern and Western traditions. In the Western tradition, the emphasis has been primarily on the outward. The approach is rational and intellectual. Consequently, the preferred method is scientific and outward focused. The result is an overwhelming concern with the physical and the outstanding achievements in understanding the physical reality. The pervasive emphasis on the physical and the rational from Heraclitus and Pythagoras to logical positivists and analytical philosophers may be traced to the Greek notion that the essence of humanness consists in reason and that man is a rational being. Different from this, the central focus in the Eastern tradition is on the inward. While reason is often used to explicate the

inwardness, it is seen as secondary to the inner experience, which has its own content different from the outward material content of reason. The two traditions with their differences in emphasis on the inward and the outward may not be seen as incompatible and conflicting. Rather they are complementary and distinct. Together they may constitute a more comprehensive and holistic approach, giving both breadth and depth to our understanding of who we are and what our place in the universe is. Especially when we are dealing with consciousness, the complementary character of Western and Eastern traditions becomes all too obvious.

There is no denying the fact that the dominant scientific notions about consciousness in the Western tradition are clearly alien to the core assumptions underlying the Eastern tradition. In the East, consciousness is regarded as an autonomous principle grounded in spiritual foundations. In the West, any such spiritual association is suspect. Objectivity of a phenomenon is considered essential for it to be scientifically studied. For example, J.B. Watson (1928), the founder of behaviorism in psychology, declared that there can be no such thing as consciousness; B.F. Skinner (1974) considered consciousness as an epiphenomenon of matter; and H. Feigl (1967) saw no more in consciousness than neural events in the brain. These notions are clearly antithetical to the assumption generally made in the East that consciousness has a capacity of its own and is involved not only in our ability to know the world but also in effecting changes in it.

In the Western tradition, those who considered consciousness as a useful concept for understanding our nature and potential differed greatly in their orientation and approach to the problems of consciousness. Some of them saw consciousness as a *process* and others as ability. For some it was a quality of experience. Some looked at it as a *state*; some regarded it as a *function*; yet for others it was reflected in the content. Consequently, the concerns of researchers also varied. Some investigators asked how consciousness *functions*, whereas *structure* and organization became the main concern for some others. A few postulated *modes* of consciousness, while some wrote about *domains* of consciousness; yet others speculated about *levels* and *degrees* of consciousness. Sometimes the answers were sought in *physiology*. In a few cases, novel neural *organizations* or special *entities* were proposed to account for conscious experience. *Metaphors* and *models* were also used. With all these cross-purposes and confusions the reader is often left wondering what precisely it is that is sought to be explained in the discussions of consciousness.

Conscious experience in the human condition is clearly dependent on certain cortical processes, because their destruction almost invariably leads to loss of awareness. This factor more than anything else is the prime justification for identifying consciousness with brain functioning. The cerebral processes accompanying a conscious experience may describe a state of the brain. They, however, are not the same as, and in fact are qualitatively different from, the experience itself. For example, it has been pointed out repeatedly that the "raw" experience of pain cannot be translated into neurobiological processes without losing something very basic in the subjective experience of pain. My thoughts and experiences are subjective in that there is, in the words of William James, "a warmth and intimacy about them." That warmth and intimacy are seen as the abiding characteristics of subjectivity and of consciousness—characteristics that we do not attribute to machines.

Again, a person may behave in many ways like a machine. Yet, one can function also as an autonomous being, exercising free will and self-determination. Individuals have intentions, goals and objectives that may not be reduced to brain states. A person is believed to be different from a machine in that

some behaviors are not seen as being constrained by the physical laws that control the functions of the brain. This proposition is best exemplified by the evidence for paranormal phenomena, such as extrasensory perception (ESP) and psychokinesis (PK), which seem to defy conventional physical laws and appear inexplicable in terms of known sensory-motor processes.

The impressive evidence accumulated over a period of one hundred years and the widespread popular belief in paranormal phenomena notwithstanding, psychical research lacks the necessary approval and support by the mainstream scientific establishments in the West. Consequently it has languished in large part as a non-academic discipline pursued by a few self-motivated part-time professionals who call themselves parapsychologists or psi researchers. The marginalization of psychical phenomena and the controversies surrounding their investigation are a reflection of the dominant scientific paradigm that renders them anomalous and incongruent events in what is presumed to be an otherwise orderly universe. However, if these events are indeed real, as the growing evidence increasingly suggests, there is at once a prima facie case for the primacy of consciousness in our being and behavior.

We may not also ignore the fact that surveys indicate that even in the Western societies, where the achievements of science play such a dominant part in the lives of their people, a solid majority believes in the reality of so-called paranormal events. Further, nearly as many attest to their occurrence in their own experience. For example, a *Newsweek* poll (Nov. 3-4, 1994) revealed that about sixty per cent of Americans feel the need to experience spiritual growth and that one third of all adults say that they have had a mystical/religious experience. Religious traditions throughout the world espouse belief in a realm of being which is entirely inconsistent with the materialistic conception of the universe as determined by fixed laws and blind chance. Many regard freedom of will as personal and private. For most of us it is intuitively evident that there is a qualitative difference between us humans and machines, which appear to lack self-awareness. There is thus a manifest incompatibility between what we think we are and the conception of man as an entirely brain driven machine.

It may not be unreasonable, therefore, to suppose that conscious experience, though dependent on neurobiological processes, may not be identical with or wholly determined by them. Mental functions resemble the operations of machines, no doubt, but at the same time consciousness may also function in a manner and mode that machines are essentially incapable of. Current "scientific" notions about consciousness embedded in the Western tradition take the machine-like functions of humans as given truisms and whatever evidence there is to the contrary is considered to be either anomalous or spurious. However, it is increasingly becoming apparent that any theory which regards consciousness as an epiphenomenon of matter, or sees in it no more than neural events in the brain, is at best incomplete, because it tends to exclude from its consideration those aspects of awareness that go beyond the categories of sense and understanding. Further, the notion that accords primacy to consciousness may have the potential to offer more satisfactory explanations for the subjective, intentional, self-determining, transpersonal and extrasensory aspects of our experience.

It is refreshing to note, however, that an increasing number of scientists, still admittedly small, appears open to the possibility that conscious experience is qualitatively different from and in principle inexplicable by neural events in the brain. They find the neurobiological models of our mental life clearly biased against those aspects of reality that go beyond what is given in sensory experience and are inconsistent with some deeply felt human needs and widespread spiritual convictions. Therefore, in order that we may gain a complete understanding of us and our place in the universe, we may do well to look at alternative models that accord primacy and causal efficacy to consciousness. At the same time, we may not ignore the fact that for all appearances we behave as if our consciousness is entirely dependent on the function of our brains. In this context, I believe that a consideration of Eastern perspectives such as the one suggested by the Samkhya-Yoga system of Indian philosophy may prove to be a heuristic model for meaningfully dealing with the complexities of consciousness.

There is of course no one perspective that characterizes all of Eastern thought, even in the area of consciousness. There are, however, shared assumptions implicit in the dominant philosophical traditions of the East. I am persuaded to think that these assumptions provide the foundation for a meaningful discourse on consciousness, a foundation on which a new comprehensive edifice of consciousness studies may be built. I find seminal ideas in Eastern thought that are indeed different from but may be truly complementary to Western approaches to the study of consciousness.

By Eastern tradition we refer to some of the salient features of the Hindu and the Buddhist thought. More explicitly, we focus on those aspects of Samkhya, Yoga, Advaita Vedanta and Buddhism that are relevant to consciousness studies. What we take to be the Eastern tradition is a composite of relevant ideas gleaned from Samkhya-Yoga, Vedanta and Buddhist thinkers. It would be legitimate to ask if what we are covering is any more than a dominant segment of Indian tradition and whether it is not an overgeneralization to label our discussions as comprising the Eastern perspective. A similar criticism can be made about our account of the Western perspective, which is equally nonmonolithic. We acknowledge at the out-set that there are other theoretically variant traditions in the East as well as in the West from those we have covered in this book. We are fully aware that even among classi-cal Indian systems of philosophy, there are powerful alternatives to what we have de-scribed as the Eastern tradition.

Our justification for using the broader and more inclusive term "Eastern perspec-tive" is twofold. First, we maintain that the ideas we present represent the dominant and theoretically powerful tradition not only in the Indian subcontinent but also in Asia generally. Second, the perspective we de-scribe is one that is in stark contrast to the dominant Western views that are discussed. Inasmuch as our objective is to highlight the limitations of the dominant Western perspective and to find a different approach that could usefully supplement it in signifi-cant ways, we feel justified in focusing on the ideas we do and treat them as an ade-quate representation of the Eastern per-spective.

As mentioned, the primary difference between the Eastern and Western approaches is the focus, whether inward or outward. In the East, the focus is on the person having the experience. Consequently, the emphasis is on the psychological rather than on the physical, and the preferred method is first-person based introspection. It is not sur-prising, therefore, that we find in classical Indian thought metaphysical theories grounded in psychological insights rather than built on physical facts. In the West, it is a different story. The focus is on the ob-ject of experience, the emphasis is on the physical, and the preferred method is third-person based observation and measurement. The intellectual exercise is more synthetic and less analytical in the East, whereas in the West it is more analytically driven and re-ductive.

In the Western scholarly tradition, we find (a) that consciousness is generally equated with the mind. If a distinction is made between them, consciousness is con-ceived as an aspect of the mind; (b) inten-tionality is regarded as its defining charac-teristic; (c) the goal is one of seeking a rational understanding of what conscious-ness/mind is. If there are any practical con-cerns with consciousness in the Western tra-dition, as in psychoanalysis, they are always limited to dealing with "disturbed" condi-tions and for restoring the individual to the so-called normal state, but not to raise one to higher levels of consciousness and being. In Eastern traditions, especially the Indian, we find, however, a different approach and emphasis. First, a basic distinction is made between consciousness and mind. Second, the existence of pure consciousness, which is believed to be nonintentional, is postu-lated whereas the mental phenomena are re-garded as essentially intentional. Third, methods of accessing pure consciousness, as well as special disciplines to deal with higher states of the mind with tangible benefits, are suggested and developed. Whereas the West-ern perspective is limited to the phenome-nal manifestations of consciousness, the Eastern tradition pays special attention to the transcendental aspects of consciousness through its concern with pure consciousness. It is therefore reasonable to suppose that an understanding of the Eastern perspective can be genuinely complementary to the Western if our goal is to have a fuller grasp of consciousness and its role in our being.

The differences between the Eastern and Western approaches are sometimes sharply contrasted to show systematic op-position between them. This need not be so. It is not an "either-or" situation. Neither of the approaches need be deemed to be false or futile; nor is it the case that we will find all the answers to the many puzzles of consciousness by pursuing any one approach alone. Rather, the many splendors of con-sciousness as reflected in our vastly complex experience may be realized only when we view consciousness from the many perspectives we have of it without overlooking any.

Consciousness studies, as mentioned, constitute a very broad field, drawing from such diverse subjects as neurobiology, neuropsychology, cognitive science, psychophysics, philosophy, physics and theology. Consequently, one cannot hope to present a comprehensive review of all the relevant literature in a single volume. What we can do instead is to organize the salient features of the relevant literature around the theme that we wish to emphasize. In our case, it is the view that there are aspects to consciousness, which do not simply fit into the restricted physical mold cast in the Western scientific and scholarly discourse. These aspects, first suggested by the spiritual and mystical traditions and now reinforced by the research findings in such disciplines as parapsychology, call for a judicious review of the connotations of consciousness and for a broadening of its scope. In this endeavor, we may be aided by the wisdom contained in the incisive discussions of consciousness in the age-old traditions of the East.

The primary focus of this study is twofold. First, we review the scholarly and scientific attempts to understand and investigate consciousness in the Western tradition and to identify their dominant features and the respects in which they appear adequate or inadequate to explain the various aspects of conscious experience. Second, we describe the main features of the Eastern tradition as represented by the Hindu and Buddhist theories and explore how they may be seen as complementary to the Western tradition for a more complete understanding of consciousness and its role. On the one hand, we expect to expose the intrinsic difficulties in casting consciousness in a wholly deterministic and reductionist mold and to explore, on the other hand, the exciting implications of the view that grants primacy and autonomy to consciousness across the entire range of consciousness studies.

In the first part of this book, we seek to understand what consciousness is by exploring the varieties of conscious experience, and reflect on the attempts to understand and explain consciousness in the Western scholarly and scientific tradition. The second part deals with Eastern spiritual traditions, and the respects in which they differ with and complement the Western viewpoints. We conclude with an attempt to reconcile the two traditions for a comprehensive understanding of what consciousness is and the respects in which such an understanding may be helpful for a cross-cultural assessment of behavior, and for enhancing human abilities and wellness.

PART I
WESTERN TRADITION

CHAPTER 1

What It Is Like to Be Conscious

Many Connotations of Consciousness

Consciousness, seen by many as the defining characteristic of the human condition, is at once fascinating and puzzling: fascinating because it is the most intimately personal aspect of one's being, and puzzling because few find it easy to say what it is and how they may define and explain it. Part of the problem is that the term "consciousness" has many meanings. In a sense, it is many concepts rolled into one. Karl Pribram (1976b) referred to some twelve different meanings of consciousness given in *Webster's Dictionary*. There are equally numerous meanings of consciousness even in the technical literature of psychology. Though psychology began as "the description and explanation of states of consciousness *as such*" (Ladd 1909), psychologists at no time were able to agree on an unambiguous definition of consciousness. Edward Titchner (1915) referred to some thirteen different connotations distinguished by Alexander Bain. Thomas Natsoulas (1978) pointed out seven distinct definitions of consciousness in every-day thought and commonsense usage as revealed by the seven entries in the *Oxford English Dictionary* and examined their counterparts in psychological literature.

That the term "consciousness" has been used to mean so many different things had led some thinkers to question the wisdom of using such a concept. For example, philosopher R.B. Perry (1904) wrote: "There is no philosophical term at once so popular and so devoid of standard meaning. How can a term mean anything when it is employed to connote anything and everything, including its own negation?" (p. 282). In a similar vein, John Dewey (1893/1886) proclaimed that "consciousness can neither be defined nor described" (p. 2). A contemporary dictionary of psychology has this to say about consciousness: "The term is impossible to define except in terms that are unintelligible without a grasp of what consciousness means" (Sutherland, 1989, p. 90). Even those who wrote about consciousness often expressed their bewilderment at the multitude of its connotations. For example, Julian Jaynes (1976) in *The Origin of Consciousness in the Breakdown of the Bicameral Mind* asked:

"This consciousness that is myself of selves, that is everything, and yet nothing at all— what is it?" (p. 1).

As aptly observed by George Miller (1987), "Consciousness is a word worn smooth by a million tongues." Over 100 scholarly books on consciousness were published in the last ten years. Since we all talk about it, and many write about it, consciousness must mean something, even if it means different things to different people and even to the same people at different times. This is not, however, unique to the concept of consciousness. No language is so precise as to consist of only words with single and unique connotations. Very often, the context makes the connotation of ambiguous words clear. A scientific concept, however, should have a shared meaning. Scientific discourse abhors ambiguity and demands precision to the fullest extent possible.

Further, the problem of unambiguously defining consciousness becomes more difficult when we recognize that the phenomena of consciousness appear to have an intrinsically subjective character and that they seem to lack objective criteria for identification and observation. They are accessible only to introspection and consequently they need to be studied from the perspective of the person having the experience (first-person perspective). Science, as traditionally practiced, ignored first-person perspective (how things appear to the experiencing subject) unless it could somehow be translated into a third-person perspective. That we are unable to reduce mental phenomena to brain states with any degree of conviction casts a blinding shadow on the prospect of finding third-person based criteria of consciousness.

The problem is further compounded when we recognize the pervasive influence of unconscious processes in our mental lives. Electrophysiological measures may indicate the presence of certain states of mind and whether the person is awake, sleeping or dreaming, but they hardly provide reliable means of measuring the subjective states and much less give us the descriptive content of such experiences. Therefore, it is not an easy exercise to define or provide sufficiently objective operational criteria for conscious events.

That consciousness in both common usage and in scholarly discussions is used to mean different things and that there are no easy criteria to identify it is no reason to think that we do not know what consciousness is and what it is like to be conscious. Consciousness as it manifests in our experience is of two sorts. It may denote a state of awareness or it may refer to certain phenomena of experience. We say we are conscious while we are awake and alert, and unconscious when in a coma. Consciousness in our phenomenal experience obviously refers to something more than alertness or wakefulness. It is an experience of being aware, aware of something. Such awareness arises when we pay attention to an object outside or to an image or feeling inside. We become aware when we selectively focus attention on anything that is cognitively accessible. What is in consciousness is available to introspection and by introspecting we gain access to the contents of awareness and become subjectively aware of them. Endowed as we are with linguistic capabilities, we are able to report what we are subjectively aware of. Consequently, consciousness is seen as intimately associated with the ability to use language; and reportability has come to be regarded as a mark of a conscious state.

Again, consciousness is seen as a state of coherent cognitive experience resulting from the organization of discrete sensations into unified and meaningful phenomena. Whether such unity and coherence is made possible by the various processes in the brain is not easily settled. However, self-perception, awareness on the part of the experiencer of being distinct from others, is a necessary adjunct to all phenomena of subjective experience. Consciousness, thus considered, is a state of self-awareness in which there is a reflexive relationship between the phenomena of experience and the experiencing person. The manifest unity and coherence in conscious experience may be regarded as an enduring self or stream of awareness. In cases where the phenomena of the mind are organized into more than one unity and channeled into parallel streams, we speak of split consciousness or multiple personality.

There may also exist states of awareness that are qualitatively and functionally different from each other. For example, awareness in dreams or in so-called out-of-body experiences (OBEs) is different from ordinary waking consciousness. Therefore, in this sense we may speak of states of consciousness. Sometimes we also distinguish between degrees of consciousness. We say we are "half-conscious," meaning that we are not fully alert. Degrees of consciousness or grades of awareness refer to organizational complexity, to differences in sensitivity, intensity of reflection, levels of creativity, originality, and so on.

In all the ways just mentioned, consciousness denotes a state of awareness. It does not refer to awareness of something, but to itself. Awareness in this sense is a subjective condition. Consciousness also means knowledge, however. It conveys information. It contains data. We are conscious when we are aware of this or that, when we have awareness that such and such is the case. This aspect of awareness is referred to as intentionality. In this sense, awareness is always awareness of something, and that "something" is part of the phenomena of our experience. When we think, doubt, remember, or perceive, there is usually something to which our thoughts, memories, etc., refer. We remember or perceive something. For example, John, who is sitting in the front row attentively listening to a lecture, is aware of the speaker and what the speaker is talking about. Similarly, he is aware of

the name of the book he read last night, which he recalls in the context of the lecture. John is also intermittently aware of the distracting pain in his mouth where the dentist earlier pulled out a tooth. In all these ways, John is conscious and has phenomenal awareness. We may label such phenomenal awareness object-consciousness, as distinguished from subject-consciousness, which refers to a state of awareness independent of its content.

In a significant sense, the distinction between subject and object consciousness is arbitrary and nonintrinsic in that they refer to two aspects of the same phenomenon. In its objective aspect, consciousness is about something, and, in its subjective aspect, it is an experience of sensing something. Therefore, we may legitimately ask of consciousness, *what is it about* (information) *and what is it like* (subjective experience).

Consciousness as Awareness

Whether consciousness is conceived as a state or knowledge, the reference is always to awareness. Thus, awareness appears to be coextensive with consciousness and may be useful to explain consciousness. Natsoulas (1978, 1983) also suggests that consciousness in all its seven meanings refers to awareness phenomena. As he points out first, consciousness as *mutual knowledge* is reflected in Skinnerian behaviorism, which regards consciousness as a social product, as well as in the psychoanalytic notion of consciousness as *expression*. Second, consciousness as *conviction* may be seen in G. H. Mead's theory of social origins of individual consciousness. The third usage of consciousness as awareness is perhaps the most important one. Fourth is *direct* awareness, as implied in statements that speak of something being accessible to consciousness. In the fifth sense, consciousness means *internal unity* and continuity of awareness. The sixth and perhaps the most general usage is that consciousness is a *general state* of being aware. The seventh usage may be seen in descriptions of *double consciousness* or split awareness, when one discusses dissociated states and multiple personality. Natsoulas argues that *awareness* is implied in all seven meanings of consciousness described above. "If the awareness phenomena" writes Natsoulas, "is as ubiquitous psychologically as our ordinary concepts of consciousness consistently imply, then modern objective psychology inherits a major responsibility, namely the development of a scientific understanding of the common element that makes awareness a distinct kind of occurrence" (1983, p. 122).

VARIETIES OF AWARENESS

As Natsoulas has noted, awareness is ubiquitous in all the senses of the concept of consciousness. Clearly, consciousness in its primitive sense refers to awareness, whether of a phenomenon or a state. Regrettably for our purpose, however, awareness is also a very complex concept admitting a variety of forms that need to be appropriately distinguished. Awareness is essentially an information state. In its most general form, it is information concerning the environment or us, our bodily and mental states. Thus, we are aware when we experience pain, perceive an object, visualize an image, recall a memory or engage in a thought. Such awareness is simple, straightforward and easy to analyze. There are, however, other and more complex forms.

Awareness of Awareness: According to G. E. Moore (1922), there are two elements in every sensation. For example, when you have the sensation of blue, one element of the sensation is the blue object and the other is the awareness of that object. While it is difficult to discern the element of awareness in your experience of sensation, Moore be-

lieved that if you look "attentively enough" you can "see" the consciousness of the blue object. In other words, according to Moore, not only can the object be conceptually distinguished from the consciousness of it, but the latter also can be directly observed as a distinct element. The awareness of awareness in this view is not merely an inference derived from self-consciousness, but it can be an object of experience as well.

Awareness of awareness may also be understood in the sense of knowing that one knows. Sometimes such knowledge may not be available to introspection. John says that he knows the woman who is talking to a man on the sidewalk, even though he is unable to recall how he knows her, where and when he met her, and who she is. John also says that he does not know the man she is talking to. In this sense, one is aware whether he is aware of it or not.

Another way of looking at it is that when people are aware that they are aware of something they are exercising some kind of inner sense that gives them such awareness. D. M. Armstrong (Armstrong & Malcolm 1984), who considers that all consciousness is consciousness of something, calls such awareness "introspective consciousness" as distinguished from "perceptual consciousness," in virtue of which one is able to perceive the external world. Perceptual consciousness without introspective consciousness, in this view, gives one no conscious awareness. Sleepwalkers, for example, are unaware of what they are doing.

Self-Awareness: We may also speak of self-awareness, awareness of I-ness, i.e., my being distinct from others, as a kind of phenomenal consciousness. However, according to some thinkers like René Descartes (1911/1969), who identify consciousness with the subject, self-awareness is implied in all awareness. This possible reflexivity between my consciousness and me makes it difficult to classify self-awareness either as subject-consciousness or object-consciousness. It seems to fit into either of the two categories, depending on how we understand it. Consciousness in this sense may also indicate its self-manifesting function, which implies not only the potential to be aware of an object or event but also awareness of itself.

Whether or not there is an enduring self that underlies all conscious experience and to which the experiences relate, it is completely unproblematic to refer self-awareness to the self-concept, one's sense of personal identity. There is substantial evidence to suggest that the self-concept has a powerful influence on our conduct.

In psychological literature, self-awareness is generally assumed to be part of the basic structure of consciousness itself. In the developmental process, self-consciousness arises with the infant gaining the necessary linguistic skills to meaningfully use the first-person pronoun. In this view, infants lacking the necessary competence to use meaningfully words "I" and "me" also lack self-consciousness. J. L. Bermudez (1998) argues, however, that such a notion involves a paradox and that it is circular. He points out that one cannot have mastery of the first-person pronoun without having first-person thoughts. The latter are not possible without the use of the first-person pronoun. Bermudez argues that first-person content exists even in the prelinguistic infants, albeit in a nonconceptual form. He presents some interesting empirical evidence from developmental psychology in support of his contention.

Dreaming and Altered Awareness: We began with the assumption that we are conscious when we are awake. Clearly, what we have described under various categories of awareness so far refers to awareness when one is awake. However, all of us more or less regularly have an awareness experience while asleep. We dream and we are conscious in the dream. Like in waking awareness, in dreams we have a subjective experience of events and objects in the form of vivid life-like images. The imagery can be as complex and organized as in the waking state. But it may also be different, bizarre and incoherent. Dreams often tell a story. There is change and temporal movement. However, contradictory things may appear together without creating any dissonance. Scenes and characters may shift and change in ways unlike what we encounter in the waking state. Dream experience is in a sense translogical. Rules that govern rational thinking are often ignored in dream mentation. Dreams are quasi-perceptual phenomena, in that the dreamer has the subjective experience of perceiving an object or event when in fact there is no corresponding object or event other than the imagery itself. In most, during dreams the experience appears real. There are, however, some exceptions. John has lucid dreams. In such a dream he is aware that he is dreaming. Dream experience fades out rather quickly. Unless rehearsed soon after waking, much of dream content tends to be forgotten. Given all these differences between awareness in the waking and dream states, it may be appropriate to distinguish dream awareness from waking consciousness. Dreams are generally regarded as a distinct altered state of consciousness; altered because the experience appears to be organized differently from the normal awareness we are accustomed to in our waking lives. In the case of dreams, alterations are normal and natural phenomena. Some altered states, however, are induced by such manipulations as hypnotic suggestion, drugs, sensory deprivation or meditation practices.

Daydreaming and Hypnagogic Imagery: Between waking and dream states are two others that may be mentioned as distinct awareness states: daydreaming and the hypnagogic state. Our thoughts may be stimulus-related and oriented to the task on hand; or they may be spontaneous, involuntary, directionless and stimulus independent. John, waiting in the classroom for the teacher to arrive and reading the notes from his previous class, suddenly recalls the Publishers' Clearing House sweepstakes and wonders what he would do if he did indeed win a million dollars. Then he thinks of the woman who had won a big cash prize in the previous round. His thoughts now turn to the sports car he would love to have and the pretty woman he saw driving the latest model. It occurs to John that Japanese cars are better made and now they are a good buy because of favorable exchange rates. John's thoughts further drift and he is worried about the Asian economy and the stock market in the US. Mentation of this sort is referred to as daydreaming. Psychologists define daydreaming as stimulus-independent mentation (Singer, 1975) as distinguished from mentation in which attention is paid to stimuli in the environment. The Freudian distinction between primary and secondary process thinking points to a somewhat similar categorization. Primary process mentation is considered irrational and not reality oriented. It occurs in the id and is therefore unconscious and directed toward gratification of instinctual drives. The secondary process, on the other hand, is ego driven, conscious, volitionally guided, rational, and oriented to reality. Daydreaming is a normal activity, and most of us daydream in characteristic ways. Personal preoccupations and stress-related factors are known to influence the content of daydreams, which serve a variety of purposes such as goal setting, strategy planning, and wish-fulfilling fantasies.

Similar to dreams in many ways is the physiologically identifiable state called the hypnagogic state that occurs just before a person falls asleep. It is a state characterized by vivid and sometimes distorted imagery of hallucinatory quality in which the experiencing person is usually a participant. There is, however, one important difference between dreams and hypnagogic hallucina-

tions. The images in the hypnagogic state tend to be static like still pictures, unlike dream imagery, which is dynamic as in a movie (Foulkes & Vogel, 1965). If the person in the hypnagogic state is awakened and asked about the depth of her sleep she is likely to say that she had been merely drowsy, whereas a subject awakened during dreams tends to report that she had been in deep sleep (Foulkes et al., 1966).

Pathological Awareness: Dreams, daydreams and hypnagogic imagery thus involve largely stimulus-independent mentation. Even though it is known that application of external stimuli may influence the contents of a dream, by and large the imagery is generated internally. Attention to internal imagery is normal and it goes on all the time in our wakeful states as well. Frequently such imagery is guided. It is stimulus-induced or task-relevant. Similar volitional direction is, however, frequently lacking in the spontaneous imagery of dream, daydream and hypnagogic states. Whatever function or functions mentation in these states may or may not serve, their natural occurrence suggests that they do not disrupt our normal cognitive functioning. The dreamer, on waking, recognizes that his dream experience is not real and that the events experienced do not correspond to or represent the reality outside. Without discrimination of this kind, awareness may become dysfunctional and disruptive, giving rise to inappropriate behavior. Hallucinatory awareness, for example, can be an instance of dysfunctional or pathological awareness. So, too, are paranoid beliefs and psychotic pseudo-revelations examples of pathological awareness.

Hallucination is a perceptual experience in which one becomes aware of a nonexistent object or event. Hallucinations may be of any sensory modality and can be produced in normal individuals by hypnotic suggestion or by applying electrical stimulation to certain parts of the brain. Schizophrenic patients frequently report hallucinations, mostly of the auditory type. Sensory deprivation is also known to cause hallucinatory awareness. Drugs like LSD induce hallucinations. However, some experts in this area suggest that the so-called psychedelic drugs may enhance one's awareness by adding new nuances to perceptual experience.

Unconscious and Unawareness: By this usage, unconscious means being unaware of something. We are unaware of lots of things happening in the world all the time. "Unconscious" does not in its normal usage refer to all instances of such nonawareness. There is a basic distinction between being unconscious and non-conscious. A man in a coma is unconscious; the stone is non-conscious. There is also a difference between unconscious and non-conscious in another sense. John, who is listening to the lecture, did not notice that the woman sitting next to him left the room a few minutes ago. We may say that John was not conscious of the woman leaving the hall. John in the lecture hall was also not aware that his wife at home had an unexpected visit from his mother. It does not seem to be a natural use of the language to describe the latter as John's being unconscious of his mother's visiting his house. John's being unaware of the woman next to him leaving the hall is in some sense different from his being unaware of his mother's visit. In the former case, the event is in the normal range of accessibility to John's sensory system. He could have noticed the woman's leaving if he had paid attention to it, but he did not. John, sitting in the lecture hall away from home could not, however, be sensorially aware of his mother's visit. Thus, consciousness in this sense implies a relationship between the person who has the experience and the object of his experience; a relationship governed by the latter's accessibility to selective attention. John also has no awareness of the processes in his brain that make him aware of the things around him. Such nonawareness may be distinguished from the following experience of John.

John meant to ask the lecturer a question about which he thought the night before. He was, however, unable to recall what it was. He was acutely aware, though, that he had a question to ask, but the question itself eluded him at the moment. He felt that the question was somewhere in his mind, but he was simply unable to become aware of it at the time. John's teacher, who also practices hypnosis, demonstrated in the class earlier how John could recall under hypnosis an experience that he had completely forgotten and could not recall. While John has all kinds of conscious experiences, he has no immediate awareness of the processes in his brain that make it possible for him to have such an experience. Such nonawareness is clearly different from the unconscious items that John was unable to recall. The former is in principle unavailable to awareness whereas the latter could be brought into awareness with some effort and help.

Implicit Awareness: What has been said of awareness so far relates mainly to reportable, explicit awareness of thought, perceptions, images, etc., that are available for introspection. Then, there is more to awareness than what is currently in focus. Apart from the fact that the processes responsible for our thoughts, images and feelings are themselves not available for introspective awareness, there are also thoughts and images, which are not in the focus of awareness but are nonetheless available for focal attention. These include so-called preconscious material and readily retrievable memories. Further, there are images, memories and perceptions that are simply beyond the reach of selective attention and are inaccessible for introspection. Though the subject reports no awareness of them, the subject's knowledge of them may be legitimately inferred from his/her behavior. This inaccessibility could be due to a variety of factors, such as injury or insult to the brain, low intensity or nonclarity of the stimulus, and so on. It may be a rare condition, as in blindsight, or a very common phenomenon like the following experience of John.

While John was attending to the lecture and taking notes, a fly flew over his forehead and his right hand spontaneously chased the fly away. But John was not subjectively aware of the fly or of his hand chasing it. Clearly, at some level John must have been aware of the fly flying by. Otherwise, he would not have waved his hand the way he did around his forehead at that time to drive the fly away. Thus, we have a paradoxical situation, a case of apparent awareness without explicit awareness: John's purposive and discriminating behavior indicates that he was aware of the fly even if he was unable to recollect the event. Sometimes awareness is in focus (John's awareness of the lecture) and sometimes it is on the fringe (John's encounter with the fly). Our actions are sometimes consciously initiated, and at other times they occur automatically without any sense of awareness. When we infer awareness from the behavior of the subject who reports no awareness whatsoever, we have a case of implicit awareness, different from explicit awareness, which is available for introspection.

It no doubt sounds paradoxical to speak of unconscious awareness, especially when one equates consciousness with awareness, as we have done. There are, however, compelling reasons for inferring awareness when, for example, a subject in a subliminal perception study systematically responds to stimuli while reporting no awareness of them.

Natural and Induced Awareness: In a sense, what breathing is to the body, awareness is to the mind. Awareness is a natural and incessant phenomenon that appears to go on all the time. There is evidence to suggest that the mind is active in nondream sleep states as well (Foulkes, 1962) and that awareness is biologically necessary, even for a resting individual. We know that awareness is not always directed. There is reason to believe that spontaneous awareness such as in daydreaming or fantasy may be rhythmic and cyclical, like nocturnal dreaming (Kripke & Sonnenschein, 1978). It may be noted, however, that naturally occurring awareness is not uniform. As was described earlier, awareness in ordinary waking and dream states has significant differences.

In addition to or in place of naturally occurring awareness, awareness may also be induced or altered by certain conditions. The examples include certain psychic development or awareness enhancing techniques, like practice of meditation, manipulations as in hypnotic suggestion, and ingestion of drugs. Such mind influencing conditions may enhance the quality of awareness or disrupt it. Meditation, for example, may induce paranormal awareness, as is widely believed by those who practice meditation. The psychedelic drugs may cause psychotic states, as sometimes alleged.

Anomalous Awareness: While John was struggling to recall the question, he became very uneasy and anxious. He suddenly felt that something was wrong at home and that he must return at once. The feeling was so strong and disturbing that he excused himself from the class and rushed home to find his mother suffering from a massive heart attack, an event he could have hardly imagined, as his mother was believed to be in excellent health. Is it possible that John had somehow become aware of his mother's condition at some level of his consciousness, even though no sensory information emanating from it was available to him? Such awareness, if it exists, is anomalous awareness because we find no discernible causal link between the subject and the event. In parapsychological literature it is referred to as extrasensory perception (ESP), one type of psi phenomenon. As we will discuss in a subsequent chapter, there is substantial evidence to suggest that it is possible to have knowledge of objects and events that are not sensorially accessible. Such extrasensory awareness may be explicit or implicit. It is, however, distinguished from implicit awareness implied in subliminal perception in that the latter presumes sensory contact with the stimulus, whereas in ESP such a contact is expressly prohibited.

Awareness-as-Such or Pure Consciousness: John was initiated into transcendental meditation (TM) a few years ago, and he has been practicing it twice daily for about twenty minutes. He thinks that during the practice of meditation he enters, on occasion, a state of "transcendental consciousness," a state wherein he loses all contact with the outside world and experiences a state of bliss and "unity with the universe." It is, according to him, a state of ineffable experience devoid of any phenomenal awareness. In fact, several meditative traditions speak of "pure consciousness" without any content. The Hindu sage Ramana Maharshi, who is reputed to have experienced such a state of awareness, says: "when all thoughts are stilled, pure consciousness remains over." Such an experience of pure consciousness appears basic to most mystical traditions. The state of pure consciousness, awareness qua awareness, is variously described as a state of blissfulness, *samadhi, nirvana, satori,* cosmic consciousness, peak or transcendental experience of great personal significance, and so on. One important aspect of such experience is that it has great personal significance to and transforming influence on the one who has such an experience.

Criteria of Consciousness

The above descriptive usages of awareness suggest that consciousness may refer not to one but to several things. If these things constitute a cluster of consciousness, we may then ask how the components of the cluster are related and whether they are conceptually coherent. Are there any features that characterize all the varieties of conscious experience? Franz Brentano (1973/ 1874), possibly the first person to attempt a comprehensive psychological analysis of the concept, saw three basic features characterizing consciousness. First, in his view, intentionality is intrinsic to consciousness, and it is what distinguishes the mental from the physical. Intentionality implies reference to the content of awareness, direction towards an object. Consciousness is *about* something. It is always directed at something, real or imaginary. It may be mentioned that for Brentano all mental phenomena are conscious; "no mental phenomenon is possible without a correlative consciousness" (p. 121). Second, consciousness has a self-revealing character. According to Brentano, mental states are about themselves; they apprehend themselves. As with Descartes, consciousness is considered intrinsic to all mental acts. Others described this aspect of consciousness as self-luminosity or transparency. Conscious experience is the one, as Thomas Metzinger (1995) puts it, that is "infinitely close" and the one most familiar to us. Third, consciousness manifests an underlying unity. This is what Immanuel Kant called "transcendental unity of apperception." At any moment of awareness, all the simultaneously occurring mental events are unified to give rise to one integrated conscious experience.

There are others, like William James (1890) and J. R. Searle (1992), who have attempted to describe the general features of consciousness. James emphasized the subjective, noetic, and attentional aspects of consciousness. Searle adds qualitative and unified criteria to the subjective and intentional as the defining characteristics of consciousness. According to Searle, conscious states arise as parts of a unified field of consciousness. "This unified field of conscious, subjective awareness is not reducible to any third person phenomenon. It has a first-person ontology, in the sense that it only exists as experienced by some 'I', some human or animal that has the experiences" (Searle 2000, p. 4). Here Searle is echoing Thomas Nagel (1974) who also called attention to subjectivity as the essential feature of consciousness that appeared to him impervious to third-person observation. However, Searle, unlike Nagel, believes that a naturalistic understanding of first-person subjectivity is possible. As with Brentano, the criteria and descriptions of consciousness given by James and Searle may be appropriate for the kind of consciousness they were discussing, but not adequate when we take into account all the forms of conscious experience that we have discussed. For example, Brentano's account is clearly inadequate if we include implicit awareness as a form of consciousness, because such awareness is not self-revealing. Again, attributing intentionality to implicit awareness and undifferentiated feelings requires an extension of the meaning of intentionality beyond what Brentano really intended. The unity of conscious field as emphasized by Searle is also clearly inappropriate to states of pathological awareness.

In yet another attempt, Bernard Baars (1988) suggests that a *verifiable, immediate consciousness report* is the objective criterion of consciousness. He writes, "we will consider people to be conscious of an event if (1) they can say immediately afterwards that they were conscious of it and (2) we can independently verify the accuracy of the report. If people tell us they experience a banana when we present them with a banana but not with an apple, we are satisfied to suppose that they are indeed conscious of the banana" (1988, p. 15).

Baars offers the above criterion as the first step and he is obviously aware of its limitations. For example, dreams and subtle feelings are not "conveniently verifiable," and yet we cannot doubt that they are conscious events. Baars, however, justifies such limitations by arguing that he has deliberately set a high criterion. "We prefer to risk the error of doubting the existence of a conscious experience when it is actually there, rather than the opposite error of assuming its existence when it is not there" (p. 15). Even granting this argument, the adequacy of the criterion is questionable. If a machine can say "banana" when presented with a banana but not with an apple, can we say that the machine is conscious? It is intuitively evident that my conscious experience of a banana, when presented with one, is different from the ability of a machine to recognize a banana. A machine may discriminate between the banana and the apple, but it has no feel for the experience of seeing a banana. It does not know what it is like to have a banana.

Functions of Consciousness

What function does consciousness serve in our being and behavior? Does it have any evolutionary contribution to make? As with the criteria of consciousness, so with the functions of consciousness there is little unanimity. What the functional role of consciousness is, appears to depend to some extent on the meaning one ascribes to consciousness. For those who use consciousness in a general and more inclusive sense, there is little reason to doubt its important role in evolution and our every day thought and action. No one would question the survival value of our ability to sense, remember, reflect, believe, expect, plan, and execute action. Humans trade in information more than other species do. Consciousness, as involved in all forms of awareness, plays a pivotal role in reception, transmission and storage of information. We could hardly function the way we do without the abilities inherent in our rational thought and action.

The answer, however, would be very different indeed if one were to restrict the meaning of consciousness to focal attention and subscribe to the view that consciousness is an epiphenomenon. In the epiphenomenalist view, consciousness has no causal efficacy and no functional role to play. It is seen as a useless appendage or, in the words of Frank Jackson, "an excrescence" (1982, p. 135) which has no survival value or explanatory relevance. Thomas Huxley, an early champion of this notion, described humans as "conscious automata." Consciousness in this view is incidental to human condition. It is like the whistle of a locomotive run by steam. For Huxley, consciousness has no more role to play in the life of a person than the steam whistle has in the working of the steam engine. William James refers to Huxley's account of consciousness in his *Principles* and rejects it as "unwarrantable impertinence." Such a view is of course inconsistent with James' notion of "will to believe," that belief makes a crucial difference to the outcome of an event in the life of an individual. James also argued that consciousness would not have survived if it had no evolutionary function.

Cognitive psychologists have attempted to identify the role of consciousness in information processing. Various suggestions have emerged from their work. (1) Consciousness is necessary for the analysis of novel stimuli (Bzork 1975; Posner & Snyder 1975). (2) Consciousness enables us to choose amongst the stimuli competing to reach the awareness threshold (Mandler 1975, 1985). (3) Consciousness is necessary for memory (James 1890; Underwood 1979). (4) Consciousness plays a role in voluntary response, monitor-

ing and planning and in processing flexible stimuli (Mandler 1975, 1985; Underwood 1982). (5) Consciousness enables us to interact with the environment in a reflective rather than in a reflexive or automatic mode (Dixon 1979; Mandler 1975; 1985).

Max Velmans (1991) argued, however, that many of the functions attributed to consciousness could be performed without consciousness. Raising the question "where does consciousness enter into human information processing?," Velmans answers that it does not itself enter into any form of information processing. Owen Flanagan (1997) among others criticized the epiphenomenalist implications of the above assertion that consciousness serves no function in human information processing. That many forms of information processing can be accomplished without consciousness entering into them, he argues, does not warrant the conclusion that, when consciousness does enter information processing, it does not play any role in it. On the contrary, Flanagan (1997) points out that there is solid evidence to suggest "that consciousness facilitates performance on many activities, despite being not absolutely necessary for those activities" (p. 364). Some others expressed similar views, ascribing a role for consciousness in rational thought and action (van Gulick 1989, 1993; Marcel 1986, 1988). Philosopher Armstrong (1980) suggests that consciousness facilitates integration of different states and activities of the brain. Introspective consciousness, the term he uses for subjective awareness, scans the brain to achieve such integration. John Searle, cites the observation of Penfield (1975) that epileptics under seizure could routinely play the piano or drive a car without being subjectively aware of their actions. The lack of flexibility and creativity that characterizes such activities suggests, according to Searle, that flexibility and creativity are functions of consciousness.

It would not be correct if we assumed

that all those who consider consciousness an irreducible and fundamental feature of reality ascribe to it important functional roles. For example, David Chalmers who regards experience (subjective awareness) as fundamental as mass, space and time, concedes that it is best to accept that phenomenal consciousness "does not need to have a function to be central to our mental lives" (1997, p. 423). A number of philosophers and a few psychologists consider the inherent subjectivity of consciousness interesting in and of itself, whether or not it has any functional role in information processing. Ulric Neisser, who was himself in the forefront of the cognitive psychology movement wrote: "Consciousness is an aspect of mental activity, not a switching center in an intrapsychic railway" (1976, p. 105).

Categories of Consciousness

A number of writers have seen double aspects in consciousness. They called them by different names and discussed them in different contexts. Consciousness does indeed appear to dichotomize itself at various levels of analysis.

MENTAL 1 AND MENTAL 2

Pratima Bowes (1971) has distinguished between two kinds of mental phenomena, mental 1 and mental 2. Mental 1 refers to those kinds of discriminatory and purposive activities where we can *infer* awareness from one's behavior, as in implicit awareness, even though the person concerned is unable to recollect any awareness of these activities. Mental 2 is involved when one *experiences* awareness of an object, whether or not his or her behavior reveals it. We share with animals mental 1. Mental 2 is considered by some to be unique to humans. We generally assume that inanimate things are devoid of consciousness because they give us no evidence of mental 1 or 2. There are, however, those like the French philosopher Henri Bergson (1913) who thought that consciousness is coextensive with life. Few, however, would attribute consciousness to plants, which are not regarded as having a system of vital relations that give the experience of the sort we humans have. Animals, unlike plants, respond to stimuli in a manner suggesting that they have sensations of them. Those who deny consciousness to animals do so by affirming that their reactions are mechanical and nonreflective and that they are not self-determined. Again, those who attribute consciousness to plants see a certain degree of sensibility in them.

There is thus a sense in which mental 1 may not be regarded as conscious phenomena at all. For example, the British philosopher John Locke (1689/1989) regards consciousness as the perception of what passes through one's own mind. It is reflection contained in the different acts of the mind such as perception, thinking, and willing. Therefore, in this view the notion of unconscious thought or perception without awareness would be self-contradictory. In a similar fashion, René Descartes argued that it is self evident that there can be nothing in the mind that one is not aware of. The Cartesian and Lockean views of consciousness had such a pervasive influence that, until the advent of Freudian psychoanalysis, the notion of unconscious thought or perception was considered self-contradictory. In fact, this view is implied in most attempts to restrict the usage of the concept of consciousness to reportable experiences alone.

SUBJECT-OBJECT AND IMPLICIT-EXPLICIT DIMENSIONS

In our own analysis, we have depicted consciousness on two bipolar dimensions (see Figure 1). They are (1) the subject-object dimension, which has, at one extreme, phenomenal awareness of concrete objects,

Consciousness as Awareness

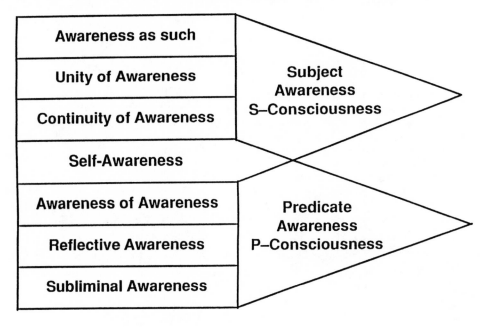

Figure 1

memories and images, and at the other extreme pure consciousness or awareness as such; and (2) the implicit-explicit dimension, which extends from focal awareness readily available to introspection to total absence of awareness. These two dimensions, which are conceptually distinguished, do not necessarily run parallel to each other. In fact they mix at various levels to produce a variety of conscious experiences. At higher levels, they appear remarkably alike and indistinguishable.

The explicit-implicit and the subject (being) and object (knowing) dimensions give us a four fold division of awareness (see Figure 2). At the explicit or liminal level, we have reflective awareness and self-awareness. At the implicit or subliminal level, there are subliminal or paradoxical awareness and awareness as such. Reflective awareness and paradoxical awareness are representational and have the characteristic of being known. Self-awareness in the sense of subjectivity

and awareness-as-such are nonrepresentational and unmediated. It is self-certifying awareness, which is being itself.

From the subject-object perspective, we have identified seven kinds of awareness (see Figure 3). Primary awareness is the most transparent and is sometimes distinguished from reflective awareness (Farthing, 1992). Primary awareness is confined to the direct experience of sensory percepts and feelings, including spontaneous thoughts, memories and images. Reflective awareness is seen as subjective awareness in which one's thoughts, images, etc. become the objects of awareness instead of the external objects and events. As we have seen, this distinction is not wholly tenable because even the so-called primary awareness in the human condition is processed against a background and in a context making it to a degree reflective.

In addition to awareness of the world around us and the discrete pains, feelings,

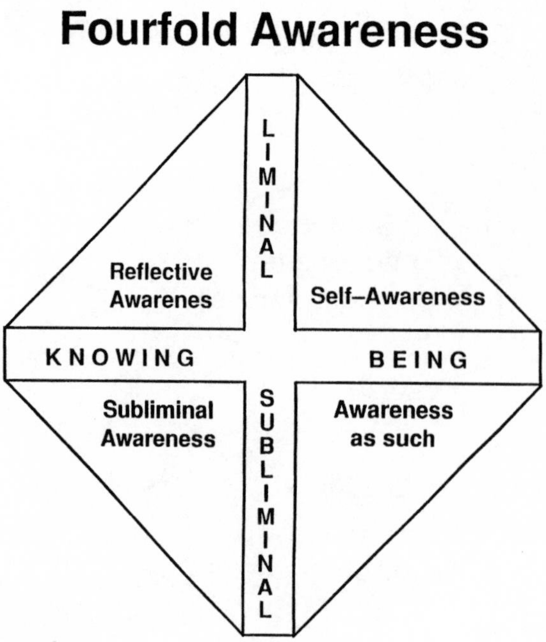

Figure 2

thoughts and images we experience, we also have a sense of identity, of being different from others. We believe that the experiences we have uniquely belong to us. Whether underlying this sense of "I-ness" there is an enduring self over and above the specific experiences is arguable; but there can be hardly any doubt that at a phenomenological level there is an experience of the self and that one's self-concept has a powerful influence on his/her being and behavior. It is also obvious that we routinely experience unity and continuity in awareness. Whether they are aspects or characteristics of consciousness itself or a form of conscious experience is not obvious. Awareness of awareness in the sense of being aware of "the element of

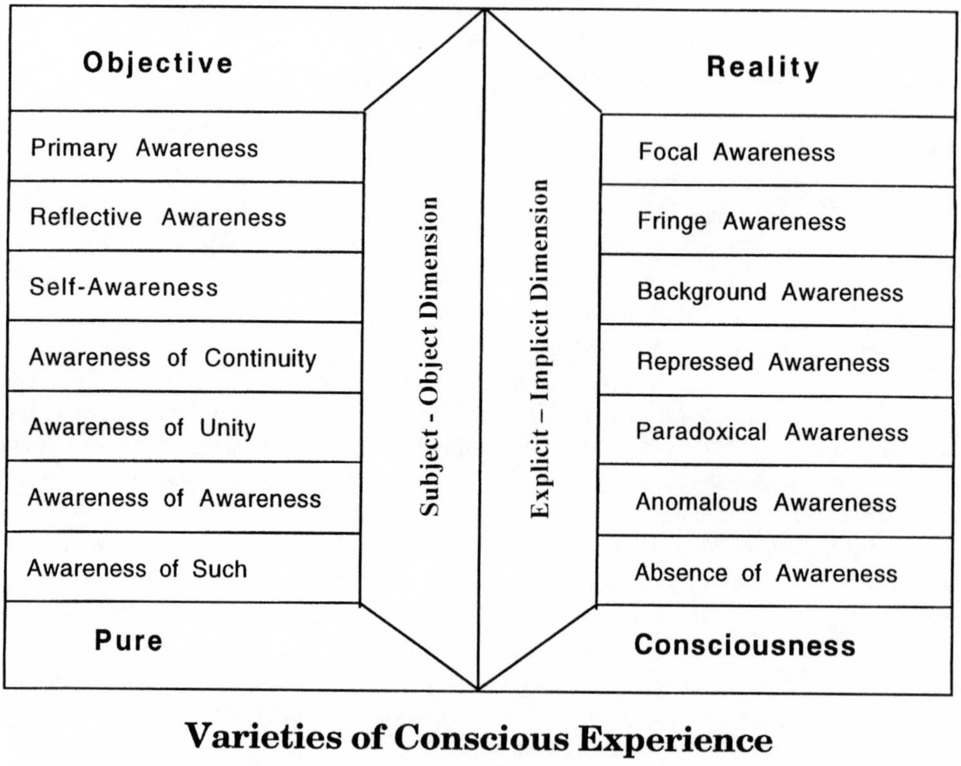

Figure 3

awareness" is more problematic. It is clear, however, if such awareness is possible, it is an outcome of disciplined practice. But in a more mundane sense, awareness of awareness refers to the subjective experience of being aware. In several contexts, such an experience is considered to be the basic characteristic of consciousness. Awareness-as-such refers to the reported experiences of mystics and yogis, and we will have more to say about it in Chapter 4.

Along the implicit-explicit dimension, we have also identified seven levels (Figure 3). *Focal* awareness is awareness readily available for introspection. *Fringe* awareness is awareness in the periphery that is vague and nonattentive. *Background* awareness includes retrievable memories as well as those that give us a sense of familiarity in a conscious experience. *Repressed* awareness represents hard-to-retrieve memories that continue to influence conduct. *Implicit* awareness is awareness without subjective experience. In the case of implicit awareness there is a manifest contradiction between self-reports of subjective experience and the attendant behavior. For example, a person may report no awareness of a stimulus when there is in fact behavioral evidence suggesting otherwise. *Anomalous* awareness is awareness received in an inexplicable manner as, for example, when there appears to be a causal discontinuity between awareness and its presumptive source. Consider, for example, the case noted by the renowned German philosopher Immanuel Kant. Emanuel Swedenborg, a versatile scholar, visiting a friend in Stockholm, had a "vision" of a raging fire at that very moment in Gothenburg about 300 miles away. He described it in great detail to about fifteen people gathered at the house and how it was extinguished at the "third door" from his house. A messenger arrived much later from Gothenburg and in the "letters brought by him the conflagration was described as Swedenborg had stated it" (quoted in Inglis 1977, p. 132). Clearly there

was no way Swedenborg could have seen the raging fire. Nor was there any other means at that time by which he could have known in any normal way about the fire. There could be thus no causal link between his veridical knowledge about the fire and the occurrence of the fire. Anomalous awareness, however, may be implicit, unlike in Swedenborg's case. Typically in most ESP experiments, the successful subject has no explicit awareness of the target (the object of his guess). Even in real-life situations, ESP may manifest in the form of a compulsive relevant action from which we infer awareness. The subject, however, may be totally ignorant of why she acted the way she did: for example, the mother who took her child away from the crib for no reason just seconds before a picture fell on the crib. Finally, we conceive of a state of awareness in which one simply has no awareness of anything, explicit or implicit. The existence of such a state is controversial and debatable, like anomalous awareness. If, however, we give any credence to the reports of practitioners of such disciplines as yoga, the possibility of such a state is indicated. *Awareness-as-such,* which is contentless and nonintentional, may be identical with pure consciousness as implied in reported mystic states. It is of course possible that in the mystic and yogic states one may also have anomalous awareness. In a state of awareness-as-such, however, the awareness contains no information. It is believed to be a state of consciousness bereft of any content.

The dual aspects of consciousness may be viewed from other angles. For example, consciousness may be seen from the perspective of its contents, as mentioned earlier, and we may ask what consciousness is about. Alternatively, we may focus on the functions of consciousness with a view to understand its processes. The subject-object dimension is primarily about the content categories, including lack of content at the level of pure consciousness. The implicit-explicit dimension involves various processes that give us different states, degrees, or levels of awareness. Again, the subject-object aspect is about the phenomenology of consciousness, whereas the second aspect is about the structure and functions of consciousness. David Chalmers (1996a), in a similar vein, distinguishes between the *phenomenal* concept and the *psychological* concept of the mind. The former refers to conscious experience and the latter is the explanatory basis for behavior. "On the phenomenal concept, mind is characterized by the way it *feels*; on the psychological concept, mind is characterized by what it *does*" (Chalmers 1996b, p. 11).

The distinction Chalmers makes is somewhat similar to the one made by Ned Block (1995). Distinguishing phenomenal or P-consciousness from access consciousness or A-consciousness, Block suggests that the conflation of them, which he believes to be ubiquitous in the writings on consciousness, is the root of many fallacious arguments. P-consciousness refers to the subjective and experiential aspect of consciousness, whereas A-consciousness has to do with information processing. "P-consciousness," he writes, "is experience. P-conscious properties are experiential properties. P-conscious states are experiential states, that is, a state is P-conscious if it has experiential properties. The totality of the experiential properties of a state are 'what it is like' to have it" (p. 380). Access consciousness is the state that underlies our reasoning, thought and action, and is available for reporting. As Block puts it, "A state is A-conscious if it is poised for direct control of thought and action" (p. 382). Block goes on to argue that "P-conscious content is phenomenal, whereas A-conscious content is representational" (p. 383). Even those who do not find the distinction between the two kinds of consciousness find it necessary to make related distinctions. For example, Owen Flanagan (1992) attributes to consciousness two kinds

of sensitivity (informational sensitivity and experiential sensitivity), which closely parallel A-consciousness and P-consciousness.

Another dual aspect of consciousness is indicated by the distinction sometimes made between phenomenal and transcendental consciousness. If the reality of anomalous phenomena and pure consciousness is conceded, this distinction becomes even more fundamental than the others.

The Four P's of Awareness

MENTAL 1 AND MENTAL 2

Awareness in the abstract is a state of knowing. It relates the knower to that which is known. Depending on the nature of the relationship between the knowing agent and the object of knowledge, awareness may be seen as falling into four broad categories—(1) primary awareness, (2) paradoxical awareness, (3) pathological awareness, and (4) paranormal awareness. I call them the four P's of awareness.

Primary awareness is what we have in the subjective acts of perception, thought, feeling and volition. Included in this category are percepts, images, inner speech, feelings such as pain and the like, which have sensory qualities, but also abstract concepts, beliefs, intentions and expectations. The basic characteristics of primary awareness are the information content and its subjective quality and accessibility to introspection. The relationship between the knower and the known is one of representation. Information flows from the object to the subject. *Paradoxical* awareness is neither accessible to introspection nor does it have the subjective feel. It is paradoxical in that it is "knowing" without knowing. There is information flow from the object, but the subject has no subjective awareness of it. Primary awareness is the most familiar and pervasive form of awareness, whereas paradoxical awareness is the least familiar and possibly the more primitive of the two. *Pathological* awareness is aberrant and dysfunctional awareness. Awareness primarily serves the function of relating us to the world by faithfully reflecting the world either in concrete or abstract forms, in actual or imaginary situations. However, awareness may sometimes misrepresent the world and lead us to indulge in behavior inappropriate to the occasion. Hallucinatory experiences and other forms of cognitive abnormalities are examples of pathological awareness. Consciousness at the primary level is coherent and continuous, whereas pathological awareness tends to be incoherent, fragmented and clouded. Finally, *paranormal* awareness involves nonconventional knowing, such as nonsensory awareness and knowing without representation. In states of paranormal awareness, the relationship between the knower and the known is one of identity. Unlike in other forms of awareness, there appears to be no information flow from the object to the subject. Paranormal awareness in a sense extends the range of awareness beyond sensory and representational knowledge. It may manifest in a form similar to primary awareness, paradoxical awareness, or pathological awareness. Veridical intuitions are very much like ordinary thoughts, except that they contain information that is in principle inaccessible to normal cognitive activity. Often paranormal awareness is implicit, but it is different from paradoxical awareness because, unlike in the latter, there is no identifiable channel of communication, i.e., no causal link, between the subject and the object of awareness. Again, a paranormal experience may occur in the form of a hallucination. However, unlike pathological awareness, the paranormally produced hallucination conveys valid information. Sometimes paranormal awareness may also be misleading (psi-missing) or even dysfunctional. At the extreme end, paranormal awareness is a contentless state of pure consciousness experience.

Summary

Attempts to classify and categorize consciousness in any systematic manner tend to be quite complicated and frustrating. First, in commonsense usage as well as in scholarly discourse consciousness has acquired multiple connotations. Second, there are no generally acceptable criteria to identify consciousness in all its forms and aspects. Third, consciousness appears to be intrinsically subjective and impervious to third-person observation and objective measurement. Viewing consciousness in all its forms is more like looking at a mountain than a non-hierarchical flat terrain. Consequently, consciousness may appear to have different characteristics as we view it from different angles, explore it at different levels and examine it from different perspectives. What may indeed seem to be appropriate criteria from one perspective may turn out to be inappropriate when looked at from another. The conceptual maps and the methodological tools needed to explore the terrain of consciousness may have to be different as we move from one level to another.

If consciousness does indeed refer to a number of things, it is arguable whether all the things it connotes constitute a conceptually coherent cluster. There appears, however, to be a fair amount of consensus among the students of consciousness studies that consciousness implies awareness. Awareness may be explicit or implicit. It may refer to a state of being or to an item of experience. As a state, awareness is subjective and appears to be essentially a first-person item. As an item of experience, consciousness has third-person ramifications and is open for shared observation. Addressing these two aspects of consciousness, we may ask of consciousness *what is it like* and *what is it about*.

The dual aspects of consciousness involving the subjective (what it is like aspect) and the objective (the information content of experience) are variously described by the scholars in this field. Chalmers (1996a) called them phenomenal and psychological aspects of the mind. Block (1995) referred to them as phenomenal consciousness and access consciousness, whereas Flanagan (1992) regarded them as information and experience. When we are conscious, we generally have both information and experience. Therefore, we may consider information sensitivity as the hallmark of consciousness. To be conscious is to be information sensitive.

This notion, however, is not unproblematic. We have attempted to show that consciousness may be depicted on two bipolar dimensions—(1) explicit-implicit dimension and (2) subject-object dimension. The former extends from implicit awareness with no subjective awareness to focal awareness that is accessible to introspection. We locate such phenomena as blindsight and subliminal perception at one extreme and consciousness-as-such or pure conscious experience at the other. Implicit awareness is utterly lacking in subjectivity, whereas a pure conscious state is believed to be completely devoid of any phenomenal content. Thus both the extreme states are paradoxical if consciousness is defined as information sensitivity, a composite of information and experience. This paradox is generally avoided on the one hand by denying consciousness to implicit awareness and by questioning on the other hand the reality of pure conscious states.

The subjectivity aspect of consciousness has troubled those who wish to make scientific studies of consciousness. The search for physiological correlates of conscious experience and the attempts to reduce or translate subjective experience into brain states and processes have not been very successful. In the recent past, there has been an increasing recognition of the possibility that subjective states may be simply irreducible into objective phenomena. The intrinsic difficulties involved in investigating subjective phenomena have led some writers to consider it as the "hard problem" (Chalmers 1996).

A few philosophers have wondered whether we could ever have a natural understanding of subjectivity because we currently have no conception of how an event can have both subjective and objective aspects (Nagel 1986). Colin McGinn (1991) has argued that we will never have a scientific explanation of consciousness because we are "cognitively closed" to observe the link between the subjective and the objective in our experience.

At least one psychologist, writing like a philosopher, suggested that a science of consciousness is possible. Max Velmans in his reflexive model suggests that the subjective and the objective in human experience are not radically different aspects but are essentially reflexive of each other. He argues that there are no observed phenomena that are not subjective. No observed phenomena are observer-free. Objectivity of phenomena, according to Velmans, consists in their intersubjectivity and sharability. Subjectively experienced phenomena can be shared inasmuch as people have similar experiences. He writes, "experienced phenomena may be *public* insofar as they are *similar are shared private experiences*" (Velmans 1999, p. 304, original emphasis). Thus, in this view, the subjective can be rendered objective by intersubject validation.

Consciousness as awareness appears to fall into four broad categories, which we designate as the four P's of consciousness—(1) primary awareness, (2) paradoxical awareness, (3) pathological awareness, and (4) paranormal awareness. Awareness as an information state involves the knowing agent and the known object. The four P's refer to four different kinds of relationships between them. Primary awareness is essentially representational. The object is represented in sensory awareness in the form of reportable subjective awareness. In paradoxical awareness, the representation does not reach the threshold of subjective awareness. Awareness becomes dysfunctional in states of pathological awareness because of aberrations in the structure or function of the processing agent. In all the above, the relation between the subject and the object is representational, whether strong, weak or aberrant, whereas in paranormal awareness it is one of identity.

In the chapters that follow we will examine in some detail the four P's of awareness in their natural and induced states with the hope of gaining better insight into the nature and function of consciousness. In this discussion, the model of consciousness as an information sensitive state that we have attempted to develop will guide us.

CHAPTER 2

Primary Awareness

The immediate conscious experience with which we are most familiar is what James called the "first concrete fact." It is awareness at its more transparent level, the level of primary and focal awareness. For this reason of immediate transparency, writers such as John Locke restricted the usage of consciousness to reflective awareness. Primary awareness may be regarded as the base of the "pyramid" of consciousness. As we look up, conscious phenomena appear less and less obvious at the higher levels of elevation. For this reason, they have become more and more controversial, as in the case of anomalous awareness and awareness-as-such. Few scientists have paid proper attention to them; and consequently we have less and less scientific understanding of them. At the same time, it may seem that the knowledge we have of awareness at the ground level is knowledge that is generalizable to consciousness in all its forms, and that the characteristics of consciousness observed at the primary level are applicable to consciousness in general. Such a temptation is hard to resist. Even the radical William James, whose broad vision and widespread interests had taken him on a variety of non-conventional routes such as studying medi-

umship phenomena firsthand and exploring religious consciousness in great depth, had in his scientific writings, for example in *The Principles of Psychology*, limited himself mainly to discussions of primary consciousness.

In many ways, James is the most influential writer whose ideas continue to influence a wide spectrum of psychological theorizing in the area of consciousness. His writings are extensive, covering nearly all aspects of consciousness studies. His discussions may not be the last word, but they appear to be the most appropriate to introduce any major topic related to consciousness. He is the guru, in the best sense of that word, of many who have sought to understand the multiple facets of consciousness. Therefore, we can do no better than follow in his footsteps while surveying the varieties of conscious experience.

We include all normal explicit awareness, whether thoughts, perceptions, feelings, or beliefs, in the category of primary awareness. We do not make any distinction between primary awareness and reflective awareness or what is sometimes described as phenomenal consciousness. Primary awareness does not refer to pure awareness of simple sensations. We hold that there can be no such "pure" awareness states, because all felt awareness is experienced. All experiences at the phenomenal level involve, in addition to cognitive content, affective and conative aspects in various degrees and forms.

Characteristics of Primary Awareness

Primary awareness is what James discusses as consciousness in *The Principles*. He regards consciousness as synonymous with thought. "*The first fact for us*," writes James, "*…is that thinking of some sort goes on.* I use the word thinking … for every form of consciousness indiscriminately" (1890/1952, p. 146, emphasis in original). James discusses five primary characteristics of consciousness. They are: (1) consciousness is personal and subjective; (2) it is changing and (3) continuous; (4) consciousness has the function of knowing (noetic); and (5) it involves selective attention. Let us examine them in some detail.

CONSCIOUSNESS IS SUBJECTIVE AND PRIVATE

The first and possibly the foremost characteristic of primary awareness is that it is personal. Each item of consciousness belongs exclusively to the person who has the awareness. Our thoughts are our own. We may keep them to ourselves as private and personal. We do not experience others' thoughts. "Absolute insulation, irreducible pluralism, is the law. It seems as if the elementary psychic fact were not *thought or this thought or that thought, but my thought,* every thought being *owned*" (James 1890/1952, p. 147, original emphasis). In a different context James writes about the "warmth and intimacy" of thoughts we experience. Warmth and intimacy are the marks of sub-

jectivity, and subjectivity is an unmistakable quality of primary awareness. In a similar manner, John Searle (1992) associates familiarity with consciousness. Subjectivity is the first-person familiarity that is exclusively available to the person experiencing awareness.

We may consider subjectivity as the sine qua non of primary conscious experience. When we see an object in the field or feel the pain in a joint, it is not merely the information conveyed to us that constitutes our consciousness of the object or of the pain. We experience the pain; and the perception of the object is not a mere pattern of neural events in the brain but an experience of seeing the object. The experience itself is entirely personal and no one other than the experiencing person has direct access to it. When I have pain, I feel the pain; when I see the red in the rose there is a feel to it. The phenomenal qualities we experience in our feelings and perceptions, which are often stated as qualia, are embedded in our subjective awareness.

Our ability to perceive, react, reflect, possess images and use them as representations, to control and plan programs of action, to project into the future, to use language, to process information, and to perceive our own state are taken as the general functions of consciousness. We are told, however, that a cleverly designed computer can also perform all the above functions. This may or may not be the case; but few among us would accept the idea that computers have subjective experiences as we do. We have an inner life that computers simply do not have; and this is intuitively evident to most of us.

In a highly influential paper "What is it like to be a bat?" Thomas Nagel (1974) provides a brilliant analysis of the subjective character of experience. An organism, he points out, has conscious experience, if "there is something it is like to be that organism." It "has conscious mental states if and only if there is something it is like to be that organism—something it is like *for* that organism" (p. 166). We do not know if a bat has consciousness because all the physical characteristics of a bat do not give us the knowledge what it is like for a bat to be a bat. "What it is like to be" is essentially a subjective feel and it is intrinsically impervious to outside observation. In other words, consciousness in the sense of subjective awareness is comprehensible only from the first-person perspective, and it is doubtful that we could ever know the physical basis of consciousness or have a naturalistic understanding of it because it is not accessible for third-person observations.

Following Nagel, Frank Jackson (1982) argued that Mary, who grew up entirely in a black and white room and bed and had never seen any other colors, would never know what it is like to see red even if she knew every conceivable fact about the neurophysiology of color vision. Nagel, Jackson and others who agree with them are essentially arguing two things. First, the experience of awareness is not identical with the concomitant brain states. Second, a naturalistic (physical) explanation of subjective states of consciousness is not conceivable. Interestingly, Nagel himself is a naturalist philosopher. He does not think that physicalism is false. Rather he feels that we are in no position to know how it might be true in relation to subjective awareness. "We have at present," writes Nagel, "no conception of how a single event or thing could have both physical and phenomenological aspects, or how if it did they might be related" (1986, p. 47). Therefore, Nagel prefers to profess agnosticism on this matter at this time. Going a step further, Colin McGinn (1991) asserts that we will never find a naturalistic explanation of subjective experience because our cognitive resources are essentially incapable of understanding its nature in physical terms. We are "cognitively closed" to understand the link that

accounts for the relation between subjective awareness and the brain state.

There are two other kinds of naturalistic approaches that deal with subjectivity in conscious experience. One is to eliminate subjectivity altogether as a useful concept. The other is to attempt to find a suitable naturalistic explanation. Those who tend to dismiss the notion of subjectivity altogether do so because they consider it to be too vague and inchoate to be scientifically useful. Any phenomenon that is not available for third-person observation is believed to be devoid of any significance and is therefore of no interest to science. What cannot be objectively verified, of which we can have no third-person knowledge, cannot be real in any fundamental sense. If there is anything meaningful and relevant in subjective awareness it will be ultimately explained in neurophysiological terms.

Even though this is the easiest route for circumventing the problem of subjectivity in our experience and the one preferred most by naturalists, a sense of uneasiness is increasingly felt by those naturalists attempting to understand consciousness. Very few now are ready to defend a position that eliminates subjective awareness altogether. Even such diehard naturalists as P.S. Churchland (1986), and P.M. Churchland (1989) have written about the subjective aspects of consciousness, albeit in physical terms.

Subjective awareness, as Owen Flanagan has aptly remarked, is phenomenologically robust and it is even more ubiquitous than light and sound. Therefore, it does call for an explanation. Flanagan, who calls himself a constructive naturalist, regards consciousness as one of the three greatest perplexities and proposes a naturalistic explanation of subjectivity within the overall framework of neo–Darwinian theory of evolution. He specifically questions the assertion that because the first-person experience is closed to third-person observations that no naturalistic account of subjective experience is plausible. He writes, "there is no reason to infer that the failure to capture the relevant first-person phenomenology third-personally, undermines the naturalist's hope of isolating the specific properties that subserve first-person experience" (Flanagan, 1991, p. 343). Just as we can make a reasonable inference that a blindsighted person "sees" the object that she is subjectively unaware of because she makes appropriate responses suggesting her awareness of the object, Flanagan points out, subjective experience or lack of it may have concomitant behavioral/neural states. Phenomenological experience and physiological observations may be no more than viewing the same thing from two different perspectives. "Mind and brain are one and the same thing seen from two different perspectives" (Flanagan, 1991, p. 365).

Raising fundamental objections against finding a purely physical explanation of subjective experience, David Chalmers (1996b) argues that in principle no reductive explanation of subjective experience is possible. Physical explanations may provide suitable accounts of physical structures and functions, but cannot explain subjective experience that is not entailed by anything physical, because "it is conceptually coherent that any given process could exist without experience" (Chalmers, 1996b, p. 15). Whereas it may be possible to find suitable physical explanations of the structure and functions of awareness and the cognitive processes involved, argues Chalmers, no such explanation could be found for subjective experience. That subjective experience cannot be reduced to simpler or more elemental processes suggests that it is fundamental in its own right, like mass and space-time. Thus, taking experience as fundamental, Chalmers attempts to develop a theory of subjective awareness that, like Flanagan's, emphasizes the dual aspects of awareness, the subjective and the structural. Subjectivity is a basic

characteristic of primary awareness. It cannot be wished away as unreal because of its exclusive first-person accessibility. Any satisfactory explanation of consciousness should address the problem of subjectivity in phenomenal experience.

Michael Tye (1995) identified ten different problems associated with phenomenal consciousness. Any one who wishes to hold that phenomenal conscious states are physical will find them challenging and perplexing. They include, first, the problem of ownership. All phenomenal conscious states are items of experience. They belong to individuals. Kathy's experience of pain is personal, private and unique to her. I do not feel it. Unlike the items of experience, physical events are public. Therefore, a physical explanation of experience of pain, for example, must provide a satisfactory answer to the question why I do not feel Kathy's pain and vice versa. A related problem is the problem of subjectivity, which we discussed at some length above. I know what pain is only when I experience it. No amount of knowledge of the physiology of pain experience or even unlimited observations of one in pain gives me the same awareness of pain that I have when I experience pain.

Another problem is the problem of mechanism. How do physical states of the brain generate subjective feelings of experience? T.H. Huxley expressed it this way: "How is it that anything so remarkable as a state of consciousness comes about as a result of irritating nervous tissues, is just as unaccountable as the appearance of Djin when Aladdin rubbed his lamp" (quoted in Tye 1995, p. 15). This is what Joseph Levine (1983) called the problem of "the explanatory gap."

The problem of the duplicates raises the question of whether another being, who does not have any subjective component but is identical in all other respects to me (my zombie twin!), can function exactly the same way as I do. If zombie replicas are indeed possible, what does it mean to have phenomenal consciousness? In a similar manner, we may ask: Can two people who are functionally identical undergo experiences that are phenomenally inverted but functionally identical? For example, let us assume, a person has an inverted visual system so that what appears green to us registers red to him. But he shares with us the same vocabulary with us and learns to describe grass as green, even though the light spectra registered in his sensory system are red. Thus his inverted vision makes no functional difference in relation to others. What does this tell us about phenomenal consciousness?

Other problems mentioned by Tye include the problem of location (Is the pain of a burned finger in the finger or in the brain?), the problem of transparency (Why is phenomenal consciousness so transparent and diaphanous?) and the problem of phenomenal causation (Why do my subjective feelings make a difference to my behavior?).

CONSCIOUSNESS IS IN CONSTANT CHANGE

The second characteristic of consciousness, according to James, is that it is in perpetual change. No conscious *"state once gone can recur and be identical with what it was before"* (James, 1890/1952, p. 149, original emphasis). Thus there is no item of consciousness that is immutable. *"A permanently existing idea,"* wrote James, *"which makes its appearance before the footlights of consciousness at periodical intervals is as mythological an entity as the Jack of Spades"* (p. 153, original emphasis). James was cautious, however. He did not assert that "no one state of mind has any duration." By change James refers to that "which takes place in sensible intervals of time" (p. 149).

The emphasis by James on the changing nature of consciousness has two purposes. First, it reinforces the subjective character and the first-person aspect of consciousness.

Second, it is used to question the atomist view that consciousness is composed of elementary sensations or simple ideas. Each conscious state is one unique experience. No two sensations are identical, even if they arise because of the same object. What we perceive and experience is different each time. "Every thought we have of a given fact is, strictly speaking, unique, and only bears a resemblance of kind with our other thoughts of the same fact" (p. 151). If each state of consciousness is thus unique, there can be no exact copy of it that we can objectively study later. Uniqueness, like being a private experience, is an aspect of subjectivity. Uniqueness of subjective sensory experience has physiological as well as psychological bases. No two brain states can be identical. "Every brain-state is partly determined by the nature of this entire past succession. Alter the latter in any part, and the brain-state must be somewhat different" (p. 152). Our conscious experiences are affected not only by brain states but also by a host of other factors. "We feel things differently according as we are sleepy or awake, hungry or full, fresh or tired; differently at night and in the morning, differently in summer or winter, and above all things differently in childhood, manhood, and old age" (p. 151).

If change and uniqueness thus characterize each item of conscious experience, what then becomes of the experience of being me, myself and my identity as the one and the same person from birth to death? The concept of self is closely linked with consciousness. If consciousness is equated with primary awareness, which is in perpetual change, self itself may have no greater permanence than the fleeting thoughts. In any case, we all have a sense of being the same person despite the many changes that befall us. What accounts for this feeling of continuity and sameness? This brings us to the third characteristic of primary awareness.

Consciousness Is
Sensibly Continuous

Despite its constant change, each normal person's consciousness is "sensibly continuous." This continuity is felt even when there are time-gaps such as those caused by sleep. The continuity is indicated by a sense of inner connectedness among conscious events, a sense that they belong together in one's consciousness. "Such words as 'chain' or 'train' do not describe it [consciousness] fitly as it presents itself in the first instance. It is nothing jointed; it flows. A 'river' or a 'stream' is the metaphor by which it is most naturally described" (James, 1890/19521, p. 155). To quote James again, "The transition between the thought of one object and the thought of another is no more a break in the *thought* than a joint in a bamboo is a break in the wood. It is a part of the *consciousness* as much as the joint is a part of the *bamboo*"(p. 156, original emphasis).

The stream of consciousness contains substantive and transitive states. The former are relative resting-places in the flow of consciousness. "The resting-places," writes James, "are usually occupied by sensorial imaginations of some sort, whose peculiarity is that they can be held before the mind for an indefinite time, and contemplated without changing; the places of flight are filled with thoughts of relations, static or dynamic, that for the most part obtain between the matters contemplated in the periods of comparative rest" (p. 158).

Even after a long night's rest, when we wake up, we remember who we are and we reconnect effortlessly with our past through our memories. We experience an unbroken continuity despite the awareness of the time-gap between the present and the past interrupted by a state of no awareness. Therefore, notwithstanding the gaps, consciousness is "for itself unbroken. It *feels* unbroken" (James 1890/1952, p. 154, original emphasis).

James speaks of a *fringe* as well as a *focus* of consciousness. While our attention is usually focused on a center and around a theme there is also a vast surround of impressions and sensations at the periphery. The fringe in a sense is the transitive, floating backdrop of substantive states that are the focus of attention. "One may admit," James says, "that a good third of our psychic life consists in the rapid premonitory perspective views of schemes of thought not yet articulate" (1892/1900, p. 164). The "fringe" of consciousness is the "halo of relations" around the conscious image. In the metaphor of the stream: "Every definite image in the mind is steeped and dyed in the free water that flows round it. With it goes the sense of its relations, near and remote, the dying echo of when it came to us, the dawning sense of whither it is to lead. The significance, the value, of the image is all in this halo or penumbra that surrounds and escorts it" (James, 1892/1900, pp. 165–166). Thus, the "fringe," according to James, is what surrounds every object of thought and gives it "psychic overtures," its "halos."

The fringe is not the same as the unconscious. It is embedded in all primary awareness in the form of extended relations and vague background knowledge that give meaning to the objects of awareness (Galin, 1996). The fringe is what provides the context and the network of past experiences and future expectations that give the meaning to the contents of present awareness. It often accounts for individual differences in perceptions. Illustrative of the role of fringe phenomena in our awareness are feelings of familiarity, the tip-of-the-tongue experience, feelings of affinity, being right and being on the right-track.

The distinction between the fringe and the focus of awareness is sometimes taken to mean two levels of cognitive organization. The notion of two levels of organization of conscious experience is prevalent from the very beginning of psychological studies of

consciousness. One level is attentive awareness and the other is the field of fringe consciousness through which attention moves.
Wilhelm Wundt (1896) postulated, in addition, an "inner subjective fixation point"
at the center of attention. In contemporary
psychological discussions the same two levels are variously described and labeled. For
example, Donald Broadbent (1958) refers
to them as the selection and perceptual systems, whereas Ulric Neisser (1967) labels
them as focal attention and preattentive
process. Bernard Baars (1988) makes a related distinction between conscious experience and conscious access, the former referring to what is in the *focus* and the latter
to what is in the *periphery* of awareness. It
is important to note, however, that the
fringe-focus distinction of James is different
in important respects from the above usage,
especially his emphasis on the fringe as a
possible determinant of personal meaning
and significance.

The stream metaphor is a powerful
one; and it has had a profound influence on
subsequent discussions of consciousness, as
it captures many characteristics of conscious
experience. Like a stream, consciousness appears serial, moving from one point to another, and it has length and width. Each
stream is different and so is each person's
consciousness. Like water in the stream,
which is accumulated from various sources,
conscious experience comes from various
modalities and combines the past accumulations with the present as it moves forward.
Again, conscious experience, like the flowing stream, is influenced by what is under
and around it.

It is unlikely that anyone would deny
the experience of continuity of consciousness. Phenomenologically there is no denying of the fact that consciousness feels continuous. However, there are those who look
at the brain to explain consciousness and
find no such continuity. For example Dennett (1991) considers it a mistake to take

continuity as a basic characteristic of consciousness. Instead, he argues that one of
"the most striking features of consciousness
is its discontinuity" (p. 356). Considering
the neurological processes underlying our
awareness, he does not find a single stream
but "multiple channels" of specialized circuits. Dennett may well be correct in his assertion of a network of specialized circuits
working in "parallel pandemoniums" to give
rise to awareness, but this does not necessarily contradict the reality of my experience of continuity of my consciousness,
which incidentally is not peculiar to me but
appears common to almost every person experiencing consciousness. As Flanagan points
out, "the phenomenology of the stream is
robust. The reality of a conscious stream is
not incompatible with anything that the science of the mind thus far needs to say. Discontinuities in the neural underpinnings of
conscious awareness, the binding problem,
and massive parallelism neither undermine
nor compete with the description of consciousness as a stream" (1992, p. 175).

**Flowing Consciousness and Endur-
ing Self:** As mentioned earlier, the notions
of consciousness and self are closely linked.
In the Western mind-set, largely a legacy of
the Cartesian tradition, consciousness,
mind and self are not sharply distinguished.
One merges into the other at some point
and they are seen alike. According to Descartes, all mental events and processes are
forms of thinking. Thinking or consciousness is the essence of the mind. I, the self,
am the mind and the mind is that which
thinks. Personal identity theorists such as
Jestus Butler further enrich this theory of
the self. Butler (1736/1897) argued that the
self endures as one and the same entity because of reflection on the self now and myself in the past gives me the conviction that
they are the same self. In a similar fashion,
Thomas Reid (1785/1941) reasserted fifty
years later that thoughts belong to a self that

is permanent and enduring. It is in virtue of the self that I regard my thoughts as "mine."

Such a notion of self fits well with the general use and the commonsense worldview. However, notably David Hume (1978) raises fundamental philosophical doubts, whether one indeed has a certain notion of an enduring self to which consciousness and thoughts belong. What is self, Hume asked, beyond the thoughts themselves? Unable to find an impression of self, he argued that since our thoughts and perceptions are separable from each other, it is not at all clear how one's thoughts belong or are related to the so-called mind or self. Self seemed to be no more than a "bundle" of one's thoughts and perceptions. In Hume's view, the self is never an item of one's experience. No amount of introspection enables one to have the awareness of the self. What one finds instead are only experiences tied together by association. Thus, in Hume's view, the concept of consciousness has no empirical content. Consequently, there is no justification for positing a cognizing self over and above the experiences themselves.

In the transcendental idealism of Immanuel Kant (1929, 1948, 1956), the mind/self reappears. Kant accepts that there exists a totally independent reality outside of us. But that reality, the things-in-themselves, is forever unknown. What is known is the phenomenal world of appearances, which is a construction of our minds. The mind with its *sensibility* and *understanding* gives us the experiences of the world. Time, space, and causality, which condition our perception of natural objects, are not given in experience, but are presupposed by it.

Kant agrees with Hume that the self is not an item in our experience. He argues, however, that it has to be presupposed as a condition for our experience. Kant points out that experience is not a mere bundle or juxtaposition of distinct events or sensations. Rather it is a coherent and integrated whole spread over time. It is a sequence of related events. When, for example, one hears a melody, what is heard are not discrete notes played one after another but notes as related to each other. The experience of melody then exists as notes related over time as a meaningful whole. Kant argues that the experience of the sequence of discrete events as wholes, such as the experience of melody from a sequence of notes, requires an underlying subject to whom it is a sequence. This requires that we presuppose a synthesizing transcendental ego, an enduring self, to account for the "phenomenological spread and coherence" of experience, which Kant calls "the transcendental unity of apperception."

The self can hardly be regarded as a category of the mind in the way time, space, and causality are. Even though we can understand how space and time are constructions of the mind, it is difficult to see the sense in which the self itself can be its own construction. Kant therefore finds it necessary to accord a noumenal status to the self. If the self belongs to the noumenal world, then, in principle, it should be unknowable. Kant is thus driven to a position in which he holds that we know no more about our noumenal nature than that we are conscious. The transcendental apperception denotes the unity of self-consciousness at the noumenal level, whereas the apperception at the empirical level denotes phenomenal self-consciousness. Thus, the self is seen as belonging to two worlds. The phenomenal self as envisaged by Kant is something that essentially fits the descriptions of Hume.

What is interesting is the fact that whether one believes in a substantive, noncorporeal entity called mind or self, as Descartes did, or dismisses mind as no more than a collection of fleeting thoughts and perceptions in the manner of Hume, some kind of an identity between thoughts, i.e., consciousness, mind and self, is assumed.

For Descartes consciousness is the incorporeal essence of mind and for Hume mind is no other than our thoughts and perceptions. In neither case is there a sharp distinction between self, mind and consciousness. Similar equation of self with the mental characterizes much of Western philosophical discourse since Descartes.

James also falls in line with the above tradition. At the outset, James makes a distinction between the empirical self and the pure self. The latter is the inner principle of personal identity. James divides the former into three constituents—material self, social self and spiritual self. My material self is the possessive aspect and refers to such things as the body, clothes and family that I claim as mine. The social self is the recognition received from significant others and includes shared values. As James points out *"a man has as many social selves as there are individuals (groups) that recognize him"* (original emphasis, 1890/1952, pp. 189–190). The spiritual self is the source of self-knowledge and one's "inner subjective being." It is the executive "me," which controls my perceptions and feelings. "It is the source of effort and attention, and the place from which appear to emanate the fiats of the will" (p. 192).

If there is a pure self beyond the phenomenal self in virtue of which we experience a sense of personal identity, what is its nature? James dismisses the spiritualistic notion of embodied soul and rules out also any transcendental principle of unity on the ground that we can give no positive account of either. At the same time, we cannot ignore personal identity as no more than passing thoughts because such a view runs counter to "the entire common-sense of mankind" (p. 213). James applies his pragmatic test and finds the criterion of personal identity in the feelings of "warmth and intimacy" that characterize one's thoughts as distinct from those of others. The philosophical certainty that Descartes attributes

to one's thinking, the first-person uniqueness, finds a psychological translation in James as the feelings of warmth and intimacy. We may note that the various categorizations of self by James closely correspond to the characteristics of consciousness enumerated by him. Self itself becomes no more than the stream of consciousness. He concludes his lengthy chapter on "the consciousness of self" in *The Principles*: "*If the passing thought be the directly verifiable existent which no school has hitherto doubted it to be, then that thought is itself the thinker, and psychology need not look beyond*" (original emphasis, 1890/1952, p. 259). This conclusion by James is hardly different from Hume's notion; we find once again the assertion of the identity between self and consciousness, the thinker and the thought.

Even in the social behaviorism of such thinkers as G.H. Mead (1934) we find a similar equation of the self and the mind. Whereas in James the self and mind emanate from and are the expressions of experience and the stream of consciousness, they are for Mead generated by the social process, i.e., within "the matrix of social interactions." This is accomplished through the instrumentality of language and in the form of vocal gestures. Mind consists in the ability for reflective thought. "Reflexiveness," as Mead puts it, "is the essential condition, within the social process, for the development of mind" (1934, p. 134). Self is constituted when one develops the ability to make himself/herself the object of reflection, i.e., when one becomes self-conscious. Mind is, then, consciousness and self is self-consciousness. "The unity of the mind," however, "is not identical with the unity of the entire rational pattern of social behavior and experience in which the individual is implicated, and which is reflected in the structure of the self; but many of the aspects or features of this entire pattern do not enter into consciousness, so that the unity of the mind is in a sense an abstraction from the more inclusive unity of the self" (Mead, 1934, p. 144 n).

The writings of William James and George Mead have had profound influence on subsequent psychological investigations of the self. Self is increasingly seen as object rather than as subject. Consequently, the concern has been more with the understanding of how one comes to perceive himself or herself to be and how such perceptions influence behavior, rather than with the self as an agent of our thoughts and actions. It is believed that it is one's perception of himself or herself that is relevant to behavior and conduct, and not the self per se. Thus in psychological discourse, "self-concept" displaced "self." The former, as D. W. Hamlyn aptly describes, is "the picture that people have of themselves" (1977, p. 172). Psychological theories of self in general are no other than attempts to explain how self-concept is formed, how it guides one's behavior, and how it can be assessed as a criterion for conduct (Gergen 1971). The self-concept, following Mead, is thought of as socially constructed. To use C. H. Cooley's phrase (1902), the "looking glass" in which people see themselves and discover their self-concept is provided by the society, the attitudes and expectations others have of us.

But, then, there are good reasons to believe that the self-concept may not be the same as the self and that the picture people have of themselves may not amount to self-knowledge (Hamlyn 1977). The self as an agency endowed with such unique human characteristics as freedom, responsibility and spontaneity in thought and action can hardly be seen as a socially given image of one self.

The transition from the self to self-concept, it would seem, is a natural extension of the view that equates self with the mental. If self is mind and mind is no other than thought or consciousness, the self translates itself into no more than the awareness we have of ourselves. The self then is not something we are aware of. Rather, it is the awareness itself that is thought of as the self. Whether such awareness is *sui generis* or a product of social construction is a matter of philosophical preference. In the age of science and positivism, the latter appears to be more compelling; and, therefore, not surprisingly it is clearly the favored view among psychologists.

CONSCIOUSNESS IS NOETIC

The fourth characteristic of consciousness is that it is noetic. It has the cognitive function of knowing. Consciousness is always about something. This is what is technically called the intentionality of consciousness. In other words, consciousness has content. Inasmuch as we experience many thoughts, each with the same objects, we are led to believe that there are objects outside corresponding to our thoughts. We not only have the knowledge of objects in our consciousness, by playing the "psychologists," as James puts it, i.e., by reflecting on the cognitive function, but we become aware of our awareness. James also emphasizes that no matter how complex an object of consciousness is, the consciousness of it is always unitary, "one undivided state of consciousness."

Intentionality: That consciousness is intentional, always of or about something, is widely accepted in the Western tradition. Conceiving mind as the substance with the essential attribute of subjective awareness, Descartes pointed out that the contents of consciousness, the ideas, represent to us the objects in the world and that the mind is essentially intentional. This notion of intentionality is further and more systematically developed by Franz Brentano, and James was familiar with Brentano's work. He commends in a footnote that Brentano's chapter on "the unity of consciousness is as good as anything" with which he was acquainted (James, 1890/1952, p. 156). Brentano (1973) points out that intentionality is the characteristic of thought which sets apart the mental from anything that is physical. Conscious phenomena, he argues, intentionally contain an object within themselves. That object may be real or imaginary and nonexistent. That a nonexistent object can be represented in thought is unique to conscious phenomena, a feature, which is unlike anything one finds in physical phenomena. Therefore, the intentionality of consciousness, according to Brentano, proves that it is immaterial. Whereas this implication of intentionality is not accepted by many, including James, the view that intentionality is a basic characteristic of consciousness is broadly based in the Western tradition.

Cognition: Our cognitive awareness has certain structural features and a developmental history, becoming more and more complex with maturation. Perceptual and emotional awareness (feelings) are among the first to emerge, followed by mental imagery and verbal thinking. With cognitive development we not only experience sensory percepts, feelings, images and thoughts, but we also develop the ability to reflect on them. Such a reflection enables us to judge, evaluate, plan and program our thoughts, feelings and actions. In this we are greatly aided by the acquisition of linguistic and reasoning skills.

Some writers, as mentioned earlier, equate consciousness with reflective awareness, arguing that mere perceptual sensations devoid of discriminating knowledge do not involve consciousness. This argument rests on the questionable assumption that perception is no more than a passive reception of inputs from the senses. Inasmuch as memories, expectations and prior assumptions actively affect even the most rudimentary perceptions, a certain amount

of organization and reflection is inherent in all kinds of primary awareness. For the same reason no clear distinction can be made between primary consciousness and reflective awareness.

Even though psychologists in general tend to be realists, i.e., believe in the reality of the world corresponding to the perceptions we have of it, few would question the importance of the processes within the organism in determining and shaping our perceptions of the world. Therefore, it is not entirely unreasonable to believe that our perceptions and images may not be precise copies of the world they represent, but the world itself, as perceived, is a cortical construction built out of the energy spectra channeled through appropriate sensory systems. Cognitive psychologists have attempted to postulate the processes that appear to be involved in such a construction of the world. A. L. Blumenthal (1977), for example, provides a useful description of the processes believed to be involved in our awareness.

In brief, at any given time in our waking life, we are confronted with a mass of sensations and memories. But our ability to process them is severely limited by the fact that we can fully deal with only one event at a time. Our immediate experience, however, is not a series of discrete events, but is unitary and coordinated. We may, therefore, assume a central processor that rapidly integrates the events occurring during a short span of time. Our immediate experience is generated by such rapid attentional integrations. The temporal span of integration is estimated to average about 100 m.sec, with a range from 50 to 250 m.sec. All the temporally discrete events occurring during a period of integration are fused, resulting in a unitary impression. In cases where the events are too different and incompatible to be fused, the dissonant ones may be masked and simply omitted. It should be mentioned that the time interval for attentional integration, though determined to some extent by biological and evolutionary factors, is not rigidly fixed but varies depending on various other factors such as the intensity and complexity of the stimulus and the states of the person at the time, including dispositional, intentional, and semantic factors.

Unity of Consciousness: Now, we may ask how does one have a continuity and flow of awareness from these intermittent integrations? If attention is a single-channel process capable of dealing with a single event during a short span of time, how is it possible to become aware of significant other events that may occur during that period? It is suggested that there are buffer processes that briefly delay raw inputs and hold them in a crude form for brief periods of time for possible attentional integration subsequently. It is estimated that such delays may range between .5 and 2.00 seconds, the typical being about .75 seconds. The buffer processes may hold, unlike rapid attentional integration, more than one event at a time. Again, impressions of immediate experience are held in short-term memory, which provides a working background and a directional context for attentional integration. The typical interval for short-term memory is about 10 seconds, with a range from approximately 5 to 20 seconds. The impressions held in short-term memory will decay within that period, unless they are rehearsed, i.e., attentionally refocused. The pre-attentive buffer delays and the post-attentive delay of short-term memory enable us to experience perceptual unities and are fundamental for the perception of sequence and multiple events simultaneously. The ratio of buffer delay time to the interval of rapid attentional integration is the number of simultaneous events one can experience from a single exposure, which is called the span of attention. Similarly, "the number of sequential impressions that can be grouped together in momentary consciousness is

limited by their duration in short-term memory" (Blumenthal 1977, p. 90).

Using a spatial metaphor, philosopher John Searle (1992) speaks of "horizontal" and "vertical" dimensions. The horizontal dimension is the organization of conscious experience "through short stretches of time," whereas "The vertical unity is a matter of the simultaneous awareness of all the diverse features of any conscious state" (p. 130).

Longer Temporal Integrations: What have been described so far are some of the processes involved in a moment of consciousness. They define the psychological present. The human cognitive process is, however, not limited to them. Long-term memory, for example, is an aspect of longer temporal integrations, and involves the summation of distinct impressions experienced over time. Separate cognitive bits such as perceptions, thoughts and memories may be pulled together in short-term memory, and their common attentional patterns may themselves become autonomous items of experience. It is through such a process of longer temporal integrations that we form concepts, rules, schemata, expectations and so on. Frequent repetition of an attentional pattern makes it automatic and habitual, requiring very little effort to manifest. It is the longer temporal integrations that help us to form images, concepts, feelings of familiarity and recognition and in the development of the self-concept, which give us the experience of continuity in action and thought.

CONSCIOUSNESS INVOLVES SELECTIVE ATTENTION

Consciousness as primary awareness is the result of constant choosing, of discrimination and of organization. Selective attention to a few of the multitude of potentially available stimuli is basic to our awareness.

In the words of James, "the mind is at every stage a theater of simultaneous possibilities. Consciousness consists in the comparison of these with each other, the selection of some, and the suppression of the rest by the reinforcing and inhibiting agency of attention" (James, 1890/1952, p. 187). The selection is not limited to one area or one level of processing. It extends from rudimentary attention to sensory data to the ethical choices that profoundly affect one's being. The selection, according to James, takes place not once but in several hierarchical stages. "The highest and most elaborated mental products are filtered from the data chosen by the faculty next beneath, out of the mass offered by the faculty below that, which mass was in turn shifted from a still larger amount of yet simpler material, and so on. The mind, in short, works on the data it receives very much as a sculptor works on his block of stone" (*ibid.*).

Attention is not only one of the main characteristics of consciousness, but it is also the central processor in our cognitive activity. James in *The Principles* devoted an entire chapter to a discussion of attention. Several of his contemporaries also paid special attention to this topic. For example, E. B. Titchner (1908) regarded attention as "the nerve of the whole psychological system." Similarly, his teacher W. Wundt emphasized the role of attention and wrote extensively on attention as a psychological structure. Again, W. B. Pillsbury (1908) published a voluminous book on attention.

The interest in studying attention has been coextensive with interest in consciousness studies. When psychology began as the science of consciousness, understanding attention was a priority pursuit. Later under the influence of behaviorism, when the interest in consciousness was eclipsed by an obsession with publicly observable aspects of psychological phenomena, little weight was given to the study of attention as a psychological process. With the advent of cognitive psychology, however, the interest in the investigation of consciousness and the process of attention was rekindled, notably due to the work of Donald Broadbent (1958).

Like consciousness, attention has enjoyed a variety of connotations largely because of its highly complex nature. In his little book *The Psychology of Attention*, the French experimental psychologist T. Ribot (1898) distinguished between *spontaneous* or natural attention and *voluntary* or artificial attention. In addition to these two, James (1890/1952) divided attention into four more categories: *sensorial* attention, *intellectual* attention, *immediate* attention and *derived* attention. Again, E. L. Thorndike (1907) conceptualized attention in five different ways. N. Moray (1969) mentioned six kinds of attention (concentration, selective attention, vigilance, search, activation and set), whereas M. Posner (1975) called our attention to its three dominant usages, viz., alertness, selection and effort.

Attention, wrote James, "is the taking possession by the mind, in clear and vivid form, of one out of what seem several simultaneously possible objects or trains of thought. Focalization, concentration of consciousness are of its essence. It implies withdrawal from some things in order to deal effectively with others…" (1890/1952, p. 261). The idea that the function of attention is to select one message to the exclusion of others among the multitude of simultaneously available messages continues to be a favorite theme among researchers in this area, especially since the publication of *Perception and Communication* by Broadbent (1958). Emphasizing the selectivity aspect of attention, Broadbent postulated a filtering mechanism, which selects from among the multiplicity of inputs received through the senses. Following the analogy of communication theory, he suggested that there is a single channel in the brain with a limited capacity to process inputs received simultaneously from different sensory channels. The organism selects only one sensory input channel at a time, while the others are held in short term memory for a few seconds. In other words, the filtering mechanism serves to block sensory inputs from reaching higher levels of information processing. Broadbent cited the results of his "split-span" experiment and "speech-shadowing" studies as evidence of his concept of a single-channel limited-capacity processor. However, the evidence from these and other experiments is not that clear. The results of speech-shadowing experiments, for example, have also shown that information from unattended channels was not completely blocked and that subjects had access to emotionally important (Moray, 1959) and contextually relevant information (Mackay, 1973) available through other channels.

In order to accommodate results of her speech-shadowing experiments, which showed that information contained in the unattended sources is processed enough to be identified and that such processing is not limited to sensory messages but extends to semantic information, Anne Treisman (1960) was constrained to modify Broadbent's filter theory and to suggest in addition to the primary channel, a secondary channel that processes semantic information from other incoming sources in a somewhat attenuated manner. Anthony Deutsch suggested further modifications to the filter theory by proposing that incoming messages are processed to a degree even before blocking by the filtering mechanism takes place. Yet others postulated a "parallel processing" model to explain automatic skills, the spectacular increases in performance following practice, and the influence of one's dispositions and intentions on attention (e.g., Kahneman, 1973).

Bernard Baars (1988) points out that the filter model serves little purpose if we assume that information is processed by attended as well as unattended channels, since the model was proposed essentially as a way of saving the processing capacity of the mind (Broadbent 1958). To circumvent this "filter paradox," Baars, therefore, argues that the filter is not an input filter, but a distribution filter, and suggests that attention controls access to consciousness. (See Chapter 7 for further discussion of Baars' theory of consciousness).

In addition to the control function of selective attention, two other functions of conscious activity may also be mentioned. First is the integration function, a function that appears to "glue" together separable components of perception such as color and shape. It is arguable whether the separable features are serially processed and glued or whether they are processed in parallel and integrated. Second is the constructive function that enables the unification of divergent features into a coherent perception (Mandler, 1983).

Volition: In the choosing activity of the mind James includes volition. "The phenomena of selective attention and deliberative will," he writes, "are of course patent examples of this choosing activity" (1890/1952, p. 184). In a sense volition is one aspect of attention, as far as cognitive activity is concerned. As James puts it, "attention with effort is all that any case of volition implies" (1890/1952, p. 815). We may recall that James conceives attention to be either passive or voluntary. Voluntary attention with effort is *the essential phenomenon of will*" (original emphasis, 1890/1952, p. 816).

Among all the processes involved in generating conscious experience, volition is considered by many as the essential ingredient. Mind, says psychologist D. O. Hebb (1974), "is the capacity for thought, and thought is the integrative activity of the brain—the activity up in the control tower that, during waking hours, overrides reflex response and frees behavior from sensory dominance." Volition as the "control tower," the self-regulation process, takes center stage in all conscious activity. Volition essentially consists in the selective deployment of attention to focus on one thought or action rather than another. At the same time, volition maintains coherence of thought and goal directedness among its activities. There are two basic aspects to attentional deployment. One is *focusing* attention selectively on certain items of experience while excluding the others. The other is *scanning*, which involves the movement of attention from one item of experience to another.

Thus, following James, we have noted that the main features of primary awareness include (1) subjectivity, (2) change, (3) continuity and stream-like nature, (4) intentionality, and (5) selectivity. By and large there is a fair amount of agreement among contemporary writers on the subject that these are the general characteristics of consciousness at the primary level. We may, however, find differences in emphasis on one or more of them. Some writers have elaborated and specified a few more. For example, J. R. Searle (1992) adds to subjectivity and intentionality four other characteristics. He points out (a) that consciousness is "situated" in that it has boundary conditions that envelop it even though one is not aware of them, (b) that it involves mood, i.e., has a flavor or tone that pervades the experience, (c) that conscious experiences are "characteristically structured" in a gestalt fashion such that the experience goes beyond "the structure of the actual stimulus," and (d) that it has an aspect of familiarity. Like James, Searle makes a distinction between the center and the periphery of consciousness, but prefers a field metaphor to the stream metaphor of James. As we have seen, the fringe of consciousness in James includes the aspects of familiarity, mood and situatedness treated as special characteristics by Searle.

Summary

Consciousness at the ground level is phenomenal experience. It is comprised of the multitude of precepts provided by the various sensory modalities such as vision, touch and smell, feelings and emotions like pain, joy and anger, internal imagery, thoughts and beliefs. Consciousness refers not only to the awareness of the contents contained in them but also to the subjective quality they possess, a sense of "what it is like." In addition to subjectivity, the first-person aspect, consciousness has the characteristics of changing and yet being continuous, like a flowing stream. It is noetic and has the cognitive function of knowing in the sense that it is about something. In being selective it attends to some inputs while ignoring others. The phenomena of primary awareness are generally accessible to introspection in human subjects.

Basically, consciousness at the primary level appears to have two components, the subjective and the objective, as suggested by the two characteristics of consciousness, viz., subjectivity and intentionality. These two features are sometimes described as phenomenal and functional aspects (Chalmers, 1996a) or P- and A-consciousness (Block, 1995). From a methodological perspective, primary awareness is both a first-person and a third-person phenomenon. The peculiarity and possibly the uniqueness of conscious experience (primary awareness) are that it purports to reveal objective reality but is always observer relative. An adequate understanding of consciousness at this level must address this issue.

Several cortical processes are associated with conscious experience. Basically two stages of processing are distinguished. They are preattentive processing of the inputs and focal attention. A central processor appears to rapidly integrate the events occurring during a short span of time. The impressions of immediate experience so generated are held in short-term memory, and further integration gives us unity and continuity of experience. Volition seems to play a significant role in the attentional process, influencing conscious experience in important ways.

Cognitive science promises to unravel many mysteries of consciousness, especially by giving us an understanding of the various functions of consciousness and the cortical processes involved in them. It is, however, highly arguable whether in principle it can provide explanations to the subjective "feel" of conscious experience.

The subjective character of primary awareness makes it person-centered. Only the experiencing person knows what it is like to have that experience. That knowledge may be communicated through verbal reports or other behavioral indices. Such communications, however, are at best descriptive translations but can never be the same as the actual experience itself. Whether the information obtained through such translations is sufficient to understand and explain the nature of consciousness is arguable. The answer rests on the weight one is prepared to accord to subjectivity as an essential ingredient of consciousness, whether it is peripheral or central to consciousness.

Unlike the subjectivity factor, the cognitive function and the attentional process are available for third-person observation. Therefore, they can be studied behaviorally and neurologically. Again, whether such studies, which do not take into account the person-centered subjectivity factors of experience, would ever tell the whole story about consciousness is debatable. At this point we may simply note that primary awareness has both subjective and objective aspects. Which one is more fundamental is difficult to discern. The possibility that both of them are fundamental features of consciousness may not be ruled out.

CHAPTER 3

Paradoxical Awareness and Pathological Awareness

William James, as we have seen, was concerned mainly with primary awareness in *The Principles of Psychology*. However, he was neither unaware of nor disinterested in other forms of awareness. His emphasis on the "fringe," the "halo of relations" around each thought, is a recognition of the importance of the context in shaping conscious experience that is not the immediate focus of awareness. James was familiar with the work of Pierre Janet and others that provided evidence for the existence of multiple centers of consciousness under hypnotic trance. In 1890, James published in *Scribner's Magazine* an article entitled "The Hidden Self" in which he reviewed the experimental evidence for the existence of subconscious mental states. In trance states a patient may reveal thoughts and emotions of which he/she appears to be completely unaware during normal waking states. In *The Principles* James also discusses hypnosis, methods of induction, theories, and characteristics of hypnotized subjects. He notes that amnesia is a pervasive characteristic of a deep state of hypnosis. The subject appears to have complete loss of aware-

ness of things that occurred during the trance period unless instructed specifically to remember them. James recognized also that the subconscious states have the potential to manifest in or influence overt awareness. All these point to mental activity at the subconscious level. James looked favorably on the reality and importance of these states, which differ from normal awareness in important respects. At the subliminal level we do not find the unity and continuity in a transparent stream of consciousness that James noted with regard to primary awareness. Instead there is a subterrain of multiple streams, which may influence one's behavior without being recognized. In normal states, awareness is unified, with a focus and a periphery. The "buried ideas" in the subconscious terrain may hang together as constellations and manifest in pathological forms, as in hysteria, tics, and in extreme cases, multiple personality.

In primary awareness, as we noted, the subject is aware of his/her awareness. Primary awareness is awareness experienced and felt. When I am aware of something, I sense that the awareness is my experience and I know what it is like to have that experience. There are, however, other situations in which such a sense is absent. For example, in cases of implicit awareness one does not know that he/she knows. Such "awareness" without awareness may appear paradoxical and self-contradictory, but it seems to be very real. There are compelling reasons for inferring awareness when, for example, a hypnotized person carries out a posthypnotic suggestion apparently without being aware of it, or when a subject in a subliminal perception study systematically responds to stimuli without reporting any awareness of them. So there is good reason to expand the connotation of consciousness beyond subjective awareness to include nonreportable awareness such as subliminal perception, implicit memory, blindsight and the like. In fact, the existence of nonconscious mentation has been widely known at least since the time of Sigmund Freud.

Implicit Awareness

Paradoxical awareness, as in subliminal perception, is a normal phenomenon, except that it is implicit. There is nothing pathological about it. It need not be induced by such manipulations as hypnosis. Normal people under ordinary circumstances manifest behavior that leads us to infer that they are aware of certain things of which they say they have no subjective awareness. In other words, subliminal perception is a normal event, and we need postulate no brain pathology or psychological dysfunction when we find dissociation between perception and subjective awareness in subliminal perception. Perception may be explicit or implicit. Whereas implicit awareness is a normal phenomenon under certain situations, in some other circumstances it may result from pathological con-

ditions such as brain damage. For example, in the case of blindsight, a patient with a damaged primary visual area reports no subjective awareness of a stimulus falling in the damaged visual field. He may be able to respond to that stimulus, however, in much the same way as a subject in a subliminal perception experiment responds. The blindsighted patient does not have explicit awareness of the stimulus falling in the damaged visual field; she may, however, have implicit awareness of it.

Paradoxical awareness, as mentioned, is not pathological awareness. Pathological states may bring about partial awareness including paradoxical awareness and dysfunctional awareness. Pathological conditions of the brain that disrupt normal explicit perceptions may leave intact processes that give rise to implicit awareness. However, brain pathologies or other abnormal conditions may in some cases constrain or distort awareness so as to render it dysfunctional and disruptive. Such dysfunctional awareness, pathological awareness as we called it, may characterize mental illness as in hysterical blindness and schizophrenia. Brain pathologies therefore may be associated with the manifestation of either paradoxical or pathological awareness.

SUBLIMINAL PERCEPTION

Subliminal perception refers to the possibility that people might be influenced by objects and events of which they report to have no perceptual awareness. Research in the area of subliminal perception has produced some interesting results. There is impressive evidence that stimuli presented at low energy levels, or in masked forms so that they cannot be recalled, recognized, or discriminated from other similarly presented stimuli, can nevertheless produce detectable cognitive, affective, or other behavioral effects (Bornstein & Pittman 1992). Even though several of the claims made and popularized in the media, such as the subliminal audio tapes for better health and well being, continue to be controversial, there is compelling evidence to suggest that people do indeed respond to stimuli that they are not subjectively aware of. In fact, such a possibility was noted even before the advent of psychoanalysis. As Kihlstrom et al. (1992) point out, the distinguished American philosopher and the founder of pragmatism Charles Pierce and his student Joseph Jastrow were the first to provide laboratory evidence for subliminal perception. Pierce and Jastrow (1884), using themselves as subjects, carried out a weight discrimination task in a psychophysical experiment. The subjects' task was to feel the pressure of the two weights and choose which one of them was heavier and to rate on a scale of 0–3 how confident they were that their choices were correct. A zero rating indicated "absence of any preference for one answer over its opposite." The results showed that both Pierce and Jastrow were able to discriminate between the weights beyond chance level, even on the zero-confidence trials. For example, in one series, Pierce succeeded guessing correctly 436 times out of 706 trials with zero rating, registering a success rate of 61.8 percent when 50 percent is expected by chance. Such a result is a clear indication of the subject's ability to discriminate between stimuli in the absence of any subjective awareness.

In another interesting early study, Otto Poetzl (1917), a Viennese neuropsychologist who was somewhat influenced by Freud, exposed a complex stimulus to the subject for 10 ms tachistoscopically. The subject was asked to produce a complete reproduction of what he had seen in the form of a drawing. The experimenter further instructed the subject to have a dream that night and report the dream the following day. Twelve subjects participated in the study. An examination of the dreams convinced Poetzl that the elements of the stimuli that were not found in the drawings were contained in the content of the dreams, implying that more information is registered and processed than is explicitly available to perception. Following Poetzl, Allers and Teler (1924) among others showed that free associative imagery could be as effective as dream content in recovering subliminal information.

There are a number of other psychoanalytically inspired experiments since Poetzl. For example, R.N. Haber and M.H. Erdelyi (1967) carried out a study with three groups of subjects. The first group, the experimental group, was exposed to a stimulus drawing for 100 ms. Following the exposure they drew what they had seen in the flash and labeled the details in the drawing (pre-fantasy recall). The subjects in the experimental group were engaged in a free-association fantasy task for 35 minutes after which they produced word strings as well as narrations of free association (post-fantasy recall). On the completion of the free association task, the subjects drew again as much of the content of the original stimulus as they could recall. The second (control) group of subjects did everything the experimental group did except that, instead of engaging in a free-association task, they threw darts during that period. The subjects in the third "yoked" group, unlike the experimental group, were not exposed to the stimulus picture. Instead they copied one of the pre-fantasy drawings of the experimental subjects. The rest of the procedure was the same as for the experimental group. The results showed that among the subjects in the experimental group, the post-fantasy recall contained significantly more stimulus content than the pre-fantasy recall. There was no such difference between the two recalls of the other two groups. An analysis of the free-association material for its semantic relatedness to the stimulus picture revealed significant differences between the experimental and the yoked groups. The stimulus content that was not revealed in either of the recalls emerged to a significant degree in the free associations of the subjects in the experimental group compared to the free associations of the yoked group.

Somewhat more controversial than the above are studies carried out by J. Weinberger and associates in which subliminal (4ms) exposure to the message "Mommy and I are one" was shown to have beneficial effects on those undergoing psychotherapy (Silverman & Weinberger 1985). In these studies, referred to as subliminal psychodynamic activation (SPA), typically the subject is exposed for 4ms to unmasked stimuli, which is believed to be psychodynamically active (Mommy and I are One, MIO). At this exposure level subjects report that they see no more than flickers of light. In the control condition the subjects are exposed to a neutral stimulus (People Are Walking) in a manner identical with the experimental condition. Subjects undergoing psychotherapy and also treatment for addictions, etc. participated in these experiments. The results of double-blind studies have repeatedly shown that the treatment was more effective in the experimental condition than in the control, suggesting the influence of psychodynamically relevant subliminal stimuli. What is even more interesting is the observation that the effects obtained under subliminal conditions were greater than those obtained when the subjects reported seeing the stimulus message (Bornstein 1989). Even though the results are clearly unambiguous about the genuineness of the SPA effect, the finding itself met with considerable resistance because of the "magical" nature of the effect. It was shown, however, that MIO stimulation induces a positive affect or mood, which in turn may aid therapy (Weinberger, Kelner, & McClelland 1990).

In a study by Spence and Holland (1962), the subjects were presented with a list of twenty words to memorize. Ten words had remote associations with the word cheese, whereas the rest were neutral. One group of subjects was presented the word cheese subliminally; another group was exposed to a blank; and the third group was actually shown the word "cheese." The results showed that the subliminal group recalled more words associated with cheese than did the subjects in the other two groups, including the one who actually saw the word.

A variety of other subliminal effects have been demonstrated under fairly rigorous conditions. These include the subliminal mere exposure effect and the subliminal lexical priming effect. The former refers to a subject's affective response to the subliminal stimulus, whereas the latter involves cognitive responses. W.R. Kunst-Wilson and R.G. Zajonc (1980) have incorporated in their subliminal studies Zajonc's "mere exposure effect" hypothesis, that mere exposure to a stimulus enhances one's attitude to that stimulus. In an important experiment, each of their 24 subjects was exposed to a series of 10 irregular polygon stimuli. Each polygon was presented to the subject five times, for a duration of 1 ms. Following the presentation of the subliminal stimuli, the subjects were shown pairs of polygons, each pair consisting of one of the previously exposed (subliminal) polygons and a novel one. Each pair was exposed for 1 second and the subject was asked (a) to identify the previously exposed polygons and (b) to state which one in the pair they preferred. The results showed that the subjects were unable to identify the previously exposed polygons to any significant degree. However, they expressed preference for the subliminally exposed stimuli 60 percent of the time, suggesting that they were indeed responding to the previously exposed stimuli even though they were unable to identify them. The subliminal mere exposure effect has since been replicated several times (see Bornstein 1992).

The *pattern masking procedure* is used in several well-controlled experimental studies of subliminal perception. In this procedure the subliminal stimulus is flashed for a fraction of a second. After a brief delay, a masking stimulus (e.g., a jumble of broken letters) is flashed. The masking stimulus has the effect of clouding the recognition of the subliminal stimulus, which would otherwise be recognized explicitly. Masking is of course a function of the duration between the flashing of the subliminal stimulus and the masking stimulus. If the duration is too long, the subject becomes subjectively aware (explicit awareness) of the stimulus, i.e., the stimulus is no longer subliminal. If the duration is too short the subject may have no awareness of any kind. Therefore, a *detection threshold* needs to be found which determines the necessary delay between the flashing of the stimulus and the mask for subliminal perception to occur. The threshold may be measured in two ways. First, the subject may be asked whether he is able to see the stimulus word, varying the duration between the flashes. The longest duration at which the subject reports no awareness of seeing the stimulus is the detection threshold. A threshold so determined is called the *subjective threshold*. Second, the threshold may be measured following a forced-choice procedure in which the subject is shown either the stimulus or a blank in a random order and asked to say whether the stimulus is present or not. The longest duration at which the subject correctly detects the presence of the stimulus at no better than chance levels (50 percent) is the detection threshold. A threshold determined in this or a similar manner is called the *objective threshold*. In the following well-controlled subliminal experiments, objective thresholds are used to mask the stimulus. J. Cheesman and P. M. Merikle (1984) found that for prime words the objective threshold averages about 30 ms whereas it is about 56 ms for the subjective threshold.

If the subjects are shown a word stem, e.g. ELA, after they are exposed to a related word, plastic (prime), and instructed to complete the stem ELA with either *elated* or *elastic*, they are more likely to choose the word elastic rather than elated. This phenomenon is called the priming effect and the word plastic in this case is the prime. Lexical priming studies by A. Marcel (1983a; 1983b) and others have provided evidence for subliminal perception of masked words in experiments involving lexical decision-making. In one study, subjects saw a string of letters (target) that were either words or nonwords. The target was presented for 1000 ms. On some trials the target presentation was preceded by a masked prime (another word) semantically related or not to the target. The subject's task was to push one of two buttons as fast as possible to record his response whether or not the letter string is an English language word. The results showed that the reaction time to the target word "nurse" was shorter when the prime was the word "doctor" and not "butter." Interestingly, the priming effect is about the same whether the prime is masked or not, even though the subjects could not detect the masked prime.

In a study by Merikle and Reingold (1990), the subjects were presented with a word or a blank for 50 ms preceded and followed by a masking stimulus. Then they were shown two words and asked to answer "yes" or "no" to the question "was either word presented?" This was the detection task. After the subjects made the detection decision, the two words were shown again with the question "which word was presented?" (recognition task). Similar tests were also done with nonwords in place of words. Merikle and Reingold found that when stimuli were *detected* both words and nonwords were *recognized*, but when they were not *detected* only words were recognized to a significant degree. Thus, when the subjects felt that they had no awareness of the stimulus, they appeared to have sufficient information to recognize the correct stimulus when it was a meaningful word. In other words, stimulus *detection* and stimulus *recognition* may be dissociated in that subjects may be able to *recognize* the stimuli even if they are not able to detect them, especially when they are meaningful to the subjects.

In a study by Greenwald, Klinger, and Liu (1989), the subjects were asked to indicate whether the target words had positive or negative connotations to them. The target words were masked by primes that had strong positive or negative connotations. The masking was so complete that the subjects were unable even to detect where the prime appeared on the screen. The results provided significant evidence to suggest that positive primes accelerated the pace of positive judgments and retarded the pace of negative judgments, whereas the negative primes did the opposite. There is thus evidence for subliminal perception under extremely conservative detection thresholds.

D. Holender (1986) criticized the subliminal experiments in general, stating that they did not accurately measure the objective threshold. He argued that the objective threshold must take into account any discriminative response, not merely the detection of the presence or absence of the stimulus. We can see, however, the use of such a criterion effectively rules out the possibility of subliminal perception altogether, because we measure subliminal perception in terms of discriminative behavior, in the absence of which one can only presume no awareness, subliminal or otherwise. If we make certain that the subject is unable to make any discriminating response to a stimulus, in a determination of objective threshold as suggested by Holender, we leave no room for the occurrence of any kind of awareness, explicit or implicit, that can be detected by any objective measure. In other words, if one insists on an objective thresh-

old that leaves no room for any kind of discriminatory behavior, he by the same token rules out the possibility of implicit awareness. What we are concerned with is a lack of subjective awareness and not of awareness itself. By ruling out all awareness, one does not settle the question of whether awareness is possible without being subjectively aware of that awareness.

Considering the extensive evidence gathered by numerous researchers utilizing a variety of experimental paradigms, the existence of subliminal perception may no longer be questioned in any reasonable manner. As Robert Bornstein (1992) pointed out, "leading researchers in this area are no longer debating whether or not perception without awareness occurs. Instead, we have turned our attention to elucidating the parameters of subliminal effects and trying to understand the conditions under which stimuli perceived without awareness significantly influence affect, cognition, and behavior" (p. 4). In addition to the fact that subliminal perception is real, we also know that subliminal perception can have emotional as well as cognitive effects. Subjects in subliminal studies successfully respond in lexical decision-making tasks (Marcel 1983), as well as in tasks that elicit affective reactions (McGinnis 1969). Subliminal stimuli can bring about attitude and mood changes (Kunst-Wilson & Zajonc 1980; Weinberger, Kelner & McClelland 1990). Subliminal stimulus effects may manifest not only in terms of subject's responses and changes in attitudes and moods, but also be revealed in free associations and dream images of the subjects, even when the subjects are unable to recognize them as such (Haber & Erdelyi 1967; Poetzl 1917).

There are a number of suggestions made to account for subliminal perception and to specify the cognitive and neurological processes involved. Yet, there is no one theory that seems to explain the different aspects of the subliminal effects. It is possible that in perception there is more than one process involved. For instance, perception with subjective awareness and perception without such awareness (subliminal perception) may be due to the operations of two different perceptual systems. It is yet an unsettled question whether there is a non-conscious channel of information processing distinct from a conscious processing system, or whether explicit and implicit perception reflects no more than different levels of experiences of one and the same system.

It is generally believed that in subliminal perception the stimulus is too weak or exposed too briefly to register in consciousness. But then there are cases in which the stimulus is well above perceptual threshold and yet the subject reports no awareness. In such cases we must assume certain subject factors inhibiting access to focal awareness and subjective experience. It is suggested that subjective (conscious) awareness is made possible by the self acting as the agent or experiencer (Kihlstrom et al. 1992). The self, a psychological representation of one's perception of himself or herself, is contained in the working memory as an "organized knowledge structure" and routinely comes into contact with information obtained through regular cognitive activity. Such a contact between the perceived event and the self gives the sense of subjective awareness. However, in cases such as subliminal perception, the sensory information does not enter the working memory and thus makes no contact with the self. Nevertheless, such information may interact with other memory structures and thereby cause phenomena like subliminal perception and implicit memory.

Brian Lancaster (1991) advanced a similar hypothesis. According to Lancaster, when an event is experienced, its representation in memory includes a reference to the self of the experiencing person, which he calls the "I-tag." By making a connection with the I-tag a subsequent recall of the event is effected. In the case of subliminal perception, Lancaster suggests, no connection is made between the self, the "I," and the stimulus information. Consequently, there can be no subjective (conscious) awareness of the stimulus. Whatever is not accessible to the self is unconscious and the subliminal stimulation is not accessible to the self, because the "I" does not connect with the stimulus information. These ideas are consistent with Jung's characterization of focal awareness as ego consciousness, Freud's contention that consciousness is the psychic sense organ that transforms unconscious excitations into conscious experiences, and James' insistence that consciousness is personal.

We should keep in perspective, though, that we sometimes have no subjective awareness even in the presence of strong stimulation well above what is considered normal threshold. In hypnotically induced negative hallucinations, for example, the stimulus is by no means subliminal. Similarly, it has been shown that surgical patients under anesthesia may be aware of what is being said during surgery (Levinson 1965). C. Evans and P.H. Richardson (1988) reported that anaesthetized patients undergoing hysterectomy showed better recovery and required less post-operative stay in the hospital when a tape containing positive and reassuring suggestions was played during surgery, compared to a control group.

SUBLIMINAL MEMORY

Analogous to subliminal perception is the phenomenon of subliminal memory, memory without subjective awareness. Unlike in subliminal perception, the subject in a subliminal memory task has subjective awareness of the stimulus when it occurs. The subject is unable, however, to deliberately recognize or recollect it subjectively. Yet, the effect of the stimulus is seen in the performance of the subject in a manner similar to the influence of subliminal stimuli in subliminal perception studies. For example, subjects tend to show appreciable saving in relearning items that they could neither recall nor recognize (Nelson 1978). Such residual, subliminal memory is known as implicit memory or indirect memory.

Subliminal memory has been investigated primarily with word completion and perceptual identification tasks. In the word completion task, the subject is provided with a word stem such as *ELA-* or *WIN-* and is asked to complete it with the word that first comes to mind. In repetition priming studies, the subjects may read a word, e.g., *ELASTIC*, during the experiment. Later when they are presented with a stem, e.g., *ELA-* and are asked to complete it without any reference to their reading, they are more likely to complete it as *ELASTIC* rather than *ELATED*. Similarly, if the subjects are asked, without any reference to what they had read, to complete *-A-DV-K,* they are more likely to complete it as *AARDVARK* if they had previously read it; (Tulving, Schacter, & Stark 1982). Utilizing a perceptual identification task, Jacoby and Dallas (1981) found that prior study of an item increased the likelihood that it would be identified on a subsequent perceptual task even if the subject were unable to recognize the word as an item in the list.

Similar repetition priming effects were obtained with normal subjects with posthypnotic amnesia (Kihlstrom 1980) and surgical patients under general anesthesia (Kihlstrom and Schacter 1990).

Subliminal Memory in Amnesic Patients: There are a number of studies that show subliminal memory among amnesic patients. It is known that damage to certain midline structures in the brain can lead to serious amnesia in humans, with the result that they are unable to remember their experiences beyond a few seconds. For exam-

ple, a person suffering from amnesia who just solved a jigsaw puzzle is typically unable to remember how she did it. However, when asked to solve the same puzzle the next day, she would solve it faster, suggesting that there is residual memory inaccessible to overt awareness but available enough to facilitate faster relearning of the same task.

Warrington and Weiskrantz (1974) reported a study of patients with anterograde amnesia. Such amnesics cannot remember events occurring after they suffered bilateral damage to the medial temporal lobe, including the hippocampus. These patients in the study were unable to recall or recognize the words in a list that they had read. However, when asked to complete subsequently a word stem, it was observed that they were more likely to complete it when the stem was related to the word they read than when it was not. A comparison of the performance of amnesic patients with control subjects on recognition and stem completion tasks revealed that the normals and amnesics performed at about the same level on the stem completion task, even though the normal subjects did significantly better on recognition tasks.

In a repetition priming study by Schacter (1985), subjects were shown pairs of related words such as "sour-grapes." Later, they were shown just the first word of the pair and were instructed to write down another word that first came to mind. The results showed, as with normal subjects, that the amnesic patients responded with the correct matching words more frequently in the case of pairs that they had studied than with the new ones. What is even more interesting is that when the experimenter presented the word and asked them to explicitly *recall* the matched word in the pair (instead of merely asking them to respond with a word that first came to mind) they did poorly. In other words, when the instructions were to recall the previously studied paired associates, they failed. However, when the instructions did not refer to the prior study, the amnesics gave evidence of the repetition priming effect.

Subliminal memory studies of normal and amnesic subjects revealed several interesting differences between memory when it is subliminal and implicit and when it is explicit and the subject is able to recognize and/or recall (Berry & Dienes 1993). First and foremost, there is no significant correlation between the performance on subliminal memory and explicit memory tests (Hayman & Tulving 1989; Graf & Schacter 1985; Tulving, et al. 1982). Second, priming effects in subliminal memory are less affected by delays of days and months than explicit memory for recognition (Jacoby & Dallas 1981; Tulving et al. 1982). Third, performance on subliminal memory tests is not affected by variations in the study task, which affect performance in explicit memory tests. Fourth, subliminal memory, unlike explicit memory, is adversely influenced by modality shifts (such as a shift from auditory to visual) between learning and testing (Jacoby & Dallas 1981; Graf, Shimamura, & Squire 1985). Finally, as we have noted, amnesics perform successfully on subliminal memory tasks and not on explicit memory tests.

SUBLIMINAL AWARENESS IN BRAIN-DAMAGED SUBJECTS

As in the case of the amnesic syndrome, brain-damaged patients show a variety of deficiencies of awareness, depending on the location and severity of the damage. The deficiencies include inability to see objects falling in the damaged visual field, failure to recognize familiar faces, and disruption in reading ability. There is, however, evidence to show that when such a perceptual loss occurs at the explicit level of subjective awareness, some patients continue to retain the ability to have implicit or sub-

liminal awareness in a manner similar to what we have noted with amnesics.

Blindsight: It has been observed that some people who are cortically blind because of damage to primary visual areas (striate cortex) can respond discriminatively to different stimuli, even though they report no subjective awareness of the stimuli. Lawrence Weiskrantz, among others, carried out extensive investigations of such people and called the phenomenon blindsight.

Complete or near complete loss of vision in one visual field due to damage to the contralateral striate is called hemianopia. D.B., one of the patients extensively investigated by Weiskrantz, had left hemianopia consequent to the removal of a tumor from the right visual cortex. D.B. was neither able to name nor describe any object that was presented to his left visual field. However, when he was asked to guess in one study whether the stimulus was "x" or "o," D.B. guessed correctly in 27 of 30 trials, suggesting that his ability to discriminate between the two stimuli was indeed preserved despite the lack of subjective awareness that he could do so. Other studies revealed that D.B. could correctly point to stimulus location, detect movements and discriminate between vertical and horizontal lines (Weiskrantz 1986).

Blindsight is also tested by using *indirect* methods (without forced-choice guessing) by taking advantage of bilateral interaction of the visual fields. For example, in a visual completion test, when a circle was flashed centered on the fixation point, the hemianopia patient responded that he saw the full circle even though the right half of the circle fell in the damaged field. When only the left half of the circle was flashed, he responded seeing a half circle; and when the right half was flashed he reported seeing nothing (Torjussen 1978). In a study by Marzi et al. (1986), it was found that hemianopia subjects, like normal subjects, responded faster in a reaction time task in which two stimuli instead of one were presented, even when the second stimulus fell in the damaged field.

Whereas the phenomenon of blindsight is adequately demonstrated in several studies, the mechanism of blindsight has not been decisively established. Some researchers have argued that blindsight is no different from normal vision in that they are both mediated by the primary visual cortex and that blindsight is a degraded version of normal vision (Champion, Latto, & Smith 1983). This, however, is a minority view and does not adequately account for all the available empirical data. A number of studies (Kentridge et al., 1999) have shown that blindsight and degraded normal vision are qualitatively different. For example, there are data indicating that in some cases of blindsight the stimulus detection is better in the damaged area than in the intact area, suggesting that the visual response in some respects is not degraded at all. As Martha J. Farah (1997) notes, "although some dissociations between visual performance and subjective awareness may be mediated by spared primary visual cortex, it seems fairly clear that the range of abilities documented in blindsight does not result from degraded normal vision…"(p. 210).

Blindsight is considered to be of special significance to philosophy of mind because of the apparent dissociation between experience and awareness, that one may have access to visual information without having a visual experience of it. There is now evidence that some blindsight patients may have conscious awareness of moving stimuli (Weiskrantz et al. 1995). That is, however, not considered sufficient to discredit the dissociation hypothesis. R.W. Kentridge and C.A. Heywood (1999) have argued persuasively that there is still good evidence for the dissociation hypothesis. They "conclude that the status of blindsight

as an example of the dissociability between access to visual information and phenomenal consciousness remains intact" (p. 10). (For an informative series of papers on blindsight, see the special issues of the *Journal of Consciousness Studies*, 6 (5), 1999.

Covert Awareness in Prosopagnosia: Prosopagnosia is a kind of memory disorder following brain damage, where the patients report no sense of familiarity for faces and appear to lack any subjective awareness of recognition for faces of people, including their own family members. In some cases the patients not only claim a lack of subjective awareness, but their performance on standard face recognition tests also shows the loss of their ability to recognize faces. However, it can be seen by some indirect measures that the face recognition is preserved to a degree.

In a study by R. M. Bauer (1984), a prosopagnosia patient was shown photographs of familiar faces. While the subject was viewing a photograph, he heard a list of names read aloud, which included the name of the person in the photograph. Simultaneously the patient's skin conductance responses (SCRs) were monitored. The results showed that while the patient was unable to select the correct names to the photographs of familiar faces, his SCRs significantly correlated with familiar faces. Elevated SCRs were also found with normal subjects when they heard the name of the person in the photograph. In two other studies by Tranel and Damasio (1985) and Tranel, Damasio and Damasio (1988), it was observed that the patients' SCRs to familiar faces were higher than their SCRs to unfamiliar faces, even though their ratings of familiarity did not differ significantly between familiar and unfamiliar faces. When asked to match simultaneously presented pairs of faces, a prosopagnosic patient was found to match familiar faces faster than unfamiliar faces (de Haan, Young & Newcomb 1987).

It is clear that prosopagnosic subjects, though unable to overtly recognize familiar faces, have implicit awareness of them. There is thus dissociation between their introspective reports, as well as their manifest inability to succeed on standard face recognition tests on the one hand and their performance on tacit (indirect) recognition tasks on the other. If there is dissociation between overt and covert recognition of faces, what is it due to? As in the case of blindsight, explanations for the covert recognition of faces by prosopagnosic subjects are controversial. Some (de Haan, Bauer, & Greve 1992) have favored the view that the face recognition system as such is intact but there is a disconnection between it and other brain mechanisms necessary for subjective awareness of recognition. Some researchers have suggested that there are two neural systems capable of face recognition, but only one of them (ventral cortical visual areas) is capable of giving subjective awareness of recognition, whereas the other (dorsal visual areas) is capable of visual recognition without subjective awareness (Bauer 1984). Farah (1997) has argued, however, that the difference between overt and covert face recognition is simply the quality of representations activated by the face, and that the residual processing capabilities of the damaged brain may be sufficient to facilitate covert recognition.

Subliminal Awareness in Unilateral Neglect: Neglect is a disorder of space perception following damage to the posterior parietal lobe, usually the right parietal lobe. Neglect patients report no subjective awareness of stimuli occurring on the side of space contralateral to the damaged area. If asked to draw a scene, the neglect patient with right parietal lobe damage will only draw the right side of the scene; if asked to bisect a line, he will do so to the right of the center. The behavior and the subjective reports of neglect patients lead us to the conclusion

that they do not perceive neglected stimuli. There is, however, significant evidence to suggest that the patients do indeed possess considerable information about the neglected stimuli.

In one study, Volpe, Le Doux and Gazzaniga (1979) presented 4 neglect patients with right parietal damage pairs of visual stimuli (drawings and three letter words), one to the right and the other to the left visual field. When asked to state whether the stimuli are the same or different, they were correct most of the time (88–100 percent) in their responses. However, when asked to name the stimuli, they were unable to identify the stimuli on the left.

In a dramatic demonstration of neglect, Marshall and Halligan (1988) presented to a patient two line drawings of a house, one above the other. The two drawings are identical except that one of them has flames coming out from the left side of the house. The patient claimed that she saw no difference between the two houses. However, when asked to indicate which of the two houses she would prefer to live in, she chose repeatedly the house with no flames. A further study by E. Bisiach and L. L. Rusconi (1990) did not replicate this finding. There was, however, convincing evidence that the patients did possess information about the stimuli falling in the neglected areas.

Hemineglect is considered by some as a disorder of attention. Even though the neglected stimuli are potentially available to subjective awareness, the attention, it is suggested, is systematically turned away from it. Those who postulate separate systems for conscious and unconscious processing see "a breakdown in the flow of information between conscious and non-conscious mental systems" (Volpe, Le Doux, & Gazzaniga 1979). M. Kinsbourne (1988), however, sees no such blockage. Instead he argues that neglect weakens or degrades the representation of the stimulus to a degree that it fails to generate integration among different neural systems, which is necessary to cause subjective awareness of the stimulus.

SUBLIMINAL AWARENESS AND COMMISSUROTOMY

Commissurotomy is surgical cutting of the corpus callosum, which connects the two hemispheres of the brain and is necessary for communication between them. Commissurotomy is sometimes performed to control severe seizures in intractable epilepsy. Extensive studies of commissurotomy (split-brain) patients by Roger Sperry and Michael Gazzaniga, among others, has shown some very interesting psychological effects bearing on consciousness. In a typical tachistoscopic testing of the split-brain subject, a picture is projected to either the right or the left side of the screen while the subject focuses on a dot at the center of screen. If the projected picture falls in the right visual field, the subject is able to identify it correctly; because of contralateral organization of the cortex, it is accessible to the left hemisphere. However, if the same picture is projected to fall in the left visual field, not only is the subject unable to identify it, she reports that she saw "nothing." In one experimental set-up there were several objects hidden on the shelf under the screen of the tachistiscope, which the subject could reach without being able to see them. When the subject was asked to feel with the left hand the objects which were visually hidden from her, she was able to pick the object that matched the projected picture on the screen, even when the picture was projected to fall in the left visual hemisphere (Gazzaniga 1970). It is clear from this that the right hemisphere of this patient was able to process the visual images and had awareness of them, but was unable to verbally identify them because it lacked the necessary verbal skills. In other words, the right hemisphere can have implicit awareness of an object even when it does not have subjective or explicit awareness of it.

In another study with a female subject, when a picture of a nude female was projected to the left visual field the subject blushed as if she was embarrassed, even though she reported that she saw nothing but a flash of light. On further questioning why she had laughed she remarked, "Oh Dr. Sperry, that's some machine you have!" It is reasonable to assume from the emotional reaction of the subject that she was indeed aware of the picture. Her right hemisphere had not only recognized the picture but also triggered the autonomic response to it. Since the right hemisphere did not possess the necessary verbal skills, she was unable to recognize and name the picture. The left hemisphere of course did not have any awareness of the picture; but in the remark about the machine we can notice that it is attempting to interpret, rationalize, and make sense of the emotional response.

Now, we may ask whether the above findings imply that there are two centers of consciousness within the same brain, one in each hemisphere, since both the hemispheres are capable of becoming aware of the objects presented to them. Again, there is sufficient evidence to suggest the superiority of one hemisphere over the other in a particular kind of task. For example, it is generally agreed that the *left* hemisphere of right-handed people is superior to the *right* hemisphere in verbal skills, whereas the latter has superiority for nonverbal, especially visuo-spatial tasks. Since subjective awareness and reportability are linked to linguistic skills in which the left hemisphere excels, is it reasonable to associate consciousness with left hemisphere activity alone? The answers of the researchers in this field vary depending on their own assumptions as to what constitutes consciousness.

Gazzaniga suggests that consciousness is associated with left hemispheric activity, especially the interpreter system. "Consciousness in my scheme of brain events," writes Gazzaniga (1985), "becomes the output of the left brain's interpreter and these products are reported and refined by the human language system" (p. 135). John Eccles regards the left hemisphere as the seat of consciousness for a different reason. Eccles postulates the existence of an immaterial entity, the self-conscious mind, which alone has subjective experiences. The left hemisphere, with its prefrontal lobe and the linguistic circuits of the temporal lobe, constitutes what Eccles calls the "liaison cortex" that transmits the knowledge of the self-conscious mind.

Roger Sperry, however, is inclined to credit both hemispheres with consciousness. Taking intelligent behavior involved in all flexible thought processes as an acceptable criterion of consciousness, Sperry (1984) favors the notion of dual consciousness in cases of unconnected and undamaged independent hemispheres. He observed that the mental performances of the right hemisphere after commissurotomy are "superior and dominant to that of the speaking hemisphere in a series of nonverbal, largely spatial tests." In the light of such superior performance, Sperry concludes, "one finds it most difficult to think of this half of the brain as being only an automaton lacking in conscious awareness" (p. 666). In fact, there is evidence to suggest that at least some split-brain patients may show linguistic abilities in the right hemisphere as well (Zaidel 1976). All these facts, however, do not warrant the conclusion that there are two distinct entities inhabiting the same body or that there are two self-contained conscious processing systems in the brain. In day-to-day activities, the commissurotomy patients do not behave as if they have two minds. Instances of one hemisphere working in opposition to the other (such as conflict between the right and the left hand) are exceptions and not common phenomenon among split-brain patients. Consider-

ing the extraordinary coordination between and complimentary processing of the two hemispheres in normal people, any generalizations from split-brain research that postulate dual consciousness is premature. The most we can say at this time is that both hemispheres have access to awareness.

FUNCTIONAL BLINDNESS AND HYPNOTIC PHENOMENA

Implicit awareness as implied in blindsight and subliminal memory is not limited to cases where there are cortical defects. Similar phenomena are reported to occur even in the absence of any damage to brain structures, e.g., functional blindness and hypnotically induced negative hallucinations. Pierre Janet, the French pioneer of psychodynamic psychiatry, reported that hysterical patients reporting blindness or deafness gave evidence suggesting that they were able to see and hear despite their claims to the contrary. He concluded that in cases of hysterical blindness what is affected are "attentive" perceptions while the elementary sensations remain intact (Janet 1907). Janet rejected the notion that the hysterical patients who claim to be blind or deaf are merely pretending and simulating their insensibility and argued that there is genuine dissociation between the subconscious sensations and focal awareness. Since Janet's time, a number of studies of conversion disorders (hysteria) involving self-reports of blindness or deafness have been carried out (e.g., Hilgard & Marquis 1940; Brady & Lind 1961; Grosz & Zimmerman 1970; Bryant & McConkey 1990), but the controversy continues whether or not the patients reporting functional blindness was merely malingering.

An analogous situation prevails even in the more rigorously investigated area of hypnotically induced perceptual distortions, positive and negative hallucinations, and analgesia. It is now well established that about 10 to 15 percent of the population who are highly hypnotizable may be rendered insensitive to painful stimulus by hypnotic suggestion (Hilgard & Hilgard 1983). Also, striking perceptual changes, such as reports of "seeing" things that are not visually present and of not seeing things that are actually there, are observed following hypnotic suggestion (Kihlstrom 1979, 1984). Interestingly, psychophysiological measurements of subjects in whom analgesia was induced by means of hypnotic suggestion showed that the subjects were responding to the painful stimulus, suggesting that some kind of perceptual processing occurred even though the subjects report no awareness. Further evidence that the subjects have in fact registered the stimulus comes from the so-called "hidden observer" studies. When the analgesic subjects under hypnosis were given the suggestion that there was a part hidden in them that could recall the true level of pain, some of them were able to report pain at levels comparable to those obtained in the waking condition (Hilgard 1986). Thus there can be little doubt that the stimulus was indeed processed even though the analgesic hypnotic subject denied any awareness of the stimulus. It is arguable, however, whether the disparity between the subject's report of no pain and the contrary evidence of stimulus impact as measured by the psychophysiological measures or the "hidden observer" recovery of the memory of the experience of pain is sufficient evidence for the existence of two distinct streams or levels of perceptual processing. N. P. Spanos, B. Jones and A. Malfara (1982), for example, argue that hypnotic deafness is no more than the subject reporting incorrectly the perceptual experience following the hypnotic suggestion and that such cases do not establish dissociation between two perceptual processes.

Pathological Awareness

So far we have discussed how awareness may be constrained by injury or insult to the brain, by masked stimuli and stimuli present at low energy levels, and by hypnotic, anesthetic and other interventions. The constraint is primarily one of losing subjective awareness of certain perceptions and memories. The studies reviewed demonstrate some kind of dissociation between subjective experience and awareness in that the subjects may be aware even when they have no subjective experience of such awareness. Paradoxical awareness as in subliminal perception or blindsight is not dysfunctional; but pathological awareness is. Hallucinatory awareness, for example, may be dysfunctional inasmuch as it is a misleading representation that may give rise to inappropriate responses.

Subliminal perception, implicit memory, and blindsight do not by themselves constitute abnormality of consciousness, whereas a hallucinatory vision or a delusional thought is an abnormality. The dream experience, though hallucinatory, is considered normal because we assume certain relationships between types of processing and wakefulness. We infer abnormalities of consciousness when a type of processing appears incompatible with the associated level of wakefulness. Such incompatibilities play a role in the psychiatric description and evaluation of patients. Pathologies of consciousness resulting from inappropriate processing may be seen as more than useful descriptors of psychiatric disorders. They may be helpful in understanding and explaining certain mental disorders in terms of disconnection, dissociation, or conflation between different levels of processing awareness. For this reason, the taxonomy of possible pathologies of consciousness constructed out of psychophysiological factors associated with awareness could prove beneficial.

In cases of clouding of consciousness such as amentia, a subacute delirious state in which the patient engages in haphazard associations and random performance of old habits and shows total lack of thought, it is reasonable to suppose a dysfunctional higher-order conscious system. The failure of such a system to control the thought processes and link the automatic actions and associations together may explain the clouding of consciousness in its various forms.

Again, we find among schizophrenic patients hallucinations, (usually in the form of hearing voices), delusions (often involving claims by patients that their thoughts are controlled from outside), and thought disorders (seen in fluent but abnormal speech which makes little sense). These symptoms are sometimes attributed to abnormal processes. They may be seen also as abnormal perceptions. It is often suggested that the schizophrenic suffers from a defective filter such that the patient is overwhelmed by excessive stimulation and is no longer able to separate the relevant from the irrelevant stimuli. It is equally plausible to argue that schizophrenic symptoms constitute abnormal perceptions. It may be seen in the schizophrenic patient that the screen separating explicit and the implicit awareness, with or without subjective experience, may become defective, with the result that the patient may attend to automatic processes and normally opaque and hidden thoughts and images. Such a situation slows one down and makes response selection more difficult and less fluent. Paying attention to trivial events, which would normally have been unnoticed, may lead people to read new and hidden meanings into events and become delusional. Again, failure to focus on one meaning to the exclusion of the alternative meanings of words may result in thought disorders.

Implicit and explicit awareness may have different functional roles. We are structurally constrained to have at any given moment subjective access to a very limited amount of information imbedded in the vast surround of awareness. There are mechanisms in place that allow this to happen. Defects in these mechanisms may block access to available information as in blindsight, or provide uncontrolled subjective access to normally inaccessible information resulting in "buzzing chaos" of thought and behavior. Therefore, it is for a good reason that subjective awareness is such a limited capacity and that much of mentation is implicit and non-conscious.

DISSOCIATION AND MULTIPLE PERSONALITY DISORDER

Dissociative disorders, such as multiple personality disorder, are a clear example of dysfunctional awareness. Dissociation implies discontinuities and disunity in the stream of consciousness. Dissociative states are not necessarily pathological. As we observed, paradoxical awareness provides pervasive evidence that awareness and its awareness may be dissociated. Injury or insult to the brain may bring about such dissociation. Also, certain stimulus conditions, e.g., subliminal exposure, may result in awareness without awareness. Hypnotic phenomena like analgesia and negative hallucinations suggest that dissociation between awareness and sensitivity to it may be manipulated by external interventions. Over learned habits such as driving may also involve dissociation; we may pass cars and change lanes without being subjectively aware of these acts. Insensitivity to pain when fully absorbed in another activity like watching a movie thriller is an instance of dissociation. In a sense, items in perceptual periphery, which we do not experience but could be recovered under suitable circumstances, may be considered dissociative phenomena. According to some, several instances of forgetting may be cases of dissociation. It may be argued that some degree of dissociation may be required to concentrate and focus attention in an intense way.

It follows from the above that dissociation itself is not a pathological state, but a natural process. C. A. Ross (1989) states, "dissociation is an ongoing dynamic process in the normal psyche" (p. 87). It may lead to a variety of states that range from simple, trivial and mundane adaptive forms to complex, idiosyncratic and profoundly maladaptive states like fugue and multiple personality disorder (MPD). As Stephen Braude (1995) points out, what dissociation does is that it erects a barrier between mental states. Though subjectively hidden or psychologically isolated, a dissociated experience or mental state is not obliterated but only banished from the main stream. It is so because a dissociated experience is potentially retrievable.

Pierre Janet, who is generally regarded by historians of psychology as the originator of the concept of dissociation, held a different view. He regarded dissociation as a phenomenon of psychopathology. He thought that it arose from a failure to integrate and maintain unity of consciousness. Also, dissociated states were considered earlier to be isolated and autonomous from and noninterfering with each other. Dissociated mental states in some cases appear, however, to overlap or have common elements (Braude 1995). *Diagnostic and Statistical Manual of Mental Disorders* (3rd edition, revised, DSM-III-R) describes dissociation as a "disturbance or alteration in the normally integrative function of identity, memory or consciousness."

Dissociation suggests, then, that the conscious stream is not always continuous and unified. There may be discontinuities and breaks, which are not necessarily pathological. They may in some cases be quite adaptive and serve as natural defenses against disturbing things. In extreme forms, however, dissociation is clearly worrisome and dysfunctional. Janet (1907/1920) at-

tempted to explain personality disorders in terms of dissociation and deep divisions of consciousness. In DSM-III (1980) multiple personality is listed as a separate disorder (MPD) under the general category of "dissociative disorders." We find a change in DSM-IV. Multiple personality disorder is replaced by dissociative identity disorder (DID). The change seems to reflect no more than some conceptual concerns with the term "personality." The diagnostic criteria for MPD and DID are quite similar. There are four suggested criteria for diagnosing DID. (1) Two or more distinct identities exist in the person. (2) They recurrently control the behavior of the person. (3) The person is unable to recall important personal information too extensive to be attributed to normal forgetting. (4). The condition is not due to physiological effects of substance use or general medication.

MPD subjects tend to be highly hypnotizable. Very often, they are victims of abuse as children. In 75 percent of the MPD cases, child personalities under the age of 12 manifest as alternates. According to surveys, the average range of multiples in MPD subjects is between 6 and 16. Some reported cases exhibit 100 or more distinct identities. In some instances, alternate personalities claim continuing existence even when not in control of subject's body. There is evidence suggesting that an alternate may influence behavior and experience subjective states when not in executive control. It is observed that earlier the trauma in the developmental process of the child, the more likely it is that that dissociation would result in MPD. Any significant trauma after the major developmental stages are completed tends to manifest less drastic forms of dissociation like hysterical amnesia and fugue states (Braude 1995)

Stephen Braude's book, *First Person Plural*, is an important contribution to the literature on the philosophy of mind in the context of multiple personality. In it Braude provides an incisive analysis of the concepts "dissociation" and "multiple personality." He points out that the crucial difference between MPD and other forms of strong dissociation is that each of the alternate personalities in MPD has a distinctive "apperceptive center." By apperceptive center Braude means a reference point characterized by autobiographical states, which are also indexical, i.e., the subject believes that these states are her own. "Whereas multiples seem to have more than one distinctive apperceptive center at a time, this does not seem to be the case for other strong forms of dissociation" (Braude 1995, pp. 78–79) such as the hidden observer in hypnotized subjects. The autobiographical states include the usual mental phenomena like perceptions, thoughts, memories, beliefs, desires, and dispositions. An apperceptive center is assumed when these states are indexical, that is, they have self-reference. In other words, they are first-person experiences. In the case of hypnotic analgesia, for example, the hidden observer has the experience of pain, which the hypnotized subject does not have. This means that the pain state is not autobiographical to the hypnotized subject but only to the hidden observer, even though the pain state is indexical to both. This kind of asymmetry characterizes non–MPD forms of dissociation.

Dissociative phenomena in general and MPD cases in particular suggest that autobiographical states may not be indexical and vice versa. Nonindexical awareness lacks self-reference. It is more like the third–person observation and less like a first-person experience. In a normal person, the successive mental states are "autobiographically and indexically continuous" whereas in the case of multiple personality they appear to be autographically and indexically discontinuous. Such discontinuities suggest, according to Braude, the existence of more than one conscious entity existing in one body. An alternate personality, who appears

to be aware of some mental states of another alter, refers to them as "his" or "hers" and not as "mine." In other words, in a multiple, the alternate personalities observe each other as a normal person would other individuals from the perspective of an outsider.

Does it follow from the above that each distinctive apperceptive center is a separate mind/self? Does the MPD patient have more than one mind? The answer depends on that we mean by mind or self. In Braude's view, despite the split and divisions of the conscious stream of a multiple, there is an underlying unity at a deeper level. Citing the observation of K. V. Wilkes (1988), Braude argues that we may not postulate the existence of multiple minds "on the grounds of mental disunity and discontinuity" (1995, p. 165). Dreamless sleep, memory gaps and the hidden observer phenomena, for example, imply discontinuities that do not warrant any supposition of multiple minds. Recall also that, though alternate personalities indicate deep divisions of consciousness in some areas, they tend to overlap each other in important respects and share with each other linguistic skills and some idiosyncrasies. Such overlaps and common qualities between alters, Braude points out, signify the existence of a "single underlying synthesizing self." The functional and adaptive aspects of dissociation make sense only as the working of a unifying self or mind. Braude writes: "it seems compelling to appeal to an underlying synthesizing subject who simply evolves into a multiple as a complex and creative response to various life situations" (1995, p. 173).

Primary awareness in normal individuals appears to be continuous and unified. It is subjective and has self-reference. Humans have a capacity to break that continuity and unity in various forms of dissociation. These forms range from simple, normal adaptive responses to complex and profoundly maladaptive states. The latter signify dissociation disorders of consciousness. Multiple personality disorder is an extreme form of such dissociation.

Consciousness and the Unconscious

Once we accept that paradoxical or implicit awareness is a species of awareness, consciousness and unconscious phenomena may no longer be seen in opposition to each other. Also, the characteristics we have associated with primary awareness need not be generalized and attributed to other forms or awareness. Implicit awareness is not only unavailable to introspection, but it also does not share several other characteristics of felt awareness. As pointed out by Baars and McGovern (1994), "consciousness [subjective awareness] is serial, *limited in capacity and internally consistent*, while unconscious processes may operate in parallel, have *very great capacity* when taken together, and allow for the coexistence of mutually *inconsistent* representations" (pp. 690–691, emphasis in the original). Thus, primary awareness, with its attribute of subjectivity, flows like a "stream," coherent and continuous, whereas paradoxical awareness lacks such order and unity.

It would be unproductive, however, to regard primary awareness available to introspection and implicit awareness as two different domains. To quote Baars and McGovern (1994) again, "Conscious and unconscious processes cannot be even conceptualized *as such* if they are kept entirely separate. Further, there is robust evidence for the closest imaginable interplay between conscious and unconscious events at all times" (p. 694). The unconscious events are of two sorts, as suggested in the previous section. In the psychoanalytic tradition, they refer to those items of experience that are inaccessible to introspection but in principle could be brought into awareness with some effort and discipline. The unconscious mental processes postulated by the cognitive theorists, however, are in principle inaccessible to awareness. In other words, the processes that are believed to be involved in our cognitive behavior are themselves unconscious and unavailable for introspection. This situation has led some cognitive theorists to postulate a computational mind capable of unconscious symbolic computations. The computational mind is thus distinguished from the phenomenological mind, which has conscious cognitive experience (Jackendoff 1987).

Neurophysiological Basis of the Unconscious

Viewing consciousness and the unconscious from the perspective of explicit and implicit awareness, several observations may be made. First and foremost, availability to introspection is not a necessary characteristic of awareness. John Searle (1992), who correctly questions any intrinsic relationship between introspection and consciousness, however, suggests that "accessibility to consciousness" is a necessary attribute of all conscious events whether or not they are currently available to introspection. Accessibility here means the possibility of focal awareness. In other words, according to Searle, there can be no conscious events that are in principle inaccessible to subjective experience, and conversely that no events that are potentially incapable of focal awareness may ever be regarded as conscious. Consequently, in this view, the physiological processes in the brain that may be involved in generating awareness may not be regarded ipso facto as mental unless they satisfy the other essential characteristics of consciousness.

Two questions arise from this notion. First, what is the ontology of the unconscious events referred to as implicit awareness, such as repressed memories and subliminal awareness? Searle locates the ontology in the purely neurophysiological phenomena that are capable of causing subjective conscious experience. In other words, underlying all conscious events there are corresponding neurophysiological states and processes that are capable of generating states of awareness. However, circumstances may arise that prevent the manifestation of subjective awareness in a manner that makes awareness available to introspection. In such a situation what we have is unconscious awareness, awareness that is not focal and explicit.

The second question is, if the neurophysiological events in the brain are the basis for the unconscious what then is the nature of unconscious mentation? Searle finds it in unconscious intentionality. He points out that unconscious intentionality refers to "*a latency relative to its manifestation in consciousness*" (1992, p. 161). The unconscious intentional state is the potential cause of focal awareness. It is of such nature that it "*can be brought to consciousness because its ontology is that of neurophysiology characterized in terms of capacity to cause consciousness*" (p. 160, original emphasis).

The reason for Searle to equate the unconscious at the ontological level with neurophysiological processes in the brain rests on the following assumptions. (1) Intentionality is the defining characteristic of the mind. (2) The mind is comprised of both the conscious and the unconscious. (3) Consciousness is limited to focal awareness. It follows, then, that we must assume unconscious intentionality to account for unconscious mental events. Since the source of all awareness is the brain, we must look in the brain to find unconscious intentionality. So Searle argues: "There is nothing going on in my brain but neurophysiological processes, some conscious, some unconscious. Of the unconscious neurophysiological processes, some are mental and some are not. The difference between them is not in con-

sciousness, by hypothesis, neither is conscious; the difference is that the mental processes are candidates for consciousness, because they are capable of causing conscious states" (1992, pp. 161–162).

Let us consider briefly some of the neurophysiological aspects of awareness that may give us an understanding of the neurological basis for implicit awareness. Following a presentation of a stimulus such as a flash of light, a change in the electrical activity of the brain cells occurs. A peripheral sensory stimulus normally elicits a large electrophysiological response, called a primary evoked potential, which begins at about 20 ms after a stimulus is applied and lasts about 50 to 100 ms. A primary evoked potential is normally accompanied by later event-related potentials. Among these is the P300 wave, which is a positive deflection and occurs about 300ms after the stimulus presentation. It is, in a sense, a late comer, because there is electrical activity preceding it. Its latency suggests that it is the result of a later stage of information processing, possibly suggesting that the subject is evaluating the stimulus.

Primary evoked potentials can be elicited without eliciting later-event related potentials by applying a single stimulus pulse to the somatosensory pathway in the brain. The same thing also happens when the intensity of the stimulus is below the threshold of sensory awareness. It is observed that stimulus durations of up to 500ms are required in the cerebral sensory system to produce a sensation. If the stimulus intensity is below the threshold or the duration of the neural response of the cerebral cortex is less than about 500ms, the subject reports no subjective awareness of the stimulus. A single stimulus pulse, however, may cause a prolonged train of neural responses to elicit a sensation, which the subject may become aware of (Libet 1993).

In a study by Libet et al. (1967), an electrical stimulation to the skin, which varied from an intensity that was felt (supraliminal) to one that was too faint to be recognized (subliminal), was applied to subjects. A comparison of the evoked electrical responses to the two kinds of stimuli revealed that the late components of the evoked response were suppressed in the subliminal stimulation condition. It is suggested that conscious experience (focal awareness) is thus related to the late components of the evoked response. Donchin et al. (1983) also point out that the presence of the late components represented by the wave is an indication that the subject is conscious (focally aware) of the information relative to the eliciting stimulus.

Similar findings of suppression of the late components of evoked responses were reported in the case of subjects under anesthesia who were exposed to auditory stimuli (Pickton & Hillyard 1974), and hypnotized subjects (Spiegel et al. 1985). In the latter study, subjects under hypnosis, who were watching a colored grid flashing on and off on a screen, were given a suggestion that they would see a cardboard box obscuring their vision of the screen when in fact there was no cardboard box to see. At the same time, the experimenters monitored the visual evoked response as the subjects watched the screen with the colored grid flashing on and off. It was observed that the highly hypnotizable subjects tended to suppress the later components of the evoked response in a manner similar to the findings of Libet et al. in the case of subliminal perception. The early components of the evoked response were again relatively unaffected.

Now, what are the implications of these findings for our understanding of the unconscious? It is obvious that the sensory input is processed in various stages, possibly by several processors working in parallel, and that suppression, distortion or simple absence of processing in one stage or in one processor may result in systematic changes in the information reaching us.

When processing at the later stages does not take place, as indicated by the blocking of the late components of the evoked response, information relative to the input remains unconscious. This may be because of cortical defects or manipulations such as anesthesia or hypnotic suggestion, or because of the low intensity of the input, psychological repression, fatigue, or lack of necessary attention. Thus, on the assumption that the brain processes correlate with evoked responses monitored from the brain in a meaningful way, there is a reasonable case for looking for the ontology of conscious and unconscious experiences in the neurophysiological events in the brain.

Now, accepting that the electrical activity and the late components of the evoked response in the cerebral cortex are correlated with the subjective experience of awareness, can we move on to find appropriate explanations of non-conscious mentation and a firm neuroanatomical basis for subjective awareness? As may be seen from some of the explanations of blindsight and hemineglect we discussed, there are three broad types of approaches in neuropsychology to relate subjective experience to brain states. One approach is to conceive of particular brain systems as mediating subjective awareness; another is to suggest that subjective awareness is not an outcome of the activity of particular brain systems, but of integration among different neural systems. The third approach associates subjective awareness with the "higher-quality end of the continuum of degrees of representations" involved in information processing (Farah 1997).

The first approach is seen in Daniel Schacter's (1989) DICE (Dissociated Interactions and Conscious Experience) model. Schacter postulates a cognitive module, labeled as the conscious awareness system (CAS), which mediates subjective awareness. The CAS is separate from the brain systems associated with different cognitive activities, which are called knowledge modules. It is also different from the executive system, which makes decisions and initiates actions. The CAS is a monitoring system, which on the one hand integrates and relates information from different knowledge modules and provides on the other hand inputs to the executive system whose outputs it in turn receives. The CAS also constructs a "global data base" for sharing information between modules. When the CAS is disconnected from other brain systems mediating perception and memory, those perceptions and memories remain implicit. Thus implicit memory and subliminal perception are understood in terms of disconnections between the CAS and the memory and perceptual systems. For instance, the failure to subjectively recognize familiar faces by prosopagnosics is due to a disconnection between the CAS and the facial knowledge module. Schacter believes that the neuroanatomical basis for the CAS is in the posterior cerebrum, involving the lower parietal lobes and the cingulate area in the posterior corpus callosum. The lower parietal lobes are known to receive inputs of highly processed perceptual information, whereas lesions in the cingulate area are associated with thought disorders and breakdown of selective attention.

Similar to Schacter's view is the one advocated by Gazzaniga (1988). Gazzaniga attributes to the interpreter mechanisms in the left hemisphere the task of mediating subjective awareness. On this view, implicit awareness may be accounted for in terms of the failure of representations to access critical areas of the left hemisphere, which houses the interpreter mechanisms and language skills.

The second approach is represented by the integrated field theory (also known as multiple drafts theory) of Marcel Kinsbourne (1988), according to which subjective awareness is not the property of particular neural systems, but rather a state of integration among different systems in the brain. Various modality-specific perceptions, memories, action plans and so on arising from disparate brain systems interact to bring about a mutually consistent and integrated state. This state is continually revised and upgraded to reflect all the information available in different parts of the brain. "All perceptual operations, and indeed all operations of thought and action, are accomplished by multitrack processes of interpretation and elaboration that occur over hundreds of milliseconds, during which time various additions, incorporations, emendations, and over-writings of content can occur, in various orders" (Dennett & Kinsbourne 1997, p. 144). It is possible, however, because of damage to one or more brain systems as in prosopagnosia or neglect, that normal integration of the output of the different systems involved may be weakened or disrupted, thus preventing the updating of the contents of awareness. Consequently, the person lacks subjective awareness of the information that fails to be incorporated into the integrated state. Absence of subjective awareness of a perception is thus a result of the failure on the part of the perceptual system to participate in the integrating activities of the rest of the brain. In a similar vein, Francis Crick and Christof Koch (1997) suggest that firing of relevant neurons in semi-synchrony at a frequency in the range of 40–70 Hz enables both integration and subjective awareness of the stimuli by activating the appropriate parts of the working memory.

The third approach draws its support from the fact that information in neural networks is not represented in an all-or-none fashion. The information may be represented partially or in a degraded manner. If the quality of a representation does not reach certain levels of clarity and intensity, then that representation may lack subjective awareness. For example, as we have noted, in subliminal perception experiments the subliminal stimuli are degraded either by presenting them at low energy levels, by suitably masking them, or by dividing the attention of the subject. When a representation is thus rendered low in quality, it may not arouse subjective awareness. Following David Armstrong (1984), one could argue that subjective awareness arises from scanning the neural representations in the brain. When these representations are too weak to be scanned, we have no subjective awareness of them.

On a closer examination, however, one wonders whether the above observations are any more compelling than simple commonsense that the person in a coma is unconscious and that injury to the brain alters one's conscious experience. No one denies that conscious experience in the human condition depends decisively on cortical processes. The real question is, are they sufficient to account for all of conscious experience?

Schacter's model is admittedly speculative. We need to have more evidence in support of the conscious awareness system before we can take it more seriously. Dennett, among others, has raised pertinent doubts as to why we may look with skepticism at any view that attempts to find a role for any functional center in the brain that modulates subjective awareness. The multiple drafts theory advocated by Dennett and Kinsbourne may have some merit in that awareness may be an outcome of integration among different brain systems instead of being the property of particular cortical systems, but the theory itself has little to say about subjective awareness as such. Damage to a brain system or a disconnection between systems may indeed be responsible for the loss of information associated with particular systems, but they do not explain in any adequate measure the absence of subjective experience alone. In fact, most functional and reductionist accounts of consciousness end up either leaving out

subjective experience or denying it altogether.

Those who are unconvinced that brain processes can in principle account for all conscious experience find hardly compelling any of the theories or models we have discussed as appropriate explanations of subjective awareness. The very fact that volition, either self-generated or initiated by suggestion is capable of causing changes in the physiological states of the brain may indicate its primacy over the brain processes in causing conscious experience. Whether volition itself can be explained satisfactorily as an essential cortical phenomenon is a different matter.

Summary

Nonintrospective awareness is implied in a variety of mental phenomena such as subliminal perception, implicit memory and blindsight. There may be significant differences in the way paradoxical awareness is processed, for example, between subliminal perception and blindsight, but a commonality that binds them all is that they are not experienced; they lack subjective awareness. It is a legitimate question whether the phenomena of paradoxical awareness should be regarded as a conscious phenomenon at all. If consciousness is seen as awareness, as we have, paradoxical awareness may be properly termed as one category of conscious phenomena. If, on the contrary, we restrict the usage of consciousness to subjective awareness, paradoxical awareness is out of the bounds of consciousness. The latter usage severely restricts the connotation of consciousness and renders it a mere subjective quality of experience. Subjective awareness is not only subjective but also awareness; and the latter needs an explanation.

Flanagan (1991) makes a useful distinction between experiential sensitivity and informational sensitivity. The person who experiences no difference in the taste of Coke and Pepsi is experientially insensitive to the difference. However, that person may be able to reliably pick Coke by taste in a blind forced-choice condition. When this happens, the experientially insensitive person may be said to be informationally sensitive. This situation is analogous to the blindsighted person who is experientially insensitive but informationally sensitive to the object in the visual field.

Studies of paradoxical awareness and pathological awareness strongly suggest that awareness is a continuum and that there are various shades and grades of awareness, which, however fall into two categories: the explicit and the implicit, the subjectively experienced and the nonexperientially processed. Further, awareness is clearly linked to brain systems. Different modalities of awareness are linked to different systems and localized in different parts of the brain. Damage to or dysfunction of the particular systems results in concomitant changes in awareness appropriate to those systems. The observed correlations between the forms of awareness and the states of the brain clearly indicate that they are closely linked. May we conclude from this that the brain processes are necessary and sufficient conditions for all awareness, including subjective awareness?

Loss of subjective awareness of the stimuli falling in the damaged visual field of the patients with blindsight, the covert awareness of faces by the prosopagnosic patients with bilateral lesions to the occipital-temporal regions of the cortex, and the implicit perceptions of neglect patients with posterior parietal damage provide persuasive arguments in favor of cortical necessity and sufficiency to modulate and constrain awareness. We may not ignore, however, the fact that similar phenomena may be observed without relevant cortical defects, as in functional blindness and hypnotically induced negative hallucinations. Again, psy-

chosomatic disease, the placebo effect and psychokinetic phenomena leave open the possibility of the primacy of consciousness as irreducible to brain states. Changes in brain states indeed cause changes in awareness. It is also possible for awareness to cause changes in brain states. The case against such "reverse direction" from consciousness to cortical states has not been made with any degree of conviction.

Lacking subjective awareness, phenomena of paradoxical awareness are readily available for third-person observations. Hence cognitive psychologists and neuroscientists carry out much of the research in this area. They have been able to discern in important respects the functional and structural aspects of awareness and provide reasonable explanations for them. The question remains, however, whether these explanations of awareness may be generalized to all awareness, including subjective awareness. A number of alternate views are advocated. First, as mentioned earlier, subjective experience may be denied any reality and treated as an epiphenomenon of simpler brain states. Second, subjectivity involved in experiential awareness may be ignored as inessential for explaining awareness. Third, assuming that subjectivity is in principle irreducible to physical processes, one may acknowledge helplessness in explaining it in satisfactory naturalistic terms. Fourth, one may postulate a more inclusive principle that accounts for subjectivity as well as awareness, a fundamental order that encompasses both experience and information.

Cognitive and neuropsychologists and other scientists who view consciousness from the perspective of paradoxical awareness have by and large ignored subjectivity, treating it as an inessential aspect of consciousness. When confronted with the reality of subjective awareness as something unaccounted for by the cognitive theories of awareness, a few researchers have tended to postulate a separate domain for experiential awareness, such as the phenomenological mind distinguished from the computational mind (Jackendoff 1987). Then the problem of the relationship between the two domains arises. If the subjectivity factor is inexplicable in functional and structural terms, then the relationship between the two remains insoluble, and we must wonder with Nagel how physical and phenomenological aspects cohere in a single event of subjective awareness.

CHAPTER 4

Paranormal Awareness

The Principles of Psychology deals, as we have noted, almost exclusively with "such things as sensations, desires, emotions, cognitions, reasonings, decisions, volitions and the like" (1892/1900, p. 1), With the beginning of the twentieth century, James moved increasingly toward the other forms of awareness, which he barely mentions in *The Principles*. His Gifford lectures at the University of Edinburgh are a full-blown account of what he called "nonrational forms" of awareness. He wrote in *The Varieties of Religious Experience* "that our normal waking consciousness, rational consciousness as we call it, is but one special type of consciousness, whilst all about it, parted from it from the filmiest of screens, there lie potential forms of consciousness entirely different" (1902/1914, p. 298). Following the British psychical researcher F.W.H. Myers, James credited the subliminal region of the mind as capable of leading to pathological as well as paranormal states and transcendental experiences. The pathological dimension reinforced his conviction that in certain cases mental illness is psychogenic. It is, however, the paranormal dimension of the subliminal that interested James most. In fact, James took serious interest in psy-

chical research and was involved in the investigation of mediumistic phenomena. He served as the president of the Society for Psychical Research (SPR) based in England, which sponsored systematic research into anomalous psychical phenomena, and was closely associated with the establishment of its American counterpart, the ASPR. (For James's contributions to psychical research, see Murphy and Ballow 1960/1969 and Taylor 1996).

The paranormal aspects of the "nonrational forms" of consciousness are what we now discuss in this chapter on paranormal awareness. Two kinds of paranormal awareness may be distinguished. One form is anomalous awareness involved in ESP and other parapsychological phenomena and the other is awareness-as-such or pure consciousness, indicated by the mystic and yogic experiences of transcendence.

Anomalous Awareness

The excursions of William James beyond the ordinary waking consciousness into nonsensory forms of consciousness are somewhat incongruous with the Western scientific tradition, which considers consciousness as bound to individual cortical structures and consequently as having no existence independent of the brain. It is assumed to be self-evident that to have awareness of a physical event or a material object without being in sensory contact with it is impossible. It is equally impossible for the mind/consciousness to cause any changes in the material world other than changes in one's own brain (Broad 1953). These assumptions, which C.D. Broad labeled as basic limiting principles, rule out the possibility (a) that one can have information about objects and events that are shielded from the senses, (b) that mind/consciousness can directly influence external objects and events, and (c) that consciousness can survive bodily death.

There is, however, growing scientific evidence to suggest the possibility of acquiring information that is apparently received independently of the sensory processes, as in extrasensory perception (ESP), and of direct action of mind over matter independent of the motor system, as in psychokinesis (PK) (see Rao & Palmer 1987). The phenomena with which scientific parapsychology deals are designated as psi. Psi includes both ESP and PK. There are also a number of cases in which a person is believed to remember events that are alleged to have occurred in a previous life (Stevenson 1974, 1975, 1984).

Parapsychology, which deals with the phenomena of ESP and PK, is a controversial subject. It has accumulated negative connotations among academic ranks, resulting in less than objective assessment of the parapsychological claims by the scientific community in general. However, because of the important implications of psychic claims to consciousness studies, we will discuss in some detail parapsychology and its findings.

The Existence of Psi

SPONTANEOUS CASE STUDIES

Evidence for ESP and PK is of two kinds. One source of evidence is the body of reported personal experiences that suggest the operation of an extrasensory process. Such reports are widespread. A systematic collection of them began with the establishment of the Society for Psychical Research in 1882. Edmund Gurney and colleagues (1886/1970) published several hundred of these cases in their book, *Phantasms of the Living*. According to these investigators, their authenticated cases provide *prima facie* evidence for telepathy, a form of psi in which there appears to be communication between two persons without the mediation of any sensory processes.

There are, however, two intrinsic difficulties in placing any reliance on reported personal experiences as evidential material. First, they are not precisely quantifiable. One cannot know whether an ostensible paranormal occurrence is in fact a case of psi or a mere chance occurrence. There are no generally acceptable methods that give reliable probability figures either in support of or against the hypothesis that a given experience is paranormal. The second difficulty is the question of the authenticity of the reported experiences. How true are the reports? What criteria should one use in determining their truthfulness? Human testimony is notorious for its unreliability. Actual experiences are often mixed with imaginary ones. Reality is sometimes distorted to satisfy personal whims. How, then, can the residuum of truth be disentangled from the complicated web of anecdotal material?

These difficulties led towards the formulation of a somewhat different policy from the SPR exercise of collecting "authentic" cases. "If the case studies are taken as merely suggestive at best and in no sense relied upon for evidential value," wrote J. B. Rhine, "they can furnish new hypotheses for the research worker that he might otherwise never obtain from any other source" (1950, p. 164). It is in this spirit that his wife, Louisa E. Rhine, studied her vast collection of spontaneous cases. When large numbers of cases are analyzed, she believed, the emerging patterns are more likely to represent the actual aspects of the cases because they are less likely to be caused by individual whims, fancies, and predispositions. These suggestive aspects may be put to appropriate experimental tests with necessary controls.

L. E. Rhine (1961) analyzed these cases systematically and found that people appear to receive information in a nonsensory manner from another person's consciousness (telepathy), from a remote object or event (clairvoyance), and from an event that has not yet happened (precognition). Some of her cases involved puzzling physical effects (i.e., PK), such as inexplicable stopping of a watch at the exact time of its owner's sudden death and unexplained physical occurrences such as poltergeist phenomena. L. E. Rhine's collection of several thousand cases is now deposited in the Duke University archives.

Her analyses of spontaneous cases led L. E. Rhine to believe that psi is a two-stage process (L. E. Rhine 1965). The first stage is a nonphysical process by which psi information is acquired at the unconscious level. The second stage involves the psychological processes of projecting unconscious information onto awareness. Her analyses further revealed that there are essentially four different forms in which psi information manifests itself in our awareness, which she called mediating vehicles. They are (a) realistic dreams, (b) unrealistic dreams, (c) hallucinations, and (d) intuitions. The realistic experiences are in pictorial form and occur mostly in dreams. On rare occasions, however, someone may see something in his or her "mind's eye" that is later found to correspond to an actual event. The unrealistic experiences contain imagery that is fictitious or symbolic, and they seldom occur in combination with realistic elements. Hallucinatory ESP experiences are vivid, sensory-like experiences and occur when one is awake. These are the least frequently observed. Unlike the other forms, intuitive experiences do not involve imagery. An intuitive experience is a hunch, a sudden "just knowing" feeling. The vehicles by which psi is mediated are thus "*normal, ordinary,* and *familiar* forms of mental life.... ESP has no distinctive form of its own*" (L. E. Rhine 1961, her emphasis). The processes by which the unconscious ESP information finds its way into overt behavior is understood by Rhine to be the same as in other psychodynamic functions.

EXPERIMENTAL EVIDENCE

The second kind of evidence is quantitative and experimental. Not withstanding the controversial nature of the subject in the mainstream of science, there is a consensus among the researchers in this area that there is compelling evidence in support of ESP and PK. This does not mean that there is general acceptance of psi research in mainstream science. If the commentary following a position paper on this subject published in the journal *Behavioral and Brain Sciences* (Rao & Palmer 1987) is any indication, the opinion on the subject among informed scientists is divided equally between those who favor and those who oppose it. A survey of "elite" scientists in general by Jim McClenon (1982) shows, however, much greater skepticism. I may add that those who find the evidence utterly unconvincing do so more for subjective reasons based on the antecedent improbability of the phenomena rather than the weakness of the evidence. Referring to J. B. Rhine's ESP experiments, psychologist D. O. Hebb

(1951) wrote: "Personally I do not accept ESP for a moment, because it does not make sense. My external criteria, both of physics and physiology, say that ESP is not a fact despite the behavioral evidence that has been reported. Rhine may still turn out to be right, improbable as I think that is, and my own rejection of his views is—in a literal sense—prejudice" (p. 45).

S. Moss and D.C. Butler (1978) summarize the reasons for rejecting the case for ESP on six grounds. (1) The test procedures are so inadequately reported and the experimental designs are so informal that the evidence generated by parapsychological experiments cannot be regarded as establishing the existence of ESP. (2) Replication by a qualified nonsympathetic observer is essential before results should be accepted, and no such replication has been successfully carried out in parapsychology. (3) In order to accept the existence of ESP we must discover at least one lawful relationship involving ESP, and there are no supposed "ESP laws" that cannot be accounted for more parsimoniously by existing psychological laws. (4) ESP is not in harmony with established laws and therefore it must be rejected. (5) We do not encounter ESP in the marketplace; therefore, it must be spurious. (6) There is no need to have an open mind on the question of ESP if the evidence has not yet established it.

(Rao 1979) argued against all the six criticisms. First, the reporting style and experimental design of good experiments in parapsychology are just as good and they are as carefully carried out and reported as any in the behavioral sciences. Second, replicability cannot be a primary criterion for demarcating the genuine and the spurious in every controversial area and, in any case, some parapsychological findings have, in a significant sense, been replicated. Third, failure to find lawful relationships does not logically negate the existence of a phenomenon and, in any case, there is

sufficient evidence in ESP data to suggest such relationships. Fourth, lack of perceived harmony with the "established laws" does not warrant the rejection of evidence and, in any case, it is by no means certain that psi phenomena are outside the scope of all physical laws. Fifth, the "marketplace" test is irrelevant to the question of the existence of a phenomenon. Finally, the evidence for ESP is strong enough to compel an unbiased observer to take it seriously.

Indeed, parapsychology can boast of a number of well-controlled experiments (Rhine & Pratt 1954; Schmidt 1973; Jahn 1982; Honorton & Bem 1994), which have provided strong evidence that psi occurs. There is significant evidence that ESP manifests in a variety of forms such as telepathy, clairvoyance and precognition and that PK acts on different systems, including quantum physical processes and explicit and implicit mental events.

Even though the first major experimental investigation of ESP in the US is by John Coover (1917) at Stanford University, it is J.B. Rhine (1934/1973) of Duke University who is generally acknowledged as the father of modern parapsychology. He made a sustained scientific claim for the existence of ESP and PK, gave the field "a shared language, methods, and problems" (McVaugh & Mauskopf 1976). He provided "radical innovation and a high potential for elaboration" (Allison 1973, p. 34). In short, Rhine turned psychical research, hitherto an amateur endeavor, into parapsychology, a professional scientific study of anomalous psychological phenomena. Rhine's experimental procedure was simple and easy to repeat. He asked his subjects to guess the randomized order of the cards in a deck of twenty-five containing five each of five symbols: circle, cross, wavy lines, square, and star. His testing procedures were such that the subjects were well shielded from the target cards, to rule out the possibility of their gaining any sensory access to the symbols or enabling them to make correct calls by logical inferences. By August 1, 1933, he collected 85,724 trials with an average score of 7.1 correct guesses per 25 guesses. The probability such a result could occur by chance is extremely small indeed (Rhine 1934/1973).

The Pearce-Pratt Experiment: The Pearce-Pratt series by Rhine is a methodological culmination of the early attempts to obtain laboratory evidence for ESP. This series, which had special precautions to exclude all possibilities of error, that included two experimenter controls, independent records and several hundred yards of distance between the target cards and the subject, gave highly significant results supporting the ESP hypothesis.

C.E.M. Hansel published a brief critique of the experiment in 1961 and an expanded version later (Hansel, 1966, 1980). Hansel does not find fault with the analyses of the data or the statistical significance of the results. He accepts that "something other than chance obviously was operating in each of the four subseries" (1980, p. 112). Hansel argues, however, that the subject, Pearce, could have cheated to obtain the high scores. There is of course no evidence of cheating by the subject. Hansel describes imaginary scenarios, such as drilling a hole in a trap door located in the ceiling and later filling in the hole without being observed, that would have permitted the subject or his accomplice to obtain sensory information of the targets. Rhine and Pratt (1961) pointed out how implausible the above argument is.

In his book of 1966 and its subsequent editions, Hansel (1980, 1989) expands on his criticism. He makes the following points to discredit the Pearce-Pratt experiment: (1) It was not reported in adequate detail at the time it was carried out. (2) There were discrepancies in its different published versions. (3) The experimental conditions were

such that the subject, Pearce, could have cheated in a number of possible ways.

Let us consider the fraud issue first. Neither Hansel, nor anyone else for that matter, presented any evidence or circumstances that suggest even remotely that Pearce did cheat. The best Hansel (1980) was able to say was his concluding statement in the book, "A further unsatisfactory feature lies in the fact that a statement has not been made by the central figure, Hubert Pearce. The experimenters state that trickery was impossible, but what would Pearce have said? Perhaps one day he will give his own account of the experiment" (p. 123). Pearce did make a statement in which he unequivocally asserted that he did not cheat (Stevenson, 1967).

The implausible scenario imaginatively described by Hansel that Pearce could have sneaked out of the library and peered through the transom at the top of the door to Pratt's room and obtained target information, based in part on a distorted architectural plan (Stevenson, 1967), highlights the fact that a determined skeptic can always call attention to certain features of the experiment to make it look less than definitive. In the case of the Pearce-Pratt experiment, Hansel's exercise is one of arguing that Pearce's whereabouts during the experiment were not completely monitored, leaving the possibility that he could have cheated, however improbable that may seem to be. Even if we assume that the conditions of the Pearce-Pratt experiment were such that the subject could not have possibly cheated, it could still be argued that the subject and the experimenters conspired to falsely obtain the results. In the final analysis, it can be seen that fraud can never be completely eliminated. Consequently, the fraud hypothesis becomes essentially non-falsifiable, in the sense that we cannot absolutely rule out fraud in any given experiment. A specific hypothesis of fraud can be subjected to a test of falsification, but fraud as such can never be completely ruled out. Inasmuch as one can always imagine after the fact some hypothetical fraud scenario, attempting to eliminate fraud will lead to an infinite regress, carrying out experiment after experiment without ever rejecting absolutely the possibility of fraud.

Conceding that "it is difficult to see how either Rhine or Pratt, unaided, could have cheated to bring about the result," Hansel goes on to raise questions about the competence of Rhine and Pratt as experimenters. He makes much of two observations (1) that the original report of the Pearce-Pratt experiment did not give all the details of procedure and experimental conditions that may be considered necessary now and (2) that there are some discrepancies between the various published reports of the experiment. Even some parapsychologists have accused Rhine that the first reporting of the results of the Pearce-Pratt experiment was inadequate. Stevenson (1967), for example, writes, "Rhine had already published informal reports [of the Pearce-Pratt experiment] in two of his popular books and it is doubtful procedure in science to announce one's result first to the general public and then (in this case many years later) present a detailed report for scientists" (p. 259).

It is not the case that Rhine announced his results first to the public. The results of the Pearce-Pratt experiment were first published in *The Journal of Abnormal and Social Psychology* (Rhine, 1936) and were only subsequently mentioned in his popular books. (The first of these, *New Frontiers of the Mind,* appeared in 1938.) *The Journal of Abnormal and Social Psychology* is a respected journal in mainstream psychology and Rhine had no editorial control over it. The fact of the matter is that the additional details that we now consider necessary were not then considered so by the psychologists who refereed his paper and the editor who published it. If the *Journal of Parapsychol-*

ogy was in existence at that time and if Rhine had published his report in it with inadequate details, we might have had some reason to blame him for not giving all the details. The details of the sort that we now require of parapsychological reports were simply not found necessary then. When it became increasingly clear that further details of the experimental procedure were called for, Rhine and Pratt published a more detailed report in 1954.

Finally, the discrepancies between various published accounts of the experiment pointed out by Hansel are trivial and clerical, and none is sufficient to call into question the veracity of the experiment or the credibility of the experimenters. Interestingly, Hansel makes more errors in his very brief review of the experiment than do the authors in their report (see Rao, 1981, 1992).

There were of course other critics of Rhine's experiments (Pratt et al., 1940; Rao, 1982). Some of the criticisms were constructive. They enabled Rhine and others who attempted to replicate his early experiments to improve the methods of collecting data and their analyses.

J. B. Rhine also conducted experiments to test the PK hypothesis. His experiments were again fairly simple. He asked his subjects to concentrate on obtaining a randomly predetermined face of the dice to test whether the movement of the dice could be influenced by the subject's volition, without any physical influence on them. He reported several experiments (Rhine 1946), which provided statistical evidence suggesting the possibility of direct influence of volition on physical processes

Since the publication of Rhine's monograph *Extra-sensory Perception* in 1934, there have been literally hundreds of experimental reports that provided evidence for psi. There were, of course, several other experiments that gave null results and no evidence for psi. There were criticisms of various kinds leveled against Rhine's experiments, but none that convincingly argued against the evidential nature of the overall results without a presumption of fraud on the part of the investigators, an unlikely possibility. In view of the fact that Rhine's results were not uniformly replicated, there were calls for a conclusive experiment, a "foolproof" study that would control for all conceivable kinds of error, including experimenter fraud. As we have argued elsewhere (Rao & Palmer 1987), the concept of a completely "conclusive" experiment in controversial areas of human science is an impossible goal, a tempting mirage, because in retrospect one can always speculate on a possible source of error. If by "conclusive" we make a more modest claim that it is highly improbable that the result of a successful experiment is due to some artifact, then a good case can be made for more than one such experiment in parapsychology.

Schmidt's REG Experiments: The REG experiments of Helmut Schmidt (1969a; 1969b), a physicist at Boeing Scientific Research Laboratories at the time of conducting these experiments, may be cited as an example of sufficiently well controlled experiments that can be accorded the status of a conclusive experiment. Schmidt's experiments were carried out with the help of specially built machines that controlled against all known artifacts such as recording errors, sensory cues, subject cheating, and improper analysis of data. The Schmidt machine, as it has come to be known, randomly selected the targets and automatically recorded them and the subject responses. The subject's task was to select which of the four lamps would light in a panel in front of him and press the corresponding button to indicate the selection. After the subject made his selection, random lighting of the lamps was achieved, by a sophisticated random event generator (REG) that used a radioactive source, strontium 90. After extensive testing in control trials, the REG

was found not to deviate significantly from chance. The results of all three experiments gave highly significant results suggesting ESP on the part of the subjects. For example, the three subjects in the first experiment did 63,066 trials and selected the correct lamp 16,458 times, i.e., 26.1 percent or 691.5 times more than mean chance expectation. The probability that such a result could occur by chance is less than 2×10^{-9}.

REPLICABILITY OF ESP EXPERIMENTS

Whereas the call for a conclusive crucial experiment appears to be somewhat misconstrued, the emphasis on the need for replication when controversial empirical claims are made is well placed. If the parapsychological phenomena were not replicable, though genuine, they would hardly excite any scientific interest. Isolated facts and unique events ordinarily hold little interest for science, unless they lead to, or are capable of leading to, some kind of general law. ESP as a laboratory effect must be observed repeatedly with reasonable ease in order that it can be studied and understood as a natural phenomenon. Also, the necessity of a foolproof experiment recedes into the background, as the phenomenon becomes increasingly replicable. What can we say about the replicability of parapsychological experiments?

Replication may be understood in two senses. Absolute replication requires that a finding be reproduced on demand. Statistical replication considers an experimental effect replicated if a series of replication attempts provides statistically significant evidence for the effect. Whereas absolute replication is easy to achieve in physical science, it becomes more complex and difficult in behavioral science experiments where perfect duplication of conditions in two independent experiments is nearly impossible in practice. Consequently, absolute replication, or even strong replicability, eludes delicate behavioral phenomena such as the experimenter expectancy effect and the placebo effect.

There is sufficient evidence to suggest that several parapsychological phenomena are replicated in the statistical sense. For example, there have been a number of attempts to replicate the REG experiments of the kind carried out by Schmidt. Schmidt himself utilized his procedures and apparatus to carry out successfully a number of experiments to test whether his preselected subjects could influence quantum processes by PK, specifically, to bias a random event generator controlled by a radioactive source. Radin, May and Thomas (1985) conducted a survey of all the binary REG experiments published from the time Schmidt first published his results in 1969 to 1984. Their review included 332 individual experiments carried out by 30 principal investigators. Seventy-one, or 21 percent, of the 332 experiments yielded statistically significant results in favor of the PK hypothesis, compared to 5 percent to be expected by chance hypothesis. The combined binomial probability for all the studies is 5.4×10^{-43}.

The most prominent of the REG replications is the series of experiments conducted by Robert Jahn and associates at Princeton University (Jahn 1982; Nelson et al. 1984). The REG used by the Princeton group is based on a commercial electronic noise source. The subjects were asked to influence the device by means of sheer volitional effort (PK) to produce the desired effect, i.e., excesses of hits or misses. The results showed that the subjects were able to bias the REG to a statistically significant degree ($p=3 \times 10^{-4}$). Extensive testing in control conditions before, during, and after the PK trials yielded essentially chance results, suggesting that the REG device itself had no bias and that the observed bias in the experimental trials may be attributed to PK on the part of the subjects.

Replication of parapsychological effects is found in several other areas such as belief and ESP (Palmer 1971; Lawrence 1993), extroversion and ESP (Sargent 1981; Honorton et al. 1998), ganzfeld and ESP (Honorton 1985), hypnosis and ESP (Schechter 1984; Stanford & Stein, 1997) and ESP in dreams (Child 1985).

Some Aspects of Parapsychological Phenomena

Parapsychological research has gone well beyond the question of the existence of psi. There has been experimental demonstration of various forms of psi such as ESP and PK and the discovery of lawful regularities between psi and other psychological and physical variables. One of the most important finding is that ESP unlike any known physical phenomena, is apparently unconstrained, by space/time variables or the complexity of the task.

Quite early in his experimental investigations, J. B. Rhine found that distance between the subject and the target in ESP experiments made no significant difference in the success rate of his subject (Rhine 1934). Similarly, Russian physiologist L.L. Vasiliev (1963) reported that he was able to hypnotize his subject telepathically during randomly determined periods of time from a distance of about 1,700 kilometers. He found also that his attempts to shield any possible electromagnetic wave transmission between the hypnotist and the subject by placing them in separate Farady cages did not diminish the success rate of telepathic induction of hypnosis. Marilyn Schlitz and Elmar Gruber (1980) successfully carried out transcontinental remote viewing experiments in which the subject attempted to describe, totally unaware sensorially, a randomly selected location on another continent being visited by an experimenter.

There is also experimental evidence to support the precognition hypothesis. As in spontaneous cases in which people have reported their experiences of gaining information about future events apparently without any other means of knowing them, experimental studies have also shown that it is possible to gain information about a target to be selected at a time in the future. For example, it was found in some remote viewing experiments that the subjects were able to successfully describe the location of an experimenter at a predetermined future time (Jahn 1982). Earlier, J. B. Rhine (1938) had reported significant results suggesting that his subjects were able to guess correctly the target order in a deck of ESP cards randomized after the subjects made their calls. A meta-analysis of precognition experiments carried out between 1935 and 1987 involving 309 studies carried out by 62 experimenters provides strong evidence in support of precognition. The cumulative probability that such a result may be obtained by chance is close to zero.

Among other parapsychological findings are the successful attempts to relate psi to subjects' beliefs and attitudes (Schmeidler & McConnell 1958), personality and motivation (Eysenck 1967; Honorton & Schmeidler 1986), and to cognitive variables like memory (Rao et al. 1977) and visual imagery (Kelly et al. 1975).

Another significant aspect of psi appears to be the relative ineffectiveness of task complexity in constraining it. Rex Stanford (1977) has reviewed the relevant literature and concluded that the efficiency of the PK function is not reduced by increases in the complexity of the target system. Thus, psi, which is believed to involve no sensory mediation, is also found not to be constrained by the variables of space and time or by the physical properties of the items of information. There is nothing to indicate from the research results available to date that any energy patterns emanating from the target objects reach the subject in ESP tests. It would seem that somehow the subject has access to information under conditions that simply do not permit any known physical energy transmission from the target. Such a possibility raises serious questions about the subject-object distinctions in cognitive processes and the representational theory of knowledge in general.

It would seem that C. G. Jung (1955) had a better insight into this problem than his critics did when he described ESP in terms of synchronicity or acausal relationships. Similarly, Polanyi's (1958) concept of tacit knowing appears to be more appropriate than conventional perceptual models to conceptualize paranormal awareness. Tacit knowing, according to Polanyi, consists in the "capacity for attending from one thing to another"—that is, from a *proximal* term to the *distal* term. The perceptual process, for example, consists in the tacit integration of perceptual clues into comprehensive entities. He describes perception as transposition of feelings. The way we see an object is mainly determined by our awareness of certain events inside our bodies, which are not observable in themselves. In a perceptual process, then, we are attending from the internal processes to the qualities of things outside.

Now, if the tacit integration or structuring of perceptual clues that results in meaningful experiences is fundamental for perceptual knowledge, there is no sense in which we can say that the perceptual experiences are produced primarily by the action of material things on our senses. While the perceptual clues may be necessary, on occasion, to have veridical perceptions, they are not sufficient. It is important to note that the clues of the steps involved in tacit knowing need not be identifiable or in some instances may not even be discernible. As Polanyi puts it, "Tacit knowing will tend to reach conclusions in ignorance of the steps involved."

Likewise, ESP seems to involve a sort of tacit knowing in ignorance of the clues involved. In an ESP experience we are not merely ignorant of the clues involved, but the clues themselves do not appear to have any sensory base. It is more like stage I processing speculated by L. E. Rhine, which is believed to be unlike other cognitive processes. At this stage, the individual psyche resembles a microcosm, potentially capable of obtaining all information in the cosmos. "ESP" as L. E. Rhine (1967) put it, "is not limited by inherent unavailability, but by the person, the individual himself, through whose psychological structure it must be filtered into consciousness" (p. 264).

REMOTE VIEWING STUDIES

Russell Targ and Harold Puthoff were the first to carry out successful remote viewing experiments at Stanford Research Institute. The remote viewing protocol simply consists of having an experimenter (the outbound experimenter) visit a randomly selected target site and ask the subject, who is sensorially unaware of the location, to describe to a second experimenter the place which the outbound experimenter is visiting at the time. A judge later attempts to match the subject's description to a predetermined pool of target sites. The results of the Targ-Puthoff experiments were published in their book *Mind Reach* (1977). A more technical version of it may be found in Puthoff and Targ (1976). Successful attempts to replicate the Targ-Puthoff experiments include those by J. Bisaha and B. J. Dunne (1979), Robert Jahn and Brenda Dunne (1987), and Marilyn Schlitz and Elmar Gruber (1980).

Some of the remote viewing experiments were severely criticized with some justification. D. Marks and R. Kammann (1978, 1980) criticized the Targ-Puthoff ex-

periments on the ground that the subjects' transcripts, which were used to match with the target locations, might have contained clues relating to the order of the trials. These clues could have been helpful to the judges in successfully matching the target locations with the subjects' descriptions. Targ and Puthoff attempted to counter this criticism by conducting new judging and fresh analysis after the presumed clues were edited out (Tart, Puthoff, & Targ, 1980). Marks and Scott (1986), however, were not satisfied with the adequacy of the editing. It turns out that their skepticism of the revised judging is hardly justified because in the new judging procedure the target sequence was also randomized. This procedure rules out the possibility of any clues in the transcripts helping the judges to make correct matches of targets and transcripts. In the Bisha-Dunne experiments, the judges were provided with pictures of the target location. It is argued that the pictures may have contained cues such as weather condition and seasonal variations that might have provided for an artificial match of the target location and the transcript (Marks, 1986). Again, some of the experiments by Jahn and Dunne were criticized on the grounds of nonrandom target selection (Hansen, Utts, & Markwick (1994), but this was disputed by Dobyns, Dunne, Jahn & Nelson (1994).

The remote viewing experiments by Targ and Puthoff at Stanford Research Institute were funded for several years by US government agencies. The support continued for this line of research by the federal government to SRI International and later (1992–94) to Science Applications International Corporation (SAIC). Edwin May and associates conducted at SAIC several ESP studies, which they prefer to call anomalous cognition experiments. These experiments are somewhat procedurally different from the original remote viewing studies and are more like traditional ESP tests, with distance intervening between the targets and the subject. For example, in the study by Lantz, Luke, and May (1994) there was no sender. The main finding of this study is that free-response ESP studies can be conducted successfully without a sender and that free-response targets can be used even in clairvoyance experiments.

As a member of the panel asked to review the ESP research at SAIC, statistician Jessica Utts reviewed the work of May and associates within the broad framework of contemporary psi research. Utilizing eight methodological criteria, Utts found significant evidence for the existence of psi in these experiments. Ray Hyman (1996), another member of the panel, who did not agree with the assessment of Utts, also found little to criticize in the SAIC experiments. His main concern was that the main investigator, Ed May, served as the judge and that he could have biased the results in that role. May, however, was completely blind to the targets when he performed the judging. Therefore, it is difficult to see how he could have biased the results. Hyman prefers, however, to withhold his judgment on the significance of these results as evidence for psi because, in his view, they may contain hidden biases and subtle errors that may come to surface in due course. Thus, it would seem, as Douglas Stokes (1998) pointed out, "Hyman and other critics are starting to absolve themselves of the need to point to possible flaws in an experiment when they fail to find any. It is now evidently sufficient merely to state that there may be undetected flaws" (p. 166). More recently, Richard Wiseman and Julie Milton (1998) pointed out some possible pathways for information leakage and other weaknesses in the conduct of some of these experiments. May (1998), however, questioned the possible leakage hypothesis of Wiseman and Milton and argued that they simply ignored contradictory evidence in their criticism of the Lantz, Luke, and May (1994) experiment.

ESP IN DREAMS

According to some surveys (L. E. Rhine, 1962a, 1962b), 65 percent of spontaneous psychic experiences occur in dreams. A number of psychoanalysts have reported what appear to be paranormal dreams in therapeutic setting (Devereux, 1953). Therefore, it is only natural to consider the dream state as psi-conducive. As Robert Van de Castle (1977), pointed out, the earliest experimental effort to paranormally influence a dream was reported by H. M. Weserman in 1819.

With the advent of dream-monitoring techniques made possible by the discovery of such physiological correlates of the dream state as rapid eye movements (REMs), the opportunity has come about to study ESP dreams in laboratory settings. Montague Ullman and associates were quick to avail themselves of it. The full account of a decade-long study of ESP and dreams at the Maimonides Medical Center in Brooklyn, NY is to be found in the book *Dream Telepathy*. Other publications by the group include Ullman, Krippner, & Feldstein (1966), Krippner (1969), Ullman, & Krippner (1970), Honorton, Krippner, & Ullman (1971), Krippner et al. (1971), Krippner, Honorton, & Ullman (1972), Krippner, Honorton, & Ullman (1973), and Ullman, Krippner, and Vaughan (1973), and Krippner and Persinger (1996).

The experimental procedure used in the Maimonides dream research involved free response ESP testing with two-experimenter controls. In each testing session, the subject and the agent spent the night in the sleep laboratory. The subject was wired up for monitoring brain waves and eye movements. He/she spent the night isolated in an acoustically shielded room. The agent, who was to send the "telepathic" message, under the supervision of a second experimenter, was located in another room. When the subject entered into a period of REM sleep, the monitoring experimenter buzzed the agent to begin sending the telepathic message. The agent in turn concentrated on the target picture given to him by the second experimenter. The target picture enclosed in a packet was randomly chosen from a pool. The agent did not open the packet until he/she was securely isolated in the sending room. Around the end of each REM period, the experimenter monitoring the subject awakened the subject and asked him/her to describe the dream. This procedure was repeated all through the night. At the end of the night session, the subject was again asked to give the impressions about the night's target picture. At this point, both the experimenter and the subject were completely blind to the target.

The dream reports and the subject's morning impressions were transcribed and sent for judging along with the potential targets in the pool. The judges were completely blind and had no clue what the target was for a given night, when they rated the similarity of the night's dream reports and impressions against the potential targets. Under a variety of conditions and with different subjects, the over all results obtained by the Maimonides group over a period of ten years showed that the dream reports were judged to be more similar to the actual target pictures than the controls to a statistically significant degree. Michael Persinger and Stanley Krippner (1989) reported that in the Maimonides dream studies, the 24-hour periods in which the most accurate telepathic dreams occurred had significantly quieter geometric activity than the days before or after.

Among the failed attempts to replicate the Maimonides dream studies is the one carried out by Belvedere and Foulkes (1971) at the University of Wyoming, which did not give significant ESP results. A comprehensive review of research on ESP and dreams is to be found in a chapter by Robert Van de Castle (1977) in Wolman's *Hand-book of Parapsychology*. The review, in Van de Castle's words, "offers very encouraging evidence that telepathic incorporation of stimuli into dreams can be demonstrated under good experimental conditions" (p. 494).

Yale psychologist Irvin Child (1985) examined the research on ESP in dreams. After a careful review of the Maimonides research of Ullman and colleagues and the attempted replications of it, Child examines incisively the manner in which psychologists represented the Maimonides research in books. Pointing out numerous distortions and misrepresentations of ESP research in these books, Child argues, "psychologists are ill served by the apparently scholarly books that seem to convey information about the dream experiments." In Child's view the Maimonides dream–ESP experiments "clearly merit careful attention from psychologists who, for whatever reason, are interested in the question of ESP."

ESP and Subliminal Perception

There are interesting similarities between ESP and subliminal perception (SP) that encourage us to consider them as two species of implicit awareness. In fact, a number of researchers were sufficiently impressed by these similarities as to undertake research relating SP and ESP (Rao & Rao 1982; Kreitler & Kreitler 1973). The French philosopher Henri Bergson (1921) pointed out the relevance of implicit awareness to psychical research. J. B. Rhine (1977) also observed: "It is here in the common unconscious functions of both sensorimotor and extrasensorimotor (or psi) character, that parapsychology comes closest to psychology." He added that it would therefore "be advisable to keep our attention on all the psychological research on unconscious mental activities, watching for similarities and differences" (p. 171).

In our attempts to understand consciousness, the relationship between ESP and SP may be instructive. It is, indeed, interesting to note that there are studies in the areas of SP disguised as studies of ESP (e.g., Calvin & Dollenmayer 1959; Miller 1940) and that there are parapsychological investigations disguised as experiments on SP (Tart 1963). As Beloff (1974a) argued, an analogy between ESP and SP applies only after the target has been apprehended by ESP, because the problem of how information is acquired through ESP is as yet unsolved.

There are several interesting commonalties in the attempts to study SP and ESP. In both cases, the stimulus and the target are presumed to have been accessible to the individual without his or her awareness, and their effects are looked for in recovery tasks, which involve some mode of behavior. In SP, as in ESP research, both intentional and nonintentional methods are utilized. For instance, forced-choice and free-response materials are used in both areas (Dixon 1956, 1971; Miller 1939, 1940; Spence & Holland 1962), and in both, autonomic responses are employed to detect the phenomena (e.g., Davis & Braud 1980; Dean 1962; Dixon 1958; Lazarus & McCleary 1951).

A number of investigators in the two fields have speculated that the same underlying psychodynamic factors may influence both SP and ESP to some extent. Dixon (1979b) considered SP to be a compromise between the restrictive demands of selective attention and the need of the organism to monitor a wide range of stimuli. Beloff (1974) suggested that ESP might also be regarded as "a compromise between the exclusiveness of the Bergsonian filter and the cosmic capacity of the mind to transcend the limits of the senses" (p. 105).

According to some writers (Dixon 1979; Eisenbud 1970; Kreitler & Kreitler 1973; Ehrenwald 1978) ESP and SP may both represent primitive brain functions.

Psychoanalytically oriented researchers have suggested that the primary process, as described by Freud (1900/1953), manifests itself in the phenomena of subliminal perception and perceptual defense (e.g., Hilgard 1962; Klein 1959; Klein & Holt 1960; Shevrin 1973). Freud himself (1925/ 1953) expressed the view that telepathy "comes about particularly easily at the moment at which an idea emerges from the unconscious or, in theoretical terms, as it passes over from the 'primary process' to the 'secondary process'" (p. 89). The phenomenon of psi-missing in ESP research (the tendency of some subjects to miss the target when they are aiming to hit) is regarded by some parapsychologists (e.g., Beloff 1974; Tart 1975) as analogous to perceptual defense. Ehrenwald (1977) remarked that "psychoanalysts have found that they [psi phenomena] obey the identical psychodynamic laws as those governing unconscious mental processes, including those of subliminal perceptions" (p. 716).

Norman Dixon (1979a) identified several areas of contact between subliminal perception and parapsychology. He pointed out that a number of variables like motivation, memory, altered states of consciousness such as relaxation and dreams, right-hemispheric modes of functioning, etc., have similar influence on both SP and ESP. Gertrude Schmeidler (1971) also remarked that "whatever psychological laws apply to the processing of ambiguous sensory material will apply also to the processing of ESP information" (p. 137). Another psi researcher, Charles Honorton (1976), wrote: "Both subliminal and psi influences are facilitated by internal-attention states, both are subject to subtle experimenter effects and situational factors, and both involve the transformation and mediation of stimulus influence through ongoing mentation processes" (pp. 215–216).

One may, however, point to an important difference between an ESP target and a subliminal perception stimulus. The latter is considered to be in sensory contact with the subject, even though it is masked or is at too low an intensity level to cause explicit awareness. The subject in ESP tests is, however, presumed to be completely isolated from the target with no possibility of any sensory contact whatsoever. These assumptions are by no means obvious. In what respect does an ESP card concealed in an opaque envelope differ from a masked stimulus the subject is unable to recall, recognize, or discriminate from other similarly masked stimuli? It is difficult to conceive that a subliminal stimulus presented at or below objective threshold, where the information is actually discriminated at no better than chance levels (Cheesman & Merikle 1984; 1985), is in any kind of sensory contact with the subject. In subliminal perception, sensory contact is inferred from the observed behavior of the subject because it is assumed that such a contact is necessary. In ESP, however, though similar behavior is observed, no sensory contact is inferred because it is not believed to be necessary. In neither case do we have a clear understanding of the process by which the subliminal stimulus or the ESP target causes these behavioral effects from which we infer subliminal or extrasensory perception. Therefore, it may not be unreasonable to believe that similar, if not the same, processes are at work in some forms of SP and ESP.

Even granting that there is sensory contact between subject and the subliminal stimulus, we are left with the problem of explaining how such contact, which causes no explicit awareness, has an influence on the behavior of the subject. It is clear that subliminal perception, like ESP, presumes some kind of dissociation between sensory inputs and higher level processing. In SP, the subject receives sensory inputs but is unable to process them at a level to have explicit awareness, whereas in an ESP experience higher level cortical processing may

take place in the absence of sensory inputs. The latter would sound paradoxical in the absence of a meaningful theory.

INFLUENCE OF BELIEFS AND ATTITUDES ON ESP SCORES

Gertrude Schmeidler, then a professor of psychology at the City College of New York, asked her subjects if they believed ESP to be possible under the conditions of the experiment. On the basis of their replies, she labeled as "sheep" those who believed in the possibility of ESP, and as "goats" those who rejected such a possibility. She found that sheep generally tended to obtain more hits in ESP tests than goats did. The sheep-goat effect, as it is now known, is one of the more widely researched topics in parapsychology. Schmeidler's first report was published in the July 1943 issue of *The Journal of American Society for Psychical Research*, and a comprehensive account of the sheep-goat experiments is available in the book by Schmeidler and McConnell (1958). One of the strong independent confirmations of the sheep-goat effect may be found in the report of Bhadra (1966). Reviews by Lawrence (1993) and Palmer (1971, 1972) suggest that sheep tend to obtain higher ESP scores than goats. Palmer's review, for example, has shown that, of the 17 experiments that used standard methods and analyses, the sheep obtained better scores in 13 of the experiments, with 6 of them achieving statistical significance. Also suggestive was that none of the four experiments giving results in the opposite direction were significant.

As Palmer (1978) points out, the effect of belief on ESP scoring is more complex than it appears. In contrast with Schmeidler's sheep-goat classification, which was based on the subject's belief or disbelief that ESP would occur specifically in the testing situation, some other investigators classified their subjects on the basis of their belief in ESP in the abstract. The latter classification generally failed to obtain significant differences between the scores of the sheep and the goats. Results further suggest that the sheep-goat effect may interact with other variables. Again, manipulation of belief and expectancy factors seems to produce predictable effects (Taddonio, 1976; Lovitts, 1981).

Inspired by the work of Dutch parapsychologist J. G. Van Busschbach (1958, 1955, 1956, 1959, 1961), American researchers Margaret Anderson and Rhea White carried out a series of experiments with students. They used a clairvoyance technique for group testing and attempted to explore interpersonal dynamics between the experimenters who administered the test and the subjects. Anderson and White (1956, 1957, 1958) reported results suggesting a significant relation between teacher-pupil attitudes and the clairvoyance scores of the pupil subjects. In these studies, the teachers gave the tests to their students. By means of questionnaires, the attitudes of pupils to their teachers and those of teachers to their pupils were ascertained. Anderson and White found that significantly positive scores were associated with a positive attitude on the part of the teacher towards the students and negative scoring was associated with a negative attitude. When the teacher and pupil attitudes were combined, it was found that mutually positive attitudes were associated with highly significant positive results and mutually negative attitudes with significant negative results.

The results of these studies are extremely interesting because they point to an important dimension of the experimenter-subject relationship. It is likely that mutually agreeable relationships and favorable attitudes between the teacher and the pupils help to create the experimental context necessary for the successful manifestation of psi, and that in a contrary situation, conditions favor psi-missing.

ESP and Personality Variables

In the search for those characteristics associated with hitting and missing in psi tests, researchers have also explored the subjects' moods (Nielsen 1956; Humphrey 1946a, 1946b; McMahan 1946), interests (Stuart 1946), and a variety of personality measures. Neuroticism, defined as a tendency "toward maladaptive behavior caused either by anxiety or by defense mechanisms against anxiety" (Palmer, 1978) is an area that has received considerable attention. Parapsychologists have used inventories such as Taylor's Manifest Anxiety Scale (Rao, 1965c; Freeman & Nielsen, 1964; Honorton, 1965) and Cattell's 16PF or the HSPQ (Kanthamani & Rao, 1973a; Kramer & Terry, 1973) as a measure of anxiety/neuroticism, and have attempted to correlate these scores with ESP scores. After listing a large number of these studies, Palmer (1978) concludes, "there is a clear trend" for subjects with relatively good emotional adjustment to score better on ESP tests than their counterparts do.

The Defense Mechanism Test (DMT) is a projective test developed in Sweden by Ulf Kragh and his associates (Kragh & Smith, 1970). It involves rapid exposure to the subject images of human interaction situations. The subject is then asked to imagine and report what these situations represent. Inasmuch as the subjects tend to project their own feelings on the images they have seen, the test can be used as a measure of subject's defensive reactions. In fact, the DMT test is used for screening suitable people for selection as airline pilots. An early experiment by Johnson and Kanthamani (1967) found, as one would expect, a negative relationship between DMT scores and ESP scores. Since the publication of this report, as Haraldsson (1978) noted, there have been seven series of experiments, all but one of which have given statistically significant results in support of a negative relationship. Considering the specialized training required to administer and score the DMT, training that only a few in parapsychology have had, one can be reasonably confident that Haraldsson's review covered all the studies up to that time. Subsequent reviews of DMT-ESP studies by Johnson and Haraldsson (1984) and by Haraldsson and Houtcooper also confirm the relationship between ESP and DMT scores. DMT-ESP studies thus seem to show a fairly stable, replicable effect, suggesting that less defensive subjects tend to obtain better ESP scores.

PHYSIOLOGICAL STUDIES OF PSI

Biofeedback studies in the sixties and seventies have raised the hope that a number of internal responses that are normally considered to be beyond the range of voluntary control can be brought under such control. By receiving instant information about heart rate, blood pressure, muscle tension, brain activity, and the like, human subjects, as well as some animals, learn to regulate these internal responses (Miller et al., 1974). Joe Kamiya (1969) and Barbara Brown (1970), among others, have successfully trained subjects to regulate their own brain-wave patterns through biofeedback. Kamiya's subjects, when trained to produce high levels of alpha activity, reported feelings of relaxation and passivity. Also, studies of yogins (Anand, Chhina, & Singh, 1961) and Zen meditators (Kasamatsu & Hirai, 1969) have shown that yogic and meditative states produce EEG patterns characterized by alpha abundance. Traditionally the yogins are credited with psychic abilities, and there is experimental evidence to suggest that relaxation as well as meditation facilitates ESP manifestation (see Honorton, 1977; Rao et al., 1978; and White (1964), for a review of these studies). It is,

therefore, reasonable to suppose that there may be a positive relation between alpha activity of the brain and ESP scores. If such a relation should exist, the ability to self-regulate brain wave activity opens up the possibility of achieving greater predictability, if not control, of ESP performance.

Among the EEG-ESP studies of interests are those by Honorton (1969); Honorton, Davidson, & Bindler (1971); Stanford & Stanford (1969); Stanford (1971); Stanford & Stevenson (1972); Stanford & Palmer (1973); Morris, Roll, Klein & Wheeler (1972); and Rao & Feola (1979). Even though the results of these studies are not uniformly significant, the bulk of the evidence is suggestive of a positive relationship between ESP and alpha activity.

There have been a number of other attempts to find physiological correlates of psi. S. Figar (1959) and Douglas Dean (1962), among others, utilized plethysmographic recordings as ESP indicators. Soji Otani (1965) and K. Tenny (1962) employed a skin resistance measure to monitor psi. William Braud and others examined autonomic detection of the phenomenon of "staring at" using the electrodermal response. A review of the earlier work on the physiological correlates of psi is found in Beloff (1974b).

More recently, Norman Don, Bruce McDonough and Charles Warren have attempted to study event-related potentials (ERPs) as indicators of psi. ERPs are minute fluctuations in the voltage of the EEG recordings from the scalp following sensory stimulation. In one study with the psychic Malcolm Bessent, Warren, McDonough, and Don (1992a) recorded ERPs elicited by target and nontarget stimuli in forced-choice ESP tests. They observed that P100, a positive spike at about 100ms after the onset of the stimulus, and NSW (a negative slow wave 400–500 ms after the stimulus is applied) were significantly larger in response to target stimuli than to nontarget stimuli.

In an attempted replication of the above with the same subject (Warren, McDonough, & Don, 1992b), the P100 effect did not occur, but there was evidence of the NSW effect. In a more recent study, Don, McDonough, & Warren (1998) attempted to test the NSW effect in 400–500 ms range as well as in 150–400 ms range. The subjects in this study were unselected volunteers. The results confirmed the NSW effect in the 150–400 ms range. For the NSW in the 400–500 ms range, the results fell short of significance (p=.085). The authors interpret the results as evidence of unconscious psi.

MEMORY AND ESP

There are a number of interesting similarities between ESP and some cognitive processes, such as memory. Memory, like ESP, involves representations of objects and events with which the organism is not directly in sensory contact. We know something about the way memory representations are stored and retrieved, as well as their biochemical and physiological basis. However, our knowledge of ESP does not provide any evidence that psi representations have a cortical base. Further, much of our memory material is accessible for introspection, whereas most ESP phenomena, being unconscious, are unavailable for any introspective analysis. These important differences not withstanding, memory and ESP seem to have a good deal in common as psychological processes, and the understanding of one may aid the understanding of the other. Therefore, it is not surprising that from the time of F. W. H. Myers (1915/1903) to that of J. B. Rhine, a role for memory in ESP was anticipated. As J. B. Rhine wrote in *Extra-sensory Perception* (1973/34): "It (ESP) is simple cognition... but it uses memory, visual or other imagination ... in its functioning" (p. 191).

Hermann Ebbinghaus (1964/1885), who pioneered quantitative studies of mem-

ory, wondered, as have most experimental psychologists since, how to control "the bewildering mass of causal conditions which, insofar as they are of mental nature, almost completely elude our control, and which, moreover, are subject to endless and incessant change." The challenge for him was how to "measure numerically the mental processes which flit by so quickly and which on introspection are so hard to analyze" (pp. 7–8). He attempted to solve the problem by inventing nonsense syllables that the subject may learn and recall under controlled conditions, a tradition which is strikingly similar to the one heralded by early ESP testers who used forced-choice card-guessing methods.

Considerable similarity is also found in the topics for research chosen for study by memory researchers and parapsychologists. Just as memory researchers are concerned with the effect on recall of differences in the material to be remembered, so are parapsychologists concerned with the effect of target differences on subjects' ESP scores. Individual differences are extensively investigated in studies of psi as they are in studies of memory. The search for states favorable to improved ESP scoring bears similarity to the research into the conditions for optimal memory. Whereas the classical card-guessing tests are like the methods used by Ebbinghaus and those following him, the open-ended, free-response studies of psi remind us of the Bartlett (1932) tradition in memory research. Again, the position effects, the differential effect, and psi-missing seem to have their analogs in memory, e.g., U curves in serial learning, retroactive inhibition, and parapraxes. If both memory and ESP involve information-processing mechanisms, as some hold, memory psychologists and parapsychologists may find common points of theoretical interest. For example, the "retrieve-edit" model of William James (1890), or its later development in Underwood's (1969) notion of retrieval and discrimination attributes, may be applied to the ESP process for a better understanding of the nature of psi. Also, some of the concepts found in the memory literature, such as short-term and long-term memory, episodic and semantic memory, and productive and reproductive memory may be relevant not only in suggesting new lines of ESP research but also in clarifying some of the questions already raised. The memory psychologist also has much to gain by reflecting on such concepts as psi-missing and the methodological advances parapsychology has made in recent years.

The first significant attempt to relate memory scores with ESP scores was made by Sara Feather (1967). In two series of preliminary tests, each subject was first shown a list of ESP symbols or digits for 15 or 20 seconds. She was then given a card-calling ESP test, and following it was asked to recall the symbols or numbers seen initially. Feather found that the subjects whose recall was better also performed better in the ESP test than did those whose recall was poorer. In a confirmatory experiment consisting of three series, she again obtained significant positive correlations between memory and ESP scores. Other studies that explore the memory–ESP relation include those by Stanford (1970; 1973), Kanthamani and H.H. Rao (1974), Rao, Morrison and Davis (1977), and Rao, Morrison, Davis, and Freeman (1977).

Psi-Missing and the Differential Effect

Another significant area of psi research is psi-missing and the effects associated with it. Psi-missing is the tendency to miss a target when attempting to hit it. Even though systematic study of psi-missing is a later development, the phenomenon of psi-missing was encountered quite early in experimental parapsychology. We find it, for example, in the 1927 experiment of George Esta-

brooks (1961). In a series of tests in which distance was introduced as a variable, his subjects averaged 4.06 hits per run of 25 trials, where the mean chance expectation is 5.00. The negative deviation in this series of experiments is statistically significant, suggesting that the subjects were for some reason missing the targets to a degree that chance is not a reasonable explanation. Rhine (1952) himself found that some of his outstanding subjects (e.g., Linzmayer and Pearce) produced strong negative deviations when they were inadvertently kept overtime, or when they were exposed to unpleasant experimental conditions. As L. E. Rhine (1965) noted, the early investigators considered psi-missing to be "a kind of nemesis which could catch up with an ESP experimenter and trip him unawares" (p. 263).

It was J. B. Rhine who first recognized the importance of psi-missing and the need to study it systematically. In two of his articles (Rhine, 1952, 1969) he discussed at length the question of psi-missing, described the different situations in which psi-missing is likely to occur, and suggested two hypotheses to account for it. Extensive discussions of psi-missing appear also in articles by K. R. Rao (1965a, 1965b) and J. C. Carpenter (1977).

In much of the process-oriented research, psi-missing occurs in one form or another. In the attitude–ESP studies, for example, the goats tended to significantly psi-miss. In the personality studies, the subjects with high scores on neuroticism and introversion also gave significant negative scores. It would seem that a successful experimental strategy for obtaining reliable evidence for psi, especially among unselected subjects, is one that separates hitters and missers.

One of the more frequently observed psi effects is the tendency of subjects to score differentially when tested in two contrasting conditions, such as two sets of targets or two kinds of response modes. This tendency I called the differential effect (Rao, 1965a, 1965b). A survey of the literature bearing on this question done a few years ago revealed 124 series of experiments involving differential conditions. Sixty-five percent of them showed differential scoring when it would be expected by chance to be just one half. More striking was that over a third of the studies provided significant evidence for the differential effect. For experimental reports on the differential effect, see Rao (1962, 1963a, 1963b, 1963c, 1964a), Sailaja and Rao (1973), Sanders (1962), Freeman (1969), Kanthamani (1965), and Carpenter (1971).

Psi and Sensory Noise Reduction

CORTICAL AROUSAL AND ESP

Several parapsychologists consider ESP "an ancient and primitive form of perception" (Eysenck, 1967). Therefore, it is suggested that conditions of high cortical arousal may inhibit ESP, whereas a state of relaxation and reduced sensory input may facilitate its occurrence. British psychologist H.J. Eysenck (1967) surveyed a surprisingly large number of studies that have bearing on this. Pointing out that introverts are habitually in a state of greater cortical arousal than extroverts, Eysenck hypothesized that extroverts would do better in ESP tests than introverts. Indeed, there is much evidence in support of this hypothesis. For over fifty years, extroversion-introversion has been one of the most widely explored dimensions of personality in relation to ESP. Carl Sargent (1981) reviewed all the English-language reports bearing on the extroversion–ESP hypothesis and found that significant confirmations of a positive relationship between ESP and extroversion occur at over six times the chance error.

Honorton, Ferrari, and Bem (1998) report a comprehensive meta-analysis of 60 independent studies of the ESP-extroversion relationship involving 2,963 subjects. The overall weighted mean correlation for all the studies is significant. Honorton, Ferrari, and Bem report, however, that, when the order of presentation of the ESP test is taken into consideration, only the free-response studies showed significant overall correlation between extroversion and ESP. When the personality tests were administered first and the subjects did not have any knowledge of their ESP scores at the time they took the personality test, the results of forced-choice ESP tests do not correlate significantly with extroversion scores. This observation led them to raise the possibility that the significant correlations observed in forced-choice studies may be an artifact of the subjects' knowledge of their ESP scores. The report also contains the results of a new confirmation of the ESP/extroversion relationship in a free-response study.

John Palmer and James Carpenter (1998) question the conclusion of Honorton, Ferrari, and Bem that the extroversion/ESP relationship is limited to free-response studies. They point out that (a) personality scales are not generally susceptible to situational biases and that (b) additional analyses show that the extroversion–ESP relationship for forced-choice tests is a genuine psi effect. Extroversion-ESP studies used in the meta-analysis include both group testing and individual testing for ESP. Most of the free-response studies employed individual testing whereas many of the forced-choice studies were done in groups. This is more likely the confounding variable, rather than testing by forced-choice or free-response methods. Palmer and Carpenter show that a significant relationship between ESP and extroversion scores is present in the data of individual tests and not in the group test data. When group-testing studies are removed from the analysis, the extroversion–ESP relationship is found to be of comparable magnitude for forced-choice and free-response ESP tests. Palmer and Carpenter refer also to a study by Krishna and Rao (1991), which showed that feedback of ESP scores does not bias the responses of the subjects to a personality questionnaire as the hypothesis of Honorton et al. assumes.

There are a number of other studies, which shed direct light on the hypothesis of ESP facilitation via sensory noise reduction. There is substantial evidence to suggest that the occurrence of ESP may be enhanced by procedures that result in the reduction of meaningful sensory stimuli and proprioceptive input to the organism. In fact, many of the traditional psychic development techniques such as yoga appear to employ sensory noise reduction procedures, as do a variety of relaxation exercises and altered state of consciousness. Psi researchers have explored some of these.

RELAXATION AND ESP

Several subjects who have done well on psi tests have claimed that they did their best when they were physically relaxed and their minds were in a "blank" state. Mary Sinclair, whom her husband, novelist Upton Sinclair, found to be an outstanding subject, gave the following advice: "You first give yourself a 'suggestion' to the effect that you will relax your mind and your body, making the body insensitive and the mind a blank" (Sinclair, 1930, p. 180). Rhea White (1964), who reviewed the early literature on this topic, also concluded that attempts "to still the body and mind" are common among the techniques used by successful subjects.

There are 33 ESP studies in which progressive relaxation procedures have been used. Seventeen of these gave significant results. William Braud and associates carried out the most extensive work in this area. In the first experiment (Braud & Braud, 1974) there were 16 subjects and the subjects self-rated their degree of relaxation. Braud and Braud report that those who performed well in the ESP tests rated themselves as more relaxed than the poor psi performers. The second experiment consisted of 20 volunteer subjects who were assigned randomly to "relaxation" or "tension" conditions. Those in the relaxation condition went through a taped, progressive-relaxation procedure (an adaptation of Jacobson's) before taking an ESP test, which was to guess the picture being "transmitted" by an agent in another room. The subjects in the other group were given taped, tension-inducing instructions before they did the same ESP test. Each subject's level of relaxation was assessed through electromyographic recordings. The EMG results showed a significant decrease in the EMG activity among the subjects in the "relaxation" group and a significant increase among those in the "tension" group. As predicted, the ESP scores of the subjects in the relaxation group were significantly higher than those of the subjects in the tension group.

Other reports of interest are Braud and Braud (1973), Braud (1975), and Altom and Braud (1976). Confirmation of Braud's results may be found in Stanford and Mayer (1974). Honorton's (1977) summary of studies on relaxation and psi shows a 77 percent success rate. Ten of the 13 studies involving induced relaxation achieved statistical significance at the 5 percent level in support of psi.

PSI IN HYPNOTIC STATES

The idea that the hypnotic state may be psi-conducive is as old as scientific parapsychology. A French physician, Azam, observed that one of his patients in a hypnotic state responded to an unspoken thought. Pierre Janet was reportedly successful in inducing a somnambulistic trance state 16 out of 20 times by mere mental suggestion (Podmore, 1894). Eleanor Sidgwick (Sidgwick et al., 1889), at the Society for Psychical Research in England, experimented with hypnotized subjects by using two-digit numbers and colors as targets. The Russian physiologist Vasiliev (1963) was highly successful in inducing hypnotic trance by telepathy from a distance. Within the card-calling paradigm, J. J. Grela (1945) reported the first ESP experiment with hypnosis.

Jarl Fahler (1957) carried out experiments in Finland, which gave significant results when the subjects were under hypnosis. He replicated the results in experiments carried out at Rhine's laboratory at Duke University, with the involvement of other experimenters collaborating with him (Fahler & Cadoret 1958). L. Casler (1962, 1964) also reported important work in the area of hypnosis and psi. Casler went a step further than Fahler by giving explicit suggestions to the subjects for improvements in their ESP scoring. Milan Ryzl (Ryzl & Ryzlova, 1962) claimed that he trained the outstanding subject Pavel Stepanek with the help of hypnosis. Charles Honorton's (1977) review lists 42 psi studies using hypnosis, 22 of which gave significant evidence of psi.

Ephraim Schechter (1984) published a review and meta-analysis of the experimental studies of ESP and hypnosis. The analysis confirms the hypothesis that subjects tend to obtain higher ESP scores in the hypnotic state than in a controlled waking state. That the hypnotic state is psi conducive fits well with the observation that people who report spontaneous psychic experiences tend to have dissociative tendencies (Pekala, Kumar, & Marcano, 1995). Hypnotic susceptibility, like psychological absorption, is a dimension of dissociative processes.

A more recent meta-analysis of ESP studies involving hypnosis and contrasting conditions is reported by Rex Stanford and Adam Stein (1994). Included in the analysis are 25 studies by 12 chief investigators. Claiming that their attempt was to extend and refine Schechter's work, Stanford and Stein also report cumulative ESP-test scores significant for hypnosis. They, however, caution that we may not draw any substantive conclusions from the current database, because the difference in ESP scores between hypnosis and contrast conditions is significant only when the comparison condition preceded hypnosis. They point out also that there is significant psi-missing in the contrasting condition.

MEDITATION AND PSI

The practice of yoga, it is said, enables one to develop psychic abilities. In the third century before Christ, Patanjali wrote a treatise on Raja Yoga (Woods 1927) detailing the processes and procedures involved and the varieties of supernormal abilities one may obtain by practicing this discipline. Meditation is the most important feature of yoga. It is pointed out that the practice of intensely focusing attention on a single object and following this by meditation enables the practitioner to hold his focus for an extended period of time, which results in a standstill state of the mind (*samadhi*). The *samadhi* state is the one in which psychic abilities are believed to manifest. Unfortunately, there are very few systematic studies of yogins to test for their psi, even though there is a vast amount of anecdotal material concerning their extraordinary psychic claims. However, a number of exploratory studies in which some kind of meditation procedure was used seem to suggest a positive relationship between meditation and ESP. Honorton (1977) reports a survey that shows 9 out of 16 experimental series involving meditation giving significant psi results. Some of these experiments are discussed in Chapter 11.

ESP IN THE GANZFELD

Finally, a number of well-designed experimental studies looked at the effects of reduced external stimulation on subject's ESP scoring by utilizing the ganzfeld. The ganzfeld is a homogeneous visual field produced, for instance, by taping two halves of a ping-pong ball over the eyes and focusing on them a uniform red light from about two feet. The subject may also be given "pink" noise through attached earphones. After being in the ganzfeld for about one half hour, subjects typically report being immersed in a sea of light. Some subjects report a total "black out," a complete absence of visual experience (Avant 1965). Continuous uniform and unpatterned stimulation in the ganzfeld, it is believed, produces a state that, in the absence of meaningful external stimulation, enhances the possibility of attention to internal states, which in turn facilitates the detection of ESP signals.

In a typical ganzfeld–ESP experiment, the subject while in the ganzfeld for about 30 minutes is asked to report whatever is going on in his/her mind at that time. The subject's mentation is monitored and recorded by an experimenter in another room via a microphone link. In most cases a second experimenter, acting as an agent, located in a different room isolated from the subject and the experimenter monitoring the subject, looks at a picture for about 15 minutes, attempting to "transmit" it to the subject in the ganzfeld. At the end of the ganzfeld period, the monitoring experimenter gives the subject four pictures with a request to rank them 1 through 4 on the basis of their correspondence to the subject's mental images and impressions during the ganzfeld. The monitoring experimenter of course does not have any knowledge as to which one of the four pictures is the one looked at by the agent. After all the four pictures are ranked, the subject is shown the target picture. The rank the subject gives to that picture provides the score for a statistical analysis of the matching of the subject's mentation with the target. Sometimes a judge, in addition to or in place of the subject, does the ranking.

Honorton and Harper (1974) reported the first ganzfeld–ESP experiment, which provided evidence that the subject's mentation during the ganzfeld matched significantly with the target picture. Between 1974 and 1981 there were in all 42 published ganzfeld–ESP experiments of which 19 gave significant evidence of psi; this it seemed that psi in ganzfeld is a highly replicable effect. However, at the joint conference of the Society for Psychical Research and the Parapsychological Association held at Cambridge University during August 1982, psychologist Ray Hyman made a presentation raising serious questions about the replicability of the ganzfeld psi experiment. Subsequently a comprehensive critical appraisal of ganzfeld ESP experiments was published in the *Journal of Parapsychology* (Hyman, 1985). In this paper Hyman (1) challenged the claimed success rate of replication, (2) argued that possible flaws involving inadequate randomization and insufficient documentation vitiate experiments reporting significant psi effects, and concluded that (3) the ganzfeld–ESP data base is "too weak to support any assertions about the existence of psi."

Charles Honorton, who responded to Hyman's critique, points to examples of inconsistent or inappropriate assignment of flaw ratings in Hyman's analysis. He presents his own meta-analysis that eliminates multiple analysis and other problems mentioned by Hyman and argues that neither selective reporting nor alleged procedural flaws account for significant psi effects reported in the ESP ganzfeld studies.

Hyman and Honorton (1986) issued a "joint communiqué" on the psi ganzfeld debate. In it they agree that such considerations as selective reporting or multiple analyses cannot reasonably explain the over-all significance of the effect away. They disagree, however, on the degree to which the effect constitutes evidence for psi. More important are the recommendations they make for conducting future experiments in this area.

Very significant in ganzfeld–ESP research is a report of a replication of the psi ganzfeld effect by Cornell psychologist Daryl Bem and Honorton (1994), published in the mainstream psychology journal, *Psychological Bulletin*. This study, consisting of 11 experiments, utilized computer control of the experimental protocol. It complied with all the guidelines Hyman and Honorton recommended in their joint communiqué. The new setup is called the autoganzfeld. Interestingly, the results of the autoganzfeld studies strongly support the existence of a psi effect in the data and replicate the ESP ganzfeld effect, meeting the "stringent standards" requirement as recommended by Hyman and Honorton in their joint communiqué.

Since the publication of Bem-Honorton experiment there have been a number of other studies of ESP in the ganzfeld. Julie Milton and Richard Wiseman (1999) published a follow-up meta-analysis of 30 more ganzfeld ESP studies conducted between 1983 and 1997. Their analysis did not provide significant cumulative evidence for the ganzfeld effect, raising again the question of replicability of the ganzfeld experiment.

Subsequently, Bem, Palmer and Broughton (2001) further updated the ESP ganzfeld database by adding ten more studies published after 1997 and not included in the meta-analysis by Milton and Wiseman. When these 10 additional studies are included, the meta-analysis yields a mean effect size that is statistically significant, though smaller than the one observed in the earlier studies. Bem et al. observed, however, that some of the experiments included in the new database appeared to deviate

significantly from the standard protocol of the ganzfeld experiment. Therefore they arranged for three independent raters unfamiliar with the studies involved to rate the degree to which each of the 40 studies in the new database deviated from the standard protocol. As expected they found that "the effect size achieved by a replication is significantly correlated with the degree to which it adhered to the standard protocol." They point out: "Standard replications yield significant effect sizes comparable to those obtained in the past." It seems reasonable, therefore, to say that we now have a broad range of replications covering over a period of 25 years. They involve over 90 experiments by a wide range of investigators scattered around the globe and showing a fairly robust effect comparable across studies that adhere to the standard ganzfeld protocol. It may also be noted that correlational studies have shown greater effect sizes when the subjects say that the ganzfeld produced an altered state of consciousness in them, further strengthening our argument that sensory noise reduction is conducive to the manifestation of ESP.

The results from ESP studies involving meditation, relaxation, hypnosis, and ganzfeld thus meaningfully converge to suggest that a reduction of ongoing sensorimotor activity may facilitate the manifestation of ESP in laboratory tests. Whatever may be the mechanism involved in ESP, it is reasonable to assume that ESP is a weak signal that must compete for the information processing resources of the organism. In this process, any reduction of ongoing sensory activity should improve the chances of detecting and registering the ESP signal. It would therefore seem reasonable to conclude that (a) psi exists; (b) psi effects are replicable, and (c) sensory noise reduction through such procedures as the ganzfeld is psi conducive.

The Case for Postmortem Survival

Research on survival of human consciousness after death or outside of the body, such as reincarnation studies and out-of-body experiences (OBEs), has a direct bearing on consciousness studies, inasmuch as any evidence for such survival is against any theory that locates consciousness in the brain. Many of the early psychical researchers were drawn to OBEs because of their relevance to the problem of survival.

PHENOMENA BEARING ON SURVIVAL

There are a large number of cases in which a deceased personality is alleged to have communicated a piece of information to a living person. Apart from the question of the genuineness of the reported cases as evidence for survival, the possibility that these experiences can be explained on the basis of known parapsychological abilities of the living, without assuming the survival of a deceased personality, renders them less than convincing.

L. E. Rhine (1961) analyzed the cases bearing on survival in her huge collection. She tried to find out whether the initiative for the experience rested primarily with the living agent or with the deceased person, assuming that if the latter is the case it must be that the communication comes from the deceased. She found several spontaneous experiences that seemed to suggest on the surface that the deceased personality had induced the experience. But, on further analysis, it appeared that in most of the cases bearing on survival, the initiative of a living agent could not be completely eliminated. She recognized, however, that there were a few cases in which the initiative of the deceased person seemed the only possible explanation.

Recurrent Spontaneous Occurrences: Recurrent occurrences of the poltergeist type involving physical disturbances associated with a particular house or place and occurring over an extended period of time are sometimes regarded as the mischief of discarnate spirits. But unfortunately, most of the poltergeist reports are inconclusive as to the agency responsible for these affects. In some instances, it is reasonable to assume that some maladjusted person in the family or in the neighborhood is responsible for the disturbances. In some others, natural causes, such as underground water, may have caused them. And in those few cases in which the effects are more likely psi-mediated, it is not possible to eliminate the hypothesis that these occurrences are due to the exercise of psi abilities by living persons rather than the dead.

The Alleged Controls of Mediums: The essential feature of a medium that enters into a trance-like state is a kind of dissociation. In the majority of cases, the normal personality of the medium seems to be obliterated and a secondary personality takes it place. Many mediums claim that during the entranced state they are possessed by some discarnate agency in the form of one or more controls, which are alleged to give the ostensible paranormal information. One cannot really take these claims too seriously because, first, there were mediums like Madame Morel (studied by Osty) who never claimed to have had any controls. Second, there is much evidence to show that the alleged spirit controls are only psychological constructs of the medium. Finally, most of the mediumistic material can be explained more parsimoniously if we assume that the medium has ESP.

There are, however, cases like the "Lethe" case, in which the deceased spirit of Myers was alleged to have communicated through Mrs. Piper. The case is indeed impressive as to the detail and richness of the material received in the form of allusions that did not certainly seem intelligible to the medium or the sitters at the time of receiving them. Considerable research had to be done in the "Lethe" case to discover the bearing of these allusions on the message in point. These cases are indeed intriguing, if true, and deserve careful study.

Cross-Correspondences: The cases of cross-correspondence are often cited as evidence of survival. The cross-correspondence cases are those in which the same message purported to come from a single discarnate agency may be obtained through the automatic writings of several sensitives. What one sensitive has written may be a continuation, repetition, or illustration of what some other sensitive has produced in her automatic writing. One main difficulty with the cross-correspondence cases is that it is difficult to evaluate the significance of the correspondences, since a certain number of them can always be expected by chance alone.

Two scripts written at random may contain many similarities if the interpreter takes the trouble to find them. The reported studies of cross-correspondence cases seldom had any controls to eliminate this possibility. It is also very difficult to eliminate the hypothesis of telepathy from some living agent. The fact that these messages were often communicated in a disguised, symbolic fashion does not give them any special status different from ESP, since ESP is reported to manifest in a number of disguised forms.

Apparitions: The most dramatic kind of spontaneous psi experience bearing on survival is the apparitional type. Most genuine apparitions may be explained as telepathically induced hallucinations. There are, however, some that seem to be so realistic and impressive that they are taken as some sort of transported spirit images involving true exteriorization. Here again it is not theoretically necessary to assume another type of objective existence indicating a personality that can survive outside one's body, unless the observed effects cannot be explained by assuming parapsychological abilities.

Out-of-Body Experience (OBE): OBEs are fairly widespread among the normal population (Monroe 1971; Rogo 1978). Some who have experienced them take them as evidence for survival. If one believes that she is a composite of spirit and body, any experience of feeling out-of-body for her is an instance of the existence of a spirit independent of the body. But then others who do not subscribe to such a belief may reasonably demand public manifestation of these experiences, because there is the need to rule out the possibility that the OBEs are simply due to one's active imagination. There is indeed a limited amount of evidence that the OB experience could not have been born out of sheer imagination (Tart 1968; Osis 1978). Even when such evidence exists, however, it is difficult to rule out a parapsychological explanation such as ESP, which appears to be more parsimonious than the spirit hypothesis.

Near-Death Experiences: There is a lot of folklore in many cultures testifying that people at the hour of death have remarkable and unusual experiences that give them visions of dead relatives, religious figures, and glimpses of what is believed to be the after-world. Osis (1961) and Osis and Haraldsson (1977) surveyed deathbed observations of physicians and nurses. Their findings show that (a) the duration of the experiences was short; (b) the apparitions were seen coming from another world and were usually of relatives; (c) most patients appeared to "go" to the other world and (d) the most frequent emotional response was one of peace and serenity, and a religious experience.

With the advances in the practice of medicine, it is no longer very rare to revive a person who has been found to be clinically dead for a while. Such near-death cases have been a subject of study (Kübler-Ross 1969; Moody 1975; Ring 1980). Many near-death cases do not reveal any experiences. However, what is interesting is that when they do, they appear similar. For example, it is common for persons who had a near-death experience to report that they traveled through a dark passage, emerging into a brilliant light. Meeting a luminous person of tremendous personal significance is also not uncommon. What is even more remarkable is that some of them report significant transformations in their lifestyles after they had the experience.

V. Krishnan (1985; 1988) made some important theoretical observations on near-death experiences. First, he critically examined near-death experiences as evidence for survival of consciousness beyond physical death. Second, he made empirically verifiable suggestions for understanding out-of-body visions. Pointing out that out-of-body experiences tend to occur under conditions of sensory deprivation, Krishnan (1993) suggests that out-of-body vision may be a way of satisfying the need for information or stimulation. It may be "useful therefore to investigate whether sensory deprivation, or the stress that it causes, has biochemical or other concomitants that can alter receptor sensitivity" (p. 259).

REINCARNATION STUDIES

Reincarnation is an active belief among many in various parts of the world. The doctrine of *karma* and rebirth is one of the pervasive themes of Indian thought. Numerous reports of ostensible cases of reincarnation have appeared in the popular media. However, the credit for pioneering

systematic research in reincarnation-type cases goes to Ian Stevenson of the University of Virginia, who earned his reputation first as a psychiatrist with a special expertise in clinical interviewing. His initial step in researching reincarnation was to examine the published reports of several hundred cases of claimed memories of past lives. Among them, he found 44 cases in which there were apparent recollections of specific people, places, or events relating to a person who was deceased before the birth of the subject. As may be expected because of the widespread belief in reincarnation in that part of the world, a majority of these cases were from India and Burma. After examining possible alternative hypothesis to reincarnation, including fraud, cryptomnesia, racial memory, ESP and possession, Stevenson concluded that reincarnation is "the most plausible hypothesis for understanding the cases of this series" (1960, p. 108). He was cautious, however, in pointing out that he did not consider them to "prove reincarnation either singly or jointly."

The second phase of Stevenson's research was to personally investigate the alleged cases of reincarnation himself instead of depending on the reports of others. This took him to various parts of the world. His research results were first published in his book *Twenty Cases Suggestive of Reincarnation.*

Stevenson (1974) concludes his review of the cases he himself investigated "without opting firmly for any one theory" as an explanation for all cases. He believes, however, that the evidence in support of the reincarnation hypothesis has increased since his first review. "This increase," he points out, "has come from several different kinds of observations and cases, but chiefly from the observations of the behavior of the children claiming the memories and the study of cases with specific or idiosyncratic skills, and with congenital birthmarks and deformities" (p. 384).

The behavioral features associated with the children believed to be reincarnations of previously deceased persons include:

> (a) Repeated verbal expressions by the subject of the identification; (b) repeated presentation of information about the previous personality as coming to the subject in the form of memories of events experienced or of people already known; (c) requests to go to the previous home either for a visit or permanently; (d) familiar address and behavior toward adults and children related to the previous personality according to the relationships and social customs which would be proper if the child really had the relationships he claims to have had with these persons; (e) emotional responses, e.g., of tears, joy, affection, fear, or resentment appropriate for the relationships and attitudes shown by the previous personality toward other persons and objects; and (f) mannerisms, habits, and skills which would be appropriate for the previous personality, or which he was known to possess. [Stevenson 1974, p. 360]

C.T.K. Chari (1967) published a critical review of Stevenson's *Twenty Cases.* He argued that Stevenson's inability to understand the local languages and his dependence on interpreters was a major weakness in his studies. Chari pointed out the disparity in the frequency of cases reported in North and South India and the time trends in the occurrence of these cases, which, according to him, are due to social and cultural factors. "The South Indian cases that I have been able to investigate personally," he wrote, "have been very, very few and far too unconvincing" (p. 218). Chari also called attention to some discrepancies between the earlier reports of these cases and Stevenson's report, thus raising the question of the reliability of the recorded statements. Chari also expressed skepticism about birthmarks as evidence of reincarnation. He wondered further how reincarnation could be a viable explanation in cases where the alleged reincarnated person was still living after the in-

dividual carrying the "memories" was born. Finally, he concluded that the reincarnationist interpretation of these cases fails to appreciate the possibility of the operation of what he calls general psychometric ESP, which could in principle account for the alleged paranormal events in these cases.

The third step in Stevenson's reincarnation studies was to involve others, not merely as interpreters and translators, but as independent investigators so as to enhance the reliability and authenticity of the reports. One of Stevenson's Indian collaborators, Satwant Pasricha of the National Institute for Mental Health and Neuro-Sciences, points out that her data are similar to Stevenson's in numerous and important respects. She argues that such cross-cultural regularities in the data indicate that the reincarnation experience may be genuine and one that is not due to cultural expectation or fraud (Pasricha 1990).

An important case investigated by Stevenson and others is the case of Sharada, which in many respects is very unusual. Uttara was born on March 14, 1941, in Nagpur. She had a normal childhood, attended college, and obtained postgraduate degrees in English and Public Administration. When she was about 32 years old, she began behaving strangely and spoke in a language other than Marathi (her mother tongue), which was later identified as Bengali. Beginning in March of 1974, there were periodic alterations in Uttara's personality. These episodes occurred more than fifty times, each episode varying in duration from over forty days to just a couple of hours. In the altered state she called herself Sharada, the daughter of a Sanskrit scholar who lived at Burdwan in Bengal. She claimed that she was the wife of a physician by the name of Viswanath Mukhopadhyaya of Shivapur in Bengal and that she died of snakebite at the age of 24, when she was in the seventh month of her pregnancy.

According to the investigators, Uttara,

in Sharada phase, wrote, spoke, and conversed in Bengali, a language she did not understand or speak as Uttara. As Sharada, Uttara manifested behavioral characteristics appropriate to a Bengali woman of the nineteenth century and gave information about people and events that she could not have normally known.

The case of Sharada is different in some important ways from typical reincarnation-type cases, which normally appear during the childhood years of the subject. When Sharada emerged, Uttara was already 32 years old. In some cases of xenoglossy (the apparent ability to recite or converse in an unlearned language), the alleged paranormal linguistic ability has manifested under hypnosis. In the case of Uttara, it manifested naturally, even though there is some reason to believe the early Sharada episodes occurred when Uttara was in an altered state of consciousness following meditation.

Prof. V.V. Akolkar, a social psychologist, investigated the Sharada case completely independent of Stevenson, using his own method. Akolkar interviewed a large number of people associated with the case, including Uttara, and observed the Sharada phase several times. Apparently he had an excellent rapport with Uttara. She spent two days in Akolkar's house in Poona; and the Sharada phase appeared there as well. Apart from the usual interviewing associated with cases such as these, Akolkar (1992) was able to obtain considerable psychological information that seemed to suggest that there was some overlapping between the two personalities. Akolkar, like Stevenson, appears to favor reincarnation as more appropriate explanation of the Sharada case than alternative hypotheses.

Stephen Braude (1992) has criticized Stevenson and associates for not adequately going beyond the surface characteristics into the psychodynamic factors influencing the behavior of Uttara and important persons associated with her. As he puts its, "the reader gets no feel whatever for Uttara and other relevant individuals as persons. We have no idea of what moved them or what their needs and desires were... In fact, it is quite remarkable how little effort Stevenson apparently made to dig beneath the surface of their concerns, either in the actual course of investigation or in his subsequent evaluation of the case material" (pp. 135–136).

The involvement of several independent, well-qualified investigators, like Akolkar and Pasricha, who clearly have the necessary understanding of the cultural factors, greatly enhances the credibility, authenticity, and reliability of the Sharada case. There is no doubt that Uttara in her Sharada phase was able to read, write, and speak Bengali, a skill that she was not known to possess as Uttara. Also, there is little doubt that some of the information that Sharada gave corresponded in significant measure to persons who lived in Bengal during the early nineteenth century. Beyond this, the interpretation of the case at this stage remains very much a matter of one's preference based on prior inclination.

Stevenson's preference for a survivalist explanation of past life memory cases, especially those involving the manifestation of skills such as speaking in unlearned languages, is based on his assumption that skills require practice and that therefore they may not be acquired paranormally without practice. S.E. Braude (1992) contests this position. He argued that "cases of multiple personality suggest that dissociation facilitates the development or acquisition of personality traits and skills which might never be developed or displayed under normal conditions" (p. 139). Further, he points out "suddenly emerging skills of child prodigies often far exceed anything displayed by the subjects investigated in xenoglossy cases or other cases suggesting survival" (p. 141). Stevenson (1992) counters by arguing that he knows of no evidence that child prodigies "manifested the skills without practicing them. If they did, perhaps they brought the skills from a previous life" (p. 149).

There may be those who reject altogether any paranormal explanation of this or similar cases. Stevenson (1984) himself refers in his book to the newspaper reports containing allegations that Uttara learned Bengali in a normal way. He also acknowledges that a "vociferous critic," who was "sure that Uttara had taken extensive lessons in Bengali," (p. 141) gave him the names of persons who could provide the necessary information. The search led Stevenson and Pasricha to T.K. Waghmare, who said, "he had seen Uttara taking a test in Bengali" (p. 141) Stevenson believes, however, that Waghmare may have mistaken Shailaja, Uttara's sister, for Uttara. Both Stevenson and Akolkar discuss other possibilities of Uttara learning Bengali in a normal way. For example, a friend of Uttara claimed that he and Uttara studied Bengali during their final year in high school and "progressed enough to read a Bengali primer" (Akolkar 1992, p. 215) and that Uttara's older brother told Akolkar "Uttara had learned Bengali" (p. 215). Stevenson mentions that two of Uttara's relatives have some knowledge of Bengali, including her younger brother, Satish. He also mentions that Uttara in a Sharada phase was reading a Bengali book when Bhattacharya and Sinha visited her. Both Stevenson and Akolkar remain unconvinced, however, that Sharada's skills in responsive xenoglossy could be explained even if we grant that Uttara had learned how to read Bengali.

At this stage of anecdotal evidence, which is somewhat strengthened by systematic studies by a few serious scientists, the most we can say in favor of survival research in general and of the reincarnation hypothesis in particular is that a case is made for survival. There are, however, several plausible alternative explanations that should be addressed in future research. (For a review of reincarnation studies see J.M. Matlock [1990]).

Awareness-as-Such or Pure Consciousness Experience

"Out of my experience," wrote James, "one fixed conclusion dogmatically emerges, and that is this, that we with our lives are like islands in the sea, or like trees in the forest. The maple and the pine may whisper to each other with their leaves, and Conanicut and Newport hear each other's foghorns. But the trees also commingle their roots in the darkness underground, and the islands also hang together through the ocean's bottom. Just so there is a continuum of cosmic consciousness, against which our individuality builds but accidental fences, and into which our several minds plunge as into a mother-sea or reservoir. Our normal consciousness is circumscribed for adaptation to our external earthly environment, but the fence is weak in spots, and fitful influences from beyond leak in, showing the otherwise unverifiable common connection. Not only psychic research, but metaphysical philosophy, and speculative biology are led in their own ways to look with favor on some such 'panpsychic' view of the universe as this" (Murphy & Ballou 1960, p. 324).

When James writes about religious and mystic experiences, the concept of consciousness takes a form very different from the one we are familiar with in *The Principles*. It becomes broader and more inclusive. James was of the view that religious experiences should be treated in the same manner as any other experiences. Just as our reflective awareness reveals certain states, mystic awareness may also reveal other forms of consciousness. James mentions four marks by which we can justifiably distinguish a mystical experience from non-mystical ones. Mystical experiences are ineffable. They defy any adequate expression in words. They are more like the experiences of feeling than of intellect. Second, they possess a noetic quality. Unlike the experiences of feeling, they are experiences of knowledge. They carry with them a kind of conviction. "They are illuminations, revelations, full of significance and importance" (James, 1902/1914, p. 330). Transience and passivity are the other two less sharply marked criteria of a mystical state.

James argues that if a mystical truth comes to a man with such a force that he cannot help but live by it, no one has any legitimate right to interfere with his way of living. The mystic has the same kind of evidence in favor of his convictions as any of us in ours. "Mystical experiences are as direct perceptions of fact for those who have them as any sensations ever were for us" (James, 1902/1914, pp. 423–424). However, he cautions, mystics have no right to convert us to their creed if we do not feel their way. So, James' thesis is that nonmystical states and rational thought are not the sole dictators of faith, and there may well be other "orders of truth."

As the interests of James moved from ordinary awareness to mystic awareness, the stream metaphor gave way to the metaphor of the ocean, "mother-sea." Whereas the stream metaphor reflects the flow of phenomenal awareness, the ocean metaphor catches the inherent interconnectedness of personal consciousness in a fundamental way at a deeper level of commonality. It is interesting to note that James considers mystic awareness as essentially noetic. Thus, what he calls "cosmic consciousness" is also basically intentional. In other words, it has content; but that content is clearly of a different form. It is in the form of illumination and revelations. They carry with them a sense of conviction and a state of realization rather than mere understanding.

Awareness-as-such is also understood in the sense of pure consciousness. The metaphor of light conveys the nature of consciousness in this sense. For instance, the French thinker Jacques Maritian (1953) sees in us "a spiritual sun ceaselessly radiating which activates everything in intelligence, and whose energy permeates every operation of our mind" (p. 98). Meditators and those claiming to have achieved higher states of awareness speak about pure consciousness. L. Oliver (1987) writes: "Pure consciousness is utterly simple. Meditation makes it possible to reach this simplicity and hold it. Consciousness resting in itself could be compared to the flame of a candle. Every time a thought or feeling arises, and your consciousness attaches to it, it is as if the flame breaks up and scatters, diminishing the power of that central focus" (p. 50).

As an example of a pure consciousness event, Robert Forman (1990) quotes the account of a practitioner of TM who describes how the boundary that ordinarily separates "individuality from unbounded pure consciousness began to dissolve." Once he was able to "let go of the veil of individuality, there is no longer 'I perceiving' or 'I aware.' There is only that, there is nothing else there. In this state, the experiencer is not experiencing as he/she normally does. It is there ready to experience, but the function has ceased. There is no thought, there is no activity, and there is no experiencer, but the physiology after that state is incredible. It is like a power surge of complete purity" (p. 28).

Allan Smith describes in the following words his own "cosmic consciousness experience" (CC), which occurred while he was watching "a particularly beautiful sunset."

The CC experience began with some mild tingling in the perineal area, the region between the genitals and the anus. The feeling was unusual, but was neither particularly pleasant nor unpleasant. After the initial few minutes, I ceased to notice the tingling or did not remember it. I then noticed that the level of light in the room as well as that of the sky outside seemed to be increasing slowly…. It soon became extremely bright, but the light was not in the least unpleasant.

Along with the light came an alteration in mood. I began to feel very good, then still better, then elated. While this was happening, the passage of time seemed to become slower and slower. The brightness, mood-elevation, and time-slowing all progressed together…. Eventually, the sense of time passing stopped entirely. It is difficult to describe this feeling, but perhaps it would be better to say that there was no time, or no sense of time. Only the present moment existed. My elation proceeded to an ecstatic state, the intensity of which I had never even imagined could be possible. The white light around me merged with the reddish light of the sunset to become one all enveloping, intense undifferentiated light field. Perception of other things faded. Again, the changes seemed to be continuous. At this point, I merged with the light and everything, including myself, became one unified whole. There was no separation between myself and the rest of the universe. In fact, to say that there was a universe, a self, or any "thing" would be misleading—it would be an equally correct description to say that there was "nothing" as to say that there was "everything." To say that subject merged with object might be almost adequate as a description of the entrance into CC, but during CC there was neither "subject" nor "object." All words or discursive thinking had stopped and there was no sense of an "observer" to comment or to categorize what was "happening." In fact, there were no discrete events to "happen"—just a timeless, unitary state of being.

CC is impossible to describe, partly because describing involves words and the state is one in which there were no words. My attempts at description here originated from reflecting on CC soon after it had passed and while there was still some taste of the event remaining.

Perhaps the most significant element of CC was the absolute knowingness that it involves. This knowing is a deep understanding that occurs without words. I was certain that the universe was one whole and that it was benign and loving as its ground [Smith and Tart 1998, pp. 100–101].

Smith was a different man after this experience. A trained physician with national recognition for his research, Smith's interests shifted away from becoming a famous academician to an explorer in such areas as theology, psychology, and mysticism. Smith's CC gave him an experience of a "unitary state of being." It appeared timeless, ineffable and devoid of subject-object distinctions. Nevertheless, it involved knowing, a deep nonverbal understanding that was sufficiently strong to change the course of his life. Thus Smith's CC experience fits well with James' description of a mystic state as noetic, transient, ineffable, and so profoundly important as to modify the inner life.

The experience of unity in all things, the oneness of being, appears to be the bedrock of all mystic states. As W.C. Stace (1960) writes: "The most important, the central characteristic in which *all fully developed* mystical experiences agree, and which in the last analysis is definitive of them and serves to mark them off from other kinds of experience, is that they involve the apprehension of an ultimate non-sensuous unity in all things, a oneness or a one to which neither the sense nor the reason can penetrate. In other words, it entirely transcends our sensory-intellectual consciousness" (original emphasis, p. 14). Stace distinguishes between introvertive and extrovertive mysticism. Unlike the extrovertive mysticism, in which the experience of unity is between the world and the self, in introvertive mysticism the unity is contained in the experience of self, with no awareness of the external world. An elemental form of introvertive mysticism, which is more transient and less complex than the extrovertive form, according to Robert Forman (1990), is the pure consciousness event (PCE). The PCE is defined as "a wakeful though contentless (nonintentional) consciousness" (p. 8).

What is contentless consciousness?

How is it different from the deep sleep state in which one has no awareness at all? What difference does wakefulness make to consciousness in a mystic state that gives one no awareness of objects, events, feelings or images? It is possible that the sleep state and the mystic state are physiologically different—even if the claim that the so called transcendental state achieved by advanced meditators produces a physiologically unique state, quite different from wakefulness, drowsiness or sleep, lacks solid basis in fact (Davidson 1976). For example, we may assume a greater degree of alertness and the absence of slow wave (delta) EEG activity in mystic states compared to sleep states. Our concern here, however, is consciousness and not physiology. Phenomenologically or experientially, what is the difference between the contentlessness in a deep sleep state and the lack of content in the PCE? Mystic awareness must mean more than absence of awareness. Mere "blackout" periods, whether brief or prolonged, hardly qualify to be called a state of pure consciousness.

Perhaps nonintentional consciousness is a more appropriate description of the PCE than characterizing it as contentless. Nonintentional consciousness is awareness that is not *of* or *about* anything. There is no directedness about it. It is objectless and nonreferential. The possibility of nonintentional consciousness presupposes dissociation between awareness and the objects of awareness, that consciousness can be experienced outside of any relationship with an object. We have already seen how some such dissociation appears to manifest in the case of implicit awareness, which is awareness without subjective awareness of that awareness. May we, then, regard the PCE as an analogous phenomenon in which there is subjective awareness (awareness of the self) without the awareness of any object, thought, or image? Such an interpretation is not inconsistent with the notion of introvertive mysticism. If we consider, however, contentless awareness as an elemental form of mystic experience, the question arises as to how the more complex mystic states, in which the self is not screened off from the external world but experiences unity with it, as in extrovertive mysticism, are constructed out of contentless awareness.

In primary awareness we postulate the existence of (1) a subject who has awareness, (2) an object of awareness, and (3) the process of awareness. The external object is related to the subject through sensory mediation and the processing in the brain. The experienced awareness is thus constructed to represent the world. In such a situation the subject and the object are seen as *divided but related* by the mediation of the senses and the brain's functions. If our senses and the brain were to be different from what they are, our relation with the world would be different, i.e., reality would be constructed differently. Now, consider the possibility that on occasion the subject can make direct contact with and has unmediated access to the world outside. Such unmediated awareness would indeed look different from ordinary awareness and would not be subject to the transformations and distortions that are brought about by sensory processing. The world would no longer be *represented* through sensations, images and thoughts but would be *revealed* the way it is. We then would know "things-in-themselves." Such revelations could be a source of absolute certainty and ultimate truth, to which knowledge obtained through sensory mediation could never make a credible claim. Further, nonmediated, direct association of the subject and object might also engender the experience of unity between them. The ineffability of revealed truth might be attributed to the absence of linguistic skills and verbal facility that are grounded in brain functions. The conviction of certitude may be a consequence of direct and unmediated access to reality.

Awareness as distinct from the awareness of certain contents is seen by some as that aspect of the mind that is in complementary relationship with the brain in the manner of wave- and particle-like properties of matter. Psychiatrist Arthur Deikman (1973) suggests, "awareness, as distinct from the contents of awareness, is not a special form of sensation, with a particular receptor organ or some other neurological system responsible, nor is it any kind of neural response at all. Rather than being the product of a particular neural circuit, awareness is the *organization* of the biosystem; that is, awareness is the 'complementary' aspect of that organization, its psychological equivalent" (p. 319, emphasis in the original).

Pure consciousness is sometimes understood to refer "to the ground of being" (Lancaster 1991, p. 18). In fact, Brian Lancaster terms pure consciousness itself as being, distinct from consciousness limited to representational awareness. This view is not much different from the Vedic notion of identifying *sat* and *chit*, being and consciousness. The attainment of a state of pure consciousness appears to be the goal of most mystic traditions, Eastern as well as Western. It is a state in which one experiences the unity of all things, one's own identity with reality. It is unmediated and nonintentional. It is not described in terms of sensory experience or mental images (Smart 1965).

The reports of such mystic experiences are legion. However, the question of whether the reports themselves are sufficient grounds to believe in the possibility of pure and unmediated consciousness is much debated. For example, Steven Katz (1978), among others, argued vehemently *"There are no pure (i.e., unmediated) experiences. Neither mystical experience nor more ordinary forms of experience give any indications, or any grounds for believing, that they are unmediated"* (original emphasis, p. 26). The notion of unmediated, pure consciousness, according to Katz, is "empty," if not

self-contradictory. Mystical experiences have content, which is determined by the religious traditions in which the one who experiences them is situated. The form and content of the so-called mystic consciousness are shaped by traditional beliefs and practices, one's concepts and expectations and the wider cultural background. Consequently, there are as many varieties of mystical experiences as there are religious traditions. "The Buddhist experience of *nirvana*," writes Katz (1978), "the Jewish of *devekuth*, and the Christian *uniomystica*, the Sufi of *fana*, the Taoist of Tao are the result, at least in part, of specific, conceptual influences, i.e., the 'starting problems' of each doctrinal, theological system" (p. 62). What a mystic experiences, then, "is the experience he seeks as a consequence of the shared beliefs he holds through his metaphysical doctrinal commitments" (p. 58).

Those who subscribe to the possibility of genuine mystic experiences dismiss, however, any suggestion that all mystic experiences are wholly formed and constructed by one's beliefs, expectations, and backgrounds. Robert Forman emphatically rejects Katz's arguments on the ground that they are systematically incomplete and do not specify how a given concept enters into a claimed mystic experience. Moreover, the history of mysticism is replete with instances, such as Buddha's enlightenment, in which expectations, models, and previously acquired concepts were transformed beyond recognition to constitute radically new and innovative ideas. In fact, Forman points out, an examination of mystical texts reveals quite the opposite of Katz's assertion. The path to mystical awakening may be seen as one of forgetting all those things and their images one has absorbed from his/her culture and turning away from traditional ideas and conceptual forms. Indeed yoga, seen as a means of achieving mystic awareness, seeks systematic cessation of thought and control of sensory processes. Again, if the

PCEs do indeed occur, contrary to the contention of Katz, they certainly do not fit into the thesis that mystic experiences are shaped or formed by previously held concepts. As Stephen Bernhardt points out, "it is hard to see how one could say that the pure consciousness event is mediated, if by that it is meant that *during the event* the mystic is employing concepts, differentiating his awareness according to religious patterns and symbols, drawing upon memory, apprehension, expectation, language or accumulation of prior experience or discriminating and integrating" (1990, p. 232).

Katz and other constructivists, as they are sometimes called, point to interesting differences between various accounts of mystic experiences, suggesting that the lack of unanimity among them is a further confirmation of their contextual origin. If mystic accounts are the result of direct and unmediated experiences of reality, they should be the same for all mystics, whether they are Christian, Sufi, or Hindu. That they are not is proof enough that they are not unmediated. Critics of constructivism, while accepting that there are a variety of phenomenologically distinct mystical experiences and that to a degree they correlate with the cultural and conceptual setting in which they originate, argue that the correlation is contingent and not an essential one. On the one hand, it is suggested, there is essential unity in mystical awareness, but when interpretations get built into the experiences of that awareness differences among them manifest (Smart 1983). It is argued, on the other hand, that mystic experiences may be *contentful* or *contentless*, "that all contentful mystical experiences are context-related and that contentless mystical experiences, although arising out of appropriate contexts, are qua contentless context-free" (Almond 1990, p. 216). That the descriptions of mystical experiences tend to be different is no argument against the underlying uniformity of mystical states, because

the descriptions may have common origin in pure conscious experience. It would seem that mystical experience might involve a two-stage process. The first stage is one of making direct and unmediated contact with reality. That is what we mean by the PCE or contentless consciousness. The second stage is its phenomenological expression in awareness, which obviously is one that is subject to mediation and contextual influence.

Whether or not genuine mystical experiences do occur may not be answered conclusively on a priori considerations or by simple logic. However, it might be helpful to identify a pragmatic criterion of pure consciousness. The "cash value" of having a pure consciousness experience may be seen in the effect it has on the one who has that experience. It has been repeatedly observed that the PCE produces significant personal transformations and simply changes one as nothing else does. The play of pure consciousness is possibly indicated when an individual undergoes a profound personal transformation following a claim of having such an experience. Psychologist Richard Mann (1984/1991), in his insightful study of Swami Muktananda, who is reputed to have experienced such states of pure consciousness, emphasizes also their transforming power. He suggests that realization of pure consciousness would help transform not only the person having experience but also others associated with him in a guru-disciple relationship. Apart from the fact that a claim of experiencing awareness as such has been made on behalf of several sages and saints in the East as well as in the West, there seem also to be similar, though less striking, events in the lives of lesser known persons. For example, people with near-death experiences (NDEs) often report significant lifestyle changes following NDEs.

Abraham Maslow also observed similar transformation among self-actualized persons and people who had what he called peak experiences. Self-actualization means: "What a man *can* be, he *must* be" (Maslow 1973, p. 162, original emphasis). According to Maslow, self-actualizing people have greater access to reality; they see reality more clearly. They are spontaneous, nonconventional, detached, autonomous, and democratic. They are problem-centered and not ego-involved. They focus on ends rather than on means. What is even more interesting in the present context of "mystic experience," the "oceanic feeling" appears to be a common experience among self-actualized persons. They have, in the words of Maslow, "feelings of limitless horizons opening up to the vision, of the feeling of being simultaneously more powerful and also more helpless, the feeling of great ecstasy and wonder and awe, the loss of placing in time and space with, finally, the conviction that something extremely important and valuable has happened, so that *the subject to some extent is transformed and strengthened in his daily life by such experience*" (1973, p. 190, emphasis added). The loss of self or transcendence, intense concentration and self-forgetfulness also characterize the self-actualized person.

Summary

There is evidence to suggest that awareness may occur without being mediated by sensory processes, as is believed to be the case in extrasensory perception. Psi awareness may occur in the form of realistic or unrealistic dreams, hallucinations, intuitions or physical effects. Such awareness may be explicit or implicit. Consequently, it shares some of the characteristics of both primary and paradoxical awareness. It's defining characteristic, however, is that it manifests no causal connection with the presumed source, the object of awareness, and is therefore considered acausal. Further, the evidence for precognition and the success of ESP experiments over long distances suggest that, unlike in the case of phenomenal awareness, space and time do not appear to be limiting conditions for psi awareness. In the case of phenomenal awareness, there is the "accessibility" factor, that is, the object of awareness should be accessible so as to make a sensory contact with the subject. In the case of psi such accessibility is presumed to be nonexisting, and the role of sensory processes is limited, at the most, to making explicit the implicit psi awareness.

The mainstream sciences tend to ignore or reject parapsychological claims primarily on the ground of their antecedent improbability. For the same reason even those who have taken a serious scientific interest in them dub them as anomalous. However, if the claimed phenomena are genuine, as they seem to be, their relevance to understanding consciousness is paramount.

In light of the claimed experiences of mystics and yogins, one may conjecture that it is possible to experience awareness-as-such. The defining characteristic of such an experience is that it has no contents. It is simply a state of being essentially indescribable. The difficulty of conceptualizing such an ineffable state of awareness is obvious. However, the accounts available to us from those who claim to have experienced awareness as such, inadequate though they are, provide some glimpses into its nature. In such a state, the dichotomy of subject and object appears to disappear. The individual having such an experience is believed to realize the oneness and unity of all being. More importantly, experiencing awareness-as-such is seen to influence people profoundly and to bring about in them powerful changes and transformations, suggesting that knowing and being become so integrated in that state that they form into a single process.

It is likely that mystic awareness is a

two-stage process. In the first stage, there is unmediated access to reality. It is a state of pure consciousness. The second stage is the phenomenological expression of the pure conscious event, a mystical experience which may manifest as a noetic revelation, or, as a realization of unity and identity with the universe, may result in feelings of joy, elation, and tranquillity and bring about personal transformations of enormous significance.

There is thus a fundamental difference between awareness as such and phenomenal awareness. The former, which is called by some writers transcendental consciousness, is regarded as nonlocal. It does not involve any sensory processes, has no representa-

tional content and yet is believed to be involved in important ways in the governance of our lives. Does this imply that they are two different, separate domains in our being? Not necessarily. They may be no more different and discontinuous than explicit and implicit awareness, the conscious and the unconscious experiences. Just as explicit and implicit awareness may be helpful in defining each other, phenomenal awareness and transcendental awareness may be useful in understanding each other. Anomalous awareness, which occupies an intermediate place between the two, is best positioned to give us helpful clues for understanding the interplay between phenomenal and transcendental awareness.

CHAPTER 5

Consciousness, Mind and Intentionality: Philosophical Discussions

The relationship of being to consciousness has been a perennial problem for philosophers. The discussions of it, though extensive from Plato to the present, are highlighted by the radical dualism of René Descartes in modern Western Philosophy and are centered on what is generally known as the mind-body problem.

What is the relation between mind and body and between mind and consciousness? Are the mind and the body distinct entities? If they are, how do they interact? If not, how do mental phenomena arise from the bodily processes? How, in other words, does conscious experience arise from the processes in the brain?

Mind and Body

It is quite apparent at the outset that there are some basic differences between what we regard as mental, the "*inner*" experiences, and the physical objects of the outside world. First, the objects in the material world occupy space, they are extended, whereas the mental appear to lack the size and shape that physical objects have. Second, mental states, one's conscious experiences, seem to possess qualities that are utterly unlike the qualities we could conceivably attribute to physical objects. The agony of pain and the ecstasy of love have little in common with the weight of a rock or the fluidity of water. Third, there is what is described as an epistemological asymmetry between the mental and the physical. Conscious experiences are "*private*" in that they are directly accessible only to the experiencing person. We can only have a first-person perspective of them. In the case of physical objects, however, we have "*public*" access to them. If I observe a physical object, any similarly situated person would be able to observe it. The above differences make a *prima facie* case that minds and material objects are indeed very different sorts of things.

Common sense takes for granted that human beings are endowed with a body and a mind, which interact to form functioning persons. In their attempts to analyze the nature of the mind and the body and their interaction, philosophers have arrived at a variety of views. Their speculations fall broadly into two categories: (1) those that assert the reality of both mind and body as constituting two fundamental substances, and (2) those that deny such reality of one in favor of the other. The former are the dualist theories. They build on the commonsense notion that the mind and the body are two different and mutually irreducible but interacting things. If mind and body are like the two opponents in a tug-of-war, as D. M. Armstrong (1988) aptly observes, then we have materialist theories that attempt to drag mind into the camp of body and the mentalist theories attempting the opposite. Dualist theories are those that attempt to maintain an equal balance between them.

René Descartes (1596–1650) is the chief proponent of a full-blown mind-body dualism. He argues that it is intuitively evident that we have minds and bodies, which are essentially distinct. Cartesian dualism, which has come to be a commonsense worldview throughout the Western world, considers mind, the *res cogitans,* as utterly independent of the brain and its existence a self-evident truth. The mind is so self-evident that it requires nothing to explain it. In his celebrated *Discourse on Method,* Descartes affirmed his resolve to arrive at the certain and the indubitable by first rejecting every assumption and supposition that admits of the least doubt. This led him to the famous dictum "*cogito ergo sum*" (I think, therefore I exist) and the notion that whatever is conceived to be a coherent experience, representing clear and distinct ideas, must be regarded as true. Descartes' mind-body dualism is based on three basic arguments. First, I cannot doubt my existence as a "*thinking thing.*" Second, I have clear and distinct ideas of mind as an unextended thinking thing and of body (matter) as unthinking and extended. Third, my body is divisible, where as the mind is indivisible. Therefore, it is evident that my mind and my body are two different kinds of things. Marleen Rozemond (1998) states in the following way the argument of Descartes that mind and body constitute two distinct substances. The defining attribute of a substance cannot be conceived to exist without asserting the existence of that substance. There can be no such attribute as thinking without a thinking substance, whereas we can conceive of thought without assuming an extended substance. We have clear and distinct ideas of body and mind with their respective attributes of extension and thought. Each of the two attributes can be conceived to exist without presupposing the other. Therefore, body and mind must be two distinct substances.

Cartesian dualism accords well with our intuitive sense that we, as purposive and free-acting agents, are different from mechanical and non-conscious material things. It is morally attractive because it elevates humans with autonomous minds above the automata, the mindless mechanical things that lack freedom of the will and are governed by causal necessity and determinism. Notwithstanding these advantages, there are serious problems with such dualism. Foremost of them is the matter of interaction between two entirely dissimilar entities. How does a nonphysical mind interact with physical body? Any kind of causal interaction between them, which is presumed by most dualist theories, comes into conflict with the physical theory that the universe is a closed system and that every physical event is linked with an antecedent physical event. Thus the possibility that a mental act can cause a physical event is preempted unless the mental act itself is presumed in some sense to be physical.

Gilbert Ryle (19490 in his celebrated book, *The Concept of Mind* raised important concerns about the notion of a substantive mind. The mind appears to be an "ontological excrescence," to use the colorful phrase of William Lycan (1987). Also, the evolutionary theory suggests that the human brain, though far more complex and advanced than the brains in other species, does appear to be a continuation of the process of evolution. There seems to be little reason to suppose then that immaterial minds inhabit humans and not other animals. There are of course further arguments from dualists to counter the above criticism.

Parallelist theories, such as the one advanced by the German philosopher G.W. Leibniz (1646–1716), attempt to circumvent the problem of interaction by assuming that physical and mental processes run parallel without influencing each other. Another way to bridge the gap between mind and body is the double aspect theory that regards the physical and the mental as two aspects of a single underlying reality. A related doctrine is panpsychism that accords mental properties to all physical things. A modern version of this is found in David Griffin's panexperientialism. According, to Griffin (1988), consciousness is not a function of a distinct entity called mind, or of the brain but a property of everything that may be considered to be a coherent entity.

In contrast to dualistic theories, monistic theories postulate only one kind of substance, mind or matter. Thus we have theories like the subjective idealism of George Berkeley (1685–1753), which eliminates matter in favor of mind, and materialism, which denies mind in favor of matter. Whereas Berkeley regards material objects as no more than assemblages of sensations, which are called ideas, materialists hold that all mental phenomena are in the final analysis reducible to physical proper-

ties and explained by the laws and principles of physics (Armstrong 1968). There are of course various shades of idealism and materialism.

Between dualism and materialism we have functionalism. In theory, functionalists differ from materialists by denying that mental states are identical with the physical. At the same time, they do not agree with the dualists that mind and body have separate and independent existence. In practice, however, the functionalists are also physicalists in that they see the emergence of mental phenomena in the complex organization of the physical substance (Shoemaker and Swinburne 1984; Shoemaker 1991).

DENIAL OF THE MATERIAL

Idealists, as mentioned, reject the materialistic dimension of being and assert only the reality of minds and their contents. An extreme view, solipsism, limits reality to a single mind and its contents. It should be recognized, however, that the denial of reality to the material world is based on the assumption that any notion that the external objects exist independent of the mind is simply unintelligible. By his famous dictum *"to be is to be perceived,"* George Berkeley attempts to show that the notion of mind-independent objects is simply vacuous and unthinkable. The existence of a tree, for example, consists in one's perceptions of it. A tree outside of the perceptions of it is completely empty of any significance. A mind-independent tree is merely a thought that has no content. The idealistic rejection of a material tree is not, however, the rejection of trees, but the rejection of a mind-independent tree. By denying the materiality of the world, idealism thus circumvents the problem of interaction between minds and material things. However, the problem with such a notion is the difficulty in finding a suitable criterion of personal identity. Idealism, though elegant by its simplicity, is counter-intuitive. It has few adherents in the contemporary Western tradition, which appears to favor the materialistic monism that attempts either to deny the existence of mind altogether, or reduce it to physical states in the brain and the nervous system.

DENIAL OF MIND

Materialistic denial of the existence of mind takes on several forms. (1) One may deny outright reality to mind and anything termed mental, including consciousness that does not translate itself into objective behavior or performance. (2) Accepting the existence of mental phenomena, one may attempt to argue that they have no causal efficacy on their own on the ground that they are only by products of physical processes. (3) Without disputing that mental states are not without causal effects, one may seek to identify mental states with, or reduce them to, events and processes in the brain. Materialist accounts of mind currently fashionable fall into two main categories— peripheralist materialism as exemplified by (a) behaviorism and (b) epiphenomenalism and central-state materialism.

Philosophical Behaviorism: The common expression of the English language treats the word "*mind*" as a noun, which denotes a thing. Questioning this notion, behaviorism proceeds with the assumption that the mind is not a thing like the brain or body. Minds, it is argued, are not entities and consciousness is not a quality inherent in them. Mental states are not the states that are privately lodged in substantive and nonphysical entities called minds. The entity notion of the mind, in this view, is the result of the "*language games*" we play. We are misled by the grammar of language to regard the mind, like the brain or butter, as a substantive noun (Wittgenstein 1922/1961).

Gilbert Ryle (1949) argued, as men-

tioned, it is a category mistake to postulate the existence of a substantive mind over and above certain behavioral states and dispositions. Just as there is no "*team*" over and above the players in it, there can be no entity called mind apart from the phenomena we designate as mental. If you were to ask, "*where is the university?*" after seeing the different administrative and academic buildings, the library, the students and the faculty, you would be making a category mistake in thinking that the term "*university*" is a physical entity like Holt Hall. It is mistaking something as belonging to one "*logical type or category*," when in fact it belongs to another. Ryle thus credited himself with exploding the myth of the ghost in the machine, the illusion of the mind residing in the body and controlling our perceptions, beliefs and actions.

Now, the question arises, what precisely are those mental states that we mistake for minds? According to the behaviorist, the so-called mental states are none other than the manifest behavior or the dispositions for such behavior. The mental state of fear, when you see a snake in the grass, for example, is the behavior that ensues following the belief that you saw a snake and that it is dangerous. It consists in the appropriate measures you take to escape, such as running away and the like. To say a man is creative is to say that he finds novel solutions to problems and that he comes up with new ideas or new combination of ideas, and so on. The anger in a man is the difference we find between his behavior and the behavior of one who is not angry. When you groan in pain, it is suggested, it does not mean that there are such things as pains, which you experience. Rather, pain is a complex description of your behavioral condition when you are in pain. States of mind, in the behaviorist view, are thus what those in those states do or would do. In other words, behaviorism asserts that all statements about the mental may be shown to be statements about behavior or dispositions to behave. It may be noted that behaviorism finds it necessary to extend the translation or reduction of mental statements beyond manifest behavior to include dispositions as well, because an angry man may not shout or do anything to show that he is angry. Once we introduce dispositions and beliefs into the equation the whole exercise becomes open-ended and there is no limit to what one may be disposed to do, when in anger, for instance.

Attempts to translate statements about mental states into dispositions have even more basic problems. Your disposition to run away when you see a snake is contingent on your belief that this snake is poisonous. Even if you believe that the snake in question is poisonous, your follow up action may depend on other beliefs you may have such as your belief that it is safer to attempt to kill it than run away from it. Or you may be disposed to catch it and turn it over to the local reptile protection agency. What you do or are disposed to do thus depends on your other beliefs or desires. In our attempts to analyze away mental states into behavioral states, we are thus led back again to reintroduce mental states. Further, it is reasonable to think that some statements of mental states may not be translatable into statements of behavior or dispositions. The experience of pain is hurtful, and the hurt is not represented by the so-called dispositions to pain-behavior. A good actor may display behavior of a person in pain without experiencing the pain, and the feeling of being hurt. Again, one may experience pain without manifesting it in the behavior. There are thus important differences in our experience of events that are not found in behavioral analysis.

It is clear that by denying the subjective states behaviorists are simply overlooking striking characteristics of sensory experience, the felt phenomenal qualities that are so obvious to all of us. Again, as pointed

out by several writers, the conceptual possibility of "inverted spectrum" argues against behaviorism. Let us suppose that a person was born with a peculiar neurological condition that he sees green when we see red. This congenital condition was not diagnosed. The person learns the color words as we all do and calls red things "red," even though the color that actually registers in his brain is green and not red. Consequently, there is no difference behaviorally between us and the person with inverted spectrum. He stops appropriately when the traffic signal is red. He is able to label colors correctly. Since his behavior is indistinguishable from normal people, we must conclude, following behaviorism, that the inverted spectrum person has the same phenomenal experience as we do. This is obviously false. Therefore, behaviorism can not be correct.

Epiphenomenalism: Epiphenomenalism, like behaviorism, rejects the notion of a substantive mind, but accepts that consciousness and states of mind exist. They are, according to epiphenomenalism, by-products of what are essentially brain processes, and they have no causal efficacy whatsoever. They are not seen as involved in controlling our behavior or actions. As B. F. Skinner (1971) put it, "*they are by-products and not to be mistaken for causes*" (p. 14). In essential respects, epiphenomenalism is no different from behaviorism because what is left of consciousness and mental states in the epiphenomenalist view is so impotent and irrelevant that it can be ignored. There is no plausible way of specifying different states of consciousness because the theory denies a priori any links between them and behavior. Contemporary refutation of epiphenomenalism is reflected in what is known as "*the problem of Zombies*." If consciousness has no causal influence, conceivably there can be no difference between two organisms, which are identical in all respects, except that one has conscious experiences and the other does not. Suppose there is another creature like me, my Zombie twin, who is identical to me in every other respect except that he has no real conscious experience. If the epiphenomenalist is correct, not only are Zombies theoretically possible, but they are essentially indistinguishable from those who do experience the feel of phenomenal awareness. (For a more detailed discussion of the Zombie problem see Chalmers (1996a) and Block (1995).

In a significant sense the peripheralist views attempt to eliminate "consciousness" altogether in psychological discourse by asserting its futility as a psychological concept. Contemporary resonance of such a radical and uncompromising view may be seen in assertions like the one by Stanovich (1991). He writes: *"Every issue in psychology that has touched 'consciousness' has become confused; and every bit of theoretical progress that has been attained has been utterly independent of any concept of 'consciousness'"* (p. 647, original emphasis).

Central-State Materialism: Central-state materialism, unlike the peripheralist theories, does not deny that the mind is a thing. Further, it regards mind as causally efficacious. The mind, however, is not considered a spiritual, nonphysical or immaterial thing, as dualist theories tend to postulate. Rather, it is seen as located in the brain and the nervous system. What causes our behavior is the brain; the goings on in the central nervous system are in this view sufficient to explain completely all forms of behavior. Thus central-state materialism is a causal theory of mind. All the facets of behavior, which are presumed to be the manifestations of the mind, are caused, according to this view, not by any mysterious entity but by natural processes in the central nervous system and are therefore explainable in neurophysiological terms. As D.M. Armstrong (1968) puts it, "mental states are not simply *determined* by corresponding states of the brain, but they are actually identical with these brain-states, brain-states that involve nothing but physical properties" (p. 182, original emphasis).

Now, what does the statement that mental states are physical states of the brain mean? Armstrong answers by what he calls, "the causal analysis of the mental concepts." According to this analysis, "the concept of a mental state essentially involves, and is exhausted by, the concept of a state that is *apt to be the cause of certain effects or apt to be the effect of certain causes*" (p. 182, original emphasis). Mental concepts get their meaning either by the effects they produce, e.g., the term poison gets its meaning by its effect in causing ill-health and even death, or by a consideration of how they are caused. The effects caused by mental states are the correlated patterns of behavior of the person in those states. The causes of the mental states, according to this view, are the objects and events in the environment of the person. The mental state, for example, the desire for food, is a state of food-seeking and food-consuming behavior. A sensation of green "is the characteristic effect in a person of the action upon his eyes of a nearby green surface" (p. 183).

Armstrong distinguishes between three kinds of mental states. First, there are unconscious states as when one is in deep sleep. An unconscious person obviously does not perceive, has no sensation of hunger or pain. We cannot deny, however, certain mental attributes to that person. We may credit her with certain abilities, knowledge, beliefs, character and temperament. This state, according to Armstrong, is one of *minimal consciousness*, in which the mind is causally quiescent. Second is *perceptual consciousness*, which arises when the mind is active and becomes aware of what is currently going on in the immediate environment. Such awareness, however, need not be explicit. Consider, for example, the case of a long-distance truck driver who after driving for many hours may find that he does not recall doing anything for some time past. Clearly there was mental activity during that period, because without it he could not have successfully driven the truck. So, it is argued, the driver had *perceptual consciousness* even though he did not have *introspective consciousness,* which is the third and possibly the most complex kind of consciousness. Introspective consciousness is much like Kant's *"inner-sense."*

There are well-known objections to all the above renderings of the mind and mental states into behavioral or neural terms. As a fact of immediate experience, consciousness as it manifests in explicit mental states cannot be denied. The phenomenological experience of pain, it is argued for instance, is qualitatively different from neural excitations in the brain. The pain experience is homogenous and continuous whereas the neural events accompanying pain are heterogeneous, discontinuous, and spatially discrete. In other words, unlike felt experience, brain activity is *"grainy"* (Sellars, 1963; Meehl, 1966). Mental states may involve phenomenal properties that appear in principle incompatible with materialism in general and central-state materialism in particular. This is the problem of the subjectivity of conscious experience that we discussed as a basic characteristic of primary awareness. The arguments of Thomas Nagel (1974), Frank Jackson (1982), Colin McGinn (1991), and Ned Block (1995) against all attempts to find a physical explanation of subjective experience of consciousness may be seen as convincing refutations of materialism as a philosophy of the mind.

In an incisive and critical analysis of contemporary materialism, John Searle (1992) points out that materialism in all its incarnations ranging from logical positivism and Watsonian behaviorism to identity theories and strong artificial intelligence is essentially guilty of leaving out the mind. He

writes, "it has left out some essential feature of the mind, such as consciousness or 'qualia' or semantic content" (p. 30). Behaviorism, for example, in denying the existence of any inner mental states goes counter to our experience of "what it is like to be a human being."

Searle (1992) further argues that an identity theory, which identifies the properties of our subjective experience such as pain with neurophysiological properties in the brain, either "leaves out the mind or it does not; if it does, it is false; if it does not, it is not materialism" (p. 37). The properties of pain are either mental or they are not. If identity theory asserts that the experience of pain is mental, then it is no longer a materialistic theory. If the theory, however, leaves out the subjective feature of the pain, unable to name a subjective feature of certain neurophysiological events, it essentially leaves out the mind.

The irreducibility of mental phenomena to the physical is, however, according to Searle, "a trivial consequence of the pragmatics of our definitional practice" (p. 122). He illustrates this by pointing out that the reduction of phenomena such as heat to the kinetic energy of molecular movements is based on a distinction made between the third-person "objective reality" and the first-person "subjective appearance." Since the reality of consciousness is its appearance, argues Searle, "The point of the reduction would be lost if we tried to carve off the appearance and simply defined consciousness in terms of the underlying physical reality" (p. 121).

While thus upholding the view that mental phenomena with their essential characteristic of subjectivity are irreducible according to standard ways of reduction, Searle, nonetheless, regards consciousness as essentially a biological phenomenon produced by processes in the brain. Mental phenomena, according to Searle, are supervenient on the physical, in the sense that the same neurophysiological states cause the same mental phenomena. David Chalmers (1996a), among others, questions the notion of the supervenience of the mental on the physical and narrates a number of compelling reasons why consciousness is not logically supervenient on the physical.

Functionalists like Putnam and Fodor argued that the identity theory implies that only the physiochemical states in the brain realize consciousness and that it would not be possible for dissimilar structures to give rise to similar mental states. There is no logical reason, however, why silicon based electronic circuits, instead of carbon based neural networks, may not realize mental states. What matters in the manifestation of mental states are not the structures of the brain states but their functional properties.

The materialist theory of mind in all its forms stands refuted if paranormal phenomena are considered genuine. For example, the reality of ESP is at once evidence against the materialist conception of the mind (Beloff 1962). Inasmuch as the brain's capacity to receive information is strictly limited to that which is received via the neural pathways, ESP is beyond the reach of the brain. Again, PK demonstrates that minds can do things that no brain can do. One may hope that new advances in physical theory may accommodate psi phenomena. However, as Keith Campbell remarks: "The doctrine that some science, we do not know which, is adequate to support the Central-State doctrine of the mind, is so vague and so weak that it is not worth holding or discussing" (1970, p. 97).

FUNCTIONALISM

Like materialism, functionalism comes in various versions. All of them claim, however, that all mental states are functional states and that they can be defined in terms of sensory inputs and behavioral outputs (Shoemaker and Swinburne 1984). Functionalism attempts to sidestep the issue whether mental phenomena are reducible to the physical. It accepts the behaviorist assumption that mental terms can be defined in operational terms. However, in the functionalist view, mental states are not mere states of behavior disposition. Nor are they brain states, as identity theorists assert. Rather, a mental state is a functional state, a result of a certain functional organization. As Hilary Putnam argues, "pain is not a brain state, in the sense of a physical-chemical state of the brain (or even the whole nervous system), but another kind of state entirely. I propose the hypothesis that pain, or the state of being in pain, is a functional state of the whole organism" (1991, p. 199). Though many functionalists tend to be materialists, functionalism is not in principle incompatible with dualism (Putnam, 1991). There is no a priori reason why the functional states that are regarded as mental are necessary manifestations of physical processes alone. What are relevant to a proper understanding of mental states are their functional roles and not their structure.

Functionalism, like central-state materialism, embraces a causal theory of mind. Mental states are defined in terms of the functional roles they play in a complex cause-and-effect, input-output network. The organism receives inputs (sensory and other) and in turn delivers corresponding outputs. The organism may be seen as a system composed of several subsystems. Consequently, the inputs and outputs may be from one subsystem to another. These subsystems, however, may not correspond to physically distinct components of the organism; rather they may represent different modes of functioning, without necessarily involving a different physical structure (Lockwood, 1989).

The input-output model of functionalism is clearly the favorite of cognitive psychologists engaged in abstract modeling of cognitive processes independent of their neurophysiological basis and the researchers in artificial intelligence occupied with writing computer programs that perform functions analogous to those performed by the human mind. The relationship between the brain and the mind is considered to be similar to the one between the hardware and software in the functioning of a computer. Consciousness is the software program running on the hardware brain. Though we may know much about the program from the system that is running it, the program itself can never be fully understood, much less experienced, by the hardware. Understanding the brain may give us much information about consciousness and mental states, but it will never tell us everything about them. An understanding of their functional roles alone, it is believed, can give us an understanding of mental phenomena (Dennett, 1991).

From the functionalist viewpoint, it is not inconceivable that nonorganic entities such as computers may have mental states. What are relevant here are the functions that a system performs and not the substance or material that constitutes it. If machines carry out the kinds of actions human minds are credited with performing, then, in this view we may ascribe mental states to them. Whether a machine such as a computer can indeed perform what the brain does is, however, arguable. Some functionalists hold that a structure such as the brain, with complex, multiple and parallel connections, is necessary to produce mental states and that computational models of the mind are simply inadequate to this task (Bechtel & Abrahamsen 1991).

There are well known objections to functionalist theories of consciousness. Like other materialist theories of mind, functionalism provides no viable explanation of subjective and qualitative aspects of experience, which we discussed in chapter 2. The qualia, the phenomenal properties of mental states, appear too elusive to be captured in a functionalist theoretical framework. They defy attempts to define them in terms of their functional roles. "The subjective character of experience," as Thomas Nagel points out, "is not captured by any of the familiar, recently devised reductive analyses of the mental, for all of them are logically compatible with its absence. It is not analyzable in terms of any explanatory system of functional states, or intentional states, since these could be ascribed to robots or automata that behaved like people though they experience nothing" (1974, pp. 166–167).

Ned Block (1991) describes the "troubles of functionalism" as chauvinism on the one hand and liberalism on the other. He argues that the functionalist theories of the mind are *chauvinistic* in that they deny with no sufficient reason mental attributes to certain systems, which may well possess them. They are liberal in ascribing mental properties to systems that do not have them. Any description of mental states in terms of inputs and outputs, as functionalists attempt to give, necessarily excludes other systems that do not satisfy that description from the class of mental states. Imagine, says Block, an alien whose inputs and outputs do not match the descriptions we specify for mental states. Can we on that ground deny all mental ascription to it? Again, Block argues, imagine a situation in which the billion inhabitants of China establish with each other connections via appropriate radio links to functionally simulate a human brain. Now suppose they can communicate with each other like neurons in the brain do. "It is not at all obvious," writes Block, "that the China-body system is physically impossible. It could be functionally equivalent to you for a short time, say an hour" (1991, p. 216). However, "there is prima facie doubt whether it has any mental state at all—especially whether it has what philosophers have variously called 'qualitative states,' 'raw feels,' or 'immediate phenomenological qualities'" (p. 217).

Some philosophers of a functionalist persuasion have gone as far as denying the very existence of qualia. For example, Daniel Dennett categorically asserts, "there simply are no qualia at all" (1997, p. 620). Taking the features of qualia to be "ineffable, intrinsic, private and directly or immediately apprehensible in consciousness," Dennett attempts to show that there are no properties in our conscious experience that match such a description. He concludes, "'qualia' is a philosopher's term that fosters nothing but confusion, and refers in the end to no properties" (p. 623). Even the Churchlands (1982), who subscribe to the identity thesis, disagree with such a blanket rejection of qualitative states of awareness. "The functionalist need not and perhaps should not," they counsel "attempt to deny the existence of qualia. Rather, he should be a realist about qualia" and hope that their nature would be revealed "by neurophysiology, neurochemistry, and neurophysics" (1952, p. 31). Patricia Churchland argues that subjective consciousness is analogous to heat. When we keep something in the microwave to heat, the molecules of the food in the microwave start to move faster and faster. The motion of molecules does not generate heat; it is heat. Likewise, consciousness is not produced by the functions of the brain. Rather functions of the brain *are* consciousness.

Paul Churchland (1989, 1995) continues the same line of argument when he suggests that we do away with "folk psychology" by replacing all discussion of mental events such as desires and beliefs with neural descriptions of behavior. In fact he goes so far as to argue that all scientific theories should be stated in terms of neuron networks and patterns of connections between neurons instead of sentences. This extreme view flies in the face of all our experiences. Also, the presumed identity between mental events and brain states, their perfect correlation, is not a fact that is established by empirical research. There is, of course, substantial evidence for the dependence of mental states on the events that take place in the brain. That evidence, however, falls far short of establishing a one to one correspondence between the items of experience and brain events, as required by the identity thesis. Even granting a perfect correlation between them, the theory implies the existence of two distinct categories that appear to be empirically correlated. The identity theorist would argue that the distinction between the two is only linguistic and that a complete understanding of the causal dependence of one on the other would obliterate that distinction in due course. This is, however, highly unlikely. Most people would consider their personal experiences more authentic than the events in the brain and the nervous system, even if one becomes aware of the latter.

Another related question is whether machines like computers can be credited with minds. Are they conscious? If all mental events are neural connections, it should be possible to simulate them in machines. It is suggested that the advances in neuroscience, computer simulation of human thought, artificial intelligence, and cognitive psychology increasingly threaten the notion that consciousness is an especially human prerogative. Recent attempts to design representational schemes by which computers may be able to generate global understandings have left many with the belief that the human mind may be no more than an information-processing machine and that all information is diffused in the brain. The distinction between conscious experience and the brain, it is suggested, may be the same as the logical-structural distinction in the Turing machine (Turing, 1950).

The Turing test is a proposal to determine whether computers can be credited with consciousness. Turing (1950) suggested that if a computer can successfully mimic human performance, so that a person communicating with a computer and a human being through a teletype terminal is unable to discriminate between the remarks of the human being and those generated by the computer, then the computer may be credited as being conscious. There are several objections to the Turing test. Roger Penrose (1989, 1994) argued persuasively that human thought cannot be considered as all algorithmic, and that it involves more than following fixed mechanical procedures in producing the output. For example, to prove the truth of Godel's incompleteness theorem requires more than algorithmic reasoning. Even Paul Churchland (1995) appears to agree with this contention.

Consciousness and Mind

Consciousness as a psychological concept had its origins in the writings of the seventeenth century philosophers René Descartes (1596–1650) and John Locke (1632–1704). Descartes, as noted earlier, is possibly the most influential Western thinker and much of the philosophy of mind has since been devoted to discussing the crucial issues raised by him.

CARTESIAN IDENTITY OF MIND AND CONSCIOUSNESS

According to Descartes, let us recall, the mind is different from the body, including the brain and the nervous system. The essential feature of physical reality is that it has extension, occupies space and is visible. Consequently, it admits of precise mathematical description and explanation, and it can be accurately described in geometrical terms. Unlike material reality, the essential characteristic of mind is not spatiality, but thinking. Mind, according to Descartes (1985), is: "A thing that doubts, understands, affirms, denies, is willing, is

unwilling, and also imagines and has sensory perceptions." The notion that thought is the essence of mind is a corollary of Descartes' basic postulate that "I exist because I think." One can doubt the existence of everything except itself. My knowledge of my thinking is thus far more certain, clear and distinct than my knowledge about anything else.

Descartes believed also that we have awareness of all our thoughts and that nothing is hidden from our minds. He wrote: "The fact that nothing can exist in the mind, in so far as a thinking thing, of which it is not conscious, seems to me self-evident because we conceive nothing to exist in it, viewed in this light, that is not thought, and something dependent on thought; for otherwise it would not belong to the mind, in so far as it is a thinking thing. But there can exist in us no thought of which, at the very moment that it is present in us, we are not conscious." (Descartes 1952, p. 162). Descartes did not limit thinking to higher cognitive activities. All mental activities, according to him, are forms of thinking; otherwise they are not mental at all. The perception of seeing something, for example, is thinking that it is a particular object. Mere sensations that do not involve thinking are manifestations of the body and are not mental. By 'thought,'" Descartes understands everything in our awareness. *Thinking* is more than understanding, willing and imagining; it includes "sensory awareness" as well. Sensing in humans is thus a form of thinking.

Descartes believed that physical reality, unlike the mental, is amenable to complete mathematical description. The properties we attribute to physical objects such as weight, sound and color, can be stated in mathematical terms. However, the experience we have of them, their qualitative aspect, is beyond mathematical description; and therefore, they should be considered nonphysical. This led Descartes to consider all sensory experience as a form of thinking.

Descartes is very clear that only humans have minds and are capable of thinking. Animals do not have minds; they do not think. The behavior of animals, in Descartes' view, can be explained in essentially physical and mechanical terms. Even in humans, such activities as digestion and muscular reflexes do not involve the mind because they can be accounted for in strictly mechanical terms. Animals are "natural automata." Since the essence of mind is thought and, since all thought is transparent to itself, we are led to assume a reflexive relationship between thought and subjective awareness. What we know of the mind is the awareness underlying its activities, such as doubting, willing, imagining and so on. Thus we find Descartes espousing a conception of mind as consciousness. Consciousness in this view is not merely coextensive with the mind; it is the mind. That mind and consciousness are synonymous and interchangeable terms has since come to be a dominant aspect of the Western philosophical tradition. This appears to be the case whether or not one believes in the substantiality and nonphysical nature of the mind as Descartes did.

Even though Descartes deduced his certainty of the existence of consciousness on rational rather than empirical grounds, i.e., from the indubitability of its existence inherent in the very nature of consciousness, his conception of mind has a crucial distinguishing characteristic. He assumed mental phenomena to be essentially devoid of any corporeal quality. If, for example, all mental phenomena can be accounted for in physical terms, and if the presumed activities of the mind such as thought, volition, and so forth are shown to be governed solely by mechanical principles, as Descartes recognized in the case of reflex actions, there would be hardly any empirical justification for assuming that humans, unlike animals,

have mind/consciousness. Also, consider the logical weakness in Descartes' assertion that his inability to doubt that he is doubting is sufficient ground for believing in the independent existence of mind. Although it is self-evident that you cannot doubt your doubting, it is not so evident that you can do the doubting independent of the body. Thus the importance of attesting to the existence of what Descartes called "ideas of pure mind" that have no corporal base becomes more relevant.

There are two aspects in Descartes' thought that are especially significant to our discussion of consciousness in the Western tradition. One of them is methodological and the other is substantive. Methodologically, Descartes was concerned with arriving at things whose existence cannot be absolutely doubted. He found such indubitable knowledge in the act of cognition itself. At the substantive level, he not only conceived of the universe as sharply and irreducibly divided into mind and matter, but he also regarded the mind essentially as nonphysical consciousness, consisting of thought, desires and all forms of perception and knowledge. These ideas continue to have a profound impact on the Western mindset.

THE BRITISH EMPIRICISM

John Locke (1632–1704) did not commit himself to dualism or the nonphysicality of the mind, as Descartes did. He, however, like Descartes, asserted that the mind is transparent to itself. He argued that it is "altogether as intelligible to say, that a body is extended without parts, as that any thing *thinks without being conscious of it*, or perceiving, that it does so" (Locke 1975, p. 592 emphasis in original). "Consciousness," wrote Locke, "is the perception of what passes on in a Man's own mind" (p. 592). It is reflection contained in the acts of perception, volition and thinking. The mind, however, is to begin with a *tabula rasa* or white paper. It has no ideas of its own. Whatever ideas it acquires are furnished in experience by reflection.

Again like Descartes, Locke makes no distinction between mind and consciousness. They are used synonymously. This fact becomes very clear when he discusses the question of personal identity in his classic *Essay Concerning Human Understanding*. Asserting that consciousness always accompanies thinking, Locke points out that it is consciousness that gives one the identity, the sense of self that distinguishes one from others and provides continuity between the past and the present and the present and the future. Humans have reason and reflection and are therefore able to think of themselves as separate selves. The self or mind can consider itself "the same thinking thing in different times and places; which it does only by that consciousness, which is inseparable from thinking, and as it seems to me essential to it: It being impossible for any one to perceive, without perceiving that he does perceive" (Locke 1975, p. 134).

Since Descartes and Locke, the discussion of consciousness in the Western tradition is dominated on the one hand by the presumption that mind and consciousness are synonymous, if not identical, and by the apparent duality between mind and body on the other. Much of the subsequent scholarly discourse on mind/consciousness was dominated by these concerns. Either the duality of mind and body is asserted, or it is denied to be real by arguing that one can or cannot be reduced to the other. This debate continues to this day, despite the widely known claim of Gilbert Ryle (1949) that he exploded the myth of "the ghost in the machine" by showing that it is a category mistake to postulate the existence of mind over and above certain behavioral states and dispositions.

We find, therefore, that those of the materialist persuasion argue, as we have discussed previously, that there is nothing in conscious experience that cannot be accounted for in strictly physical terms. Again, it is not surprising that contemporary defenses of dualism from an empirical perspective fall back on those mental phenomena that seem to defy materialistic explanations. John Beloff, for example, argues that physicalism in principle is inconsistent with phenomena like ESP (see Smythies & Beloff 1989).

As mentioned above, according to Descartes, all sensing is a form of thinking. This had become necessary for him because qualities we attribute to objects such as color do not admit mathematical description, which he conceived as a necessary condition of being physical. For Locke, however, sensing and thinking are distinct. Qualities in his view are of two kinds—primary qualities such as size and form, which are considered by Descartes as amenable to mathematical description, and secondary qualities such as color and taste that are ideas in the mind produced by combinations of primary qualities. Primary qualities are in "things themselves, whether they are perceived or no; and upon their different modifications it is, that the secondary qualities depend" (Locke 1975, p. 136). So, according to Locke, we have two kinds of ideas depending on whether they relate to primary or secondary qualities. The ideas of primary qualities are the resemblances of objects and they inhere in them, whereas the ideas produced by the secondary qualities have no resemblance to the objects and they do not exist in those objects.

The Irish philosopher George Berkeley (1685–1753) argues that we cannot really separate the two kinds of ideas. Consciousness, according to Berkeley (1975), is an aspect of all ideas. Sensations or ideas exist only in the mind perceiving them. The existence of all sensible things is in the perceptions we have of them. "Their *esse* is *percipi*; nor is it possible they should have any existence out of the minds or thinking things which perceive them." Thus, Berkeley asserts the primacy of mind over matter. The existence of the latter is reduced to the mental observations of them.

British empiricism reaches its logical culmination in the writings of the Scottish philosopher David Hume (1711–1776). Hume wrote, "what we call mind is nothing but a heap or collection of different perceptions, unified together by certain relations, and suppos'd tho' falsely, to be endow'd with a perfect simplicity and identity" (1978, p. 207). Just as Berkeley saw nothing in material objects except the perceptions we have of them, Hume noted nothing in the mind except its perceptions, impressions and ideas. "To hate, to love, to think, to feel, to see, all this is nothing but to perceive" (1978, p. 67). The mind that constitutes one's identity is not an immaterial substance. In fact, it is constituted by "successive perceptions only," which are related by resemblance and contiguity. In Hume's view, "personal identity *arises* from consciousness; and consciousness is nothing but a reflected thought or perception" (p. 635). Thus, according to Hume, there is no substantive mind apart from consciousness. Causality is not a logical relation, nor is it an item of experience. Rather, it is based merely on the association of perceptions. According to Hume, perceptions are of two distinct kinds: impressions and ideas. The difference between them consists in the "force and liveliness" with which they enter our thought or consciousness. What is certain is that which is given in experience; and what are given in experience are impressions or sensations. Consequently, Hume argues, metaphysical speculations can never be rationally demonstrated as ultimately true. There can be no rational certainty for empirical knowledge, either on the grounds of causation or of induction. The espousal of such a skeptical outlook has had enormous impact on the subsequent philosophy of mind.

In Hume's epistemological skepticism, empiricism reached its logical conclusion, denying that there is any compelling reason to attribute substantiality to the mind and that there are any rationally demonstrable laws, including causality. All that we know is what is given in experience; and what is given in experience are only sensations and impressions. Therefore, Hume (1978) saw no reason to assume an enduring self. The mind lost its substantive dimension, but its essential nature at the level of experience, in the form of thought, reflections, images and feelings, was retained.

TRANSCENDENTALISM

The German philosopher Immanuel Kant (1724–1804) credited Hume as the one who awakened him from his "dogmatic slumber" to see the limits of reason. This "awakening" led Kant to question, on the one hand, the possibility of having a priori knowledge independent of experience and to reject, on the other hand, the notion that all knowledge is based on empirical data. Thus disagreeing with both continental European rationalism as well as British empiricism, Kant attempted a remarkable synthesis of the rational and empirical aspects of knowing. He argued persuasively that empirical investigation based as it is on sensory data can give us only knowledge of appearances, i.e., the way things appear to us, and not knowledge of things-in-themselves. Our inherent features condition the appearance of things. These features, according to Kant, have two main sources in our constitution: the sensibility and understanding. The former is the receptive feature of the mind, which enables us to have representations of things that affect us. Kant distinguishes between the "inner" sense of time and the "outer" sense of spatiality, which locate and order objects in time and space. Understanding is that aspect of the mind which, building on sensibility, enables us to have conceptual knowledge. It is the source of the categories, the principles that govern the classification of reality as it is represented in the phenomena of our experience, principles without which no knowledge is possible.

In Kant's transcendental idealism, the mind as an entity reappears (1929, 1948, 1956). Also, the reality of objects outside of us is asserted. However, that reality, the things-in-themselves, is forever unknown. What is known is the phenomenal world of appearances, which is a construction of our mind. The mind with its *sensibility* and *understanding* gives our experience of the world its subjective features. The subjective features themselves are not given in experience, but are presupposed by experience. They include time, space, and causality, which condition our perception of natural objects, including us.

Kant agrees with Hume that the self is not an item in our experience. He argues, however, that it has to be presupposed as a condition for our experience. The self, however, can hardly be regarded as a category of the mind in the way time, space and causality are. Even though we can understand how space and time are constructions of the mind, it is difficult to see the sense in which the self itself can be its own construction. Kant, therefore, finds it necessary to accord a noumenal status to the self. If the self belongs to the noumenal world, then, in principle, it should be unknowable. Kant is thus driven to a position in which he holds that we know no more about our noumenal nature than that of which we are conscious. The transcendental apperception denotes the unity of self-consciousness at the noumenal level; whereas apperception at the empirical level denotes phenomenal self-consciousness. Thus, the self is seen as belonging to two worlds.

The conscious states of our experience are phenomenal, and they are therefore conditioned by categories of time, space, and causality. At the transcendental level, however, the self is free from them. Thus, whereas determinism holds at the level of appearances, the noumenal self at the transcendental level is wholly free and can act independently of any cause. According to Kant, it is morally imperative that the "will" be autonomous, i.e., a law unto itself. The will in its pure form is independent of being determined by sensory impulses or stimuli. The freedom of will consists in the "absolute spontaneity" of pure will. The causality of natural phenomena is one of physical necessity determined in time. The causality of free will, which belongs to the world of supersensible things, operates independently of the temporal conditions of natural causality. The causality of free will, according to Kant, is capable of producing effects independently of and even in opposition to the power of natural causes. Thus, volition is seen to be capable of *spontaneously* originating a series of events.

We see in Kant two aspects of consciousness, the phenomenal and the noumenal, which in the abstract correspond to the distinction we made between phenomenal awareness and transcendental awareness, or consciousness-as-such. While asserting that we cannot know much about consciousness-as-such, Kant clearly recognizes that it is autonomous and capable of influencing our phenomenal being. Kant was intrigued by the anomalous phenomena of the kind attributed to Swedenborg. He left open the possibility of spirits communicating with each other and with humans. The embodied soul is considered a member of both the material and the spirit worlds. Altruism, benevolence, and felt moral obligations signify the indissoluble relationship between spirits. (For a discussion of Kant's views on the paranormal, see Broad, 1953).

Kant's critique of Cartesian rationalism and British empiricism is well taken, and his arguments in favor of transcendental apperception are persuasive. Locke's separation of primary and secondary qualities and Hume's distinction of impressions and ideas find their echo in Kant's characterization of the faculties of sensibility and understanding. Also, Descartes' assertion of the autonomous mind is retained. However, Kant's assertion of the essential unknowability of transcendental consciousness virtually leaves out any possibility of our understanding the way the so-called pure will can influence our mental states. The nature of the dual citizenship of the self in the world of spirits and that of the senses remains forever utterly unknown, like the mysterious interaction of mind and body in Descartes.

The French philosopher **Henri Bergson** (1859–1941), in his postulation of pure memory, attempts to deal with this issue. Bergson's philosophy is indeed a notable attempt to overcome the Cartesian impasse without denying the reality of matter or mind. For Bergson (1911, 1912, 1913), consciousness is ever changing and yet unified, whereas the world of objects is static. The interaction of matter and mind is explained by postulating that their distinguishing feature is not spatiality, as Descartes posited, but duration, or temporality. Consciousness partakes of duration and matter does not. Duration does not consist of discrete, indivisible, and homogeneous instants. Instead, time is qualitative, heterogeneous, and non-discrete, in that it is a qualitatively ever-changing flow that is experienced subjectively. No moment repeats itself. Hence, time may not be reduced to quantifiable discrete units but can be understood only as a psychological phenomenon beyond the scope of complete mathematical treatment.

Perception, according to Bergson (1913), is not a process of representation whereby sensory images are communicated to the brain. It is a process of selective action that limits the percepts. Of the numerous objects that are capable of being *virtually* perceived, the perceptive process, by

immobilizing the universal becoming, isolates one object in time and space. The distinction between subject and object in perception thus becomes a temporal one rather than a spatial one.

The past is a dimension of the present and is preserved as memory. Memory is not a weakened perception because it is not a function of the brain. As Bergson puts it, "the cerebral organ prepares the frame; it does not furnish the recollections." According to Bergson, the higher mental functions cannot be accounted for by the workings of the brain. "Brain is no more than a telephonic exchange." Thus, consciousness is not a function of the brain but is merely maintained by the brain. "The state of the brain," says Bergson, "continues the remembrance; it gives it a hold on the present by the materiality which it confers upon it; but pure memory is spiritual manifestation. With memory we are in very truth in the domain of spirit" (1913, p. 320).

Consciousness, it would seem, is where body and spirit meet. It is coextensive with life; but it is seen in the freedom to act, in the transition from *virtual* activity to real activity. Where there is no difference between the two, as in purely instinctive phenomena, there is hardly any room for consciousness. The increasing complexity of the brain and nervous system as a product of creative evolution provides greater choice to retain the past better and organize its activity in richer and more profound ways. "Spirit borrows from matter the perceptions on which it feeds, and restores them to matter in the form of movements which it has stamped with its own freedom" (Bergson, 1913, p. 332).

In a sense, then, consciousness is at the interface of spirit and matter, or memory and the brain. Bergson distinguishes between pure memory and memory image. The latter is "nascent perception." Insofar as it partakes of pure memory, it begins to materialize memory. Though independent, pure memory is inert and devoid of action unless it manifests itself in a living image. Pure memory is essentially detached from life. It is latent and without subjective awareness. When it is actualized in an image, it becomes a present state. As Bergson puts it, "the chief office of consciousness is to preside over action and to enlighten choice" (1913, p. 182). It is in the exercise of choice that we see the definitive role of consciousness, which is the actualization of experience through attention and expectation.

Pure memory, then, is like Kant's transcendental consciousness and, in our terms, consciousness-as-such. It is essentially noncorporeal, but its manifestation or actualization in life is temporal. In the process of actualization, experience acquires material properties. Consciousness, which makes this actualization possible, is able to go beyond time and space. In its exercise of free choice, consciousness is able to anticipate the future and draw on the past. Consciousness has thus the possibility of constituting pure memory and playing its role in both worlds, the virtual and the actual.

In the Western philosophical tradition, whether rationalism or empiricism, monism or dualism, we thus find that the concepts "mind" and "consciousness" are not sharply distinguished. They are used somewhat interchangeably as if they were synonymous terms that refer to the same thing. Even when a distinction is implied, one of the terms is ignored as if it has no special role to play. For Descartes the mind is the immaterial substance and consciousness is its essence. Though the mind interacts with the body, it has its own realm of being. Thus the focus in Descartes is on the mind *as such*, i.e., the disembodied mind. In Locke, no such dualism is emphasized, but the mind continues to be the "thinking thing." The mind is understood in its embodied condition as giving rise to thoughts and experiences. The mind in Hume's philosophy

loses its substantive dimension but retains its essential character of consciousness. Consciousness, however, is no more than what underlies the impressions, our thoughts and experiences. The differences among them consist in their conceptions of the mind whether it is that which causes consciousness or it is consciousness itself, or whether it is the thinking thing or a bundle of thoughts. Kant, unlike Descartes, focuses on the embodied mind with its sensibility and understanding. Unlike Hume, Bergson is concerned with consciousness independent of its existential predicaments as pure memory in its transcendental state.

The failure to make a more marked distinction between mind and consciousness, it seems to me, is related to interesting developments in their philosophies. Descartes' uncompromising dualism divorces the mind from the natural world of objects, and elevates to a separate realm of being in an attempt to find an appropriate place for those aspects of thought that simply do not fit into mechanistic postulations that seem to govern the physical world. For a similar reason, Locke found it necessary to distinguish between primary and secondary qualities, Hume between impressions and ideas, and Kant between sensibility and understanding. Mind as consciousness denotes something more than what intrinsically inheres in the natural world of objects; it reveals or encompasses aspects that may not be attributed to physical objects. Call it subjectivity, free will, or whatever; there is a dimension to our being, manifested in thought and experience that appears to go beyond physical causation and determinism. In a sense, Bergson's concept of pure memory and Kant's transcendentalism may be seen as their attempts to find the right place for this dimension of our being.

INTENTIONALITY AND
THE PHENOMENOLOGY
OF CONSCIOUSNESS

In the European phenomenological tradition, consciousness has a special place; and intentionality takes the center stage in the discussions of consciousness. Intentionality in philosophical discourse is a technical term, and its meaning varies widely from its nontechnical usage. For example, intentionality does not refer to one's motivation or intentions to do something deliberately or on purpose. The philosophical concept of intentionality arose from medieval discussions that were concerned with distinguishing mental phenomena such as thoughts from physical objects such as books. Physical phenomena are believed to have *natural* existence, whereas the latter have only *mental* existence. To have an idea or thought is to think about something, to direct one's attention to an image or thought. Mental phenomena contain thoughts and objects. Thus intentionality has come to be referred as the "directedness" or "aboutness" that appears to characterize mental existence.

Franz Brentano (1838–1917): The concept of intentionality has a checkered history in Western philosophy beginning with the Scholastics in the middle ages. It was, however, the Austrian philosopher and psychologist Franz Brentano who gave it an essentially original formulation and called attention to its centrality in the philosophy of mind (Mohanty 1972). Brentano's concern was to identify the distinguishing feature or property of mental phenomena (with which psychology deals), a feature that is not present in physical phenomena. Brentano (1973) found it in the scholastic concept of "intentional inexistence." Intentional inexistence means that conscious phenomena "intentionally contain an object within themselves." In other words, mental phenomena require reference to a context. Brentano asserted that this property of "aboutness" is distinctive to psychical states and is absent in all non-mental phenomena. Thus the act of seeing a rose is a mental phenomenon, but the object rose is not. The former is an act of representation whereas the latter is the represented object. Brentano speaks of intentionality as "the relatedness to a content" and "directedness towards an object." In an intentional situation then we have (1) the act of intention, (2) the mental representation or content and (3) the object of which it is a representation. According to Brentano, the object can be real or imaginary, such as the one that appears in fantasy. Inasmuch as the object can be fictitious and need not exist at all, it does not enter into an analysis of the mental act. Brentano is not clear, however, as to the relationship between the act of intention and the content of cognition. In his earlier writings he seems to hold that there is indeed the intended object, content or representation, and the object of thought, the thing itself, whether real or imaginary. In his later writings, as J. N. Mohanty (1972) points out, he tended to abandon the notion of representation and not make any distinction between the object in thought and the object itself. In addition to intentionality, Brentano pointed out two more distinguishing characters of consciousness. They are (1) its self-revealing (inner perception) character and (2) its intrinsic unity. These, according to Brentano, are characteristics that are not found in physical phenomena.

Brentano was a realist and a naturalist. His interest in the concept of intentionality was that of a psychologist. He found in intentionality a common characteristic that distinguishes all mental phenomena from all physical phenomena. Thus, for him, along with self-revealing reflexivity and the binding unity, intentionality became a defining characteristic of consciousness. As a realist, Brentano could not ignore the object of consciousness as having existence independent of consciousness. As a naturalist he was committed to a causal explanation of our cognitions, beliefs and desires. Consequently, he was confronted with the problem of relating in an intentional act, the mental act, its content and the objects. In this context the following questions arise. How does the object enter consciousness? How does consciousness contain its object within itself? The object does not exist in the mind. The actual physical existence of the object outside is irrelevant because it can be an imaginary item. Then how is consciousness able to refer to its object? These questions are not answered in Brentano's discussion of intentionality. As Mohanty points out: "If the concept of intentionality is to serve any purpose, it should be able to dispense with the content *as a medium of reference*: consciousness should be able to refer to its object by virtue of some inalienable power of its own" (1972, p. 8). Despite the many problems in Brentano's formulation of intentionality, his thesis that intentionality is an irreducible feature of consciousness is often cited as reason to reject the notion of mind-brain identity.

Edmund Husserl (1859–1938): It is, however, in the German philosopher Husserl that we find a thorough phenomenological expression of the concept of intentionality as a consummate theory of subjectivity. Unlike Brentano, Husserl was not interested in using intentionality as a demarcating criterion for mental phenomena. Rather, his interest is in intentionality on its own. Further, Husserl has abandoned completely the causal approach to understanding conscious phenomena. Instead, he championed a phenomenological attitude, one that accepts phenomena as given. Husserl saw that conscious states do not cause each other, as physical states do. The unity that characterizes consciousness consists in that conscious states imply each other; they internally refer to each other.

According to Husserl, the intentional act has two functions. It does not merely refer to an object; it essentially constitutes the object. It does so by *synthesizing* the various aspects of the object revealed in different acts and by *identifying* that it is the same object intended in all the acts. The intentional act constitutes the object qua object involving a process of phenomenological reduction by which we "bracket" or put aside our natural attitude and attend to phenomena as they are intended. Thus, the reduction accomplished by a transcendental mode of analysis leads us to the essence of our subjective experience.

Husserl (1931, 1960, 1971, 1982) shared Descartes' concern for a method to arrive at those things that are absolutely evident so that no doubt can be entertained about their existence. He considered it truly "epoch-making" that Descartes found such evidence in the act of cognition. Husserl felt, however, that Descartes did not carry his method far enough. He, therefore, proposed his own method by which we can seek what he called "*apodictic evidence*," which carries with it absolute indubitability. "It discloses itself, to a critical reflection, as having the signal peculiarity of being *at the same time the absolute unimaginableness* (inconceivability) of their *non-being...*" (Husserl 1960, pp. 15–16, original emphasis). Further, the critical reflection itself will have in such cases the sense of indubitability, of being *apodictic*.

Fundamental to Husserl's passion for absolute evidence is his conviction that our prejudices and presuppositions generally taint our knowledge of the world and of us. Whereas we meet and exchange views and ideas concerning things about which we presumably agree, our ideas themselves seldom have universal acceptance because we are predisposed to observe and interpret those observations in accordance with our biases, intellectual or otherwise. Therefore, as Husserl observes, at philosophical congresses and such gatherings the "philosophers meet but, unfortunately, not the philosophies" (1960,p. 5). Descartes, Husserl suggests, who rightly started on the course of doubt, became a victim of his own prejudice when, for example, he equated the act of thinking with a thinking substance, *substantia cogitans*.

The essential step in Husserl's method of absolute universal doubt "is abstention from all positions that already give anything existent, must first create for itself a *universe of absolute freedom from prejudice*" (1960, p. 35). In the course of arriving at such *apodictic* evidence, one must establish oneself as a "disinterested onlooker' so as "to see and to describe adequately what he sees, purely as seen, as what is seen and seen in such and such a manner" (1960, p. 35). According to Husserl, such transcendental experience and reflection give us knowledge "intuitively," knowledge that is free from prejudice and all interpretations, read into them beyond the genuinely observed. By means of such intuitions we comprehend the "essence" of objects.

Husserl's method involves a specific procedure for examining the structures of consciousness and intentionality. This procedure called *époch* (bracketing) incorporates a "transcendental" mode of analysis. The "natural world" that we normally take for granted and the "natural attitude" of its independence from our cognitions of it are deliberately "bracketed," or put aside, so that we can closely observe the experience itself. When one does this and consciousness reflectively considers its own cognitive acts, there is then, according to Husserl, the emergence of "the transcendental ego," described as "the principle of subjectivity." Adopting this procedure to arrive at the structures of consciousness, Husserl claims that his method enables us to understand the contents of consciousness experienced internally and to see how they are generated from those structures.

According to Husserl, the external object, the content of consciousness, and our awareness of it are directly related by the intentionality of consciousness. Our knowledge of the world is not via the sensations we receive, but is a consequence of the logical process of intention. The common world we share with each other is not made possible by the sensations we have of them, which tend to be discrete and private and cannot therefore reveal the universal and unitary character of their objects, but by a "constitutive function" of consciousness that intuitively grasps their essence. The constitutive function of consciousness lies in the intuiting of the essence of objects so that we may understand their significance and meaningfulness to us. The unitary character that objects have as phenomena of our experience can only be understood in terms of their essences, and not as a summation of their shifting qualities.

There are at least three aspects to Husserl's procedure. First, by putting aside the "natural attitude," an attempt is made to focus attention on phenomenal experiences instead of on the externally conceived world. Second, the internal focus is on the contents of consciousness, since consciousness is always directed to something. Such a focus is understood to give us intuitively the essence of objects experienced in consciousness. Third is that aspect in which the focus is on the enduring subject who has the experience. Just as the "constitutive function" gives us the uniqueness and sameness of objects despite the infinitely varied mosaic of "sensory states," the "transcendental" function gives us the sense of subjectivity and personal identity amidst the ever-changing contents of the stream of consciousness.

While postulating the "transcendental ego" as the principle of subjectivity, Husserl falls short of accepting pure consciousness or consciousness-as-such, which could display the transcendental ego as it is in itself.

This is so because of his commitment to the intentional view of consciousness. If consciousness is conceived to be always consciousness of something, as the intentional view of consciousness requires, there can be no pure consciousness, which has no content. When consciousness itself becomes an object of awareness, then it ceases to be pure consciousness.

Others have criticized Husserl for his final step, which ended in logical abstractions, rather than staying rooted in experience, as he intended and claimed. Varela, Thompson and Rosch (1993, pp. 16, 17) write:

> He began with a solitary individual consciousness, took the structure he was seeking to be entirely mental and accessible to consciousness in an act of abstract philosophical introspection, and from there had great difficulty in generating the consensual, intersubjective world of human experience. And having no method other than his own philosophical introspection, he certainly could not take the final move that would return him to his experience, back to the beginning of the process. The irony of Husserl's procedure, then, is that although he claimed to be turning philosophy toward a direct facing of experience, he was actually ignoring both the consensual aspect and the direct embodied aspect of experience.

Martin Heidegger (1884–1976): Husserl's student and fellow German philosopher Heidegger addressed several of these issues. In Heidegger (1962, 1982, 1984), intentionality of consciousness, divested of its theoretical and abstract look, comes closer to the practical and existential human concerns. Phenomenological reduction, which is an indispensable condition in Husserl's understanding of intentionality, is abandoned; and Dasein replaces the transcendental ego, the source of intentionality (Mohanty 1972). *Dasein* (literal meaning "being there") refers to human existence, the being in the world. Heidegger located

intentionality in *Dasein*. His phenomenological account of intentionality is given in the context of finding the meaning of Being. The *Dasein* is not an abstract or neutral being. It is in the world and yet it is outside of it by self-transcendence. Being-in-the-world, Mohanty points out, "is Heidegger's substitute for intentionality" (1972, pp. 129–130).

According to Heidegger there are three structural features of being-in-the-world. First is the pre-given in human experience. The second is its comprehension, which makes the world meaningful. This is the self-transcendence feature of *Dasein* and the one that bestows meaning to an intentional act. *Dasein* "projects itself to others in order to seize and manipulate them, and, in so doing, give(s) them meaning and significance" (Mohanty 1972, p. 130). The third is speech, which articulates. These three features of being-in-the-world together locate *Dasein* in the past, the future and the present. *Dasein* is also characterized as "radical openness to Being." It makes it possible for beings to manifest Being. (For an in depth discussion of the concept of intentionality in Husserl and Heidegger, see Mohanty 1972; Hopkins 1993).

Jean Paul Sartre (1905–1980): The existential philosopher Jean Paul Sartre once again emphasizes the centrality of consciousness in the human condition. Sartre regards Heidegger's notion of *Dasein* as unsatisfactory, because it is seen as excluding consciousness. Like Husserl, Sartre locates intentionality in consciousness. He, however, questions the Husserlian method of transcendental reduction, or "bracketing," which puts aside the natural world in order to deduce the transcendental ego as a consciousness function. Sartre points out that no such ego is phenomenologically apparent. Nor is it logically necessary to account for the unity of experience. With the aim of drafting an architectonic of being, Sartre inquires into the structure displayed by consciousness. He argues that both consciousness and the objects of our consciousness are facts given in experience. They enjoy two distinctive kinds of reality. Since the very nature of consciousness is intentional, the essential characteristic of consciousness is the *revelation* of the thing to which it is directed. Its reality is functional and not substantive. Therefore, it cannot be described as this or that. It is not a thing; nor is it a container in which the phenomena of our experience are deposited. Its sole reality consists in its revelatory function.

Consciousness is defined in Sartre's existentialism in terms of intentionality and translucence. Like John Locke, consciousness for Sartre is self-luminous and wholly transparent; and nothing in it is hidden or opaque. Even pre-reflective awareness, according to Sartre, is transparent. Pain is pain because we are aware of it. Mere sensation cannot be an element or aspect of consciousness. Intentionality is not conceived as constituting the being of its object. Rather, the basic feature of intentionality is transcendence. By transcendence Sartre means reference to something outside of itself and also the tendency to bestow meaning on being. By its very nature, consciousness is *of* something other than itself. The things consciousness reveals are outside of it. Consciousness is thus distinct and distant from the intended objects. The distinctiveness, however, consists merely in intending an object, without itself being an object. Consciousness is thus nothing other than its intentional function.

The notion that consciousness is both intentional and translucent leads to his well-known theory that characterizes consciousness as signifying "nothingness." But by "nothingness," Sartre clearly does not mean complete void, but merely lack of content or corporeality. It signifies the contrast with the objective world that is "being." By "being," Sartre does not mean the phenomena of our experience that derive their significance by virtue of their appearance in consciousness. Being refers to "the in-itself" whereas consciousness is a "for-itself."

The "nothingness" of consciousness may be understood only in the sense of lacking content and not as being unreal. Consciousness is completely transparent; it is not a substance but a form or appearance. "The existence of consciousness," says Sartre, "comes from consciousness itself" (1956, p. lxvi). There is nonbeing in its being, for it can transcend itself and intend an object. That is why consciousness, unlike objects of experience, is a being-for-itself.

The concept of nothingness may be better understood in the context of Sartre's psychology of imagination (Sartre, 1948). When we imagine, for example, a book, we do not, according to Sartre, form an image of the book in consciousness. Consciousness is not a container, not a canvas on which the images are imprinted, and not a stage on which objects are displayed. Both in imagination, as well as in perception, the object always remains external to consciousness. The difference between the imagination of a book and the perception of it consists in the manner in which we intend the book. When we imagine something, we have an imaginative consciousness of it that reveals at once its non-presence. In perceptual consciousness of the book, we intend its presence. Therefore, the image, perceptual or imaginative, is not an entity, but merely a function of consciousness. Consciousness in signifying "nothingness" is beyond being. Inasmuch as we can go beyond being in our imagination we are able to grasp the synthetic unity and totality of the world.

It is interesting to note that for Sartre consciousness is both intentional and at the same time it has no content. How can consciousness, be of something and at the same time be devoid of content? In *The Transcendence of the Ego*, Sartre answers: "consciousness can be self-conscious only by means of which it is conscious." In Sartre's discussion of consciousness, one may find several contradictory statements. Sometimes he speaks of consciousness as if it is not an autonomous something, but dependent on the objects it reveals. On other occasions he asserts that consciousness is absolute and autonomous, which being a for-itself, cannot be derived from that of objects, the in-itself. When he asserts its autonomy and freedom, consciousness becomes the principle of subjectivity, as in Husserl. In his introduction to *Being and Nothingness,* we find Sartre describing consciousness as "the first being to whom all other appearances appear...; it is subjectivity itself, the immanence of self itself" (1956, p. lxvi).

When criticizing Husserl, it is apparent that Sartre falls back on the more restrictive conception of consciousness as not being absolute but dependent on objects. But he himself finds it necessary to use consciousness in a broader sense. The transcendental ego, distinguished from the empirical ego, which is the principle of subjectivity in Husserl's philosophy, is not very different from Sartre's conception of consciousness in its absolute sense. Again, Sartre's *revelatory* function of consciousness is similar to Husserl's *constitutive* function, not withstanding Sartre's criticism of the latter. In both, it is the intentional nature of consciousness that is stressed as its essential characteristic. Both Husserl and Sartre find it logically necessary to postulate consciousness as a principle of subjectivity to account for the manifest unity, meaning, and significance of the phenomena of our experience, even though Sartre's view of consciousness as "nothingness" goes beyond the epistemological to an ontological formulation.

Our discussion of intentionality has been confined largely to the phenomenological tradition that dealt with intentionality in a metaphysical context. There are, however, other attempts to explain intentionality within the Anglo-American analytic tradition and cognitive and computational psychology. These attempts are largely influenced by what W. Quine (1960) called "semantic ascent," which, putting aside the epistemological and metaphysical questions about intentional phenomena, focused on the analysis of the way we talk about the phenomena.

Concluding Discussion

What is consciousness? Does it exist as a fact of its own, autonomous and irreducible? If it does, can we have a naturalist understanding of it? We have attempted in this chapter to answer these questions by exploring the relationships between mind and body, consciousness and mind, and intentionality and consciousness in the Western tradition. Focusing mainly on the rationalistic, empiricist, and phenomenological traditions in Western philosophical discourse, we have examined from a philosophical perspective the spectrum of views expressed by a few prominent thinkers who believe in the usefulness of the concept "consciousness" to understand our nature and potential. To be sure, it is a highly select and relatively limited account. Our discussion of those philosophies that accord little or no role to consciousness in our being is admittedly scanty and we make no excuse for it, because our primary concern here has been with consciousness and its place in the universe.

We may note, however, notwithstanding the resurgence of interest in studying consciousness is recent years, the dominant trend among academic thinkers is one of relative skepticism. There are several reasons for this state of affairs (Flanagan 1992). First, the concept of consciousness is considered too vague and simplistic to refer to phenomena that can be empirically investigated. If there are any genuine phenomena that consciousness denotes, it is believed, they would be explained when we have a complete understanding of the brain. In the meantime it is best to eliminate the concept, which can only help to further confusion and provide false leads. Second, it is argued that consciousness is "terminally mysterious" and impervious to naturalistic understanding. This is so, not because consciousness is a supermaterial or nonnaturalistic phenomena, but because we are "cognitively closed" and are intellectually ill equipped to grasp and explain its properties. Third, it is pointed out that consciousness is essentially subjective and that we simply do not know how subjectivity may be objectively rendered. The intrinsic asymmetry between the subjective and the objective leaves consciousness outside the scope of naturalistic understanding. Finally, arguably the most persuasive argument advanced by cognitive scientists is that all mental states can be accounted for in terms of information flows and networks, without bringing in consciousness. In other words, minds do not require consciousness to function as minds.

Each of the above arguments has its adherents. Together they make a formidable case for skepticism. Further, as some spectacular advances in neuroscience increasingly unravel the mysteries of the brain, the hope of finding neurological correlates of all mental states is greatly reinforced. If minds do not require consciousness and if minds are understood as brain states, the case for materialism appears unassailable. On the other side, it may be pointed out, neuroscience, with all its evidence for the dependence of mental states on brain states, is not anywhere close to finding a one to one correspondence between mental phenomena and neural events. The case for consciousness is phenomenologically robust; and the subjectivity of conscious experience cannot be simply wished away. "Conscious awareness," writes philosopher-

psychologist Owen Flanagan (1992), "is as ubiquitous as light, sound, heat, and color. Indeed, one might argue that it is even more ubiquitous than any of these, since there is light and sound and heat and color only insofar as these phenomena are revealed in experience." (p. 34).

The logical possibility of silicon brains, and the "absent qualia" and "inverted qualia" arguments are persuasively against all forms of identity thesis. Again, if we take paranormal experiences with any degree of seriousness, and, as we have noted, there is substantial evidence to warrant doing so, any assumption of total dependence of awareness on one's cortical structures becomes less convincing, as are materialistic attempts to reduce consciousness to brain states. Thus, the question, whether consciousness is the "quicksilver of phenomenology" better left to philosophers, who are not afraid of making fools of themselves (Dennett 1978), or whether it exists as an autonomous and irreducible aspect of our being that no serious thinker can afford to ignore, has not been answered with any sense of finality at this time.

Are there any common features that characterize the Western tradition in consciousness studies even if there is a lack of consensus on the main question of how fundamental consciousness is to our being? It is clearly hazardous to embark on an exercise to identify commonalties among such a diverse mix of ideas as we have seen. The Western tradition is not monolithic, in that we have outstanding thinkers who have championed conflicting viewpoints. We can always find a forceful argument and a prominent philosopher to cite a counter point of view. The Western tradition has had varied development. There is no single character or set of characters that can be attributed uniformly to all strands of philosophy in the West. Without disputing this fact, I believe, it is possible to make a few generalizations concerning the Western tradition in the area of consciousness, such as the following. They may not be seen, however, as unexceptional features, but as dominant trends.

The discussion of consciousness in the Western scholarly tradition appears to be dominated by (a) the presumed dichotomy or identity of mind and body, (b) the presumed identity of consciousness and the mind, (c) an emphasis on intentionality as the defining characteristic of consciousness/mind, and (d) a lack of practical orientation and goals for applying our understanding of consciousness to elevate the human condition and enhance our potential. In a sense, all four aspects may be seen as remnants of the Cartesian legacy.

MIND-BODY DICHOTOMY

The mind-body dichotomy is possibly the most important and persistent, and the least tractable, of all problems in the history of Western philosophy (MacGregor 1989). Whether the duality of mind and body is asserted or denied, the problem tends to take the center stage. Beginning with Plato, who sharply distinguished mind (spirit) and body, dualism is a favored view of most philosophers until recently. A radical and forceful enunciation of dualism by Descartes has had such a pervasive influence that mind-body dualism has come to be the commonsense worldview in the Western tradition. The main problem with dualism is the difficulty in relating mind and body to account for their interaction. This has led to the elimination of one or the other, as in idealism or materialism. These attempts, however, have had only limited success. An outright reduction of one to the other appears to leave out something very basic in the world of one's experience. Neither the argument that the sensible qualities may be reduced to neural excitations in the brain nor the reasoning that physical objects are no more than collections of sensible qualities appears feasible. The latter has little currency in contemporary thought. The former is increasingly under pressure to account for subjective experience. Therefore, the more recent attempts to reformulate materialism seem to bring in qualia and subjective experience through a backdoor. Whether it is logical behaviorism or the identity thesis of materialism, mental attributes are ascribed to certain physical objects, even though the attributes themselves are taken to be physical. Dualism in one form or another, whether of entities or of properties, persists even when a philosophy professes to reject such dualism.

An important consequence of the persistent dualist debate is the ubiquitous subject-object distinction in the Western discourse, which takes on several forms. Just as the mind-body dichotomy has given rise to the perennial problem of their interaction, the subject-object distinction has led to the problem of their relationship at different levels. Conceptually, does the subject contain the object or vice-versa? Methodologically, do we understand the subject better by studying the object, or conversely does an inquiry into the nature of the subject facilitate the study of the object? Substantively, it is the question of primacy of one over the other: what is the role of the subject and the objective world in our being and knowing? In philosophical inquiry, the problem has taken the form of attention to and emphasis on the "inwardness" or "outwardness" of being. In his comparative study of Eastern and Western philosophical traditions, P. T. Raju (1992) focused on this distinction. He wrote, "the general tendency of western philosophy is to disentangle outwardness from inwardness, ignoring or even rejecting inwardness, at least for philosophical purposes" (p. 86). Even Descartes, who found certainty in the "I," conferred that certainty on the ability to doubt and think. The essence of the "I," the mind, is thought. In other words, the existence of mind is predicated on thought and not the other way around. It is not that we think because we have a mind; we have a mind because we think. Again, for Locke, the mind is a *tabula rasa*. It is the objects outside of the mind that imprint the mind, and we have impressions. The situation is not very different in the phenomenological and existential traditions that profess fundamental opposition to the positivistic obsession with naturalism. By emphasizing that intentionality is the defining characteristic of consciousness, the phenomenological tradition asserts the primacy of the object without which there can be no awareness. This approach reaches its logical end in Sartre's characterization of consciousness as "nothingness."

IDENTITY OF CONSCIOUSNESS AND MIND

As mentioned above, many writers in the West use "mind" and "consciousness" interchangeably to convey the same meaning. It was Descartes who explicitly promoted this trend by asserting that the mind is the thinking thing (*res cogitans*). This tradition has since continued to characterize the Western mindset. For example, since the decline of behaviorism, the eclipse of positivism, and the respectable reemergence of consciousness in psychological and philosophical discourse, a large number of books have appeared on the subject. The titles of these books are almost equally divided between "consciousness" and "mind." Consider some of the recent titles: *The Nature of Consciousness* (Block, Flanagan & Guzeldere, 1997), *Conscious Experience* (Metzinger, 1995), *The Science of Consciousness* (Velmans, 1996), *The Embodied Mind* (Varela, Thompson & Rosch, 1993), *Consciousness and Experience* (Lycan, 1996), *Consciousness Explained* (Dennett, 1991), *The Rediscovery of the Mind* (Searle, 1992), *Shadows of the Mind* (Penrose, 1994), and *The*

Conscious Mind (Chalmers, 1996). Interestingly, Flanagan's book in 1991 is titled *The Science of the Mind*. His 1992 book has the title *Consciousness Reconsidered*. Again, some authors used both mind and consciousness in the same title. For example, Dennett's 1996 book has the title *Kinds of Minds: Towards an Understanding of Consciousness*. Alwyn Scott titled his 1995 publication *Stairway to the Mind: The Controversial New Science of Consciousness*.

True to the Cartesian legacy, E. B. Titcherner (1909) stated explicitly: "Consciousness is identified with mind and 'conscious' with 'mental'" (p. 18). Even those who rejected consciousness as a usable concept in a scientific discourse, like J. B. Watson (1928), regarded it as another word for "mind." More recently, J. R. Searle (1992) pointed out: "The study of the mind is the study of consciousness, in much the same sense that biology is the study of life" (p. 227).

When Descartes and Locke wrote about the mind as consciousness, there was little appreciation of non-conscious mentation and the unconscious. But now, as we have discussed in Chapter 1, implicit awareness is widely seen as an aspect of the mind. So we find in a recent textbook on the psychology of consciousness (Farthing, 1992): "Consciousness is not the same as mind. Mind is the broader concept, it includes both conscious and unconscious mental processes."(p. 5). Interestingly, this book, which discusses in just as much detail unconscious mental processes as it does conscious states, is titled *The Psychology of Consciousness* and not "the psychology of the mind." Thus, we see again the Western mind set of treating consciousness and mind as identical and interchangeable concepts. If consciousness is the proper subject matter of the book, the non-conscious processes should recede into the background. Alternatively, if the book deals with both conscious and non-conscious mentation, the appropriate title would be "the psychology of the mind."

Farthing is, however, not alone in suggesting that we restrict the meaning of the concept "consciousness" to subjective or introspective awareness. In fact, such a restriction is not uncommon in psychological discussions of consciousness and mind. However, we find striking inconsistencies in the use of the concept even among those who presume a distinction between mind and consciousness, as we have pointed out in the case of Farthing. The reason for this rests possibly in the fact that subjectivity is only a qualitative aspect of consciousness, which manifests in various degrees and a variety of farms. Awareness in dreams, hypnagogic imagery and other forms of conscious experience in altered states suggest that focal awareness is not fundamental to and a necessary condition for consciousness, and that such a characterization does not capture the totality of its connotation. As mentioned above, the problem did not exist for Descartes and Locke, who did not consider the possibility of non-conscious mind or mentation without subjective awareness. Though in a sense the failure to make the distinction is a Cartesian legacy, the problem is possibly deeper than that. It may be traced to the general problem of determinism versus free will and the disjunction of the individual and society. Naturalism and science on the one hand, and freedom of will and choice on the other, are the twin anchors of the Western intellectual and social tradition. Whereas science and the naturalistic attitude foster a belief in determinism, social institutions and ethical practices are founded on the belief in free will, that we are born free and can act free. Similarly, individualism and corporate culture characterize the Western emphasis on the individual as well as the society. The vocabulary of the mind suggests the deterministic aspect as well as the individuality of human beings, whereas consciousness is more open to free choice and social obligations. Together, connoting the same, "mind" and "consciousness" cater conveniently to satisfy naturalistic determinism on the one hand and moral imperatives on the other. Thus the mind/consciousness ambiguity helps to blunt the dilemmas of the individual and society, and free will and determinism.

INTENTIONALITY OF CONSCIOUSNESS

Another feature of the Western conception of consciousness is that *intentionality* is its defining characteristic. Consciousness is *of* or *about* something. We are aware of this or aware that such and such is the case. Descartes regarded mind essentially as subjective consciousness. The contents of consciousness, the ideas, represent to us the objects in the world. Consequently, mind is regarded essentially as intentional. This notion of intentionality, as we have seen, was further and more systematically developed by Franz Brentano (1973). He wrote in his inimitable style, "intentional inexistence is excessively peculiar to psychical phenomena." Brentano distinguishes between content and act in mental phenomena, and asserts that all mental acts have meaningful content. Such an assertion appears to be independent of one's prior philosophical assumptions and is not tied to metaphysical dualism as espoused by Descartes.

That consciousness always points to something, i.e., mental phenomena have a *directedness* about them, is a notion that is endorsed by a diverse mix of philosophers and psychologists in the Western tradition. For example, D. M. Armstrong, a philosopher of a materialistic persuasion, argues that all consciousness is consciousness of something (Armstrong & Malcolm, 1984). Similarly, J. R. Searle (1983) emphasizes that intentionality is the essence of mind/consciousness. Intentionality of consciousness is of course central to all phenomenology. Husserl attended Brentano's lectures and fully subscribed to the latter's view that consciousness is essentially intentional. Freud and Sartre, among others, have emphasized the intentional nature of consciousness.

The intentional view of mind/consciousness entails in some form the representational theory of cognition and knowledge. Whether it is the "input-output" model of cognitive scientists or the more traditional notion that the mind is a mirror of nature, we are led to believe that there is a pre-given world of which our cognitions are representations. Inasmuch as every act of consciousness intends something and every thought has an object, we are inescapably led to the notion of subject-object duality and the known-knower distinction. Even those who are vehemently opposed to such a dichotomy on ontological grounds have difficulty in circumventing the duality of the knower and the known. William James, for example, wrote: "The attributions subject and object, represented and representative, thing and thought, thus signify a practical distinction which is of the utmost importance but which is only of a *functional* order and is not of an ontological order as classical dualism presents it. In the final analysis things and thoughts are not fundamentally heterogeneous. They are instead made of the same stuff, a stuff which cannot be defined as such, but can only be experienced and which can be called, if one so desires, the stuff of experience in general" (James, 1912/1947, pp. 232–233). Thus, while rejecting dualism in its interactionist mode, James locates both mind and matter, the knower and the known, in experience-as-such. But what that experience is remains as elusive as the interaction of mind and matter in dualistic postulations. In fact, James is more explicit and concedes some kind of epistemic dualism in the *Principles*. "*The psychologist's attitude toward cognition...*" he writes, "*is a thoroughgoing dual-*

ism. It supposes two elements, mind knowing and thing known, and treats them as irreducible" (James 1952, p. 142, original emphasis).

Again, the existential philosopher Sartre, as we noted, observed that consciousness by its very nature is consciousness of things other than itself. The objects of consciousness are characterized as being, the in-itself. Consciousness, the for-itself, is dependent on the objects for being. The being of conscious, according to Sartre, consists in its intentionality, to posit a transcendental object. Sartre wished that the subject-object duality would "disappear from philosophical preoccupations" (Sartre, 1957). But it remains completely mysterious how by being intentional, consciousness transcends itself in relating the knower and the known, as Sartre believed. In distinguishing the conscious self (subject) from the world (object), Sartre creates for himself an inescapable dualism.

The emphasis on the intentionality of consciousness in Western tradition thus highlights, on the one hand, the distinction between subject and object, whether functional or foundational, and entails, on the other hand, a disbelief in consciousness-as-such, consciousness devoid of content. If consciousness is inseparable from its phenomenal content, we can have no direct knowledge of the world except through its phenomenal representations. Even those who conceived of transcendental aspects of existence, such as Kant, had to admit that things-in-themselves are essentially unknowable. The paradox of such veiled existence is no better illustrated than in the philosophy of Husserl.

NEGLECT OF THE PRACTICAL ASPECTS

The third feature of Western discussions on consciousness is their almost total concern for rational theory and abstraction, undermining the practicality that is again so evident in Husserl. It is indeed paradoxical that the Western tradition, so steeped in the development of science and its application to human condition in the realm of the physical world, is so overwhelmingly theoretical in the area of the mental. If there were any practical concerns about consciousness in the Western tradition, as in psychoanalysis and certain psychotherapies, they were always limited to dealing with "disturbed" individuals and for restoring them to a normal state, but not to raising them to higher levels of awareness. Husserl himself felt that his own European intellectual tradition stood in sharp contrast with the Indian, Chinese and other Eastern traditions that foster a mythical-religious attitude that sets practical goals (Husserl 1965). It is therefore not surprising that Western philosophies, even when they emphasized experience, as in Husserl's phenomenology, remained essentially intellectual pursuits.

This aspect constitutes both the pride and the problem inherent in the Western tradition. The pride is the remarkable progress of science; and the problem is the need for a philosophy of the whole life. The Western emphasis on rational thought led inevitably to an overwhelmingly scientific attitude. This began with the ancient Greek conception that the essence of man, the soul, is reason, and culminated in positivism, physicalism and contemporary materialism. The predominance of reason and objectivity in science resulted in a chasm between science and religion, between belief and behavior. So we have professors teach evolution during weekdays in classrooms and offer prayers to the creator in the church on Sundays!

CHAPTER 6

Consciousness, Brain and the New Physics

What is the nature of consciousness? What are its genesis, ontology, and role in the human condition? Who has consciousness? Where is it located? How does it arise? What purpose does it serve? These questions may be answered from a variety of disciplinary perspectives. For example, a physicist may seek to know how consciousness is a part of physical reality, whereas a biologist may attempt to understand its relationship to the brain, considered the seat of awareness. It is natural to assume from a physical or a biological point of view that consciousness is contained in the physical world and that the mechanics of the brain would account in principle for all forms of conscious experience. Obviously such a view would be the most parsimonious, necessitating the postulation of no new entities or processes that have not already been incorporated into physical theory. The scientists' task then is to reduce the varieties of conscious experience to their physical equivalents, such as the events in the brain.

As we have seen, there are several basic difficulties with this approach. First, experiential subjectivity appears irreducible to its apparent physical underpinnings. Second, the human mind functions in ways that appear in principle to be beyond the capability of physical machines such as computers. Third, there is significant empirical evidence purporting to show the primacy of consciousness, the influence of consciousness in the physical world. At the extreme end of such influence are the data of psychokinesis, the effects of consciousness on physical events. If the integrity of the claimed evidence for psi is intact and the skeptical explanations of it unsatisfactory, we are confronted at once with a very perplexing anomaly, one that physics cannot simply ignore. Recognition of the reality of psi leaves two possible courses of action to the physicist. First, one may suitably amend and expand physical theory to account for the anomalies of psi. Second, one may abandon the notion that all reality is physical, accept the possibility of the primacy of consciousness, and assert that it is autonomous and essentially irreducible to and independent of physical reality. The latter assertion does not entail that the physicist has no role to play in consciousness studies.

In the human condition, consciousness is associated with and even constrained by the events in the brain and other physical and physiological circumstances. In other words, consciousness does seem to coexist and interact with physical events. Such an interaction would be as much of interest to a physicist as it is to a psychologist.

Consciousness in Physics

Jean Burns (1990) reviewed various contemporary attempts to explore theoretically the relationship of consciousness to physical laws. She concluded that they fall broadly into four categories—(1) those that consider consciousness as something that emerges from the physical and is therefore not in principle different from it, (2) those that regard consciousness as belonging to a realm different from and independent of the physical, and yet capable of interacting with it, (3) those who consider them independent and yet see no causal but, only a synchronistic relationship between the mental and the physical, and (4) those who make no assumption about the independence or dependence of consciousness on the physical. Clearly, most physicists belong to the first category, even though few of them have made any systematic attempts to account for consciousness in strictly physical terms.

Until recently, physicists generally treated consciousness either as nonexistent or as totally unrelated to their discipline. The Cartesian legacy of the separation of the physical substance governed by inviolable laws within a deterministic framework as different from the thinking substance had pervaded much of classical physics. Newton's mechanical model of the universe, composed of solid and indestructible particles moving in space by means of gravitational force and guided by a set of immutable laws, left no room for consciousness in the woof and warp of the physical web of

the universe. Therefore, from a physicist's standpoint, it seemed, either there is nothing to consciousness or, if there is, it is completely outside the purview of the physicist.

However, some thoughtful physicists throughout history who have paid attention to the subjective awareness that underlies their being have wondered what the basic relationship is between consciousness and the physical processes. A few have doubted that consciousness can ever be understood completely within the framework of physical theory. At the same time, it seemed to them that attempts to dismiss phenomena that have no apparent physical base are misguided and that there may be another principle, distinct from the material, involved in our conscious experience. As Arthur Eddington (1978) wrote, "If those who hold that there must be a physical basis for everything hold that these mystical views are nonsense, we may ask ... what then is the physical basis of nonsense? (p. 344).

In recent years there have been attempts to reconcile the so-called mystical traditions, which seem to accord primacy to the phenomena of consciousness, and the physical sciences, which claim to deal exclusively with objective data. For example, Fritjof Capra (1983), who surveyed the mystical traditions of the East and contrasted them with ideas underlying contemporary physics, concluded: "Eastern mysticism provides a consistent and beautiful philosophical framework which can accommodate our most advanced theories of the physical world" (p. 12). The developments in quantum physics, such as Heisenberg's uncertainty principle relating to the inherent indeterminacy of position and momentum of a subatomic particle, and the EPR paradox throw up the possibility of nonlocal relationships between electrons. These possibilities provided inspiration for writers like Capra (1983) and others (Davies, 1983; Talbot, 1981; Zukav, 1979) to draw parallels between physical theories and the notions of the universe contained in the Chinese and Indian mystical traditions.

Brain Josephson, a Nobel prize winning physicist, argued in favor of taking subjective experience seriously in our attempts to understand nature, because the events naturally occurring in the real world may be too subtle and elusive to admit of precise description. As suggested by Niels Bohr, the very act of describing a naturally occurring system within a quantum mechanical framework will alter that system so that by the time it is described, the description becomes obsolete. Similarly, Josephson points out that chaos theory (Gleick 1988) sets limits on our ability to precisely pin down nature to exact descriptions. These observations lead Josephson (1988; 1992) to speak of nature's resistance to being grasped by the conventional methods of science, which tend to keep subjectivity and consciousness out of its precincts. He goes on to suggest that in order to come to terms with that resistance, science should ask the help of direct experience. In other words, for a complete and all-round development of science, the first-person perspective of consciousness is needed to supplement the third-person perspective of physical science. Josephson points out that the first-person approach has been found to have useful application in arts and mystical traditions. He thus emphasizes the complementarity of the two approaches for a fuller understanding of human nature.

QUANTUM THEORIES OF CONSCIOUSNESS

From the very beginning, some of the founders of quantum mechanics such as Erwin Schrödinger considered consciousness as an essential principle in the universe, which is necessary as much as any physical principle for its proper understanding. Eugene Wigner (1972), another Nobel Laureate in physics, wrote: "when the province of physical theory was extended to encompass microscopic phenomena, through the creation of quantum mechanics, the concept of consciousness came to the fore again; it was not possible to formulate the laws of quantum mechanics in a fully consistent way without reference to the consciousness..." (p. 133). Consequently, many of the modern attempts to understand consciousness by physicists make use of quantum concepts and theory.

The Metaphor of Complementarity: Attempting to explain the behavior of light that appears like a set of waves in one situation and as particles in another situation, Niels Bohr (1934) proposed the principle of complementarity. He pointed out that light is potentially both wave-like and particle-like. It manifests in one of the two forms only after an observation is made. The form it takes depends on the conditions accompanying the observation. The wave/particle complementarity is now seen to apply to a variety of phenomena at the quantum level.

Princeton physicist Robert Jahn and his associate parapsychologist Brenda Dunne (1999) draw on their empirical data to conclude: "consciousness has the capacity not only to absorb and process objective information, but to *create* it, in rigorously measurable quantities" (p. 206). In attempting to understand the interactions between consciousness and the environment, they (1987) use as a metaphor the formalism of quantum theory and the complementarity principle. While clearly recognizing the limitations of the metaphor, they point to several interesting points of its relevance to understanding consciousness. Referring to wave/particle paradoxes in physical theory and the "irreducible complementarity" of wave/particle explanations, Jahn and Dunne suggest that it is our consciousness that "imposes such a dichotomy ... it is imposed by the process of consciousness interacting with its physical environment" (p. 211). They go on to argue that consciousness itself may have the option of "wave-like or particulate" function. The conventional conceptualizations of consciousness are essentially particle-like, localizing consciousness in physical space and time. Such conceptions, they argue, are clearly inadequate to account for, and certainly inconsistent with, such phenomena as precognition. If however, we allow the wave/particle duality to apply to consciousness, then "consciousness could employ a host of interference, diffraction, penetration, and remote influence effects to achieve normally most of the anomalies of the particulate paradigm" (p. 212).

The quantum metaphor, according to Jahn and Dunne, may provide insights into a variety of behavioral paradoxes and anomalies. For example, in mystical traditions the dichotomy between subject and object is obliterated at certain stages of mental development. This may be similar to bonding in physical systems explained by the indistinguishability principle. Also, the principles of uncertainty and complementarity may have counterparts in a variety of dichotomous relationships seen in consciousness, such as reason and intuition, the individual and the collective, and so on. All this suggests to them that consciousness is a *proactive* agency in the establishment of reality (1999).

Jahn, who had set up a laboratory at Princeton University to carry out experiments to study the influence of consciousness on quantum systems and what he calls remote perception, a form of ESP, also emphasizes the information aspect to build a link between consciousness and the material world. Jahn and Dunne (1987) suggest that reality in a significant sense "is constituted only at the interface between consciousness and its environment" and that "the sole currency of reality is *information*" (pp. 203–204). Any form of creative human

experience, they contend, is characterized by (1) an unfocused *environment*, (2) *consciousness* guided by intention or purpose, (3) *information* that flows between consciousness and the pertinent environment, and (4) a nurturing *resonance* between consciousness and the environment. Assuming that consciousness is a *proactive* agency in the establishment of reality, they find the "Copenhagen" interpretation of quantum mechanics a helpful physical theory to include consciousness explicitly to encompass both objective and subjective components of information. "Like elementary particles (a form of matter), and physical light (a form of energy)," they write, "consciousness (a processor and generator of information) enjoys a 'wave/particle duality' which allows it to circumvent and penetrate barriers, and to resonate with other consciousness and with appropriate aspects of its environment" (Jahn, and Dunne 1999, p. 213).

Stapp's Model: As mentioned, nature at the quantum level seems to exist more as potential rather than as definite individual events we are normally familiar with at the macroscopic level, to which classical physics generally applies. Consequently, the transition from the probabilistic quantum state to an actual event observed in the classical sense needs to be explained. In quantum mechanics a number of interpretations are offered. According to one of these interpretations, both the probabilistic universe and the deterministic physical world are ontologically separate but real domains. What is needed is an understanding of the means by which the probable becomes actual, the potential becomes the manifest.

Henry Stapp (1982, 1990, 1992) utilized Werner Heisenberg's conception of the physical universe to develop a model to account for both consciousness/mind and matter. In the context of describing the behavior of a quantum measuring device, Heisenberg thought of an atom not as a real entity in the sense that it represents no actual or substantive quality, but only as objective tendencies related to the occurrence of events. In addition to the deterministic quantum state mechanically generated by the Schrödinger-equation there is a disorderly process of "quantum jumps" that is not *individually* subject to the precise laws of physics but *collectively* conforms to statistical estimates. Heisenberg considered these quantum jumps to be nature's actual events. An actual event is an actualization of an objective tendency that involves the selection of one possibility and the elimination of the others. This interpretation differs from the more orthodox interpretation of quantum theory. As Stapp (1992) puts it, "Heisenberg's picture allows quantum theory to be viewed as a coherent description of the evolution of the entire physical reality itself, rather than a set of stark statistical rules about connections between human observations" (p. 212).

Stapp suggests that we look at the human brain as similar to Heisenberg's measuring device. The brain represents the world to us in the form of physiological and psychological schema at a macroscopic level of experience. However, it is very much a quantum process involving micro-chemical events. For example, the question of whether or not a given synapse will transmit a signal should be treated as a quantum event. Following Heisenberg, we may assume that the actual events in the brain involve quantum jumps. Stapp argues that in the absence of such quantum jumps, brain states will continue to evolve "into a superposition of a set of increasingly disparate macroscopic possibilities" (p. 214). Consequently, it is reasonable to suppose, following Hesenberg's picture of the world, that an actual event must select and actualize one of these observable states and eradicate the others. Stapp identifies "each such actual brain event with a conscious event" and "conversely, each conscious event with an

actual brain event of the particular kind" (p. 215). Not all actual brain events are, however, conscious events. Only those that select one of the possible configurations among the many routinely generated by the Schrodinger equation are actual conscious events. "Each consciousness event is, therefore, an entity that supervenes over the quantum mechanical laws analogous to the laws of classical physics. It corresponds to a Heisenberg event that actualizes one classically describable, metastable, quantum state of the brain, chosen from among the many alternatively possible macroscopic metastable states generated by the strictly mechanical part of the quantum law of evolution" (pp. 215–216). The actual event may not be limited to firing a single neuron. It may initiate a large-scale integrated pattern of neural activity corresponding to conscious thought. Inasmuch as a conscious event is an entity that supervenes to actualize a quantum state of the brain among the many possible alternative states, Stapp's model provides for a top-level process that controls brain processes. Stapp does not specify, however, whether that process itself is entirely physical or nonphysical.

In his book *Mind, Matter and Quantum Mechanics*, Stapp (1993) attempts to deal with the question of how the content of thought is related to the relevant functions in the brain. Making use of the ideas of the physicist Werner Heisenberg and the psychologist William James, Stapp focuses on the concept of wholeness. The wholeness does not consist in the existence of separate physical parts that are dynamically linked by field forces, as classical physics postulates. Rather, it is the wholeness implied by quantum theory, the unity of all things, including the mind, brain and consciousness. In this view, the mind can influence the activities of the brain, and our thoughts may guide our actions. Consequently, the determinism of classical physics is derailed. Equally untenable is the notion that considers matter as the primary constituent, the building block of physical reality. Matter is no more than an "objective tendency" or "potentiality" as understood in quantum physics. The human brain, then, may not be seen as made up of interacting parts; rather it is "one unified body/brain/mind system observing itself." The observer is the body/brain/mind system and it is an integral part of the quantum system. In addition to the physical line that deterministically unfolds a physical event, "there is a mental line of causation that transfers the experiential intention of an earlier event into an experiential attention of a later event. These two causal strands, one physical and one mental, join to form the physical and mental poles of a succeeding quantum event" (Stapp, 1999, p. 157). What permits the interaction between the physical and mental aspects is the informational character of the physical aspect as represented in quantum theory.

The Observer Model: In the observer model, the quantum object is described by the multiple possibilities generated by the quantum mechanical wave function until one possibility becomes actual in the presence of an observer. While the role of the observer varies in different interpretations, most interpretations accept that an observer is associated with the collapse of the wave function into a distinct state. The brain, which is the base for conscious experience, is a quantum mechanical system. In time, a brain state develops from one configuration into a number of potential states. The development of brain states is thus probabilistic, and which of these states manifests in an observation is not determined by any known physical variables. However, when a state is observed, the multiple potential states collapse into a single state. It is assumed that this collapse is brought about by hidden variables.

Evan Harris Walker equates these hidden variables with consciousness. His (1970, 1977, 2000) quantum theory of consciousness is indeed a bold and innovative attempt to understand consciousness in relation to the processes in the brain. Contrary to the views of most physicists, Walker assumes the existence of consciousness as a distinct entity. Inasmuch as it is apparently immeasurable in quantitative terms, it may even be regarded as nonphysical. Since consciousness is obviously involved in a variety of behavioral phenomena to which the brain is linked, it is likely that consciousness is associated in some manner with the electrochemical processes in the brain. Therefore, it should be possible to study the interaction between consciousness variables and the variables of physical phenomena in those cortical processes that seem to mediate consciousness. According to Walker, such an interaction is quantum mechanical. He postulates, "there must exist a quantum mechanical process operating within the brain that is ultimately involved with the data processing function of the brain" (1970, p. 131).

In Walker's model, consciousness and the physical world are coupled by means of the quantum mechanical wave function. The linking or coupling is maintained by the hidden variables via the "will" channel. The "will," according Walker, is "that part of man's conscious experience postulated to allow him to exert some control over physical events" (1975, p. 9). Walker argues that the "will" can effect changes not only within one's brain, but also in the world outside, because the brain through its sensory inputs is connected with the external world and is therefore a part of a larger system.

Walker worked out a detailed mathematical model to explain the quantum mechanical tunneling at the synaptic cleft and various implications of this theory for the structure of the synapses and brain functioning, which he believes can be empirically examined. Walker's theory implies, among other things: "A nonliving computer that is capable of both thought and consciousness would be a real possibility. Consciousness may also exist without being associated with either a living being or a data processing system. Indeed, since everything that occurs is ultimately the result of one or more quantum mechanical events, the universe is 'inhabited' by an almost unlimited number of rather discrete conscious, usually nonthinking, entities that are responsible for the detailed working of the universe" (1970, p. 176). Clearly, Walker talks here more like a metaphysician than a physicist, but then, someone must bridge the gulf between the two.

Amit Goswami (1989, 1990), a physicist at the University of Oregon, goes even beyond the "pragmatic dualism" of Evan Harris Walker to an outright idealistic ontology in the Upanishadic tradition. Suggesting in the manner of Walker that consciousness is involved in the collapse of the quantum wave function, i.e., the actualization of many quantum possibilities of an event into a unique observed event, Goswami argues that consciousness, not physical matter, is the ground of all being. The actual reality, according to Goswami, is consciousness, and matter is no more than the quantum possibilities. When an observation is made, it is consciousness that recognizes and chooses one of the possibilities, thus bringing into being an actual event. Thus, consciousness provides a way out of the quantum measurement paradox. Goswami does not, however, limit consciousness to individual observers. He regards consciousness as transcendental, thus providing for the collapse of the wave function in the absence of individual observers.

Goswami (1995) argues that quantum physics and the Copenhagen interpretation of it developed by Heisenberg and Bohr, which enable us to treat quantum objects as waves and to interpret them in probabilistic terms, warrants the rejection of the philosophy of material realism. The notion of naive objectivity implicit in realism is contradicted by the role of observation and measurement in collapsing the quantum wave packet to a localized particle. The quantum uncertainty principle shows the limits of determinism, another hallmark of materialism. Finally, if waves, spread over vast distances, collapse instantly without the mediation of any local signal, i.e., if quantum objects display the character of nonlocality, materialism stands refuted. Again, if it is accepted that consciousness is instrumental in collapsing the wave of a quantum object, Goswami observes, not only is idealistic monism compatible with quantum mechanics, but also it is essential for a proper interpretation and understanding of quantum physics.

Goswami adapts the model of Henry Stapp (1982) that the brain is an interacting system with quantum as well as classical components. He goes on to suggest that the quantum component is "the vehicle for conscious choice and creativity," and that the classical component is the one associated with memory and all that constitutes the point of reference for one's experience. Creative mental acts are discontinuous, like quantum jumps. The *content* of thought is like the *position* of a physical object, whereas the *association* a thought generates is akin to *momentum*. *Awareness* may be seen as the *space* in which thoughts appear. Goswami goes on to suggest that between manifestations thoughts may exist as "transcendent archetypes," in the manner of the quantum objects with their wave and particle aspects. "Just as ordinary matter," writes Goswami (1995), "consists ultimately of submicroscopic quantum objects that can be called archetypes of matter, let us assume that the mind consists ultimately of the archetypes of mental objects.... I further suggest that they are made of the same basic substance that material archetypes are made of and that they also obey quantum mechanics"

(p. 167). The quantum component of the brain has causal efficacy, which is made possible by consciousness. Consciousness is nonlocal. It collapses the brain's wave function and at the same time experiences the outcome of the collapse.

Goswami does not distinguish between the brain and the mind. The so-called mental states are the states of the quantum system in the brain. Most of the brain is a measuring apparatus. It is important for him, however, to distinguish between the mind and consciousness. Mental phenomena, such as thoughts, are similar to material things; and they are likewise objects of consciousness. It is consciousness that chooses the outcome of the collapse of the quantum state of the brain/mind. We experience the resultant state but are unaware of the process. This lack of awareness creates the illusion of the separateness of the self. In reality, consciousness, according to Goswami, is one, unitive and nonlocal. If consciousness is one, how does it differentiate itself into the subject and objects of awareness? We may recall that in this theory brain events are considered quantum states, i.e., probability structures. These are collapsed by the choice of consciousness in the "field" of awareness. Objects of experience arise in awareness as a consequence of the choice consciousness makes. The question whether awareness or choice comes first cannot be answered in any noncircular way. We are in a situation of "tangled hierarchy," says Goswami. As consciousness finds itself identified with the "I," self-consciousness arises. "*The self of self-reference and the consciousness of the original consciousness, together, make what we call self-consciousness*" (Goswami, 1995, p. 187, original emphasis).

If physicist Walker was speaking like a philosopher, we find Goswami writing more like a mystic but in the language of quantum mechanics. As he frankly admits, he is not attempting to understand consciousness within the framework of science. Rather, by taking a quantum jump as it were, he seeks to formulate a new physics "based on consciousness as the building block of everything."

Only a few physicists are prepared to travel as far as Goswami to the dizzying heights of the transcendental realm. However, there is growing conviction among physicists (Margenau, 1984; Squires, 1990; Leggett, 1987; Penrose, 1989, 1994) that functions of the brain may be better understood in terms of quantum mechanics than as the output of a classical system of neural assemblies. Indeed, there is increasing recognition that quantum theory itself cannot be completely defined without reference to consciousness (Squires, 1994). The so-called measurement problem, which suggests the dependence of material states on observation, and the little understood non-locality of quantum systems, suggest powerful links to connect consciousness with quantum processes (Hodgson, 1991).

IMPLICATE ORDER AND HOLOMOVEMENT

The models we have discussed above have attempted to understand the interface between consciousness and the physical world and their possible interactions. Another quantum physicist and Nobel Laureate who looked for an interface between consciousness and matter is David Bohm. He found no such relationship. Instead, he saw them acting synchronistically, having a common source in a hidden order of reality characterized by "undivided wholeness." According to David Bohm (1980), there is an *implicate* realm of existence with energy of extraordinary magnitude and potential. The implicate order is the ground for the *explicate* world of matter and experience, to which quantum mechanical descriptions apply. The relationship between the two is one of *unfoldment* and *enfoldment*. The whole of the universe, says Bohm, is "in some way enfolded in everything and that each thing is enfolded in the whole" (1986, p. 114). In other words, everything "enfolds or implicates everything." At the same time, the explicate world order is continually unfolding. These processes are not static, but basically dynamic. This dynamic nature is what Bohm calls the *holomovement*. All the things that we find around us, the objects of our observation and experience, constitute the unfolded explicate order, and they emerge from the holomovement of the implicate realm in which "they are enfolded as potentialities" (1986, p. 115).

Bohm, unlike Goswami, is a realist, and the divide between the classical and the quantum, the von Neumann legacy, does not appeal to him. Measurement in his view is just another physical interaction. It has no fundamental role to play in formulating a new theory. Consequently, the concept of consciousness is not required for a coherent interpretation of quantum mechanics. Bohm favors a quantum theory that can be understood without reference to observers and measurement. At the same time, he sees some connection between consciousness and matter in the implicate order (Bohm & Hiley, 1993).

Consciousness, like matter, is a process in the implicate order. Like matter, it manifests in some explicate order. The only difference between matter and consciousness is that the latter is a more subtle form of matter, a more subtle aspect of the holomovement. Bohm finds a common relationship between consciousness and matter in the concepts of meaning and information. In his causal interpretation of quantum mechanics, Bohm postulates that a thing such as an electron is an inseparable union of a particle and the field. The field contains objective and active information that at the subjective level of experience signifies meaning. Thus, "meaning is simultaneously both mental and physical in nature." This meaning aspect, according to

Bohm, helps to link the mental and physical, which "are two sides of one overall process that are (like form and content) separated only in thought and not in actuality" (1986, p. 129).

Interestingly, Bohm allows for different levels of information and mental activity. Subtler mental activity can lead to subtler information. The meaning that they generate bridges the different levels of information. Thus, Bohm is led to believe that "a rudimentary consciousness is present even at the level of particle physics. It would also be reasonable to suppose an indefinitely greater kind of consciousness that is universal and that pervades the entire process" (1986, p. 131). The multiplicity of objects and events we experience in manifest reality are but "ripples," whose meaning depends on the understanding of the ground that underlies them. If consciousness could empty itself of its contents, the ripples, then it could become an instrument or vehicle for the operation of the wholeness that is contained in the implicate realm. Time and space emerge from the implicate order, as do consciousness and matter. The interaction of consciousness/mind and brain is merely an appearance that reflects their common origin in the implicate order and their proneness to act synchronistically.

The transition from the implicate order to the explicate order in Bohm's model reminds us very much of Bergson's account of the virtual and actual activity embedded in our experience. Also, Bohm's two orders of reality appear analogous to the distinction between the transcendental and phenomenal realms of being as discussed by Vedanta philosophers like Sankara.

CALL FOR NEW PHYSICS

Roger Penrose, unlike Goswami, does not believe that "consciousness can be rooted in anything outside physical reality"

(Penrose, 1994b, p. 24). However, in his "search for the missing science of consciousness" (1994a), he is led to look *beyond* quantum mechanics and physics as now understood. Quantum mechanics, Penrose argues, is not a complete theory, because "it does not explain why the macroscopic world behaves the way it does. So there is something profoundly missing here" (1994b, p. 21). In his recent book *Shadows of the Mind*, he argues that we must go beyond mere computation to account for mental abilities such as mathematical understanding. Basing his argument on Godel's incompleteness theorem, which asserts the intrinsic algorithmic unprovability of a true mathematical axiom, Penrose maintains that the capabilities displayed by the human mind in understanding mathematical truths and linguistic meanings cannot be wholly algorithmic. Inasmuch as understanding involves conscious awareness and at least some aspect of understanding is beyond computation, consciousness may be basically noncomputational. The present-day physics, whether quantum or classical, is essentially computational. Therefore, we must look outside of "known physics" for an explanation of consciousness.

Is there anything in physics, Penrose asks, that is conceivably noncomputable? By noncomputability Penrose does not mean randomness, or a highly complex or chaotic state, but something that is in principle nondeterministic. Classical physics is essentially deterministic, full of computational laws. Even quantum physics is deterministic insofar as the Schrödinger equation provides a description. So, Penrose points out that there is no indeterminacy either at the classical or quantum levels of physics. However, quantum indeterminacy arises at the level of transition from the quantum to a classical state. The so-called "collapse of the wave function" or "reduction of the statevector" is a mere stop-gap arrangement and reveals nothing essential to a theoretical understanding of what is going on here as illustrated by the predicament of Schrödinger's cat that exists in a superposition between life and death. Penrose believes it is in this context that we need a new theory in physics to provide for "objective reduction that goes beyond wave function collapse." Such objective reduction, according to him, would be nonlocal and noncomputational. It would not be random, as current quantum theory postulates, but "what it is in detail we do not yet know; because it is in the part of fundamental physics we have not yet understood" (Penrose, 1994c, p. 249). Penrose speculates, however, that objective reduction is likely to be a gravitational phenomenon. Chris Nunn et al. (1994) report an experiment that provides statistically significant evidence that the task performance of the subject may be influenced by taking an EEG from his/her relevant brain areas. The results of this experiment provide support for Penrose's suggestion of possible gravitational link with the occurrence of quantum coherence.

Now, coming to the specifics of the theory, Penrose suspects that microtubules of neural cells are possibly the place where subtle quantum effects take place. Following on the proposal of Stuart Hameroff (1994), Penrose speculates that water molecules in the microtubules forming the cytoskeletons of widely separated neurons may exist in a coherent quantum mechanical state. The nonlocally correlated changes in cytoskeleton configurations may influence synaptic connections between neurons. Such nonlocal influence may account for the unity of conscious experience as well as the notion of free will. According to Penrose, free will is nothing other than the quantum mechanical, noncomputational influence on the configurations of the microtubules in a quantum-mechanically coherent state.

Penrose's proposed solution to the enigma of consciousness is criticized as an unsuccessful attempt to explain one mystery by another. Bernard Baars (1994), for example, severely indicts Penrose for ignoring the real living aspects of consciousness in favor of more abstract notions such as the Platonic view of mathematical intuition. Penrose's quest for the "quantum soul," as Baars put it, simply sets aside much of the empirical literature on conscious experience, and he bases his argument mainly on refuting the capability of Turing machines to engage in creative activities. Again, Penrose's formulation, alleges Baars, has nothing to offer about unconscious mental processes.

CONSCIOUSNESS IN PHYSICS: A SUMMARY

The question whether consciousness/ mind is a manifestation of higher order, more subtle physical processes is not yet answered with any convincing degree of assurance. Quantum physics appears, however, to open up possibilities for resolving some of the inconsistencies between subjective experience and physical reality. Whereas a strictly Newtonian physicalist view excludes the possibility of consciousness/mind supervening to influence physical processes, the developments in quantum physics appear to leave room for postulating an interface between consciousness and the physical world, i.e., between subjective experience and objective events. The wave/ particle duality is fundamental in quantum theory. Unobserved, a subatomic particle is like a wave of possibilities. Observation, it is assumed, collapses the wave function and we have the particle. Quantum coherence or inseparability suggests that physical objects at the micro level may have nonlocal connections, with the result that what happens to one may influence another with no signal passing between them. There is credible experimental evidence for nonlocal connections that take place instantly, independently of space and impervious to shielding

(Aspect & Grangier, 1986). These are weird, bizarre, and puzzling characteristics at the quantum level. They are inconsistent with our intuitive sense as well as classical physics. At the theoretical level, physics itself is thus confronted with the problem of reconciling what appear to be in principle indeterministic and probable events at the microscopic quantum level with the entirely predictable events at classical level. This transition from indeterminate quantum states to actual events, measured and observed, need to be explained. It may not be out of place, then, to conjecture that consciousness may be crucially involved in that process of transition.

How consciousness may be involved is not quite clear, however. The precise nature of measurement/observation that is central to the collapse of the wave function is not described with any degree of specificity. We hardly have any understanding of it. Is the observation a part and parcel of the mind/brain system, as some assume? In other words, is it the case that the mental and the physical are two aspects of the same system, or are they the outcomes of two distinct systems? We are back again to the monist and dualist dilemma. The question of the relationship between the two "worlds," as it were, of quantum and classical physics is crucial, and it is not answered with any degree of conviction. We are still confronted with the issue of whether the measurement itself is a physical interaction and whether we need a new physics beyond quantum mechanics to understand the problems associated with measurement and observation.

Physical events at certain levels of subtlety are seen to manifest nonlocal characteristics. For example, in the case of two widely separated electrons, the observed spin of one electron appears to determine the spin of the other in the absence of any conceivable physical interaction between them. Therefore, it is not unreasonable to speculate that there may be greater inter-connectedness among events in the vast universe that is unbounded at subtler levels by space-time constraints. Such interconnectedness, implicated by quantum coherence, and the inseparability that is inexplicable by current theories in physics may call for bold speculations and new theoretical advances to provide the missing links between conscious experience and physical reality, between micro and macro physical events. The jury is still out. We do not know if those advances would come from physics as such, without going beyond the currently accepted theory to postulate a new domain of consciousness. It remains to be seen whether physics needs consciousness to fill the gap of the transition from quantum to classical physics, or whether a physical explanation of the interaction would provide a satisfactory solution to the problem of consciousness.

Consciousness in Physiology

In both physics and philosophy, the ultimate resolution of the problem of consciousness seems to rest, as we have seen, on the role of the brain in generating awareness. The tenability of the identity thesis and our understanding of the physical basis of consciousness crucially depend on the extent to which consciousness is contained in the functions of the brain. It is thus the question of identity or otherwise of conscious experience and neural activity that is central to a discussion of consciousness. Consequently, one would hope that research in brain sciences would hold the key to a proper resolution of the consciousness problem. That injury to the brain affects conscious experience makes a prima facie case for the dependence of consciousness on the brain. But then what is the nature of such dependence? Is it the case that all conscious experience, qualia and subjectivity

included, has appropriate correspondence in neural coding in the brain? How do neurons in the brain cause conscious experience? What are the brain structures that are necessary for one to have conscious experience? Are these structures localized or distributed globally in the brain? Can studies of the brain provide in principle a complete understanding of the neural correlates of consciousness that are necessary and sufficient to account for the "hard problems" of phenomenal awareness? If, on the contrary, consciousness can act independently on physical systems and process information outside of the brain, what is its relationship to the brain and the nervous system?

Folk psychology, unlike neuroscience, accords comparable reality to subjective experience, regarded as mental, and the observable physical world, considered as material, and takes interactive dualism as a given fact of experience. Contrary to this view, however, a preponderant majority of brain scientists hold that there is in principle a one-to-one correspondence between what we consider to be mental phenomena and the events occurring in the brain. The identity hypothesis in one form or another is the favorite among scientists and for this reason it merits characterization as "the official brain doctrine" of consciousness (Kelly, 1979).

There are a number of reasons why the identity hypothesis continues to be a favorite of brain scientists. At the common-sense level, we are familiar how the development of complex behavioral patterns is correlated with the development of the brain and the nervous system. Again, it is also commonly observed that variables affecting the functioning of the brain such as fatigue, drugs, and injury or damage to the brain have concomitant effects on behavior and subjective experience. More than half a century ago, G. Moruzzi and H.W. Magoun (1949) proposed the reticular activating system (RAS) as causing and maintaining arousal and wakefulness. Their studies suggest that the RAS originates in the reticular formation of the pontine region of the hindbrain. Wilder Penfield (1958) observed irreversible coma among patients with pathological legions in arousal-related structures in the brain, even though extensive damage to the cerebral cortex produced no such coma. This led Penfield to propose that consciousness is localized in the "centrencephalic" system of the brain stem.

We now have a great deal of information about neuronal activities that correlate with cognitive states. Electroencephalographic recordings are one such. Slow EEG activity (1–2 Hz range) correlates with deep sleep, faster activity in alpha range (10 cycles per second) with a wakeful conscious state and so on. Event related potentials (ERPs) are known to correlate more directly with conscious experience. The early components of ERPs correlate with stimulus intensity, stimulus repetition, the area of stimulation, etc. The late components (beyond 150 ms) seem necessary for conscious experience (Libet 1993). There are indeed several important advances in neuroscience that have given us significant understanding of the structural organization of the brain and the complex operations of neurons, as well as the role of different structures of the brain in generating and organizing awareness both in its content and its form. These advances, especially in the area of vision, have reinforced the conclusion that "properties of minds can ultimately be explained entirely by those of brains" (Kelly 1979, p. 3).

Neurological studies make a strong case for the dependence of conscious experience on cortical structures and processes. It is not clear, however, whether these are both necessary and *sufficient*. Some investigators in this area are not at all convinced that we could ever establish that certain neuronal activities are sufficient causes for

conscious experience (Libet 1996). Some have argued that correlations of the kind observed so far between conscious experience and cortical activity are not sufficient reasons to equate mental events, with brain events because the brain may be simply a receiving mechanism, a *detector* rather than a *generator* of the mind (Eccles 1953).

THE ASTONISHING HYPOTHESIS OF FRANCIS CRICK

Francis Crick won the Nobel Prize in medicine (1962) along with James Watson and Maurice Wilkins for the discovery of the structure of DNA. Since moving into neuroscience, Crick has made important contributions to an understanding of visual awareness. In his recent book, Crick (1993) proposes what he calls the "astonishing hypothesis." His ideas are strictly in the materialistic tradition, advocating strong reductionism as an explanation of consciousness. In his words, the astonishing hypothesis is that "You, your joys and sorrows, your memories and ambitions, your sense of personal identity and free will, are, in fact, no more than the behavior of a vast assembly of nerve-cells. As Lewis Carroll's Alice might have phrased it: 'You're nothing but a pack of neurons'" (Crick, 1993, p. 3). What is interesting here is that Crick, unlike some other reductionist thinkers, is willing to accept the reality of consciousness, our fears and sorrows, but hopes to account for them by identifying their neural correlates.

Convinced that the problem of consciousness can be solved only at the neural level, Crick and his associates have attempted to explore the neural basis of awareness. Even though their studies are largely confined to the visual area, they believe their approach and the theoretical base they suggest can be extended to other areas of awareness as well. This is so because, in their view, all the different aspects of consciousness employ a "basic common mechanism or perhaps a few such mechanisms." An understanding of these in one area will lead, they hope, to understanding the rest of them.

According to Crick and Koch (1990), consciousness basically depends on short-term memory and serial attention. The attentional process enables the relevant neuron sets to fire in a coherent semi-oscillatory fashion. They suggest the oscillations to be in the frequency range of 40–70 Hz. Such coherent firing of neurons helps to impose a temporary global unity on neurons in several different parts of the brain. The oscillations thus generated activate short-term memory. Crick and Koch locate the source of operations that correspond to consciousness mainly, if not exclusively, in the neocortex and paleocortex. They refer to the binding problem (the need to account for the perception of a unitary object possessing different characteristics such as color, shape and movement that involve the activity of numerous neurons widely separated in the brain). Crick and Koch credit a serial binding mechanism with the task of effecting unified awareness. In their view, attention and awareness are intimately tied together. The attentional mechanism temporarily binds together the relevant neurons "by synchronizing their spikes in 40 Hz oscillations." These oscillations help to join together existing information to constitute a coherent percept.

Crick has in his "astonishing hypothesis" an idea and a program for research, but not a detailed model or theory of consciousness. He has deliberately chosen to limit himself to simpler issues where neural connections of consciousness are more apparent, leaving out more difficult issues such as the problem of qualia. It is significant that a scientist of Crick's stature finds it necessary to look at consciousness instead of dismissing it as some others have done. It is likely that the program of research he suggests would yield important information about the relationship between the brain and consciousness and about the neural correlates of some aspects of consciousness. Herms Ramjin (2002) has proposed that subjectivity may be a fundamental property of omnipresent virtual photons.

NON-IDENTITY APPROACHES TOWARD UNDERSTANDING CONSCIOUSNESS

There are other models in addition to those that assume the identity of conscious states with neural states or a perfect correlation between them. Some of them regard conscious events as irreducible to brain events. These models claim support from the weakness of the identity models in adequately explaining certain aspects of conscious experience, such as subjectivity, qualia, the experience of self-consciousness, free will, and the holistic information processing abilities of humans. Paranormal phenomena like ESP, and any evidence of the possibility of postmortem survival such as memories in the putative cases of reincarnation, would render the identity models even less plausible, if not totally false.

Among the mind-brain models that consider consciousness/mind as capable of acting on its own, some postulate that mind and brain belong to two ontologically separate realms, whereas others locate the source of consciousness, with capabilities to act independently of the brain, in the brain itself. Here, physiological accounts of consciousness parallel those in physics.

Philosopher John Searle (1983, 1992), for example, asserts that mental states are real and that they have properties of their own. In other words, consciousness is irreducible to brain states. As Searle puts it, "we all really do have subjective conscious mental states and that these are not eliminable in favor of anything else" (1992, p. 3). Subjectivity, the first-person perspective of awareness, is the crucial feature that distinguishes mental from non-mental phenomena. At the same time, these states, according to him, are not dissociated from the brain. On the contrary, they are biologically based. Searle says that mental phenomena "are both caused by the operations of the brain and realized in the structure of the brain. On this view, consciousness and intentionality are as much a part of human biology as digestion or circulation of the blood. It is an *objective* fact about the world that it contains certain systems, viz., brains, with *subjective* mental states, and it is a *physical* fact about such systems that they have *mental* features" (1983, p. ix). Again, "Mental events and processes are as much part of our biological natural history as digestion, mitosis, meiosis, or enzyme secretion" (1992, p. 1).

Searle goes on to argue that consciousness, inasmuch as it is a product of biological processes, cannot cause anything that is in principle unexplainable in terms of the behavior of neurons, i.e., in the causal language of the brain. In other words, though conscious experience cannot be reduced to brain states, the functions attributed to consciousness may be explained by the causal behavior of neurons. David Hodgson (1994) has argued that the above two assertions are incompatible and that it is more reasonable to reject the latter rather than the former.

Combined Brain Activity: In the mainstream of neuroscience is the Russian neuropsychologist A. R. Luria who, following L. S. Vygotskie, holds that consciousness is a complex structural system with a semantic function that is amenable to proper scientific investigation. He rejects the dualistic postulation that consciousness/mind is fundamentally different in principle from material objects. At the same time, he views the attempts to locate the mechanisms of consciousness inside the brain as equally misguided. Consciousness, according to

Luria, is the ability "to assess sensory information to respond to it with critical thoughts and actions, and retain memory traces in order that past traces or actions may be used in the future" (1978, pp. 5–6). This ability is not a function of any one part of the brain. Rather, it "must be sought in the combined activity of discrete brain systems, each of which makes its own special contribution to the work of the functional system as a whole" (p. 31). Among the brain systems that are involved in conscious mental activity, according to Luria, are: (a) the brain-stem reticular formation that controls the levels of wakefulness, (b) secondary zones of the posterior (afferent) cortical areas that are involved in the recording of incoming information, and more importantly, (c) the medial zones of frontal lobes, which intimately participate in the formation of intentions and action programs, and play an essential role in the conscious regulation of goal-directed behavior.

Luria's account thus limits consciousness to what Locke called reflection. His rejection of the view that we can localize consciousness in some brain cells is well taken. Also, the notion that consciousness is an emergent property of complex interactions of some major functional systems in the brain is an advance over the identity theory. But he has little to say about how these interactions and processes differ to produce different states of consciousness. It is likely that the brain systems he identifies as involved in conscious activity may be necessary but not sufficient conditions for consciousness.

Holism and Holographic Processing: Karl Pribram, while agreeing that the variety of conscious states experienced by individuals may be produced by the operation of processes in the brain structure, recognizes that the analyses of these operations reveal little about the states themselves. He believes, therefore, that the studies of consciousness may provide valuable insights into the "tools" required for understanding mental states. Pribram (1971, 1976a, 1976b, 1984) published extensively, attempting to adapt his theories of memory and attention to account for some of the phenomena associated with consciousness, such as self-awareness, intentionality, and even mystical experience.

In his attempt to find the brain processes operative in one's experience of self-consciousness and intention, Pribram makes use of the distinction between feedback and feedforward operations. In a feedback situation, an operation continues until congruence between two settings is achieved, e.g., between a thermostat and room temperature. In a feedforward control, an operation proceeds until a predetermined point is reached, e.g., heating for a fixed time period without regard to room temperature. In the human system, homeostatic processes such as biological rhythms involve feedback organization. But when an external bias is applied to them, such as through biofeedback, feedforward organizations of feedback joined into parallel processes are constituted, which give the experience of conscious attention. "The bias, maintained with effort," according to Pribram, "produces conscious voluntary control on the system, which now is an information-processing, feedforward, openloop, helical mechanism rather than just an unconscious error-processing, feedback, closed-loop system" (1976b, p. 87). In other words, the change from the feedback to feedforward organization of the control mechanisms in the brain gives rise to conscious control. This control is achieved through attention, and consequently attention becomes central to understanding self-consciousness. Attention is the process that organizes the contents of consciousness. Reorganizations of the structure of the neural information-processing system lead to the experience of altered states, which Pribram

(1984) calls "alternate" states of consciousness.

One of the "alternate" states of consciousness referred to in several mystical traditions is the experience of transcendence, where the dichotomy of the knower and known, the "self" and "other" is transcended. Pribram suggests that such experiences may result from the changes or disturbances in the structures of the brain that control the joining of the various feedback and feedforward mechanisms. He points out that patients with "epileptogenic lesions of the medial part of the pole of the temporal lobe ... experience inappropriate *deja vu* and *jamais vu* feelings of familiarity and unfamiliarity and fail to incorporate into memory experiences occurring during an episode of electrical seizure activity in their brains. In a sense, therefore, these clinical episodes point to a transcendence of content, a phenomenon of consciousness without content, a phenomenon also experienced in mystical states..." (Pribram 1976a, p. 309).

Few who are familiar with the accounts of transcendental experience would consider that such experiences are similar to those obtained during epileptic seizures of the kind Pribram refers to. Apart from the fact that many of those reporting such experiences had no history of brain damage of the kind required, the personal transformation accompanying the transcendental experience is clearly lacking in the case of those suffering from epileptogenic lesions. Thus, there seem to be qualitative differences between the experiences of Pribram's patients and those reported by mystics.

Pribram's emphasis on the structure of the brain may be important and necessary to some extent to understand the context and even the conditions that must be met for experiencing certain states of consciousness. It does not seem, however, that the understanding of the structure of the brain itself is sufficient to explain consciousness and the phenomena associated with it.

Pribram (1971, 1978) proposed a holographic model of the brain and consciousness. According to Pribram (1978), the brain function is holonomic in that it partakes of both computer and optical information processes. "The brain is like a computer in that information is processed in steps by an organized and organizing set of rules. It differs from current computers in that each step is more extended in space—brain has considerably more parallel processing capability than today's computers" (p. 103). Again, unlike today's computers, memory storage in the brain is holographic. Pribram believes that his holonomic theory, besides providing models that would help us precisely explore in the laboratory such cognitive processes as memory, attention, and problem solving, has possibilities for the study of consciousness. Ordinary consciousness, he says, is "achieved by a mechanism (somewhat like a hologram) that disposes the organism to locate fresh experiences and performances at some distance from the receptive and expressive interfaces that join organism and environment" (p. 109). One of the reasons for this conclusion is the similarity between sensory processing and physical holography. For example, G. von Bekesy (1967) found that when a set of phase-related vibratory stimuli were applied to two of a subject's limbs, the subject pointed to a place between the two limbs as being the somatosensory source of the stimulus.

Pribram goes on to suggest that the world itself may be a hologram. Following David Bohm's (1973) distinction between explicate and implicate organizations relative to structural and holographic processes, Pribram makes a similar distinction for perceptual processes. Our current scientific analysis gives us knowledge about *extrinsic* properties of the physical world. Pribram argues that even the *intrinsic* properties (such as stoneness of stones) are knowable. In fact, he says, "they are the 'ground' in

which the extrinsic properties are embedded in order to become realized" (1978, p. 112). Again: "The intrinsic properties of the physical universe, their implicate organization, the field, ground or medium in which explicit organizations, extrinsic properties, become realized, are multiform. In the extreme, the intrinsic properties, the implicate organization is holographic. As extrinsic properties become realized, they make the implicate organization become more explicit" (p. 112). This implies that the "uncertainty of occurrence of events is only superficial and is the result of holographic 'blurring'…" (pp. 112–113). Thus, a random distribution, inasmuch as it is based on holographic principles, is not haphazard but determined. All this leads Pribram to conclude that there is "no more mystery to the mystic than to the induction process that allows selective depression of DNA to form now this organ, now that one" (p. 115).

EMERGENT INTERACTIONISM

Another neuroscientist, R. W. Sperry, goes beyond the cortical structures and to consciousness itself as a primary source of causal influence on brain processes. In doing so, he possibly provides the necessary link missing in Pribram's account. For Sperry (1969), consciousness is autonomous in its own right. It is not reducible to electrochemical processes. It is an "integral working component" in the brain. Sperry considers consciousness as a dynamic, emergent property resulting from the higher level functional organization of the cerebral cortex. As an emergent property, consciousness is in a sense determined by the neural infrastructures of the brain at the highest levels of its organizational hierarchy. But at the same time, not only does consciousness manifest characteristics that are not attributable to any of the constituent brain systems, but it also exerts regulatory control influence on brain processes. Thus, mental phenomena are "*causes*" rather than "*corre-lates*" of neural events. As Sperry puts it, "the brain physiology determines the mental effects and the mental phenomena in turn have causal influence on the neuro-physiology" (1976, p. 168). As emergent properties of cortical activity, conscious phenomena could functionally interact at their own level and also at the same time exert downward control over their constituent neural processes. Thus conscious states "supervene" rather than "intervene" in the physiological processes.

Sperry is careful to emphasize that in his view consciousness "is strictly a property of brain circuits" and that he does not see how individual consciousness could coalesce into a "megaconscious experience" or how "the consciousness of one brain could influence that of another" (1976, p. 168). He argues, however, that his emergent interactionism will help to resolve the free-will/determinism paradox, as well as ease the tensions between religion and science (1988).

Sperry's views have a certain intuitive appeal. But as Globus, Maxwell, and Savodnik (1976) point out, it is difficult to conceive how a complex organization of neural processes gives us mental phenomena that enjoy primacy and autonomy. There are obvious qualitative differences between neural events and mental activity. The analogy of water having properties that hydrogen and oxygen lack is not quite applicable to consciousness as constituted by cortical processes. Water and its elements, hydrogen and oxygen, share physical properties, whereas consciousness and brain do not. Water is essentially an organization of hydrogen and oxygen atoms.

DUALIST INTERACTIONISM

Wilder Penfield (1975), another prominent neurophysiologist, is not so reluctant as Sperry to lean toward a dualistic model of mind/brain relationship. His reasons for assuming that the mind is not contained completely in the mechanisms of the brain include his observation that movements and other somato-sensory activities produced by electrical stimulation of the relevant areas of the brain are reported to be involuntary and ego-alien. If electrical stimulation of a certain area in the brain caused a patient to raise her arm, the patient did not report any intention to raise the arm. It was involuntary and seemed to be independent of her will. Thus the lack of any sense of volition following electrical stimulation of the brain from outside is a powerful reason that led Penfield to postulate a conscious mind outside the brain structures.

If the mind and the brain are distinctly different, how does the mind interact with the brain? What is the location of such interaction? Today few would agree with Descartes' conjecture that the pineal gland is the seat of mind-body interaction. Many neurologists associate the reticular activating system of the brain stem with awareness, because damage to this area results in loss of consciousness. Penfield did not favor this view. He believed that it is not the cerebral cortex but the evolutionarily more primitive region of the higher brain stem, the diencephalon, which is crucially involved in the integration of brain activity. Injury to this area, noted Penfield, renders one unconscious. Also, it is pointed out that epileptic seizures in the higher brain stem make one behave like a mindless machine, losing awareness of one's actions. Attention, according to Penfield, is essential for storing memories. Other neuroscientists do not agree with Penfield on the location of the center of awareness in the human system. Since many parts of the brain are intimately connected with consciousness and since consciousness is understood differently and described variously, neurophysiologists proposed many different areas of the brain as possible locations of conscious activity. For example, according V. S. Ramachandran (1980) it is the frontal lobes, because legions in this area are associated with disruptions in personal identity, continuity and coherence in the sense of self. Those, like Joseph LeDoux (1985), who associate consciousness with linguistic abilities, prefer those areas in the brain concerned with language use as the neural basis of consciousness. Again, those who conceive of consciousness as consisting of forming mental representations credit the hippocampal region of the brain with manifesting consciousness (O'Keefe, 1985). James Newman (1997a, 1997b) speculates on a "core conscious system," which he calls the extended reticular-thalamic activating system (ERTAS). He argues that several models explaining our orientation to the outer world, dreaming, and the integration of sensory-motor representations converge to support this hypothesis.

Sir John Eccles, another Nobel Laureate (Popper & Eccles, 1977), unlike Sperry, comes out strongly in favor of dualism and the substantive reality of the conscious self. As a neurophysiologist, he finds it difficult to account for the unity of conscious experience in terms of heterogeneous, discontinuous, and spatially discrete neural events. Similarly, self-consciousness and human will require for their explanation an agency independent of brain processes. Phenomena such as "antedating," where conscious experience does not immediately follow stimulation but is referred backward in time, do not fit with the hypothesis of psychoneural identity. Again, we do not know the precise physiological processes involved in the synthesis of perceptual experience. Finally, Eccles argues that the surface-negative potential in the cerebral cortex preceding simple voluntary moments, called the readiness potential, takes considerable time to develop and is distributed widely over the cortex. This phenomenon, according to Eccles, suggests the action of the self-

conscious mind upon specialized modules in the cortex that are critically poised at a special level of activity to produce consciously willed actions. As Eccles explains, "The willing of a movement produces the gradual evolution of neuronal responses over a wide area of frontal and parietal cortices on both sides, so giving rise to the readiness potential. Furthermore, the mental act that we call willing must guide or mold this unimaginably complex neuronal performance of the liaison cortex so that it eventually 'homes in' on to the appropriate modules of the motor cortex and brings about discharges of their motor pyramidal cells" (Eccles, 1976, p. 117). In his (1977) address to the Parapsychological Association, he termed this action of mind on brain cells *psychokinesis* and called on psi researchers to focus on the mind rather than the brain. Eccles called those regions of the brain containing the "open modules" amenable to the interaction of the mind the "liaison brain." According to him, the liaison brain is in the cerebral cortex rather than the in mid-brain's deeper areas.

In his earlier writings, Eccles suggested that the dominant hemisphere is the "seat" of the conscious self, because the persons in whom the corpus callosum is surgically severed do not report any conscious awareness of actions programmed from the minor hemisphere. Also, language abilities, which are considered to be a prerequisite for self-consciousness, are located in this area. In his later writings, Eccles gave up this idea because research had shown that the right (minor) hemisphere in split-brain patients is capable of enabling them to recognize their faces (Sperry, Zaidel, & Zaidel, 1979).

In his last book, *How Self Controls Its Brain*, Eccles (1994) rejects outright all the recent attempts to explain away consciousness as nothing but cortical activity. The crusade of Crick and Koch is dubbed as "science fiction of the blatant kind" and Dennett's *Consciousness Explained* is described as "impoverished and empty." Now, Eccles takes the help of quantum mechanics to build a theory of consciousness and self. According to him, one of the reasons for questioning dualism is based on the belief that the body-mind interaction implicit in dualist postulations would violate the law of conservation. By invoking quantum mechanics and the Schrödinger wave function, Eccles attempts to show how synaptic transmission is influenced by quantum mechanical functions without violating the first law of dynamics. The primary mechanism that transmits nerve impulses from one neuron to another, speculates Eccles, involves quantum mechanical processes, and the Schrödinger wave function allows the mind to influence the probability of synaptic response without violating the law of conservation. Here, then, is the room for conscious control of our behavioral actions, the influence of the conscious self on mental events. According to Eccles, there are in the mind "psychons," corresponding to the "dendrons" in the brain. Dendrons and psychons interact to give us the subjective experience involved in our perceptions, thoughts, memories, feelings and so on. Along with Friedrich Beck, Eccles developed the underlying quantum theory to estimate the probability values of vesicle release. We thus have a dualistic solution for the mind-body problem, one in which separate mental units (psychons) can affect the probability of the presynaptic release of transmitters.

We thus see how a highly prominent neurophysiologist provides an unqualified defense of dualism. There are, of course, various weaknesses in his arguments (see Kelly, 1979 and Savage, 1976). There are, however, two aspects of conscious experience to which Eccles calls our attention that may not be ignored. First is the unified and integrated nature of conscious experience. The concomitant cortical activity, however, is highly localized and distributed over wide areas of the brain. This needs to be explained. Is it due to some not yet understood neurophysiological synthesis? Or, as Eccles postulates, is it due to the "integrating character of the self-conscious mind?" Second, what about our own feeling that we can control our thoughts and actions? Are these merely illusory feelings? Or, as Eccles proposes, can mental events influence and control neuronal processes?

Benjamin Libet (1994), a highly respected neurophysiologist, takes these questions seriously as in need of scientific answers. Toward this end he proposed a theory of mind-brain interaction that is testable in principle. He postulates what he calls the "conscious mental field (CMF), which is "produced by, but is phenomenologically distinct from, brain activity." CMF is not a physical field like the electromagnetic field, but operational phenomena. It cannot be observed by external physical means, but may be experienced subjectively and is accessible to introspection. The CMF, in Libet's view, is intimately related to neural processes but not reducible to them. Unlike Eccles, he does not propose a specific and fixed relationship between the mental and the physical. Rather, the local alterations in the CMF are reflected in changes in the overall conscious mental field.

How do we know that such a field exists? Libet proposes an empirical test. First, we create a situation, in which a cortical area is completely isolated from the rest of the cortex, either surgically or by an appropriate pharmacological method, so that no neuronal communication is possible. We must also ensure that no physical pathways exist between it and other parts of the brain. Then activate that area by suitable electrical and/or chemical stimulation. If such activation were followed by relevant conscious experience then there would be reason to believe in the existence of a conscious mental field. Libet describes the special requirements a test like this should meet. If positive evidence is obtained by the proposed test, he argues, it would have profound implications for an understanding of mind-brain interaction, because such a result would be completely unexpected from the present knowledge of how the brain functions. But, then, if psi is real and that if one mind can influence another with no neural connections or physical pathways between them, do we not already have the kind of evidence that Libet is looking for?

CONSCIOUSNESS IN PHYSIOLOGY: A SUMMARY

We have surveyed in this section a spectrum of the views of select neuroscientists who evinced interest in the study of consciousness. By and large most neuroscientists are unconcerned with consciousness per se. Their scientific interest is limited to understanding the cortical processes associated with mental functions. The emphasis is on the functions of the brain and not on the subjective aspects of consciousness. This is as it should be, because their business is to discover how the brain functions. However, if brain processes themselves are somehow influenced by factors other than cortical activity in the brain, and if we fail to find in neural terms satisfactory explanations of the phenomena we are attempting to understand, there is reason to go beyond the brain. It is in this context that we find a divergence of approaches. Some continue to hope that further understanding of cortical structures and processes will eventually yield scientific answers in neural terms to all aspects of awareness. Yet others have looked at the possibility of non-cortical determinants of certain characteristics of consciousness. Admittedly, the latter approach has fewer adherents, even though their number is steadily growing. At this time, it is reasonable to conclude that it is not unequivocally established that the unity of

conscious experience in the midst of heterogeneous, discontinuous, and spatially distinct neural events, self-awareness, free will, non-algorithmic or intuitive processing, and subjectivity are entirely the manifestations of brain processes. Therefore, openness to nonreductionist alternatives is not unwarranted.

The main problem in seeking a physiological understanding of consciousness, it would seem, is the lack of unanimity on the meaning of the concept of consciousness. This has led neuroscientists to investigate various areas of the brain in the search for the source of consciousness. Indeed the proposed cortical areas are too numerous to exclude any area of the brain from this search. This is not a bad thing in itself. Understanding the relative roles of different areas of brain involved in the experience of consciousness would provide valuable information about mind-brain interaction. To believe, however, that any of these individually, or several of them collectively, would give us the necessary understanding of mind and consciousness appears to be more a hope than a reasoned judgment at this time. If we wish to explain mind-brain interaction, we may have to look beyond the brain to discover the mind.

Quantum mechanics appears to be one area of relevance in this context. Quantum coherence and "nonlocality" are possibly the closest analogs to some of the essential characteristics of conscious awareness. The question of concern here is whether the indeterminacy implied in the process of "measurement" is the venue for the action of consciousness on the physiological functions of the brain. There are different interpretations of quantum mechanics. Many of the ideas proposed to link quantum mechanics to consciousness are speculative extensions of these interpretations. However, the recent attempts to better understand the mechanics of synaptic action with the help of quantum theory are important in that they suggest various empirically testable hypotheses.

The relevance of consciousness to quantum mechanics is two-fold. First, a proper comprehension of consciousness as a concept may be considered a necessary condition to have a coherent understanding of quantum theory. Second, a quantum mechanical understanding of brain function may be regarded as a necessary precondition for understanding consciousness. The first may well result in a new physics, or at least a radical extension of current physics. The second appears at this time to be the best hope for finding a neurological basis for consciousness.

CHAPTER 7

Psychologies of Consciousness

Though little acknowledged, studying consciousness is central to psychology. When psychology started as a separate discipline a little over a century ago, it was indeed considered as the science of consciousness. Subsequent developments, largely owing to the ascendance of behaviorism, moved psychology systematically away from studying consciousness. Even though there has been in recent years a resurgence of interest in consciousness and some notable attempts to study it by cognitive psychologists, it would not be wrong to say that mainstream psychology in general continues to ignore consciousness. So we have Stuart Sutherland (1989) who writes as follows in *The International Dictionary of Psychology*: "Consciousness is a fascinating but an elusive phenomenon; it is impossible to specify what it is, what it does, or why it evolved. Nothing worth reading has been written on it" (p. 90). Such deliberate "bracketing" of consciousness is not easy to understand, given that historically the founders of American psychology such as William James (1890), J. R. Angel (1908), and E. B. Titchener (1909), and even behaviorist E. C. Tol-

man (1927) discussed the concept of consciousness in a variety of its uses.

The Groundwork of James

William James begins his *Psychology: Briefer Course* (1892/1900) with the statement: "The definition of psychology may be best given in the words of Professor Ladd, as the *description and explanation of states of consciousness-as-such*" (p. 1, original emphasis). Margaret Knight (1950) and several others since noted that James' book *The Principles of Psychology* has profoundly influenced subsequent developments in Western psychology. Joseph Adelson described *The Principles* as "the single greatest work in American psychology. Among books written by psychologists, its only rival is Sigmund Freud's *The Interpretation of Dreams*" (1982, p. 52). Of the many seminal psychological ideas of James contained in *The Principles*, none is more influential than his conception of the stream of consciousness. In our own description of conscious states in the earlier chapters, we have made extensive use of James's account of consciousness as given in *The Principles*.

What is especially important in James is the fact that he did not leave out any aspect of consciousness, including its negation. His discussions of consciousness are more inclusive and comprehensive than any others by a philosopher or a psychologist on the subject. Unfortunately, however, they are somewhat disjointed. They occur in different places and contexts. This state of affairs had two consequences—(1) misreading of James and (2) lopsided and uneven emphasis on one aspect and neglect of other aspects in James' thought. At any rate, James, as we note, is the forerunner of almost all the major strands of psychological thought on consciousness. James discussed consciousness from different perspectives, and some of his statements, considered out of context, may be seen as mutually inconsistent. It is quite obvious that there are distinctive strands in James's accounts of consciousness. It is possible, however, to appreciate their interconnectedness if we place them in their appropriate contexts.

In an insightful analysis of the documents of James, the well known and the little known, Eugene Taylor (1996) attempted to trace the evolution of James' psychological work from its early positivistic beginnings in *The Principles of Psychology* (1890), through radical empiricism, and to the phenomenology of mystic experiences and religious awakening in *The Varieties of Religious Experience* (1902). According to Taylor, it is James' concern to weave a comprehensive *person-centered* science of psychology that binds the different strands found in his work. The detractors of James as well as his admirers often miss this point. They tend to focus on the strand that is consistent with their own assumptions, blow it out of proportion and reject or ignore the other strands. For example, psychologists, with few notable exceptions, paid little attention to James' writings after

The Principles, considering them as primarily philosophical, and thus failed to appreciate the true import of his contributions to psychology. "Most experimental psychologists," writes Taylor (1996), "do not read James after 1890, if they read him at all, while theologians, ministers, and psychologists of religion tend to ignore him before *Varieties of Religions Experience*" (p. 7). The supposed cleavage and the apparent contradictions in James may be better understood if we keep in perspective that consciousness manifests in many forms, and that their understanding may call for divergent conceptual schemes and methodologies.

In *The Principles of Psychology*, James, as we have noted, affirms that consciousness is the "first and foremost concrete fact" of one's inner experience. He characterizes consciousness as an activity that is personal, selective, changing and yet sensibly continuous. It has the function of choosing which objects to welcome and which to reject. Consciousness feels continuous because it "flows" like a river or a stream. Therefore, James calls it "*The stream of thought, of consciousness, or of subjective life*" (1900, p. 159). The stream metaphor, which represents the better-known strand in Jamesian thought, reflects the twin aspects of the continuous character of consciousness. First, when there is a time gap, the consciousness that follows relates itself to the one before it, as if they belong to one and the same self. Second, when there are shifts in the quality of consciousness from one moment to another, the shifts are never absolutely abrupt, because no current psychological event takes place in a vacuum without some reference to the proceeding.

In writing a textbook of psychology, an emerging science at the time, James was essentially concerned with depicting psychology as a legitimate scientific discipline, a natural science. He attempted to find, wherever he could, a scientific basis for our perceptions, thoughts and feelings. Consequently, his main focus was on what we have called primary awareness and the result is an enticing cognitive psychology of consciousness. In *The Varieties of Religious Experience* (1902/1914), James expands consciousness to include, besides thinking and other reflective functions, what he calls nonrational forms of consciousness. His explorations in these areas do the groundwork for an emerging transpersonal psychology. When we move on to his philosophical writings, we find statements sharply contrasting with those in *The Principles*. For example, in his *Essays on Radical Empiricism* we find: "For twenty years past I have mistrusted 'consciousness' as an entity; for seven or eight years past I have suggested its nonexistence to my students and tried to give them its pragmatic equivalent in realities of experience. It seems to me that the hour is ripe for it to be openly and universally discarded" (1912/1947, p. 3).

What James was discarding here is not "consciousness" as such, but consciousness as an entity or substance. The notion of substance was clearly antithetical to his stream metaphor as well as to his radical empiricist viewpoint. "I believe," wrote James, "that consciousness as it is commonly represented either as an entity or as a pure activity, but in any case as fluid, nonextended, diaphanous, spiritual, void of any content of its own but capable of knowing itself directly... I believe that this consciousness is a pure chimera and that the total concrete reality that the word 'consciousness' denotes should be given a totally different description" (1912/1947, p. 222).

What James is protesting here is the possibility of *pure* consciousness or awareness-*as-such*. His shared bias in favor of the pervasive Western notion that intentionality is the defining characteristic of consciousness is likely the basis for his a priori rejection of pure consciousness. In a way this is somewhat surprising and remarkable,

because James does not espouse a representational theory of consciousness.

We realize that there is hardly any conflict between the versions of consciousness expounded by James in the *Varieties*, *Essays*, and the *Principles* when we consider the context of these writings. In both the *Varieties* and the *Essays*, James abhors intellectualism and defends "experience" against trans-empirical agencies, whether they are matter or mind. "Consciousness, as it is ordinarily understood, does not exist any more than does matter, to which Berkeley has given the coup de grace. What does exist and form the element of truth contained in the word 'consciousness' is the susceptibility which the parts of experience have for being related and known."

When James deals with primary awareness in *The Principles*, we have the fitting metaphor of the stream. His description of consciousness as personal changing and yet continuous, subjective, selective, noetic and unified is appropriate and helpful in this context. However, when confronted with mystical and paranormal forms of awareness, the stream metaphor gives way to "Mother Sea." The description moves on to the subliminal, the multiple streams that lack unity and cohesion, and to the experiences that defy reason and logic. Yet, James recognizes that they are real and that they significantly influence our behavior and being.

We thus have three distinct strands in James' writings on consciousness. In a sense they are the bedrock of cognitive psychology as well as depth and transpersonal psychologies. The many tones in James' views on consciousness have their echoes in subsequent psychological discussions on consciousness. Behaviorists find comfort in James' rejection of consciousness in his *Essays*. Cognitive psychologists embrace the functionalist aspect of James in *The Principles* and attempt to study the processes and functions of consciousness. The metaphor, "the stream of consciousness," appeals to them as long as that stream is limited only to thought and mental activities like feelings, imagining, reasoning, remembering, and so forth. Once the stream is conceived to encompass other states, such as religious experiences and mystic awareness, they see contradictions in James. No such confusion or contradiction is seen by those who are impressed by the evidence in support of the so-called non-rational forms of consciousness. Therefore, it was left to transpersonal psychologists and parapsychologists to make use of James in his more inclusive conception of consciousness.

The depth psychology strand is possibly the least influential of James' writings. It was overshadowed by the advent of psychoanalysis and its popular appeal. In this context, we may note that the notion of the subliminal and the concept of "subconscious," which James pretty much borrowed from F.W.H. Myers, are no less important. Subliminal processes, according to James, account for mental abnormalities, supernormal experiences, and a host of other psychological phenomena. James wrote in the *Varieties*:

> If the word "subliminal" is offensive to any of you, as smelling too much of psychical research or other aberrations, call it by any other name you please, to distinguish it from the level of full sunlit consciousness. Call this latter the A-region of personality if you care to, and call the other the B-region. The B-region, then, is obviously the larger part of each of us for it is the abode of everything that is latent and the reservoir of everything that passes recorded or unobserved. It contains, for example, such things as all our momentary inactive memories and it harbors the springs of all our intuitions, hypotheses, fancies, superstitions, persuasions, convictions, and in general all our non-rational operations come from it. It is the source of our dreams, and apparently they may return to it. In it arise whatever mystical experience we may have, and our automatisms, sensory or motor; our life in hypnotic and "hypnoid"

conditions; our delusions, fixed ideas, and hysterical accidents, if we are hysteric subjects; our supranormal cognitions, if such there be, and if we are telepathic subjects. It is also the fountainhead of much that feeds our religion. In persons deep in the religious life, as we have now abundantly seen—and this is my conclusion—the door to this region seems unusually wide open; at any rate, experiences making their entrance through that door have had emphatic influence in shaping religious history [1902, pp. 483–484].

James postulates a screen that separates focal awareness from the subconscious. He identified that barrier as the hypnagogic state, which has both physiological and mental aspects. The images that break out of the hypnagogic barrier can be intense and produce psychopathic symptoms or result in ecstatic visions. James recognized that images arising out of the subconscious are on occasions luminous. Such luminous images may bring about important transformations in the lives of those who have them. When one moves below the threshold of focal awareness, the attention is no longer restricted to single items, and when "the nimbus that surrounds the sensational present" is vastly enlarged one enters a mystical state. As James puts it: "It will be transient, if the change in threshold is transient. It will be of reality, enlargement, and illumination, possibly rapturously so. It will be of unification, for the present coalesces in it with range of the remote quite out of reach under ordinary circumstances; and the sense of *relation* will be greatly enhanced. Its form will be intuitive and perceptual, not conceptual, for the remembered or conceived objects in the enlarged field are supposed not to attract the attention singly, but only to give the sense of a tremendous *muchness* suddenly revealed" (quoted from Taylor 1996, p. 145).

James thus provides us with a comprehensive map of consciousness that covers the implicit as well as the explicit, the cognitive as well as the transcendental aspects. We may or may not agree with the specifics of his accounts or the plausibility of his speculations, but we can hardly fail to appreciate the breadth and the scope of his discussions that leave virtually no aspect of consciousness untouched. In the writings of James, we find the seeds that sprouted later to give rise to a wide spectrum of interesting ideas and approaches seen and admired in the landscape of consciousness studies today.

Cognitive Theories of Consciousness

Cognitive psychology attempts to give a functional description of the mind. It does this to a large extent in information processing terms. Cognitive awareness implies (1) a subject who has awareness, (2) an object of awareness and (3) the processes of awareness. The processes themselves are inaccessible to awareness. All kinds of cognitive activity may go on without the subject having any introspective awareness. Again, cognition itself may be without subjective awareness, if, for example, subliminal perception is considered a form of cognition. There is, however, a difference between the inaccessibility of cognitive processes to introspection and the lack of subjective awareness in some forms of cognition. In one case it is the *process* that is inaccessible to introspection, whereas in the other it is the *contents* of a cognition of which we experience no subjective awareness. This distinction may be blunted somewhat, however, if we take into consideration biofeedback and the possibility of controlling internal attention states by special techniques like meditation.

The dominant trend in consciousness research among psychologists until recently was the one that is modeled after information processing (computational metaphor). During the past quarter of a century, cog-

nitive science made tremendous strides and was able to uncover many complex organizations and processes involved in our ability to acquire, store and retrieve information. Cognitive theories of consciousness attempt to relate the unconscious information processing to conscious awareness and the experience of "self," the subject who has direct access to what is going on. This generally takes the form of adapting a cognitive theory to explain some of the phenomenon associated with consciousness, such as self-awareness, intention, attention, and unity of experience.

UNCONSCIOUS INFORMATION PROCESSING

Seeking to study the place of consciousness in information processing, cognitive psychologists have attempted to determine the respects in which conscious processing differs from unconscious or nonconscious processing. The relation between subjective awareness and information processing is sought by comparing the conscious and the unconscious processes. It is suggested, among other things, that the processing of novel stimuli and voluntary response require consciousness. A widely held view among cognitive psychologists is that information is first processed at the preconscious level. Preconscious processing is automatic and involuntary, and it can go on simultaneously to process information in a parallel fashion from different sensory channels. Conscious processing, unlike preconscious processing, is voluntary, flexible and serial in nature. It processes only one item at a time. Information that is processed by the limited capacity central processor becomes accessible to consciousness. Only the messages to which we attend are processed for meaning. The built-in filtering mechanism prevents all other messages from reaching higher centers of the brain, whose activity is essential for introspective awareness (Triesman 1969). Preconscious processing is pre-attentive and conscious processing is focal attentive. Pre-attentive processing activates the memory traces of the stimulus as well as related traces. Focal-attentive processing requires intention for its operation. It takes place after the "spreading activation" of pre-attentive processing (Posner & Snyder 1975) and is a necessary condition for subjective awareness. The item on which attention is focused enters working memory, enabling its recall or recognition later. In this view, the neural mechanisms of attention and short-term memory are thus closely linked to consciousness.

There are good reasons to believe that complex mental activity, including our ability to acquire, store, and retrieve information, is carried out by operations that are primarily unconscious in that they are inaccessible to introspection. Max Velmans (1991) has reviewed evidence suggesting that consciousness in the sense of being introspectively aware need not enter into the processing of information at any level, including the organization of complex activity that requires planning, reflection, or creativity. Thus, much of mental activity seems to go on without subjective awareness, which is traditionally regarded as an essential aspect of the mind. Apart from the fact that the processes that mediate awareness are themselves non-conscious, the contents in some forms of awareness may be implicit and not accessible to introspection. We now have considerable information on a variety of phenomena indicating awareness when subjects themselves are unable to report any awareness, bringing into question the intuitive assumption that all perception is a conscious act. These phenomena, as we have discussed in Chapter 3, fall into two broad categories. The first one involves automatic processing. Here we find no conscious intention on the part of the subject. The subject cannot exercise control over the process.

There is no awareness of how the process operates or of the information processed. The second category is the area of implicit awareness observed in subliminal perception, in some cases of amnesia following brain damage, in hypnotic phenomena such as hypnotic analgesia and posthypnotic suggestion, and in prosopagnosic patients and blindsighted persons. Distinguished from these are conscious processes over which we have voluntary control. These are processes in which we are aware of the operations and have introspective access to the outputs. For many cognitive psychologists, the contrasting aspects of subjective awareness and the cognitive unconscious are important for investigating consciousness. For example, P. Johnson-Laird (1983) thinks that the conscious-unconscious distinction is the most valuable tool for understanding the mind.

THE COMPUTATIONAL MIND

Cognitive science is based on the premise that intelligence, whether artificial or human, is basically computational and that cognition can be understood as computation. Computation is the manipulation of symbols. Symbols are representations. Cognition is thus a representation of the world. It is further suggested that the representations are an outcome of operations on symbols semantically encoded with appropriate programming in the brain or suitably equipped machines. Thought is conceived to consist in symbolic computations, which involve no more than physical manipulations. The brain is seen as an information processing system that selectively processes certain features of the environment. The computer metaphor is used to generate hypotheses and model cognitive processes in terms of symbols and representations. In this formulation, consciousness acquired a degree of respectability, no longer tabooed, because it could be seen as an operational concept employed in empirical research.

That is all good. The problem remains, however. How are these brain processes actually connected to experience itself? The cognitive processes in the brain are such that we have no conscious access to them. Computational states in the brain are symbolic representations and are qualitatively different from the subjective experience we have of the environment. Consciousness is seen as something that relates to the contents of awareness. Cognition on this account is essentially an unconscious process that processes sensory inputs. If cognition and consciousness are thus separable, what then is the relation between them? This is a major problem for most cognitive theories of consciousness.

Attempting to find a place for consciousness in the information processing architecture of the brain, some cognitive psychologists tend to conceive consciousness as a special module connected to various others that severally process the inputs. One example is the CAS, or consciousness awareness system, in Daniel Schacter's model we discussed earlier. The notion that there is a single place in the brain that is the seat of consciousness, where multiple sources of information are brought together to give unity and coherence to conscious experience, is dubbed by Daniel Dennett as the "Cartesian Theater" (Dennett 1991; Dennett and Kinsbourne 1992). This notion has several problems, conceptual and empirical. First, there is no credible evidence for the existence of a single location that controls all forms of conscious experience. Second, studies of dissociated states and split-brain research suggest multiple controls rather than a single locus for consciousness in the brain.

There are a number of attempts to bypass the impasse of the Cartesian Theater and bring the multiple sources of information together without postulating one specific location for consciousness. These include the dominant action system model (DAS) of Tim Shallice (1978, 1988) and the operation system model proposed by P. Johnson-Laird (1988). In his model, Shallice attempts to link volition and consciousness by postulating the DAS, which consists of presently set goals that work together to control conscious thought and action. In this model, information processing is done by a system consisting of a large set of specialized modules that include input processors as well as highly specialized modules for information management and storage. Routine activities that require no conscious intention are run on well-learned, specific programs of the modules. Shallice conceptualizes a *supervisory system* that comes into play when the routines do not meet the demands of current goals. In addition, a language system and an episodic memory component enter into higher level cognitive and control functions of the system. Shallice suggests that consciousness does not reside in any one of these systems. Rather, consciousness arises when there is coherent and simultaneous operation of several systems. The content of consciousness is the information flow between the control systems and the rest of the cognitive system.

According to Johnson-Laird, the brain is a hierarchy of parallel processes. The operating system at the top of the hierarchy is the source of conscious awareness. It controls mental events involved in triggering thought and action, in directing attention and in planning and self-reflection. It expresses the outcome of some of the computations the brain makes, but not the details of how they are done. It is unclear, however, if there is indeed such an operating system, where in the brain it is located. There are good reasons to believe that the identification of consciousness with specific modules is flawed in a fundamental way, and that the information flowcharts of cognitive activity appear to leave the subjective or phenomenal aspect of consciousness essentially unexplained. Indeed, Ulric Neisser, a key-player in the emergence of cognitive psychology, is himself unconvinced of the usefulness of this approach. In his view, the attempt to treat consciousness as a stage in information processing is unsatisfactory. "It does justice neither to the usage of the word 'consciousness' in ordinary discourse nor to the subtleties of experience" (Neisser 1976, p. 104).

Ray Jackendoff (1987) explicitly divides cognition into symbolic computation, of which we have no subjective awareness, and consciousness. He distinguishes between what he calls the computational mind and the phenomenological mind. The computational mind is the one that does the symbolic computations. The phenomenological mind is the one that experiences and has subjective awareness. Jackendoff recognizes that the computational mind "offers no explanation of what a conscious experience is" (p. 20). The dichotomy of the computational mind and the phenomenological mind is at the base of what he calls the mind-*mind* problem, "What is the relationship between computational states and experience?" (p. 20). How does Jackendoff propose to solve this problem of the relation between cognition as computation and cognition as conscious experience? How are unconscious computational symbols transformed into subjectively experienced states of consciousness? After detailed consideration of the language system, the visual system and the music system, he is led to believe that consciousness is not associated with the highest levels in the hierarchy. Rather, conscious experiences correspond to "intermediate-level representations" in the computational mind. They are "caused by/supported by/projected from information and processes of the computational mind" (Jackendoff 1987, p. 23). One's conscious experience is thus a projection from intermediate levels of representation in the computational mind. According to Jackendoff, consciousness is "fundamentally not

unified" because it arises from different sources in different modalities. The diversity of experiences and the phenomenological distinctions we make are the consequence of modality specific projections. Each form of conscious experience is a projection from a different set of computations performed by different structures of the computational mind. Furthermore, the phenomenological mind has no causal role. It results entirely from relevant computational organization. Thus, in Jackendoff's view, consciousness has no causal efficacy. It is merely an epiphenomenon, "not good for anything" (p. 26).

CONSCIOUSNESS AND INFORMATION

E. Roy John (1976), another psychologist, regards consciousness as a process that combines information about multiple modalities of sensation and perception into a unified multidimensional representation of the state of the system and its environment. This is integrated with information about memories and the needs of the organism, generating emotional reactions and programs of behavior to enable the organism to adjust to its environment.

John (1976) postulates seven levels of information processing in the brain. They include sensation, perception, consciousness, content of consciousness, subjective experience, self, and self-awareness. Each of these levels of information processing is dependent "upon all the levels below (feedforward) and each influenced by the levels above (feedback)" (1976, p. 8). John presents extensive electrophysiological data in support of his classification. On the basis of his data, John suggests that "subjective experience is the product of a cooperative process involving both cellular and extra cellular constituents of neural tissue, most probably in the center encephalic system" (p. 76) which he calls "hyperneuron."

Parallel to John's classification is the one by John Battista (1978). According to Battista, (a) consciousness is information; (b) different forms of consciousness represent different levels of information; and (c) the intensity of a state of consciousness is a function of its informational content. In Battista's schema, there are six levels of consciousness, beginning with sensation and leading up to the "information about the process of self-awareness." In between are perception, emotion, awareness (which includes cognition as well as intuition), and self-awareness. Battista leaves room for a seventh level of consciousness "that would involve the universe's experience as a whole and refer to the interactions and coordination of all of the lower levels of information" (p. 83). The implications of this *informational holism*, as he calls it, include: (a) consciousness is present in the entire universe, including the physical systems; (b) machines like computers have consciousness; and (c) not only individuals but also groups and societies have consciousness.

GLOBAL WORKSPACE THEORY

In his book, *A Cognitive Theory of Consciousness*, Bernard Baars (1988) seeks to explain conscious experience with the theoretical metaphor of global workspace. Global workspace (GW) is a memory blackboard whose contents are widely distributed in the nervous system. Baars' theory rests on three basic constructs. First is the construct of "unconscious specialized processors." They work either autonomously or as a coalition with others. They can receive and send global messages. The second construct is the global workspace itself. Context is the third construct. Contexts are "*knowledge structures that constrain conscious contents without being conscious themselves*" (Baars 1996, p. 89, original emphasis). By examining paired comparisons between similar conscious and unconscious processes

Baars concludes that consciousness creates global access, access to virtually any part of the nervous system. He presents a wide variety of experimental studies in support of his model, which can be summarized in three statements. (1) Consciousness is like a global workspace with a distributed network of information processors. (2) The purpose of the processors is to broadcast a message through the global workspace. (3) What we experience as contents of consciousness are the contents in the global workspace. Within this framework, Baars seeks to explain several aspects of human information processing.

Conscious contents are "globally broadcast" to specialized processors, which are unconscious systems. They are limited to one particular function but can combine to become larger specialized processors. Stable coalitions of processors are called *contexts*. Contexts serve to evoke and shape messages. A coherent set of contexts that currently controls access to global workspace is labeled the *Dominant Context Hierarchy*. In order that we may have conscious experience, it is necessary that the contents are *globally broadcast, internally consistent,* and *informative*. Inconsistent global messages trigger competition, which quickly destroys the message. Informativeness means "*choice within a context of alternatives, demanding adaptation by other processors*" (p. 360, original emphasis). According to this theory, intention is the goal context "which constrains conscious information processing." Attention is the control of access to conscious experience. Self is conceived as an "enduring Dominant Context, near the topmost levels of the Dominant Context Hierarchy" (Baars 1988, p. 327)

Baars is confident that the questions raised by subjective conscious experience in the human condition can be answered scientifically and that his GW Theory is a rigorous attempt in that direction. While asserting that global access is a necessary condition for consciousness, he recognizes that it may not be sufficient and that other conditions such as access to a self-system may be necessary to account fully for our conscious experience. Baars regards consciousness as the publicity organ of the brain. It is a facility for *accessing, disseminating and exchanging information*, and for *exercising global coordination and control*" (1997b, p. 299, original emphasis).

In his recent book, Baars (1997a) uses the metaphor of theater to illustrate conscious experience. In the theater metaphor, focal awareness is the bright spot of light on the stage, which is surrounded by a fringe of "vaguely conscious events." Selective attention is the director, which controls the spotlight; "only events in the bright spot on stage are strictly conscious" (Baars 1997b, p. 303). The stage is the working memory. Behind the stage are unconscious contextual systems that "shape events in the bright spot." The audiences in the theater are those unconscious processes that mainly receive information from the bright spot.

The GW theory is clearly insightful. It is consistent with a wide body of data in cognitive science. The theater metaphor captures some nuances of conscious experience, especially the conscious-unconscious dichotomy. As Allen Combs (1997) remarked, the "simplicity and sheer appeal of the image of the stage, with conscious events acted out upon it by players moving under the spotlight of attention, makes it easy to visualize, to remember, and to think about" (p. 314). It is observed, however, that the metaphor is inadequate in some details. It is suggested, for example, that consciousness is more dynamic than the theater metaphor warrants. In conscious experience the observer and the observed are not separate, as the theater metaphor presupposes (Hiley 1997). The notion that the stage is equivalent to working memory ignores the fact that consciousness is flooded with sensory and emotional experience (Combs 1997). Francisco Varela (1997) argued, "The theater metaphor is fundamentally flawed. In Baars' description ... we are left almost entirely in the dark as to how this could possibly be more than a metaphor unless we shift away from the handy description embedded in 'actor's utterances under a spotlight.' What could this possibly mean for a brain in a body? Baars does insist that the audience addressed by the consciousness stage is distributed, but how on Earth *can* they be affected by what's happening on the central spot? ... My complaint is that it needs to be addressed more specifically to make the image of a global workspace into an explicit mechanism" (p. 345). In defense of Baars, we may note that no metaphor is a perfect analogy. He did strive to suggest certain hypotheses as possible brain mechanisms for global access and other aspects of consciousness. His explicit recognition of the observing self and the experiential component of consciousness, even though his theory has little to contribute to its understanding, go well beyond what the usual cognitive and naturalistic explanations of consciousness allow.

REFLEXIVE MODEL

British psychologist, Max Velmans, it seems to me, stands at the threshold that divides mind-brain dualism on the one hand and epiphenomenalism on the other among cognitive psychologists. In a target article in the journal *Behavioral and Brain Sciences* entitled "Is human information processing conscious?" Velmans raises several interesting issues and makes some provocative suggestions about the complimentary nature of first-person and third-person perspectives of consciousness. He argues persuasively that consciousness, as awareness, is a result of focal-attentive processing. It is a form of output "that does not enter into cerebral processing" (1991, p. 667).

In support of his contention he examines a variety of mental activities from the simple to the very complex and suggests that they are primarily unconscious. Thus consciousness on the one hand is dissociated from cerebral processing and on the other hand it is concomitant with focal attention. Whenever there is an experience of consciousness, there is focal attention. They covary and occur together. Consciousness seen in this light may be interpreted as an epiphenomenon of brain activity, which has no effect on the brain. At this point, Velmans makes a provocative suggestion that this epiphenomenal rendering of consciousness is valid only from the perspective of third-person. From the first-person perspective, Velmans asserts, "Consciousness is *central* to the determination of human action" (1991, p. 667, original emphasis). Velmans goes on to point out how the first-person accounts may be translated in principle into third-person accounts. However, this possibility, according to Velmans, does not warrant the assumption that the first-person accounts are any less real or that they are less preferable to third-person accounts.

Velmans considers his reflexive model of consciousness a preferred alternative to mind-brain dualism on the one hand and physical reductionism on the other. In this model, the external world of which we have phenomenal awareness is "viewed as *part of* consciousness rather than *apart from* it" (1993, p. 81, original emphasis). Velmans attempts to bridge the gap between physical and psychological phenomena by arguing that objectivity is no more than intersubjectivity and that public observations are shared private experiences. In the reflexive model, the phenomenal world is a representation. Our sensory system and perceptual processes help to form the representation. The phenomenal world, however, is not its representation in the brain, but "the brain models the world by *reflexively pro-jecting* experiences to the judged location of the events they represent" (p. 84, original emphasis). For example, seeing a cat out there is not merely forming a precept in the mind, which is either *different* from the neural representation (dualistic view) or identical with it (reductionist view). Rather, the experience of seeing the cat is reflexively projected by the perceptual processes in the brain to the location in which the cat is believed to be situated. The subject's consciousness of the world, in this view, "is not some ephemeral 'cloud' that requires reduction to make it respectable to science, but his *entire* phenomenal world. This is *formed* by perceptual processing interacting with represented entities and events, but does not *reduce* to such processing" (p. 90, original emphasis). Thus, Velmans asserts that the entire phenomenal world is part of consciousness and not separate from it.

Velmans suggests that his reflexive model of consciousness renders scientific study of consciousness possible. However, I find much of his analysis as essentially logical and semantic. I do not see any important deductions from this model that can give rise to significant empirical investigations the other models do not warrant. I believe, however, his assertion of first-person third-person complementarity is highly heuristic. I find it provocative when Velmans writes about items entering into consciousness, about disruption of consciousness interfering with at least some aspects of focal attention, and about dissociation of consciousness from cerebral functioning. Here it makes sense to think that consciousness is not only different in kind from neurobiological processes, but also has primacy of its own and can indeed causally influence other processes. The third-person epiphenomenalism espoused by Velmans denies all this, even though his complimentary first-person approach is not averse to according primacy to consciousness and to accepting its causal efficacy.

What does it mean to say that consciousness is causally efficacious from the first-person perspective and not from the third-person perspective? Does it mean that the effects of consciousness can be observed only from the first-person perspective? This question is not answered by the assertion that the observations from the first-person perspective are as "real" as those from the third-person perspective. If conscious states cause effects that can be observed from the third-person perspective, they cannot be explained away as a consequence of our viewing the phenomena from a mixed perspective. The causal efficacy of consciousness implies genuine interaction between conscious states and whatever they influence. Velmans does not in fact dispute that conscious and neural states interact, but he sees no need to invoke consciousness to explain neural activity or vice versa. This is fine, but insofar as consciousness and brain activity interact and causally influence each other, there arises a need to invoke one while discussing the other. They cannot be kept apart. The fact of interaction between consciousness and neural states constitutes what Velmans calls the "causal paradox," which he admits must be addressed by "any adequate theory of how consciousness relates to the brain" (1991, p. 716). His first-person, third-person mapping of our cognitive process highlights the causal paradox without addressing it.

According to Velmans, "first-person accounts can be translated into third person accounts, but they cannot be reduced to them" p. 717). It is not clear whether the third-person accounts can also be translated into first-person accounts. It is also not mentioned whether all the first-person accounts are in principle translatable into third-person accounts. If they were, their significance is lost not only for our understanding of the human information processing but also for explaining other facets of our mental life as well. The importance of complementarity is correspondingly diminished with the increasing viability of translating the first-person accounts into third-person accounts. Only if there is a residue left behind in the first-person accounts will there be a genuine complementarity between them.

Velmans says, "there will always be something lost in the translation" (p. 716). It is not stated, however, what it is that is lost in the translation and how that is relevant to our understanding of human information processing and indeed all our mental activity.

We should keep in mind that first-person accounts are themselves translations of subjective experience, which in its "raw" state, that is, without translation into some form of language, is essentially ineffable. The distinction between knowledge by *acquaintance* and knowledge by *description* (Russell (1948) is relevant here. Pain in a first-person account is not the "raw" experience of pain, but is a translation of it, as when one reports that it hurts. The experience of pain is not identical with one's expression of pain. We do not understand pain as such unless we experience it. Our understanding of pain from either first- or third-person accounts is qualitatively different from pain experience. What is lost in the translation of pain experience is the *subjectivity*, and it is this *subjectivity* and not *awareness* that is the hallmark and the sine qua non of consciousness. Subjectivity is not the construction of the brain. Rather, it is something that we must presuppose as a necessary condition of our experiences. It is the essence of self and consciousness in the most appropriate sense.

The attempts to grant reality and causal efficacy to conscious/mental phenomena and yet regard them as manifestations of brain activity (Searle 1983; Sperry 1976) are based on false analogies. It is difficult to conceive how the complex organization of neural processes gives us mental phenomena that enjoy primacy and autonomy as causal determinants and are considered to be qualitatively different from physical phenomena. There is no good sense in which we could affirm genuine human freedom and responsibility without conceiving our minds as capable of self-determination. Recognition of this has important implications for understanding mental functions, including information processing. I think it is also implied in any assertion of causal efficacy and irreducibility of consciousness to physical events in the brain and consequently is relevant to Velmans' emphasis on the complementarity of first- and third-person perspectives. Genuine complementarity between first- and third-person perspectives is possible only if we grant uniqueness to conscious phenomena, as they are manifest in our awareness, something that is not reflected in third-person accounts

In his target article referred to earlier, Velmans (1991) seemed more like one who was championing an epiphenomenalist view of consciousness. At the same time his assertion of the irreducibility of first-person experiences into brain functions or states seemed inconsistent with the main thrust of his paper. Clearly, there were two streams of thought whose confluence or complementarity was not then obvious. They appeared somewhat disparate and disjointed. Since then, Velmans has published a number of articles (1993, 1995, 1996) clarifying his position and attempting to reconcile the two streams. We find his ideas in a more crystallized and definitive from in his book *Understanding Consciousness* (Velmans 2000).

In Velmans' new vision, "there is *one* universe (the thing itself) with relatively differentiated parts in the form of conscious beings like ourselves, each with a unique, conscious view of the larger universe of which it is a part. In so far as we are parts of the universe that, in turn, experience the larger universe, we participate in a reflexive process whereby the universe experiences itself." (2000, p. 233). Velmans asserts that there are no phenomenal differences between objects *as seen* and objects *as experienced*. There is no separation between physical phenomena, presumed to exist outside, and mental phenomena believed to be inside. The only phenomenal data we have of objects, events and processes in the universe are our experiences of them. They constitute the contents of our consciousness. Our experiences are constructed in the form of cognitive and affective states and are determined by the existential context of location in time, place, community and culture. There is a "reflexive interaction" between entities, events and processes (things themselves) in the universe and our perceptual and cognitive systems. The latter are the instruments that represent the universe to us. The representations are perspectival, personal and subjective. They are translations of entities, events and processes of the universe into personal experiences. Thus our conscious experiences are unique, subjective and private. In other words, our experiences are representations of things in the universe and not things themselves. In this view, things themselves are not unknowable, but the knowledge we have of them is "incomplete, uncertain and species specific" (p. 166).

There is a basic asymmetry of access between our external observations, and our inner experiences. We have direct access to our experiences and only indirect or inferential access to the experiences of others. Our phenomenal worlds, the universe as contained in the representations we have of objects, events and processes, "arise from a reflexive interaction of attended-to entities and events with their perceptual processes" (p. 189). It depends on the focus of attention; whether one *observes* a phenomenon or *experiences* it. Observation is the third-person focus and experience is the first-person account. While there is thus an asymmetry of access between first-person and third-person perspectives there is no fundamental gap or discontinuity between them because in the final analysis all observations are experiences at some level. As Velmans puts it, "the 'phenomena' observed by experimenters are as much a part of the world that they experience as are the 'subjective experiences' of subjects" (p. 190).

From the above analyses, Velmans attempts to resolve the so-called "causal paradox" and determine what consciousness is and what it does. The causal paradox relates to the causal efficacy of consciousness. As he argued in his target article, from some accounts (first-person), consciousness *must have* important causal role in our mental life. From other accounts (third-person), it *cannot have* any such role. Viewed from a first-person perspective, consciousness may be seen as central. It appears to be involved in most forms of learning and memory. It seems necessary for novel and complex mental activities, playing an important role in various aspects of information processing. However, from a third-person perspective, Velmans points out, the causal role of consciousness is non-existent. Consciousness appears to be essentially epiphenomenal. Thus consciousness may be seem as both causally efficacious (first-person account) as well as inert (third-person account). This is what Velmans describes as the "causal paradox." The causal paradox resolves itself, Velmans suggests when we consider first- and third-person accounts as complementary and not conflicting. Viewed from first-person perspective, consciousness reveals itself in our experiences. It is embedded in what we see, feel, think and like. Our thinking appears to influence our actions. Viewed from an external, third-person perspective, consciousness may be seen as the neural events taking place in the brain. They can be described in neural or information processing terms. From this perspective, consciousness, in Velmans' view, has no role in

our mental life because our mental activities can be explained, in principle, in terms of brain states and functions. Inasmuch as the first-person conscious experiences are not reducible to third-person observations, they can be seen as complementary and not conflicting accounts of consciousness. "The information encoded in your experiences and their neural correlates," writes Velmans, "is identical. Consequently, first- and third-person accounts of the causal roles of such information need not conflict. They may simply be accounts of the same underlying process developing over time, viewed in two complementary ways" (2000, p. 254).

Velmans argues that there is no third-person role for consciousness. The fact that one is conscious of a mental process because their operations are accessible to introspection does not imply that consciousness is the cause of the outcome of that process. Similarly, the fact that consciousness accompanies the operation of a process such as focal attention does not accord any causal role to consciousness. There is little evidence to suggest, according to Velmans, that consciousness causally influences the process.

If consciousness has no third-person role, what does it add to the world? In Velmans' view, "knowing what it is like to see the beauty in some one's eyes, or hear the nightingale at dust is a distinct form of knowledge. It differs from abstract knowledge (or 'knowledge by description') in an obvious way… It is only where we *experience* entities, events and processes for ourselves that they become *subjectively real*. It is through consciousness that we *real-ise*. That, and that alone, is its function" (Velmans 2000 pp. 259–260). Thus, the function of consciousness is to confer subjectivity on data processed by our perceptual and cognitive systems. It consists in the words of William James, in the warmth and intimacy of personal experience. It follows thus that there are in Velmans' view two kinds of knowing—(1) knowing directly as felt experience and (2) knowing indirectly and inferentially when we observe others. This distinction corresponds to the basic difference between first-person experience and third-person observation. The two kinds of knowing are essentially complementary, revealing reality from two different perspectives. Velmans writes: "Conscious experiences represent what is going on in a very special way. There is a big difference between having something described to us and experiencing it for ourselves. And there is an even bigger difference between actually experiencing a given situation or state and merely having unconscious information about it (stored, for example, in long-term memory). It is only when we experience something for ourselves that it becomes *subjectively real*. In this, consciousness is the creator of subjective realities" (p. 277). He dubs this view as ontological monism and epistemological dualism.

Velmans favors the view that "evolution accounts for the different *forms* that consciousness takes. But consciousness, in some primal form, did not emerge at any particular stage of evolution. Rather it was there from the beginning. Its emergence, with the birth of the universe, is neither more nor less mysterious than the emergence of matter and energy." (p. 275).

From the above brief account of Velmans' more recent accounts of consciousness, it is clear that his understanding of consciousness goes far beyond the general accounts of cognitive psychologists. At the same time, he does not go far enough to deal with the esoteric sorts of conscious phenomena. Velmans recognizes the limitations of his theory that does not deal with "extraordinary experiences, altered states of consciousness, and the investigations of consciousness that have been pursued in Eastern traditions over millennia" (p. 263). He admits that he is constrained by Western philosophy and science. Had he allowed himself to go beyond the currently fashionable Western philosophical tradition and looked objectively and with no preconceptions into controversial areas of science dealing with exceptional experiences, Velmans' account of consciousness would have been closer, as we will discuss later, to the Eastern perspective of consciousness.

DIFFICULTIES WITH COGNITIVE THEORIES

The small sample of cognitive psychologists we have considered gives us a flavor of their approach. At the same time, it illustrates some of the limitations of this approach. Primarily concerned with finding descriptive explanations for some of the manifestation of consciousness in information processing, cognitive theorists are in danger of missing the essential aspects of consciousness, of mistaking the description of parts for the whole. In Baars' theory, for example, the question of subjectivity is not addressed at all. How does information-processing manifest as subjective experience? That the information is globally accessible is no explanation of subjective experience, which is a more relevant aspect of consciousness than its contents. There is also the problem of relating subjective awareness to the outcomes of unconscious processing. For example, if both hemispheres in split-brain subjects are apparently able to process information at the highest levels, even though only the information reaching the dominant hemisphere is consciously experienced, we are inevitably led to believe that consciousness is dependent on language. Any attempt to break with this consequence leads to notions such as rocks having consciousness because they too can exchange information. This, it seems to me, is stretching the connotation of consciousness to untenable limits.

Inasmuch as cognitive theories tend to deal with consciousness in terms of information, they enjoy the advantage of quantifying consciousness in one of its senses. This makes it less difficult to conduct scientific studies of consciousness. But, then, they also run the danger of missing the essence of consciousness, which does not appear to be so quantifiable. The essence of consciousness, as we have attempted to show, is not information, but *sensitivity* to information. Again, consider that information contained in one's conscious experience may not have a corresponding encoding in the brain/nervous system. Information and experience may be dissociated and experience may be unintelligible in physiological terms. Or there may be non-informational modalities to consciousness. All these possibilities render cognitive theories of consciousness less than complete.

It seems to me that the attempts to understand consciousness by contrasting conscious and unconscious processing are flawed by category mistakes. Consciousness as subjective awareness is fundamentally different from the cognitive processing of computational symbols. Even granting that neural processes give rise to subjective awareness, we cannot equate them as the same. One is the cause and the other is the effect. They are not identical by assumption. No one could reasonably deny that conscious experiences are associated with certain cortical states. It is, however, unclear that the latter, though necessary, are sufficient to give rise to consciousness. Even if this were so, consciousness seen as an effect cannot at the same time be viewed as having any control function over the very processes that give rise to it. It is no wonder, therefore, that consciousness is considered by some cognitive theorists as a "not good for anything" epiphenomenon.

Cognitive theories consider the process of attention as very important in our cognitive activity. This is rightly so. However, they tend to regard attention and volitional activity as mechanical and attempt to understand them mistakenly in deterministic terms. Our intentions are often determined by brain states; for example, our intention to drink water may be caused by the activity of neurons of the hypothalamus, which makes us feel thirsty. But then there are intentions, which have no neural antecedents. To believe in genuine freedom is to believe in the existence of such intentions.

Consider the case of attention. When different stimuli compete for our attention, one of them is selected. The selection may be automatic and involuntary or it may be under voluntary control. If the volition itself is determined by brain activity, then it is safe to say that attention is so programmed that there will be little choice in exercising it. Our attention, whether or not we are aware of it, is then automatically focused on a stimulus because the stimulus conditions, including their interest and importance to the subject, demand it and our brains are programmed to respond accordingly. In this view, our brains contain both the hardware and the software, and the software itself is written by the brain's hardware. That would be unadulterated psychological determinism.

A deterministic notion of attention is inconsistent with the phenomenology of attention. We experience attention fluctuating incessantly and not always in any pattern during the waking states. It requires effort to focus attention. There is a good deal of literature on meditation suggesting that attention can be voluntary and not always determined by stimulus conditions. There is reason to believe that meditative practices help to bring about the cessation of habitual brain activity. Arthur Deikman (1966) called it "deautomatization." One pointed focus in concentrative forms of meditation controls, on the one hand, the random fluctuations of attention, and, on the one hand, it renders attention impervious to environmental pressures and subject biases. Even in so-called passive meditation, the meditator learns to attend to incoming signals nonreactively for prolonged periods of time, which serves the same purpose of promoting voluntary attention, that is, attention not determined by the brain activity.

The more fundamental objections to the cognitive science approach to consciousness studies in general are directed toward the assumption that the human brain processes information essentially like a computer. For example, John Searle (1980, 1992) argues that no computer program can in principle generate the essential features of the mind. The Chinese room argument, as it has come to be known, illustrates how minds have semantic context whereas computer programs are purely syntactical. Searle's Chinese room argument goes like this: Let us suppose that a person who has no knowledge of the Chinese language is closeted in a room with complete computer facilities and an adequate program. He receives questions in Chinese symbols as input and gives answers to them as output again in Chinese symbols. Let us further assume that the answers generated are indistinguishable from those of a native Chinese speaker. Yet, we cannot reasonably say that either the person in the room, or the programmed computer or the two together understand Chinese. Searle points out that computation, as a mere physical process is insufficient to explain a mental event, because the latter involves understanding that is observer relative. It requires a person to give a computational interpretation.

Roger Penrose (1994) also provides strong arguments to suggest that understanding, which is an important ingredient of consciousness, is something that no computation can in principle accomplish. According to Penrose, computation alone cannot simulate, let alone replicate, certain aspects of conscious thinking, feelings and intentions. Consequently, the human mind

"must indeed be something that cannot be described in any kind of computational terms" (Penrose 1994, p. vi). It may be noted that both Searle and Penrose are firmly committed to a thoroughly naturalistic understanding of the mind as an integral aspect of nature.

Consciousness in Depth Psychology

The depth psychological aspects of consciousness we noted in James are more fully developed by Freud, Jung and others who followed them. As mentioned, James recognized the importance of subliminal mentation and noted how one's conscious thoughts become internal mental images and how subliminal impulses may be translated into mental images. He did not, however, analyze the content of these images as Freud and Jung did (Taylor 1996).

We must not confuse the concept of "subconscious" in James with the Freudian "unconscious." For one thing, as Taylor (1996) points out, the subconscious "contains the iconography of the transcendent, which Freud and his interpreters flatly denied" (p. 186). For another, "unconscious" implies the negation of "consciousness." Conscious and unconscious thus exclude each other. In such a sense it is difficult to attribute any awareness to the unconscious. In fact, Freud's main objection to positing multiple centers of consciousness in the unconscious stems from his understanding that the notion of "unconscious consciousness" is an absurdity and that "unconscious awareness" is an oxymoron. Again, the possibility of degrees of awareness is blunted by the dichotomy of the conscious and the unconscious; and consciousness so restricted means no more than focal awareness. The concept of the subconscious does not entail these difficulties.

THE CONSCIOUS, THE PRECONSCIOUS AND THE UNCONSCIOUS IN FREUD

The existence of unconscious mentation was known well before Freud, at least from the time of Plato. Thomas Aquinas and J. Rousseau wrote about unconscious processes (Whyte 1960). The psychotherapeutic studies of Alfred Binet and Pierre Janet and others provided strong evidence for dissociation and multiple personality disorder. William James and others wrote about subliminal channels of awareness. It was, however, the writings of Sigmund Freud that made the unconscious a household word. Freud postulated three different domains of the mind—the conscious, the preconscious and the unconscious. Being the deepest and least accessible region of the mind, the unconscious hides within it all apparently forgotten memories, repressed thoughts, and unacceptable ideas and feelings. Freud (1915) has shown how complex thought processes might occur without awareness. His studies of dreams, memory lapses, and slips of the tongue convinced Freud of the reality of unconscious thoughts and motivations. He saw meaning and purpose in the seemingly innocuous slips of the tongue, unintentional acts of misplacing objects and forgetting. It seemed, therefore, that the earlier characterization of consciousness as purposeful mental activity must be taken to apply to the unconscious as well. Freud insisted that all psychological processes that occur at the conscious level also occur at the unconscious level. These include awareness and feelings. In addition, the unconscious is believed to contain the "mental representations" of the instincts.

The preconscious is the link between the conscious and the unconscious. The repressed material of the unconscious continuously strives to find expression in consciousness. This can be achieved only through passage through the preconscious, subject to the transformations of the "primary process." The preconscious itself is the region of the mind that contains mental phenomena that are not currently in consciousness but, unlike unconscious phenomena, are available for introspective awareness and reporting. The distinction between the conscious and the preconscious is reminiscent of the distinction made by James between the *fringe* and the *focus* of consciousness, which is also reflected in some of the later discussions of cognitive psychologists. In the Freudian topography of the mind, the conscious region is the outermost and possibly a superficial part. Freud, however, credits consciousness with a function to transform merely quantitative unconscious impulses into qualitative personal experiences. Consciousness plays the part of "a sense organ for the perceptions of psychical qualities" (Freud 1900/1953).

THE COLLECTIVE UNCONSCIOUS

Hidden in the recesses of the unconscious, Freud found childhood fantasies, repressed sexual urges, and the pleasure seeking propensities that motivate much of one's behavior. They manifest in dreams and in many acts of omission and commission during waking periods. His one time associate C. G. Jung differed from Freud on this, as he saw more in the unconscious. In Jung's conception of the collective unconscious, the unconscious acquires transpersonal characteristics. Instead of being a ploy for a thorough mechanistic explanation of human behavior, as in psychoanalysis, the unconscious for Jung implies a purposeful world. Here we find Jung closer to James than to Freud.

Jung, like Freud, postulated different elements in the make up of the psyche. The first is the conscious, which includes everything that is associated with what Jung called the "ego complex." Association with the ego complex gives one the awareness that "I am conscious of it." This is sometimes referred to as ego consciousness. The second is what is generally regarded as unconscious material, which is unknown but becomes known when it touches the threshold of consciousness. The psychoid system constitutes the third element of the psyche. By psychoid, Jung refers to those contents of the psyche that are completely unknown, those that never reach the threshold of consciousness. What Jung calls the archetypes are complex psychic structures that belong to the category of the completely unknown elements of the psyche at the psychoid level. Even though archetypes are completely unobservable, they are capable of producing, at crucial moments, archetypal images, thoughts, fantasies and feelings. Archetypes are elemental ideas, feelings and fantasies that exist as structural dispositions common to all humankind, as observed in universally present folklore, myths, and religious and mythological customs.

If psychoanalysis, with its emphasis on unconscious processes, showed that the unconscious is not merely the absence of consciousness but has a domain of its own, Jung went further to blunt the distinction between consciousness and the unconscious. The unconscious is no longer seen as the dung heap of repressed thoughts and infantile sexual fantasies that Freud described; rather, for Jung, it is the consummate source of our collectivity and creativity. The collective unconscious is "an image of the world which had taken aeons to form... [It] consists of the sum of instincts and their correlates, the archetypes. Just as everybody possesses instincts, so he also possesses a stock of archetypal images" (Jung 1919/1954, p. 138). In his later years, Jung was led beyond archetypal images to the concept of the archetype-as-such and what he called the psychoid level of the unconscious. The *archetype-as-such*, is in a sense a transpsychic

concept, in that at the psychoid level matter and mind appear to lose their separate identity. The archetype is the a priori ordering principle by virtue of which we experience synchronistic events that suggest "acausal orderedness." This advance in Jung's thinking from subjectively experienced archetypal image to archetype as the a priori ordering principle obscured his earlier distinction between consciousness and the unconscious (Frey-Rohn 1974/1990). Consciousness was originally associated with a certain degree of brightness and luminosity. Jung increasingly saw that this luminosity is not limited to what is called consciousness but is also to be found in some unconscious contents. Jung came to the "paradoxical conclusion that there is no conscious content which is not in some other aspect unconscious" (1919/1954, p. 185).

The reason for attributing "consciousness" to some of the contents of the unconscious, such as the archetypes, lies in the assumption that archetypal driven images have a cognitive component that may manifest in the conscious mind as sudden flashes of insight. Such a cognitive aspect of archetypes is what Jung called "luminosity," as distinguished from the "day light" of the conscious mind (von Franz 1992). Further, archetypal images are dynamic and laden with enormous energy and emotion. Consequently, they may produce passionate impulses and convictions and also cause creative pursuits and remarkable personal transformations. In several contexts, Jung appears to accord a numinous quality to the manifestations of the collective unconscious in the form of archetypal images that seem to connect us to some universal mind. Whereas Freud credited the unconscious with all the psychological processes that are believed to govern consciousness, Jung located in the collective unconscious principles and processes that go well beyond the normal conscious mental activity to include transpersonal and nonsensory sources. Jung's conception of the collective unconscious thus provides a link between depth psychology and transpersonal psychology, a link that we noted also in James.

Transpersonal Approaches to Consciousness

Transpersonal psychology, with its openness to more esoteric types of human experience such as self-actualization, ecstasy, and mystical and transcendental experience, builds on the third strand of consciousness in James. In doing so it tends to be more theoretical and less empirical.

Intellectual and Intuitive Modes: Robert Ornstein (1972/1977), for example, makes use of James's distinction between rational and non-rational forms of consciousness. He cites a good deal of evidence converging on the notion that reality is a personal construct based largely on the sensory inputs received. Our senses do not increase information about objects, but actually limit it. Science, psychology included, tends to view the universe in essentially analytic, verbal, linear, and rational terms, with the result that we "de-emphasize and even devalue the arational, nonverbal modes of consciousness." A variety of sources that include the laboratory research on the paranormal and the testimonies of those practicing awareness-enhancing disciplines such as yoga suggest the existence of the nonlinear, intuitive mode of consciousness. They have shown that "consciousness can be extended into areas beyond those defined as the current limits of contemporary psychology" (Ornstein 1972/1977, p. 11). Thus, Ornstein sees two modes of consciousness—the intellectual and the intuitive. The ordinary mode of consciousness is predominantly intellectual. It is "analytic, sequential, and limited by the characteris-

tic of our sense organs." The second mode is "receptive and holistic, one in which all action can be perceived simultaneously" (pp. 226–227). Ornstein suggests that the highest human achievements are the joint outputs, "products of the complementary functioning of the two modes" (p. 14).

Action Mode and Receptive Mode: Like Ornstein, Arthur Deikman (1973) distinguishes between two modes of consciousness: the action mode and the receptive mode. The action mode is the one we use to manipulate the environment. It is seen in the predominance of the sympathetic nervous system and focal attention and in the striving to achieve personal goals. The receptive mode, in contrast, is involved in the intake of the environment rather than in its manipulation. In this mode, according to Deikman, parasympathetic functions tend to be prominent; attention becomes diffused, and there tends to be decreased boundary perception. For one reason or another, one of these modes may become dominant in a given culture. For example, in Western culture the dominance of the action mode can be seen reflected in almost every endeavor. Yet there are other cultures where the receptive mode is not taken as an inferior mode. Deikman believes that in the receptive mode new forms of knowledge and environmental interaction, which are not considered possible from the perspective of the action mode, may become possible.

TART'S ATTENTION/ AWARENESS MODEL

Charles Tart's concept of state-specific sciences and his studies of altered states of consciousness go well beyond reflective consciousness. Tart points out that consciousness is a "highly complex construction" and that our ordinary state of consciousness "is not a group of isolated psychological functions but a system—an interacting, dynamic configuration of psychological components that perform various functions in greatly changing environments" (Tart, 1975, p. 14). The parts constituting consciousness include awareness and structures. Awareness is an "ability to know or sense." Along with awareness goes the ability to direct it from one thing to another. Therefore, Tart designates this concept as attention/awareness. Attention/awareness can be experienced as distinct from the content of awareness. In addition, we experience self-awareness, an awareness of being aware. According to Tart, "There is an experiential continuum at one end of which attention/awareness and the particular content of awareness are essentially merged, and at the other end of which awareness of being aware exists in addition to the particular content of awareness" (1975, p. 15). Tart also keeps the possibility open that attention/awareness may stand completely separate from the content and that basic awareness may be outside the workings of the brain.

Tart considers attention/awareness as an energy source. (a) It can activate structures; (b) it may inhibit some structures from functioning; and (c) some structures can automatically or habitually draw energy from it.

According to Tart, the other component of consciousness consists of "myriad structures," which in the psychological sense refer to relatively stable organizations performing psychological functions. Some structures are essentially permanent in that they are biologically given. There are others that are the results of the developmental history of a person. In computer language, the permanent structure is the hardware, and the structure programmed by learning and enculturation processes is the software. Many structures may function independently of and some others in association with attention/awareness. The latter may also differ in the amount of attention/awareness energy required for their activation.

The interaction of attention/awareness and the structures one has determines the state of consciousness. In other words, an individual's state of consciousness is constrained by the deployment of attention/awareness energy as well as by the available structures. Since the structures can be activated or inhibited by the state an individual is in, he or she may experience different states of consciousness.

INTEGRAL PSYCHOLOGY

Ken Wilber (1993, 1997, 2000), an influential theorist in transpersonal psychology, is a prolific writer. His writings are collected in eight volumes and published by Shambhala in 1999 and 2000. In his integral psychology, Wilber draws from numerous psychological traditions prevalent in the past and the present in various parts of the world to map the immensely complex field of consciousness. In his topography, consciousness can be viewed from four distinctive perspectives, which he calls "the four quadrants." One quadrant is the way consciousness appears to us from inside. It is the familiar first-person perspective. The second quadrant comprises of the outside appearance of consciousness, the third-person perspective. It is the perspective from which most of the scientific studies of consciousness are made. In Wilber's view, consciousness is also shaped and affected in a collective manner, because consciousness exists in a "community of other selves." Thus, consciousness also exists in the plural. We may look at it within the collective perspective of the community or from the perspective outside of the community. In this view, then, the four quadrants have four different perspectives, the inside and outside of "me" and "we," the subjective and the objective perspectives in the singular and the plural.

In his integral theory, Wilber (2000) sketches the full spectrum of consciousness, detailing its types and modes. He groups them under various categories such as levels, lines, structures, and states of consciousness. Among the levels are the subconscious, self-conscious and the superconscious. The over all conscious spectrum may also be seen as a continuum ranging from "prepersonal, to personal to transpersonal" (2000, p. 147). The *levels* of consciousness are like "*waves*" and the *lines* are like "*streams*." Included in the category of lines are cognition, morals, needs, motivation, and self-identity. States of consciousness include such familiar states as waking, dreaming and sleeping. Wilber refers to four mystic or transpersonal states. He calls them psychic, subtle, causal, and nondual. The psychic state is not merely one in which paranormal events may be experienced. It is a state in which phenomenological experience of oneness with natural world occurs. For this reason this state is also referred to as nature mysticism. In the subtle state, there is the experience of identity with the source or the ground of the natural world. This state is also called deity mysticism. Individuals experiencing the causal state report being immersed in "unmanifest, formless consciousness" (2000, p. 150). In the nondual state, there is the experience of union of the manifest and the unmanifest. This state is also labeled as integral mysticism, different from the third designated as formless mysticism.

Wilber, drawing from the Indian philosopher-sage Sri Aurobindo, suggests that the manifestation of consciousness in the universe is an evolutionary process, moving stage by stage to higher levels culminating in superconscious state of realization of Spirit. While societies pass through these stages with recognizable predominance of a featured state of consciousness at a given time to progressively higher states, Wilber notes that at any given time individuals here and there may experience higher levels of consciousness like the Buddha. Even ordinary individuals without any training or esoteric practices may experience for brief periods of time higher states of consciousness. Such experiences would be more common in further evolved societies in future. Wilbur, a champion of transpersonal aspects of consciousness, recognizes the importance of objective studies of consciousness. In fact, the second and the fourth quadrants in his scheme comprise of objective understanding of consciousness. Wilbur makes several suggestions for consciousness research. They include correlation studies of conscious events that arise at different levels, lines and states to gain an integral understanding of consciousness.

There are several other transpersonal psychologists whose ideas are relevant to consciousness studies. The theme that runs through them all is that one's psychological functioning is not limited by the constraints imposed by the body. They attempt to provide for expanded boundaries of awareness beyond sense-mediated cognition. In the human condition, the mind is imprisoned, as it were, in the body and therefore all its interactions with the environment are through the windows of the senses. The embodied mind, however, has the intrinsic ability to escape from this predicament by jumping over (transcending) the physical barriers and thus have an experience of reality without sensory mediation. This is its intuitive or receptive mode, which can give us supernormal cognitions and result in transcendental experiences.

The main problem for transpersonal psychology is the difficulty in generating testable hypotheses that would support their conjectures. Tart's concept of attention/awareness is one attempt to develop a testable theory by linking the two domains of awareness with the process of attention and by allowing the possibility of dissociating content from awareness-as-such. Scientific studies of voluntary control and manipulation of attention may be quite relevant here. If transpersonal psychologists do not translate their theories into testable hypotheses, their ideas will be of little interest to many of us.

Consciousness and Psychical Research

The review of anomalous phenomena suggests: (1) It may be possible to become aware of events that do not exist now but will come into being in the future, as in precognitive experiences in which no causal or inferential links that connect us with the events are discernible. (2) Human intentions may correlate significantly with external events without any conceivable mediating physical energy source, as in psychic healing. (3) One may experience memories of a person who is already deceased, as in cases suggestive of reincarnation. Do the anomalous phenomena have plausible conventional physical explanations? The fact that they are considered anomalous suggests the implausibility of such explanations. In fact, all conventional attempts to explain them either deny the existence of psi or its anomalous aspects.

NATURAL EXPLANATIONS OF PSI

Natural explanations of psi fall into two broad categories. First are those that attempt to explain away parapsychological phenomena as no more than artifacts resulting from wrong observation and/or misinterpretation. In the second category are the attempts to otherwise explain psi within the physical framework of current science without invoking any paranormal process. The latter include those that seek to find a place for psi in the physical world, as we know it now and those that find it necessary to extend current physical theory to introduce new principles to account for psi and related phenomena.

With regard to the first, or "skeptical" category, we have discussed at some length in the chapter on paranormal awareness the attempts to explain away psi as an artifact. The paranormal experiences people report, it is alleged, are due to memory lapses, misconceptions, or simple chance coincidence of events. Some have argued (Spencer-Brown 1953; Gilmore 1989) that the statistically significant ESP results are due to inappropriate assumptions about chance expectations. Some skeptics have dismissed all the evidence on the priori grounds of possible fraud on the part of those involved in the experiment, including the experimenter (Hansel 1966). More responsible critics like Persi Diaconis (1978) and Ray Hyman (1985) looked for procedural errors in psi experiments. I have found these attempts to explain away parapsychological phenomena less compelling than the claimed evidence in support of them. It has been generally agreed that the statistical procedures employed to evaluate psi experimental data since Rhine's early experiments are basically valid (Camp 1937). The fraud hypothesis is essentially nonfalsifiable. Critics have in most cases failed to show that procedural errors can account for the significant results obtained in major psi experiments.

In the second category of natural explanations of psi are the physical theories. There are a variety of them, the more prominent being electromagnetic theories and the observational theories. The latter are derived from quantum mechanics.

Electromagnetic Theories: On the analogy of the radio, it is suggested that in telepathy some kind of electromagnetic wave transmission may take place between the subject and the agent. According to the Russian scientist B. Kajinsky, the neuron system is vibratory in nature. There are closed electrical circuits in the nervous system. Every thought in this view is accompanied by electromagnetic waves generated in the nervous system; and the waves thus generated in one brain can be afferently received by another brain resulting in a telepathic kind of experience (see Vasiliev 1976).

There are several problems with an electromagnetic theory like the above. Electromagnetic transmission between brains, if it is possible, must be subject to the inverse square law. It is not known, however, that the effectiveness of telepathic communication decreases with distance. Another Russian physiologist, L. L. Vasiliev (1963/1976) reported that he was able to induce hypnotic trance over long distances (1700 km) by telepathic suggestion, and that he found no diminishing of the effect when double metal screens were used to shield electromagnetic wave transmission. Again, ESP is known to manifest in the form of clairvoyance, where the information is not generated in the brain but comes from objects that do not have brain-like structures to transmit electromagnetic waves.

Modern versions of electromagnetic theory appear in I. M. Kogan (1966) and Robert Becker (1992). Kogan postulated the existence of "the electromagnetic field of extra-long waves excited by biocurrents" (p. 81). In a similar vein, Becker proposed that extremely low frequency (ELF) waves are involved in psi communications. The ELF waves are assumed to be of such great length that they are not impeded by physical obstructions. In Becker's view, psi signals are not processed by the neurons in the brain, but by a more primitive system involving possibly the glial cells. It is hypothesized that such a primitive communication system consisting of electromagnetic field effects may function more effectively during periods of less turbulent geomagnetic activity. Significant correlations are in fact observed between the occurrence of spontaneous ESP experiences and quiet geomagnetic activity (Persinger 1985,1989) and

between successful psi tests in the laboratory and low levels of geomagnetic activity at the time the tests were conducted (Berger & Persinger 1991; Persinger & Krippner 1989). These are cited as evidence in support of the ELF hypothesis.

The Observational Theories: In recent years several physicists have attempted to explain psi with the help of quantum mechanics. These are referred to as the observational theories of psi (see chapter 5 for quantum physical discussions of consciousness). It may be recalled that classical mechanics assumes that the future state of a physical system can be determined if we have a complete description of the preceding state of the system. In quantum mechanics, however, a given system develops into one of several possible subsequent states and, according to the widely accepted Copenhagen interpretation, the ultimate description, or state vector of the system incorporates all the potential states. However, when a measurement or "observation" of the system is made, the state vector loses this undefined probabilistic quality and gets "reduced" to one real outcome. Unfortunately, the mathematical formalism of quantum mechanics does not specify what exactly constitutes an "observation," and the resulting difficulties lead to the well known "measurement problem" in quantum mechanics.

One attempt to overcome this problem is to introduce the concept of "hidden variables," the hypothetical factors that reconcile the demands of the deterministic and stochastic conceptions of the development of the state vector. Harris Walker takes off from here and locates the hidden variables in consciousness and equates them with the "will." In Walker's view, as mentioned in the previous chapter, the will is responsible for the collapse of the state vector for a physical system. PK is an instance of such collapse brought about by human volition.

Since the hidden variables are "nonlocal" and unconstrained by space-time factors, they are capable of coupling two observers or an observer and an object separated by distance or time. In telepathy, for instance, "the will of the subject and the experimenter act together to select a particular state into which the system is collapsed" (Walker 1975, p. 10). In psi, whether ESP or PK, there is no transfer of energy; only information is transferred. The magnitude of a psi effect, in Walker's view, depends on the amount of information transferred through the will channel and the amount needed to collapse the state vector of a given system. Walker suggests that quantitative predictions of psi effects can be made based on a detailed analysis of the psi task and the estimate of the observer's abilities and will.

The observational theories of psi are stated to be experimentally testable, as they are formulated in mathematical terms. Indeed, Walker's theory and modifications of it by others did stimulate a significant amount of research, especially in the area of PK. However, the validity of any of the versions of the observational theory is yet to be established (Irwin 1999). Even in the liberal version of quantum mechanics, it is highly controversial whether the collapse of the state vector involves consciousness in the sense the observational theories require for explaining psi. Further, the question of what constitutes an "observation" that is necessary to bring about the collapse of the state vector is not answered with any degree of clarity by theorists in this area. Even granting some validity to the observational theories of psi, it is difficult to see them as mere extensions of current physical theory. Walker's theory, for example, sounds clearly dualistic. The "will" and the "hidden variables" seem to have the same ontological primacy as energy, which accounts for events in the physical world. That the "will" influences only the micro-level quantum systems is beside the point. What is impor-

tant is that even the physical theories do seem to assume principles and processes that are not a mere extension of what is ordinarily understood as physical, but things that are commonly regarded as mental in the Cartesian model. In an important sense, Walker's theory is a significant reversal of the physical model. One could even characterize it as vitalist, because the central principle that accounts for psi is located in the "will" of the subject. This shift away from the stimulus-centered approach gives Walker's theory a vitalist look. Note that Walker is not looking at the process by which the energy emanating from objects reaches the subject, but rather at the subject and his "will" variables. The development of a dualistic physics (this is what this theory attempts to develop) would indeed constitute a paradigmatic shift, and its acceptance would have revolutionary consequences for physics.

PSYCHOLOGICAL MODELS

Some attempts have been made by parapsychologists to explain psi within the framework of an information-processing model (Schmeidler 1991; Irwin 1979, 1999). In fact, the concept "extrasensory perception" presupposes a perceptual model, that psi operates in a sensory-like fashion, even if it is not mediated by any known senses. This model has shown little promise and attracted only negligible support within the parapsychological community. In a sense, it is paradoxical to consider psi as a species of perception and at the same time regard it as nonsensory. In fact, lack of any sensory orientation, and the absence of any systematic effects of color, shape size and location of the target on ESP performance, clearly suggest that no sensory processing of the kind that goes on in perception is involved in psi. For this reason, I have argued elsewhere (Rao 1966) that psi in its cognitive aspect is more like imagination than perception.

More recently, H. J. Irwin (1979, 1999) suggested that psi fits better with the information-processing model in its ideational mode than in its sensory mode. Irwin recommends a memory model of psi such as the one proposed by W. G. Roll (1966, 1987). Roll suggested that ESP is more like remembering than perceiving. The mediation of psi into awareness may involve essentially similar cognitive processing as in memory and be subject to similar laws, e.g., laws of association and frequency. In support of this theory it is claimed that exceptionally successful subjects appear to have excellent memories. At least one experimental study (Feather 1967) reported a positive correlation between subjects' memory scores and ESP scores. All this is well taken, and there may be some genuine similarities in the way memories and ESP information are mediated into awareness. The memory model, however, does not really explain ESP without invoking something more fundamental, something that is entirely beyond what memory can do. As Irwin himself recognizes, the memory model at best attempts to account for the mediation phase of psi, but not how the subject has access to extrasensory information in the first place. The latter does seem to require a paranormal process.

PARANORMAL EXPLANATIONS OF PSI

If psi phenomena are anomalous, as they appear to be, and do not fit into physical and psychological models, we will be tempted naturally to conclude that consciousness is not completely contained in our cortical structures or the rest of the nervous system. Indeed, several psychical researchers from F.W.H. Myers and William James to R. H. Thouless and Larry LeShan (1976) felt it necessary to postulate a hitherto unknown "entity" or a yet unrecognized principle operating when one has a psi experience. Though philosopher Michael Scriven (1962) complained that parapsychology is the reverse of psychoanalysis with only facts and no theory, there is no lack of speculative theorizing in parapsychology. The primary thrust of the theories in this area has been directed toward explaining how psi functions relatively unaffected by space-time constraints. Since there are too many theories to review here, we may consider only the prominent ones that have relevance to consciousness studies (see Rao 1977; Stokes 1987 for a more detailed discussion of parapsychological theories).

Subliminal Self: In his monumental work *Human Personality and Its Survival of Bodily Death*, F.W.H. Myers (1903/1915) attempted to lay the foundation for a comprehensive science of consciousness. Myers believed that consciousness is more than that of which we are ordinarily aware. Our ordinary consciousness, which Myers called *supraliminal consciousness*, "does not comprise the whole of consciousness or of the faculty within us. There exists a more comprehensive consciousness, a profounder faculty" (p. 12), which he refers to as *subliminal* or *ultramarginal consciousness*. Consciousness is like radiation beyond the visible spectrum. According to Myers, the conscious human faculty can be represented "as a linear spectrum whose red rays begin where voluntary muscular control and organic sensation begin, and whose violet rays fade away at the point at which man's highest strain of thought or imagination merges in reverie and ecstasy" (p. 18). Thus, at either end of the psychological spectrum, Myers sensed a wide variety of conscious states that go beyond sensation and intellect.

The ultramarginal consciousness that remains for the most part only as potential is what Myers calls the *subliminal self*. "I mean by the subliminal self," wrote Myers, "that part of the self which is commonly subliminal. And I conceive also that no self of which we can have cognizance is in reality more than a fragment of a larger Self,—revealed in a fashion at once shifting and limited through an organism not so framed as to afford its full manifestation" (p. 15).

In his conception of the subliminal self, Myers postulates an "inward extension of our being," as James put it, "cut off from common consciousness by a stream or diaphragm not absolutely impervious but liable to leakage and to occasional rupture" (Murphy & Ballou, 1960, p. 230). However, Myers was vague as to how the subliminal self makes contact with the "cosmic" environment to bring about paranormal events. Various alternatives suggest themselves. (1) The subliminal selves are but waves in a sea of consciousness. (2) The subliminal selves themselves are discrete and discontinuous but can interact because they are submerged or situated in a common medium of consciousness. (3) The subliminal self is a discrete center of consciousness inherently capable of interacting with others without being limited by space or time. For his time, the ideas of Myers were provocative and seminal. They inspired a number of subsequent thinkers from William James to Jan Ehrenwald (1947).

S. David Kahn (1976) plausibly argues that Myers' hypothesis can be further extended if we assume, as James did, that we are linked together in a far more fundamental way than we have hitherto imagined. The subliminal influence on our being may not be conceived of merely as the "subliminal uprush" on rare occasions. Rather, according to Kahn, it is more pervasive than that, and is, in fact, "an intrinsic component to the human condition" (p. 225). "Here the emphasis," writes Kahn, "is on a constantly impinging heteropsychic set of stimuli which occasionally may breakthrough, but which ordinarily press on the stream of thought in such a way as to steadily distort,

modify, emphasize, and deflect the ongoing process of consciousness. Here the occasional breakthrough is less important than the constant interaction between the psi level and the stream of consciousness itself, which now becomes the focus of our attention" (p. 224).

The Common Unconscious: The British philosopher H. H. Price, who took anomalous phenomena such as ESP seriously, felt that the evidence suggestive of mind-to-mind communication (telepathy) makes it foolish to argue for the plurality of minds. Between one mind and another there are no clear-cut boundaries. The division of minds is not "absolute and unconditional, either." The illusion of the individual mind arises out of the superficial nature of self-consciousness (Price, 1940, 1948).

Price thinks that the unconscious portion of one mind may interact with that of another because they share the "collective unconscious" and that the collective unconscious, which connects all the apparently individual minds, is responsible for telepathic cognition. The collective unconscious, according to Price, is not an "entity" or a "thing" but a "field of interaction." Minds are not causally isolated entities. Unconscious events in one mind may produce unconscious events in another mind.

Why then are we not aware of others' thoughts all the time? Following Bergson, Price argues that the human mind has developed a repressive mechanism that suppresses the continual flow of telepathic impact from one mind to another. There is a biological need for such a mechanism. Otherwise, everyone would constantly receive the thoughts and emotions experienced by all minds; life would very likely become chaos, and action impossible. Psychoanalysts have indicated that repressive mechanisms are partly in abeyance during states of relaxation and dreaming. If telepathic influences are suppressed by similar repressive mechanisms, the former should come through more often when the latter are in relative abeyance. Price points out that, in fact, many spontaneous cases of a telepathic nature do occur during dreams. The existence of a repressive mechanism, he says, is also suggested by the fact that most mediums known for their psychic abilities enter a state of dissociation that seems to release them from the repressive controls.

Price suggests that the unconscious part of our minds may be capable of perceiving everything, however remote in space, for the simple reason that the unconscious may be in contact with all things. However, we do not see all things at once because the nervous system and the sense organs may be preventing us from doing so and this process is, of course, biologically useful to us. Occasionally, however, when the physiological mechanism allows it, these unconscious contacts may actualize themselves in the form of anomalous experiences.

The Compound Theory: Another British philosopher with an interest in psychical research, C. D. Broad (1925/1951), proposed what he called the "compound theory" of the mind. According to this theory, the mind is not a single substance. It is a compound of two substances, and neither of them by itself has the characteristics of the mind. The two substances are the *psychic factor, psychogenic factor,* or *psi component,* as he later called it, and the *bodily factor.*

Such actions as perception, reasoning, and remembering are not the functions of either of the factors by itself. Just as a chemical compound possesses characteristics that do not belong individually to either of the constituents, the functions of the mind are not to be found solely in one or another of its constituent elements.

Broad goes on to suggest that the psychic factor could persist even after the cessation of the body at death. When a psychic factor is united with a body, it functions as a mind, and certain traces are formed. When the person dies, this factor separates. Consequently, a discarnate psychic factor does not have a mind or conscious awareness. Let us suppose that a psychic factor, after it's separation from the body with which it has so long been associated, comes into contact with the body of another living organism, as would be in the case with an entranced medium. The newly formed "mind," in virtue of the impressions this psychic factor had in the form of traces, may recall the experiences of the deceased person with whose body the psychic factor had been associated.

The Shin Hypothesis: The British psychologist R. H. Thouless and his associate B. P. Weisner advocate a radical dualistic postulation of the mind-brain relationship. Thouless and Weisner (1948) suggest that an entity, which they call "shin," is involved in all our cognitive processes, normal as well as paranormal. They argue that in all normal processes of volition and perception shin functions through the medium of the brain and the nervous system. Anomalous cognitive experiences occur when shin bypasses the brain and the nervous system and directly interacts with the environment. In this view, shin becomes aware of the brain states by a clairvoyant type of monitoring of neural activity in a manner that is similar to a theory by neurophysiologist John Eccles (1976, 1977). Similarly, the psychokinetic type of influence on neural events by shin results in volitional activity. In normal perception, stimuli from the object act on the sensory part of the nervous system. The processes in the nervous system and the brain inform shin. In clairvoyance, however, direct connections are established between shin and the objects, without the mediation of the brain and the nervous system. Thus, psi cognitions are no more supernormal than ordinary perceptions, but they are, as Thouless and Weisner put it, "exosomatic forms of processes which are normally endosomatic" (1948 p. 199).

"In normal thinking and perceiving," Thouless and Weisner write, *"I am in the same sort of relation to what is going on in the sensory part of my brain and nervous system as that of the successful clairvoyant to some external event, and ... this relation is established by the same means"* (p. 196, original emphasis). In an act of perception, they point out, we are not aware of the immediate cause of our perceptions, the cause being the changes in the brain and nervous system. So also, a successful clairvoyant is not aware of the object of his or her cognition. Thus, normal perception differs from clairvoyance only in that the brain and the nervous system mediate the former, whereas in clairvoyant perception a direct contact between the subject and the object is established.

It would appear that shin is more like the mind in the state of what we referred to as pure consciousness. The question remains, however, whether shin is a discrete center of consciousness like Broad's psychic factor or a common medium that envelops the multitude of beings with cognitive abilities. Shin, as a discrete entity, is consistent with the notion of the plurality of selves. But plurality of nonlocal selves, whose normal cognitive processes manifest only in association with particulate brain structures, will be hardly noticeable as functional plurality. At the nonlocal/transcendental level, the question of the one and the many may be meaningless if discreteness and multiplicity are the result of the union of pure consciousness with the brain.

What is important, however, is the recognition that there is another source of awareness that is different from and runs parallel to sensorially processed cognition. It involves a process that appears to give direct and unmediated access to reality. Such a process involving a transcendental transac-

tion, as it were, may be designated as the paranormal process. The paranormal process is possibly the one that leads to a state of "knowing by being." This is a state that mystics are believed to be capable of experiencing. In the case of psychical phenomena, such as ESP, we have reason to believe that the normal and paranormal processes work in a complementary manner. G.N.M. Tyrrell and L. E. Rhine, among others, recognized that psi is a two-stage process. Tyrrell (1947), for example, suggested that ESP phenomena first occur at the subliminal level and then are obliged "to pass through the bottleneck at the threshold if they are to reach the normal consciousness" (p. 331). They pass over the threshold by making use of what he called the "mediating vehicles." The second stage is a form of cognitive processing that enables the subliminally received material to manifest in awareness. An ESP experience thus seems to involve both normal and paranormal processes. Inasmuch as parapsychological phenomena involve both these processes, they may be useful in providing the bridge connecting cognitive psychology at one end and transpersonal psychology at the other.

Summary

Psychology, it is said, has no theory but only bits of theories. We have theories of learning, personality, motivation and so on, but no theory we could advance with any degree of conviction to apply to all areas of psychology. A unified theory still eludes us. We have schools and systems of psychology that seem to work pretty well in some areas and not so well in others. I believe that this state of affairs is not necessarily an indication of the immaturity of the field. Rather, it is an indication of the highly complex nature of the subject matter and the many faceted heterogeneity of human nature. There are no simple basic facts, elemental units of behavior that we could use to build a comprehensive theoretical edifice. Every statement of fact needs to be qualified and compromised at some point, because behavior has multiple causes and the context in which behavior manifests is ever changing. Therefore, here pluralism is the law.

The area of consciousness studies is no exception to this state of affairs. There is as yet no unified theory of consciousness, but many theories to explain bits of conscious experience. As we have seen, theorizing in cognitive psychology focuses on particular forms of consciousness, whereas the focus of transpersonal psychologies is on entirely different forms. Depth psychologies comfortably deal with darker aspects of the unconscious rather than with the brighter side of consciousness, even though they have attempted to map the whole field of consciousness. Cognitive psychology typically restricts its scope to mundane functions of primary awareness and the processes of the cognitive unconscious. Transpersonal psychologies take off where the others have left. Consequently, if we extend the findings of cognitive psychology to transpersonal psychology or vice-versa we land in difficulties. However, if we accept the fact that consciousness manifests in many forms and that their understanding may require different methodological approaches and theoretical models, we are on safer grounds. Thus we may have psychologies of consciousness rather than the psychology of consciousness.

Depth psychology is useful in understanding some aspects of pathological awareness. Psychoanalysis, for example, has helped us to appreciate the psychogenesis of mental abnormalities. More attention to the possibility that cognitive impairment itself may be a cause of certain psychotic states would have resulted in a better appreciation of the role of consciousness in one's well being. Indeed, the postulation of

unconscious mentation, is a significant contribution to our understanding of consciousness. Dissociation, repression and a host of other depth psychological concepts are invaluable for studying dysfunctional awareness. However, we should be cautious about over-generalizing their applicability to other forms of awareness. One example of such avoidable over-generalization is the attempt by M. H. Erdelyi (1985) to translate Freudian concepts into the information processing terms of cognitive psychology. The Freudian unconscious, as mentioned earlier, is very different from the unconscious mind in cognitive psychology. The cognitive unconscious is intrinsically unconscious and is in principle inaccessible to introspection. It is not awareness repressed from being experienced. It refers more to the *processes* of awareness than the *contents* of awareness. The computational mind is the composite of structures and processes that transform cognitive inputs into symbolic representations. The cognitive unconscious is a natural consequence of the way the cognitive mind is structured. Subjective awareness (consciousness) itself is said to be no more than a projection from these structures. Even though psychoanalysis also emphasizes the processes of the unconscious, the unconscious itself refers to the *contents* rather than the *processes* that are inaccessible to awareness. Thus, though both cognitive psychology and psychoanalysis make a distinction between consciousness and the unconscious, that distinction, however, has different significance in the two.

Cognitive psychologists, as we have seen, focus on the contrasting aspects of conscious and unconscious mental processes. Their studies of unconscious mental processes have thrown light on some aspects of consciousness and their underlying structures in the brain, especially in the areas of attention, perception and psycholinguistics. They have indeed registered remarkable success in understanding a variety of cognitive functions and, to use Jackendoff's phrase, the computational mind. Their attempts to extend their generalizations to explain the conscious or the phenomenological mind are less fruitful, however. Cognitive psychology therefore appears to be better suited for solving what Chalmers characterized as "easy problems" rather than the "hard problems" of subjective experience.

Freud modeled unconscious mentation after the conscious. In his view, the unconscious is capable of doing almost everything that consciousness does. The unconscious has images and thoughts in much the same way as consciousness does. The contents of the unconscious, like conscious thoughts and images, are intentional and fully representational. Cognitive psychology appears to be in essential agreement on this point, with one major difference. It models conscious mentation after the unconscious processes. Consequently, representations are attributed to computational outcomes in the brain. Freud, on the other hand, begins with consciousness and finds the origins of unconscious material in consciousness. The psychoanalytic goal is to return the repressed (unconscious) wishes, hostilities and so on to their original source in consciousness. Cognitive psychology locates the source of consciousness in the unconscious processes. This reversal of direction lands it in a difficult situation by creating the difficult-to-bridge conscious-unconscious duality, and what Jackendoff called "the mind-*mind* problem." This problem could only be solved either by ignoring consciousness altogether or by rendering it an impotent, "good for nothing" epiphenomenon of unconscious brain processes. The psychoanalytic distinction between consciousness and the unconscious does not entail the above difficulty implicit in cognitive psychology, because the conscious and the unconscious are seen as two aspects of experience and not of computational symbols.

Both psychoanalysis and cognitive psychology make a distinction between mind and consciousness, challenging the traditional notion of their identity. Cognitive theories go even further to deny any necessary connection between them. I tend to think, however, that the distinction is only superficial and not fundamental in either case. It is superficial in most cognitive theories because what are fundamental to mental activity are processes to which we never have conscious access. Conscious awareness itself is a quality of mentation brought about by the operation of certain unconscious cortical systems. It is superficial in psychoanalysis also because the dynamics of mentation are buried in the depths of the unconscious. The emphasis in both is on studying the unconscious processes; the difference being that psychoanalysis deals with lived experiences whereas cognitive psychology is concerned with abstract computations. In both, the unconscious mind is fundamental.

It is in C. G. Jung that consciousness emerges as the central principle underlying both the unconscious and conscious mentation. Consciousness is not seen as "daylight" or, as in Baars' metaphor, the "spotlight" on the stage. It is described as "luminosity" that underlies all cognitions, whether conscious or unconscious. The "spotlight" of subjective awareness may indeed be a manifestation of certain cortical processes. The core of cognition, however, is its luminosity. Consciousness as "luminous" does not require an outside source to make it cognizable. Rather it is self-luminous and intrinsically reflexive. Luminosity is the essence of consciousness; it is what makes cognition a cognition. Further, it is in principle irreducible to physical processes in the brain. Thus consciousness in Jung comes into its own as an equal partner, with energy embedded in archetypal activity at the psychoid level of being.

The possibility of an extra-cerebral existence of consciousness is the starting point of transpersonal psychologies. The autonomy and the causal efficacy of consciousness are taken for granted. The possibility of non-representational consciousness, consciousness-*as-such*, is upheld. The distinction between mind and consciousness becomes more fundamental than in psychoanalysis and cognitive psychology. Consciousness is regarded as transpersonal and non-local. The mind itself is understood as embodied consciousness.

Transpersonal psychology, like psychoanalysis, is more a theoretical enterprise than an empirical science. Psychical research, dedicated as it is to the tenants of empirical science, has collected a significant amount of data that gives a certain amount of credible empirical support to some of the presuppositions of transpersonal psychology. Inasmuch as ESP experience involves both the paranormal and normal cognitive processes, psi functioning may be thought of as constituting an interface between the two. Conceived as studying threshold phenomena that link the two modes of awareness, psi research may hold the promise of giving us insights into the relation between the mind and the brain on the one hand and the mind and consciousness on the other. In so doing, it may also pave the way for reconciliation between cognitive psychology and transpersonal psychology, the cognitive mind and transpersonal consciousness.

PART II
EASTERN TRADITION

CHAPTER 8

Yoga: Royal Road to Higher Consciousness

So far we reviewed some essentially scholarly and scientific attempts to study consciousness in the West. As we have noted, the Western perspective is largely focused outward with a view to understand consciousness objectively and to explain the subjective in objective terms. This focus has led increasingly either to do away with inner experience altogether as a subject of scientific inquiry or to reduce it into objective items that can be understood in the vocabulary of brain physiology and neural activity. These attempts, as we have seen, have not been entirely successful. On the one hand, there appears to be an unsettling uneasiness with an axiomatic rejection of inner experience and an increasing awareness of the primacy of subjective experience as a phenomenon irreducible into meaningful physiological events. There is on the other hand mounting evidence for the reality of phenomena that in principle appear to be beyond the boundaries of matter as we understand it now. Together, the two events make a powerful presumptive case against the physical foundations of consciousness. The assumption of essential irreducibility

of inner subjective experience into objectively observed external phenomena prompts us to look at consciousness from other perspectives. Nonwestern traditions with a focus on inwardness are obvious alternate sources to search for models that put subjective awareness in a different light and thus provide us with a better look at consciousness. The new look may have deeper consequences for understanding consciousness than hitherto acknowledged in Western scientific discourse on consciousness.

Chinese Perspectives

The major strands of the Eastern tradition are the Chinese and the Indian. If we were to make a distinction between the two, the Chinese is more humanistic and less spiritual and inward than the Indian tradition. In a sense, the Chinese tradition stands midway between the Western and the Indian. The Chinese are neither focused outward as is the case in the West nor inward as in the Indian tradition. Avoiding the two extremes the Chinese focus is on man himself. The Tao is idealized human nature. Also, extreme forms of rationalism and mysticism are avoided. The emotional nature of man is emphasized to complement the rational in understanding ethical behavior. As Chuangtzu contends, the Tao is beyond the reach of reason. Again, contemplation and absorption are not emphasized in Chinese mysticism. Rather the Chinese is a form of natural mysticism centered on human nature. Asserting that reality is none other than human nature, the Chinese avoided the exploration of the inward spirit or the outward matter and thus moved away from the extremes of materialism and mysticism. In the process, the Chinese tradition offers no systematic speculations on metaphysical or epistemological matters. (See Fung Yulan, 1952; Raju, 1992.) Both Confucianism and Taoism affirm man first. The questions relating to the mind or the world outside were raised occasionally but they were never pushed to their logical conclusions, always returning the inquiry back to human condition. Thus with the deep commitment to human affairs, the Chinese made significant contributions to social and political thought, even if they lagged in matters relating to metaphysics, epistemology and to some extent psychology of consciousness.

Even Buddhism, which found its way into China about the first century AD, and subsequently had a profound influence on Chinese life, itself became pragmatic and humanistic conforming to the traditional Chinese mold. Chinese assimilation of Buddhism transformed it into a system "built up of Taoist and Confucian elements" (Raju 1992, p. 144). The result was "to humanize, naturalize, and socialize Buddhism" (p. 145). The Buddhist concept of *Tathata* was understood as the Tao and *Nirvana* as *Wu Wei*, the Taoist doctrine of enlightenment and nonaction or natural action. The Buddhist middle path was equated with Confucian golden mean. Meditation was not seen as a means to attain Buddhahood but

to achieve sageliness. The sage, unlike the monk, participated in worldly activities, as a member of the family or the government.

The Chinese affinity with what we consider to be the essential aspect of the Eastern tradition becomes apparent, only when we consider the Chinese practices such as Qigong. Qigong, a fundamental component of Chinese tradition, refers to practices that are designed to harness inner energy that is believed to be life sustaining and vital for growth, health and harmony. The *Qigong* practices are much like yoga practices involving breathing and postural exercises for regulating and controlling one's mind. "All *Qigong* exercises," as Allen Dorcas (1997) points out, "essentially consist of the training and gradual learning of the ability to expel distracting thoughts, to focus one's entire conscious attention on a single, simple point, and to eventually attain a quiescent, meditative state in which the division between the practitioner and the world ceases to exist, a state in which he/she is one with the universe (Tian Ren He Yi)" (p. 310).

Physiological studies of *Qigong* practitioners have yielded results very similar to those on yogins. For example, electrical brain wave activity monitored during practice of *Qigong* showed increase in alpha and greater synchronization between the right and left hemispheres of the brain (Dorcas 1997). These findings are very similar to those accompanying the practice of yoga, as we will discuss later. Again, the pragmatic and humanistic orientation of the Chinese culture, led to an emphasis on the health benefits and curative effects of *Qigong* on people suffering from physical and psychological ailments. No doubt *Qigong* has its supernatural aspects in the minds of Chinese, but unlike in India little intellectual effort went into understanding the mind-body relationship and for gaining insights into the nature of consciousness. Therefore, we turn to the Indian tradition to give us the glimpses of alternative models for viewing consciousness from within.

Indian Perspectives

Clearly, there is no one perspective that characterizes all of Indian thought on consciousness. There are indeed some important differences in speculations about consciousness among the classical systems of Indian philosophy. We find, however, some basic assumptions that are generally shared. These assumptions provide the foundation on which the dominant philosophical discourse rests in the Indian tradition. Because it is impossible to cover even the major ones in this brief presentation, I will confine my discussion to what appears to be the dominant Indian tradition with special reference to Samkhya-Yoga, Advaita Vedanta, and Buddhism. What are relevant here are ideas and theories that present consciousness in a new light so that we may have a more comprehensive understanding of it. We look to Indian philosophical tradition because of the special emphasis given to consciousness. The theories of consciousness seem to determine the epistemological positions that in turn lead to the metaphysical stands taken by the various systems in Indian philosophy. As J. N. Mohanty (1993) points out, "a metaphysics of consciousness has been the destiny of Indian thought" (p. 56).

Unlike in the West, Indian thinkers tend to make a distinction between mind and consciousness. Mind in the Indian tradition is considered to be a subtle form of matter, whereas consciousness is completely noncorporal. The mind is the interfacing instrumentality that is connected at one end to the external world and to consciousness at the other end. Mental phenomena therefore manifest the influence of consciousness as subject and of the world of things as objects. The subject-object dichotomy that is implicit in our ordinary phenomenal awareness is a consequence of the stage the mind sets up for the play of consciousness and the material world as subject and objects.

As Mohanty notes, there are three fundamental issues around which Indian theories of consciousness revolve. In his words, "Does consciousness necessarily manifest itself as it manifests its object? Secondly, is consciousness, by its essential nature, of an object or not? Thirdly, does consciousness have form, structure, or content of its own, or not? (Mohanty 1993, p. 56). In addition, the Vedanta philosophers raised the question of whether consciousness belongs o someone or to no one.

The attention to the inward in Indian thought has led to an emphasis on consciousness and its primacy. The primacy is asserted either as an over arching single reality as in Advaita monism or as an irreducible aspect of reality independent of the physical as in Samkhya-Yoga. In either case, the assumption is not engendered by rational argument alone based on metaphysical presumptions. They are derived from their respective epistemological positions, which are themselves grounded in psychological assumptions based not merely on the authority of the *Vedas*, but claimed to be empirically supported. Consequently, we find that among the Indian systems of thought the discussions of consciousness end up as metaphysical assertions. They are, however, rooted in a large measure in psychological assumptions, insights and observations. Often the metaphysical discussions are carried as rational discourse like in the West, but they are founded on a psychological theory of consciousness and are related to experience.

In its quest for truth, the Indian tradition turns inward. It attempts to identify the elements that tend to distort and falsify our general understanding of the world around us. It seeks to explore methods and strategies to control them. Further, it endeavors to develop techniques that reveal truth in its pristine and unsullied condition, to formulate philosophical theories and to prescribe practices of conduct consistent with the truth so revealed. In such a scheme, the first step is to understand how we normally acquire information and the possible limitations and imperfections of such information. The beginning point then is cognitive science as systematic epistemology.

Now, the predominant mode of acquiring information is sensory processing. Such processing is known to be biased because of the manner in which the processing person is situated, whose presuppositions, attitudes and motivations constrain and bias perceptions. More importantly, the processing mechanisms themselves determine to some degree the form, the extent and situation of the content of cognitions. The way bats perceive the world is different from the way we do. Humans cannot process low auditory signals as dogs or deer can. If we were situated differently with different kinds of sensory-motor apparatus we would likely function differently and our knowledge of the world would be different in significant ways. What then is the "true" world? Answers vary depending on what one's focus is. If the focus is outward, one's perceptions of the world consists in the way it is represented to us. The representations are believed to be true inasmuch as they are seen to correspond to the external objects and events, a correspondence attested by inter-subject agreement/validation. Even though the outward reality is known only via the representations we have of it and, in Kant's terms, the thing-in-themselves are for ever unknown, our knowledge of it is true and valid to the extent we have consensual agreement on it. If the focus is inward, however one tends to view true reality as no other than awareness itself. Some philosophers in the West subscribed to this view and asserted that our perceptions con-

stitute reality. In the Indian tradition, even when reality is equated with awareness, awareness is not limited to representational perception. Rather awareness is regarded as consisting of direct and unmediated awareness of reality. Such nonrepresentational awareness in a significant sense is reality itself. Humans, it is assumed, have the ability to realize reality in itself as *consciousness-as-such*. Indeed, it is generally agreed among Indian thinkers, independent of their metaphysical preferences, that by following specified procedures and cultivating certain habits of mind, it is possible to attain a state of awareness that is reality itself. Such an understanding underscores much of Hindu and Buddhist thought,

We thus find in the Indian tradition a belief in the possibility of nonsensory source of knowledge, which by its very nature is free from the distortions, and imperfections that beset sensorially processed information. The ultimate goal of human achievement is spoken of as liberation or *moksha*. In an important sense it is liberation of the mind from its sensory bondage that is believed to be the most significant single source that screens true reality from us. For the one who realizes reality in its true form, the sensory knowledge we have of the world appears as nothing but ignorance or *avidya*, as a dream appears on waking. Freedom from such ignorance and disinformation is a necessary condition for realizing truth in one's being. The goal is to achieve perfect knowledge, because perfect knowledge makes one perfect. To know *Brahman* is to be *Brahman*. Knowing is thus realization in being. The strength of such assertion is not derived merely from rational argument. Rather it is grounded in the belief that it is possible to find such persons in real life. Realizing consciousness-as-such is considered an empirical fact experienced subjectively as well as shared by those who undergo necessary training and practice (*sadhana*) the prescribed discipline. Yoga is considered almost universally by Indian thinkers to be a useful technique for emancipating the mind from its existential condition of sensory bondage so that it can access consciousness-as-such for realization of absolute truth.

BACKGROUND

Yoga is a system of Indian philosophy. By the time of Panini, the great grammarian who lived probably before the Buddha, yoga came to be identified with a method of achieving concentration and controlling sensory inputs and responses. Although the word "yoga," in this sense of a method, appears in some of the later Upanishads such as *Maitrayani, Svetasvatara and Katha*, it was in Patanjali's *Yoga-Sutras* that we find its first systematic treatment. As Dasgupta (1922) points out, Patanjali collected the different yoga practices, systematized diverse ideas on the subject, and "grafted them on Samkhya metaphysics" (p. 229). When Yoga refers to a philosophical system, we use capital "Y" and when it denotes a method, lower case "y" is used.

There is some controversy about Patanjali's dates and whether he is the same person as the author of *Mahabhashya*, a commentary on Panini's grammar. If the authority of Dasgupta is relied upon, the grammarian Patanjali and the Patanjali of *Yoga Sutras* is one and the same, and he lived in the second century BC. J. H. Woods (1914/1988) suggests, however, that "Patanjali's sutras were written at some time in the fourth or fifth century of our era." Vyasa wrote a commentary on *Yoga Sutras*, and Vacaspati Misra and Vijnana Bhiksu provide extensive explanations on the *Vyasabhasya*. Together these works constitute the original and primary sources of much of the Yoga literature in Patanjali tradition. *The Yoga System of Patanjali* by J. H. Woods (1914/1988) contains English translations of the text as well as the commentary by Vyasa and the explanation of Vacaspatimisra.

In the *Yogatattva Upanishad*, four kinds of yoga, *raja yoga, hatha yoga, laya yoga*, and *mantra yoga*, are mentioned. *Raja yoga*, which is the subject of *Yoga Sutras*, is regarded as the highest of all. In *hatha yoga* the emphasis is on physical exercises. *Laya yoga* has to do with *Kundalini* arousal. *Mantra yoga* involves meditation on certain mystical syllables. Thus, it was recognized that different techniques could be used to achieve a state of psychic concentration, meditation and absorption, which are believed to enable the practitioner to attain all kinds of *siddhis*, or supernatural powers.

Sutras literally mean principles. The *Yoga Sutras* are concise in the extreme. They are succinct and difficult to grasp without the necessary background. The commentaries and explanations by Yoga scholars such as Vyasa, Vacaspatimisra and Vijnanabhiksu attempt to provide that background. It is still difficult to clearly comprehend the meaning and significance of the Yoga aphorisms without access to the tradition and some personal experience. I prefer to think that the aphorisms themselves are given intuitively. The commentaries and explanations are their logical elaborations and metaphorical descriptions. They attempt to address metaphysical problems, ethical issues, psychological subtleties and religious matters together in the same breadth, further complicating the matters. Therefore, it is not easy to tease out the psychological essence of yoga without bringing in one's own preferences and biases.

Yoga-Sutras is in four parts. The first three parts describe the doctrines of the yoga. The last part is devoted, among other things, to criticizing the views of Buddhists. Several scholars, including Dasgupta (1922) argued convincingly that the fourth part is a subsequent addition to the three original parts of Patanjali.

The Metaphysical Base

It should be emphasized that yoga is not merely a method having psychical and psycho-physiological implications. Together with Samkhya it is also a full-fledged system of philosophy. Therefore, to understand and grasp the full significance of Patanjali's yoga, it is necessary to be aware of its metaphysical context. Some minor differences of detail notwithstanding, Yoga as a system of philosophy shares with Samkhya the basic assumptions concerning human nature. Therefore, Samkhya and Yoga are traditionally treated as one joint system in Indian philosophy.

According to Samkhya thinkers (Sastri 1935; Raja, 1963), there are essentially two principles that govern our being—*purusha* and *prakriti*. It is difficult to translate these concepts because there are no equivalents in English vocabulary. For example, *purusha* is sometimes translated as "soul" and at other times as "spirit," "self," or "consciousness." When *purusha* is rendered by the word "soul" it acquires a religious connotation and tends to loose the metaphysical and psychological subtleties of the word *purusha*. Similarly, when it is translated as "self" the metaphysical aspects come into focus and its psychological aspects are marginalized. Since we are dealing in this chapter essentially with the psychological aspects of Yoga, it would seem that "consciousness" might be the closest concept to convey the appropriate sense of *purusha* for our purpose. *Prakriti* may be understood as nonconscious matter.

Purusha: *Purusha* is pure consciousness. It has no qualities or characteristics of its own. It is the transcendental principle that makes awareness possible. In conjunction with *prakriti*, it enables us to experience unity, coherence, continuity, and selfhood. There is a separate *purusha* for each person. *Purusha* per se cannot be perceived. It can

only be realized. However its presence can be inferred from the manifest purposiveness in the universe. Without such a transcendental principle, it is contended, it would not be possible to make sense of moral responsibility.

Our awareness of things is contained in the ideas and images we have of them. Like the worldly things, which are indeed material, the thoughts and images of them are equally physical, except that they are subtler. Like gross physical objects, images of objects are nonconscious in that they cannot be felt as experiences unless they are made conscious by the presence of the *purusha*, the principle of consciousness. The *purusha* is the light that illumines the contents of the mind. Without such an illumination, what is in the mind would remain like a painted canvas enveloped by immense darkness. Consciousness-as-such, however, has no content. It is self-luminous and capable of illuminating others. Self-luminosity (*swayam-jyothi*) implies immediacy of consciousness, which means that such distinctions as subject and object are inappropriate to it. It is in a significant sense *reflexive*. Consciousness is both self-manifesting and other-manifesting. In being self-manifesting it is a primary and irreducible principle. Consciousness is other-manifesting in that it is foundational to all awareness. In revealing itself consciousness reveals everything else. In a sense, it breathes consciousness into matter associated with it. In so doing, the distinction of subject and object is generated and consciousness is reflected in the subjective aspects of natural phenomena. As the *Samkhyakarika* (19) puts it, *purusha* differs from *prakriti* thus: "From the contrast with that [*prakriti*], there follows, the *purusha* the character of being a witness, freedom, neutrality, percipience, and non agency."

Prakriti: *Prakriti* is matter. It is the basis of objectivity. The world of objects is a consummate evolution of *prakriti*. Whereas the objects are limited in space and time, the *prakriti* itself is ubiquitous and all-pervading. It is the ground condition of all physical manifestations in the universe. Three fundamental characteristics (*gunas*) are inherent in the *prakriti*. They are *sattva* (essence/information content), *rajas* (energy), and *tamas* (mass/inertia). *Prakriti* in its primordial condition is the state in which the three *gunas* are in perfect equilibrium. The equilibrium is created by equal mutual opposition between them. Vyasa, who wrote the commentary on Patanjali's *Yoga Sutras*, describes such a state as "that which never is nor is not, that which exists and does not exist, that in which there is no nonexistence, the unmanifested, without any specific mark, the central background of all" (quoted from Radhakrishnan, 1923/1989, Vol. 2. Pp. 260–261).

Like *purusha*, *prakriti* as such cannot be perceived. It may be inferred from the manifest universe and can be understood rationally. It can be known directly, however, by the practice of yoga. According to *Samkhya*, *prakriti* is the first cause of the material universe. It is the uncaused cause of the evolved phenomena. The characteristics of *prakriti* may be understood by contrasting it with those of the evolved. As the *Samkhyakarika* (10) puts it, "The evolved is caused, noneternal, non-pervasive, mobile, manifold, dependent, emergent, conjunct, and heteronomous; the unevolved [*prakriti*] is the reverse [of all these]." Whereas *purusha* is never an object of cognition and is changeless *prakriti* undergoes change as it unfolds in the process of evolution and manifests objects of cognition.

Prakriti in its primordial state of perfect equilibrium is the ground condition of the universe. The world of objects, including the living, has evolved in different stages as the equilibrium between the *gunas* is disturbed and the *gunas* recombine in various proportions. The evolution of the manifold

is the varied mix of the essence, energy, and mass contained in the *prakriti*. It is a process where the incoherent, the indeterminate, and the undifferentiated *prakriti* manifests a coherent, determinate, and differentiated form. The order of evolution is not one of combining parts into a whole or splitting the whole into parts, but of a progression from less differentiated to a more differentiated state, from a less coherent to a more coherent condition, and from a less determinate to a more determinate whole. Evolution is the actualization of the potential; it brings about increasing differentiation within the evolving whole (Dasgupta, 1922/1988).

According to Samkhya, the first to evolve out of the *prakriti* is the *mahat* (the great one), from which the rest of the world manifests. The *mahat* is characterized by *sattva* preponderance. It may therefore be regarded as the quintessence of all things. It is the collective mind (*buddhitattva*); a concatenation of all minds (*buddhis*).

Once the *mahat* is formed, the process of its further differentiation proceeds by the interplay of the *gunas* along two lines of evolution—the *sattva*-dominant and the *tamas*-dominant lines. Both these are driven by the energy of *rajas*. The *tamas* line (*bhutadi*), helped by *rajas*, generates *tanmatras,* which are the bases of all physical manifestations. Whereas the *bhutadi* is homogeneous, inert, and characterless mass, the *tanmatras* possess physical character and the potentials for being perceived as sound, touch, color, taste, and smell. At this stage they represent subtle matter, and further differentiation generates gross matter, the atoms and their aggregates. "It is thus," as Dasgupta points out, "that the course of evolution which started in the *prakriti* reaches its furtherest limit in the production of the senses on the one side and the atoms on the other" (1988, Vol. 1, p. 253). Inasmuch as they share the same source in the *mahat*, these parallel developments manifest relationships between themselves.

In the process of evolution we have after the *mahat* and along the *sattvic* line, the minds with their triple functional aspects, *buddhi*, *ahamkara* and *manas*. The mind is termed in Samkhya *antahkarana* and *citta* in Yoga. After the mind, the next to evolve are the ten *indriyas* or senses, five for acquiring knowledge and five causing action. Following the *indriyas* are the five *tanmatras*, which are the essence of sound, touch, form, taste, and odor. The last five forms into which the *prakriti* unfolds itself are the five *mahabhutas*. They are ether (sound carrier) air, fire, water, and earth.

Thus *purusha* and *prakriti* are the two ultimate principles that together constitute the manifest world. They are in a sense the "soul and substance" of the universe (Bernard, 1947), the subjective and the objective in our being. In the manifest world, the original polarity of *purusha* and *prakriti* appear as consciousness and unconsciousness and as knowing subject and known object. They are the foundational principles and ground conditions for consciousness and subjectivity on the one hand and manifest objects and events on the other. The empirical world and the experience we have of it are made possible by their union at various levels. Neither of them, in this view, is sufficient to explain the universe and our place in it.

Psychological Assumptions

As mentioned, consciousness (*purusha*) is primary and it is in principle irreducible to any form or manifestation of matter (*prakriti*). It is self-manifesting and self-luminous (*svatah prakash*). Consciousness-as-such has no content and consequently is not an object of cognition. It is non-rational and yet foundational for all awareness and knowledge. Consciousness, which is differ-

ent from the mind, has two fundamental aspects. It manifests in two basic forms, (1) transcendental and (2) phenomenal. In its transcendental aspect consciousness is apprehended in immediate intuition where there is no distinction between subject and object. In its phenomenal form it manifests in the cognitions where there is a differentiation between the cognizing subject (*grahi*), the object of cognition (*grahya*) and the process of cognition (*grahana*). When the *purusha* gets entangled with *prakriti*, i.e., when there is an association between consciousness and *buddhi*, which is an evolute of *prakriti*, conscious mind is formed. When this happens the *buddhi*, which is by its nature unconscious, becomes conscious. Deriving its illumination from its proximity to *purusha* it manifests awareness and subjectivity. The *purusha*, however, by this entanglement loses its freedom and innate purity and perfection. By mistaking the cognitions of *buddhi* as its own the *purusha* tends to bind itself to *buddhi* and thus develops a sense of false identity with it. Thus lost in the mirage of the mind, according to Samkhya-Yoga, the quest of the entrapped *purusha* is to gain release from the shackles and the bondage brought about by its association with *buddhi*. The Yoga system attempts to explain this bondage and lays down a progressive scheme of self-realization of the *purusha*. When the *purusha* gets its release and gains freedom from the barricade of matter and the confinement of the senses, it regains its self-illumination in a state of splendid isolation (*kaivalya*). *Kaivalya* is the goal and yoga practice is a means to achieve it. Thus Yoga is both a theory of our psychological bondage and a method to escape from that bondage.

THE CONSCIOUS MIND

Consciousness as such is inert and formless. *Buddhi* and other evolutes of *prakriti* have energy and substantiality but no consciousness. Conscious mind arises with the association of the *purusha* and *buddhi*. The association does not involve genuine interaction between the two but only a relation that provides for a reflection of the *purusha* in *buddhi*. Such a reflection is made possible by the *sattva* component of *buddhi*, which resembles the *purusha*. *Sattva* aspect of matter has peculiar affinity with the *purusha* in that it is capable of reflecting consciousness, unlike *tamas*, which obstructs it. *Buddhi* is always translucent and becomes transparent in association with the *purusha*. The reflection of the *purusha* renders the *buddhi* conscious. When the *buddhi* becomes conscious, that consciousness in turn is superimposed upon the *purusha*, who gets the notion of an experiencing person by mistaking the modifications of *buddhi* as its own. Thus, it is the conjunction of the *purusha* and *buddhi* that gives us self-consciousness and the subjective experience we have of the world.

The term for the functional mind in Yoga is *citta*. The *citta* is comprised of not only the cognitive processes, the ego and the senses, but it also contains instinctual tendencies inherited from previous lives and the effects of past actions (*vasanas* and *samskaras*). The *samskaras* and *vasanas* tend to color our cognitions and predispose us to behave in certain ways. The *citta* manifests also volitional activity, which enables it to attend to some objects and not to others. In addition, the *citta* has latent power (*shakti*), which can be used to guide and control the course it would take. The *shakti* enables the *citta* to "reflect and react back upon itself and change the passivity of its transformations into active states associated with will and effort" (Dasgupta, 1930, pp. 286–287). The *citta* is thus the seat of one's cognition, volition, feelings and actions.

Three levels in the functioning of the *citta* are distinguished—*buddhi*, *ahamkara* (ego, the empirical self), and *manas*. The *manas* is the central processor, which selec-

tively reflects on the material provided by the senses and determines its character by assimilation and discrimination. The *ahamkara* appropriates what is provided by the *manas* as one's own and considers the object of perception in reference to the perceiving person. The *buddhi* then reacts to the information provided in an appropriate manner. The functions, or processes, of the *citta* are described by Vachaspatimisra thus: "Every one who deals with an object first intuits it, then reflects upon it, then appropriates it, then resolves 'this is to be done by me,' and then proceeds to act" (quoted from Sinha, 1958, Vol. 1, p. 121). It should be kept in mind that Yoga does not regard *buddhi*, *ahamkara*, and *manas* as distinct faculties. They are simply the functional aspects of the *citta*. These three functions of the *citta* are collectively referred to as the internal organ (*antahkarana*), distinct from the senses regarded as external organs. As stated in the *Samkhyakarika* (35), the senses are gateways to knowledge and the *citta* functions as the gatekeeper.

Mind is thus the instrument that interfaces the conscious *purusha* with the unconscious objects. The mind is similar as well as different from the *purusha*. It is different in the first place because unlike the *purusha* it undergoes fluctuations and modifications. Second, the mind has no set goals; it subserves and realizes the goals of the *purusha*. The mind exists for the *purusha*. Third, the mind partakes in the world of objects, taking their forms, whereas the *purusha* is always a witness and does not interact with the objects. The mistaken identity of the mind with the *purusha* may be seen in the reflections of the *purusha* in *buddhi* and the false apprehension of the states of *buddhi* as its own. According to Vacaspathimisra (1969), the *purusha* is reflected on *buddhi* to make the latter conscious. However, another Samkhya thinker Vijnanabhiksu (1909) suggests that the reflections on *buddhi* reflect back on the *purusha*. Such mutual reflection is the reason why the *purusha* mistakes the experiences of the *buddhi* as its own.

COGNITION

Cognition arises from the relation of mind, with its three-fold functions, to the object. The object manifests in the mind as a transformation of *buddhi*. The transformed *buddhi* by itself is nonconscious. Consciousness is bestowed by the *purusha's* illumination that makes *buddhi* transparent and the cognition conscious.

Thus cognition is literally reflective awareness, a reflection of *purusha* on the surface of *buddhi*. For example, in perception, when an external object registers on a peripheral sense organ (*bahyendriya*) there is a sensorial transformation of the object. The *manas* attends to these transformations and processes them by assimilation and discrimination. Then they are presented to *ahamkara* (the ego function) which appropriates them so that the sensory transformations are related to the subject. These are then carried to *buddhi*, making buddhi assume the form of the object and then react to the object of cognition in an appropriate manner. *Buddhi*, however, is not conscious by itself. It becomes conscious by its association with the *purusha*. When the light of the *purusha* shines on *buddhi*, which now has the form of the object, it reflects the object so that there is not only conscious awareness of the object, but also that awareness takes a subjective form because of the influence of *ahamkara*. The cognition therefore is a transformation (*vritti*) of *buddhi*. The *purusha* itself is not affected by this just as the sun is not affected by its image in the lake. The role of *purusha* is like that of the sun in virtue of which there is light on the moon.

If the light of the *purusha* is not reflected on *buddhi*, the cognition of the object, the *buddhi* transformation of it, remains unconscious. Thus Samkhya-Yoga

provide for unconscious cognitive states. Nontransparent *vrittis* are the unconscious states of the mind. Their existence in the mind are due to its *tamas* component. *Manas*, *ahamkara* and *buddhi* are regarded as the three internal organs. They are superior to the external senses, which are considered subordinate organs. Among the internal organs *buddhi* is the principal organ. The superiority of one organ over another is related to their functions. *Buddhi* is considered to be the chief instrument in one's cognitive activity because (1) it alone has direct access to *purusha* and is capable of becoming conscious in virtue of its predominant *sattvic* disposition to reflect the *purusha*. (2) *Buddhi* is the final point in the knowledge process. (3) It is the storehouse of latent subconscious impressions and tendencies (*samskaras* and *vasanas*) that color our cognitions and dispositions to act. (4) Finally, recollection is the function of *buddhi* (Sinha 1958). Such is the importance of *buddhi* in the functioning of the mind (*citta*) that we find Patanjali using the words *citta* and *buddhi* interchangeably in several places in his *Yoga Sutras*.

In perception, it is said, the mind goes out to the proximate objects through the senses and assumes their form. When the *purusha* is reflected in the mind that acquired the form of an object, we have an awareness of it. As this reflection is reflected back into the *purusha*, the *purusha* has the experience of perceiving the object. What does it mean to say that the mind goes out to the object? It makes little sense to assume that the mind leaves the body to make contact with the object, especially when we consider the mind to be a set of processes and functions rather than a substance. "Going out" function of the mind appears to be no more than the assertion of the freedom of the subject to choose her own objects of perception. Unlike objects with no functioning minds, which have no choice in their relationship to other objects, subjects with minds have a choice to enter into or withdraw from a relationship with an object. The notion that the mind takes the form of the objects through the mediation of the senses can only mean that in the mind we have a sensorial transformation of the objects. The transformation itself is a physical process, and the resultant form is also material, albeit subtle.

It should be mentioned here that the mind, though physical, is assumed to be nonlocal. Unlike the gross material objects, the mind (*buddhi*) is subtle and therefore is capable of reflecting the light of the *purusha*. Time and space are categories created by the mind to organize and understand sensory information. *Buddhi* itself exists beyond the constraints of space and time. The reason why *buddhi* is not in touch with or affected by all the worldly objects is that the mind has a layer of *tamas*, which acting as an opaque screen covers and conceals the objects from it. It is through the instrumentality of the external organs, which make the sensory contact with the object, that the mind overcomes the obstruction of *tamas* and finds an opening to the object. In purified minds where *tamas* is "dwindled away" the object shines forth without sensory mediation.

STATES OF THE MIND

The conscious mind is a stage of perpetually changing and shifting scenes called *vrittis*. *Vrittis* are fluctuating states of the mind that are cognitively, affectively and volitionally loaded. *Vritti* is a very important concept in Indian psychology. The classification of *vrittis*, the way they arise and influence one's behavior, the methods of channeling and controlling them are believed to be of great significance in understanding the nature and destiny of human condition. Indeed the very practice of yoga has the sublime purpose of controlling *citta vrittis*, the fluctuating states of the mind,

because they are considered to be inimical for attaining the goal of *kaivalya*, which is the true state of *purusha* in its splendid isolation. *Kaivalya* is a state of pure consciousness, free and unencumbered by the manifestations of *prakriti*, which normally cloud consciousness as it is reflected on the *buddhi*. The *citta vrittis* (fluctuating states of the mind) are many and varied. Yoga classifies them under five heads. The first category comprises of true cognitions arising from valid sources of knowledge (*pramanas*). According to Yoga there are three such sources—(i) perception, (ii) inference and (iii) verbal testimony. The second category consists of false cognition (*viparyaya*). *Viparyaya* includes also doubts and uncertain cognitions. The third is *vikalpa*, which refers to just an idea that has no corresponding material object. *Vikalpa* is, however, not false knowledge. Sleep (*nidra*) is considered to be a category of *vritti* in Yoga system. Finally, memory (*smriti*) is believed to represent a separate category of mental states. Memory involves storage and retrieval. *Samskaras* are stored impressions of *vrittis* in *citta* for later recall. Thus *vrittis* comprise of true cognitions, either perceptual, inferential or testimonial that include revelational intuitions, false cognitions including doubtful and uncertain cognitions, mental states occurring in sleep and reminiscence. If the mind is a sea, the *vrittis* are its waves. The disturbed minds are like turbulent seas and the goal of human endeavor for self-realization is one of stilling the mind by controlling its fluctuations (*vrittis*).

Basically, there are five sources of hindrance (*klesa*) that stand in the way of controlling the fluctuations of the mind. They are *avidya, asmita, raga, dvesha,* and *abhinivesa* (*Yoga Sutras* II.3). *Avidya* is the inability to discriminate between good and evil, pleasant and unpleasant, truth and falsehood, the permanent and the impermanent and the pure and impure. *Avidya* does not denote lack of knowledge. Rather it refers to a condition, the soil that nourishes all other kinds of hindrances. *Asmita* is personal identity, the I-ness generated by the wrongful identification of the *purusha* with *buddhi*. It is the self-sense that distinguishes one from others. *Raga* is passion for pleasure. It is the thirst, greed and craving for enjoyment. *Avidya* generates a sense of personal identity (*asmita*) and *asmita* underscores passion (*raga*). *Dvesha* is the opposite of *raga*. It is hatred of and aversion to anything considered painful. *Abinivesa* is indicated by the will to live and the instinctive fear of death.

Afflicted by the five kinds of hindrances and the ever-present *vrittis*, the mental field (*citta-bhumi*) manifests five levels of activity and attention. First is the fluctuating level (*ksipta*) where attention wanders. The second is the level of inactivity or forgetfulness (*mudha*) as in drowsiness and sleep. It is a state of inattentiveness. In the third, the mind becomes occasionally steady (*viksipta*) and gets temporarily absorbed in the objects of its attention. At the fourth level, the mind achieves one-pointed concentration (*ekagrata*) and gets absorbed fully and unwaveringly in the object of attention to the complete exclusion of others. In the final level of *niruddha*, all mental functions are completely restrained so that one experiences consciousness-as-such, unmediated by any mental functions.

Niruddha is the level one hopes to reach through practice of yoga. When this happens, after passing through several states of *samadhi* (complete absorption), the practitioner (yogin) overcomes hindrances and gains control over the *citta vrittis*. As a consequence, one's consciousness gets progressively detached from the *buddhi* and advances toward self-realization, i.e., a state of consciousness-as-such, pure, free and self-luminous and devoid of all material vestments.

Closely linked to the concept of *vritti* is *samskara*. J. H. Woods translates *samskara*

as "subliminal impression." There is some kind of reciprocal relation between *vrittis* and *samskaras*. *Vrittis* give rise to *samskaras* and the latter in turn generate *vrittis*. The major difference between the two is that the *vrittis* are in awareness, whereas *samskaras* are latent preconscious or unconscious states. Both are affected by the hindrances of the five *klesas*. Like *vrittis*, *samskaras* are not homogeneous. There are several grades and shades of them. Some *samskaras* are helpful and have positive influence toward self-realization and some are negative and harmful.

Samskaras are of three kinds—those generated by (1) cognition and knowledge (*jnanaja*), (2) by emotion (*klesaja*) and by volition and action (*karmaja*). The cognitive kind (*jnana samskaras*) is associated with cognitive fluctuations of the mind (*vrittis*). Every *vritti* leaves an impression on the *buddhi* in the form of a *samskara*. It is in virtue of such *samskaras* that we have memory (*smriti*). As Vachaspatimisra says in his commentary on *Yoga Sutras* (I. 11) memory is recall of a subliminal impression cast in *buddhi* with no modifications or alteration. *Klesas* (the five hindrances) give rise to *samskaras* associated with emotion. Volitional activity also generates its own kind of *samskaras*. Inasmuch as *samskaras* are imprinted on *buddhi*, the mental states one experiences have their source not only in the sensorial transformations of the material objects, but also in the subliminal deposits of *samskaras*. The latter may manifest by themselves as *vrittis* or they may color, distort or modify the *vrittis* generated by the sensory contact with objects and events. Thus one's cognitions are colored, biased, or even distorted by the *samskaras* imprinted in *buddhi*.

Samskara and *vasana* are similar concepts. Sometimes they are used interchangeably. However, as N. C. Panda (1996) points out, there is a subtle but significant difference between the two. *Samskara* is a broader concept and includes *vasana*, but all *samskaras* are not *vasanas*. For example, *samskaras* associated with memory (*smriti*) are not considered *vasanas*. *Samskaras* engendered by the five *klesas* are *vasanas* inasmuch as they act as seeds that will sprout in due course in our thought, passion and action. In a sense, they are latent dispositions and propensities and motivating influences on one's conduct. Like the hindrances (*klesas*), our actions also generate *vasanas*. The latter are called *karma vasanas* as distinguished from *klesa vasanas*. *Vasanas* are believed to be the force behind our worldly urges, sensuous passions, desires, and cravings. I am inclined to regard *samskaras* as sources of unconscious mentation, unlike *vrittis*, which refer to conscious mentation. They, however, influence *vrittis*. *Vasanas* appear to refer to deeper and more potent layers of the unconscious.

In Indian thought, one's actions good or bad deposit *karma*. Good actions produce meritorious *karma* and bad actions deposit *black karma*. Both white (meritorious) and black (demerit) *karma* cause *vasanas*. There are, however, actions that produce *karma* that is neither white nor black such as the activities of an accomplished yogin in whom the *klesas* have dwindled away. Such actions leave no *vasanas* behind. The accumulated *karma* lays dormant in the *citta* like a seed in the ground to sprout at an appropriate time. When *karma* thus leads to action, that action in turn produces *karma* again and this cycle continues indefinitely unless broken by effort toward self-realization. The seeds of *karma* can be burned and made impotent to propagate. The *samskaras* and *vasanas* the vehicles by which *karma* acts, are rooted in *klesas* (hindrances). When the *klesa* roots are cut there would be no more accumulation of *karma* and as the past *karma* plays out the individual comes progressively closer to self-realization. Thus by controlling *samskaras* that are generated by the five hindrances (*klesaja*) and consequent

actions (*kriyaja*), the cycle of *karma* may be broken for good. This is something that can be achieved, according to Yoga, by a yogin who enters states of *samadhi* by practicing contemplative meditation. Psychological implications of the possibility to burn dormant *karma* and render harmful *samskaras* impotent are indeed profound. Yoga psychology recognizes the lasting influence of unconscious mentation in the form of *samskaras* and *vasanas*, emphasizes the need to gain control of them and suggests methods to achieve such control. Whether or not one agrees with the postulated goal of self-realization and of achieving a state of consciousness-as-such, the methods suggested for controlling the influence of unconscious mental activity and the hidden motives might have beneficial application in psychotherapy.

It should be mentioned at this point that the Yoga system upholds the doctrine of reincarnation and subscribes to the notion of the cycle of birth and death. The cycle is perpetuated by the accumulated *karma* and *samskaras*. The mind, the *buddhi*, on which the *samskaras* are imprinted, survives bodily death. Mind, as the subtlest form of matter does not perish at death. The *karma* that is deposited in it causes it to take another life so that it can play itself out. *Jiva*, the functioning human being, is the embodied mind, which in the proximity of the *purusha* has access to conscious awareness. The embodied mind is a composite of subtle and gross matter, the mind being the subtle part. With bodily death the gross body disintegrates. However, the mind, subtle body, with its accumulations of *karma* and *samskaras*, survives to be born again with another gross body conceived by sexual union of a man and a woman. The cycle of birth and death continues until the existential accretions of the mind (*karma* deposits) are completely obliterated by good conduct, yoga practice (*prasankhyana*) and discriminative knowledge (*viveka jnana*).

Consciousness and Levels of Awareness

As we observed in our discussions of consciousness in the Western tradition, there is an unmistakable tendency in the West to equate consciousness and mind. If a distinction between them is ever made it is to restrict consciousness to certain aspects of the mind and to provide for unconscious mental states. In other words, mind is considered a broader concept than consciousness. All conscious states are mental states, but all mental states are not conscious states. As we noted, in Yoga, there is a clear and basic distinction between consciousness and mind. In a sense, it is a qualitative distinction that is as sharp as the distinction between mind and body in the West. Yoga, as mentioned, subscribes to a dualistic metaphysics, but the two basic substances or principles are not mind and matter, but consciousness and matter. In fact mind, we may recall, is regarded as a form of matter.

Consciousness itself is located in multiple centers called the *purushas*. Consciousness is not an attribute of the *purusha*. Rather it is the essence of *purusha*. The dualism of Yoga does not espouse any interaction between consciousness and physical mind as in certain forms of dualism. Nor does it subscribe to the notion of psychophysical parallelism. The relation between consciousness and embodied mind is one of *reflection*. The consciousness (*purusha*) is reflected on *buddhi*, the principal aspect of the mind. Consciousness of the reflecting mind is not identical with *purusha* consciousness, which is consciousness-as-such. It is only an image, a reflection. As an image it is subject to imperfections and distortions, which can be minimized and even eliminated by removing the blemishes and cleaning up the mental field so as to reflect a perfect image and thus obtain true knowledge. Samkhya and Yoga thus avoid in their dualist postulation both psychophysical parallelism and interactionism. This is made possible by a special conception of mind in general and of *buddhi* in particular as an interfacing instrumentality between gross matter and conscious *purusha*. The *purusha* whose essence is insight appears to be more like microcosmic intelligence capable of causing awareness of all conceivable things, by its very presence. It is the source of all awareness. In a significant sense we are led to think that no knowledge is possible without its illuminating insight. At the same time we recognize that in human condition, mind is the instrument of knowing. So we have on the one hand the *purusha*, which is the source of all knowledge in the form of illuminating insight, and on the other hand the mind which has the limited scope of giving us knowledge of the things with which it comes into contact.

Mind serves as a knowledge instrument because of its facility to reflect the *purusha* due to its predominant *sattva* character. *Sattva*, the subtlest and lightest component of *prakriti* (matter), constitutes the very essence of the material object comprising it. To put it somewhat differently, *sattva* is the information component of matter. As mentioned, *sattva* is considered in Samkhya-Yoga an integral constituent of matter containing its very essence (information). It is in the nature of *sattva* to reflect the *purusha* so that the information becomes manifest in awareness. In so reflecting the *purusha*, *sattva* reveals its own essence. From this we may surmise that in principle all objects, in so far as they have a *sattva* component, albeit in various degrees, can reflect the *purusha* in various degrees and thus become conscious at various levels. However, in reality only the mind is seen as capable of reflecting the *purusha* because the *sattva* content in the rest of the material objects does not rise above the threshold level necessary to register the reflections of the *purusha*. In other words, material objects other than minds are not translucent enough to have the light of the *purusha* pass through them and become transparent. The *tamas* component of matter is responsible for the obstruction. If, then, the information content of material objects other than the minds is masked by a preponderance of *tamas*, the question arises as to how one can ever have knowledge of them because on their own they cannot reflect the *purusha* and thus manifest their essence (information). In other words, how do we have information (awareness) about material objects? It would seem that in this view material objects unable to reflect the *purusha* by themselves might do so with help from the mind. In association with a mind, a gross material object may manifest its information content. The sensory apparatus that the mind makes use of in its information processing endeavor distills the *sattva* component of the object of its contact. The destilled form is processed by the *manas*, which in turn collects the information and conveys it to *buddhi* via *ahamkara*. Then *buddhi* is transformed to take on the form of the object. When the *purusha* shines on *buddhi*, there is awareness of the object. In Yoga psychology, this appears to be the normal perceptual process by which we become aware of external objects.

Perceptual awareness brought about by sensory transformation in *buddhi* is different in kind from *purusha* consciousness. First of all, perceptual awareness is imperfect because of the blemishes inherent in the very processing. Again, such awareness is contingent on the sensory contact, which limits the range, scope and form of awareness. *Purusha* consciousness, however, is not subject to such limitations. It is unblemished insight. It is *it*, consciousness-as-such in and of itself. Thus in this view we have two kinds of awareness—intuitive insight and sense mediated awareness. Intuitive insight is awareness caused by a direct reflection of *purusha* in *buddhi*, the latter faithfully reflecting the *purusha* without any modifica-

tions arising from the influence of *samskaras*. Sensory awareness is awareness caused by the *purusha*'s reflection on *buddhi* which is modified by the sensory contact.

Conscious experience mediated by the mind via its *vrittis* is phenomenal awareness. Phenomenal awareness involves three distinguishable aspects: (a) the subject, the one who has the awareness (*grahi*), a product of *ahamkara* (b) the process of awareness (*grahana*), the activity of the *manas* and (c) the object of awareness (*grahya*). All three determine the nature and context of awareness. For example, the sensory processes have their own imprint on what is known. Similarly, our predisposition, the biases and prejudices (*samskaras*) color cognitions and influence our actions. Consequently phenomenal awareness is at best a *representation* of reality subject to all kinds of limitations and distortions. Therefore, it cannot be a true experience of reality-as-such.

Experience of pure consciousness unmediated by any mental modes is transcendental awareness. Such awareness is considered supreme because it is believed to be completely unbiased. Knowledge mediated by mental functions is imperfect because the mind by its very nature has a distorting and biasing influence. Therefore, it is believed that perfect knowledge can be obtained only in an experience of pure consciousness, which is facilitated by voluntary restraining of all mental functions through appropriate discipline. This can be achieved by practicing yoga, which leads to *samadhi*, a state in which the knower merges with known by restraining the functions of the mind that cause these distinctions and distortions. By progressing through a series of *samadhi* states, one experiences pure consciousness.

Samadhi is a state of complete absorption, a state in which the natural wanderings of the mind are controlled. When one's mind by means of concentration and meditation on an object gets absorbed in it and experiences identity with it, one is said to attain a state of *samadhi*. Until the mind reaches a state of steady one-pointed concentration that results in unwavering absorption in the object of attention, the subject-object duality persists. Once such absorption is achieved, the duality of the subject and the object disappears. Knowledge obtained in states of *samadhi* is considered superior because it involves severe restraints on the mental functions that ordinarily bias our knowledge.

Two kinds of *samadhi* are distinguished: *samprajnata samadhi* and *asamprajnata samadhi*. In *samprajnata samadhi*, the *vrittis*, the mental events, are not completely annihilated. Even though the subject-object duality is transcended and the subject-object identity is experienced, consciousness in this state is not objectless. In other words, it continues to have content, albeit greatly transformed. In *asamprajnata samadhi*, one has the experience of pure consciousness. It is a state of consciousness without content. Such objectless experience is the highest state. It is a state of perfection, liberated from all existential constraints.

Other Yoga writers made further distinctions. Vacaspatimisra, for example, divides *samprajnata samadhi* into eight categories. He groups them into three classes: (1) *grahya-samadhi* in which the focus of concentration is an external object, (2) *grahana-samadhi*, where the focus is the sensory system, and (3) *grahitri-samadhi* which involves concentration on the ego or empirical self. These states of *samprajnata samadhi* seem to refer to states of consciousness obtained by a sustained one-pointed concentration on the different aspects of the knowledge process—the knower, the known (the objects of knowledge), and the process of knowing. It is believed that in different states of *samprajnata samadhi* one obtains paranormal experiences such as clairvoyance, telepathy, and precognition. A variety of such psychic experiences, it is said, are achieved as a result of concentration on

different objects. As Sinha (1958) points out, no reason is given why and how concentration on a particular object or process gives rise to a particular paranormal power or psychic experience. These are recorded simply as facts of actual experience without any explanation. These include among others clairvoyance, telepathy, and foreknowledge of past and future events.

Awareness is thus of two sorts, transcendental and phenomenal. Transcendental awareness ensues from directly accessing consciousness-as-such, which in the language of Samkhya-Yoga is realization of *purushahood*. Phenomenal awareness consists in accessing the information content, the *sattva* component of the material objects, through the mediation of the "knowledge" apparatus of the embodied mind. The *purusha* is consciousness-*as-such* which in the human condition is masked by the manifestations of the mind (*vrittis*). The human mind is the center of phenomenal awareness. At the same time, it is also associated with the *purusha* whose proximity bestows consciousness on the nonconscious contents of the mind. The embodied mind thus enjoys dual citizenship as it were in the domains of the physical world (*prakriti*) as well as in the world of consciousness (*purusha*). It has the facility to access information from material objects and the potential to partake in consciousness-as-such. The mind's dual engagement with *prakriti* and *purusha* makes it a seat of a variety of awareness states between the sensory and the transcendental. These include (1) nonconscious states, (2) unconscious states, (3) normal phenomenal states, (4) altered phenomenal states, (5) refined phenomenal states, (6) transcendental states translated into or leading to phenomenal states, (7) anomalous mental states, and (8) transcendental states-as-such.

Non-conscious states are those information states the mind is simply unaware at all its levels, those that are devoid of *purusha* reflections. This may be so because the *sattva* or information content in them does not reach the threshold level to bask in the reflections of the *purusha* or because of the utter dominance of *tamas* that veils the information. The unconscious states are those, which were once conscious but now relegated to the region of the mind that, is shielded from the light of the *purusha* such as *samskaras* and *vasanas* but capable of influencing the mind without being noticed. The phenomenal states are what are generally regarded as conscious states. The light of the *purusha* shines on them with the result that their information content is *revealed* as subjective knowledge. Phenomenal knowledge is an image of consciousness but not consciousness-as-such. The image is set in an ever-flowing flux, which is subject to all kinds off distortions and alterations. Consequently, there is no finality to phenomenal awareness and no absolute phenomenal truth. Inasmuch as phenomenal states are mediated by several mechanisms of the mind (the knowledge apparatus, *antahkarana*) any changes in the structure and functions of these mechanisms would have a corresponding effect on the processed image, i.e., the information accessed. The so-called altered states of consciousness are the sufficiently marked and distinguishable categories of alteration such as, for example, alterations that occur in dream states and states induced by hypnosis, drugs and other manipulations.

The phenomenal states mentioned so far are images of reality. These images, because of the way they are processed, are subject to a variety of distortions. Such distortions can be overcome and the images may be rendered as faithful reproductions of the original in the sensory form by controlling the biasing influences at the level of the subject and the process of cognition. The method for accomplishing this consists in entering a state of *samadhi*. The state of *samprajnata samadhi* appears to be one in which cognitions are refined to be free from distortions. Samadhi gives clarity of insight. The three kinds of *samprajnata samadhi* described by Vacaspatimisra essentially refer to the three sources of distortion. The state of *asamprajnata samadhi* is of course different. It is a state of accessing consciousness as such; a state in which consciousness does not take any sensory form. Consciousness-as-such is reality itself.

In transcendental states the reality is by assumption revealed in and of itself. The *purusha* detached completely from the mind in its sublime state of splendid isolation (*kaivalya*) is of course a state of supreme transcendence. How could such a state exist, however, in the human condition of the embodied mind? The answer, it seems to me, may be found in the inherent reflexivity of consciousness. Consciousness which is the essence of reality, in the same sense the *sattva* component of material objects is their essence, reveals itself to the mind when the mind is in a *niruddha* state and is completely devoid of any content that could become transparent in the light of *purusha*. In such a situation consciousness instead of reflecting the contents of the mind reflects itself in the mind. The mind thus partakes in consciousness-as-such and experiences transcendental states. These are the states that highly evolved yogins are believed capable of achieving. On this model, the mystic experiences transient states of transcendence in which consciousness-as-such is realized. Such a momentary realization may leave an indelible mark and manifest subsequently in the form of profound changes in the life-style, attitudes and personality of the individual experiencing such states. Inasmuch as the mystical experience occurs when the normal mental functions are in abeyance, it is not available to rational understanding and verbal descriptions. It is ineffable in this sense. Though ineffable, it is also infallible because it is consciousness-as-such. The mystic, therefore, struggles to translate his experience into common language for making sense to communicate to others. That is why the mystical utterances are often metaphorical and seldom convincingly empirical. What a mystic may not be able to communicate in words he attempts to do so in his actions. Thus nonrational forms of belief are formed. In attempting to express the ineffable experience in phenomenal terms, the mystic risks compromising infallibility for intelligibility.

Expanding the Samkhya-Yoga epistemology further, one could argue that the source of intuitive knowledge is a state of transcendence, an experience with consciousness-as-such. The mystic reveals his wisdom in his actions like a leader who shows his thought in action and translates his experience in the form of metaphorical descriptions as poets do. A scientist who intuitively encounters a scientific truth is led to trace back stepwise from the generality of the intuitively grasped truth to the specific events contingent on it. Thus in science one may go from fact to fact to weave a theory or begin with an intuitive hunch and gather relevant facts to make sense of the hunch and thus come to a discovery of a law or a relation. The former espouses the phenomenal or intellectual tradition where as the latter is in line with the transcendental approach. Inasmuch as the image of reality is inlaid in the *sattva* component of the physical universe, the human mind with its knowledge apparatus has access to that image. It is the image we can share. It is reality in the third-person. However, the transcendental transactions the mind is capable of give it the intuitions and the first-person experience of reality.

Anomalous states (A-states) of awareness stand in between transcendental and phenomenal states. They are called anomalous precisely because they do not fit into either of the two categories. They are different from phenomenal states (P-states) in that they appear to transcend sensory-

motor and space-time constraints that bind phenomenal awareness. In this aspect they are more like the transcendental states (T-states). Anomalous states are, however, different from T-states because they are intentional and carry information like the P-states. A-states are mental *qua* mental states. The mind (*citta*), as we noted in Yoga psychology, is different from consciousness, and it is physical, albeit subtle. The subtlety confers on it nonlocality in virtue of which it can relate with other minds and objects outside of it. By relating to other minds, it can acquire telepathic information. By relating to the *sattva* component of objects the minds may obtain clairvoyant information about them. The notion of the nonlocality of minds may also be seen in the concept of *mahat*, the collective mind that indeed is the first evolute of *prakriti* and therefore has nexus to all minds and all objects in existence. The *sattva* component of material objects, whether of subtle thoughts or gross objects, is the link that makes a connection between minds and objects possible.

As noted in our earlier discussions in Part I, anomalous awareness seems to involve two stages. In Stage I anomalous information is received at the unconscious level. It is extrasensory in that the A-states are not processed by the sensory-motor apparatus. For that reason, on the one hand, they lack some phenomenal properties and, on the other hand, they are not subject to some of the phenomenal constraints. Stage I anomalous states may make use of similar psychodynamic processes that are known to be involved in bringing unconscious states into overt behavior and awareness. This is the Stage II of the psi or anomalous process.

On this model anomalous awareness is different in kind from mystical awareness which involves a glimpse of the transcendental, i.e., consciousness-as-such. It is intentional and conveys information about objects and events. Anomalous awareness is phenomenal awareness without some of the limitations of the latter. It is not sensory, but may affect sensory experience and may even be carried into the phenomenal field by means of what G.N.M. Tyrrell called mediating vehicles, such as dreams, hallucinations and intuitive hunches. Anomalous awareness is not infallible even if it transcends some phenomenal limitations. Even though they are different from T-states, A-states bear some resemblance to them. Both of them are undermined by phenomenal states linked to sensory experience. The restriction and control of sensory noise appears to be conducive to the manifestation of anomalous states. The A-states are, however, considered an impediment for realizing *purushahood* (transcendence) or self-realization. Like the phenomenal states they are to be avoided if the goal is transcendence because they stand in the way of realizing that state of splendid isolation (*kaivalya*), consciousness-as-such.

Yoga Practice

What is interesting in yoga is that it is not merely a theory of mind, but also a practical discipline that claims to provide empirical support for its ideas. Patanjali tells us in *Yoga-Sutras* how the mind can be restrained to achieve a quiescent state, how the natural modifications and fluctuations (*vrittis*) of the mind are restricted and how a variety of *siddhis* (anomalous phenomena) may be obtained by the practice of yoga. According to Patanjali, fluctuations of the mind (*citta vrittis*) may be controlled by practice and by detachment in thought and action. Paranormal abilities are acquired by practicing *samyama* that leads through states of concentration, meditation and absorption. *Kaivalya* is achieved by the total eradication (*nirodha*) of the mental states. *Yoga-Sutras* narrates different hurdles in the

human condition that afflict and hinder the practice of yoga and the means of overcoming them.

Patanjali prescribes an eightfold path for reaching the highest state of consciousness, the state in which one realizes consciousness as such, unencumbered with any phenomenal awareness. The first five are preparatory and the last three are the essential stages of yoga. The preparatory stages are *yama*, *niyama*, *asana*, *pranayama*, and *pratyahara*. *Yama* and *niyama* are a set of prescriptions, "dos and don'ts" for the one who is on the path of yoga. The *yamas*, the do nots, include abstinence from injuring, stealing, lying, and lust. The *niyamas*, the dos, require cultivation of habits of cleanliness, faith, ascetic self-control, and contentment.

Asana and *pranayama* are physical exercises. Although Patanjali himself does not name any postures except to say that the correct posture is one that is stable and comfortable (2.46), his commentator Vyasa describes a few of them. *Pranayama* is regulating the flow of breath through systematic inhalation and exhalation as well as holding breath. The final preparatory step is *pratyahara*, which is the focusing of attention inward. The function of *pratyahara* is to dissociate the mind from its sensory channels so that no sensory input from the external world reaches the mind.

The essence of yoga is *samyama*. *Samyama* involves the triple effort of *dharana* (concentration), *dhyana* (meditation), and *samadhi* (absorption). The first three *sutras* in the third chapter of *Yoga-Sutras* describe them in the following way. Concentration involves focusing attention on an object, which progressively leads to the restraining of the natural wanderings of the mind. In the state of *dhyana* there is an uninterrupted flow of the mind toward the object of meditation so that the practitioner can focus the attention totally on a single object for a prolonged period of time. Such prolonged one-pointed attention to a single object leads to *samadhi*, a state of absorption. In a state of *samadhi* there is the awareness of the object alone, without an awareness of self. When the yogin thus loses self-awareness and enters a state of complete absorption in the object of meditation, he/she achieves a state of higher consciousness that enables him/her to grasp the essence of the objects in focus. The yogin thus knows the things in their true state without the biasing influence of the senses or the presuppositions and biases of the mind. Some of these experiences may appear anomalous to those who do not have similar experiences themselves. The final point of yogin's progress is complete liberation from all phenomenal constraints of the mind so that she may realize the state of *asamprajnata* as mentioned before.

Philosophers belonging to other schools may have disputed the philosophy of *Samkhya-Yoga*, but few have questioned the merits of yoga practice. It should be mentioned also that as the practitioner of yoga reaches the *samadhi* state and is able to practice *samyama* he/she is likely to encounter a variety of paranormal phenomena. In fact, Patanjali devotes a major part of the third chapter of *Yoga-Sutras* to describing the *siddhis* (paranormal powers) that one could obtain by doing *samyama*, such as knowledge of past and future, knowing other people's thoughts, becoming invisible, and so on. Thus, the anomalous states of awareness appear to be a natural consequence of yoga practice. They are, however, states that the yogin should ignore and move forward on the path to *kaivalya* to attain a state of consciousness-as-such.

Summary

To sum up, then, reality according to Samkhya-Yoga system of Indian philosophy is governed by two fundamental principles,

consciousness (*purusha*) and matter (*prakriti*). As fundamental principles, they have metaphysical and epistemological implications. In fact, Indian tradition is holistic in a very significant sense. In it the existential, epistemological, ethical, and aesthetic aspects of reality are seen to blend harmoniously. Being and knowing, the good and the beautiful are governed by the same principles. In our attempts to understand reality, we analyze it in a variety of forms, giving rise to distinctive concepts such as truth (*satyam*), goodness (*sivam*) and beauty (*sundaram*). The *Brahman* is described as *sat* (existence), *chit* (consciousness) and *ananda* (bliss or enjoyment). Thus, being, knowing and feeling are conceptually differentiated attributes of one and the same reality.

The dualism of Yoga consists in its assertion of *prakriti* and *purusha* as two irreducible but complementary principles of reality. They enable us to understand the relative roles of permanence and change in our being. These two principles are not merely the metaphysical constituents of reality, they have equally useful epistemological implications. Both *purusha* and *prakriti* are fundamental, one representing the permanent and unchanging and the other denoting the equally permanent but changing aspects of reality and knowledge. Knowledge may be processed through the route of *prakriti* or it may be obtained directly from the *purusha*. Both the avenues are available to humans even though we largely depend on the former. However, Yoga considers only that which is derived from the *purusha* as true knowledge.

Prakriti (matter) has three basic constituent elements, *sattva* (information), *rajas* (energy), and *tamas* (mass/inertia). *Sattva* is similar to consciousness in that it is translucent and allows consciousness to pass through and reflect itself in it. The images of reality are thus inlaid in the *sattva* content of *prakriti*. Each and every object that has evolved out of *prakriti*, however gross it may be, has an element of *sattva* in it. It is its essence, its information content. The human mind has evolved suitably equipped to process the information content inlaid in the *sattva* component of the objects that are in its reach. The brain, the nervous system and the sensory-motor apparatus enable the mind to process the information content in objects.

We must recognize, however, that every object in its association with the *purusha* forms a mind of its own. The minds thus formed may or may not reflect *purusha* consciousness. If the layer of *tamas* is too opaque to allow the *purusha* reflections to reflect back, the mind loses its functional character. Only when there is a conjunction between consciousness (*purusha*) and a material form capable of reflecting back consciousness, a conscious mind with subjective experiences is formed. Such a mind acts like a functional trap to catch the reflected light of the *purusha*. In the mind (a) nonconscious material forms in the proximity of *purusha* become conscious experiences, i.e., the *sattva* component of objects is processed, (b) the inert and characterless consciousness assumes form and manifests activity, and (c) the *purusha* mistakenly takes those forms and actions as its own. When consciousness (*purusha*) is thus trapped, in Yoga view, we have the ego sense and subjective experience, which tend to bind it more and more firmly to sensory processes. This is the existential context in which we find ourselves. The *purusha* finds itself cruising in the unceasing flow of cognitive states in the mental stream. At this stage, the embodied mind (*jiva*) has two options. The mental stream (*cittanadi*), as Vyasa calls it (*YS* 1.12), may through discriminative knowledge (*viveka*) flow in the direction of achieving a state of consciousness-as-such in splendid isolation (*kaivalya*) from the influence of *prakriti*. Alternatively, it may flow nondiscriminatively (*aviveka*) in the direction of increasing bondage and get further

entangled with *prakriti* and the whirlpool of material existence. One is the direction of good and the other is that of evil.

There is a reflexive relationship between consciousness (*purusha*) and the *buddhi*. *Buddhi* processes information from the *sattva* content of objects. This information by its very nature is subject to a variety of distortions, primarily because *buddhi*, though it is predominantly *sattvic*, also contains *rajas* and *tamas*. The *purusha* in its association with *buddhi* reflexively takes the contents of the latter as its own; and the embodied mind has the knowledge of the objects and events. When every trace of *rajas* and *tamas* is removed and *buddhi* is all *sattva* with no fluctuations in the mind, the *purusha* is revealed in the mind, consciousness manifests itself. This is the highest form of knowledge. Devoid of all distractions, it is sublime and infallible. That is the state of *kaivalya*, the ultimate goal of yoga practice.

From the epistemological perspective, knowledge processed from the *sattva* of material bodies via sensory channel is phenomenal. There is no finality and absoluteness about it. It is at best an informing image and in the worst case it is outright misleading falsehood. This is so because it is mixed up with *rajas* and *tamas* and the distorting influences of the human condition. When the mind is relieved of all the vestments of *rajas* and *tamas* by practice and passionlessness and is grounded in *sattva* itself, it can now have the true reflection of the *purusha* and know the difference between changing and ephemeral phenomenal awareness and self-illuminating transcendental awareness. Relational thinking gives way to insight and intuition, as the knowledge comes from the *purusha* itself. Such knowledge, Yoga thinkers believe, as many classical Indian philosopher also do, is permanent and absolutely true because there is no possibility of distortions and misunderstandings such as those that afflict phenomenal awareness. Thus, it would seem, unless we transcend the constraints imposed by the "mind trap," we could not have knowledge in its pristine form. The pursuit of liberation in this view is the quest for perfect knowledge, which is none other than accessing consciousness as such.

Mental phenomena that give us phenomenal awareness are intentional in that they are about objects. Mind experiences subject-object duality (*visayin* and *visaya*) in its normal states of cognition and action. In transcendental states, however, consciousness manifests in its pure form where there is no object to which consciousness is directed and no awareness of subject and object duality. Interestingly, knowledge can be obtained in both the intentional and nonintentional modes; but only that which is gained in the latter is considered the highest because it is direct pure and unbiased. For example, in Yoga literature a distinction is made between *savitarka* and *nirvitarka samadhi*. In both there is a direct, intuitive awareness. In the former we gain knowledge of objects in their conceptual form. The latter gives us knowledge free from any conceptual form. "The thing in this state does not appear to be an object of my consciousness, but my consciousness becoming divested of all 'I' or 'mine' becomes one with the object itself; so that there is no notion here as 'I know this,' but the mind becomes one with the thing, so that the notion of subject drops off and the result is the one steady transformation of the mind into the object of its contemplation" (Dasgupta, 1924, p. 151). In other words, yoga practice enables one to enter into a state of *samadhi* and have unbiased knowledge of objects, even when that knowledge is obtained via sensory processes. In *asamprajnata samadhi*, consciousness is completely on its own and a total transcendence from all mental states is achieved. There can also be a reverse flow. Glimpses of consciousness obtained in not so perfect a state of *samadhi* may be conceptualized and translated into phenomenal forms. Intuitions may lead to a rational reconstruction of a glimpse of direct awareness into an empirical fact.

Phenomenal awareness may be thus induced by transient transcendental states. This is clearly unlike normal phenomenal awareness, which arises from processing *prakriti*. There is yet another source of phenomenal awareness. In case of anomalous awareness such as in ESP, the information is obtained directly by *buddhi's* (mind) link up with the *sattva* of an object without the mediation of the senses. This possibility is open to *buddhi* because it is a manifestation of the universal *mahat*, like other *buddhis*. There is thus an interconnectedness of minds whether they are functional as in humans or dormant as in gross objects. Anomalous awareness is then a form of phenomenal awareness and may be seen as qualitatively different from transcendental awareness. Yoga system of Patanjali describes a variety of anomalous phenomena and how they may be obtained.

The notion of multiplicity of *purushas* in Samkhya-Yoga system poses some problems. If the *purusha* is considered to be pure consciousness devoid of individuality, form, or character, what is it that distinguishes one *purusha* from another? Multiplicity has meaning only when we can make distinctions. As Radhakrishnan (1989) points out, "Multiplicity without distinction is impossible" (Vol. 2, p. 322). It would appear more plausible, therefore, to regard the *purusha* as the foundational source, the ground condition of all conscious experience, like the *prakriti*, which is considered to be the ground condition of all material forms. The notion of individual *purusha* arises from the "mind trap" where the *purusha* apparently individuates and identifies itself with *buddhi* with which it is associated and whose experiences it considers as its own. Because *buddhi* is an extremely subtle form of matter that is in essence nonlocal, it can survive the disintegration of the body in which it is located and can contain and continue the effects of its actions beyond one life. Hence the notion of multiplicity of *purushas* appears needless.

In defense of Samkhya-Yoga it may be said, however, that without multiple *purushas* the concept of individuality would be limited to the unenlightened mind and that it would be an illusion at the level of *purusha*. Individuality cannot be attributed to the mind because without its association to the *purusha*, the mind cannot experience individuality. Samkhya-Yoga is very clear on this. It is the *purusha* that mistakes the content of the mind as its own. If there is just a single *purusha*, how is it in one case it is entrapped and has the illusion of separateness and individuality and in another instance it is free and on its own? The postulation of multiple *purushas* escapes this and similar problems associated with the notion of freedom as well.

The Indian subcontinent is the land of many faiths. Many religions arose and numerous systems of philosophy flourished here. They gave rise to a tantalizing array of opposing ideas. Yet, yoga was recognized almost universally in this part of the world as the most complete means of achieving higher states of consciousness. Even those schools of thought, which held philosophically conflicting positions, rarely questioned the usefulness of yoga practices. Such is the pervasive place of yoga in the Indian tradition. Raja yoga literally means royal yoga, and yoga as expounded in Patanjali's *Yoga-Sutras* is considered to be the majestic royal route to higher forms of awareness that include, as we have seen, anomalous as well as transcendental states of consciousness.

CHAPTER 9

Vedanta: A Philosophy of Pure Consciousness

The assertion by Samkhya thinkers of the existence of pure consciousness in their conception of *purusha* that has no form or content is pushed to its logical conclusion in the philosophy of Vedanta in general and Advaita Vedanta in particular. Advaita is the most influential among the orthodox systems of Indian Philosophy. Samkara is the philosopher who made Advaita not merely a very popular Vedanta sect but a profound philosophical system based ostensibly on the *Upanishadic* teachings. As Theos Bernard (1947) aptly observed, Samkara "was one of the great philosophers of his day, the sage of his century, the saint of his race" (p. 8). Undoubtedly Samkara is one of the outstanding thinkers of all time. His ideas have the depth of Plato and Kant, and his logic the sharpness and penetration of Aquinas and Hegel (Radhakrishnan 1989).

It is all too well known that the Indian tradition is indifferent to history. Little attention is paid to individuals, their time and place in the scheme of things. The literature is barren of biographical accounts of the philosophers and scholars of the past. Consequently we know very little of the found-

ers of the various systems of philosophy. In some cases even their identities are in question. According to tradition, Samkara dates back to 200 BC; but the orientalists generally hold that Samkara, the chief exponent of Advaita Vedanta, lived between 788 and 820 AD (Dasgupta 1963). In a short span of thirty-two years, Samkara traveled widely and wrote extensively. Born in the hills of Malabar in the southern tip of India, he is believed to have died in Kedarnath on the foothills of Himalayas. The most important of his philosophical writings are his commentaries on the *Upanishads, Bhagavadgita* and *Brahma-Sutras.*

Badarayana is credited with the authorship of the *Brahma-Sutras,* written probably in the second century BC (Dasgupta 1963). *Brahma-Sutras* essentially summarizes the philosophical thought of the *Upanishads.* Vedanta literally means the end of the *Vedas.* The end portions of the *Vedas* are called *Upanishads.* Therefore, Vedanta is the philosophy of the *Upanishads. Upanishads* are believed to be the philosophical treasure-chest of Hindus. They contain the invaluable insights of the truth seekers of India's past. They deal with the nature of and the relationship between the manifest world, the individual self and the ultimate reality encompassing the two. The fundamental reality, in this view, is the *Brahman/Atman. Atman* is the universal spirit or supreme consciousness. According to Badarayana, there is an intelligent principle behind the manifest world, which alone can account for the design and purpose of the universe. While accepting the Samkhya thesis of evolution, Vedanta raises the question: Who indeed is responsible for starting the process of evolution and how this process would end? Neither the *prakriti* nor *purusha* could in principle be conceived as primal causes for this. Therefore, it is argued, we need to postulate the existence of the *Brahman* who is the prime mover, the ultimate principle/agent that sets in motion the process of evolution first and causes its dissolution (*pralaya*) later. It would seem that Badarayana was more a theist and a dualist rather than an absolutist and monist. Until the time of Gaudapada (Samkara's teacher's teacher) and Samkara's commentary on the *Brahma-Sutras*, Vedanta was regarded as an authoritative dualist treatise (Dasgupta 1963).

There are a number of commentaries on *Brahma-Sutras*. Among them Samkara's (1890) is the foremost. Other important Vedanta thinkers are Ramanuja who propounded Visistadvaita, a system of qualified nondualism and Madhva who interpreted Vedanta in entirely dualist terms. Continuing Gaudapada's monism contained in his *Mandukyakarika*, Samkara, however, expounds his own system of nondualism, asserting that the *Brahman* or *Atman* alone is real and that everything else is an illusion and a manifestation of ignorance (*avidya*). In this view, the notion of multiple *purushas*, each *purusha* being a center of *pure* consciousness is false. According to Samkara, there can be only one center of pure consciousness and that is *Brahman. Brahaman/Atman* is the one, ultimate, absolute, and supreme consciousness, which appears as many to the ignorant.

The Metaphysics of Pure Consciousness

According to Samkara (1890), the *Atman/Brahman* is pure consciousness. It is self-manifesting and self-illuminating (*svaprakasa*). Unlike the *purusha*, the *Brahman* is one and not many; but like the *purusha* it is contentless (*nirvisaya*) and nonintentional. It is formless (*nirakara*) and rests in no other (*nirasraya*). It is suggested that the best way to grasp the *Brahman* is to strip it of all the contents of experience through a process of elimination. The process of successive denial of attributes in describing *Brahman* is expressed in the famous formula *"neti, neti"* (not this, not this). The denied attributes include all the things and relations we find in the world, including spatial, temporal, and sensory attributes. *Brahma* is neither limited in space and time nor is it distinguished from other objects. It is both the subject and the object. In a sense, it is undifferentiated subjectivity or nonobjective consciousness, and yet it underlies all persons in their experience. The *Brahman/Atman* is neither the agent of knowledge nor the object of knowledge. It is knowledge itself, consciousness undifferentiated as this or that. How then is the Brahman apprehended? According to Samkara, it is self-luminous and self-revealing. By self-luminous Samkara means that which is never the object of a knowing act. Rather it is immediate, direct and implicit in our own being. In reality pure consciousness, *Atman* (with capital A), the transcendental all pervading, self-manifesting and self-revealing absolute, and the individual self (*atman*) are the same. Myself (*atman*) is the same as the supreme self (*Brahman/Atman*). Consciousness alone is real and it is one and the same in all beings.

Atman as pure consciousness is the supreme principle in which there is no differentiation of knower, knowledge and known. It is nonintentional, undifferentiated and nonobjective. *Brahman* signifies also existence. In the *Brahman* knowing and being are one. Also, *Brahman* is regarded as absolute bliss (*ananda*). *Ananda* is freedom from all bondage and attachment. It is a state of complete emancipation from the determinations of space, time and material objects. *Brahman* is thus described as *sat*, *chit*, and *ananda*. At the ontological level, *Brahman* is *sat*, the principle underlying true existence. From the psychological perspective, it is consciousness (*citt*) encompassing all knowing. From the ethical standpoint, it is *ananda* (bliss), subjective freedom from objective determination.

Advaita attempts to establish its metaphysical thesis about supreme consciousness at three levels following the Hindu tradition. First is the level of faith or belief in what we learn/hear (*sravana*) to be the truth. For Advaita, like other orthodox systems of Hindu philosophy, the faith comes from the authority of the *Vedas*. The *Vedic* statements like *tat tvam asi* (thou art that) and *soham* (I am he) are cited in support.

The second level is the level of understanding (*manana*) truth through logic and rational discourse. Here Samkara excels. Numerous arguments are offered (a) in support of Advaita position and (b) to refute the criticisms and alternate postulations. It is argued that the existence of *Atman/Brahman* cannot be doubted because such a doubt implies the absence of he who doubts it. *Brahman* is self-revealing (*svayam prakasha*). If *Brahman* is other than consciousness, it has to be material because matter and consciousness together include everything while excluding each other. It is all too evident that nothing is known without

consciousness. Consciousness does not need something else to reveal it. A lamp does not need another lamp to make us see the lamp. Thus consciousness is self-illuminating. Consciousness dispels ignorance like light removes darkness. Since consciousness (knowledge) and ignorance are opposed like light and darkness, the lack of ignorance implies presence of knowledge. Again, that which is unconscious cannot make another conscious. If one assumes that a cognition needs a second cognition to reveal it, then a third cognition would be needed to reveal the second and so on ad infinitum. It may be argued, as Nyaya thinkers do, that a contact between individual consciousness (*atman/self*) and the inner sense, the mind (*antahkarana*), is needed for cognition to arise. Since such a contact gives knowledge of the object of cognition, Nyaya thinkers point out, why not simply assume that the contact also gives the knowledge of the self? Advaita rebuts this argument by saying that the contact between the self and the mind is a necessary condition, but not sufficient to give rise to a cognition.

The third level is the level of realization of truth by meditation (*nididhyasana*). Realization, unlike mere understanding, gives one absolute conviction because he/she at this level becomes one with reality. Realization may be accomplished by meditation and yoga practice. This appears to be the purport of the *Upanishadic* saying that to know *Brahman* is to become *Brahman*. At this level, knowing and being become one. So the ultimate test of the existence of pure consciousness, self-luminous and formless state of being, is the experience of *Brahman* and the consequent revelation of the identity of the self with the *Brahman*, an experience of consciousness without subject-object duality, nonintentional awareness.

BRAHMAN AND THE EMPIRICAL BEING

Though *Brahman* is the one supreme principle underlying all reality, undifferentiated and non-dual, reality in the human condition appears differentiated as subjects and objects located in time and space. This is so because in the existential situation, the *Atman*, the supreme being, resides as individual consciousness in the abode of *jiva*. The *jiva* is the embodied self; it is consciousness limited by the mind, intellect, senses and body.

In Advaita, the *jiva* is conceived as being encased and covered at different levels by *kosas* (sheaths). They are the *annamaya kosa* (representing the body and the material nourishment it needs), *pranamaya kosa* (the life sustaining vital breath), *manomaya kosa* (the mental system), and *anandamaya kosa* (the surround of happiness and bliss). The first *kosa* refers to the gross body. The next are the life sustaining and knowledge processing principles. The last, *anandamaya kosa*, is the state of bliss that the *jiva* seeks and strives for (see Gaudapada's *Mandukyakarika* III-2). *Jiva* comprises of the sum total of the ever changing and multifarious conscious states and the processes that give rise to them. In the *jiva*, consciousness is surrounded by the limiting adjuncts of the mind-body complex. The consciousness in the *jiva* is none other than the *Brahman/Atman*, the supreme consciousness itself.

The *Atman* in the existential context as individual consciousness is, however, covered by the effects of *maya*. *Maya* is the seed out of which phenomenal experience sprouts. As stated in *Brahma-Sutras*, *maya* is the potential cause of the empirical world of illusion. It is undeveloped and unmanifested because it cannot be defined either as that which is or that which is not (I-4.3). *Maya* is similar to *prakriti*, which we discussed earlier. From it emanate name and form. *Maya* exists in the form of ignorance in the person. When knowledge of truth dawns, it disappears. Thus it is neither real nor unreal. In his commentary on the *Bhagavad-Gita*, Samkara points out, "all emanations, fluctuations or modifications from mind to the gross body, and all qualities such as those which manifest themselves as pleasure, pain, delusion, and other mental states ... spring from *prakriti*, the *maya* composed of three qualities—goodness, passion and darkness" (XIII, 19). Maya is the mother illusion of the manifest world of the ever changing phenomena. It is an illusion that ends on the realization of the truth that we are one with *Brahman*, just as we realize the illusoriness of the dream on waking. However, the phenomenal or empirical world is not unreal like the sky flower or hare's horn. The dream is real when we are dreaming. It is unreal only after we realize it to be a dream. In like manner, the experience of the phenomenal (*vyavaharika*) world is real until one has the transcendental (*paramarthika*) experience of the nonduality of subject and object, and the experience of the unity of the individual consciousness (*jiva*) and the supreme consciousness (*Atman/Brahman*).

The statement in *Chandogya Upanishad* "*tat tvam asi*" (thou art that), referred to as the *mahavakya* or the great saying, expresses the relationship between individual consciousness (*jiva atman*) and the *Atman*, or supreme consciousness. In a sense, the supreme consciousness constitutes the ground for our individual consciousness. *Tat tvam asi* is the assertion of the common ground that links the individual to *Brahman*. Individual consciousness is a manifestation of the supreme consciousness, when the latter is clouded by *avidya* (ignorance), and limited by the functions of the mind, all being manifestations of *maya*.

The individual is thus, in Advaita view, a curious combination of both reality and appearance. Insofar as the *Atman* constitutes the ground, the individual is real; but in its phenomenal aspect with its stream of experience, the individual is mere appearance. The phenomenal consciousness as it manifests in our mental states, according to Samkara, is directed toward one object or another, whereas consciousness as such, the supreme consciousness, is pure and objectless. In other words, it is nonintentional.

The *atman* within us is the transcendental subject, "I," whereas the self of the manifest experience is the empirical subject, "me." The latter is subject to change, unlike the changeless transcendental self (*paramatma*). The *Atman* is pure cognition; the empirical self is seen as an agency actively engaged, striving towards one end or another. As Samkara states in his commentary on *Brahma-Sutras* (II-3.40), the *jiva* (individual consciousness) is essentially an agent of all activities. Its agency dwells in the *upadhis*, the limitations imposed by *buddhi* (mind). Jiva, as the *Mandukyakarika* states, "is a product of imagination and is capable of further imagination" (III-2). It is, however, more than an illusory manifesting in individual consciousness of the empirical world. Amidst the evanescent mental states, there is the abiding reality of the Atman, supreme consciousness. It is called in Vedanta *saksin* (the witness consciousness). Though it is associated with experience in the empirical world, the *saksin* is not a product of experience, but is presupposed by it. It is the continuing witness of the changing mental life of the embodied being. It is a sort of stage on which various mental events take place. There are slightly different views among the Advaita thinkers about the relation between *jiva* (individual consciousness) and *saksin* (witness consciousness). The essential difference between the two appears to be that the mind (*antahkarana*) is the attribute of individual consciousness (*jiva*) whereas it is merely a limitation (*upadhi*) of witness consciousness (*saksin*).

It is important to note that in Advaita

the individual person is neither part of, nor different from, nor a modification of the supreme consciousness. It is the *Atman* itself steeped in *avidya*, or ignorance. The *upadhis*, the mental processes, within us limit the understanding of the *Atman*. According to the theory of limitation developed by the later Advaita thinkers, known as *avacchedavada*, the individual person (*jiva*) is the *Atman* limited by his mind. There is also another theory called *pratibimbavada* to account for the relationship between the individual and the supreme consciousness, according to which the individual consciousness is a reflection of the supreme consciousness in the mirror of *avidya* (ignorance). The reflection is a function of the state of the individual. Like the reflection of a person in a pool of water which varies depending on the state of the water, whether it is clear or dirty, calm or turbulent, so does the reflection of supreme consciousness in an individual self vary depending on the state of the *avidya* of the individual person in whom it is reflected. Samkara himself used the simile of reflection. Commenting on *Brihadaranyaka Upanishad* (4.12) Samkara points out that, as the reflections of sun and moon on water is a mere appearance, so are the individual selves (personal consciousness) reflections of the one reality Atman in *avidya*. They are not truly real. On overcoming *avidya*, the reflections cease and the true consciousness alone remains.

The Mind and States of Consciousness

Mind, in Vedanta, is not the knowing self. Rather the mind is the *instrument* of knowledge. The self is the *agent* (*karta*) of knowledge. In the Advaita system, *antahkarana* is the name used to connote mind in its totality. *Antahkarana* literally means internal organ. Mind then is one's internal organ that enables him/her to know, feel, will and act. It is the totality of mental states and the processes that give rise to them. As in the Yoga system, other concepts are used, sometimes interchangeably with mind and *antahkarana* to coincide with the different functions of the mind. These include *manas, buddhi, ahamkara,* and *citta. Manas* denotes the processing aspect of the mind. *Buddhi* is the determining aspect. Ahankara is the ego or the "I" aspect of the mind.

In Advaita Vedanta, we may recall, there is one undifferentiated consciousness (*Atman/Brahman*). At the empirical level, this is seen as differentiated and particularized in the individual beings (*jivas*). The mind (*antahkarana*) is that which makes such particularization possible. It is the principle of individuation. Basically two types of individuation are distinguished. The first type is one where we attribute qualitative characteristics to consciousness. This happens in association with objects when, for example, one becomes perceptually aware of an object. The second type involves determination not by the qualifying conditions (*visesana*) of the objects but by the limiting conditions (*upadhis*). The mind is involved in both kinds of determination.

The Samkara School distinguishes between two types of *jiva*, depending upon the individuation process involved. When *antahkarana* in its role as a qualifying adjunct determines the supreme consciousness, there is one type of *jiva*, the individual empirical self. However, when the supreme consciousness is determined by the limiting adjuncts (*upadhi*) of the mind we have witness self (*jiva-saksin*). Mind is involved in the manifestation of *jiva* as well as *jiva-saksin*. In the case of the former, mind is a constituent element, a part of *jiva* and inseparable from it; whereas in the latter, it is only a limiting condition that determines the *jiva* but separable from it. Thus mind (*antahkarana*) is needed in both cases.

There can be no manifestation of *jiva* or *jiva-saksin* without a mind. The Samkara School finds it necessary to distinguish between *jiva* and *jiva-saksin* because it is assumed that without the presupposition of the latter it is difficult to account for the unity of apperception in one's awareness of external objects and of oneself. Thus in this view, *jiva* is the empirical ego/self with mind as a constituent and *jiva-saksin* is the transcendental ego not qualified but only limited by the mind. (For a detailed discussion of the relation between them *see* Sinha, 1958,Vol. I, pp. 372–375.)

In Advaita view, like in Samkhya-Yoga, the mind (*antahkarana*) is essentially material. It is preponderantly *sattva*. It is possibly the subtlest form of matter, translucent and capable of receiving reflections of the supreme consciousness. Mind is the inner medium, which in association with sensory organs takes the forms of the objects perceived. Thus mind is the main instrument that enables the essence of the object revealed by removing what is believed to be the veil of ignorance.

PERCEPTION AND COGNITION

In Advaita view, even though consciousness (*Brahman*) is one, it has three distinguishable phases and may be seen as three different aspects. First, consciousness appears to be qualified by the external objects. The resultant phenomenon is called object-consciousness (*visaya-caitanya*). The second category is cognitive-consciousness (*pramana-caitanya*). When mental modes (*vrittis*) qualify consciousness, we have cognitive consciousness. When consciousness is limited by a mind, there is self-consciousness (*pramatra-caitanya*). The first appears to correspond roughly to what we normally understand by sensation. The second and the third seem to relate to processing of perpetual awareness. In Advaita, perception is cognition and cognition is consciousness, which is essentially one but appears to *jiva* in its embodied state as many and in different forms because of the qualifying or limiting conditions. The three phases of consciousness are thus the three types of empirical modalities of consciousness as qualified by objects, mental modes or the mind. They appear to be three levels of cognition brought about by three different activities of the mind.

In perception, Advaitins believe, the mind "goes out" to the object through sensory channels and assumes the form of the object. As in Yoga, the modification in the mind brought about by the contact of the mind with an object is called *vritti* (mental mode). The *vritti* (the form the mind takes after sensory-contact with the object) is a necessary condition for perception. In inference of fire from smoke, for example, there is no sensory contact with fire, but a contact with the corresponding *vritti* of fire. In inference the mind does not reach out and come into contact with the object, it only "thinks" of the inferred object. The second necessary condition of perception is that there should be space-time contiguity between the *vritti* and the object that gives rise to it; they should be contiguous in time and place. "The *vritti*," as Jadunath Sinha (1958) describes so aptly, "is an empirical mode of the mind which takes the form of the object. Therefore, it is the meeting place, as it were, of the two substances, the mind and the object. It is not different from the mind, because it is a mode of the mind. It is not different from the object, because it is the transformation of the mind into the form of the object, i.e. it incorporates the form of the object in itself. Thus the mental mode, being identified with the object, occupies the same position in space" (pp. 132–133). If the mental mode and the object of perception are temporally apart, such as in the case of thinking about yesterday's pain, we have recollection and not perception. The third necessary condition

for perception to take place is that the object of perception must be capable (*yogya*) of being perceived. As summarized by Dharmarajadhvarindra in *Vedanta Paribhasa* "the direct perceptibility of an object consists in the fact that the subjective consciousness underlying the apprehending mental mode becomes united with the consciousness underlying the object, the object existing in the present space and time and capable of being perceived through a specific sense-organ, and the apprehending mental mode also having the same form as that of the object" (quoted from Sinha, 1958, vol.1, p. 134).

According to Advaita, mere perception of an object is different from the perception of the object *as object*. Here the distinction appears to be between, for example, (a) seeing a pot and (b) knowing that he sees the pot. There is awareness of awareness (self-consciousness) in (b) and not in (a). In (a) as pointed out in *Vedanta-Paribhasa*, an identity occurs between object-consciousness and cognitive-consciousness. In (b) there is the experience of not only this identity but also the identity of cognitive consciousness with the subject or "I"-consciousness. Vedanta assumes identity among the three phases of consciousness because there is really no difference between *vritti* and *ahamkara* (the ego aspect of the mind). *Vritti* is an *activity* of the mind, and *ahamkara* is one *aspect* of the mind. Therefore, the consciousness determined by the *vritti* and the consciousness processed by the mind in its relation to the ego cannot be different. All that is meant here, it would seem, is that the object-consciousness underlies cognitive consciousness. In other words, the perception of an object as object involves the identification of the perceived object with its corresponding *vritti* (mental mode) as well as with the perceiving subject. This is the case, in Advaita view, whether the object of perception is external, e.g. perception of a pot, or internal like the awareness of pain.

Among other divisions Advaitins make is the distinction between perception of an object (*jnaneya pratyaksa*) and perception of cognition (*jnana pratyaksa*). Perception of an object involves a *vritti* as a medium, whereas in perception of a cognition there is no involvement of *vritti* (mental mode). Again, like most other Indian thinkers, Samkara makes a distinction between determinate (*savikalpa*) and indeterminate (*nirvikalpa*) perception. Actually the two may be regarded as two distinct stages of perception. At the stage of indeterminate perception there is only an identification or apprehension of the object without any attributes are qualities imputed to it. It is simple undifferentiated, non-relational, or direct awareness. It consists of bare sense-datum with no representational content. The possibility of such non-representational perception is accepted in almost all the major systems of Indian philosophy including Buddhism, even though there is in the literature considerable discussion of significant differences among them. Determinate perception is representational in character. It is relational involving analysis, assimilation and synthesis. It involves images and associations, and can be described in words. In Samkara's view, indeterminate perception is *essentially* and absolutely indeterminate, having no qualifications whatsoever. It is limited to an apprehension of mere "being" with no concrete awareness of individual object or its qualities. Some of the neo–Advaita thinkers like Dharmarajadhavarindra suggest that indeterminate perception may involve immediate apprehension of qualities without awareness of the relations between them and the object.

Like Samkhya-Yoga thinkers, Samkara emphasizes in the perceptual process the going out function of the mind to reach out to the objects. As we have pointed out in our discussion of Yoga theory of perception, it makes little sense to assume that the mind literally goes out to meet the external object.

Rather the "going out" may mean no more than reaching out to the object, indicating the relative importance of the subject over the object. It is the subject who has the freedom to choose whether or not to have a relationship with an object. Jadunath Sinha (1958), favorably commenting on the Advaita theory of perception also argues in favor of the view that Samkara's theory of perception gives dominance to the subject and subordinates the object to the perceiving subject in their relative importance.

Advaita distinguishes between four cognitive states; (1) the waking state, (2) the dream state, (3) the state of deep sleep, and (4) the transcendental state of *turiya* or *samadhi*. In the waking state, external objects determine the content of consciousness. It is the state where consciousness is processed by the whole set of our psychophysical system. Dream consciousness is made up of the same stuff as the waking consciousness, except that its content is not empirically real and that it is not determined to a large extent by the external objects. It is illusory in the sense that on waking one realizes the unreality of what is experienced in the dream. The deep sleep sate is characterized by the abeyance of all distinctions including the distinction of the subject from the object. The *Mandukya Upanishad* describes the fourth state of consciousness thus:

> They consider the fourth to be that which is not conscious of the internal world, nor conscious of the external world, nor conscious of both the worlds, nor a mass of consciousness, nor simple consciousness, nor unconsciousness, which is unseen, beyond empirical determination, beyond the grasp (of the mind), undemonstrable, unthinkable, undescribable, of the nature of the consciousness alone wherein all phenomena cease, unchanging, peaceful and nondual.

In the fourth state of consciousness, there is a realization of the identity of the individual and the supreme consciousness and the non-reality of the world experienced in waking consciousness. Just as on waking one recognizes the illusoriness of dreams, so does the one who realizes the highest state of consciousness realizes the illusoriness of waking experience. What seems to be unique to transcendental or pure conscious state is that it is, unlike any state of phenomenal awareness, nonintentional. There is no object that one is conscious of, except consciousness itself. Pure consciousness is nonintentional and objectless and contains no ego sense. Phenomenal awareness of objects as manifested in our ordinary consciousness signifies states of consciousness brought about by the various degrees of influence of its limiting adjuncts in human mind.

Advaita thinkers generally accept Patanjali's classification of *samadhi*, including the possibility of acquiring paranormal abilities. Sadananda in his *Vedantasara* distinguishes between *savikalpa* and *nirvikalpa samadhi*. In *savikalpa samadhi* the identity of the individual consciousness with pure consciousness is experienced through the agency of the mind. Here the *vritti* has *Brahman* as the object of awareness. In *nirvikalpa samadhi* there is no awareness of the mental mode (*vritti*). The mind is completely dissolved. Whereas in the former the distinction between the knower and the known, the subject and the object, is not completely obliterated, in the later such distinctions disappear.

CONSCIOUSNESS AS UNDIFFERENTIATED SUBJECTIVITY

As mentioned before, according to Samkara, consciousness is self-luminous and self-revealing. Self-luminosity is defined as "that which is never the object of a knowing act but is yet immediate and direct with us." It means the "capacity of being always present in all our acts of consciousness without in anyway being an object of consciousness." We may interpret these statements to mean that consciousness as such is self-revealing subjectivity, the center-point to which all phenomena are referenced. It is argued that consciousness manifests itself and that it is not known as some thing other than itself. It is never an object. It is *self-revealing* (*svaprakasa*). In Advaita view, there can be no doubt, error, or contrary knowledge in respect of consciousness. Consciousness, then, is knowledge in its sublime condition free from error, doubt and misgivings. Doubt and error are a consequence of its association with the mind, the senses and the sensory objects. Progressive dissociation from them enables one to achieve a state of being in which there is realization of consciousness as such, a state of nonobjective awareness.

The discussion of the four states of consciousness in Advaita philosophy is extremely helpful in understanding the true nature of consciousness. The distinction Advaita makes between waking, dreams, dreamless sleep, and the *turiya* or *samadhi* states is pivotal and provides the reason *d'être* to interpret pure consciousness as undifferentiated subjectivity or nonobjective consciousness. Here we make use of a revealing and original interpretation of Advaita Vedanta by K. C. Bhattacharya (1909) in his *Studies of Vedantism*.

In dreams what we usually have are copies of waking percepts, that do not follow any definite rules of formation. Here imaginative construction is more free than in waking life. In the waking state, our consciousness is so deeply intertwined with objective determinations that it can hardly move of its own accord as it does in dreams. So long as we are awake we can scarcely free our consciousness from that of objects. In dreams, on the other hand, our subjectivity is almost free from this limitation, because the object-consciousness is reduced to a minimum. Sometimes it is altogether absent.

Consciousness appears to be free from the determination of the sense objects and even the body itself. When, for instance, we have the out-of-body experiences in dreams we have the experience of seeing our bodies as lying asleep. Consciousness is here almost free from all objective determinations and sometimes all objectivity disappears. Dream consciousness is not bound to any sense datum. No object manifests it. Thus, as K. C. Bhattacharya says, "dreams may be described as perceptions without sensations" (p. 2).

The self-revealing nature of consciousness is evident also in the state of *sushupti* or deep, dreamless sleep. The state of *sushupti* (deep sleep) is not a state devoid of consciousness. That it is so, Samkara argues, is evident from the awareness of the man, after he has arisen from the state of dreamless sleep, that he had a blissful sleep during which he was conscious of nothing. Of course, his knowledge is directly derived from memory. Still memory is always memory of presentation of something that was actually presented. Therefore, the bliss and consciousness, concludes Samkara, must have been experienced during the state of *sushupti*. It follows, therefore, that the self-revealing nature of consciousness is manifest in deep sleep also. The empirical consciousness determined by sensory objects lapses here altogether. What is left is none other than undifferentiated subjectivity.

But even *sushupti* (deep sleep experience) cannot give us the actuality of the knowledge of the reality of pure consciousness, though its possibility is suggested. In the state of deep sleep consciousness is the awareness of a positive blank. It consists in a "direct cognition of the absence of specific cognition" (Bhattacharya 1909, p. 14). The nature of consciousness as complete freedom from objects, nay, as conscious freedom from the determination of anything that is not consciousness itself, can be realized only in the state of *turiya*, an ecstatic state of *samadhi*. It is an experience of consciousness as such, indeterminate, undetermined and free from all objective limitations. Unlike *sushupti*, wherein consciousness lapses into a state of undetermined consciousness without striving for it, the *turiya* stage represents a complete installation in subjectivity through conscious withdrawal from objects. It represents, according to Advaita, a higher, in fact the highest level of being. It signifies realization of the reality as transcending all determinateness. It is a state where there is no duality. It is non-dual not merely because there is the absence of duality as in *sushupti*. It is non-dual because the veil of ignorance (*ajnana*) distorting consciousness and creating the illusion of empirical reality is removed, and removed for good; and even the consciousness of the removal is absent. It is a state of pure undifferentiated consciousness. Objective plurality is not only negated, even the sense of negation itself is absent. What is left is only pure consciousness in which there is the essential identity of being, consciousness and bliss.

The highest *samadhi* state is one that is thus completely indeterminate (*nirvikalpa*). The Advaita also recognizes determinate (*savikalpa*) states of *samadhi*, preceding the indeterminate state. *Savikalpa samadhi* is an intermediate state between *sushupti* (deep sleep) and *nirvikalpa samadhi*. What then is the difference between deep sleep and determinate *samadhi* state? In the words of K.C. Bhattacharya (1909): "The difference, as ordinarily given, is that in the former the (empirical) mind with all its modes lapses altogether, whereas in the latter it does not lapse but only gets concentrated into one absolute irrelative mode, which thus becomes actualized in the highest degree. The one represents the greatest *dispersion* of attention, the other its utmost *concentration*. In both, the consciousness of duality lapses; in both, the self enjoys undifferentiated bliss; in both, the timeless seeds of knowledge and action (*vidya-karma*) persist, accounting for the recognition of the past on awaking from them. But whereas on awaking from *sushupti*, the self remembers that it was in the attitude of knowing object though the object was there a blank, on rising from *samadhi* it ought to remember it *was* the object in that state and not in the object-knowing attitude at all. In the former, the self as always limited was simply isolated: in the latter, it burst its bonds, destroyed the barrier between subject and object, and became the absolute" (pp. 14–15).

As Bhattacharya points out, the stages of waking, dreams, dreamless sleep, determinate and indeterminate *samadhi* form a gradation of existence. Waking experience, where there is hardly any freedom for the subject from the object-consciousness, is one variation of this gradation. Consciousness at this stage completely identities itself with the objective world. The other extreme is constituted by the state of undifferentiated subjectivity that is completely free from all objective determinations, a state of pure consciousness. Between these stages come dreams and a deep sleep state. They reveal the ever increasing freedom from objectivity and a deepening of the installation into non-dual consciousness. The state of *samadhi* is not a stage among other stages. While almost everybody experiences the states of dream, and dream-less sleep, the state of *samadhi* is not attained by all. That is because the state has to be achieved through a conscious effort, a continual withdrawal from objects and a corresponding installation in subjectivity. Samkara points out that this realization of the ultimate truth, the identity of the self with *Brahman* comes only to a mind that prepares itself for it. Samkara adds that an initial preparation is necessary to achieve this highest level of existence. Such preparation leads to a development of the subjective attitude striving for conscious freedom from objects.

The suggestion all through the writings of Samkara is that the ultimate reality, the pure consciousness, is to be realized from within, through a withdrawal from objectivity, by prolonged and continued meditation. It cannot be grasped through discursive reason, which proceeds by way of making a distinction between the knower, the knowledge and the known, since it is free from all distinctions. A phenomenon has not merely a relational aspect, which can be understood through discursive reason, but also an intrinsic aspect that can be grasped only through intuitive insight, which is imaginative withdrawal from its non-essential attributes and installation into what is inseparable from it.

This subjective attitude of realizing consciousness-as-such which is in reality a process of imaginative isolation, or conscious withdrawal from objects is, however, helped to certain extent by rational discussion in so far as it serves as a means of detailing certain aspects of the object before the mind. But discursive reason ultimately has to make place for intuitive insight since it is not always free from doubt. In other words, reason gives understanding of truth and not necessarily its realization in one's being.

Intuitive insight prepares the path for an immediate realization of consciousness-as-such and an experience of nonduality. In Advaita view, only when in and through the process of steadfast meditation and imaginative isolation the state of *turiya* is attained that we have the experience (*anubhava*) of the non-duality of subject and object. It is then and then only that the light of consciousness, pure and without obstruction, shines forth in us as a living truth of the identity of existence, consciousness and absolute bliss.

DOES PURE CONSCIOUSNESS EXIST?

Following Bhattacharya we have attempted to interpret the different states of consciousness from waking to *samadhi* as a progressive movement away from objectivity to subjectivity until one experiences subjectivity in its indeterminate form, i.e., pure consciousness without any content. The question remains to be answered, however, whether there are any compelling reasons for believing in the existence of such consciousness, pure and indeterminate.

J. N. Mohanty (1993) in an incisive analysis of the Vedanta theory of consciousness points out three different ways of conceiving the relationship between consciousness-as-such and conscious states. First, the relation may be one between a universal and a particularized instance of it, as between redness and patches of red. Second, one may conceive the relation to be between awareness and that of which one is aware. Third, consciousness as such may be regarded as the *reality* whereas the mental states are mere *appearances* of that reality, like the moon and the many images of it reflected in different lakes and rivers. We find all these interpretations in Vedanta literature.

As Mohanty suggests, nonintentional pure consciousness is not a "phenomenological datum of non-mystical experience" (p. 59). What then are the grounds for supposing the possibility of nonintentional consciousness? According to Advaita Vedanta, first, there can be no conscious states without consciousness-as-such because the former presupposes the latter. Second, consciousness admits of no differences that necessarily belong to objects. Therefore, the subject-object differences as obtained in our conscious states should belong to the empirical world and not to consciousness as such. Third, undifferentiated awareness in pure consciousness that does not signify any object or quality accompanies all waking consciousness and even dreamless sleep. All the three arguments can be disputed, of course, as those philosophies that questioned the Advaita thesis have done. Point-

ing to the weaknesses of the above arguments, Mohanty considers the third argument more plausible than others, if we were to make a distinction between the awareness aspect and the intentionality aspect of conscious states. Awareness, he suggests, may be regarded as a universal feature present in all states of consciousness, whereas intentionality is relative to the object, the person, and the cognizing situation. Yogic literature suggests the possibility of achieving a mere awareness state with out content. Nonintentional consciousness-as-such is then a "universal detachable from the particular mental states." Mohanty considers this to be a logical possibility even though he does not within the bounds of his experience find a "foothold" from where he could conceptualize nonintentional consciousness.

Mohanty goes on, however, to suggest that pure consciousness may best be considered "as a goal to be attained rather than as an ontological reality" (p. 62). Here he makes use of an idea advanced by K.C. Bhattacharya in his book *The Subject as Freedom*. Bhattacharya (1930) argues that the subject-object relation is one-sided inasmuch as the relation is essential from the side of the object but only optional from the side of the subject. In other words, the object has no choice and is dependent upon an appropriate intentional act in order to be an object. Pure consciousness may be conceived as a goal to be achieved by exercising one's freedom to withdraw from all object-directedness. Mohanty says that "the idea of pure non-intentional consciousness is the reified, ontological equivalent of that normative goal" (p. 63).

That it is difficult, if not impossible, to conceptualize pure consciousness is clearly recognized by the Vedantins in their characterization of *Brahman* as "not this and not this" (*neti neti*). Conceptualization is a mental act that is necessarily limited to conscious states that have a directedness about them. Therefore, it would be a futile endeavor to seek any conceptualization of pure consciousness. In other words, pure consciousness may be beyond any intellectual understanding. That pure consciousness cannot be an object of conventional understanding does not entail that it does not exist.

Some who claim to have mystical experiences say that they have experienced pure consciousness. There is a conviction that goes with such experience. But then, conviction is not proof. We know that our expectations can produce convictions. It is also suggested that the experience of pure consciousness is accompanied not only by a conviction that it is an objectless conscious experience but also by remarkable behavioral changes such as those attributed to saints. It is possible that experiencing consciousness-as-such is accompanied by realization that goes beyond mere understanding, a realization where there is no dissociation between knowing and being as exemplified in the *Upanishadic* statement: *"Knowing Brahman is becoming Brahman."* We may indeed find persons who achieved such an integrated state in which there is no dissociation between their beliefs and conduct. Does this prove the existence of consciousness as such? Mohanty (1993) contends, *"To have an experience and to draw metaphysical lessons from it are two different things. No bare experience tells its own tale.* The experience concerned has to play a certain role of fulfilling a prior conceptual intention, in order to be of cognitive value. This is why mystical experiences are made to support quite different theories. They are to a large extent theory-neutral" (author's emphasis, p. 64).

Mohanty may be right in assuming that mystical insights may lend support to different metaphysical notions. Indeed if *Upanishads* contain such mystical, intuitive insights of those who are believed to have achieved higher conscious states as in *sa-*madhi, they are clearly amenable to support a variety of metaphysical theories. This is evident in the case of Vedanta itself, which harbors a number of schools with distinctive metaphysical presuppositions, all claiming the authority of the *Vedas*. What is important, however, is that none of them question the intuitions themselves, their veracity and genuineness. They differ only in the interpretation of them. Consequently it is not unreasonable to believe in pure consciousness as a datum of experience, if such experiences are indeed genuine. Their metaphysical implications, however, may be discussed at a different level.

Concluding Summary

Existence has various gradations from the *essentially* unreal like hare's horn or barren woman's son to the *ultimately* real *Brahman*. In between there are various gradations such as the illusion of silver in a shell, perception of the external world of objects, the experience of dream, dreamless sleep devoid of any imagery, and the different states of *samadhi*. In these phases of existence, there is a progressive movement away from externally driven objectivity to internally experienced subjectivity. That subjectivity in its essential form is absolutely detached from everything else. It is undifferentiated unity of being, bliss and consciousness. In that state the other forms of existence are understood as illusory and unreal in a manner similar to discovering the unreality of the dream after awakening from sleep. In Advaita view, the ultimate reality, eternal and absolute, is the pure being of consciousness-as-such. The empirical being or the individual consciousness is a phenomenal manifestation of the supreme conscious being, limited by the mind, intellect, senses, and body. The supreme consciousness not only provides the necessary support to the individual but also acts as the witnessing consciousness throughout the life history of the person. It is possible to transcend the limitations of our bodily conditions and achieve understanding of the supreme, which consists in removing the veil of ignorance and realizing the identity of the individual consciousness with the supreme consciousness. Such a realization at once reveals the illusory nature of the empirical world and gives rise to the sublime bliss of non-objective consciousness, an experience of unconditioned person, consciousness in its splendid unsullied form.

There are glaring differences in the metaphysical postulations of Advaita Vedanta and Sankhya-Yoga as we discussed earlier. One is unwaveringly absolutist and non-dualist whereas the other espouses dualism of consciousness and matter and pluralism of *purushas.* More importantly for our purpose, however, there are striking similarities between them on the notion of pure consciousness and their understanding of cognitive processes, perception and phenomenal experience. They agree that consciousness is not a quality or attribute of the mind. Consciousness is assumed to be essentially different from mind, having its own primacy of being. Further both conceive consciousness-as-such without any form or content. In Yoga, consciousness is also devoid of activity. Since Advaita discards matter at the highest level of existence, it has to provide for some kind of activity in consciousness itself. Advaita concepts of *Brahman* and *Maya* roughly correspond to *purusha* and *prakriti* in Sāmkhya. However, Advaita nondualism not only deprives matter (*prakriti*) the status of being ultimately real, but it also denies multiplicity to consciousness. In Yoga theory there are multiple centers of consciousness in *purushas,* whereas all of them are consumed in Advaita under one supreme consciousness, *Brahman.*

Again, the concept of mind and theories of perception are similar in Yoga and Advaita. They seem to agree on some of the details of how the mind works and is able to reflect consciousness to give us awareness in its various forms. Both Yoga and Vedanta agree that mind and consciousness are different and that mind is physical. In Advaita, however, the physical is only empirically real and not ultimately real. They are essential similarities in their views on perception and cognition. The bare outline of Yoga-Vedanta theory of mind may be summarized in the following way.

Mind is the composite of awareness and response systems. It may be functionally distinguished into (1) *buddhi* (executive system), (2) *ahamkara,* (self-reference system), (3) *manas* (central processing system) and (4)sensory-motor system (*Jnana-karma indriyas*). In perception *buddhi* makes contact with the object via the sensory channels. This gives rise to modifications in *Buddhi* and *vrittis* arise in the mind. The *vritti* is homogeneous and immediate. It is *indeterminate apprehension* of the object. The *vritti* then is processed by the *manas,* which with its selective attention subjects the *vritti* to analysis, assimilation, and discrimination. The *vritti* thus becomes determinate and definitive; it is broken into subject-predicate relationship; and the object is *reflectively apprehended.* In the next stage, the *vritti* is appropriated by *ahamkara,* which is the self-reference system. *Vritti* becomes associated with the person. One has the *self-apprehension* of the object. With this self-reference of *ahamkara* and the determinate form given by the *manas,* the *vritti* finds itself back in *buddhi* with all the manifest modifications.

The *buddhi* is not a *tabula rasa.* It is a storehouse of past memories, accumulated *karma,* subliminal impressions, inherited tendencies, *samskaras* and *vasanas.* The *vritti* is impacted by them and takes further transformations and finally surfaces as a form of the *buddhi.* The light of *purusha* or *Brahman* always envelops the *buddhi.* Consequently, the light that is consciousness reflects on the exposed surface of *buddhi* in its *vritti* form, resulting in the *conscious apprehension* of the object. The *buddhi,* then may choose to respond in appropriate way by initiating action through its response system, *karmendriyas*. This is the cognition-action mode in which the mind is centrally and constantly involved unless it is obscured, obstructed or covered by *tamas* as in sleep or voluntarily controlled as in meditation. *Conscious apprehension*, the final outcome of cognitive process, may be conceived as bestowing or imprinting, to borrow Nagel's celebrated phrase, the "what it is like" character on the experienced object. It is the consummation of the information content (*sattva*) of the object in the subjectivity of consciousness.

The above is a description of the empirical mode of awareness. It is the existential condition of human cognition and action. The limitedness of such awareness and its illusory nature become evident, Advaitins believe, after one awakens with the dawn of pure consciousness. When existence moves to the level of pure consciousness, one's relation with reality takes a dramatic turn. The subject-object duality experienced at the empirical level disappears. Knowledge ceases to be representational. Consciousness-as-such becomes contentless. "Contentless" means here the essential ineffability of experience. Advaitins believe that it is possible to enjoy states of pure consciousness by the embodied mind. *Jivanmukta* is one who has gained freedom from the constraints of the mind and realized in his being the true identity of his/her consciousness with *Brahman,* the supreme or pure consciousness. This is a state of transcendence where knowing and being become one, differences and distinctions are overcome and one experiences utter subjectivity and objectless consciousness. Whether such a state is ever possible may not be established on rational grounds. The claims of reality of the state of pure consciousness are not

confined to metaphysical presuppositions, but are said to be grounded in genuine experiences of a few people.

The metaphysical speculations of Vedanta apart and also leaving aside the questions about which is real and at what level, there appears to be a general agreement among Hindu thinkers that there are indeed two levels of knowing. Knowing at the empirical level does not give absolutely true knowledge, because such knowledge is essentially variable. At this level dissociation between cognition and action, conflict between what one knows and does (as for example, when one knows that smoking is bad but continues to smoke) is possible. Knowing at the transcendental level is, it is assumed, free from empirical distortions. Since the awareness system and the response system are not involved at this level, the possibility of dissociation between their outputs does not exist. At one level, knowledge is mediated; it is direct and immediate at the other level. Freedom, in Advaita view, is the goal. Perfect knowledge is the way. Meditation is a means.

At this point, it is necessary to recognize that Samkhya-Yoga-Vedanta views do not exhaust between themselves all the salient ideas concerning mind and consciousness in Hindu thought. It would be misleading to think otherwise. Even though they represent the dominant trend in the Indian tradition, there are equally important epistemological and metaphysical view points. The contributions of Nyaya-Vaisesika systems are specially note worthy in this context—Nyaya from an epistemological perspective and Vaisesika from a metaphysical view point. Nyaya views are in the dualist tradition, but different in important respects from Cartesian dualism. (For an extensive discussion of Nyaya theory of mind and consciousness see K. K. Chakrabarti 1999.)

In line with the Indian tradition, Nyaya-Vaisesika thinkers regard mind as physical. Different in essentials from the physical substance is the self or soul, which is nonphysical. Self is like *purusha* in Samkhya-Yoga except that it is not consciousness itself. It is the substratum of consciousness, like matter is the substratum of all qualities that physical objects manifest. Consciousness is not intrinsic, but adventitious. It is a quality of the self that manifests under conditions of self's contact with the mind. Thus unlike in Advaita and Samkhya, consciousness in Nyaya-Vaisesika is not a substance but an attribute of self. This is an important difference; significant metaphysical and epistemological discussions ensue from it. However, what is important from our perspective is the assertion of Nyaya thinkers that consciousness requires a nonphysical substance for its manifestation and does not inhere as a quality of physical substance. Also, "consciousness" in Nyaya is more like empirical consciousness in Advaita, which manifests as intentional awareness. Pure consciousness, however, is entirely devoid of any empirical qualities that are indeed adventitious and arise in association with the physical mind. Therefore, the differences between Samkhya-Yoga-Vedanta on the one hand and Nyaya-Vaisesika on the other do not appear crucial and fundamental to substantially alter what we have attempted to describe as the Hindu tradition.

The above observation is further reinforced when we consider Nyaya-Vaisesika views on yogic perception or the supernormal abilities of yogins. As Sridhara (1895) the author of *Nyayakandali* points out, disciplined and prolonged meditation enables one to enter a state of *samadhi* where one has super-sensuous knowledge. Another Nyaya thinker Prasastapada (1923) divides yogic perception into two kinds. In the higher kind of *samadhi,* yogins are able to have knowledge of not only of their selves, but also of others. They achieve a kind of omniscience. In them only the mind is operative and the sensory functions are held in abeyance. The Neo-Nyaya thinkers consider the yogin in the state of *samadhi* as one who has attained union with the supreme Being. This does not seem to be very different from the notion of realization of pure consciousness in Advaita and Yoga. Again, Sridhara accepts the distinction between *samprajnata* (determinate) and *asamprajnata* (indeterminate) states of *samadhi.* (See the chapter on super-normal perceptions in J. Sinha, 1958, Vol. 1.) Such a distinction clearly leads to the presupposition of pure conscious states.

CHAPTER 10

Buddhism: A Psychology of Consciousness

Buddhist psychology is essentially an attempt to understand the nature of consciousness, the variety of its states, and the methods of attaining them. In Buddhist view, normal consciousness and the psychological processes associated with it are so organized as to generate a false sense of stable and enduring ego, which in its turn influences, colors, and even determines our passions, thoughts and actions. To achieve higher states of consciousness, it is necessary to transcend the boundaries of our normal phenomenal awareness. When one attains higher states of awareness the psychological processes lose their ego-reference and bias, and one's cognition and action transcend their normal limitations. Buddhism believes not only in the existence of such transpersonal ego-absent states of awareness but also in the possibility of cultivating them by following certain practices. Buddhism describes the different stages involved in the progress from the normal to the transcendental states, from *samsara* to *nirvana*, and along the way provides us with one of the most interesting and pervasive phenomenologies of consciousness.

There are many scholars who consider Samkhya and Yoga as the earliest systematic philosophies in India and suggest that Buddhism received much of its inspiration from them. At the same time, it should be kept in mind that the systematic treatises of Samkhya and Yoga, such as Patanjali's *Yoga-Sutras*, were written only after the advent of Buddhism. Also considering that many of the classical Indian thinkers, including Samkara, were stimulated by intellectual conflicts with Buddhists (Dasgupta, 1957), it is reasonable to assume that there is a reciprocal influence between classical Hindu thought and Buddhism.

Buddhism, apart from being a major religion, is an important heterodox system of Indian philosophy. Unlike the orthodox systems such as Vedanta and Samkhya-Yoga, which accept the authority of the *Vedas*, Buddhism not only expressly disowns them, but it is also a reaction against the dominant ideas contained in them that are widely accepted. Whereas the *Upanishadic* thought sought the eternal, permanent and changeless reality, the Buddha saw reality and permanence in change itself.

Gautama the Buddha lived between 563 and 483 BC. He was born in a princely family and grew up in royal comfort protected from many of life's sorrows. When he saw, however, the miseries of life that afflict people and the suffering that goes on, Gautama was moved and driven by a steadfast determination to gain the supreme wisdom that would give him insights into the existential crisis and the ways to overcome it. He traveled widely, studied extensively and practiced intense asceticism for over six years. Finally, after seven weeks of continuous meditation sitting under a baniyan tree, Gautama felt that he had found the answers he was seeking. He became the Buddha and started preaching his insights. Thus came into being Buddhism five hundred years before Christ.

Buddha's concerns were practical, and his approach was essentially empirical. As Radhakrishnan (1989) points out, his was an attempt "to start a religion independent of dogma and priesthood, sacrifice and sacrament, which would insist on an inward change of heart and a system of self-culture" (Vol. 1, p. 357). It was an earnest ethical endeavor based on incisive psychological analysis. He shunned speculations concerning God, soul, and other ontological questions. He saw in our experience nothing permanent but only change. When asked what underlies all changes, he retorted: "It is not the time to discuss about fire for those who are actually in the burning fire, but it is time to escape from it" (*Majjima Nikaya*). The Buddha was thus against mere armchair metaphysical speculations not rooted in the problems that confront humans, speculations that are not aimed at their resolution. His goal was to find the way out of suffering, which he saw in abundance. His was an empirical approach of direct observation, observation directed outward as well as inward. His method at once revealed that this suffering (*duhkha*) encountered in daily existence is a consequence of craving, which

is born out of the illusion of permanence and ego-centering. He saw no such thing as a stable and unchanging reality. Reality is dynamic; it is a process that has continuity, but no changelessness. The pragmatism advocated by the Buddha involves taking middle positions and avoiding extremes. To assert that "everything is" is one extreme, and to argue that "nothing exists" is another extreme. The truth, he said, is in the middle. It is becoming.

As Buddhist thought developed, there came a need to answer the questions the Buddha avoided; and his disciples were divided in their answers. The result was the emergence of different schools within the Buddhist tradition soon after Buddha's death. Four of these are intellectually prominent, and they cover much of the philosophical spectrum from the naïve realism of Vaibhasika and the representationalism of Sautrantika to the idealism of Yogacara and the shades of nihilism in the Madhyamika schools.

A psychological analysis into one's own being would convince us, Buddhists generally believe, reminding us the Scottish philosopher Hume, that it is but a series of connected processes, a stream of consciousness, and that there is no unchanging or permanent soul or mind underlying them. The illusion of the feeling of a permanent entity subsisting in us is an ego-defense. It is the main source of all suffering. Therefore, the solution of the problem lies in overcoming all such defenses, obstacles, attachments, desires, and other obsessions that stand in the way of attaining a state of transcendence called *nirvana*, a state devoid of all ego-references. It is a state of fulfillment, of equanimity, of calm contentment, and of supreme intellectual insight. The transformation from *samsara* to *nirvana*, from suffering to salvation, can be brought about by means of practical training, self-discipline, and intellectual effort. Buddhist psychology is a theory of the nature and states of consciousness from the mundane and the sensuous to the supreme and the sublime. At the same time, it also describes the path and the methods of achieving the transformation of man from sensuality to transcendence.

Scope of Buddhist Psychology

Two important assumptions characterize the early Buddhist thought concerning human nature: (a) a good deal of one's conduct is determined by the *karma* accumulated by one's past actions, and (b) at the same time it is possible to exercise voluntary control and to guide actions through one's effort and volition. Thus, although man's destiny is in some sense determined by his past, it is possible to change its course by sustained and determined effort. Buddhist psychology in a significant sense is a psychology applied to this very important task. The result is a thorough introspective analysis and a useful classification of states of consciousness. Also, interesting psychological explorations into the processes of cognition and action follow.

It would seem that man's perceptions seldom fully correspond to or represent the things as they really are. They are usually seen through colored dispositions and are conditioned by habits born out of past actions. Buddhist psychology attempts to analyze our psychical processes in order to understand the various factors that influence, bias, and determine our perceptions, thoughts, and actions. It consists of a series of important steps for deconditioning the person. The goal is to achieve a state where things are seen as they really are. Transcendence is such a state of perfect knowledge, knowledge devoid of all distortions, which can be achieved, it is believed, by destroying all past *karma* (*kamma* in Pali) and by progressively annihilating the ego.

We should keep in mind that Buddhist

inquiry is guided more by ethical considerations than by the desire to investigate human nature. However, what is important is that its ethical doctrine is based on psychological principles. It is a psychology applied to ethics. Therefore, not surprisingly, the first book of the *Abhidhamma* treats *dharma* in terms of states of consciousness. As Rhys Davids points out in the introductory essay accompanying her translation of the *Dhamma-Sangani,* "the inquiry is conducted from a psychological standpoint, and, indeed, is in great part an analysis of the psychological and psycho-physical data of ethics" (1923, p. xxxii).

One could argue that, for the early Buddhists, *dhamma* (Pali for Sanskrit *dharma*) is the subject matter of psychology. Actually, the term *dhamma,* can be interpreted in more than one way. But it seems clear that, in the works that have psychological bearing, the word *dhamma* is used to denote a mental state or process. As Davids says in the *Abhidhamma,* the *dhammas*

> always prove to be, whatever their ethical value, factors of cittam used evidently in its widest sense, i.e., concrete mental process or state. Again, the analysis of rupam in Book II, as a species of "indeterminate" dhamma is almost wholly a study in the phenomena of sensation and of the human organism as sentient. Finally, in Book III the questions on various dhamma are for the most part answered in terms of the four mental skandhas of the cittani dealt with in Book I, and of the springs of action as shown in their effect on will [1923, p. xxxix].

The Buddhist definition of psychology as the science of *dharma* is not very dissimilar to the contemporary definition of psychology as the science of behavior, for *dharma* is behavior internalized. While the contemporary psychologist is mainly concerned with behavior as it manifests externally and observed by others, the Buddhist deals with behavior as it is experienced introspectively by the behaving person. Without minimizing or overlooking the obviously great difference between these two approaches, it is not difficult to see how the two approaches could supplement each other by their respective emphases on studying the person as he finds himself and as seen by others, first-person and third-person perspectives.

LITERATURE

The Buddhist Pali scriptures are contained in the three *Pitakas*. (1) *Sutta Pitaka*, (2) *Vinaya Pitaka* and (3) *Abhidhamma Pitaka*. The *Sutta Pitaka* contains five groups of collections, called *Nikayas that* deal mainly with the doctrine of *dhamma* (*dharma*). The *Vinaya* contains regulations concerning the discipline of the monks. In the *Abhidamma*, which is in seven parts, we again find the doctrines of the *Suttas*, with a good deal of psychological and philosophical interpretation. *Dhamma-Sangani*, a compendium of states of consciousness, is the first book in the *Abhidhamma Pitaka*. Mrs. Rhys Davids translated it under the title *A Buddhist Manual of Psychological Ethics*, and wrote a valuable introduction (Davids, 1923). It is generally agreed that the *Dhamma-Sangani* was compiled toward the end of the fourth century BC. Buddhaghosa of the fifth century AD wrote a commentary on it, entitled *Atthasalini*. Another book of Buddhaghosa, *Visuddhimagga*, is also an important source of Buddhist psychology. A standard book of considerable importance in Buddhism from the psychological standpoint is the *Abhidhammatthasangaha*, translated with copious notes and a lengthy introduction by Aung (1929) and published under the title *Compendium of Philosophy*. The author of this book is *Anuruddha*. It is difficult to precisely date Anuruddha. It is likely that he lived some time between the eighth and twelfth centuries AD. *Milinda Panha* (*Questions of King Milinda*) also contains valuable material, especially on the Bhuddist doctrine of "no soul" and on dreams. These works written in Pali constitute the main sources for understanding the psychological thought of early Buddhism.

The main account of Buddhist psychology described in the following pages is based on the Theravada tradition, which is the most psychological of all. However, I will also refer to two other schools, the Yogacara and the Madhyamika. Nagarjuna, who lived around the middle of the second century AD, a philosopher of the same caliber as Samkara, wrote the *Madhyamika-Sutras*, which is the main text for the Madhyamika school. Chandrakirti of the seventh century AD wrote a commentary on *Madhyamika-Sutras*.

Consciousness and Unconscious Mind

The approach of Buddhism to the understanding of the mind is basically functional. Buddhism emphatically rejects the view that consciousness is a modification or a quality of the mind and argues that there is no soul or substantive mind apart from the states of consciousness experienced.

Consciousness is defined by Buddhaghosa in *Atthasalini* as "that which thinks of its object" (p. 148). It is cognitive in character. Its function is to guide, discriminate, and inform. It manifests in a series and thus has continuity. It is caused by the psychical and endosomatic excitations as well as by physical and external simulations.

Nama and *rupa*—name and form or mind and body—are but convenient terms to depict highly complex and continuously changing processes. Reality is always in a state of ceaseless change, and both mind and body are in a state of flux. The impermanence/change is somewhat more marked with regard to the mind and states of consciousness. The mind is like a stream. It maintains one constant form, one seeming identity, even though its contents, like water in a stream, continuously change. The mind in *Dhamma-Sangani* is accounted for in entirely phenomenological terms and the analysis is restricted to the states of mind. We find no reference to the personal agent. In *Milinda Panha* (Davids 1963), Nagasena, expounding the doctrine of "no soul," quotes the *Samyutta Nikaya* thus:

> Just as it is by the condition precedent of the coexistence of its various parts that the "chariot" is used, just so is it that when the skandhas are there we talk of a "being" [Davids 1963, p. 45].

Whenever we speak of "soul," we mean one or more of the *skandhas*. The *skandhas* are groups or aggregates of bodily and mental states. These are five kinds, namely: (1) *rupa*, (2) *vedana*, (3) *sanna*, (4) *sankhara*, and (5) *vinnana*. In *Samyutta Nikaya*, *rupa* is defined as that which "manifests as the touch of gnats, mosquitoes, wind, the sun, and the snake; it manifests, therefore, it is called rūpa" (Dasgupta 1957, p. 95). Under *rupa* are included the four elements or the *mahabhutas*—the body as well as the senses. As Dasgupta (1957) points out:

> The four elements manifested themselves in certain forms and were therefore called rupa; the forms of affection that appeared were also called rupa; many other mental states or features which appeared with them were also called rūpa. The āyatanas or the senses were also called rupa. The mahabhutas or four elements were themselves but changing manifestations, and they together with all that appeared in association with them were called rupa and formed the rupa khanda (the classes of sense materials, sense data, senses and sensations (Vol.2, p. 95).

It would appear that *rupa* may mean gross matter as well as the sense data. The double meaning may not be considered inconsistent inasmuch as Buddhism makes no sharp distinction between the physical and the mental. *Vedana* is feeling; and it can be pleasurable, painful, or indifferent *Sanna* (Sanskrit: *samjna*) is sensation/perception. It is representational and includes perceptual as well as conceptual knowledge. *Sankhara* means both volition as well as a synthetic function that enables the several mental properties or elements (*cetasikas*) to function in association with each other. *Sankhara* as a *skandha*, to quote Aung, "really means the group of 'volitions and other associated factors'" (1929, p. 274). *Vinnana* is consciousness. It is referred to the stage at which the cognitive process starts as well as the resulting awareness. We shall return to a further discussion of these concepts later when we attempt to interpret the contribution of Buddhist psychology to the study of human nature.

In Buddhist view, consciousness is a relation between subject and object. However *subject* and *object* are to be understood as relative and mutually dependent; one cannot exist without the other. "Both the subject and the object are alike transitory, the relation alone between the two impermanent correlates remaining constant. This constancy of relation, which ... is consciousness itself, gives rise to the erroneous ideas of personal identity" (Aung, 1929, p. 11). Again, "life is like an ever changing river, having its source in birth, its goal in death, receiving from the tributary streams of sense constant accretions to its flood, and ever dispensing to the world around it the thought stuff, it has gathered by the way" (Aung, 1929, p. 12).

Consciousness is not a static state but a dynamic process. It is like a flowing stream, which has an identifiable form without being the same at any two moments in time. The stream of consciousness, or rather the stream of being, has both a subliminal as well as a supraliminal existence. The subliminal stream, which is a thought-free state, like the state of dreamless sleep, is called *bhavanga*. *Bhavanga* is a very important concept but a difficult one to grasp. It is described as "the cause, reason, indispensable condition of our being regarded subjectively as continuous, the sine qua non of our existence, that without which one cannot subsist or exist" (Aung, 1929, pp. 265–266). *Bhavanga* makes the passive side of our existence possible. It is also to be regarded as a state below the threshold of introspective awareness. "As such it is the sub-conscious state of mind—'below the threshold' of consciousness—by which we conceive continuous subjective existence as possible" (Aung, 1929, p. 266).

It would appear that *bhavanga* is the key concept in a system of thought that believes in continuity of existence through several births without believing in a permanent migrating entity like the soul. *Bhavanga* may be regarded as a functional substitute for substantive soul in Buddhist thought. If our present existence is a consequence of our past *karma, bhavanga*, it would seem, is the medium through which past *karma* influences one's thought and action. *Bhavanga* is a concept similar to *buddhi* in Yoga and Advaita. *Buddhi*, we may recall, is the seat of memory as well as the depository of *samskaras* and *vasanas*, the carriers of *karma*. There is, however, a significant difference between the two concepts. *Buddhi* is essentially nonconscious. It becomes conscious in the proximity of *purusha*, when the light of *purusha* is reflected on it. In Buddhism, there is no such outside source. Some of the contents of *bhavanga* become conscious when they are further processed. In other words, certain states of mind are conscious and others are not.

Mind at birth is entirely a subconscious state, like the state of dreamless sleep. It is, however, endowed with the potentiality to guide, influence, and determine our thoughts, passions, and actions. When an external stimulus or an internal thought is perceived, the stream of being is momentarily interrupted and a psychic field is cre-

ated. It is this field that results in our perceptions of the external objects as well as ourselves.

Bhavanga may be interpreted as a key psychological concept that not only provides a meaningful explanation for understanding the dynamics of behavior but also reveals the essential subjective and personal character of our knowledge of the external world. Our cognitions are but manifestations at the periphery of *bhavanga* and result from the interactions between the unconscious flow of our being, which in itself consists of myriad predispositions, and the external and internal stimulations processed through the channels of the senses and the mind. Thus, what we know about the world in our ordinary state of consciousness is in a very significant sense personal.

COGNITION

The process of sense cognition is described in the *Compendium of Philosophy* thus:

> *When,* say, a visible object, after one thought-moment has passed, enters the avenue of sight and, the life-continuum vibrating twice, the stream of that continuum is interrupted; *then* consciousness of the kind which apprehends sensations, apprehending that visible object, rises and ceases [Aung 1929, p. 126].

Cognitive process involves six steps— (1) the impinging of the sensory stimulus on our peripheral system, which is described as sense-object contact; (2) excitation of bhavanga, the stream of being; (3) the momentary arrest of *bhavanga* by the reflecting mind; (4) apperception of the object perceived; (5) registering in and retention by the mind of the object apperceived; and (6) the cessation of awareness and its submergence into *bhavanga*.

This process is described by the following simile of the mango tree:

A man, lost in the deepest sleep, is lying at the foot of a mango-tree with his head covered. A wind now stirs the branches, and a fruit falls beside the sleeping man. He is in consequence aroused from dreamless slumbers. He removes his head-covering in order to ascertain what has awakened him. He sees the newly fallen fruit, picks it up and examines it. Apprehending it to be a fruit with certain constitutive attributes observed in the previous stage of investigation, he eats it, and then, replacing his head-covering, once more resigns himself to sleep.

The dreamless sleep corresponds to the unperturbed current of the stream of being (bhavanga). The striking of the wind against the tree is like the "past" life-moment, during which the object enters the stream and passes down with it, without perturbing it. The swaying of the branches in that wind represents the vibration of the stream of being. The falling of the fruit corresponds to the arrest or interruption of being, the moment at which the stream is "cut off" by thought; the waking of the man to the awakening of attention in the act of cognition on occasion of sense; the removal of the head-covering to the sense-reaction of sight. The picking up of the fruit is comparable to the operation of receiving; inspection of it recalls the examining function. The simple apprehension of the fruit as such, with certain constitutive attributes of its own, corresponds to the discriminative or determining stage; the eating of the fruit resembles the act of apperception. Finally, the swallowing of the last morsels that are left in the mouth corresponds to the operation of retention, after which the mind subsides into mere vital process, even as the man once more falls asleep [Aung 1929, p. 30].

What has been said so far relates to perceptions that are very vivid; but Buddhists accept various grades of vividness, based on the intensity of the sense impressions. They account for these in terms of thought moments. A cognition, in order to attain an apperceptive stage, needs, to last for 17 thought moments. The 17 moments represent the duration from the moment the object enters the stream until the stream re-sumes its flow. When an object causes a less vivid impression, then, there is no retention of the object. There is no apperception at all. When the object makes a very slight impression, there is not even a sensation. Thus, there are four grades of sense-object contact: (1) full sense cognition with retention; (2) apperception without retention; (3) sensation without apperception; and (4) futile sense impression, which is too weak to be translated into sensation (that is, it fails to hold the arrested bhavanga for any length of time). The greater the intensity of the sense impression, the shorter will be the duration required for the vibration to set in after the object reaches the field of presentation.

In retentive apperception, the stream is perturbed within one moment of the object's entry into the field. In nonretentive apperception, the vibration of the stream commences only after two or three moments have lapsed since the object's entry into the stream. In nonapperceptive sensation, the object causes excitation in the stream only after five to nine moments. When the object fails to set a vibration in the stream for ten or more moments, the impressions cannot reach the state of sensation.

It needs to be mentioned that we seldom have a single isolated sense cognition. Usually there are strings of related sense impressions that go through the reflective processes of imagination, memory, conception, discrimination, and classification in rapid succession before an individual has a discernible perceptual awareness of an external event or object.

Mental reflection is made possible by the retentiveness of the objects perceived. Objects of past experience can be recalled by themselves, or in association with others. Also, new objects can be imaginatively constructed by a combination of the parts of previously experienced objects. A combination of these with the position of the object in time—that is, whether it belongs to past, present, or future—makes it possible for Buddhists to distinguish between varieties of reflective processes.

In Buddhist view, perception itself is always indeterminate. It is in a sense nameless and ineffable. It can be neither named nor recognized and is thus free from all interpretative processes of the mind. In other words, perception is pure sensation representing nothing more than what is given in experience. To have the sensation of "blue" is not the same as knowing it as blue. Perception then is immediate and "pure acquaintance." It is free from construction, name and generality as Dinnaga says in his *Pramana-samuccaya*. Perception, which is devoid of all interpretation, is therefore necessarily true because there is no possibility of being different from the object that gives rise to it.

There are four kinds of perception. The first kind is sensory (*indriya jnana*). This is bare sensation resulting from the sensory process. The second is mental perception (*mano-vijnana*). It is the successive stage accompanying sensory processing. It is a transitory stage between perception as such and thought. *Sva-samvedana* (self-consciousness) is the direct perception of mental states like pain and pleasure, which also does not involve any interpretation and therefore is free from error. The fourth kind of perception is *yogi-pratyaksa*, paranormal awareness brought about by intense practice of concentration and meditation.

PHENOMENOLOGY AND STATES OF CONSCIOUSNESS

As pointed out earlier, consciousness, according to Buddhists, is a relation between the subject and the object. The latter may belong to one of the five senses, or it may be a mental object. When an interaction between the subject and the object takes place and consciousness arises—as described above—the resultant consciousness,

which is the product of a number of variables both of the subject and of the object, manifests characteristics that can be distinguished. These characteristics form the basis for a classification of consciousness. The early Buddhists identified and distinguished 89 states of consciousness. A broader classification has 121 such states.

From the perspective of the subject, there is, first of all, the position of the person on the plane of existence. Four such possible planes are distinguished. They are (1) *kamaloka*, (2) *rupaloka*, (3) *arupaloka*, and (4) *lokuttara*. Experiences in each of these planes have their own peculiar characteristics.

The plane of pure form (*rupaloka*) has in common with the sensuous domain (*kamaloka*) the property of having forms and with the formless domain (*arupaloka*) the property of abstraction and the transcendence of the ego. In the sensuous domain (the *kamaloka* plane), the objects of consciousness are bounded by ego-centeredness; and therefore a tension between the subjects and the objects arises, resulting in desires and craving. The objects of consciousness in the *arupa* plane are free from ego entanglement, and are thus excluded from all sorts of craving. In the *rupa* plane, we find thinking, reflection, rapture, happiness, and concentration. These five factors help to eliminate the hindrances that bind consciousness to the sensuous world. Thinking helps to overcome sloth, lethargy, and indifference. Reflection enables one to overcome doubt. Rapture destroys hatred. Happiness dissipates restlessness and worry. Concentration enables one to overcome greed. Thus in the world of pure form, we find five classes of consciousness, culminating in concentration, which leads to the *arupa* plane.

At the non-*rupa* (*arupa*) plane, we have such consciousness as the awareness of the infinity of space, the infinity of consciousness, nothingness, and transperceptual and transpersonal experience. Transcendental consciousness is that which belongs to the path of *nibbana*. It is called *lokuttara*, which literally means "beyond the worlds." It involves the awareness of a path that expels the causes of rebirth and leads to *nibbāna*. *Atthasalini* distinguishes the worldly phenomenon of consciousness from an experience of transcendental consciousness in the following way:

> In worldly phenomena consciousness is the chief, consciousness is the principal, consciousness is the forerunner. In transcendental phenomena, however, understanding is the chief, understanding is the principal, understanding is the forerunner [Buddhaghosa 1920, p. 90].

It would appear that the Buddhist analysis of consciousness is essentially from the perspective of mental states without delving into substantive issues. Neither the mind nor consciousness is discussed as a ground condition, but only as states of awareness. The analysis, however, gives rise to a profound understanding of the cognitive, the conative, and the emotive factors that enter into the determination of consciousness at any given time. A given consciousness can be something that arises automatically on the presentation of a stimulus or something that is determined by volition. Consciousness of an object may be devoid of any feeling. On the cognitive side it may be erroneous or non-erroneous. It may give knowledge or may be devoid of knowledge. A permutation and combination of these give rise to a variety of conscious states. At the *kamaloka* (empirical) plane there are fifty-four such states, fifteen at the *rupaloka* (physical) plane, twelve at the *arupa* (mental) plane, and eight at the *lokuttara* (transcendental) plane.

The states of consciousness are also described as moral, immoral, or amoral. It is very difficult to understand what precisely the Buddhist notion of morality applied to

consciousness is. The good and the bad are not defined but only illustrated. We find psychology and ethics combine to account for behavior. Each conscious state is a link in a continuous chain of conscious events. A conscious state to which good or bad can be imputed is an effect of certain antecedents and the cause or part of the cause of certain subsequent effects. This chain of causation applies to most of our behavior. The moral states lead to good results and immoral states to bad or unhappy results. But there are also states of consciousness that are only results of antecedent conditions, but are not themselves causes of subsequent events or vice versa. When a physical state is only an effect or simply a cause without being both a cause and an effect, it is not moral or immoral, but a morally indeterminate state. Also, at the transcendental plane, all states of consciousness are morally indeterminate because they are unconditioned states in that they produce neither good nor bad *karma*.

KARMA

Karma (*kamma* in Pali) is the predisposing factor that is assumed to be responsible, not only for a continuing cycle of birth and death, but also for our state of being at any given time. *Karmas* are considered to be of four kinds, which are based on the effects they produce. First are those which produce impure effects and cause bad results. Second are those which produce pure effects and cause good results. Again, there are those that produce partly good and partly bad results. Finally, there are *karmas* that produce neither good nor bad effects but contribute to the destruction of past *karmas*. The root cause of *karma* is binding volition and the states associated with it that give rise to ego sense and consequent attachments and cravings. Where such volition is not present, actions cannot produce any *karma*.

Although the mental states that are

fixed and determined are the resultants of *karma*, *karma* itself is produced by apperceptual acts that are free. Man's behavior is conditioned by all sorts of circumstances, but he is still free to adapt himself to his environment through his volition. It is this exercise of volition, which is involved in reflective thinking and in representative apperception, that gives rise to *karma*. The Buddhist manuals describe the nature and the strength of volitions, and how *karma* affects behavior in this birth and the births to follow. The volition of such developed persons as the Buddha and the *arahants* does not, however, carry any *karma* with it because it is free from evil tendencies and binding attachments. It should be understood that all apperceptive acts that are of the character of inoperative thoughts do not transform themselves into *karma*.

In Buddhaghosa's *Visuddhimagga*, we find twelve kinds of *karmas,* distinguished from different viewpoints. First, there are: (1) *karmas* which bring about results in this birth; (2) *karmas* that will be effective in the next life; (3) those that will become operational in some life thereafter; and (4) *karmas* "that have been." The last mentioned is, in effect, inoperative *karma. Karma* "that has been" is so-called because "there was no fruit of *karma*, there will be no fruit of *karma,* there is no fruit of *karma*" (Buddhghosa 1923, p. 724).

Second, there are (5) weighty *karma,* (6) abundant *karma* (7) proximate *karma* and (8) outstanding *karma*. The weighty (such as killing one's mother) and abundant *karmas*—as opposed to light and slender deeds—are the first to yield fruit. The proximate *karma* is the recollection at the time of death by which, according to Buddhists, one is reborn. "That karma which is not of the first three kinds, and which has had many opportunities of repetition, is *outstanding karma*. In the absence of the other three kinds, it brings on rebirth" (Buddhaghosa 1923, p. 725).

Third, there are four other kinds of *karma*. They are in Buddhaghosa's words:

reproductive *karma*, maintaining *karma*, unfavorable *karma*, destructive *karma*. Of them *reproductive karma* is both moral and immoral, and reproduces the resultant aggregates of the mind and matter at rebirth. The *maintaining karma* is unable to reproduce a result. It maintains and prolongs the happiness or ill, which arises when rebirth has been granted, and a result yielded by another *karma*. The *unfavorable karma* oppresses, afflicts and gives no opportunity of long life to the happiness or ill, which arises when rebirth has been granted, and a result yielded by another *karma*. The *destructive karma,* though itself moral and immoral, kills some other *karma* which is weak, inhibits its result and makes room for its own results. That result, which is due to the opportunity thus given by the *karma*, is called *uprisen* result" [Buddhaghosa 1923, p. 725].

ELEMENTS OF CONSCIOUSNESS (*CETASIKAS*)

In addition to classifying consciousness into various states as described above, the early Buddhists analyzed consciousness into certain basic elements that combine to give rise to a variety of conscious states. These elements are called *cetasikas.*

There are fifty-two such elements. Of these, as summarized in the *Abhidhammatthasangaha,* seven are common to all states of consciousness. They are (1) contact (*phassa*), (2) feeling (*vedana*), (3) volition (*cetana*), (4) perception (*sanna*), (5) individuation or one-pointed concentration (*ekaggata*), (6) psychic life (*jivitindriya*), and (7) attention (*manasikara*). There are six elements that are termed particular, which are not invariably present in all conscious acts. In addition, fourteen elements present in immoral acts and nineteen elements present in moral acts are also distinguished. In other words, whereas the seven universal mental elements ought to be found in all the eighty-nine states of consciousness, the six particular elements are present in fifty-five states of consciousness. The universal elements seem to relate to the basic psychological processes.

Contact (*phassa*), which brings the object into the field of consciousness, is described in the *Atthasalini* as the pillar that supports the structure of consciousness (p. 143). Contact consists in consciousness coming into touch with the object and then producing an impact. Contact is described both as a cause and an effect. As the sense and the object come together and are in contact, there arises the potential for awareness.

The second universal element of consciousness is feeling (*vedana*). Feeling is not considered a quality of experience, but an agency of experience: "'Feeling' is that which feels. It has (1) experiencing as characteristic, (2) enjoying as function, or possessing the desirable portion of an object as function, (3) taste of the mental properties as manifestation, and (4) tranquillity as proximate cause" (Buddhaghosa 1920, p. 145). Although feeling has enjoyment as function, it is not confined to pleasurable feelings alone. It includes painful as well as neutral ones. *Vedana* approximates what we characterized as the subjectivity, "what it is like," aspect of consciousness.

The characteristic of volition (*cetana*) is coordination. It coordinates all the associated sates of an object; and, in so doing, it binds together the various states related to an object. The function of volition is conation, which is present in moral as well as immoral states, but not in morally inoperative states. Volition is the source of a good deal of energy, and it manifests in the form of directing the associated states.

Some writers on *Abhidhamma* criticize the translation of *cetana* as "volition." For example, Guenther writes that "*cetana* not only arouses mass activity, but also sustains it so that certain definite results appear. This

shows beyond doubt that the translation of *cetana* by volition is against all evidence.... *Cetana*, to state it plainly, is something that corresponds to our idea of stimulus, motive, or drive" (1976, pp. 43–44). Although *cetana* implies something more than what is normally meant by volition, neither "stimulus," "motive," nor "drive' convey its precise intent either.

Sanna is what gives us distinct cognitions. It enables us to recognize general relations between objects, and to have perceptions of all kinds—sensuous and mental. "The perception, the perceiving, the state of having perceived which on that occasion is born of contact with the appropriate element of representative intellection—this is the perception that there then is" (Davids, 1923, p. 7). Attention (*manasikara*) is what brings the mind and its object together. "Attention is like a charioteer harnessing two horses (mind and object) into a pair" (Aung, 1929, p. 282). As Buddhghosa puts it: "Mind indeed always gets at its object, its constant companion being attention (*manasikara*), without which it would be like a rudderless ship, drifting on to *any* object. With this rudder the senses arrive at their proper destination" (Aung, 1929, p. 283).

Jivitindriya is described as the faculty of life. *Dhamma-Sangani* defines *jivitindriya* thus: "The persistence of these incorporeal states, their subsistence, going on, their being kept going on, their progress, continuance, preservation, life, life as faculty—this is the faculty of life that there then is" (Davids 1923, pp. 16–17).

Ekaggata is "the stability, solidity, absorbed steadfastness of thought which on that occasion is the absence of distraction, balance, unperturbed mental procedure, quiet, the faculty and the power of concentration, right concentration" (Davids, 1923, pp. 11–12).

Thus, we find that the above mentioned seven universal mental properties are the basic psychological processes involved in all states of consciousness. First of all, there is the life process without which no psychic activity is possible. Then, there is the contact between the mind and the object, which is made possible by attention. An amount of concentration that would enable the emergence of the object into a specific space-time setting is also required. The emergence of the object into the conscious field causes both perceptions as well as feelings, which are also influenced by one's volition. We may note how similar are the universal mental elements described in Buddhism to the characteristics attributed to consciousness by William James in the *Principles*. *Vedana* is the subjectivity, the personal aspect. *Cetana* is the process that gives us the unity and coherence in conscious experience. *Sanna* refers to the noetic aspect and intentionality, whereas *manasikara* is selective attention.

Attaining Transcendence (Nirvana)

The path of Buddhism is to achieve a state of transcendence called *nibbana* (*nirvana* in Sanskrit). Transcendence results in the cessation of rebirth and attainment of perfect knowledge. Transcendence has both metaphysical and empirical connotations. In its empirical sense, it refers to the human situation where a transformation of the *person* takes place. This transformation affects one's cognitive style, emotional state, and personality. In the cognitive sphere, the discursive and the differentiating processes give way to nonrepresetational and intuitive comprehension. As Johansson (1969) puts it: "Cognition after the attainment of *nibbana* is more similar to a comprehensive Gestalt or intuition" (p. 23). Knowledge attained in this state is devoid of all distortions brought about by the existential situation of personal involvement. Because the state of *nibbana* is devoid of all obsessions

such as desire, hate, and illusion, the knowledge attained is perfect and undistorted. Subjectively, it is an experience of unity, completeness, and timelessness. In the state of *nibbana*, it is said, there is freedom from all suffering and attachment. From an emotional point of view, *nibbana* is happiness, peace, calm contentment, and compassion. The most important aspect of *nibbana* is the transformation brought about in the personality resulting in an unemotional, stable, and unobsessed mind that is devoid of ego-compulsions.

The one who has realized *nibbana* is the *arahant*, the perfect or the ideal man. Arahantship is the culmination of all psychic development. As *Samyutta Nikaya* puts it: "The destruction of desire, hate and illusion—that is called arahantship."

Achieving higher states of awareness, unobsessed states of the mind, free from the compulsions of ego and the delusion of permanence, is often described as "crossing the river." The one who "crosses the river" realizes the four noble truths. He knows about suffering, how it arises, its extinction and the way to achieve it. *Samyutta-Nikaya* (V, 199–200) mentions five steps in the path of the monk from *samsara* (sensuality) to sainthood *(arahantship)*. They are (1) faith in Buddha's teachings, (2) vigor or motivation to strive to get rid of undesirable states of mind and to acquire, maintain, preserve, and enhance wholesome mental states, (3) practice of mindfulness, (4) cultivation of concentration and one pointed attention, and (5) attainment of wisdom, which is enlightenment itself.

MINDFULNESS AND CONCENTRATION

Mindfulness and concentration are central exercises in the pursuit of enlightenment and transcendence. These two are not different and opposing practices. They are necessarily complementary. Mindfulness is recommended to the monks as a practice for purification of body and mind and for successfully proceeding on the path of *nirvana*. Mindfulness is applied in four ways— (1) contemplating the body in the body; (2) contemplating the feelings in the feelings; (3) contemplating the mind in the mind; and (4) contemplating the mental states in the mental states.

Contemplating the body in the body begins with paying attention to breathing. "Mindful he breathes in, mindful he breathes out." Similarly the monk goes through a variety of activities such as walking and eating. Then he reflects on the body itself from the head to foot, the various impurities in it, and the various elements of which it is composed and into which it would be decomposed.

Contemplating the feelings in the feelings consists in paying attention to states of pain and pleasure or lack of them. *Majjhima-Nikaya* describes how a monk lives contemplating the mind in the mind in the following way:

> He comprehends the mind which has passion and that which has none as such, which has hatred and that which has none as such, which has confusion and which has none as such; he comprehends the collected mind, the distracted mind as such; the mind which has become great and that which has not as such; the mind which has some other or no other (mental state) superior to it; the mind which is concentrated or that which is not as such.... It is thus that a monk lives contemplating the mind in the mind [quoted from Conze 1954/1995, p. 58].

Finally, mindfulness is directed at contemplating mental states in mental states. This exercise involves five steps. First, he contemplates the mental states from the point of view of the five hindrances (desire, ill will, restlessness, worry or doubt). Second, he contemplates on mental acts such as perception, feeling and awareness. Third, he contemplates on the six aspects of awareness system and the six aspects of the response system. Fourth, he contemplates on the seven steps to the path of enlightenment, when they are present and when they are not present in his experience. Fifth, the monk contemplates on the four noble truths and comprehends that "this is suffering, this is its uprising, this its stopping, this the course leading to its stopping" (*Majjhima-Nikaya* I, 55–63).

Such passive and yet incisive attention to the details of the constitution, composition and functioning of the body and mind in mindfulness exercises reminds us of the *pratyahara* phase of raja yoga practice, where the attention is focused inward. *Pratyahara* is, however, limited to the workings of the mind and voluntary control of internal attention states, whereas mindfulness is much broader and includes attention to body. Another difference is that mindfulness appears to be limited to observation and understanding rather than control of the processes involved.

Buddhism in general and Theravada tradition in particular has worked out an elaborate method to enable one to achieve transcendence. The practices involve among other things (a) scrupulous observance of moral precepts (*silas*), (b) practice of meditation (*samadhi*), and (c) realization or understanding (*panna*). Moral precepts include such injunctions as non-killing, non-stealing, chastity, refraining from taking intoxicants, from speaking falsehood and harsh words, and from indulging in malicious acts. One was asked to be truthful, keep his promises, seek harmony, and speak pleasantly. The monks seeking *arahantship* were also exhorted to overcome enviousness, hatred, pride, arrogance, immodesty, anger, and deceitfulness. These disciplinary rules are found in great detail in *Vinaya Pitaka*. The general direction of all these precepts is to overcome the basic obsessions, viz., greed, hatred, and delusions and to control the tendencies of attachment, aversion, wrong thoughts, and ego-feeling.

Panna, (understanding), is also given great prominence in Buddhism. A person who dispels ignorance through understanding may become an *arahant*. Apparently, it is believed that some may attain transcendence by understanding alone, i.e., without meditation. Such a person is called *panna-vimutto* whereas a person who achieves transcendence through meditation and mind control is called *ceto-vimutto*.

From a psychological point of view, the most important path is the path of meditation and mental training by which the mind is controlled and transformed. *Visuddhimagga* gives minute details of the processes involved in the practice of meditation from the lowest to the highest. Five kinds of variables are identified. They relate to (a) hindrances to the practice of meditation. (b) object on which meditation should be made, (c) teacher, (d) practitioner or the disciple, and (e) the process of meditation. Buddhaghosa identifies ten hindrances that obstruct the practice of meditation. Among these are interest in construction of buildings and monasteries, nepotism, greed for food and clothes, and sickness. Also included is the acquisition of miraculous powers (*siddhis*), which, when indulged in, would hinder the development of insight necessary to achieve transcendence. So we find in *Visuddhimagga*:

"Psychic powers" are those of an average man. Like a child lying on its back and like tender corn it is difficult to manage. It is broken by the slightest thing. It is an impediment to insight, but not to concentration, because it ought to be obtained when concentration is obtained. Therefore one who desires insight should cut off the impediment of psychic powers, but ... [Buddaghosa 1923, p. 113].

All meditation should have an object on which to fix the attention. Theoretically, there can be any number of objects for meditation. Traditionally, however, 40 of these are mentioned. They include the ten *kasinas*, the ten *asubhas*, ten *anussatis*, four *brahma viharas*, four *arupas*, and, finally, meditation to develop aversion to food and meditation to determine the four elements of the body. The ten *kasinas* include such things as earth, water, fire, wind, color, light, spot, and circumscribed space. The ten *asubhas* are a variety of situations in which a corpse is the object of meditation. The *anussatis* (recollections) involve meditating on the merits of the Buddha, *dhamma* (morality), *sangha* (society), *sila* (conduct), *caga* (charity), and *nibbana*. In this list is also included breath control. Breath control is given a very prominent place in Buddhist meditational practices. On this, the *Yogavacara's Manual* says:

Let the aspirant who has truly felt the dread of the stream of becoming strive hard to win Nibbāna by earnestly meditating on the way of concentration by inbreathing and outbreathing, held by Our Blessed Lord to be the chief aim of meditation, which is highly praised by Him, and has been of the greatest help to countless Buddhas, among them the last and latest, Gautama the Buddha, for the winning of the Wisdom Supreme [Woodward 1916, p. 67].

The four *brahma viharas* are friendship, compassion, joy, and equanimity. The objects mentioned so far are meant to induce the first four states of *jhana* (Sanskrit: *dhyana*), or meditation. To progress further, the meditator has to use immaterial objects (*arupa*), such as unlimited space, infinite consciousness, nothingness, and the state of neither perception nor non-perception.

The need for choosing a competent teacher is very much emphasized in Buddhist practices. The *guru* (preceptor) should have mastered the fourth and fifth *jhanas*, and have become an *arahant*. If that is not possible, the best available *guru* should be chosen; this should be at least a person of self-restraint. The guru is the guide who leads the meditator through the difficult terrain full of obstacles to a state of right concentration. By understanding the disposition, character, and personality of the disciple, the *guru* can specify an appropriate object for meditation. As Buddhaghosa puts it.

> He [the teacher] instructs beings according to their worthiness, regarding ultimate truths of the present and the future. Further, as "Teacher" he is like the man "with the goods"; i.e., the Blessed One is the caravan leader. As the caravan leader takes the goods across the desert through the dangers of robbers, across places infested by wild beasts, through famine-stricken and waterless regions, takes them over, out of, through such perils, and places them in a safe place, so the Blessed One, the Teacher, the caravan-leader, takes beings across the desert, that is, of birth [1923, p. 239].

The disciple must have absolute faith in the teacher, and should be prepared to obey instructions. The disciple should give evidence of an intention to overcome attachment (*raga*), hatred (*dosa*), and delusion (*moha*). Likewise, the disciple should have a strong desire to meditate and to ultimately attain *nibbana*. The teacher closely scrutinizes and studies the behavior and mental disposition of the disciple, and suggests a suitable object for meditation befitting the disciple's conduct. According to Buddhaghosa, "conduct is of six kinds: conduct of lust, of hate, of delusion, of faith, of intelligence, of applied thought" (1923, p. 118). Buddhaghosa further illustrates the characteristics of the six classes of individuals thus:

> Procedure of the states of mind: wiliness, deceitfulness, pride, evil desire, covetousness, discontentedness, lasciviousness, frivolity— these and other states arise abundantly in one who walks in lust…. Anger, malice, hypocrisy, rivalry, envy, meanness—these and other states arise abundantly in one who walks in hate. Sloth, torpor, distraction, worry, misgiving, obstinate grasping, tenac-

ity—these and other states arise abundantly in one who walks in delusion. Clean liberality, desire to see the Noble Ones, desire to hear the good Law, abundance of joy, absence of craftiness, absence of wiliness, faithfulness in objects of faith—these and other states arise abundantly in one who walks in faith. Docility, good friendship, moderation in food, mindfulness and comprehension, application to wakefulness, emotion over objects of emotion, wise effort due to emotion—these and other states abundantly arise in one who walks in intelligence. Talkativeness, fondness of society, want to delight in moral application, unsteadiness in work, smokiness by night, luminosity by day, running after this and that object—these and other states abundantly arise in one who walks in thoughts. Thus one may explain the kinds of conduct from the procedure of states [1923, pp. 124–25].

The teacher, after understanding the disciple's basic disposition and character, recommends suitable objects for meditation. For example, for one whose behavior is characterized by lust, the ten *asubhas*, such as involving a corpse as the object of meditation, are recommended; and for one who is characterized by *dosa*, or hatred, one of the four *brahma vihāras* is recommended. Thus, it is evident that the choice of an appropriate object for meditation has been given a very prominent place in Buddhist meditational practices.

The process of meditation involves certain preliminary practices and two kinds of exercises before one enters a *jhana* state. Eight successive states of *jhana* are distinguished. The preliminaries include offering invocations to the Buddha, *dhamma*, and *sangha*, prayers for happiness of all beings, confession of one's guilt, and faith in the teachings of the Buddha.

Sitting cross-legged and his body erect, the disciple endeavors to fix his mind on the object of meditation. The first exercise is *upacara*, which is preparatory to reach a state of absorption. This exercise has three steps. In the first step the meditator fixes his attention on the object of his meditation. The second step is visualization and the meditator is able to form a mental image of the object with his eyes closed, an image that is as vivid and distinct as the object itself. In the third stage, the meditator attempts to have the image clearer and brighter than the object itself but devoid of such characteristics as color, form, and size. It may be mentioned that in the state of *upacara* the meditator's mind has not reached a state of steady concentration. The attention of the mind still wanders.

> At access [upacara] the factors owning to their weakness, are not strong. As a baby-child on being lifted to its feet, falls down repeatedly to the ground, even so when the access arises the mind at times makes the sign the object, at times lapses into subconsciousess. At ecstasy [appana] the factors from their very strength are strong. As a strong man rising from his seat might stand even the whole day, so when ecstatic concentration arises consciousness, once it has cut off the occasion of subconsciousness, lasts the whole night, even the whole day, and proceeds by way of moral apperceptional succession [Buddhaghosa 1923, p. 147].

To attain the state of *appana,* the meditator should sever the connection between his subliminal consciousness (*bhavanga citta*) and the object of meditation so that he can reflect on the image of the object without activating the *bhavanga.* When he is able to do this and reflect on the image for a certain length of time he is said to have entered into the first stage of *jhana.*

The persons who enter such a state should continue to direct their mind to the object of meditation and engage in a steady concentration of the mind on that object. In addition, the practitioner should dissociate himself from the worldly attractions, deprive himself of physical pleasures, and free himself from mental impurities.

There are five aspects to the first state

of meditation. They are *vitakka* (discursive or relational thought), *vicara* (inquiry), *piti* (joy), *sukha* (pleasure), and *ekeggata* (concentration). *Piti* and *sukha* are the emotive factors. *Ekeggata* represents the effort involved in obtaining a state of absorption, which is the goal of meditative concentration. When the meditator enters the first stage, his worldly desires are eliminated and the undesirable mental states are removed. He develops equanimity and enjoys psychological bliss. The meditator having achieved the first stage is advised to repeat it and practice entering into, maintaining and coming out of the same state. Such a practice would lead him into the second stage, where discursive and inquiring faculties cease to function. The object of meditation, we are told, gets so integrated with the mind that the physical sensations cease. The meditator experiences complete tranquillity. He is able to concentrate his mind on the object of meditation so completely that his senses do not respond to any external or internal stimulations. The meditator at this stage attains full concentration of the mind and experiences pleasure and happiness.

When they enter the third stage, the meditators are no longer worried about such thoughts as the impermanence of the world or about theories of suffering and nothingness. They are not affected by feelings of pleasure or happiness. They enjoy perfect ease, which they realize only after coming out of the state. In the fourth stage, the meditator experiences complete freedom from physical as well as mental pain or happiness. All these four stages of meditation are attained by the practice of concentration on a suitable object to induce *upacara* and *appana.*

In addition, there are four other higher stages that are achieved by meditating on the four *arupas,* viz., unlimited space, unlimited consciousness, nothingness, and a condition of neither perception nor nonperception. By concentrating on unlimited space, the mind of the meditator overcomes all sense distinctions and attains the fifth stage. By meditating on the condition of neither perception nor nonperception he attains a transperceptual state and reaches the eighth stage. This is the highest stage of meditation one could hope to achieve. In fact, after the fourth stage of meditation, the meditator becomes emancipated and achieves a state of transcendence by overcoming all mental limitations (*ceto-vimuth*).

Despite several fundamental differences in the philosophical positions between Yoga and Buddhist systems, as we have seen, there is a great deal of similarity between the meditation practices advocated by them. The yogic *samadhi* and the Buddhist *jhana* state have much in common, including their progressive nature to achieve a transperceptual state of consciousness in which the realization of perfect knowledge and understanding is believed to be possible. What that perfect knowledge is, however, appears to be a matter of one's focus of meditation and philosophical predisposition. Each system has its own eggs (ideas) to hatch; but the method of hatching (meditation) appears to be essentially the same. In Yoga, the goal is the realization of the *purusha* consciousness in its sublime purity unsullied by its appearance in mundane mental phenomena. In Advaita Vedanta, it is the realization of the illusory nature of the world of appearance and the understanding of the essential identity of the self with the *Atman*, the undifferentiated self-manifesting, contentless pure consciousness. In Buddhism generally, it is the experience of impermanence and momentariness, and in Madhyamika especially, it is the realization of the emptiness (*sunyata*), the nonfoundational character, of all existence.

If one could gain perfect knowledge through meditation, how is it that there are these different notions on the nature of the universe among those who presumably had

access to the highest state? It is possible that the highest meditative experience may be similar to all, whether one is a Buddhist or a Vedantin, but a discursive discernment of that experience later may be determined by one's prior philosophical assumptions. Therefore, the same experience may be described differently. It may also be the case that in the highest state of consciousness, no new knowledge is revealed, but essential insights into one's concerns at the moment are obtained so that one gains clarity and conviction associated with the ideas on which the meditation is focused. In any case, what seems to be critically important to the meditator is the inner transformation, rather than mere knowledge, brought about by an integration of knowing and being, which are often dissociated in our lives. Also, meditative experience at its highest level is regarded by all systems as blissful.

Non-Theravada Traditions in Buddhism

The preceding account of Buddhist psychology of consciousness differs from that of Yoga and Vedanta. In the latter, as we have seen, consciousness-as-such is contentless and nonintentional. For Buddhaghosa, however, consciousness is "that which thinks of its object." In this sense, consciousness is clearly intentional. Buddhaghosa, unlike Samkara, for example, does not distinguish between mind and consciousness. Where he describes consciousness in the intentional sense, he is describing the mind and its cognitive functions. Buddhaghosa belongs to the *Theravada* school in the *Hinayana* tradition, which subscribed to a metaphysics of realism. In the later developments of Buddhist thought, such as in Mahayana, we find a somewhat different approach, which places a greater emphasis on consciousness as distinct from the mind.

Buddha's concerns were practical and not speculative. It is all too well known that Buddha was silent when fundamental metaphysical questions were asked. Buddha left no unambiguous answers to many questions a philosophy should answer. Consequently soon after his death differences arose among his disciples. This led inevitably to the emergence of different schools. In India, as mentioned earlier, there are four such schools with distinctive philosophies of their own. They range from the radical pluralism of Vaibhasika to radical absolutism of Madhyamika, from realism of Sautrantika to idealism of Yogacara. T.R.V. Murti (1983) points out three distinctive phases in the development of Buddhist thought. The first is the realistic and pluralistic phase of Theravada and Vaibhasika. This is partially modified as critical realism in Sautrantika. The second phase emerges with the Madhyamika of Nagarjuna (2nd century AD). With a series of *reductio ad absurdum* arguments, Nagarjuna has attempted to show the logical absurdities of all rational attempts to understand being and non-being. He has argued that one needs to rise above reason to a higher level of consciousness, where one has intuitive insight. The third phase, according to Murti, is the emergence of Yogacara idealism of Asanga and Vasubandhu (4th century AD). The salient feature of this phase is the emphasis on *vijnana*, consciousness as the sole reality. Madhyamika's *sunya* is now identified with pure consciousness. The Vaibhasika *dharmas* (momentary elements of existence) have become mental states.

Nagarjuna emphasized the *Abhidamma* distinction between two levels of truth, the empirical (*samvriti*) and the transcendental (*paramartha*) truth. *Samvriti,* which literally means a covering or a screen that shrouds the transcendental truth, gives rise to the variety of phenomena of our experience. The distinctions such as subject and object belong to this level; and reason

reigns supreme here. But once this level is transcended, one recognizes the illusory nature of the phenomena, just as one apprehends the illusory nature of the dream after waking up. At the transcendental level, there are no subject-object distinctions and no discursive thought and reflection to give us knowledge. The only source of true knowledge is by way of revelation and direct intuition. Nagarjuna does not repudiate the reality of the empirical world in any absolute sense. He denies, however, that it is the ultimate reality. As shadow reality, the world of phenomena is useful in reaching the ultimate state of *nirvana*.

Nagarjuna's philosophy is called Sunyavada. *Sunya* is not absolute nothingness, but lack of substantiality. We are reminded here of the French existential philosopher Sartre. The notion that the world is *sunya* (void or empty) is an assertion of the nonsubstantial nature of the mind and the world it is supposed to grasp; it is the essential groundlessness of the mind and the objects. The understanding one achieves in the highest state of consciousness that gives one the realization of *sunyata*, the emptiness, cannot be an act of knowing, because there is no object to know. As Varela, Thompson, and Rosch (1993) point out: "knowing *sunyata* (most accurately, knowing the world as *sunayata)* is surely not an intentional act. Rather, (to use traditional imagery), it is like a reflection in a mirror—pure, brilliant, but with no additional reality apart from itself" (p. 225).

The distinction between *samvriti* (empirical) and *paramartha* (ultimate or transcendental) is basic for Nagarjuna. He asserts in the *Madhyamaka-Karika*: "Those who are unaware of the distinction between these two truths [*samvriti* and *paramartha*] are incapable of grasping the deep significance of the teaching of Buddha" (xxiv, 9). Empirical determinations of knowledge as in *samvriti* are covered by categories of thoughts, distorted by points of view and biased by the functions of the mind. The ultimate truth is undetermined, direct and ineffable. It is "experienced by the wise in a very intimate way." Therefore, *paramartha* is the knowledge of the real without any distortions. It may be mentioned that in Buddhism perception is always indeterminate, inarticulate and nameless (Sinha 1958, vol. 1, p. 105).

The *Madhyamika* distinction between *samvriti* and *paramartha* is very much like Samkara's conception of *vyavaharika* (empirical) and *paramartha* (ultimate). The difference, however, is that Nagarjuna, unlike Samkara, does not find the need to postulate a ground, a foundation, underlying all reality. Consequently, the highest knowledge for him is not the realization of the unity with the ultimate such as the *Brahman*. Rather, it is the realization of the groundlessness of all existence. The *Brahman* devoid of any qualities in Samkara's philosophy is similar to *sunyata* in Nagarjuna. Again, the role of *avidya* in the manifestation of the phenomenal world is accepted in Advaita as well as Madhyamika philosophies. (For a comparison of Advaita and Madhyamika views on this point see Murti 1983.)

In the Yogacara school of Buddhism, also known as Vijnanavada, the intentionality of consciousness is only apparent (Mohanty 1979). When one is conscious of blue, according to this school, the blueness is a form of consciousness and not of an outside object. In other words, when one sees blue, there is no "self-transcending reference" to an object external to the cognition itself. Any such reference is due to ignorance (*avidya*). Consequently, all imputation of intentionality to consciousness is false. Consciousness in this view is self-revealing. Consciousness and its contents are identical because they are apprehended together without exception. (See Jaiswal 1999 for an evaluation of the nature of consciousness in Vijnanavada).

Vijananavada accepts *sunyata,* but with a difference. In Madhyamika the approach is *logical*, whereas the Vijnanavada takes a psychological view. According to Madhyamika, phenomena lack reality because they are interdependent, whereas in Vijnanavada the objectivity itself is dependent on consciousness. Consciousness exists by itself. Consciousness may undergo modifications, but it can overcome all superimpositions and find itself in its essential real form. *Sunyata*, then, is not devoid of reality, it is *pure consciousness* devoid of subject-object duality. Pure consciousness, which is the undifferentiated essence of all things, takes on three-fold modifications. First is *visaya-vijnana* or object-consciousness arising from sense data including introspective awareness of objects. It gives us knowledge of external objects, like books, trees and houses. The knowledge itself is a projection of consciousness. The second modification (*mano-vijnana*) is the one brought about by the mental functions of analysis and assimilation, a synthetic experience of the object perceived. The third is *alaya-vijnana*, the storehouse of consciousness. Vijnanavada asserts the existence of pure consciousness without any objective content on the basis of reported experiences in *samadhi* states.

Finally, even in the Hinayana tradition such as in Theravada, the higher states of *jhana* consciousness cannot be regarded as intentional. These are states in which consciousness transcends subject-object, matter-form distinctions. The understanding of unlimited space, infinite consciousness, nothingness, and a "neither perception nor nonperception" state, it would seem, is essentially an exercise to dissociate consciousness from its objects. *Arupa-loca* clearly refers to formlessness. *Lokottara-citta* or transcendental consciousness cannot be intentional.

We thus find in Theravada tradition of early Buddhism greater attention paid to the mind and its states without making any meaningful distinction between mind and consciousness. There is no discussion of consciousness-as-such. In this respect, the early Buddhist notion of consciousness is somewhat similar to the Western. The reason for this may be found in Buddha's empirical concerns and his general reluctance to go beyond the immediate existential concerns to the more remote metaphysical issues. Buddhism, however, can not stop with a consideration of phenomenal consciousness, because its ultimate goal is to transcend these states and achieve the state of transcendence (*nirvana*). The later developments in Buddhist thought are clearly the attempts to close the gap between phenomenal and transcendental states of consciousness. In our own discussion of Buddhist psychology, we focused more on early Buddhism because we find in it the nature and states of phenomenal consciousness discussed in greater detail and depth than the other Indian systems, which are concerned more with pure consciousness than phenomenal consciousness. In fact, the Hindu systems and the schools of Buddhism complement each other in significant ways to give us a more comprehensive understanding of consciousness.

Heuristic Summary

Buddha's teachings were meant to be a radical departure from the then prevalent Upanishadic thought of the Hindus. In a sense they were. Buddha repudiated the widespread practice of rituals and sacrifices as meaningless. He discarded the notion that permanence is the hallmark of reality. He saw permanence only in change. He rejected the existence of a substantive soul or *atman* underlying the changing states of the mind. He felt pain and suffering in abundance around him. In his statement of the four noble truths he centered on suffering,

its cause, its cessation, and the means of overcoming it. Freedom from suffering was the goal. He recommended an eight-fold path to achieve that goal. This path consisted of practicing virtues (*sila*), cultivating mind by concentration (*samadhi*) and achieving wisdom (*prajna*). This triple pronged drive of *sila*, *samadhi* and *prajna*, he believed, would lead one to *nirvana*, the goal of cessation of all suffering, the dawn of perfect knowledge, and the disappearance of ignorance. Buddha believed that knowledge about the nature of suffering would set one free from bondage and suffering. That knowledge is beyond reason and discursive intellect, a matter of immediate experience, intuitive insight.

Scholars like S. Radhakrishnan have shown a number of similarities between Buddhism and some of the Hindu doctrines and argued that Buddha was himself influenced by *Upanishadic* thought and Samkhya philosophy which is believed to antedate the advent of Buddhism. There is no question that Buddha was influenced by some of the ideas contained in the *Upanishads*. Among Gautama's teachers were Samkhya philosophers. At the same time, it is also equally evident that Buddhism influenced many of the subsequent Indian thinkers, including Samkara. Not withstanding all this, there is no denying the fact that there are fundamental differences between Buddhism and other systems of philosophy, especially Advaita. Buddhism is a philosophy of becoming whereas Vedanta is a philosophy of being. As Murti (1983) points out: "It would be difficult to find two philosophies so different as Vedanta and Buddhism" (p. 199).

Buddhism in the various phases of its development made important contributions to philosophical thought. What is important, however, for the purposes of our study is the common thread that runs through various systems of Indian thought, whether orthodox like Vedanta or heterodox like

Buddhism. The common thread appears to be the core concepts and the method rather than the content, the source of knowledge rather than its substance.

The core concepts that run through all the major systems of Indian thought and in a significant sense characterize the Indian psyche are *karma, dharma and moksha*. Different systems may use different words but the connotations are not far apart. For example, In Samkhya-Yoga we find *kaivalya*, whereas it is *nirvana* in Buddhism and *moksha* in Vedanta. It is generally agreed that one is born with *karma* and accumulates *karma* during his lifetime by his thoughts and actions. We are conditioned beings because of our *karma*. It makes us creatures of habits, biases and predispositions. It detains us, as it were, in a deterministic universe. By our true nature we are unconditioned beings. Therefore, the goal of human endeavor is to find one's freedom (*moksha*). The way to achieve this is the path of *dharma*. Understanding *dharma* and acting following its precepts one may overcome *karma* and its effects. As we have seen, Buddhism has much to say about *dharma*. It describes human nature in terms of *dharma* and the states of mind. It provides us with profound insights and an empirical psychology far more detailed and elaborate than any thing we find in other Eastern systems. This, it does without losing sight of the ultimate goal of achieving transcendence

In the search for truth, the Indian approach, whether orthodox or heterodox, is to focus attention inward, first, to identify the elements that distort our perceptions and understanding of truth. The second step is to explore the methods that help us control these elements. The third step is to develop techniques to seek truth directly without distortions. The final step is to formulate theories and prescribe practices of conduct that enable us to know and experience truth. There is a general consensus among Indian thinkers that the knowledge

we have of the world around us is tainted. This is for a variety of reasons. We find ourselves at the center of a circle covered with ignorance. Our task is to break through the circle, pierce the veil of ignorance and find truth. Meditation is a means of achieving a state where we transcend ignorance and realize truth. In this process it is assumed that there is a more secure source of truth than the tainted knowledge obtained through sensory channels and analyzed by reason and discursive argument. Buddhism, like the other Indian systems we discussed, is a quest for perfect knowledge and unsullied truth that would at once dispel ignorance and remove suffering.

We regard certain behaviors as normal because they represent to us the consensus reality—the experiential reality we all seem to agree on. Such a consensus reality is made possible by similarities in the psychical processes and structures that we humans appear to share in common. When structural or process changes occur, the ensuing experiences present a reality that may not agree with our consensus reality. Within the framework of the altered state, however, they could make sense. Difficulties arise when we seek to explain experiences obtained in an altered state of consciousness by concepts derived from experiences obtained in our so-called normal state of consciousness (Tart 1972).

Buddhism in all its forms recognizes nonsensory sources of awareness. Buddha himself attained his state of wisdom by intuitive insight and not by discursive reasoning. Like the Buddha, many Buddhist thinkers were less consumed by theoretical concerns and more fascinated by the practical applications of their understanding of consciousness to achieve higher states to know truth and to end suffering.

Even though we do not find awareness, consciousness, and mind sharply distinguished in Buddhist writings, all of them are included in the Buddhist conception of consciousness. In Buddhist view consciousness implies awareness (*vinnana*), both as a process and as the content of our cognitions. So, we find Buddaghosa saying: "Consciousness is that which thinks of its object... Cognizing object is its characteristic, forerunning is its function, connecting is its manifestation, a mental and material organism is its proximate cause" (1920, pp. 148–49). Again, "the resultant is also termed, 'consciousness' because it is accumulated (*cito*) by kamma and the corruptions" (p. 85). Thus, mind for the Buddhists is both a process and a repository for all our cognitions.

Our normal consciousness is a stabilized set of psychic structures that function to regulate our awareness. This set is reasonably stable for any individual (with predictable variations), and is normally shared by others. However, it is not unalterable. When it is modified, one enters into an altered state of consciousness. In Buddhist psychology consciousness is analyzed into various elements that unite in a number of combinations and give us a variety of conscious states. It would not be appropriate to regard all these as altered states. But the analysis itself is helpful in understanding how alterations of consciousness occur and what specific characteristics such alterations would manifest.

I find Charles Tart's (1975) analogy of the computer to be helpful in understanding the components of consciousness. He points out that some structures of our consciousness are essentially permanent, such as the biological and physiological givens. These constitute the hardware of the mind. Other structures are mainly a result of the individual's developmental history; they derive from such processes as conditioning, learning, and acculturation. These constitute the software of the human mind. Our so-called normal state of consciousness is determined by the hardware of the mind as well as by the program that appears to be common to most individuals during most of their life-time. This does not mean, however, that the program does not undergo any changes or that it is essentially identical in all human beings. While the seed program is shared largely, the program itself may be more or less complex and developed. An individual's accumulated *karma* and *samskaras* influence his cognition and action to some degree. Consequently, information processed by one mind may not be processed by another in precisely the same way. However, information relating to similar things is likely to be similar, because the two minds share the same basic program.

Buddhist psychology attempts to understand how this processing normally takes place and whether the programming can be qualitatively changed. Buddhists believe that it is possible not only to induce modifications in an individual's program, but also to bring about radical changes in the organization of given psychic structures—resulting in a qualitatively different functioning of the mind.

In Buddhist psychology, the concept "*karma*" approximates what we here call "programming." *Karma*, however, determines both the hardware as well as the software, inasmuch as Buddhists believe that even the physical form is a fruit of past *karma*. The Buddhist conception of *karma* is not merely a hypothesis. It also explains how modifications in the programming process can be brought about. Volition (*cetana*) is the key concept here.

Volition is both a source of accumulated *karma* and also an instrument to bring about changes in our program. Volition is the mental function that coordinates and closely binds other functions of the mind. It gives direction to our activity as well as provides necessary energy for action. In its *karma*-producing aspect, it creates in us the illusion of "I-ness," and all actions and experiences thus gain ego-reference. Whenever there is such ego-reference, all related actions produce *karma*, which, in turn, conditions subsequent behavior. Ego, then, is an epiphenomenon; it results from the way the volition functions to bind the various psychic structures. This means that the ego itself is not an intrinsic structure necessary for all our mental processes. Therefore, we do not find ego included among the five *skandhas* of the mind. It is not to be found even among the seven universal elements (*cetasikas*) of consciousness. Ego is merely a creation of our volition.

At the same time, Buddhism recognizes that volition can—by being directed in meditation (*jhāna*) and other means of psychic development—function in such a way that the resultant experiences do not have ego-reference. Such actions are those that are necessarily not motivated and determined by previous *karma*. All *karma*-prompted experiences have ego-reference as their basic characteristic—that is, the experiences are regarded as belonging to the experiencer. The very process of experiencing is itself processed through a program that is determined by *karma*. In such a situation, the cognitions experienced or the knowledge derived from them are personal in the sense that they are dependent on the nature and condition of the experiencing person. To transcend this personal character of cognition and knowledge, it is necessary that the knowledge process be free from the influences of *karma* and its associated habits and reflex like responses. In other words, the person in his existential context is conditioned. His freedom consists in making him unconditioned.

How can this be done? This brings us to a critically important point in Buddhist psychology. In cognitive processes, the normal flow of *bhavanga* is halted, but the *bhavanga* itself gets perturbed and goes into a state of convulsion. *Bhavanga*, it appears, is the medium through which *karma* influences our being and behavior. Buddhists believe that it is possible to eliminate *karma*

influence, so that the resulting knowledge escapes the limitations of the human condition. The human condition, which is characterized as a continuous cycle of birth and death, is a preprogrammed cognitive style and behavior disposition, which sets boundaries and limits to what we can experience and the sense that can be made of the experience. Transcendence is thus a release of the "imprisoned splendor," to use R.C. Johnson's phrase, made possible by the breaking of ego shackles and *karma* influences. We are told, for example, that a meditator in attempting to reach the *appana* state seeks to reflect the image of an object without stimulating *bhavanga*. If he is successful, he enters the *jhāna* states, which leads him progressively to transcendence. Cognitively, a state of transcendence is one where the person is able to image and reflect on an object without stimulating *bhavanga*. The resultant knowledge is perfect in the sense that it is unbiased, objective, and impersonal.

We may note here the interesting difference between Samkhya-Yoga and Advaita Vedanta on the one hand and Buddhism on the other. *Bhavanga* is a concept specific to Buddhism. As mentioned earlier, it is similar to *buddhi*, but also quite different from it. *Bhavanga* is the unconscious stream of awareness and the carrier of *karma* like the *samskaras* and *vasanas*. The *samskaras* are, however, are part of the *buddhi* and do not constitute a separate stream of subterranean flow of consciousness. In Yoga, we presuppose the existence of *purusha*, a center of consciousness, without which no conscious awareness is possible. The light of consciousness shines on the *vritti* of the *buddhi* to render the mental states subjectively experienced. In Buddhism no such separate source of consciousness is assumed. Consciousness is considered an intrinsic aspect of mental states themselves. In *bhavanga* it is subterranean and in phenomenal states it is overt and associated with subjective experience. In transcendental states, it is nonrepresentational and devoid of sensory content. This notion is somewhat similar to the subconscious/subliminal self of F.W.H. Myers and the analogy of the light spectrum. At one end of the spectrum is the *bhavanga* mentation. At the other end are the transcendental states of *jhana*. Buddhists, however, will not accept the notion of subliminal self.

The differences between the Hindu systems we discussed and Buddhist schools are at the metaphysical level. For example, Yoga subscribes to the notion of substantive *purusha*. Similarly, in Advaita, *Brahman/ Atman* is the ground condition of consciousness. Buddhism rejects the notion of any such substantive ground reality, whether mind or matter. However, by accepting the reality of transcendental states of consciousness, which are essentially devoid of content and therefore nonintentional, Buddhism does not reject the notion of pure consciousness. In fact, pure consciousness is implied in the higher states of *jhana*. This point is mute in early Buddhism, but becomes more explicit in the later writings of Madhyamika and Yogacara thinkers.

To sum up, then, we postulate the existence of a stream of consciousness which, functioning at the subliminal level, is the basis of the subjective feeling of continuity and identity and which is the binding influence on our perceptions, thoughts, actions, and feelings. This stream, which operates below the threshold of normal awareness, carries with it the imprints of a person's life history—predisposing him to behave in certain ways. These imprints motivate, condition, and drive an individual to behave in set ways; but they lose their strength and may even disappear soon after they have activated a set behavior. However, the resultant experience will, in its turn, produce another imprint. And so, the chain of causation continues. The imprints are formed when the mind functions in such a way that

the resultant experiences have ego reference and entanglement. But it is possible for the mind (1) to function so as to destroy the imprints, and (2) to function without precipitating new imprints. Attainment of a state where all these imprints are destroyed or disarmed and where the mind functions independently of the processing medium is the state of psychological transcendence. This is basically a transego state engendered by a reorganization of the psychic structures with the help of such devices as meditation.

Much of what has been said is admittedly speculative. But the medium that Buddhist psychology finds necessary to postulate is no more mysterious than the Freudian unconscious or the Jungian archetypes. What is interesting, however, is the explanatory model that extends psychology's scope to account for normal, abnormal, and paranormal behaviors. The implications of the theory to paranormal psychology are obvious. The state of transcendence is one in which new cognitive relationships are established and where subject-object dichotomies cease. It is necessarily a state where our experience and knowing are not limited by space-time barriers or our normal sensory thresholds. The theory also fits well with several of the psychodynamic factors studied by depth psychologists. In fact some aspects of the theory have test implications, and permit empirical verification.

I find the Buddhist ideas particularly helpful in planning empirical studies of meditation. They provide a rich phenomenology for understanding the changes in consciousness accompanying meditation, which could be utilized to determine the associated psychophysiological states. Such a determination would not only give us the needed objectivity to describe these phenomena, but would also permit a more precise application of the meditative techniques to aspects perhaps less significant than transcendence but more immediately relevant—

such as mental health. For example, much psychoanalytic groundwork is aimed at scanning the patient's life history to identify those critical past experiences that seem to be causing the present symptoms. But the treatment itself only touches the periphery of the problem. What could be more important in psychotherapy than to find a method of disarming or, even better, for destroying the disruptive effects of such past experience? Certain aspects of Buddhist meditation do promise to accomplish just that. More importantly, Buddhist psychology presupposes a state of transcendence, which in important respects resembles the state of pure consciousness in Samkhya and Advaita Vedanta philosophies.

Setting aside the speculative, metaphysical and sacred aspects of the Hindu and Buddhist thought, one may focus on the secular, psychological assumptions of the concept of pure consciousness in Samkhya-Yoga-Vedanta and the concept of void (*sunya*) in Buddhism. Pure consciousness is stated to be in principle characterless and without content. As an experiential state, and not as a metaphysical presupposition, *sunyata* or pure consciousness may mean one of two things. It may be essentially in-

describable or ineffable in terms of communicating what it is like to experience it. Language may be an incompetent tool here. Empirically derived characteristics, the qualities that we are familiar with in *vyavaharika* or *samsara* mode, may be utterly inadequate for that purpose. Alternately, the state of pure consciousness may be literally "void," a complete blank, a state like profound sleep with no mentation taking place. In either case, it would seem, achieving a state of pure consciousness is not inconsequential. If it is an ineffable state, it may be inexpressible but can be shared. In other words, it would still have inter-subject validity because people who achieve that state may share essentially similar and experientially meaningful outcome. Even assuming that pure consciousness is a complete blank state of the mind, we may recall, in Hindu thought it is an extremely blissful state and in Buddhism it leads to an end of suffering. In either case, it is a very desirable state. Even occasional excursions into the region of pure consciousness may have remarkable consequences, as suggested, at a secular level. They may be even amenable for intersubject validation and empirical verification.

CHAPTER 11

When East and West Meet: The Case of Meditation

Rudyard Kipling wrote: "East is East and West is West, and never the twain shall meet." This celebrated statement is often interpreted to mean that Eastern and Western traditions have distinctive identities and that they do not influence each other. In our attempts to study consciousness from Eastern and Western perspectives and to explore their complementary characteristics we may learn some historical lessons from an examination of the past interactions between East and West. If two cultures with distinct identities meet, it is possible: (a) a synthesis of them may emerge, a melting pot situation, (b) one may displace the other by domination, (c) both may coexist with mutual isolation, or (d) they may form a mosaic complementing each other.

West came to East by the route of trade and then spread its political wings to colonize and rule much of Asia. Western presence in Asia was obviously a meeting point between East and West. It had a double effect. East had an intense Western exposure and West had gained firsthand familiarity with Eastern traditions. As West ruled East, it attempted to impose its values and establish its institutions on Eastern soil. It was largely successful in that. At the same time, Eastern thought and literature attracted the attention of some Western scholars who translated several of the Eastern classics. These have fascinated a few Western thinkers who paid attention to them. Yet, in a very important sense, both in East and West there was little tangible evidence of reciprocal influence. In the East, Western type of institutions by and large displaced the native structures. The latter either languished in isolation or were abandoned altogether. In either case they had little impact on the existing type of institutions. The West was too proud and protective of its own heritage to allow itself to be influenced in any significant way by its exposure to the East. Even those in the West with curious and open minds, who had some familiarity with Eastern thought and who were indeed fascinated by its depth and contrast to their own had some difficulty in dealing with it. They in some ways appear to have been afraid that they might be swept away by the powerful currents of the Eastern stream if they attempted to pay attention to it.

Consider, for example, what happened to the distinguished psychologist C. G. Jung. Jung went to India in December of 1937 and spent about three months there. He was overwhelmed by "the impact of the dreamlike world of India." The biographer Gerhard Wehr (1987) tells us that in order "not to lose himself in the hypnotic quality of Eastern religiosity," Jung took with him the first volume of *Theatrum Chemicum*, a book on alchemy that he read from beginning to end during the trip to India. What appears to be a prelude to Jung's leaving India was a great dream he had, which he evaluated in the following way:

> Imperiously, the dream wiped away all the intense impressions of India and swept me back to the too-long-neglected concerns of the Occident, which had formerly been expressed in the quest for the Holy Grail as well as in the search for the philosophers' stone. I was taken out of the world of India, and reminded that India was not my task, but only a part of the way—admittedly a significant one—which should carry me closer to my goal. It was as though the dream were asking me, "What are you doing in India? Rather seek for yourself and your fellows the healing vessel, the *salvator mundi*, which you urgently need. For your state is perilous; you are all in imminent danger of destroying all that centuries have built up" [quoted from Gerhard Wehr 1987, pp. 288–289].

Jung was of course a great admirer of Eastern spirit. He pleaded for "understanding openness, beyond any Christian resentment, beyond any European arrogance." Yet he asked: "What good is the wisdom of the Upanishads to us, and the insights of Chinese yoga, if we abandon our own foundations like outworn mistakes, to settle thievishly on foreign shores like homeless pirates?" (quoted from Wehr, 1987, p. 463). This predicament of Jung reinforces the notion that East and West as two distinct traditions tend to stay separate, possibly fear-ful of each other and lends support to Kipling's dictum.

West Came to East

Centuries before the Portuguese, the French and the British came East to trade and then to rule, India, for example, had a long intellectual tradition with vast literature, highly developed languages, rich philosophical thought and well-trenched native religious life styles. Two centuries of British rule had changed India in many ways; and yet India remained essentially the same in some ways. The religious outlook, native belief systems, the values of *dharma*, *karma*, and *moksha* (freedom) remained in the Indian psyche with little change through centuries.

Indians during the two centuries of Western colonial rule were exposed to European languages, Western science and values. European education displaced the native learning both in content and method. The British established universities in India nearly one and half centuries ago. They were created to teach European literature and science, to instruct Christian morals and Western jurisprudence, and to train a class of persons qualified "for high employment in the civil administration of India." The British rulers saw little that is valuable in native literature, whether Sanskrit or Arabic. In the process, there was not merely a neglect of the native tradition by the rulers, but an unscrupulous attempt to displace it.

The main objective of promoting higher education in India by the British was to Westernize elite Indians with whom they could communicate and through whom they could administer and control their empire. Western education was intended to stabilize their hold on Indian people and continue their control with clear imperialistic designs. The silver lining, however, was the intrinsic benefit of education, whether

Indian or Western. In fact some Indians welcomed the introduction of Western type of education. For example, Raja Rammohan Roy protested against the establishment of a Sanskrit college in Calcutta on the ground that he did not want the new generation of Indians to ponder over "the vain and empty subtleties" of the speculative thinkers of a bygone age. From the other side, some of the British leaders opposed the introduction of Western education in India for the fear that it would be difficult to rule India when Indians have Western education. One of them lamented that they had just lost America because of their folly in having allowed the establishment of schools and colleges and that it would not do for them to repeat the same act of folly in regard to India.

Some times, Indians uncharitably depict Lord Macaulay as the villain who foisted on Indians a system of Western education with the sole purpose of keeping India as a British colony forever. They attribute to him all the ills of the present education in India. I believe, this is unfair in some ways because Macaulay's motivation was more cultural than political. He was more interested in spreading Western cultural dominance than continuing the political empire. Consider what he said in the British Parliament years before he wrote his famous Minute.

Are we to keep the people of India ignorant in order that we may keep them submissive? Or do we think that we can give knowledge without awakening ambition? Or do we mean to awaken ambition and to provide it with no legitimate vent? ... It may be that the public mind of India may expand under our system until it has outgrown that system, that by good government we may educate our subjects into a capacity for better government that having become instructed in European institutions. Whether such a day will ever come I know not. Whenever it comes it will be the proudest day in English history.... The scepter may pass away from

us. Victory may be inconsistent to our arms. But there are triumphs, which are followed by no reverse. There is an empire exempt from all natural causes of decay. These triumphs are the pacific triumphs of reason over barbarism: that empire is the imperishable empire of our arts and our morals, our literature and our laws.

So what Macaulay was advocating is not political imperialism, but cultural colonization, replete with British arts and morals, English literature and laws. Education was the force that would create and preserve that cultural empire. Education, for Macaulay, was an instrument for making native Indians "thoroughly English scholars," not just docile subjects.

The governor-general, Lord William Bentinck and his council approved Macaulay's minute on 7 March 1836. Consequently "the promotion of European literature and science amongst the natives of India" became the sole object of the British initiative to aid education in India. Supporting students in colleges of oriental learning was discontinued and no funds were allowed to be spent on printing oriental works. Thus the foundation was laid for building a lasting edifice of Western education on Indian soil. The intentions are very clear. The British rulers were bent on foisting their culture and traditions, paying no attention to the local conditions

Independent India has thus inherited from the colonial rule an alien system of education, functional and deeply entrenched, and universities which flourished with the task of disseminating Western science, literature and values. With the transfer of political power on August 15, 1947, there were enormous changes in the economic and political conditions of Indian society. There were new challenges and responsibilities confronting the Indian people. The social and cultural relevance of education became more apparent and pronounced than ever. The universities needed to assume new duties and manifest a new outlook. They needed to be instruments of change and provide the necessary leadership in politics and governance, in industry and commerce and in promoting and creating knowledge. Yet the universities established and nurtured for preserving and promoting Western science and values remained essentially the same in independent India. England chose to end its political empire, but left intact the cultural empire that Macaulay and those who followed him sought to preserve through the educational institutions they had created.

The peaceful transfer of power in India gave no cause for hasty actions to overthrow the institutions the British rule had created. There was little effort to replace the Western type institutions by indigenous ones. As far as education is concerned, the reasons for this are not difficult to fathom. First, there existed a system that was fully functional and in some ways useful. Second, political power to change the system rested with those who were themselves the products of that system. People like M. K. Gandhi who paid close attention to the dangerous and damaging consequences of an alien system of education kept themselves out of the Government.

Thus West came to India with trade and political ambitions, but they also sought at the same time cultural supremacy. Political compulsion led to a peaceful liquidation of colonial rule. However, the spread of Western education has come to stay and the Western intellectual tradition survived with undiminished influence on the growing minds. Unfortunately, the influence was one way and it did little to enrich the British culturally. When Europeans ruled India, there is no question that they exploited her wealth and natural resources but when they left they hardly took anything from India's treasure chest of ideas and her rich intellectual tradition. The British rule transplanted Western political ideas, European lan-

guages, and some science on Indian soil, which was not bad. However, it was unfortunate that native thought and tradition were treated as weeds to be wiped out rather than as sources that can enrich their own intellectual landscape. Thus, not withstanding centuries of association with East, West remained essentially West. British colonies like India did overcome England's political dominance but did not come out of the intellectual dominance of the West. So, India in a sense lost itself, its intellectual identity.

It would be wrong to say, however, that the association with the West was all bad for India or that the Western colonization had completely wiped out the native ethos. The classical Indian tradition is too strong and has too long a history to be completely displaced. It is true that it lost state patronage for the most part during the colonial period; and it has become less fashionable since to write in native languages or quote the native sources. At the same time, the exposure to Western science and an appreciation of what it stands for, and a measure of proficiency in European languages, especially English were welcome developments that opened up windows of opportunity for many Indians. If these were seen as tools used to harness the natural wealth of native ideas to serve national needs, they would have served a great purpose. Regrettably, they have become ends in themselves. So we have tradition and science staring at each other rather than coming together to address the national issues. As a consequence, science in general and social sciences in particular have become largely irrelevant in the context of national development. The country itself has continued to endure the aches and pains of a "split soul," as it were, caught between acquired "modernity" and inherited tradition. The development of the discipline of psychology in India is an excellent illustration of the schismatic split-soul phenomenon. A discussion of it, I believe, would provide a link with the central concern of inquiry in this book, viz., East-West perspectives of consciousness.

From our discussion of Hindu and Buddhist contributions to our understanding of consciousness in chapters 8, 9, and 10, it is clear that India has a long tradition of psychological theory and practice. Since the time of the *Upanishads*, a thousand years before Christ, there have been fascinating speculations about human nature. It is of course true that the psychological insights contained in *Upanishadic* thought and in several classical systems of Indian philosophy were not born out of experiment and observation as required in contemporary psychology. The classical Indian tradition in psychology is, however, conceptually rich, methodologically different and substantially theory-loaded. This fact is little appreciated in the mainstream psychology, even in India today. Few students of psychology know of the distinct native psychological traditions in India.

Most of the standard psychology textbooks, and even scholarly books on the history of psychology, make no mention of Indian psychology. An exception is the erudite three-volume classic, Brett's *History of Psychology*, which devotes a section in Chapter 18 of Volume 1 to Indian psychology under the heading "Indian writings." Even this section is omitted in the now available abridged edition. Another exception is the latest edition of *Theories of Personality* by Hall and Lindsey, which has a section on Indian theories on personality. Of course, it does not necessarily follow from this that there is no such thing as classical Indian psychology, any more than the non-inclusion of any material on Indian philosophy in a standard book on history of philosophy implies the nonexistence of Indian philosophy. What it does mean, however, is that the native Indian psychological tradition has little influence on what is now regarded as psychology. This is not, however, unique to

psychology. Until Bertrand Russell published his *History of Western Philosophy*, all major books purported to be histories of philosophy were merely histories of Western philosophy, implying that there is no philosophy worth the name except what is available within the Western tradition. Obviously, that state of affairs was due to the pervasive influence of Western intellectual tradition on the rest of the world, owing largely to the West's political and economic dominance during the past couple of centuries.

Psychology as taught in India now is no different from what it obtains in the Western countries, except that it is less original and more imitative. Western psychology came to India in 1916 when the first department of psychology was started at Calcutta University under the leadership of N. N. Sengupta, who had his training under Munsterberg at Harvard University. The inspiration for introducing psychology as a university study came from a staunch nationalist, Brajendra Nath Seal, the great historian of Indian science. Seal helped to draft the first syllabus for the experimental psychology course at Calcutta University (S. Sinha 1963) and he was the main inspiration to Jadunath Sinha (1958; 1961) the author of the monumental work on classical Indian psychology. The founders and promoters of psychology as an academic discipline were thus not unfamiliar with the relevance of classical Indian thought to psychology.

The subcontinent had enjoyed a long line of religio-philosophical tradition that is characteristically Indian. Yet, psychology in India remains today blissfully aloof from its native culture, content to be confined to the narrow boundaries drawn from the borrowed models of the West. It has been said that Indian research in psychology is largely imitative that relies heavily on Western models and concepts (Pandey 1988). As H.S. Asthana (1988) lamented: "The concerns of Western psychology of yester years are the current interests of the Indian psychologists" (pp. 155–156). Durgananda Sinha and Henry Kao also observed how psychological researches in Asia "were largely imitative and replicative of foreign studies. Psychologists in these countries became recipients rather than exchange agents of knowledge. The culture of imitation and replication in research reached a peak when local problems were conceptualized in Western frameworks" (1997, p. 10). Consequently psychological knowledge has played little role in the process of national development in countries like India. Psychological services are simply nonexistent in much of the country. Where they are available, they are little appreciated. This unflattering situation is not confined to psychology alone. The situation in several of the social sciences is no different in many of the developing countries in Asia.

There are many reasons for this state of affairs. First, it is clear that there is little interest among Indian psychologists in classical Indian thought. Few of them have even modest familiarity with the sources. Most of them received their psychological training within the Western tradition and had little exposure to and understanding of classical Indian ideas. Also, with some justification they have grown suspicious of what is paraded in the name of Indian heritage and orthodoxy, which seems to be no more than unwarranted perpetuation of superstition and dogma.

Second, there are understandable difficulties in studying Indian texts that have psychological insights even if this interest is there. In the words of S. K. Ramachandra Rao (1962):

> The field of philosophical inquiry was structured into numerous interests, orthodox and heterodox, so that the compilation of relevant reflections of all interests concerning a specific problem was almost impossible; psychological speculations were extant in diverse and even disparate disciplines (like

metaphysics and medicine, logic and sexology, religion and poetry) so that no writer could be expected to have a competent acquaintance with all of them sufficient to sieve out the psychological contributions; and the multiplicity of languages in which Indian works are written (as, for example, *Vedas* in archaic Sanskrit, the *Upanishads* and later scholastic works in classical Sanskrit, the early Buddhist books in Pali, the Jaina texts in Ardhamagadhi and mixed-Sanskrit) prevented a writer who was not versatile from attempting such a psychological compilation [p. vii].

Third, there is so little of classical thought that is meaningfully presented to a student of this subject. In fact, the available writings are extremely limited. The few that are available suffer from one of two shortcomings. The writer, if he is familiar firsthand with the original sources, has little understanding of psychology as an intellectual discipline. If, on the other hand, he is a trained psychologist, he has no more than superficial knowledge of the scholarly sources of native psychological ideas. In other words, the two traditions stay separate.

Fourth, there appears to be a sharp polarization of viewpoints on the importance and significance of classical thought. At one end are those who extol sanctimoniously the wisdom and virtues of all that is ancient and native. At the other extreme are those who naively reject with utter contempt anything that smacks of a return to the old, which is considered, *excathedra*, superstitious and unworthy of any serious note. What is not covered adequately in the books that are available is the middle ground.

What is needed, therefore, is a systematic and dispassionate rendering of ideas, with emphasis on logical analysis and empirical study. Uninformed rejection as well as undocumented assertion must be equally avoided if we were to arrive at that which is academically and intellectually credible. In a sense, Indian psychology suffers the lack of a Radhakrishnan, who could present a credible and intellectually coherent account, an account that is both systematic and comprehensive, and one that meaningfully interprets Indian thought to students of psychology with clarity and authority.

As the historian of psychology, R. S. Peters (1962) observed:

> Ever since Francis Bacon people have supposed that knowledge is acquired by studiously collecting "data," storing them under a variety of headings, and then cautiously making generalizations which do not go beyond the data. There is, as it were, a Book of Nature, which is being laboriously compiled with chapters set aside for different scientists to write. The material for each chapter is the "subject-matter" of a special science [pp. 25–26].

The above notion, Peters points out, is defective for at least two reasons. First, knowledge seldom arises afresh; it is built on a tradition and a set of assumptions. Psychology, as we understand it today, is a product of over 2,300 years of speculations about a variety of things. It just did not begin in Germany with W. Wundt's establishing a psychological laboratory, or in America with William James's publishing *The Principles of Psychology*. Second, there is no inquiry that is not based on some assumptions. Peters writes, "We are never without interests in and attitudes towards our environment just as we are never without expectations of it and assumptions about it. Patient, passive, presuppositionless enquiry is a methodological myth" (p. 26). Therefore, it is the questions we ask and not the answers we give that are important in the development of a discipline, whether it be physics or psychology. What is known as psychology today, says Peters, is "just an amalgam of different questions about human beings which have grown out of a variety of traditions of enquiry" (p. 27).

As Brett's history shows, Western psychology is built on the inheritance of a tradition of a long line of religio-philosophical and medical writers. In India too, the thinkers of various systems of philosophy and the men who practiced Indian medicine, like their counterparts in Europe, had expectations about human nature and asked questions that showed profound insights into the dispositions of men and women and the causes and the consequences of their behavior.

Unfortunately, however, the psychology we do in India today bears no relationship to this hoary tradition of rich psychological wisdom that could have been an integral part of the psychology we teach and research in India. Instead we have a transplant, an alien tradition replete with concepts that are hardly compatible with our intellectual inheritance. Yet, it survives without any significant modifications. The heavy doses of Westernization that were injected into the main body of our university system have successfully numbed the native cultural sensibilities.

It is true that the psychological insights of our ancestors are not born out of experiment and observation. Much of their thought may be essentially metaphysical and not subject to quick empirical verification. But this should not automatically disqualify them from receiving the academic and intellectual attention they deserve both as a historical backdrop and intellectual heritage and as a theme for further exploration. What are considered to be metaphysical at some point in history may turn out to be empirically verifiable at a later time. Again, concepts such as "instincts" "unconscious" and "mind" may be considered metaphysical from one point of view and empirical from another. Again, there are indeed culture-specific factors that deserve attention in all attempts to understand and explain behavior. Divorced from the native ethos, psychology becomes not only stale and insipid, but also positively irrelevant. Psychology may be a science in the sense that it uses the scientific method, observation and experiment, which may have universal relevance. At the same time, psychology is also like philosophy because it involves organization of data with an orientation and around a worldview. Psychological theorizing involves prior assumptions. For that reason we have theories in and schools and systems of psychology. The assumptions themselves are not data driven but are derived from one's *weltanschauung*. Psychology in India, I believe, is found impotent in being meaningfully involved in the shaping of India's social thought and action because of its alien antecedents and lack of roots in the national ethos.

In recent years, there appears to be an increasing realization of the need to pay more attention to the indigenous traditions. There have been lone voices earlier (e.g., Nandy 1974), but the disenchantment with Western type of psychology among Indian psychologists is becoming more widespread (J.B.P. Sinha 1993). Along with the disenchantment with Western models, there is also a greater appreciation of the usefulness of Eastern models.

Durganand Sinha (1981) for example has been emphatic in asserting the universality of knowledge as well as its cultural relativity. He pointed out that Indian thought contains valuable conceptual, methodological, and theoretical ideas and insights that could provide alternative hypotheses concerning human nature. These could be genuinely complementary to the "Western approach to the subject rooted in materialism, modeled on physical science and taking almost wholly a mechanistic view of man" (p. 3). He pointed out that, unlike in the Western tradition, the dichotomous distinctions of religion and science, material and immaterial, conscious and unconscious do not exist in Indian thought. Similarly, the Indian tradition is not obsessed by the distinction of subject and object. Further, in

the Indian tradition, psychological knowledge is not pursued for its own sake or for exploiting nature seen in opposition to us, but it is applied for self-realization and self-fulfillment. Therefore, we find in Indian psychology, as Sinha (1981) says, searching for "techniques for controlling body and mind, relaxation, meditation techniques for self-control, the ultimate aim being the highest well-being of man" (p. 6).

Paranjpe (1981) also emphasized the complementary character of distinctive Indian ideas to Western scientific psychology. He pointed out how the barriers created by the dichotomies of mind and body, science and religion, conscious and the unconscious were over come by the Yoga and Vedanta thinkers. He suggests that *samadhi* "provides a moment of self-realization, brings about a valuable existential transformation of personality, and also gives a direct, transcognitive experience of reality" (p. 12).

Asian Contributions to Psychology edited by A. C. Paranjpe, D.Y.F. Ho and R. W. Rieber (1988) highlights the indigenous psychological thought of Asian cultures. The volume includes contributions by Eastern and Western scholars, who discuss classical ideas and contemporary research with an emphasis on native traditions. As the editors acknowledge, the volume is a modest contribution to the extremely rich intellectual traditions of Asia. It is, however, an important attempt to draw the attention of psychologists to a highly neglected field of studies they consider significant and relevant not merely to psychology as practiced in Asian countries but to psychology in general. More recently H.S.R. Kao and D. Sinha (1997) brought out another volume entitled *Asian Perspectives on Psychology*. The main theme of this volume is to emphasize culture-specific psychological theory and research. Kao and Sinha point out that psychology as practiced in Asian countries is a "transplant" of psychology developed in the West and that it has little relevance to the realities of Asian life and experience. They attempt to make a case for Asian psychology as distinguished from Western psychology.

Many of the contributors to this volume stress the culture-specific aspects of psychology. They deplore (a) the tendency to borrow alien concepts of questionable relevance to Asia, (b) the uncritical use of methods and tools developed and standardized in Western cultural settings and (c) the lack of indigenous perspectives in the theories and models advanced to understand the behavior patterns of Asian peoples. Such criticism is not unreasonable. The question, which was not unanswered with any measure of success in the volume, however, relates to what really constitutes Asian psychology as distinct from other psychologies, apart from its geographical circumscription. In other words, what is the "identity" of Asian psychology?

Valiant attempts were made by Durganand Sinha and Mala Sinha (1997) in the lead chapter, "Orientation to Psychology: Asian and Western," to sketch the respects in which Asian psychology is different from psychology in the West. They point out that Asian and Western psychologies differ in significant ways in their objective, content and methods. However, the contents of the book are hardly reassuring that the suggested differences do indeed characterize Asian psychology. For example, Sinha and Sinha rightly point out that dichotomies such as subjective and objective, mind and body, theoretical and applied, and so on characterize the Western approach, whereas such dualisms are avoided in the Eastern approach. But, then, several of the discussions in the book are based on essentially similar dichotomous distinctions. A sharp distinction between individualism and collectivism, for instance, characterizes important analyses of Western versus Asian approaches as reviewed in this volume. Thus psychological investigations that are presumed to

address culture specific issues in Asian countries are themselves not free from Western conceptualization.

It would seem that the only heuristic sense in which we may conceptualize region-specific psychologies is the one that refers to psychological models inherent in a native culture. It is the same sense in which we speak of Asian or Eastern philosophy. Of course, such conceptualization presupposes the existence of a distinct psychological tradition in a given culture. In cases where such native traditions exist, it does not follow that they are culture-specific in the sense that the psychological models derived from them are inappropriate to other societies. For example, yoga psychology is relevant not only to Indian society, but also to all humankind. Its relevance consists in enlarging the scope of psychology for a fuller understanding of human nature. We may note in this context that today there are more psychologists interested in yoga in the West than in India. Recall also that all the three authors of the chapter on Vedic psychology in the volume referred, David Orme-Johnson, Eva Zimmerman and Mark Hawkins, are not from the East.

There is no denying of the fact that some of the Asian countries have native psychological traditions that could be genuinely complementary to the currently dominant Western tradition. For example, Houston Smith (1966) contrasts the Western psychology and Indian psychology in the following way:

> Atman, karma, reincarnation, maya ... it may be impossible to prove that objective counterparts to these momentous concepts exist; but has a conceptual schema been devised which is more effective in inspiring the human will in times of need and decision? To compare Indian and Western psychology, one must see Western psychology as the psychology of empirical causation and Indian psychology as the psychology of freedom. In therapeutic terms, Western psychology asks

what can be done to help men; Indian psychology asks what men can do to help themselves [p. 251].

Pratima Bowes (1971; 1981) has written also on the complementary aspects of the Indian and Western views. The dominant Western view, she points out, is that consciousness is localized in a person and that it is a state of mind that occurs in relation to something, the object of awareness. According to this view, there can be no objectless consciousness except as a pure abstraction that has no reality in the world. In Indian thought, consciousness is conceived to be a self-existing, self-luminous, and self-transparent autonomous principle.

T. R. Kulkarni (1972, 1978) attempted to interpret *Upanishads* and Yoga in contemporary psychological terms. He suggested that contemporary trends in psychology help to provide the necessary background for a better understanding of classical Indian psychological ideas. Kulkarni is among the few experimental psychologists in India who paid special attention to Indian psychology. In an article on Yoga psychology, Kulkarni (1968) points out the empirical basis for Yoga. He also suggests that "the type of perceptual learning underlying the highest achievement in Yoga is but a special case of the operation of the general principles which account for perceptual learning in all human individuals irrespective of whether they do or do not practice Yoga" (p. 4). He further argued that "Yoga does provide a rich material that can be subjected to a rigorous experimental scrutiny and investigated in the same manner as common psychological problems are studied in modern laboratories.... Postural fixation, breath-regulation and withdrawal of organs seem fully capable of lending themselves easily for quantification, repetition and various other kinds of experimental manipulation" (p. 9).

One of the early attempts to make a scientific study of yoga with a Western psychological background was by K. T. Behanan (1937). Behanan was a doctoral student from India at Yale University in the U.S. when he undertook this work. He studied under and worked with Swami Kuvalayananda in India. His book, *Yoga: A Scientific Evaluation*, which was in part his Ph.D. thesis, contains an account of his research with himself as a subject. The book is mostly a theoretical analysis of yoga practice and its relation to psychoanalysis and personal psychology. H. S. Brar (1970) attempted to show the similarities between Yoga and psychoanalysis. However, Paranjpe (1984) pointed out that, whereas psychoanalytic free-association facilitates the flow of ideas in the stream of consciousness, Yoga makes no effort to interpret the meaning of the contents of the stream of consciousness. (See also Chakraborty1970.) J. C. Malhotra (1963) reviewed the relation of yoga to psychiatry in a paper. H. C. Coward (1983) called attention to the parallel between the concept of *karma* in Patanjali's *Yoga-Sutras* and modern psychology of memory. In a comparative study of Patanjali yoga and Jung's analytical psychology, Coward (1979) calls our attention to a significant difference between the two. "Whereas in Jung's view the mystic experience of reality required the continued existence of an ego in order to be known, for Patanjali's yoga the ego was nothing more than a limiting and distorting emotional obscuration which had to be removed if the real was to be fully known" (p. 334).

The approach taken by some of the psychologists as above, who think that classical Indian thought has something to offer to the science of psychology, is to relate a few statements found in classical texts to some aspects of contemporary psychological theory or research. Such comparisons may be of interest for historical reasons but can hardly be expected to advance psychological science in any significant manner.

Any attempt to gain legitimacy to classical Indian psychological ideas by making them appear to look respectable because they seem to have some justification, however farfetched, in some laboratory research or contemporary theory is somewhat misguided. Such comparisons hardly give us fruitful programs of future research. The justification for discussing classical ideas in contemporary context must be primarily based on their potential for generating new hypotheses and programs of research that are either complementary or alternative to the existing ones. Contemporary research has little to gain by ad hoc comparisons with classical ideas. The latter do not become respectable simply because they bear some similarity to a contemporary theory.

East Goes West

The meeting of East and West on the Asian soil with Western political and economic dominance, as we have seen, did not help to diminish the great divide between the two. Western type of education had no doubt become deeply rooted and institutionalized in countries like India. The influence was, however, one sided. Thus West came to East, but the two did not really meet. The native ideas and practices had become more isolated and less fashionable, but they were not obliterated altogether. Nor were the Western patterns influenced in any significant way by the native traditions. Kipling's statement is thus vindicated, even though some in the East are now beginning to see the wisdom of asserting their intellectual identity.

The movement of East to West is less conspicuous and spectacular than the latter's entry to East. It was not a collective effort. Rather, it is a few individuals who, by the force of their personality and strength of their ideas, captured the imagination and attention of some in the West. For example,

Swami Vivekananda, who was first presented by his hostess Kate Sanborn at "Breezy Meadow" in Massachusetts more as "a curio from India" than a serious sage, radiated the Parliament of Religions in Chicago with his rhetoric and brilliance and stood out as the greatest single attraction. "It is undeniable ... that the American people had not been merely intellectually impressed by the nobility and supreme wisdom of Eastern doctrines ... but that they had been touched by and had responded to the tremendous power of living spirituality that Swamiji embodied. Something far more important and more far-reaching had taken place than an intellectual appreciation of Eastern religions. It was as though the soul of America had long asked for spiritual substance and had now been answered" (Burke 1958, p. 83).

There are others like Aurobindo Ghosh, a thinker of tremendous depth, Yogananda, the author of the *Autobiography of a Yogi* and the founder of self-realization fellowship in California, and J. Krishnamurti, a nonconventional philosopher. Each of them in his own way, brought Eastern traditions to the Western attention. Perhaps the most pervasive, not necessarily profound, influence is that of Mahesh Yogi of the transcendental meditation fame. Millions of people around the globe were initiated into transcendental meditation (TM) practice. TM, I venture to suggest, is the single most important influence of East on West.

The relevance of Eastern thought to scientific psychology was not completely lost sight of in academic circles. A few prominent Western psychologists like Gordon Allport and Gardner Murphy (Murphy & Murphy 1968) urged psychologists in the West to pay attention to Eastern psychological thought. For example, Allport (1946) says: "It is inexcusable that we who think in the Western frame of thought should be as ignorant as we are of the frame of thought of the East" (p. ix). Introducing Akhila-nanda's book, *Hindu Psychology: Its Meaning to the West*, Allport writes: "In some respects, I am convinced, American psychology would improve in richness and wisdom if it accommodated in some way the wise things that the author says about meditation and the necessity for an adequate philosophy of life" (1946, p. x).

Humanistic tradition in American psychology is influenced in some ways by Eastern thought. For example, the person-centered Eastern perspective is incorporated into client-centered therapies championed by some humanistic psychologists. Again, transpersonal psychologists generally have drawn from the classical ideas of the East. The writings of Ken Wilbur, Charles Tart and Robert Ornstein bear testimony to this. Even among the mainstream cognitive psychologists interested in consciousness studies there is some awareness of possible relevance of Eastern concepts, methods and models. In a few of them, the awareness is explicit. For example, Francisco Varela has creatively adapted some of the Buddhist ideas in Madhyamika tradition in his writings and research. I suspect that many more are covertly influenced by Eastern ideas, even though it is not easy to pinpoint the exact source of contact. It would seem that Max Velmans, whose views on consciousness we discussed in a previous chapter at some length, is one of those caught between an explicit commitment to main stream cognitive psychology and a subterranean current of Eastern ideas. Velmans' proposal for the marriage of first-person and third-person perspectives in his reflexive model, it seems to me, is a clear attempt to amalgamate Western positivism with Eastern personalism. As I find Velmans' recent writings an interesting example of covert Eastern influence on Western scientists, I am tempted to consider in some detail the similarities between his views (Velmans 2000) as with the Eastern perspective we discussed.

Meeting of East and West in Velmans

Max Velmans (2000) writes, "we participate in a process whereby the universe observes itself—and the universe becomes both the subject and object of experiences. Consciousness and matter are intertwined in mind. Through the evolution of matter, consciousness is given form. And through consciousness, the material universe is *realised*" (pp. 280–281, original emphasis). These concluding lines from Velmans' book state more elegantly than we have the purport of what we have described as the Eastern perspective of consciousness. Such a notion of consciousness as it comes from a cognitive psychologist, a scientist steeped in the Western tradition, who was once dubbed as espousing epiphenomenalism, is indeed provocatively nonwestern.

I will be surprised if Velmans on his own sees in the traditional Indian ideas of consciousness any more than superficial resemblance of his views. He may with some justification insist that the Eastern ideas are mere speculations extending beyond what is warranted and that his own are more empirically rooted, down to earth surmises and submissions. Indeed, Velmans is clearly restrained by his Western tradition and training in academic psychology and experimental science. He does not push his analysis of consciousness to its logical conclusion. He is more like John Locke, who barely dipped in the stream of empiricism, than David Hume who sailed in it to its logical destination. Velmans' thoughts are important for two reasons. First, they signal the dead end to which the Western reductionism has led consciousness studies. Second, Velmans sketches thoughtfully the new directions the science of consciousness should take, which appear to be entirely consistent with what we have stated as the dominant perspective in the East.

Vemans' theory as far as it goes is

entirely consistent with Eastern views. The latter contain much more that Velmans leaves out. In fact, where Velmans' accounts lack clarity or are inconsistent, it seems to me, it is largely due to the constraints that he placed on himself bowing to the dominant Western mind set. The following is a summary of the salient features of Velmans' theory and Eastern (Yoga) views.

Understanding Consciousness A Comparison of Samkhya-Yoga and Velmans

Samkhya-Yoga

1. *Prakriti* (matter) and *purusha* (consciousness) are two basic principles underlying the universe.
2. Consciousness is fundamentally different from matter and is essentially irreducible to material forms.
3. Each *purusha* is distinct and has unique experiences in its association with the mind-body complex.
4. The *purusha* illuminates the material forms of the universe through the instrumentality of the mind.
5. Consciousness (*purusha*) and mind (*citta*) are different. Mind is not the same as the brain.
6. Mind is the interface between consciousness and the brain. The distinctions such as subject and object arise in the mind's interactions with the brain and the sensory system.
7. Consciousness as such has no form. In the human condition, it takes the form of material objects by illuminating them in the mind.
8. By accessing consciousness as such the mind *realizes* the universe.
9. Consciousness as such is undifferentiated subjectivity. Subjectivity of experience arises from the mind's association with consciousness.
10. Consciousness as such has no content. Intentionality is the characteristic of the mind and not of consciousness.
11. There are two ways of knowing—(1) direct

knowing without sensory involvement and (2) mediated knowing with sensory involvement.

Velmans

1. There exist in the universe matter (our bodies) and consciousness (our experience) as integral parts.
2. Consciousness may have neurological correlates and certain processes in the brain may accompany it, but consciousness and bodily states or functions are not ontologically identical. Consciousness is irreducibly distinct from brain states and functions.
3. Each of us has "a unique conscious perspective of the larger universe."
4. We are part of a process by which the universe observes itself, creating the subject-object distinction.
5. "Consciousness," "mind" and "brain" are distinguishable concepts, but mind includes consciousness and certain states of the brain.
6. "Consciousness and matter are intertwined in the mind."
7. Matter gives consciousness its form.
8. "Through consciousness the material universe is *real-ised*."
9. Consciousness bestows subjectivity to phenomenal awareness. Consciousness renders perceived objects, events and processes subjectively real. "That, and that alone, is its function."
10. Intentionality is a characteristic of consciousness. Consciousness is always *of* or *about* something.
11. There are two fundamental ways of knowing—(1) knowing directly (by acquaintance) and (2) knowing indirectly (by description).

As we may note from the above, there are many similarities between Samkhya-Yoga and Velmans' views on consciousness. There are also profound differences between them. Samkhya-Yoga is traditionally regarded as a dualist system. Considering the similarity of its views to the Advaita of Samkara, which is unqualified monism, the question whether the universe is composed of one or more substances seems to hardly matter for our discussion of consciousness.

Velmans calls his theory reflexive monism and he is uncompromisingly adverse to dualist postulations. He is troubled by the problem of interaction between the mental and the physical in dualist theories. Since the physical part of the universe is causally closed, in his view, there is no room for the mental to intervene. However, Velmans regards consciousness as irreducibly distinct from material forms. Consequently, while rejecting ontological dualism, he embraces epistemological dualism. He believes that his notion of reflexivity overcomes the problem of interaction that afflicts the metaphysics of dualism. However, epistemological dualism is not without its share of problems. These become apparent when we consider Velmans' distinction between consciousness and mind.

In the Eastern view we described, as well as in Velmans' theory, our knowledge of the universe is perspectival in the sense that it is relative to the observer. It is subjective and personal. The *purusha* as the center of consciousness is distinct and has unique experiences through its associated mind-body complex. Such observer dependent relativity, in Yoga as well as in Vedanta, is not absolutely given but a transient condition that can be overcome by disciplined practice. The *purusha* finds itself reflected in the mind illuminating the material forms of the universe. Thus mind becomes an instrument through which the universe reveals itself. Subject-object distinction is not fundamental. It is a contingent manifestation of the mental process by which the universe is revealed. Both the views agree that the mental representations are not things themselves. Whereas Velmans is content with "the incomplete, uncertain and species specific" representations we have of the universe, the Eastern view provides for the possibility of attaining complete and certain knowledge.

The Indian theories as well as Velmans' make a distinction between consciousness and mind. In the Indian view, the distinction is fundamental and primary in the sense that one is not reducible to the other. In Velmans' view, the distinction is secondary and holds good at the epistemological level and not at the ontological level. Thus consciousness becomes a subcategory or species of the mind. Velmans acknowledges that consciousness is not reducible to brain states or functions. Yet, he considers consciousness an aspect of the mind. The mind in his view is broader to include nonconscious mental activities as well. Here rests the real problem. Consciousness (subjective experience) is irreducible to neural states or brain functions, whereas the nonsubjective states of the mind are reducible in principle. In the light of such a fundamental difference between mind and consciousness, it is hardly plausible to argue that consciousness is a species or an aspect of the mind. The irreducibility of consciousness to physical states entails that the difference between conscious and nonconscious aspects of the mind is one of kind, primary and fundamental. Reducibility or otherwise of one category into another is an ontological matter and not an epistemological issue.

The inclusion of consciousness as a subcategory of the mind leads Velmans to equate consciousness with phenomenal data. There appears to be some confusion here between the contents and the container, between substance and form. It is not obvious that consciousness and its data are not distinguishable. Nor is it axiomatic that consciousness is always intentional; i.e. it is about or of something. The data as such are common to both conscious and nonconscious mentation. Intentionality characterizes nonconscious states as well. Conscious mentation has an additional characteristic of being subjectively experienced. Velmans agrees that experiencing data means bestowing consciousness and subjectivity on them, but considers consciousness as merely a characteristic of certain mental states. The tendency to incorporate consciousness as a part or aspect of the mind is consistent with the Western equivocation of mind and consciousness. This serves well reductionism, which in the final analysis leaves out consciousness all together. It is ill-suited, however, for those that accord primacy to consciousness, as Velmans does from its first-person perspective. By regarding consciousness as a subcategory of the mind, Velmans puts himself in the uncomfortable position of limiting consciousness to a role that in functional terms is utterly insignificant.

Again, the distinction between first-person consciousness and third-person consciousness adds little to the clarity of the concept of consciousness. Consciousness is consciousness whether we look at it from a first-person or the third-person perspective. It may manifest different characteristics at different levels of observation, but it is something that underlies all awareness, whether that awareness is awareness of one's own experience or of others. Consciousness is what makes awareness possible. It is the ground condition for all forms of awareness, like matter which is the ground condition of all the material forms we experience. Velmans himself does not seem to be excited about the notion that consciousness is something that emerged at a certain point in the evolution of the brain. Rather, he appears to favor the view that consciousness is in some primal form is there from the beginning of the universe and that evolution only accounts for the different *forms* that consciousness takes and not for consciousness-as-such. If one accepts the notion that consciousness in some form is coextensive with the universe, then it is likely that it is fundamentally different from anything that is essentially reducible to physical forms, including the mind.

The Indian views we considered make this point emphatically and insist that the distinction between mind and consciousness is fundamental. The mind, unlike consciousness, is physical in that it can be described in material forms and accounted for in physical terms. Therefore, the interaction of the mind with other physical systems poses no special problems. The reflexivity is not between the mind with its cognitive and perceptual systems and the physical objects, events and processes. Rather, it is between mind and consciousness. Consciousness does not causally interact with the mind. It has a reflexive relation with the mind. Again, the mind with its cognitive and perceptual systems is peculiarly human. The presence of mind in a rudimentary sense in other forms of life or matter in general may not be ruled out. The notion that *sattva* component in varying proportions is believed to exist in matter implies the existence of mind in less developed forms than in humans. Velmans views appear to be consistent with the Eastern accounts on this point, when he suggests that the different forms of consciousness may have an evolutionary origin, with the difference that what evolves in the Indian view is not consciousness but the mind.

Velmans' analysis of the causal efficacy of consciousness is quite similar and yet very different from Eastern viewpoint. In Yoga as well as in Advaita Vedanta consciousness has no causal role. It is inert and undifferentiated subjectivity. In its association with the mind, however, there arises personal experience. The mind with its person-centered subjectivity, in the Indian view, has both first-person and third-person causal roles. I am not persuaded by Velmans' arguments that consciousness as subjective experience has no causal efficacy at the level of third-person. His reasoning relates primarily to the information processing aspect of consciousness. Inasmuch as all kinds of mental processing may be shown to take place at the nonconscious level, it is argued, consciousness may not enter into information processing at all. As we pointed out earlier, the observation that many or all of the mental functions can be performed at the nonconscious level does not warrant the conclusion that consciousness does not enter into information processing. It is all too obvious that we process information with greater efficiency and better control when we are conscious than when we are not conscious.

Again, Velmans does not seem to take proper note of other avenues where subjective awareness (consciousness) does seem to have a first-person causal role. For example, it is now an accepted fact that placeboes bring about somatic change observable at the third-person level. The practice of psychoanalysis and much of psychotherapy is based on the assumption that subjective awareness of unconscious conflicts, motivation etc. have tangible effects on mental health observed from a third-person perspective. Further, human intentions seem to correlate with the output of random event generators. In the absence of any other relevant variables in these experiments, it is reasonable to assume that consciousness influences physical states. Therefore, there is really no "causal paradox." Consciousness appears to have a causal role both from first- and third-person perspectives.

Both Velmans and the Samkhya-Yoga emphasize the role of the mind in connecting consciousness with the brain. We described the role as one of *interfacing*. Velmans describes it as *intertwining*. There may be subtle differences between the two phrases, but they do not seem to be significantly different. However, the differences in the connotations ascribed to these two concepts, mind and consciousness, in the two theories have far reaching implications. As mentioned, Velmans seems to equate consciousness with phenomenal data; and he leaves no room for possible dissociation between consciousness and contents of consciousness. The Western bias that emphasizes intentionality as the defining characteristic of mind/consciousness has limited Velmans taking the next step of accepting the possibility of pure conscious experience and the existence of consciousness-as-such. If consciousness can be dissociated from sensorially processed data, as provided for in the Samkhya-Yoga view, all kinds of possibilities that give us knowledge of different sorts will open up. Paranormal awareness is one such form.

Velmans, like in Yoga, speaks of direct and indirect knowledge. He points to the asymmetry of access in the two forms. We have direct access to our experiences and only indirect access to the experiences of others. This seems to be so because one's consciousness is bound to and associated directly with his/her brain and not with the others. In Yoga theory, even the so-called first-person experience is indirect, because what the mind presents to consciousness are representations mediated by the perceptual and cognitive systems. Consequently, awareness arising from such mediation is also indirect. In other words, in Velmans, the direct acquaintance is with the representations whereas in Yoga it is with the things themselves. Direct knowledge results when the mind detaches itself from the sensory inputs and makes contact directly with the objects, events and processes in the universe. This is the paranormal process distinguished from the normal process in which there is the involvement of the sensory processes. The assumption that consciousness can exist apart from phenomenal data leaves the possibility for the existence of pure conscious states and extraordinary experiences that are not constrained by the limits of sensory processing.

In Velmans, the material universe is *real-ized* through consciousness. In the Indian view, the universe is *realized* by accessing consciousness-as-such. In the former the universe becomes *subjectively real*. We have representations that are at best incomplete approximations to things themselves. In the latter we become one with the universe and have perfect, complete and direct acquaintance with the things themselves and not merely their representations.

In sum, Velmans took one important step forward in bridging East-West views on consciousness by asserting the irreducibility of consciousness to the physical states and the brain functions and by pointing to the immediacy and directness of conscious experience. If he took another step to provide for consciousness-as-such and its existence apart from its contents, his views would have been a lot closer to the Eastern view we have attempted to develop from Yoga, Advaita and Buddhist systems of thought. Such a step would have extended his theory to account for extraordinary experiences, including the paranormal, and at the same time made sense of the Eastern disciplines for cultivating consciousness such as yoga practice that have gained in recent years a measure of acceptance in the West. Also, the additional step, it seems to me, is needed to avoid some of the inconsistencies in Velmans' account of consciousness and to render the distinction between mind and consciousness more meaningful. Moreover, his obvious enthusiasm for first-person consciousness would have been better served if he considered the possibility of separating consciousness from its contents. At any rate, the step he did take is a giant step for the one with the Western mindset, indeed a welcome step for bridging the gap between East and West.

Meditation: An East-West Link

The strongest link that connects Eastern and Western psychologies is likely the one that comes out of meditation research. Meditation, I believe, is an area that promises to be a genuine meeting ground for East-West traditions in psychology. If the distinctive orientations of East and West are "subjective inner discipline" and "external objective science" respectively, meditation may be the link to bridge the inner and the outer.

We have discussed in the previous chapters the practice of meditation in Buddhist and yogic traditions. Today there are many forms of meditation practiced in India as well as in the Western countries. Daniel Goleman (1978) surveyed fourteen different techniques and argued that all of them employ essentially one or two methods described in *Visuddhimagga*. These are concentration (focusing attention on one object) and mindfulness (focusing attention on bare sense impressions), both involve redeployment or, as he termed it, "retraining" of attention. Goleman (1978) writes: "The need for the meditator to retrain his attention, whether through concentration or mindfulness, is the single invariant ingredient in the recipe for altering consciousness of every meditation system" (p. 111).

C. Naranjo describes meditation as "the pursuit of a certain state of mind ... a mental process rather than a mental content." He points out that its practices "generally involve an effort to stop this merry-go-round of mental or other activity and to set our attention upon a single object, sensation, utterance, issue, mental state, or activity" (Naranjo & Ornstein, 1971, p. 10). Naranjo distinguishes three kinds of meditative practices. His classification is based on the object of meditation rather than on any intrinsic differences in the meditative process itself. In concentration meditation, the meditator focuses on "externally given symbolic objects ... attempting to interiorize an externally given form." In absorptive meditation, the object of focus is any of the "spontaneously arising contents of the mind." The third kind, which is neither "outer-directed" nor "inner-directed," involves an effort "to attain a stillness of the mind's conceptualizing activity, a withdrawal from external perceptions and internal experience alike" (p. 18). Naranjo is merely paraphrasing the final three steps of raja yoga practice, *dharana*, *dhyana*, and *samadhi*. They are not different inasmuch as one practice may lead to the other. Successful meditation involves a combination of the three practices, as presumed to be the case in raja yoga when one practices *samyama*.

Ornstein discusses two general varieties of meditation: "those exercises which involve restriction of awareness ... and those which involve a deliberate attempt to" open up "awareness of the external environment" (Naranjo & Ornstein, 1971, p. 144). An essential element in many meditative practices is the actual "restriction of awareness" to a single, unchanging stimulus. Ornstein finds the object of meditation much less important than maintaining it "as the single focus of awareness over a long period of time" (p. 161). In concentrative meditation, the focus on an unchanging stimulus causes a diminished awareness of the external environment, leading to a "blank out" that permits expanded awareness of faint signals that otherwise would go unrecognized. An analogy is that of the dark night when the stars are visible.

Taking a totally secular view of meditation, psychologist Jonathan Smith (1986) sees it "not so much as a technique but as a set of skills" (p. 4). According to Smith, the essence of meditation is to learn how to (1) avoid physical tension and be physically calm; (2) overcome distraction and be able to focus attention on a task for a period of time; and (3) give up over-control and let yourself be "fully and restfully involved in what you are doing." Smith apparently brings an eclectic approach to a clinical application of meditation by combining it with other techniques of relaxation. However, it is not difficult to see why avoiding tension and distraction are considered in

yoga to be essential preliminaries for successful meditation. Meditation proper, however, is limited to the attentional part, whether it is achieved via concentration on an object, external or internal, or passive and effortless awareness of spontaneous mentation.

For any kind of controlled study of meditation it is necessary that we have a standardized technique or techniques so that we may make meaningful generalizations and comparisons. Though we still do not have a single technique that most researchers could use, there are a few that have been used for studying meditation.

TRANSCENDENTAL MEDITATION

Maharshi Mahesh Yogi's transcendental meditation (TM) is probably the single most extensively researched meditative technique (Orme-Johnson & Farrow, 1977). This is because: (1) Mahesh Yogi, himself a student of science, is not averse to subjecting his technique to scientific scrutiny, and therefore his organization has encouraged and even supported such research; (2) the large number of TM practitioners available for research is an attraction for many researchers; (3) the technique itself is simple and easy to practice; and (4) more important, because it has been uniformly taught by those trained in the TM organization, it appears to be a standardized technique.

Basic to TM is the premise that in addition to the known states of wakefulness, sleep, and dreaming, there is a transcendental state of consciousness that is blissful (Mahesh Yogi 1963a; 1963b). It is a state that is psychologically necessary, like sleeping and dreaming, to relieve stress and rejuvenate our whole system. Meditation is a means of reaching the transcendental state.

It is claimed that Mahesh Yogi's system is different from others, especially the classical ones, in two crucial respects. First, there is no need for elaborate preparation for practicing TM, because virtuous life is a consequence of the experience of transcendental consciousness rather than a prerequisite for attaining it. Second, the transcendental state is blissful, and the natural tendency of the mind is not to wander aimlessly, but to move in the direction of experiencing bliss. Therefore, the movement toward the transcendental state can be effortless and natural. Meditation, then, need not involve special effort to hold our attention steadfast. It happens easily if we allow ourselves to experience it.

In TM, each initiate is given a Sanskrit *mantra* by the teacher, and meditation consists in repeating this mantra mentally. In the words of its founder, one turns "attention inward towards the subtler levels of a thought until the mind transcends the experience of the subtlest state of the thought and arrives at the source of the thought." Meditation is described as the process of developing systematic contact with the source of thought, pure awareness. TM meditators are told to avoid any mental effort to concentrate on the *mantra,* but to gently bring their attention back to the *mantra* when it wanders. The teacher apparently decides which of the various *mantras* is the most appropriate for a given individual. The *mantra* itself remains a secret, and the practitioner is asked not to reveal it to anyone.

The initiation to TM involves a series of two orientation lectures in which the benefits of meditation are explained and positive expectations are built up. Then the would-be meditator is instructed on how to passively attend to the *mantra* while covertly repeating it. Follow-up meetings clear up questions the novice meditator may experience. The meditator is advised to practice twice daily with the eyes closed sitting comfortably in a quiet environment for about twenty minutes. According to an estimate, over a million people were initiated into

TM in USA alone (Orme-Johnson & Farrow, 1977).

BENSON'S TECHNIQUE

Herbert Benson was among the first, along with R. K. Wallace, to carry out some well-known research on TM, which is cited as evidence that its practice can help lower the metabolic rate (Wallace, Benson & Wilson, 1971; Wallace & Benson, 1972). Benson later developed his own technique of meditation which, he claimed, produces similar effects but is non-cultist (Beary & Benson, 1974). The "relaxation response," as he called it, is a low-arousal hypometabolic state that can be produced by a wide variety of techniques. Physiologically, it is described as an integrated hypothalamic response with parasympathetic dominance and decreased sympathetic activity (Benson, Beary, & Carol, 1974). The relaxation response may be obtained without any *mantra* or *puja* rituals associated with TM. In Benson's method, the meditator, after some muscular relaxation exercises, sits in a quiet environment and passively concentrates on breathing, counting "one" each time she exhales. When distracting thoughts come up, the meditator attempts to ignore them and count "one," coordinating with outer breath. Benson's contention that all meditation techniques produce a common pattern of physiological changes is questioned by Schwartz, Davidson, and Goleman (1978), who maintain that more specific patterns of physiological responses may be superimposed upon the relaxation response by the particular meditative technique employed.

CARRINGTON'S CSM

Patricia Carrington felt that there were several disadvantages in using TM for research. First, because TM is associated with a quasi-religious movement with strong support groups and high expectations built into its practice, it is difficult to assess accurately the extent to which the observed effect is contributed solely by meditation, and not by other factors. Second, TM followers claim that the *mantra* is very important for meditation, but the *mantra* itself is kept secret. This makes it very difficult to study TM scientifically and assess the role of the *mantra*. Third, to obtain the cooperation of the TM organization, the research proposals must first be submitted to them for approval. They seldom grant permission for comparing TM with any other technique, which makes it difficult to carry out comparative studies of different meditation techniques. For these reasons, Carrington (1977) devised her own type of *mantra* meditation, Clinically Standardized Meditation (CSM) that could be used in clinical practice and research.

CSM is similar to TM without the latter's expectations and mystery surrounding the *mantra*. In CSM, the choice of the *mantra* is left to the individual, who chooses one among the sixteen *mantras* in Sanskrit that Carrington collected. It is even possible for the meditator to concoct her own *mantra* by following some simple rules.

Similar to TM, the instructions for CSM dwell on the effortlessness of meditation. The meditator is asked to choose a *mantra* and first say it aloud with the eyes open. Repeating it more softly, one then drifts gradually, with the eyes now closed, into a state where one simply listens to the *mantra* repeated internally. The meditator, sitting peacefully, thinks the *mantra* without saying it. Carrington writes:

> That is all there is to meditating, hearing the mantra in your mind, allowing it to change any way it wants—to get louder or softer—to disappear or return—to stretch out or speed up...Meditation is like drifting on a stream in a boat without oars—because you need no oars—you are not going anywhere [1977, pp. 79–80].

AUTOGENIC TRAINING AND PROGRESSIVE RELAXATION

There are two other techniques, which are extensively used in psychotherapy which have close affinity with meditation. One of them, autogenic training, is a technique developed by a German medical doctor, J. H. Schultz. This technique (Schultz & Luthe, 1959) is derived from many years of Schultz's studies of yoga and meditation. Autogenic training is described as a meditation technique that is psycho-physiologically rationalized systematic yoga. Another passive meditation technique is progressive relaxation developed by Jacobson (1938), a technique in which one is taught to become aware of tension and relaxation in each muscle.

The meditation techniques just described are at best preliminary steps and approximations to those practiced traditionally. Meditation, in classical terms, is a pursuit of transcendence from the constraints of the human condition. It is a quest for perfection, a quest to experience reality in and of itself, unblemished by the sensory modalities. As one travels on this path to perfection, it is believed that she finds herself on new frontiers of unfolding human potentials that hitherto have lain dormant and hidden. It is hardly a concern of the traditional meditator to lower anxiety or control blood pressure. In fact, such concerns are considered preparations for meditations.

In the traditional yoga system, for example, cultivation of certain attitudes, habits, and the practice of physical and breathing exercises precede meditation. They are preliminary steps that enable one to practice meditation more efficiently. If the purpose of yoga is to gain control over one's mind through meditation, all distractions that hinder such concentration and attentional focus must be overcome. It seems, therefore, that the goals of contemporary meditative systems to help achieve psychosomatic well-being seem to be somewhat misplaced.

The following appear to be some important differences between classical and contemporary approaches to meditation: (1) Classically, meditation is a rigorous discipline practiced for many years before one considers himself to be proficient; (2) teaching meditation in traditional systems requires close supervision, personalized attention, and constant guidance; (3) meditation is preceded by several preparatory steps that are considered necessary; and (4) good health and well-being are not effects but necessary conditions for practicing meditation.

Empirical Research

As mentioned earlier, Yoga means both a system of Indian philosophy and a set of practices. Meditation is the central focus of yoga practice. Yoga is equated, however, in the public mind with a physical culture involving bodily exercises and breathing, which are included in Patanjali yoga among the preliminary steps leading to meditation. Some of the *hatha* yogic exercises date back to antiquity. But many are added over the years and a variety of benefits are claimed for them (Swatmarama, 1933). Inasmuch as the exercises are designed for the purpose of controlling mental states, it is clear that there has been an explicit recognition that bodily processes influence mental states. Consequently, a study of the effects of these exercises on human psyche and soma is of interest on its own, independent of the goals of yoga.

Empirical research on meditation is vast, some of it is well done and much of it lacking in conceptual clarity and methodological rigor. Since it is not possible to review comprehensively all the studies in this section, we will focus on some of the main trends. We will not only refer to the good

studies, but also include a sample that illustrates some of the shortcomings of research in this area.

The interest in scientific study of yoga and meditation is worldwide (Pratap 1971). It is one area where classical Indian ideas inspired an immense amount of research. In fact, much of this research, though based on Indian concepts and practices, is carried out in other countries. A bibliography on meditation and related states included in *Meditation: Classical and Contemporary Perspectives* (Shapiro & Walsh, 1984) contains a little over seven hundred items. Of these, less than seven percent are by those with Indian names. Many of the Indians listed are working in the Western countries. A smaller bibliography of 452 items compiled by Peo of Scandinavian Yoga and Meditation School (1978) has about 14 percent of the items by authors of Indian origin. A more recent *Yoga Research Bibliography* (Monro, Ghosh, & Kalish, 1989), with over 1,350 authors, lists some 20 percent Indian authors. If we consider only those studies that are published in refereed journals or cited in articles published in scholarly and scientific journals, the number of Indians who are engaged in meditation research would be very much smaller. However, there does appear to be awareness among Indians that techniques based on yoga and meditation could be beneficial for reducing stress. In an interview survey of 100 male executives in India, Dubey and Kumar (1986) found that yoga, TM, autosuggestion, and relaxation therapies are among the techniques believed to be effective in reducing stress.

There are a number of excellent reviews of meditation research (Andresen 2000; Bogart 1991; Jeving, Wallace & West 1987; Holmes 1984; Beidebach, 1992; Shapiro & Walsh, 1984; Schuman 1980; Davidson 1976). Meditation refers to a discipline or technique for psychic development and physical well being. Some times it is regarded as a state of mind. Much of scientific research on meditation has assumed that it is a state. As Schuman (1980) notes: "Based on research involving practitioners of Yoga, Zen or Transcendental Meditation (TM), meditation has been considered a unique psychophysiological state, associated with a distinct configuration of autonomic and electrocortical changes" (p. 333). Studies on meditation have explored the physiology and psychology of meditation. They attempted to investigate whether the practice of meditation produces a unique physiological state that lowers arousal, and whether it is conducive to better health and well being. The available evidence falls into three categories, anecdotal, casual research, and controlled experiments. Even though casual studies outnumber controlled experiments, on balance, meditation appears to be a powerful tool to alter states of mind.

ELECTROPHYSIOLOGICAL EFFECTS AND CORRELATES

A French cardiologist, T. Brosse (1946) traveled to India in the mid-thirties and took electrophysical measurements of yogins. She reported that a yogin stopped his heart for a while. A similar observation was made by Bhole and Karambelkar (1971). There are other anecdotal reports of pit burial, where yogins are said to stay alive when they are buried underground for several days. Casual studies by Vakil (1950) and Hoenig (1968) seemed to confirm this. In studies by Bhole, Karambelkar, and Vinekar (1967a, 1967b) the subjects were observed when they were buried in an air-tight pit. The subjects showed reduced consumption of oxygen compared to basal requirements. In a somewhat better controlled study by Anand et al. (1961b) with Ramananda Yogi sealed in an airtight box, low pulse rate and lower consumption of oxygen were observed. Anand and Chhina (1961) reported a case in which a yogin was believed to stop his heart. They found that there was still

electrical activity of the heart even though it was too reduced to be heard even with a stethoscope.

Wallace (1970b) concluded his study of twenty-seven TM meditators with the assertion that "transcendental meditation produces a fourth major state of consciousness which is physiologically and biochemically unique" (p. 107). Wallace reported significant decrease in oxygen consumption, carbon dioxide elimination, cardiac output, heart rate, and respiration rate during meditation as compared to pre- and post-meditative periods in the same subjects. Significant increases in skin resistance, changes in certain EEG frequencies, and marked decrease in arterial lactate were also noted during meditation.

The findings of Wallace were considered to be the first major scientific confirmation of some of the claims made for TM. They are cited in support of the contention of Mahesh Yogi that there exists a transcendental state identifiable by measurable physiological changes, a state easily accessible to those practicing a simple technique of meditation. Wallace's findings have become the basis of a good deal of further research. A recent review of meditation research by Murphy and Donavon (1997) suggests that a variety of meditation practices appear to reduce respiration rate, carbon dioxide elimination and oxygen consumption.

Earlier there were several sporadic efforts to identify physiological correlates of meditative practices. Das and Gastaut (1955) tested seven practicing yogins and observed an increase of EEG alpha frequency by 1 to 3 Hz with a decrease in amplitude, and beta wave activity appearing in the range of 15 to 30 Hz. These appeared to correlate with subjectively experienced "mystical" states. This observation was largely ignored until another Frenchman, J.P. Banquet (1973), using a more sophisticated EEG analysis, found in four of his TM subjects a stable and continuous beta activity at 20 Hz against a persistent background of alpha and theta activity as they approached deeper states of meditation. These results find further confirmation in the more recent work of Benson et al. (1990) with advanced Tibetan Buddhist monks.

Bagchi and Wenger (1957) did not find any changes in the alpha activity of 14 Indian yogins between the meditation and rest periods. However, they did find decreased respiratory rate and increased skin resistance that indicated a state of deep relaxation of the autonomic nervous system without drowsiness or sleep (Wenger & Bagchi, 1961). Anand, Chhina, and Singh (1961a) reported that their meditating Indian yogins who produced persistent alpha activity did not show any alpha blocking to external stimuli. The dominant alpha activity, present during meditation, was not disturbed by loud noises or flashes of light. It was not disturbed even when the yogin's hands were immersed in ice-cold water. Working with the Zen meditators in Japan, Kasamatsu and Hirai (1966) also observed an increase of alpha activity during meditation. But their subjects, unlike those tested by Anand et al., showed EEG patterns that resembled the alpha-blocking response of the waking state when external stimuli were applied to them. However, they showed no evidence of habituation to recurring stimuli that we find in normal subjects.

The remarkable difference in the findings of Anand et al., and Kasamatsu and Hirai may be due to the differences between the two meditative practices of their subjects. Yogic meditation is a concentration type of meditation, whereas in Zen meditation one allows the free flow of all sensory inputs to which one passively attends. In other words, the concentrative meditative practices may lead to decreased reactivity to external stimuli, whereas "mindfulness" or insight meditation helps to maintain alertness at an unusual level (Johnson, 1970; Mills & Campbell, 1974). If this interpretation is correct, one could regard the two types of meditation, Zen and raja yoga, as physiologically distinct.

However, this interpretation is problematic on several grounds. In an early review of the physiology of meditation, Davidson (1976) pointed out that the alpha-blocking responses of the Zen meditators in the study by Kasamatsu and Hirai (1966) are essentially uninterpretable. The Zen masters meditated with their eyes open, and the control subjects were tested with their eyes closed. Consequently, the EEG measurements of the latter cannot be regarded as true controls. In addition, there were too few subjects in these studies—three subjects in the Zen study, and four in the study by Anand et al. (1961). Until replications with refined methodologies are made, it would seem premature to conclude that a case has been made for differential reactivity to external stimuli by Zen and yogic meditators. The study of Banquet (1973), which is sometimes cited as a confirmation of the finding of Anand et al. regarding the failure to elicit alpha blocking in meditators, was carried out with TM practitioners. However, TM is more like Zen than the concentrative meditation of *raja yogins* tested by Anand. Schuman (1980) concludes:

> Even assuming the basic effects to be replicable, it does not follow that changes in the alpha-blocking response are necessarily due to the meditative ASC achieved through mindfulness and concentration practices. Differences in cognitive set during meditation might account for differences in alpha blocking apart from the induction of an ASC [p. 360].

In an attempt to replicate the findings of Anand et al. and Kasamatsu and Hirai, Becker and Shapiro (1981) tested thirty experienced Zen, yoga, and TM meditators, along with twenty college-student controls. They found that both EEG alpha blocking and skin conductivity response showed clear habituation in all groups without any significant differences between them.

There are a number of other studies that investigated the EEG correlates of meditation. These include West (1980), Fenwick (1987), Orme-Johnson (1988), Sim and Tsoi (1992), and Deepak et al. (1994). Whatever the type of meditation, there seems to be a general tendency for meditating subjects to produce greater alpha activity (Anand, Chhina & Singh, 1961a; Akishige 1968; Kasamatsu & Hirai 1966; Bangquet 1973; Glueck & Stroebel, 1975). Also, Banquet (1973) as well as Kasamatsu and Hirai (1966), found theta activity, especially among the advanced practitioners of meditation. Another interesting finding is the intrahemispheric coherence of EEG during meditation (Banquet 1973; Rogers 1976; Orme-Johnson 1977). Gaylord, Orme-Johnson, and Travis (1989) reported global increases in alpha and theta coherence among central and frontal leads following a period of TM compared to eyes-closed condition. No such coherence was seen in subjects practicing progressive relaxation. Orme-Johnson characterized such coherence as "the EEG signature of the transcendental state."

More recent research focused on possible physiological correlates of the experience of a pure consciousness state that is free from all thoughts and mentation (Austin 1988; Shear 2001). Taking the clue from *Yoga-Sutras* and other writings on meditation, which suggest a possible link between breath control and higher states of awareness, a number of experimental studies were conducted to test whether breath suspension episodes among meditators are associated with subjective reports of pure conscious experience. For example, J. T. Farrow and R. Hebert (1982) report several studies in this area. The results of these studies show that (a) meditating subjects report 10 times the number of periods of respiratory suspension than the control non-meditating subjects and that (b) the subjective reports of pure consciousness experience by meditating subjects highly correlate with the occurrence of breath suspension episodes. Badawi et al. (1984) published studies that provide further support to the findings of Hebert and Farrow. The results showed strong correlation between the thought-free or pure conscious states of subjective experience and respiratory suspension periods. Badawi and associates also reported increased EEG coherence during the periods when the subjects indicated that they had an experience of pure consciousness. After reviewing the relevant literature, James Austin (1998) concludes: "These studies of TM subjects link clear, thought-free consciousness with two quite different sets of physiological evidence. The most impressive of these events suspends respiratory drive and causes a relative hypoventilation. The second cluster of associated findings are more subtle and variable. They include peripheral autonomic changes and tendencies toward increased EEG coherence" (1998, p. 97).

In a study of autonomic patterns of TM practicing subjects during periods of respiratory suspensions and subjective reports of experiencing pure conscious states, Frederick Travis and Keith Wallace (1997) found that skin conductance responses and heart rate deceleration occurred at the onset of respiratory suspension and experience of transcendental or pure consciousness. In a second study, when the above autonomic pattern associated with respiratory suspension and pure consciousness experience is compared with forced holding of breath, they observed that phasic autonomic activity was significantly higher at the onset of respiratory suspension in meditation than at the onset of breath holding. In another study Travis and Wallace (1999) compared autonomic and EEG patterns of subjects during TM practice and eyes-closed rest condition. The results of the study lead them to conclude that the practice of TM appears to produce fundamentally different state from the eyes-closed rest condition. Travis and Pearson (2000) reported certain phenomenological as well as physiological correlates of experience of pure consciousness. The phenomenological correlates include the absence of time, space, and body sense, and content qualities of perception that characterize normal waking experience. The physiological measures associated with pure conscious experience, as observed in this study, are apneustic breathing, autonomic orienting at the onset of breath changes and increases in the frequency of peak EEG power.

IS MEDITATIVE STATE A UNIQUE PHYSIOLOGICAL STATE?

As mentioned earlier, the presence of slow-wave EEG activity, reduced oxygen consumption and carbon dioxide elimination, reduced heart rate, and increase of skin resistance during meditation were claimed by Wallace as indicating a unique physiological state of profound relaxation, a wakeful hypometabolic state. Dhanaraj and Singh (1977) and Corey (1974) obtained results similar to those reported by Wallace et al. (1970a; 1971; 1972) suggestive of the hypometabolic state believed to be unique to meditation. Fenwick et al. (1984), who also observed in their studies a drop in oxygen consumption and carbon dioxide production, suggested that the drop could be attributed to muscle relaxation. They conclude: "No evidence has been found to support the hypothesis that TM produces a unique state of consciousness or metabolic functioning. Both the metabolic changes and the EEG phenomena observed during TM can be explained within the framework of accepted physiological mechanisms" (Fenwick et al., 1984, p. 462).

Again, many of the same autonomic-metabolic changes are found also during

sleep and drowsiness. In fact, in a study by Pagano et al. (1976), the EEG records of five male subjects who had been practicing meditation for over 2.5 years were obtained when they were meditating TM and when they were taking a nap while sitting. Analyses of the data showed that, "(1) during TM, meditators spent 39.2 percent in stage W (wakefulness), 19.2 percent of time in Stage 1 EEG sleep activity, 23.0 percent of time in Stage 2, and 16.8 percent in Stages 3 and 4; (2) there were no significant differences between meditation and nap sessions in the amount of time spent in sleep Stages 2, 3, or 4" (Pagano & Warrenburg, 1983, p. 156). This study thus raises questions about the physiological uniqueness of the meditative state. In fact, the experiments of Wallace were criticized on the grounds that he did not have non-meditating control subjects. Some of the results Wallace found in his original study, such as a large 16 percent decrement in VO_2 during meditation, appear to be exaggerated because the baseline values of his subjects in the resting period were 9 percent above the expected value. Davidson (1976) pointed out:

> That (a) TM represents a state of profound physiological rest, greater than that attainable with sleep of much longer duration; and (b) the specific changes in consciousness and the unique (and, in my opinion, unquestionable) benefits of meditation are somehow linked to the physiologic changes discussed above still seem to lack a solid basis in experimental fact [p. 354].

Davidson's assessment has been supported by later reviews as well. On the basis of the results of their own experiments and a review made by others, Pagano and Warrenburg (1983) concluded:

> We regret to report that our search for a unique or dramatic effect directly attributable to meditation thus far has not been successful.... Our experience has been that when good scientific methodology has been

used, the claims made have been extravagant and premature [p. 203].

The work of R. A. Jevning and associates involving the study of blood hormones suggests that there may be other parameters that may distinguish physiologically the meditation state from sleep state. Their results seem to indicate that "long-term regular practice [of TM] is associated with development of a psychophysiological response of decreased pituitary-adrenal activity during meditation" (Jevning & O'Halloran, 1984, p. 467).

In an important review of early experimental literature on meditation and somatic arousal reduction, Holmes (1984) concluded that across experiments or measures there is no evidence that meditating subjects show lower levels of arousal than resting subjects. He wrote, "the most consistent finding was that there were not reliable differences between meditating and resting subjects" (p. 5). Holmes pointed out that the studies fall into three groups: (1) case studies, (2) experiments in which the subjects served as their own controls, and (3) experiments with independent control groups. Case studies, inasmuch as they lack controls, cannot serve as empirical tests of a hypothesis. Experiments in which the same subject served as his or her own control at best provide equivocal evidence. Much of the evidence in support of the hypothesis that meditation lowers somatic arousal, according to Holmes, comes from experiments with the subjects serving as their own controls. Such evidence, however, is not sufficient to prove that meditation lowers arousal more effectively than simple resting, because the subject's expectations may be critical. Meditators generally believe in the efficacy of meditation over resting, and this may be sufficient to cause the observed differences. Holmes points out that none of the experiments in which proper controls were provided gave evidence that

meditation reduces somatic arousal significantly better than resting. He concluded that "not one experiment provided consistent evidence that meditating subjects were less aroused than resting subjects.... Indeed, there does not even appear to be one bad experiment offering consistent evidence that meditation reduces arousal more than sleep" (p. 6).

Dillbeck and Orme-Johnson (1987) argued persuasively, however, that the reviews such as those by Holmes do not take into account significant effect size differences between meditation and typical resting conditions. Their own meta-analysis of 31 studies they were able to locate showed that the effect size for TM was almost twice the size found with a simple eyes-closed rest condition across several indicators of reduced somatic arousal. Dillbeck and Orme-Johnson also cite a number of studies such as the one by Warshal (1980) suggesting that TM involves improved reflex response and therefore greater alertness.

A few studies do show that there are indeed observable differences between a meditative state and drowsiness. In one study by Ikemi (1988), it is reported that the changes in EEG frequencies during the practice of self-regulation based on meditation could be distinguished from those in a drowsy state. The results also showed reduction of amplitude in contingent negative variations during meditation practice. A review by Jevning, Wallace, and Beidebach (1992) also suggest an overall effect of "wakeful hypometabolic response" during meditation.

PSYCHOLOGY OF MEDITATION

It is of course well known that there are differences in the meditational practices, the techniques used and the length of practice. Therefore it is not surprising that there is no uniformity in the results of all these studies. Clearly tantric type of meditation is different in essential respects from TM. Therefore, we may not expect comparable physiological correlates accompanying these two kinds of practices. It is also clear that the effects of long term meditation are different from the effects obtained with beginners (Mason et al. 1997; Jevning et al. 1992). Added to this, there are individual variations, whether it is metabolic rate or EEG. As Austin (1998) aptly observes: "we know that people's EEGs differ, that an individual's EEGs vary, and that meditation is not one state but a series of dynamic physiological changes. So it comes as no surprise to find that may different EEG changes have been recorded during meditation, and that most studies are open to criticism" (p. 88).

Even granting that certain physiochemical states correlate significantly with some meditation practices, it does not follow that meditation produces a unique physiological state. What appears to be the case is that meditation practices give the meditator an ability to voluntarily control autonomic activity and a variety of internal attention states that include respiratory drive, metabolic rate, arousal levels, and EEG activity. However, to equate meditation with any of these is neither implied in the classical accounts of meditation nor warranted by empirical research. In a study of tantric yoga meditation, Corby et al. (1978) observed increased autonomic activity among proficient meditators during meditation and decreased autonomic response among inexperienced meditators. The assumption that meditation is a state of relaxation is clearly challenged by the findings in this study. Meditators may achieve different kinds of physiological states depending on their orientation and the type of meditation practiced. The goal of meditation is not to gain control of bodily functions, but to transcend them to achieve higher states of consciousness, which are believed to be impeded by the mundane activities of the mind-body complex. Patan-

jali is explicit in stating that yoga is a means of controlling the activities of the mind. The emphasis is on the *mind* and not on the *body*. What is unique to meditation is the state of the mind and not the condition of the body. The latter are relevant to the extent they influence the mind. The attempts to find unique physio-chemical states of meditation are a reflection of the Western mindset that equates mental phenomena with brain states. The connection between the two, the mental and the brain states, is a necessary one in the Western scientific tradition whereas in the Eastern tradition, which believes in the existence of pure conscious states, such connection, where it exists, is contingent and epiphenomenal rather than intrinsic and essential.

Discussions on the psychology of meditation fall broadly into three different categories. First, there are studies that regard meditation as a self-regulation strategy that has clinical relevance for managing stress, hypertension, and drug addictions. Second, there are studies that consider meditation as an altered state of consciousness (Shapiro & Giber, 1978). In this category there are a number of studies that have attempted to test the role of attention in meditation and the issues relating to training. There are also phenomenological studies that deal with the reported experience during meditation. The third category includes studies with normal subjects that are designed to test the effects of meditation on psychological processes.

There are a number of studies that seem to suggest that meditation has the effect of reducing stress (Goleman & Schwartz, 1976; Linden, 1971; Patel, 1993). Vahia et al. (1973) reported results suggesting that a therapy based on Patanjali yoga is more effective than pseudotherapy in treating some psychiatric outpatients. In one study the subjects were outpatients at the K.E.M. Hospital in Bombay aged between 15 and 50 years who were diagnosed as suffering from psychoneurosis. The subjects were randomly assigned to two groups. In the experimental group, the patients went through a five-step treatment process that included *asana, pranayama, pratyahara, dharana,* and *dhyana.* The patients were treated for one hour daily on all weekdays for a minimum of four weeks. In the pseudotreatment (control) group, the patients were asked to relax and do some exercises resembling *asanas* and *pranayama.* They were also asked to write all the thoughts that came to their minds during that period. Both groups were administered the Rorschach, the MMPI and Taylor's Manifest Anxiety Scale and were clinically assessed before, during, and after the treatment. The subjects in the two groups were matched on a number of relevant variables. The clinical assessment as well as psychological testing were done by those who did not know to which group the subjects belonged. The results showed statistically significant differences between the two groups. The experimental group improved significantly in comparison to the control group. There was a significant reduction in the anxiety scores of patients in the experimental group and not in the control group.

Clearly, this study is a well-controlled study compared to many others in this area. However, there is one weakness. The fact that the same therapist treated both the groups leaves open the possibility of an experimenter expectancy effect (Smith, 1975). Because the therapist knew whether a patient belonged to the experimental or control group, he could have had a differential influence on the patients.

Kocher and Pratap (1971; 1972) found that their subjects obtained significantly lower scores on neuroticism and anxiety scales after they went through a series of daily yogic practices including *asanas* and breathing practices carried out over three weeks. Again, the main methodological problem with these studies is that there were no control groups to guard against confounding variables such as expectation.

In a study of the effect of yoga practices on the neuroticism and anxiety scores of subjects, Kocher (1972) found that the subjects who practiced yoga obtained significantly lower scores on neuroticism, anxiety, and general hostility after eight months of practice consisting of *asanas, pranayama,* and *kriyas* (cleansing exercises). No such effects were observed in a control group of subjects who did not practice yoga. According to the author, both groups were matched for intelligence, education, sex, age, and socioeconomic status. It should be pointed out, however, that the subjects in the experimental group were selected from G. S. College of Yoga whereas those in the control group came from Poona University. It is not unreasonable to consider the yoga students to be different from the average university students. Their expectations may indeed play a role that may be just as important as yoga practice.

Kocher (1976a) confirmed these findings in a subsequent study with students who enrolled in a certificate course in yoga and practiced yoga daily ninety minutes for over three weeks. This study did not have a control group. In a study by Girodo (1974), patients diagnosed as "anxious" and "neurotic" practiced TM-like meditation. Anxiety-symptom questionnaires administered every two weeks revealed a significant reduction of anxiety symptoms after the eighth session of meditation. Because the patients served as their own controls, the possibility that their expectations rather than meditation was responsible for reduction in anxiety is not ruled out. Linden (1971) also reported significant decrease in anxiety scores from pre- and post-treatment conditions involving Zen meditation. No such effect was found in control subjects.

In a well-controlled study with college students, Smith (1976) found that the subjects who practiced TM obtained significantly lower trait anxiety scores than the control subjects. The anxiety scores of TM meditators did not, however, differ significantly from the scores of subjects in control treatment groups who simply sat with their eyes closed. Oak and Bhole (1982) also reported a decrement in neuroticism and anxiety scores among asthmatics undergoing yogic treatment. No analyses of the data were provided to know whether the observed results are statistically significant. Anantharaman and Kabir (1984) found no significant changes in the anxiety scores of their subjects after three months of yoga practice, which included simple *asanas* and *pranayama*. They, however, found significant changes in other variables, including blood pressure and pulse rate.

In a more recent study involving a sample of 356 nonclinical subjects. Vinod, Vinod, and Khire (1991) reported a significant effect of yoga on reducing anxiety. The report, however, raises a number of questions. The subjects were given "comprehensive training" in yoga for two hours each day for one month. The training consisted of "meditation, thorough understanding of the practical applications of the philosophical concepts of yoga through 'Brain Storming' sessions along with usual physical training and relaxation" (p. 26). The subjects were administered a paper and pencil test (Sinha's Anxiety Scale) before and after the one-month training period to determine their anxiety levels. Finding significant statistical differences between the pre- and post-training anxiety scores, the authors conclude among other things that the "Yoga Training Programme had produced significant reduction in anxiety level over a period of 5 years" (p. 27).

It is unclear how the pre- and post-training anxiety scores, which were presumably obtained within the duration of one month, could lead the authors to generalize their finding to a five-year period. Apart from this obvious puzzle, any dis-

cerning reader finds the entire report quite confusing. First, there is a lack of adequate reporting. How did they select the sample? What kind of physical training and relaxation techniques were used? Did all the subjects complete their training? Because of the way the paper is presented, one can hardly draw any meaningful conclusions. Not only does one find the vital data links missing for sustaining their conclusion, the design itself is faulty and self-defeating. It makes sense to consider that the so-called brain storming sessions may be responsible for the apparent anxiety reduction in the subjects and that the practical training and so forth may have nothing to do with the results. Confounding of variables is a major drawback of many studies of similar nature. Apart from the statistical and methodological cleanliness that is required, conceptual clarity is equally important. If we wish to find a relationship between practice of yoga and anxiety, we must have a precise understanding of yoga and anxiety. One cannot jumble up meditation, physical relaxation exercises, counseling sessions, and so on, and then proceed to conclude that the obtained result is due to yoga. The whole purpose of empirical research is one of relating precisely defined variables. In the absence of clearly circumscribed variables we can hardly be expected to have any understanding of the claimed relationship. Much of research of this type coming from India is clearly lacking in necessary methodological controls and conceptual clarity.

In a cross-sectional study of some attentional and affective concomitants of meditation, Davidson, Goleman, and Schwartz (1984) administered the Telligen Absorption Scale, the Shor Personal Experience Questionnaire, and the Spielberger State-Trait Anxiety Inventory to four groups of subjects: non-meditating controls, beginners, and short-term and long-term meditators. The results showed "reliable increases in measures of attentional absorption in conjunction with a reliable decrement in trait anxiety across groups as a function of length of time meditating" (p. 229).

Eppley, Abrams and Shear (1989) did a meta-analysis of approximately 130 studies they were able to locate that attempted to study the effects of meditation on trait anxiety. The analysis revealed differential outcomes. Practice of TM appeared to reduce trait anxiety more than other procedures including Benson's relaxation response. The mean effect size observed in TM-anxiety studies is 170 per cent larger than the effect size observed in studies that used relaxation response. The latter were found to be no different from the effect size obtained with placeboes. Surprisingly, other forms of meditation such as those involving concentration fared far worse. The mean effect sizes in these studies were less than those observed in placebo studies.

In addition to anxiety, a number of other psychological variables were explored in relation to practice of meditation. Pelletier (1984) reported a study in which one group of subjects practiced standard TM for three months whereas the second group was instructed to sit quietly for 20 minutes each morning for three months. The subjects in both groups were administered tests before and after three months of practice to measure autokinetic perception. The results of meditators showed a shift in the autokinetic effect toward increased field independence. No such effect was observed in the control group. Pelletier concludes:

> Since deployment of attention is the critical factor in determining performance on these perceptual tasks and since it is the expressed goal of meditation to achieve an inward, focused attention, it is suggested that these observed differences can be attributed to an alteration in the individual's deployment of attention due to meditative practice [p. 225].

In a well-designed study in which two comparable groups of subjects were tested, one before and the other after yogic training, Jhansi Rani and P.V.K. Rao (1990) found no significant difference in the self-ideal disparity scores of the two groups.

Kocher (1976b) reported two studies in which he attempted to investigate the effects of yogic training on short-term memory. In the first study he administered a battery of memory tests to a group of 30 subjects before and after they underwent three weeks of yoga training. Similar tests were also administered to another group of 30 subjects drawn from the same school and matched for age, intelligence, and initial memory scores. The latter group did not practice yoga. The results showed a significant improvement in the short-term memory scores of the subjects in the experimental group and not in the control. The second study, which did not have a control group, also showed that the memory scores of subjects after they practiced yoga for three weeks improved significantly from heir initial scores. Even assuming that the necessary precautions were taken in collecting and analyzing the data accurately, we cannot rule out in these studies the possibility that the subject's expectations and motivation to do better after yogic training may be responsible for improved memory scores. Also it is not mentioned whether those who administered the memory tests were blind to the experimental conditions. If they were not, as it appears likely, their bias may be responsible for the observed results.

M.B. Kolsawalla (1978) investigated the effectiveness of meditation and yogic exercises on personality. She tested three groups of subjects, each group consisting of 16 subjects. All the subjects were first administered Rokeach's "D" scale and Cattell's 16 PF Questionnaire. Then, the subjects in Group 1 practiced meditation and yoga *asanas* for 75 days and Group 2 did only the *asanas*, and Group 3 did neither meditation nor yoga *asanas*. All the subjects were again give the "D" scale and 16 PF

Questionnaire. The results showed significant changes in the scores on the "D" scale of Group I subjects only. The subjects in the experimental group tended to be more open minded after 75 days of meditation practice. Also there was a significant reduction of tension level and increase of emotional maturity among the Group I subjects and not in other groups. Kolsawalla points out, "The subjects [Group 1] unanimously reported feeling at peace with themselves and had developed a relaxed and positive attitude to life, leading to more efficient problem solving, an urge to reach out to people, an attempt to understand another's point of view, deep and restful sleep, and general sense of well being" (p. 64). Kolsawalla's research is clearly important in support of the benefits of meditation. One possible limitation of the study is that the experimenter's expectations could have biased the results in favor of the meditation group. The problem of experimenter expectation is not controlled in many studies on meditation.

YOGA AND HYPERTENSION

In a study Datey et al. (1969) explored the effect of *shavasan* (lying down posture with awareness of breathing by attending to stomach movements) on hypertensive patients. They found that a group of subjects who took no drugs showed a significant decrease in their blood pressure after practicing *shavasan* 30 minutes daily for 30 weeks.

Extensive studies on the effect of meditation (relaxation response as they called it) on hypertensive patients were reported by Benson and associates (Benson 1977; Benson, Alexander & Feldman, 1975; Benson, Marzetta, & Rosen, 1974: Benson et al., 1974). They report in one study that patients who practiced meditation showed significant decrease in systolic as well as diastolic blood pressure during the experimental period of 20 weeks compared to the

control period of 5 weeks when the patients did not meditate. The results of these studies clearly show a significant reduction in blood pressure. However, one methodological problem relates to the possibility that the subject expectation might have contaminated the results because the same subjects served as controls. This is a problem that vitiates a good deal of research in this area.

Chandra Patel (1973; 1975; 1977) published a number of experimental reports on the effect of meditation on hypertension patients. In these studies the subjects practiced *shavasana*, meditation on breath, muscle relaxation, and a concentrative form of meditation. They also received biofeedback of their GSR through audio signal. The results show that there is a significant improvement in blood pressure over a period of three months. It is not clear, however, the extent to which meditation is responsible for the reduction of blood pressure because among other things the patients received biofeedback and had contacts with the therapist.

In a study of elderly American origin, Schneider et al. (1995) found that practice of TM significantly reduced systolic and diastolic blood pressure from their baseline levels and that the effect produced by TM is significantly larger than the one observed with progressive muscle relaxation.

Selvamurty et al. (1983) found that six months of yogic exercises resulted in a trend toward relative parasympathetic dominance, improvement in thermo-regulatory efficiency, and orthostatic tolerance among the 30 physically healthy men they studied.

In an exploratory study of 20 patients suffering from migraine and tension headaches, Latha and Kaliappan (1992) divided the subjects into two groups. One group of ten patients received yogic therapy consisting of *asanas* and breathing exercises while the other group (control) received no such training. They reported significant reduction in headaches and medication intake among the patients in the yoga therapy group.

Sharma, Kumaraiah, Mishra, and Balodhi (1990) studied the effect of *vipassana* meditation on 10 patients with tension headaches. The patients were assessed on two physiological and three behavioral measures along with a self-report during, before, and after 20 daily sessions of meditation. Significant decrease in frontalis muscle tension and reduction in skin conductance after meditation were observed. Also, intensity, frequency, and duration of headaches were reduced, and there was improvement in the anxiety symptoms. Follow-up studies after five and twelve months showed that the improvement in the condition of the patient was maintained.

John Astin (1997) examined the effects of mindfulness meditation on undergraduate students, who participated in an eight week stress reduction program involving mindfulness meditation. A comparison of the experimental subjects with the control group revealed significantly greater changes in the reduction of overall psychological symptoms. From these results, Astin concludes that mindfulness meditation is a powerful technique for transforming the ways in which one responds to life events and for preventing the relapse of affective disorders.

Miller and associates studied the effect of mindfulness meditation on patients diagnosed as suffering from anxiety disorders. They found that 20 of their 22 patients showed significant reduction in subjective and objective symptoms of anxiety following eight weeks of treatment based on mindfulness meditation. A follow up study after three years confirmed the long-term beneficial effect of reducing anxiety symptoms (Miller et al. 1995). Earlier studies that suggest the possibility of anxiety and stress reduction following practice of meditation include Davidson, et al. (1976); Puryear & Cayce (1976); Davies (1977); and Lazar et al. (1977). There are of course a few other studies, which reported no effect of meditation

on anxiety reduction. For example, Goldman et al. (1979) found in their study involving 72 subjects that practice of Zen meditation had no effect on reducing anxiety.

A number of studies were carried out in India to study the therapeutic effects of yoga on patients suffering from asthma and other diseases (Bhole 1976; Bhagwat, Soman, & Bhole, 1981; Bhole 1982). The results generally show improvements in the condition of the patients. From a strictly scientific perspective, the results are essentially uninterpretable because the studies lack necessary controls for ruling out other possible explanations. Among the better-controlled studies that show promise in this area are by Nagaratna and Nagendra (1985) and Nagendra and Nagaratna (1986).

Among the studies that investigated the biochemical changes brought about by yogic (physical) exercises, mention may be made of those by Udupa and co-workers at Banaras Hindu University (Udupa & Singh 1972; Udupa et al., 1972; 1975a; 1975b; 1975c; 1975d). In one of their earlier studies it is reported that normal subjects (12 youths) who practiced physical yoga exercises for six months showed lower cholesterol and blood sugar levels. They found also increased adrenocortical activity, which seemed to indicate greater resistance to stress. The analysis of urine indicated larger testosterone excretion. In another study with 42 subjects, they observed the rise of catecholamines and secretion of 17-hydoxycortiosteroids and reduction in 17-ketosteroids, which, according to Udupa, indicates a vitalizing effect of yoga. In a study by Settiwar et al. (1983), it was observed that the neurohumoral substances in urine came very close to normal in 15 of their patients with essential hypertension after 15 to 20 weeks of yoga treatment.

From a review of therapeutic uses of meditation Delmonte (1986), however, concludes that there is little clinical evidence to support the usefulness of meditation except in areas of anxiety and hypertension reduction.

Just as a number of attempts were made to reduce meditation to a simple technique that could be studied in controlled laboratory studies, efforts were also made to stimulate some *kriyas* and *pranayama* practices of yoga as simple laboratory procedures. Very often the efforts appear to miss the essential aspects of yoga. For example, Novak, Lepicovaka, Dostalek, and Hajek (1990) carried out a sophisticated study, even though it involved only two subjects, to test the effects of *kapalabhati*. *Kapalabhati* is a yogic exercise of inhalation and exhalation by voluntary rhythmic contraction and relaxation of abdominal muscles. It is traditionally regarded as a *kriya*, a cleansing technique. Even though I was unable to find a clear-cut definition or an unambiguous description of *kapalabhati* in any of the texts I was able to consult, it stands to reason to consider it as something that emphasizes exhalation as distinct from *bhastrika*, which lays more emphasis on inhalation. In the study mentioned above the Czechoslovakian scientists attempted to simulate the affect of *kapalabhati* by a simple periodical air insufflation into a select nostril by rhythmically puffing air current into the left or right nostril. Finding that such air insufflation has a concomitant effect of increased theta activity in the EEG mapping in the two subjects they tested, they conclude that the effect is due to *kapalabhati*.

The above observation, with its admittedly limited generalizability, because there were only two subjects, may be of some interest on its own. But, to suggest that puffing air into one nostril is equivalent to the practice of *kapalabhati* is, however, quite naive. Considering the prevailing view that *kapalabhati* is a cleansing process and therefore its emphasis is on exhalation, puffing air may have a contrary effect.

Moreover, the central part of *kapalabhati* is flexing abdominal muscles, inward pressure of the abdomen in the navel area with sudden exhalation. This part is conspicuously missing in the modeling of *kapalabhati* by the Czechoslovakian scientists.

The credit for a tremendous explosion of research interest in yoga and meditation, as mentioned earlier, is largely due to the popularity of TM and the support of Maharshi Mahesh Yogi and the TM organization. It is true that much of research on TM suffers from a lack of necessary controls, over-generalizations, and above all the positive expectations of the researchers themselves who are TM enthusiasts. I, myself criticized TM as instant meditation only remotely resembling classical meditation (Rao 1989; 1992). It must be admitted, however, that not only the sheer quantity of reports claiming positive effects for TM (Orme-Johnson & Farrow, 1977) but also some of the recent studies with very sophisticated designs do make a claim in favor of genuine benefits of TM that could not be ignored.

An important study by Alexander et al. (1989) provides clear evidence that suggests the beneficial effects of meditation compared to simple resting and control conditions. In this study, 73 elderly subjects with a mean age of 81 years were randomly assigned to four groups. One group practiced TM 20 minutes twice daily. The subjects in the second group were instructed in mindfulness involving a guided attention technique (MF). The third group (MR) consisted of the subjects who were required to sit comfortably with eyes closed, repeating to themselves any mental stimuli they found to be pleasant or comfortable. The fourth was a no-treatment, control group (NT). The subjects were randomly assigned to these groups and pre-tested on a number of measures, including cognitive flexibility, blood pressure, behavioral flexibility, and aging. They found no significant differences between the groups on any of these variables in the results of pre-testing.

The subjects then practiced the assigned treatment for three months. After the completion of the three-month period, they were again tested on the same measures. The results showed significant differences in the cognitive performance scores of the subjects of TM and MF groups compared to MR and nontreatment groups. There were also significant differences in systolic blood pressure following the three months' practice with TM group having the lowest followed by the mindfulness group. The most spectacular finding relates to the mortality rates observed during the following three-year period. It is reported that all the subjects in the TM group survived, whereas the survival rate in the MF group was 87.5 percent, and 65 percent for the MR group. The average survival rate of the residents of these homes for the elderly was 62.6 percent. This finding is quite consistent with the results of a field study in which it was found that TM practitioners had approximately half as many hospitalizations or visits to the doctors as nonmeditating matched groups as revealed by the insurance claims (Orme-Johnson 1987).

Alexander et al. (1994) did a meta-analysis comparing TM with other forms of meditation and relaxation techniques. The results showed that TM is significantly more effective in (a) reducing psychological and somatic arousal, (b) decreasing trait anxiety, and (c) promoting positive mental health on measures of self-actualization. Alexander and associates also point out that epidemiological studies show that people practicing TM had significantly lower inpatient and outpatient visits and expenditures than comparable groups. Therefore, it does not seem that the practice of meditation in general and transcendental meditation in particular has beneficial psychological and somatic effects.

DOES MEDITATION HELP TO DEVELOP PSYCHIC ABILITIES?

As we have noted in the chapter on "Paranormal Awareness," there is suggestive evidence for a positive relationship between meditation and psi. Schmeidler (1970) reported that her subjects scored higher on an ESP task following a brief instruction in and practice of meditation and breathing exercises guided by a *swami* compared to their scores before the meditation session. The results of the study showed that while the performance in the pre-meditation run was close to chance expectation, the scores after they meditated were significantly more than chance, suggesting that meditation may have been responsible for psi-hitting in the second run.

Osis and Bokert (1971) carried out three correlation studies and found meditation and ESP to be related in a complex manner. The meditative practices of the subjects in this study varied; they were encouraged to use their own preferred techniques. Some subjects employed Zen and raja yoga methods, while others adopted self-hypnosis and depth imagery concentration. The ESP tests employed were both forced-choice and free-response tasks. The forced-choice test was a version of Brugman's checkerboard test with a close-circuit TV adaptation. The free response test involved guessing pictorial slides. Questionnaires designed to measure changes in the state of consciousness were administered before and after each session. The ESP tests themselves were given after a period of meditation.

A factor analysis of the questionnaire material revealed three stable factors. Of these, the factor of "self-transcendence and openness to experience" was found to be associated significantly with ESP scores. The investigators concluded that, among possibilities, the meager correlation between meditative experiences and ESP might be due to the subjects' experiencing the ESP tests as interruptions to their meditation, thus causing "task rivalry" and possibly a preferential effect.

In a PK study by Matas and Pantas (1971) subjects who had experience with some form of meditation meditated for 15 minutes before they attempted to influence by PK a random event generator. The results of the meditators were found to be significantly better than those of control subjects who performed identical tasks without meditating. In three series of experiments, Schmidt and Pantas (1971) found that a single subject performed significantly on a PK task after practicing Zen meditation for 20 minutes prior to the test.

At Andhra University, Rao, Dukhan, and Rao (1978) carried out a series of forced-choice and free-response ESP tests to see whether subjects would obtain higher ESP scores after meditation than in pre-meditation sessions. The same subjects were tested in pre- and post-meditation sessions. Thus, the same subjects acted as their controls. Fifty-nine subjects who were practicing a nonstandardized form of meditation at Anandashram in Pondicherry participated in this study. The ESP tests involved matching cards with ESP symbols and guessing concealed pictures. In both the tests the results showed that subjects obtained significantly better ESP scores in tests administered immediately following meditation than in tests carried out before the subjects meditated. Interestingly, the subjects obtained significantly fewer hits in pre-meditation sessions than would be expected by chance.

While the results of the above studies do suggest ESP on the part of the meditating subjects, it is difficult to argue that these experiments support the hypothesis that meditation enhances one's psychic ability. Like the studies of meditation in other areas, ESP-meditation studies suffer from a lack of appropriate controls.

WHAT HAVE WE LEARNT FROM MEDITATION RESEARCH?

There are indeed severe methodological problems in several of the meditation studies. These include (a) the widespread practice of the same subject designs in which each subject acts as his own control and (b) the failure to control for individual differences in personality, attitudes, expectations, training, and duration and quality of meditation practice of the subjects tested. Also (c) meditation research is beset with a good deal of conceptual confusion and over generalizations. Conceptual confusions stem from (a) a failure to distinguish between meditation as a state and as a method, (b) lack of adequate criteria to identify a meditative state and to measure its quality and depth, and (c) the simplistic notion that sitting cross-legged and chanting a *mantra* is qualitatively the same as the classical discipline of meditation. These problems not withstanding, the widespread interest in meditation has some useful consequences. First, despite the numerous well-taken criticisms, it is difficult to deny that practice of meditation has certain benefits for one's health and well being. The criticism that a meditative state is similar in some respects to a state of drowsiness or sleep does not make meditation any less important. We may recall that in Vedanta, for example, sleep state is closer to a transcendental state than the waking state. Higher states of consciousness appear to depend on controlling sensory inputs. Meditation does seem to be an useful tool for reducing sensory noise. Second, meditation research is a good example of how a concept considered esoteric can be empirically studied in a controlled setting. Third, meditation studies open up windows of opportunity to look at Eastern psychological traditions. Meditation research may prove that Rudyard Kipling is wrong after all and that East and West do meet in some special ways.

As mentioned, there are glaring differences between contemporary practices of meditation and the classical prescriptions for practicing meditation. There is, however, a good deal of common ground between them. The core commonality among all systems of meditation past and present undoubtedly has to do with attention. Most reviewers of the varieties of meditation practices seem to agree on that (Goleman 1978, Naranjo & Ornstein, 1971). Attention seems to be the essence of yoga, if by the latter we mean the control of normal mental functions (*citta vrittis*). In his commentary on *Yoga-Sutras*, Vacaspatimisra defines attention as one-pointedness. It is the focusing of the mind on one object to the exclusion of others. According to Buddhaghosha, attention narrows the focus of consciousness and makes the object of attention distinct. Inasmuch as attention involves the absence of distraction, it leads to peace and equanimity, to growth, fulfillment, and perfection. Bhatta Akalanka mentions the following conditions as necessary for focusing attention:

(1) a congenial environment, which is neither too hot nor too cold, which is free from the scorching sun and rain, which is not infested by wild beasts, birds and reptiles, that divert the internal organ and the external sense-organs to improper objects; (2) a favourable posture of the body; (3) inhaling and exhaling slowly and steadily; (4) inhibition of distracting bodily actions; (5) suppression of attachment, aversion and delusion; (6) fixation of the mind without wavering on a desirable object; and (7) suppression of lethargy, sleep, attachment, sex-love, grief, mirth, fear, doubt, desire and aversion [quoted from Sinha, 1961].

Commenting on the *Yoga Sutras* of Patanjali, Vyasa explains how distractions that inhibit attention may be overcome. Detachment, compassion and love for all, regulation of breathing, good company, concentration on agreeable and pleasing ob-

jects, and covert or overt repetition of the mystic sound OM or any name of God are among those recommended for overcoming distraction. Different meditative practices seem to involve essentially similar approaches. As Davidson and Goleman (1977) suggest, meditation appears to be one of the oldest techniques for self-regulation of attention. The two apparently distinct forms of meditation—concentrative meditation and passive meditation—both involve manipulation of attention. The object of attentional focus may be different, but attentional deployment seems to be at the core of all meditation practices.

Meditation is not a psychic development technique as is often assumed. Rather, it is a process initiated by focusing attention for a prolonged period on an object or a mental or bodily state. Sustained one-pointed attention is believed to lead to a state of absorption in which one experiences expanded awareness that transcends the limitations imposed by the normal psychobiological processes—an awareness that gives unbiased knowledge. In order to attain such an intentional focus and sustain it, it is suggested that one should avoid distractions, both psychological and biological. As a consequence, other benefits such as psychological and biological well being may accrue. They are, however, not a direct result of meditation. Inasmuch as meditation enables selective deployment of attention, it may be possible to gain control over certain psychobiological processes over which we normally lack volitional control. Thus, it would seem that if meditative practices help gain volitional control of autonomic processes or achieve psychic abilities, the latter may not be regarded as the essence of meditation. Classical systems warn us against pursuing those ends because they become hurdles on the path of perfection. This leads me to make a distinction between secular and sacred uses of meditation. The secular meditation is applied meditation.

Sacred meditation is pure meditation whose sole objective is the transcendence, and not the control of our psychobiological processes. The latter may be necessary for achieving the former, but they are not identical. Much of contemporary research has dealt with meditation in the secular sense, both in its practices, which emphasized the technique rather than the attitude, and in its application which aimed at mundane benefits rather than for cognitive perfection. Westernization of meditation has led to its secularization.

Meditation is a process that involves manipulation of attention. A variety of techniques may be used and diverse state effects or even trait effects may be obtained. It may be, therefore, a futile attempt to look for a unique psychophysiological characterization of meditation. Instead we should be looking at attentional phenomena. It is likely that meditative practice enables selective deployment of attention to arouse or depress specific cortical areas. I tend to agree with Schuman (1980) that cognitive variables may be more important than physiological correlates of meditation. As she points out, "the available evidence supports the notion of specificity in cortical activation and suggests that EEG correlates in meditation may, in fact, be explicable in terms of specific cognitive behaviors, that is, in terms of the content rather than the context of meditation" (Schuman, 1980, p. 361). Discovering physiological correlates of meditation, if they exist, is not sufficient to understand the meditation process. The urgent need now is to define the psychological roots. This can only be done by carefully studying the subjective experiences of highly proficient meditators and not by questioning the "instant" meditators or recording their physiological measures.

Attention may be a key factor in understanding mind/matter interface. Ordinarily attention either fluctuates randomly or is determined by environmental conditions and subject dispositions. The subject conditions that influence attention are themselves the products of environmental or genetic determinants. For this reason, much of cognitive behavior can be understood and explained by deterministic models. If, however, we construe consciousness as an independent principle, there should be nondeterministic aspects to human volition and intention. Meditation, it would seem, is a process of promoting such voluntary attention.

Whether in perception or action, attention is not always under voluntary control, it may be automatic. Consider, for example, the distinction between what William James called *ideo-motor* and *willed* actions. The latter, in contrast to the former, require *will*. The will may exercise control by activation or inhibition of available signals/impulses so that they receive attention. While the will often succeeds in its modulating role to activate some and inhibit other signals when they are competing for attention, the stimulus characteristics of signals, themselves are quite powerful in triggering their activation. Again, the will itself may be influenced by subjective conditions, interests, attitudes and dispositions. Thus, in principle, given the subjective characteristics of the individual and the stimulus properties at a precise point in time, it should be possible to predict the focus of one's attention—what one would perceive, do or think at a given moment. For this reason, much of our cognitive behavior can be understood and explained by deterministic models. Where we are unable to find a reasonable explanation we assume that our present knowledge and instrumentation are insufficient at the moment to record and monitor the minute and complex brain processes. Alternatively, it may be argued that some of the brain processes are random and because of that some aspects of human behavior remain unpredictable. It would appear, then, that attentional fluctuations are either determined or random. If so, there is hardly any room for free will.

Such is the general wisdom born out of determinism promoted by advances in physical science. However, meditation research seems to suggest something different. If meditation is a process of promoting voluntary attention, meditators may reveal nondeterministic aspects of human volition and intention that have discernable effects distinct from others modulated by subjective bias and external pressures. There would be, then, reason to believe in free volition and consciousness as an independent principle.

It is likely that one-pointed attentional focus in concentrative forms of meditation controls on the one hand, the random fluctuations of attention, and, on the other hand, it renders attention impervious to environmental pressures and subjective bias. Even in the so-called passive meditation, the meditator learns to nonreactively attend to incoming signals for prolonged periods of time, which serves the same purpose of promoting voluntary attention or pure volition. In other words, meditation brings about cessation of thought-evoking habitual brain activity which normally has the effect of masking pure volition.

Enhancing pure *volitional activity* may have the effect of bringing mind/matter or consciousness/environment interface into focus in ways that are not explicable in terms of current scientific constructs, which deny or ignore nondeterministic role of mental functions such as free will. Consequently, if anomalous effects could be obtained by manipulating volition and attention as in meditation, we may come closer to having a more accurate understanding of mind/matter interface in the human condition. Even such phenomena as man-machine interaction, psychic and spiritual healing may be scientifically studied in the light of the findings from meditation research. There, then, is the importance of studying meditation in relation to paranormal phenomena.

Summary

Two centuries of European presence helped to create Western type of political and educational institutions in India. The new institutions were meant to replace the traditional ones. Little effort went into integrating the two or promoting them separately. The consequences are two-fold. Western type of education spread in India at the expense of the traditional and native institutions. The colonial powers also had benefited little culturally and intellectually by their long association with Asian countries, providing ground for Kipling's assertion that East and West will never meet. Exposed to Western traditions and the political patronage given to them, Eastern scholars were tempted to appropriate them, ignoring their own native thought and tradition. The result in Indian psychology, for example, is the blind and uncritical adoption of Western concepts, methods and models. This state of affairs has continued unabated for over one half a century after the colonial rule had ended.

There is some reason to believe that things are beginning to change. There is on the one hand a greater appreciation in the East of the relevance of their own roots, culture and tradition for a balanced and sustained growth, both economic and intellectual. On the other hand, there is also some awareness in a few areas of endeavor in the West that the Eastern traditions may supply some of the missing links in their own. This trend was heralded first by a few thinkers, men of excellence and energy like Swami Vivekananda, Aurobindo Ghosh, Yogananda, and J. Krishnamurti and later popularized by Mahesh Yogi and other Eastern *gurus*. Their thoughts and actions were able to open up windows for the West to see the rich spiritual and philosophical heritage of the East, that sharply contrasts with that of the West. The Eastern tradition has focused on the inner, subjective discipline whereas the West has emphasized the external, objective science. There is some hope now that we may find a common ground where East and West can meet with their own traditions in tact. The area of meditation appears to be one such common ground. Meditation as a discipline for inner exploration is deeply rooted in Eastern traditions. Researchers have shown that meditation is eminently amenable for scientific investigation, which is West's important concern. Meditation is an area in which both first-person and third-person methodologies could be beneficially applied. More importantly, in the context of this study, meditation studies may provide the main foundation on which a full-fledged science of consciousness may be built.

The difficult methodological and conceptual problems that beset scientific studies of meditation not withstanding, the investigations in this area are beginning to yield some important results. It is clear, for example, that practice of meditation has some somatic and psychological benefits. In our view, it is not important that the meditative state represents a unique physiological state. All subjective states may not have the corresponding physiological states. It may be less relevant, therefore, that the subjective experiences of meditation are translated into precise physiological descriptions than it is to intersubjectively validate them by shared experiences of meditating subjects. Again, drowsiness, dream state, deep sleep, and meditation may have some important things in common and, therefore, may produce similar effects to some extent. In the view of some Indian thinkers, like Samkara, they appear to be distinctive points in an essential continuum that involves a progressive reduction in the influence of the sensory-motor system on our mind and freedom from the objective determination of one's behavior and being. Contemporary researches have indeed shown that sensory noise reduction is conducive for achieving higher states of awareness, including the acquisition of psychic abilities. Of course, any discovery of dependable physiological correlates of meditative experience would be important and useful for scientific research of meditation. For example, the observation of significant correlation between thought-free subjective states and corresponding suppression or cessation of breathing may render the belief in the existence of pure consciousness more credible and at the same time allow for scientific research of the so called mystical states (Shear, 2001).

The above is not simply a wish of an Eastern psychologist. There is an increasing number of Western scholars interested in consciousness studies and are familiar with Eastern meditative traditions that share the above view. For example, Jonathan Shear and Ron Jeving (1999) have called our attention to the complementarity of first-person and third-person accounts in meditation research and the need for "some combination of objective and subjective approaches" (p. 189). Drawing from the traditional accounts of meditation in the East and the modern scientific investigations in the West, they make a case that certain physiological measures (third-person items) such as reduction of pulse, circulation and metabolic rate, and cessation of respiration, correlate with reports of pure conscious experience (first-person item). Such findings open up avenues for East-West meeting. Promising to be a valuable tool to achieve higher states of awareness, meditation may well hold the key to unlock the mysteries of consciousness. Meditation studies require, however, highly sophisticated and well-controlled scientific research in which the West excels and equally well-cultivated and organized first-person strategies implicit in the meditative traditions of the East.

CHAPTER 12

Confluence of Two Streams:
East-West *Sangamam*

Edward Titchner (1915) quoted James Ward approvingly that consciousness is "the most treacherous of psychological concepts" (p. 323). We have seen why this is so. In the Western scholarly tradition, discussions on consciousness are vitiated by its multiple connotations. It would seem that consciousness is many concepts rolled into one. We have noted, however, that a common thread seems to run across the many meanings it connotes. Consciousness appears to refer always to some form of awareness. We distinguished between four basic forms of awareness. Paradoxical awareness is implied in a variety of mental phenomena such as subliminal perception, implicit memory, hypnotic analgesia and negative hallucinations, blindsight and other forms of impaired awareness due to brain damage. It is nonsubjective and unrecognized awareness. The information conveyed by such awareness is inaccessible to introspection. Primary awareness is what we have in the acts of perception, thinking, feeling and volition. Included in this category are perceptions, images, inner speech, feelings as well as abstract concepts, beliefs, intentions and expectations. The basic characteristics of primary awareness are its subjective quality, accessibility to introspection, and immediate transparency. Pathological awareness is aberrant and dysfunctional awareness. Cognitive abnormalities, multiple personality and thought disorders as in schizophrenia are examples. Paranormal awareness is nonsensory and nonrepresentational awareness as in ESP and mystic experiences of pure consciousness. Parapsychological phenomena are acausal and show no casual link between the subject and the object of awareness. Mystical experience has no representational content. Many psychologists who see no problem with the first three forms of awareness have difficulty in accepting the fourth as genuine. We have seen, however, that there is credible evidence supporting the existence of psi.

We have also noted how consciousness appears differently as we look at it from the perspectives of its different forms described above. At the level of primary awareness, the stream metaphor appears to be the most appropriate as it captures the sense of subjectivity reflected in the unity and continuity of phenomenal awareness. The metaphor of the stream, however, is of little help in the discussions of paradoxical awareness, which lacks subjective awareness. We find therefore philosophers like Daniel Dennett (1991), who are uncomfortable with subjective aspects of consciousness, go as far as dismissing all the qualitative aspects of awareness (qualia) as imaginary and unreal and question the appropriateness of the stream metaphor. Even William James, as his interests moved away from primary awareness in *The Principles of Psychology* to paranormal awareness in *The Varieties of Religious Experience*, replaced the stream metaphor with the metaphor of the "Mother Sea" to describe consciousness. Again, psychologist Jung, who was more concerned with transpersonal aspects of consciousness, likened consciousness to the luminosity and brightness of light (Jung 1919/1954).

So we see why we need different conceptual maps in order to explore different areas of consciousness. Also, it follows that we require diverse methodological tools to explore the different regions of consciousness. Clearly, the subjective aspects of conscious experience require a first-person approach. Paradoxical awareness, however, may be fruitfully investigated with objective methods and from the perspective of the third-person. It is entirely possible that neurobiological studies may provide a complete description and explanation of implicit perception. When we move on to the area of paranormal awareness, however, we need an altogether new approach and very different strategies to capture its essence.

I am persuaded that exclusive concern with some forms of consciousness and the neglect of others, or their conflation, is at the root of much controversy and confusion in consciousness studies. Consciousness, it would seem, is much like a multi-story structure, a building with several floors. Primary awareness is like the ground floor, whereas paradoxical awareness is the basement. Other forms of consciousness look like the upper floors; and the terrace at the top, open and unenclosed, is analogous to pure consciousness or awareness as such. The differences between Western and Eastern perspectives of consciousness appear to stem from their primary concerns with one or another level of consciousness. They use different conceptual maps and methodological strategies. They also set different goals and have different objectives in investigating consciousness.

What Is Consciousness?

In the Western tradition, as we have seen, the concepts "consciousness" and "mind" are not sharply distinguished. In fact, they are often used interchangeably. John Locke meant by consciousness what goes on in one's mind. Predominantly this is the sense in which consciousness is used in most discussions even today. Consciousness thus refers in Western discourse essentially to primary awareness. Since the time of Locke, however, there is an increasing recognition of mental activity of which one is not subjectively aware. We now recognize implicit awareness and unconscious motivations as facts of life. There is mentation of which one is subjectively aware of and mentation that goes on beneath the threshold of consciousness. This calls for a clear distinction to be made between mind and consciousness, because the mind is also the container of information that is not in focal awareness or is not accessible to it. This has led some in the West to use the concept "mind" to include explicit awareness as well as covert mental activity and implicit awareness and restrict the use of "consciousness" to subjective awareness accessible to introspection. In this usage consciousness refers to a quality of experience and becomes a species of awareness. .

Cognitive psychologists like Bernard

Baars who wish to accord a greater role to consciousness in our mental life, attempt to contrast the brain states that are accompanied by consciousness with those that are not. By contrasting conscious and unconscious mentation they hope to isolate those brain states and functions that are critically correlated with explicit awareness and not with implicit awareness. Again, there is such great interest in the study of blindsight because it is considered to be evidence for awareness without consciousness. This exercise, it seems to me, would succeed only if the mental phenomena, including subjective experience, are ultimately reducible to brain states either as functions of separate systems or integrated activity of different systems in the brain. There are weighty considerations that render this a very unlikely possibility. There are good reasons to assume that a naturalistic understanding of the subjective aspect of consciousness may be in principle unobtainable. An increasing number of philosophers like Thomas Nagel consider subjectivity an "irreducible feature of reality" along with matter, space, time, and numbers. As Nagel states, subjectivity "is not captured by any of the familiar, recently devised reductive analysis of the mental" (1974, p. 167). There are of course those who find subjectivity a useless appendage of mental activity, a vacuous concept we are better without, and others who consider it irreducible and fundamental but essentially impervious to rational scrutiny and objective understanding. In either case, we have in the West scientists who have little interest in studying consciousness because, as a subjective phenomenon, it is either inessential and unimportant or intractable in principle. Those who do study consciousness tend to limit themselves to the nonsubjective aspects of the mind, as if that is all there is to consciousness. The exceptions are the few who regard consciousness as something primary and fundamental that can be empirically studied and rationally discussed.

The main thrust of the cognitive psychology of consciousness has been to study the nonconscious mind with the hope that somehow that would account for consciousness. This has not worked. This approach is flawed, conceptually and empirically. At the conceptual level, it is all too obvious that we need to make a basic distinction between mind and consciousness, whatever we may mean by them. At the empirical level, an equivocation of consciousness and mind has lead in the West to what appears to be a dead end with no fruitful avenues of exploring subjectivity in consciousness. Consciousness becomes either a vacuous concept or one that is simply beyond objective and scientific study.

Contrary to the scientific world view, the commonsense conception accords primacy to consciousness/mind, conceived as falling completely outside of naturalistic postulates. Yet its presence is considered necessary for the phenomena of our experience. This Cartesian world-view of mind-body dualism continues to be the commonsense mindset in the West. However, dualism of the sort advocated by Descartes stands discredited as a viable theory by the mainstream science as well as by the dominant philosophical traditions currently fashionable in the West. The reason for opposing Cartesian dualism is the problem of mind-body interaction, which has become too difficult to resolve. How do two entities so fundamentally different as the incorporeal mind and the physical body influence each other without violating the well-established law of conservation of energy?

The equating of mind and consciousness has another important consequence in the Western tradition. In general, intentionality has become the defining characteristic of consciousness. Whether one is a materialist (Armstrong & Malcolm 1984), a naturalist (Searle 1983), a phenomenalist (Husserl 1960), a psychoanalyst (Freud 1915) or an existentialist (Sartre 1957), the tendency is to assert that consciousness is always *of* or *about* something. All mental phenomena are believed to have a directedness about them. Even William James, who championed a very inclusive view of consciousness to encompass paranormal awareness, was not spared the pervasive influence of this notion. As we have observed, the emphasis on the intentionality of consciousness highlights on the one hand the fundamental distinction between subject and object, whether functional or foundational, and entails on the other hand a representational theory of knowledge. Moreover, it rules out a priori the possibility of pure conscious states. If consciousness is conceived to be inseparable from phenomenal content, there can be no direct knowledge of things except through their phenomenal representations. Even those who conceived of transcendental aspects of existence, such as Kant, admitted that things-in-themselves are essentially unknowable.

If consciousness as awareness in its broader sense includes explicit as well as implicit awareness, no fundamental distinction between consciousness and the unconscious can be sustained. Similarly, the attempts to restrict consciousness to focal attention, short-term memory or reflective awareness, i.e., awareness accessible to introspection, and to regard the mind more broadly to include implicit awareness and unconscious processes (Farthing 1992) is unsatisfactory.

The question then is whether consciousness is merely a quality of mental representations, as implied in the notion that equates it with focal attention or other brain processes. Alternatively, do mental phenomena as they manifest in our experience involve an independent factor or process without which experience of awareness is not possible? The Western approach favors the notion that consciousness is merely a quality of certain mental states. The Eastern perspective, however, takes the alternative position that leads us to regard consciousness as an independent source that which makes subjective awareness possible in the human condition. In other words, in the Eastern view, cortical processes alone cannot give us subjective awareness. Here a basic distinction is made between consciousness and mind, a distinction that helps to resolve the problem of interaction between mind and body in some important aspects. In Buddhism, however, consciousness is not seen as an outside source, something different from the mental states. At the same time, all schools of Buddhism recognize the existence of transcendental mental states and provide for nonintentional states of pure consciousness. In the Madhyamika and Yogacara schools, this point becomes more explicit in the concepts of *sunya* and *alaya-vijnana*.

In the Advaita system as well as in Samkhya-Yoga, consciousness is considered a fundamental principle that lies outside of physical things. It does not, however, interact with material objects, events and processes, but its presence makes them knowable. Consciousness is the light that shines on the objects of the universe and makes them subjectively realized. Since consciousness has no direct influence on physical things and does not interact with them, no physical laws are violated. The mind is conceptualized as the interfacing instrumentality that is connected at one end to consciousness and with the objects of cognition and action at the other. It processes information from objects and events accessible to it, making use of the brain and the sensory system. When consciousness shines on the processed information, there is sensory awareness of it. In this view, the relation between consciousness and the mind, at one level, is like the relation between the mirror and the image it reflects. The material forms processed in the mind lack subjectivity. They are mere images, which the mind may become aware of only in the presence of consciousness. The reflected images become the objects of sensory experience in the mind of the experiencing person. Subjective awareness thus involves (a) the presence of consciousness, (b) a functional mind capable of processing the sensory and proprioceptive inputs it receives and of experiencing their images in the medium of consciousness, and (c) the inputs themselves. All three are necessary conditions for phenomenal awareness to manifest.

In the Hindu systems, there is more to consciousness than being a mere light source for the apprehension of images and sensations processed in the mind. It is considered to be the ground condition without which no awareness is possible. It is the knowledge side of the universe. When the mind withdraws itself from participating in sensory processes by conscious choice and empties itself of all sense data and associated effects, it would be in a position to access consciousness-as-such. When the mind is able to access consciousness-as-such, there arises unmediated and direct knowledge, which is what consciousness is in itself. To the mind filled with sensory data, consciousness is a reflecting source. When the mind is emptied of sensory contents and partakes in pure consciousness it experiences a realization of knowledge in a direct and unmediated way. Such an experience by its very nature is ineffable and beyond verbal descriptions because it is nonrepresentational. However, such an experience may have immediate behavioral and attitudinal consequences for the experiencing person. The person may be transformed in important ways. Also, acts of creativity, value insights and intuitive apprehension of the working of the universe may manifest following the experience of a pure conscious state.

The above view may not be considered as contradicting the Western tradition in its positive aspects or as questioning the remarkable contributions of Western science to our understanding of a variety of mental functions. The role of the different constituents of the brain, their processes and functions, the cortical connections of mental phenomena, are duly acknowledged. Buddhist psychology, which discusses in some detail the mundane states of consciousness at the *kamaloka* and *rupaloka* planes, is a good example. While overcoming the limitations inherent in the Western assumptions, the Eastern view suggests the possible ways of expanding them to include other forms of awareness that appear anomalous. Also by asserting that there is more to mental phenomena than what goes on in the brain, the Eastern view takes us beyond the brain and the mind to consciousness-as-such. Thereby it offers a reasonable explanation of subjective experience, which neuroscience and cognitive psychology find too difficult to fathom and which continues to be an intractable problem for naturalism in the philosophy of mind.

If consciousness is an autonomous principle irreducible to material forms, as is claimed in the Eastern tradition, we may ask, how is it then different from the mind as postulated in Western dualistic doctrines? In the Eastern formulations, as we have noted, a distinction is made between consciousness and the mind. The mind is conceived as an interface between consciousness and the brain. Such an interface is considered possible because certain characteristics attributed to the mind are akin to consciousness, e.g., the *sattva* element in Samhkhya system. This suggests that there might be some value in looking for new forms of matter and material functioning to resolve traditional puzzles of the mind-body relation. It is interesting to note that in recent years a few scholars in the Western scientific tradition, who are dissatisfied with all attempts to reductively explain consciousness in familiar physical terms, appear to be embarking on a similar course (Penrose, 1994; Chalmers, 1996).

It is in line with the Cartesian legacy of mind-body duality that Western philosophical discourse is replete with disparate conceptual oppositions and difficult disjunctive categorizations such as subject-object, physical-mental, and so on. The nature of the opposition between them is such that the assertion of one implies the negation of the other. Thus, physical implies nonmental, and mental implies nonphysical; the object implies nonsubject, and so on. What is of special interest is that these categorizations are shared irrespective of one's philosophical affiliations, for example, whether one is a dualist or a materialist. John Searle (1992) has complained repeatedly that this Cartesian mindset is at the base of the misunderstandings of his own ideas by other philosophers.

The Eastern conception of mind as the interface and gateway between consciousness and the objective world, I am persuaded, frees us from the compulsions of such disjunctive categorizations as mentioned above. Mind in the Eastern tradition is the tool of awareness; it is our reality connection. When it connects with the objective world through our sensory system, we have phenomenal awareness. When the connection is to consciousness, we have transcendental realization. We make here an important distinction between states of awareness that give us representational knowledge on the one hand and those that bring about direct realization of unmediated knowledge on the other. While experiencing *awareness* it is possible to have dissociation between cognition and conduct. A state of *realization* is one where there is no room for such dissociation. Knowing and being become inseparable. The lives of true saints and those who had genuine "peak" or self-actualizing experiences are cited as instances of realization. Realization on the one hand removes any dissociation between belief and behavior. On the other hand, it has immediate transformational consequences.

Accessing consciousness-as-such is achieving a state of realization, which is believed to have a remarkable impact on one's life, conduct and values. Such a transformational possibility has important implications for our well being. The implications of such a claim to psychotherapy are all too obvious.

Now, contrast this with the dualism of Descartes, where mind is consciousness and it is nonphysical. How then do mind and the physical body interact? We all know how unsatisfactory are the attempts to answer this question. The essential feature of the mind, according to Descartes, is consciousness, and consciousness is thought. Indeed it is self-evident that one cannot doubt that he is doubting; but can one doubt without the brain? If the brain is necessary for thought and awareness, how can thought be the essence of consciousness? Inasmuch as experience manifests at the phenomenal as well as transcendental levels, there is need for a concept like mind, distinct from consciousness-as-such, which can be the bridge between consciousness and material reality.

We should keep in perspective that the Eastern model is not presented as a mere intellectual abstraction or a philosophical postulate, but as an empirical claim. The entire gamut of psychic development disciplines in the East are based on that claim. Therefore, the question of whether consciousness-as-such really exists should not be settled on mere theoretical grounds, because pure consciousness is not a logical presupposition. Its existence is considered a fact of experience. There are numerous instances of claims in the East of those who are believed to have achieved states of pure consciousness. The practice of yoga, for example, is considered to be an important technique for reaching higher states of awareness and for accessing consciousness qua consciousness.

The problem of interaction is then a non-issue from the Eastern perspective because mental phenomena are not conceived as resulting from an interaction of consciousness with the mind or the brain. Minds or brains do not interact with consciousness. The relation between consciousness and mind is not causal, one influencing the other. Rather it is reflexive, projecting one on the other. In the Eastern tradition, consciousness is assumed to be an autonomous principle inexplicable in terms of brain states. It does not cause mental phenomena nor does it influence the physical states of the brain. The mind, however, influences and is influenced by the brain states and by its own actions. Thus, consciousness-as-such has no causal role, but mind participates in upward as well as downward causation. The distinction between consciousness and mind thus circumvents the problem of interaction between nonphysical consciousness and physical body. They coexist, but do not interact. The interaction is between mind and body. Both are material forms. Mind, like the brain and unlike consciousness, is physical. Like consciousness and unlike the brain, it has nonlocal aspects.

There are good reasons to assume that one form of attentional activity, volitional effort, may be involved in bringing about the interface between the mind and consciousness. Control of sensory inputs and brain activity may help in this. The importance of volition as the connecting link between thought and action, the mind and the brain, is recognized as early as Plato. Recall Plato's division of the soul into three parts—reason, spirit and appetite. Spirit is what influences the conduct without which reason alone will be unable to guide our actions. Spirit is the volitional aspect that seems to cause reason to influence conduct.

I find Immanuel Kant's discussion of free will quite relevant here. Kant regards the "will" as autonomous, that is, as a law unto itself. The will in its pure form is independent of being determined by sensuous

impulses or stimuli. The freedom of will consists in the "absolute spontaneity" of pure will. According to Kant, there are two modes of causality. The causality of natural phenomena is one of physical necessity determined in time. The causality of free will, which belongs to the world of supersensible things, operates independently of the temporal conditions of natural causality. The causality of free will, in Kant's view, is capable of producing effects independently of, and even in opposition to, the power of natural causes, and of *spontaneously* originating a series of events.

Can we empirically deal with those issues of mind-brain interaction that apparently seem to refer to a transcendental domain? I believe we can. For example, the literature on psychic development techniques in general and meditation in particular seems to suggest that pure volitional activity can be facilitated by controlling habitual brain activity, which normally has the effect of masking pure volition. One-pointed attentional focus in concentration forms of meditation controls the random fluctuations of attention and at the same time renders attention impervious to environmental pressures and subjective bias. Even in passive meditation, as mentioned, the meditator learns to attend to incoming signals nonreactively for prolonged periods of time, which serves the same purpose of promoting voluntary attention and enhancing the pure volitional function.

NORMAL AND PARANORMAL PROCESSES

The conceptual distinctions between "consciousness," "mind" and "brain," and the notion that the mind is the interfacing instrumentality of consciousness and the brain activity warrants the assumption that there may be two distinct processes of awareness, the normal and the paranormal. In normal awareness, such as perceptual awareness, we postulate (1) a subject who has awareness, (2) the object of awareness, and (3) a process of awareness. The object is related to the subject through the instrumentality of sensory mediation and the processes in the brain. The resultant awareness is thus constructed to represent the world to us. In this situation the subject and the object are seen as divided and separate, but related by the mediation of the senses and the brain's functions. If our sensory mechanisms and cerebral processes were different from what they are, our perception of the world would be very different indeed. What we have in our perceptions of the world are the appearances of reality in the form of representations and not the reality itself. In that sense "things-in-themselves" remain forever "unknown."

Now, consider the possibility that a subject is in direct contact with and has unmediated access to the object. Awareness arising out of unmediated access would be an instance of what we referred to as paranormal awareness. Such awareness would indeed be different in kind from normal awareness. In normal perceptions, for example, the object is represented, and it is these representations and our reflections on them that give us the "knowledge" of the object perceived. Since all of us have similar sensory systems and cortical structures that process the energy patterns emanating from the object in similar ways, we have shared representations that give us a sense of objectivity about them. Also, we make assumptions about reality as it is represented to us and we test these assumptions by means of other representations and thus attempt to verify and validate our assumptions about the objects of representations and the nature of reality. Our knowledge of reality is thus indirect, mediated and in a sense inferential. On the other hand, the awareness we would have if we had unmediated access to the object would be direct and not represented via sensations, images and thoughts. Instead, such unmediated awareness would acquaint us directly with the object and we would have an awareness of the object in itself. This is what we termed as knowing-by-being.

Awareness via sensory representations is "knowing" by *description*; unmediated awareness is awareness by direct *acquaintance* or awareness by being. The former approximates to what we generally label as information. The latter may be thought of as *revelation* or *realization* as distinguished from *knowing* or *understanding*. Information is cognitively processed awareness whereas realization or revelation is awareness-as-such, an experience by being. In paranormal processes, then, there is no information flow; and in a significant sense it is contentless awareness, in the sense that it is devoid of any sensory content. When consciousness-as-such is described as having no content or form, it is likely that the reference is to sensory content and form. When the relation between the mind and the object of awareness is one of *identity* rather than of *representation,* the resultant awareness may be considered to be devoid of form and content.

In Eastern thought, such as in *Samkhya-Yoga*, it is assumed that there is a primordial existential state, the ground condition, an amorphous and undifferentiated state in which knowing and being are indistinguishable. They are seen as coalescing into a single state. With the development of the sensory and the cortical systems, knowing and being branch off and are differentiated. Awareness becomes a state of knowing instead of a state of being, and we tend to increasingly become dependent on cortically processed and sensory mediated awareness, and lose touch with awareness by being. Normal awareness is awareness of representations; paranormal awareness is awareness of reality-as-such. The latter involves reflexive identity between the subject and the object. The former involves the subject's reflection and the object's representation, and the subject-object relationship is *causal*.

If paranormal awareness is thus conceived to be awareness-as-such without sensory content, how is it different from a state where there is no awareness at all? Accustomed, as we are, to depend almost exclusively on mediated awareness, it is only natural to think that it is the only kind of awareness there is. Recall that our perceptions are only appearances, and their genuineness is tested by appeal to inter-subject consensus and other assumptions we make of reality. Awareness as such, on the other hand, does not require such cross-validation, because it is unmediated awareness of being, a relationship of identity and direct acquaintance as distinct from descriptive awareness by representation. Its validity is reflexive, apodictic and self-certifying unlike cognitive awareness. Awareness as such, by assumption, does not involve any sensory processes, has no representational content, and yet it influences, as mentioned earlier, our lives in important ways. We may consider the lives of true saints and those who had genuine near-death and "peak" experiences that were life transforming as examples of states of unmediated awareness or realization.

Considered in this manner, the normal and the paranormal may indeed be complementary processes. We may speculate further that the validation of our perceptual appearances as reality may itself be grounded in the paranormal. The basic principles underlying fundamental discoveries, the seeds of creativity and the inspiration for artistic excellence may have an intuitive genesis. Their validation via scientific formulation or evaluation by art criticism, however, is a consequence of rational reflection. In fact, we may conceive that the basic values that govern our conduct in general and seem to pervade across cultures and persist over the ages are likely given to us intuitively. We may also adhere to the notion

that there is nothing purely random in nature or in our behavior. It is not unlikely that all our behavior and indeed the entire course of nature is determined by normal or paranormal processes or a combination of both. It is possible that apparent random behavior, where we find no normal causation, may have a paranormal source. Take for example the case of evolution. There are no generally agreed upon probability formulae among mathematicians and biologists to satisfactorily explain how our biosphere has evolved the way it did by random mutation and selection. The inherent difficulties in the classical Darwinian position has led at least one eminent biologist, Sir Alister Hardy (1965), to suggest that a paranormal system may interact with a normal physical system in the evolutionary process and thus account for some of the gaps left by classical selection theory and some of the strange "jumps' in evolution. Again, the distinction between explicate and implicate organizations made by David Bohm (1973) is similar to the one we have made between normal and paranormal processes.

THE INTERMEDIARY PLACE OF PSI

So far, we have been concerned with the paranormal as contentless awareness, partaking in pure consciousness. Parapsychological phenomena, though regarded as paranormal because they do not seem to involve sensory-motor processes, manifest content. A parapsychological event, such as an ESP experience, is not a pure conscious state, because it has content. It is also not a sensory phenomenon, because the sensory processes do not mediate it. There is a good deal of evidence that such factors as time, space, and task complexity, which constrain sensory experience do not constrain ESP. ESP appears anomalous when viewed from the perspective of either of the two processes. Therefore, it is conceivable that ESP may be an instance where both normal and paranormal processes are in play, or that an altogether different process is at work.

In the Indian tradition, parapsychological events are expected to occur when one practices yoga. The practitioner of yoga is warned against indulging in them because they may become an impediment to the goal of attaining *kaivalya*, the pure conscious state free from sense-object contact. It is assumed that the mind consists of the subtlest form of matter. At that level of subtlety, matter has nonlocal characteristics and it has access to information that is remote in space and time. Its nonlocal functions are severely constrained by the fact that it is bound by the cortical structures that are local. When the mind moves away from the sensory processes and holds in abeyance the normal sensory and proprioceptive inputs, it is believed that it will be in a position to exercise its nonlocal functions, such as acquiring information from remote objects and events. Thus, in this view, when the mind successfully steers clear of sensory-motor activity and makes a direct contact with an information source, there is anomalous awareness. Anomalous awareness is necessarily implicit unless the light of consciousness illumines it. Therefore, many psi events do not involve subjective awareness. The kind of ESP evidenced in laboratory experiments is typically implicit. The common ground anomalous events such as ESP share with pure conscious states is the fact that sensory noise reduction facilitates their manifestation. As we have seen, yoga and meditation involve exercises that appear to enable the practitioner to gain voluntary control of internal states. There is also significant evidence suggesting that the reduction of sensory noise is conducive for the occurrence of psi. The common ground between anomalous awareness and ordinary sensory awareness is that the resultant awareness in both instances has content and

is in some sense representational. Then the question arises, how does anomalous awareness acquire the properties that are generally attributed to processing in the brain? There is reason therefore to postulate the involvement of the normal processes of the brain in the occurrence of ESP events.

Psi may be seen then as an interactive phenomenon, a combined product of normal and paranormal processes. The paranormal in this case being the mind's direct contact with the object of awareness. Though ESP has content, which means that it conveys information, unlike in normal process, in ESP there is no information flow from the target to the subject. The ESP subject does not receive information from the target in the manner one receives information from the stimulus object in perception. The information is generated from within. A reverse of the normal process appears to be in play here. In normal processes, the sensory inputs reach the mind after being processed in the brain. In the case of anomalous awareness, it would seem that the brain receives its inputs from the mind. It is a case of downward causation. The paranormal thus finds expression in normal cognitive processes.

ESP then needs to be explained at two levels—the level of nonlocal mind and the level of mediated knowing. The paranormal process establishes the source of psi in the subject's mind. Then at the level of knowing psi is cognitively processed so as to manifest in one of its familiar forms. L. E. Rhine's analysis of spontaneous cases revealed four basic forms of psi occurrence. They are (1) realistic dreams, (2) unrealistic dreams, (3) hallucinations, and (4) intuitions. In addition, laboratory studies have shown that ESP may manifest in a covert fashion as awareness does in subliminal perception; and sometimes psi information is revealed via physiological changes in the subject without any cognitive awareness (Figar 1959; Tart 1963; Dean & Nash 1967).

G.N.M. Tyrrell and L. E. Rhine, among others, recognized that psi functions at two levels. Tyrrell (1947) suggested that ESP phenomena first occur at the subliminal level and then they are obliged "to pass through the bottleneck at the threshold if they are to reach the normal consciousness" (p. 331). They pass over the threshold by making use of what Tyrrell called the "mediating vehicles," which according to him include dreams, sensory hallucinations, automatic writing, mental images, and strong emotions. Following Tyrrell, L. E. Rhine (1965) hypothesized that psi involves a two-stage process. First is the paranormal stage, about which we know so little. The second stage involves normal cognitive processing, similar to the psychodynamic processes by which unconscious material finds its way into subjective awareness. She points out that cases of incomplete and distorted psi information, including psi-missing in which the subject significantly misses the target (beyond chance expectation) while attempting to hit, are better understood in terms of the two-stage process.

In this context it is of interest to note the striking similarities between ESP and subliminal perception (SP), which we discussed in Chapter 4. Significant research exploring possible relationship between ESP and subliminal perception has been carried out (Rao & Rao 1982; Kreitler & Kreitler 1973). Norman Dixon (1979), Gertrude Schmeidler (1971) and Charles Honorton (1976), among others, identified several areas of contact between SP and ESP. Freud himself (1953) expressed the view that telepathy "comes about particularly easily at the moment at which an idea emerges from the unconscious or, in theoretical terms, as it passes over from the 'primary' process to the 'secondary' process" (p. 89). In a similar vein, Jan Ehrenwald (1977) suggested that ESP and subliminal perception might represent primordial brain functions.

DOUBLE ASPECTS OF CONSCIOUSNESS

By accepting, then, that there are normal and paranormal processes and that the latter are intrinsically incapable of being explained within a physical system, are we favoring radical dualist metaphysics of substantive independence of body and mind? It need not be so. That normal and paranormal processes appear to be two aspects of psi suggests that they may be complementary aspects of one and the same reality, without either of them being reduced to the other. Characterizing them as physical and nonphysical or material and immaterial is something that is better avoided at this point, because such a dichotomous characterization will create additional problems without helping to solve any. However, the reality of psi decisively stands against all materialistic doctrines, whether state-central materialism or neural identity theory, as they are formulated now. At this stage, a double aspect theory appears in a better light. Whether the underlying reality of which the normal and the paranormal are two fundamental aspects is material or nonmaterial is, as Douglas Stokes (1997) says, "a matter of semantics rather than substance" (p. 140).

The British philosopher C.D. Broad (1925/1951) proposed a theory of mind that incorporates the normal and the paranormal processes into a single system. According to his compound theory, the mind is not a single substance, but a compound of two factors—the psychic factor and the bodily factor. In other words, the mind is the composite of consciousness and the brain. He suggests that mental functions such as perception, reasoning and remembering are not the products of either of the factors alone. Just as a chemical compound possesses characteristics that do not belong individually to any of the constituent elements of the compound, the functions of the mind are not found solely in one or another of the constituent elements. In functional terms, the two factors in Broad's theory are the normal and paranormal processes of the mind. The shin theory proposed by Thouless and Weisner (discussed earlier), and leaving aside its dualistic overtone, may be interpreted as a dual process theory. Shin is the Hebrew word for mind. It simplifies matters considerably if the normal and paranormal aspects are regarded as two processes of the mind, instead of assuming that the shin is a nonphysical entity in virtue of which psi becomes possible.

A similar point has been made more forcibly in some of the classical Indian theories of the mind (see Channakesavan 1991). In the Samkhya-Yoga system, for example, reality is seen as governed by two fundamental principles—consciousness and matter. When there is a conjunction between consciousness and a material form, a mind is formed. The mind is a functional trap where nonconscious material forms become conscious experiences, and inert and characterless consciousness assumes form and manifests activity. When consciousness is thus trapped, we have subjective experience, which tends to bind consciousness more and more firmly to sensory processes. The mind functions via *vrittis*, the sensory modes. This is, however, not an irreversible process. By rendering the sensory and related systems quiescent through meditation and other techniques one can attain a state of *samadhi* in which the mind can experience consciousness as such, without the limitations imposed by the sensory system.

Even in Buddhism we find a similar approach. In Buddhism there is, of course, no substantive soul or mind. What we have is only consciousness, which is seen as a dynamic process. Consciousness is the stream of being, has subliminal and supraliminal existence, and is governed by paranormal as well as normal processes. The supraliminal is our normal cognitive stream. In the manifest stream, consciousness, in the words of

Buddhaghosa (1923), is "that which thinks of its object" (p. 148). It gives us discriminative information. The subliminal stream, the *bhavanga*, on the other hand, is a thoughtless or thought-free state. It is described as "the cause, reason, indispensable condition, the sine qua non of our existence, but without which one can not subsist or exist" (Aung 1929, pp. 265–266). The cognitive consciousness and *bhavanga* are thus the two aspects of the functional mind corresponding to the normal and paranormal distinction we made.

So, we see in Indian thought, whether one subscribes to dualism of the sort espoused by Smkhya-Yoga theorists or the monism of Advaita Vedanta, the mind is considered an interface between the normal and the paranormal, the phenomenal and transcendental aspects of being. Mind is the instrumentality of our experience; it is, to repeat, our reality connection. In its normal phase the mind with its associated cortical and sensory-motor systems connects us to the objective world, and we have cognitive awareness of it. In its paranormal phase, the mind participates in pure consciousness and becomes one with reality, giving rise to transcendental realization.

A meaningful distinction between mind and consciousness may be heuristic. It may even suggest new models to study consciousness and mind. The Samkhya-Yoga views on consciousness and mind are one such possibility. Let us recall that in the Yoga system a sharp distinction is made between consciousness and mind. The latter is in a sense physical and acts as an interfacing instrumentality between consciousness and physical reality. Physical reality, *prakriti*, though not conscious, contains the element of *sattva*, which is its essence. It is the *sattva* component of physical objects and events that enables us to know them, to have awareness of them. For this reason, we have considered the *sattva* of an object its information content. *Sattva* is not consciousness but the subtlest constituent of matter that is capable of reflecting consciousness. The *purusha* is undifferentiated and unmanifest consciousness, the ground condition of all information. It is a microcosmic quintessence of all knowledge. In other words, the *purusha* is the knowledge side of the universe inasmuch as the universe is reflected in it. The universe is its image. The mind is the knowledge instrument. It is, as we described, information sensitive. The sensitivity is a function of the mind's association with consciousness.

In gross physical objects, as mentioned before, *sattva* is mixed up with *rajas* and masked by *tamas*. Consequently, they fail to catch the glimpses of the *purursha* and remain essentially unconscious. The mind, however is predominantly *sattva*. Therefore, it is capable of reflecting the *purusha*. In addition, it has the ability to process sensorially the proximate objects by distilling as it were their information content, the *sattva* component. When the light of the *purusha* shines on this distilled information there is awareness of the object. The mind, unlike gross physical objects, is subtle, with very little *tamas* in it. It is thus translucent to let through the light of the *purusha*. When an association is thus established with consciousness, the mind manifests self-awareness and the ego-sense (*ahankara*) as well as the awareness of whatever information content there is in its focus. Without consciousness shining on the mind, the latter would have neither awareness of the objects nor of itself. The subjectivity in the experienced content of information is thus a joint function of mind and consciousness. The cognitive mind functions at three levels. First is the level of the *manas*, which processes the sensory inputs. At the level of *ahankara* the processed inputs are referred to the ego and become subjective and personalized. *Buddhi* transforms the processed self-appropriated inputs into mental forms that are displayed in the light of the *purusha* that shines on them.

The mind in association with consciousness is like a rainbow. The colors and the form of the rainbow are the phenomenal qualities experienced in the mind of a person. Consciousness is that which emits light. Rather it is "light." When the light passes through critically poised subtle matter (the substratum of the mind) the rainbow is formed. The characteristics and the colors displayed by the rainbow, the phenomenal qualities of experience, are different from the material substratum of the mind as well as from the consciousness that shines through the mind. Consciousness itself is without any characteristics of its own.

Subjectivity manifests in one's experience when the *purusha* is reflected in the ego function of the mind. Subjectivity consists, in the Indian view, in the identification of the *purusha* with the information content processed by the *manas*, appropriated by the *ahankara* and transformed by *buddhi* into *vrittis*. Subjectivity arises when *purusha* mistakenly regards the mental content *vritti* as its own.

The mind normally holds in focus the *sattva* of an object processed by its sensory-cortical adjuncts manifesting as sensory data (*vrittis*). When the latter are restrained, it can make direct contact with the *sattva* component of the object. When consciousness (*purusha*) is reflected on the former (*vrittis*) we have normal, sensory awareness. When there is direct contact between the mind and the *sattva* component of any material object or form (material reality) without the mediation of the senses, there arises anomalous awareness. Thus there are in principle two basic processes by which the mind obtains information, one by direct contact with the object or event and the other through the mediation of the sensory system. In either case, however, the mind is involved in accessing/realizing information. In case of paranormal awareness, the mind directly partakes in consciousness as such and experiences pure consciousness without any content. However, as in the case of anomalous awareness, it may be possible by later reflection to translate it into representational vocabulary. Such a translation is likely to be more imperfect and embellished than the recall of a dream experience on awakening.

The normal processes of awareness are those in which awareness is mediated by sensory processes, the nervous system and the brain. They admit of naturalistic explanations, within the framework of a physical system. However, without consciousness there will be no awareness of awareness, no subjectivity in experience. The paranormal processes, however, call for fundamentally different assumptions. In paranormal awareness there is no sensory mediation. The awareness is direct. The subject and the object have an identity relationship. The subject realizes the object in his/her own being, a process we called awareness by *being*, distinguished from awareness by *knowing*. Awareness by being involves accessing pure consciousness. It is contentless and nonrepresentational. Spontaneously on rare occasions and often by disciplined practice (if we may trust the yogic claims), a pure conscious event may manifest in a cognitively processed form. Parapsychological phenomena appear to take an intermediary place between pure conscious events and sensory experiences. They appear to involve both normal and paranormal processes.

If ESP and PK are real and can be investigated by employing scientific methods, psi research may have profound conceptual, methodological and theoretical implications for consciousness studies and vice versa. The fundamental distinction between awareness by *being* and awareness by *knowing* can play a crucial role in adding a new dimension to consciousness studies. Once there is such recognition of the dual play of the normal and the paranormal in our being, many of the anomalies cease to be the puzzles they

have been. An understanding of the interaction between the two would help to explain the subjective, "what it is like," experience and other aspects of consciousness that seem to defy physical explanations. As researchers learn more about the physical and psychological variables related to the occurrence of psi experiences, useful common ground between psi and other forms of awareness will be found.

Also, recognition of the reality of psi would take the wind out of the sail of central-state materialism and neural identity theories. Whether this necessarily leads us to favor radical dualism is, however, doubtful. A double aspect theory of mind, which does not commit to either materialism or spiritualism, could account for all types of awareness, including psi, without the additional problems that radical dualism entails. Thus, process dualism appears to be less problematic than entity dualism. Many classical Indian theories of mind consider the mind as matter in its subtlest form, with normal and paranormal attributes.

The Western objective approach to study consciousness from the perspective of brain states and functions has been very promising in unraveling many secrets of the mind that do not involve subjective awareness. For example, we know a great deal about the role of the different systems of the brain in processing information. Phenomena such as paradoxical awareness that lack subjective awareness appear to admit plausible physical explanations. The Eastern perspective we described here is not inconsistent with the known dependence of awareness on our cognitive and perceptual systems with their cortical connections. It is recognized that consciousness by itself cannot give rise to sensory awareness. Only when the mind opens its window to let consciousness shine on the processed information manifest in the mind do we have phenomenal awareness. Without the mind's ability to process the sensory inputs it receives, there can be no normal perceptual awareness. Similarly in the case of pathological awareness, insofar as the dysfunction is due to injury or insult to the brain, the Western approach is highly useful.

We may recall, however, that as far as we know subjective awareness does not appear to be mediated by a single brain system or several systems working together. We know that loss of awareness may occur when there is damage to different regions in the brain. For example, blindsight is a consequence of damage to the visual cortex and hemi neglect is caused by damage to the posterior parietal region of the brain. Again, in cases of functional blindness and hypnotic analgesia there is no known physical damage to the brain. Therefore, it is not unreasonable to assume that the loss of subjective awareness may arise when there is dissociation between consciousness and the information available to the mind. The dissociation may occur because of problems with the processing systems in the brain or because the window of the mind is not open for consciousness to reach the processed information. If conscious awareness is sensitivity to information, as we have pointed out, sensitivity is provided by consciousness, and information is supplied by the mind acting through the cognitive and perceptual systems of the brain. The conception of autonomous consciousness, as distinct from the mind, has the added advantage of providing possible explanations for extraordinary phenomena that appear anomalous when looked at from the Western perspective.

The ten problems of phenomenal consciousness mentioned by Michael Tye (1995) are less perplexing and troublesome from the Eastern view we sketched than from the Western perspective. By assuming that consciousness lies outside the postulates of physical reality, the hurdles that physical interpretations of consciousness entail are easily overcome. Consciousness in

this view is not caused by the physical states of the brain. Therefore, there is no need to look for a mechanism. Again, consciousness does not cause awareness; there is no interaction between consciousness and physical states, and hence no problem of the explanatory gap. Machines may have awareness, but they can not have conscious awareness unless they are credited with having minds. Minds are formed out of the subtlest forms of matter that enjoy nonlocal characteristics. We seem to know so little about this aspect of matter. Future revolutionary advances in physical sciences may well be in this area.

First-Person and Third-Person Perspectives

We have noted that the defining characteristic of primary awareness is subjectivity, which gives the phenomenal feel to awareness. Subjectivity involves exclusive accessibility to and ownership of a state of awareness by the experiencing person. For example, the experience of pain is uniquely personal to the one having it. Others may observe a person in pain. They may infer that she is experiencing pain from her behavior or physiological state, but they can not directly experience that pain. In this sense, felt pain is an exclusive experience of the one in pain and it is not directly accessible to outside observers. However, the pain behavior, the pain report or the concurrent brain states of the person in pain are accessible to everyone who cares to attend to them and has the competence to read into them. In other words, the experience of pain is what it is like for one to have the pain, which is different from observing a person in pain. The former, the *experience* of pain, has only first-person accessibility, whereas the latter, the *observation* of pain, has also third-person accessibility. Thus, awareness of pain has two contrasting aspects or perspectives. Between the two there is thus an epistemic asymmetry, in that the *experience* of pain is uniquely personal and subjective and the *observation* of pain is public and shareable.

From the Western perspective, which relies on third-person observations as criteria of objectivity and validity, there is the problem of "the explanatory gap" between first-person experience and third-person observation. Consequently, the thrust of the Western quest for understanding consciousness has been one of finding how changes in the brain (observable phenomena) cause subjective experiences. The search then is for the mechanism that generates the "what it is like" awareness that characterizes subjectivity in experience. As we have seen, there is, in the Western tradition, an obsessive concern with observation and objective verification. Truth is ascribed to that which is objectively verified. To observe is to be objective, to experience is to be subjective. In the Eastern tradition, it is different. The traditional Indian outlook, for example, is consumed by the concern with the individual and his transformation. In this view, true knowledge is not abstract and impersonal but is individually experienced and subjectively *realized* awareness. In the Eastern tradition, the focus is on the person. The goal of knowledge is not a mere understanding of truth but its realization in one's being. Consequently, the most appropriate starting point of inquiry is believed to be from the first-person perspective.

In the West, even when a first-person methodology is employed, such as introspection, the concern is to observe and not to experience. The attempt is to obtain an impersonal and objective account of what is going on within oneself. The introspecting individual is ideally one who reports a given state of mind in much the same way a machine records whatever it is monitoring. Critics of the use of introspection as a viable method, such as Auguste Compte, argue that it is an essentially impossible task for the experiencing person to be an observer of his/her own experience. "The thinking individual," wrote Compte, "cannot split himself in two, one part of which would think while the other would watch the former thinking. The organ observed and the organ observing being, in the case, identical, how could any such act of observation take place? This supposedly psychological method is therefore radically faulty in principle" (quoted from Vermesch, 1999, p. 19).

It is of course obvious that, endowed as we are with linguistic skills, we can report what we think is going on in our minds. What is not so obvious, however, is whether such reports are the same as experience per se. Few would consider the descriptions of experiences incorporated into those reports to be entirely observer independent. Vermersch (1999) observed: "The influence of observation on what is observed is a major epistemological problem, but it is a problem which extends throughout the sciences. For it is obvious that the idea of an observer who had somehow succeeded in situating himself outside the system he is engaged in studying is an epistemological fiction" (p. 19). The attempts to refine introspection are essentially measures to minimize and overcome, when possible, subjectivity and variability, and render the introspective accounts more objective and reliable across subjects. The exercise is thus one of converting subjective experience into objective observation.

Can experience per se be observed? In other words, is it possible to reduce first-person experiences to third-person observations? It is questionable. In fact, such reduction appears nearly impossible. The alternative is to render a faithful translation of first-person accounts into observable events. Even here it is not easy to find the necessary third-person vocabulary for first-person experiences. Perhaps some cognitive aspects of experience may be transformed into the third-person vocabulary. Our thoughts may be shared, but similar thoughts may evoke variable experiences. The point we have attempted to stress is that there can be no pure thoughts independent of the thinking person. All thoughts are experiences in a significant sense. An abstract thought is as mythological an entity as the Jack of Spades, as William James would say. It is conceptually real, but existentially empty. Therefore, any attempt to make introspection a credible method of transforming first-person experiences into first-person observations is doomed at the outset. There can be first-person observations, but they are not the same as first-person experiences. A person may report that she is in pain. This is a first-person observation. Reporting pain and experiencing pain are, however, two qualitatively different things. A report of pain is different from pain itself in much the same sense as the firing of a subset of neurons (c-fibers) in the brain is different from an experience of pain.

Many of the methodological improvements to introspective techniques undertaken since the time of Brentano and James in the name of "systematic introspection" and "experimental introspection" by psychologists such as Binet in France, Külpe in Germany and Titchner in the United States are important. They have a place in psychological research. However, they are all aimed at making introspective reports intersubjectively reliable by transforming experience into observation. Even the so-called method of phenomenological reduction is one of making observations out of experience. In all these cases the basic difference between observation and experience is not adequately appreciated. It is assumed that attentive experience bereft of expectations, assumptions, biases, and prejudices is observation. It is questionable, however, whether a mere intellectual exercise could in principle enable one to effectively suspend the "natural attitude" so as to observe the phenomena in their pure state. Even if it were possible to arrive at such phenomenal data via reduction or by suitably refined methods of introspection, do such data capture the "what it is like" character of experience? In other words, can one ever transform an experience into an observation even at the level of the first-person?

The real source of the problem, it would appear, is the basic distinction made between 'subject' and 'object' in the Western tradition. Such a fundamental dichotomy between the two does not allow any adequate transformation of one into the other. In the area of consciousness studies, this has led to unsuccessful attempts to reduce consciousness to its contents by regarding intentionality as the defining characteristic of consciousness. The contents are mistaken for the container, and consciousness is confused with the data it contains. With the spotlight on phenomenal data, the possibility of pure consciousness is lost sight of. This is the major lacuna in the Western conception of consciousness.

In the Eastern tradition, no distinction between subject and object is made in any fundamental way. The manifest dichotomy between them at the empirical level is regarded as an unreal appearance. At the more profound level of being, accessible with disciplined effort, the subject-object distinction disappears. Knowing truth in a representational form gives way to a different mode of realizing truth intuitively. In this view, the former gives us only the appearance of reality whereas the latter involves experiencing reality as such in an unmediated mode. The endeavor here is to seek and participate in pure conscious experience and realize truth in one's being. Realization involves participation and entering into a relation of identity with consciousness-as-such. A green leaf is not a juxtaposition of two different things, green and leaf. The two, which can be conceptually distinguished, inhere in one and the same thing, the green leaf. Subject and object are integral to experience as green and leaf are to a green leaf.

Observation implies a relation between the observer and the observed. That relation is subject to distortion and variation because what observation gives is a representation, an image and not the thing itself. As Varela and Shear (1999) observe, "A phenomenon, in the original sense of the word, is an appearance and therefore something relational. It is what something is for something else; it is a *being for* by opposition to a being in itself independently of its appearance by another entity" (p. 3, original emphasis). Observation, therefore, needs intersubject validation for its reliability. It is different with experience. Experience is participation. It is knowing something directly. It does not involve subject-object separation. As William James pointed out, "we have every right to speak of it [experience] as subjective and objective both at once." The question of intersubject validity becomes moot and in a significant sense irrelevant. The problem of intersubject validation, a necessary adjunct of observational procedures, is thus sidestepped and bypassed in dealing with experience. However, the problem of validation itself is not resolved. How do we validate the authenticity of pure conscious experience?

It is asserted that a pure conscious experience is intrinsically authentic; it does not require external validation. In experiencing pure conscious states, there is *realization*, which is distinct from *understanding*. We have called attention to the basic difference between the two modes of knowing. Realization engenders instant conviction of certainty. Its validity is reflexive. What about other experiences that do not entail such conviction or give a false sense of conviction? Let us consider the case of one seeking to achieve a state of pure consciousness. It is believed that a state of pure consciousness can be attained by a disciplined practice of yoga. How does the practitioner know whether the variety of experiences she has, as she progresses in the path, which are different from her ordinary experiences, are indeed genuine steps that lead to pure conscious states? How does she know if she did not mistakenly consider a non-pure conscious experience as a pure conscious experience? How can she identify pseudo states so that she can pass beyond them? Therefore, some kind of validation beyond self-conviction is necessary in all cases of experience with the possible exception of genuine pure conscious experiences.

This problem is not unlike the one the introspective techniques in general face. The resolution of this problem in the Indian tradition is achieved by the second-person role of the teacher as a mediator. As we have noted in the Chapter on Buddhist Psychology, the *guru* (preceptor) is an important and indispensable part of any training program to reach higher states of consciousness. The *guru* should be the one who traveled the path before. He serves as the reference point and provides a second-person position. He is the "caravan leader" who guides his pupil mindful of checkpoints and signposts in transit. The *guru* thus plays an important role of guidance, helping the practitioner to improve and progress along the path he knows. Thus the *guru* occupies an intermediate position between first-person experience of the practitioner and the final self-certifying state of pure consciousness, playing an indispensable role of mediation and providing a second-person perspective.

It is interesting to note that a similar effort is underway in the West to accord legitimacy to introspection as a viable research tool in human science. A special issue of the *Journal of Consciousness Studies* edited by Francisco Varela and Jonathan Shear (1999) entitled "The View within: First-Person Approaches to the Study of Consciousness" is a case in point. Varela and Shear argue that it is futile to use first-person accounts in isolation. They commend the notion of the second-person position as a necessary link between first-person and third-person perspectives. They also call attention to a necessary distinction between content and process of a mental act, which is common to all first-person methods. "Not keeping this fundamental distinction in view is a source of much confusion" (Varela & Shear 1999, p. 8). Pierre Vermersch (1999) makes a similar distinction between the content and the act by which an image is given. He also emphasizes the need to supplement first-person accounts with second-person points of view, the latter playing a mediating role. These developments echo the basic distinction made between consciousness and its content and the role accorded to the *guru* to supplement the first-person experiences. In this connection, we may point out why it is extremely helpful to have researchers in areas such as meditation, which is essentially a first-person exploration, who are themselves advanced practitioners of these disciplines. If they know the art themselves, they can provide the second-person position so essential to link first-person experiences with third-person accounts.

Goals and Objectives

There is a fundamental difference between the Eastern and Western concerns in consciousness studies. The Western concern is to have a rational understanding of what consciousness is. The Indian perspective, as we have seen, is not only theoretically rich, but also highly oriented toward practical aspects. Akhilananda (1950) wrote, "Indian psychology is not merely conceptual or theoretical. Its therapeutic value is in its teaching various methods of mental integration" (p. 20). In classical Indian psychology there are significant attempts to develop and standardize techniques for developing higher states of consciousness for tangible benefits

to practitioners. The development of yogic exercises and a variety of meditation practices along with impressive descriptions and exquisite phenomenology of higher states of awareness are important outcomes of the Eastern emphasis on the practical side of consciousness. It is indeed surprising and somewhat paradoxical that the Western tradition, so steeped in the development of science and its application to better the human condition in the realm of the physical world, is so overwhelmingly theoretical in the area of consciousness. Husserl (1965) himself felt that his own European intellectual tradition stood in sharp contrast with the Indian, Chinese and other Eastern traditions that foster a mythico-religious attitude and set practical goals. It would be instructive to compare Husserl's method with yoga practice, because such a comparison may illustrate the pathways that link in some fundamental way the Eastern and Western perspectives of consciousness.

HUSSERL AND YOGA

These are clearly some striking similarities between what has been said above about the Eastern perspective and Husserl's reductive phenomenology. As we have seen, Husserl's goal is to obtain "*appodictic* evidence" which entails absolute indubitability. Such knowledge can be obtained only when one, in the words of Husserl, is in a "*universe of absolute freedom and prejudice.*" We can agree that it is possible to place oneself in such a universe by practicing the procedure he described as epoché, which brackets the "natural attitude." We can also agree that such a practice enables one to understand intuitively the contents of consciousness experienced internally, and that the intuitive experience so generated is what gives us the essence of the object in our consciousness.

Several scholars have already called attention to the similarities between Husserl's method and yogic meditation. (For an interesting discussion of similarities between Husserl and yoga, see Paranjpe and Hanson, 1988; Puligandla, 1970; Sinari 1965). Clearly, the yogin is also in search of perfect knowledge that is self-validating and based on no suppositions. Whereas the phenomenological epoche remains essentially a theoretical speculation and at best a logical exercise, it is claimed for yogic techniques that they are capable of freeing one from all previously held attitudes and other hindrances and eventually leading to an intuitive, direct grasp of reality. Heidegger perhaps was attempting to do something similar in advocating that we go beyond "bracketing" to hidden meaning.

As we have seen, in addition to the three essential stages of *dharana* (concentration), *dhyana* (meditation), and *samadhi* (absorption), yoga has five preparatory steps that include moral observances (*yama* and *niyama*) and physical exercises (*asana* and *pranayama*), which enable the practitioner to control bodily disturbances, desires and emotions that distract the mind from the practice of one-pointed concentration. The fifth preparatory state is focusing internal attention (*pratyahara*). As Puligandla (1970) points out:

> The function of *pratyahara* is to detach the sense-organ from the mind, thus cutting it off from the external world and the sense-impressions it produces on the mind. The subject's mind is now completely isolated from the world and is therefore ready to practice concentration and meditation without any distraction, bodily or mental. This preparatory stage is the yogic counterpart of phenomenological epoché, the act of suspending the natural attitude. Freed from all kinds of hindrances, be they beliefs, desires, emotions, theories, feelings, the mind now is in a position to direct full attention to any object whatever and grasp it in its primordiality. But before the subject can arrive at the imaginary or primordial intuition, he has to pass through three stages of concentra-

tion, namely, *dharana, dhyana,* and *samadhi,* the last three *angas* of Patanjali's yoga.

The essence of yoga is *samayama. Samayama* involves the triple effort of *dharana* (concentration), *dhyana,* (meditation), and *samadhi* (absorption). The first three *sutras* in the third chapter of *Yoga Sutras* define them in the following way. Concentration involves focusing attention on an object, which progressively leads to the restraining of the natural wanderings of the mind. In the state of *dhyana* there is an uninterrupted flow of the mind toward the object of meditation so that the practitioner can focus the attention totally on a single object for a prolonged period of time. Such prolonged one-pointed attention to a single object leads to *samadhi,* a state of absorption. *Samadhi* is a state in which there is the awareness of the object alone, without an awareness of the self. With the suspension of self-awareness and complete absorption in the object of meditation, the practitioner achieves a state of being that enables one to grasp the essence of the objects of his focus. The yogin thus knows the things in their intrinsic state without the biasing influences of the cognitive and perceptual systems, the *vasanas* and *samskaras.* In addition, we are told that a variety of supernormal phenomena manifest when the triple effort of *samyama* (concentration, meditation and absorption) is directed at select things. These extraordinary experiences appear anomalous to those who have never experienced that state. The final point of a yogi's progress is, however, beyond this; it is complete liberation from all constraints so that she may realize pure consciousness.

"Husserlean yoga," the *epoché*, unlike Patanjali's yoga, falls short of reaching its logical end of realizing pure consciousness. Husserl criticized Descartes for not carrying his method of universal doubt to its conclusion. It would seem that Husserl himself did no better and became equally a victim of his own presuppositions. In assuming that consciousness is always intentional, he ruled out the possibility of experiencing pure consciousness. Husserl believed that phenomenological intuition gives us the *essence* of things, a possibility ruled out by Kant. It is not clear, however, how such an intuition is possible on rational grounds without making some basic assumptions. It would seem that phenomenologists by treating Husserl's method as a logico-epistemological tool rather than a practical method tended to regard intuition as an intellectual abstraction, an outcome of reflection rather than being a genuine experience. By failing to appreciate the possibility that transcendental subjectivity goes beyond suspending the natural attitude, the Husserlean method stops in practice with the *pratyahara* stage, as it were.

Puligandla notes, "whereas phenomenology merely talks of bracketing, ideating, and performing reduction, Patanjali's yoga provides a stepwise procedure for actually accomplishing them" (p. 33). In fact, yoga does more, as it is believed to lead one to the realization of pure consciousness, a trans-cognitive state that alone is regarded as capable of giving absolutely certain, direct and self-validating knowledge. If pure consciousness exists, as the Indian theories postulate, it cannot be *experienced* through the normal sensory processes or their variants. It can only be *realized* in a very special way, as the yogins and seers testify.

CULTIVATING CONSCIOUSNESS

Yoga, then, is a way of cultivating consciousness to reach higher states of awareness and well being. As we have discussed previously, meditation seems to involve control of internal states, which involves appropriate deployment of attention. Attention helps first to restrain and control habitual sensory activity, and second to achieve spontaneity and freedom. Sensory activity

binds the mind to processes that leave little room for spontaneity and freedom of choice. Unless the mind achieves a state in which it can voluntarily dissociate itself from normal sensory processing, it cannot activate the paranormal processes involved in higher states of awareness. In other words, in higher states of consciousness, attention shifts away from normal to paranormal processes. When attention reaches the domain of consciousness-as-such, the "will" regains its intrinsic spontaneity. When this happens, the mind is no longer controlled by the processes in the brain, and it becomes impervious to sensuous impulses and stimuli. At the same time, the mind begins to exercise control over the cortical processes and to influence the world of objects.

Meditation, as mentioned earlier, fits very well with this model for cultivating consciousness. Yoga is designed essentially to cultivate consciousness by controlling the natural wanderings of the mind. Patanjali defines the objective of yoga practice as the cessation of *citta vrittis*, mental fluctuations. According to the Sankhya-Yoga school, as we have noted, the mind is material and is constantly under the pressure of internal and external influences. These influences need to be controlled so that access to consciousness-as-such can be gained. The object of all the physical exercises and other preliminaries before practicing meditation is to control somatic and psychological distractions so that one can concentrate. Concentration, or *dharana*, along with *dhyana* and *samadhi*, produces a state in which the natural wanderings of our thoughts, the fluctuations of the mind, are brought under control. As the practice of concentration and the expansion of attention are continued for prolonged periods, one is led to a stand-still state where the mind's wanderings come under volitional control. When this happens, one has direct access to consciousness-as-such. Such an access enables one to experience events and to cause affects that appear anomalous from the perspective of the sensory-motor processes.

Focusing attention narrowly on an object for a prolonged period may have the effect of regulating sensory input by appropriate attentional shifts and dissociating the mind from competing (distracting) sensory impulses. Such dissociation and withdrawal of the senses and shutting-off of attention to some impulses, while focusing it on others, seems to be an essential aspect of meditation practice.

The similarities between meditation and hypnotic states have led some to think that yoga involves some sort of autohypnosis (Zorab, 1963). Indeed, the similarities seem to stem basically from their dissociative nature. Meditative practices as well as hypnotic induction procedures involve attentional shifts, selective attention and inattention, the disruption of memories, and the critical feedback that characterize dissociative experience. One-pointed concentration and the effort to meditate may indeed stimulate imagination and cause disorientation, loss of experience of the body, and detachment in the same manner as hypnotic induction does. Reports of yoga practitioners do suggest that yogic concentration in its early phases generates hallucinatory imagery similar to that obtained under hypnosis. Obviously, yogic meditation is more than a hypnotic state. It does not stop with achieving dissociation from the competing sensory impulses, but goes on to a standstill state in which the mind, severed from its sensory connection, apparently enjoys spontaneity and volitional freedom. The goal of meditation is not one of achieving a dissociative state as such, but of gaining and exercising volitional freedom to reach out to any object, event or process in the universe to have *direct* and *unmediated* knowledge of it. The path the meditator travels is one where shifts of attention take place in a controlled manner, to the point where there is

simply attention with no object to attend to, a state of consciousness-as-such, a microcosmic state of omniscience. It is a state of knowing by being. Emptying the mind, as it were, appears to be an essential aspect of gaining volitional spontaneity and freedom in the meditative state. Such an emptying, it seems to me, is possible only when one's attention is withdrawn from sensory impulses and stimuli, and much of the cognitive backdrop, the host of memories and habitual dispositions, are held in abeyance. I do not believe we are wrong in assuming that the practice of meditation prepares one for a state of dissociation from sense-mediated experience so that one may focus on experiencing awareness in a direct way. What is important is the facility with which the meditator refocuses her attention. Such a facility seems to be clearly enhanced in a state where the usual cognitive controls are in abeyance or become inoperative. Such a state seems to be a necessary condition for enhancing volitional spontaneity and freedom and for gaining access to consciousness-as-such.

In this context we may refer to a study by Arthur Deikman (1963), which shows how intentional deployment of attention may lead to enhanced awareness. Deikman called it *deautomatization*. Deautomatization, according to Deikman (1966), is an essential aspect of meditation. In an interesting study, he instructed his subjects to focus their attention on a blue vase to the exclusion of all other thoughts. After a series of these intense concentration sessions, his subjects reported seeing things about the vase that they never did before. One subject felt that she had "merged" with the vase. Deikman felt that deautomatization as achieved through selective deployment of attention may permit a new and perhaps more advanced experience.

It will be of interest to note that several other techniques of cultivating consciousness seem to involve a state of dissociation from sensory processes. James Hall (1991), one of the foremost Jungian analysts in the United States, has called our attention to the Jungian insight into "the dissociability of the psyche" and how in hypnotherapy it can be made use of "in an intentional and controlled way" to treat psychopathology.

Jung also spoke of "active imagination," which allows images to develop by themselves. It seems to me that such an autonomous function of images is clearly consistent with the concept of volitional spontaneity achieved in the play of consciousness-as-such. Again, active imagination is a manifestation of the dissociability of the psyche and the temporary abeyance of the usual cognitive controls. It has been shown that free imagery is an effective means of circumventing a variety of controls that restrain behavior.

Several therapeutic techniques such as psychosynthesis and autogenic training involve guided imagination, which is another way of preparing for the loosening of controls to achieve a state of dissociation from routine sensory processes. Recall Ernest Hilgard's observation that dissociation involves essentially the suppression or alteration of the usual controls of conscious activities. "The modification of controls can be described as dissociation if the usual controls are inoperative, and are replaced by new ones" (Hilgard, 1977/1986, p. 228). Again, the so-called enactment techniques, such as painting, dancing, group rituals, shamanistic trips, and the visualization procedures to enhance the immune system to fight or prevent diseases, as Hall points out, utilize the dissociability of the psyche.

I hardly need to mention that dreaming, especially lucid dreaming, and out-of-body experiences, being natural dissociative states, could be utilized for cultivating consciousness. Similarly, automatic writing, mediumship and channeling all involve some form of dissociation from the sensory controls that normally constrain our conscious functioning.

Dissociation of the mind from normal sensory inputs and processes is possibly the most significant and pervasive method to achieve access to consciousness-as-such. Though yogic practice may manifest dissociation-like states, its goal is some kind of higher-order integration where the mind becomes progressively free from cerebral chores to function on its own and to reflect consciousness faithfully so as to give one perfect knowledge in a state of realization.

EMBODIED LIBERATION (*JIVAN-MUKTI*)

Freedom of being is the goal one must strive for. This is the message the Indian tradition widely disseminates. In the human situation, the mind-body complex conditions our being and behavior. Our values are tainted by the circumstances we live in. Our thoughts are influenced by our biases and prejudices, acquired and inherited. Perceptions are determined by one's perceptual system and are influenced by a number of variables, internal and external. Consequently, the conditioned person has neither perfect knowledge of the world nor of himself. The goal of freedom or liberation is to overcome this existential predicament and impasse and restore the being to its natural unconditioned state, which is described as an integral state of truth (*satyam*), goodness (*sivam*) and beauty (*sundaram*).

Being in the world necessarily involves embodied existence. The inherited mind-body complex through which being manifests is an instrument of knowledge and action. The mind is so situated as to essentially limit what one can know and do, and knowledge itself is processed by the perceptual and cognitive systems it is endowed with. If these were different, as is the case with some other species, the knowledge of the world we have would be different. Our knowledge then is relative and species specific. It is constrained in a number of other ways. Ignoring these fundamental features of our existence, we tend to attribute certainty and finality to our knowledge of the world and of ourselves revealed by the limited-capacity sensory processes. Thereby we see perfection, beauty, and happiness and act to further reinforce these thoughts and impressions in our being. In this view, being in the world is thus tainted by ignorance (*avidya*). We live in bondage, our existence is confined to the imprisoned condition of limited by being biased awareness. The essential feature of being is, however, freedom from all constraints, a state of unconditioned existence, of perfect knowledge and of unmitigated bliss. The human endeavor should therefore be one of achieving the state of such unconditioned being. That state itself is variously termed, for example, as *kaivalya* in Samkhya and Yoga, and as *nirvana* in Buddhism. Its essential feature is, however, freedom. It is liberation of the conditioned person to experience an unconditioned state of being.

Now, the question is whether such a state can be achieved by embodied beings such as us. Inasmuch as our being is intertwined with the mind-body complex, which is the root cause of our existential predicament and bondage, how can we achieve the unconditioned state while being thus caged? In the Indian tradition, the belief in reincarnation is pervasive. The goal of liberation is seen as an escape from the cycle of birth and death. In the final analysis, then, it would seem that a disembodied state of being is a precondition for complete liberation. The individual who achieves a state of liberation is no longer caught up in the vortex of *karma* currents and the cycle of birth and death. Therefore, some Indian thinkers have argued that liberation is a post-mortem phenomenon that could occur only upon death. For this reason Indian thought is often spoken of as otherworldly.

While few have questioned the ulti-

mate freedom of unconditioned being in the disembodied state, several Indian thinkers, including *Samkara*, have argued persuasively that liberation is indeed possible in the embodied state of being in the world. Liberation, it is pointed out, has meaning only when it is experienced. Without such experiential certainty, liberation is vacuous and would be devoid of any conviction, because after-life experience of liberation is at best conjectural. In this view, freedom of being is possible not only in the disembodied state (*videha-mukti*), but it is also achievable being in the world (*jivan-mukti*).

The notion of embodied liberation (*jivan-mukti*), the belief that it is possible to enjoy freedom while being in the world, is found in the *Upanishads* and the *Bhagavad-Gita*. Badarayana discusses it in his *Vedanta-Sutras*. The Samkhya and Yoga systems clearly recognize the possibility of embodied liberation. Vyasa in his commentary on *Yoga-Sutras* states explicitly "the wise man becomes liberated even while he is alive" (IV, 30). Buddhism and Advaita enthusiastically endorse the notion of *jivan-mukti*. Samkara develops the doctrine of *jivan-mukti* in its essential details. M. Hiriyanna, an eminent historian of Indian philosophy, considers the notion of *jivan-mukti* a landmark in the history of Indian thought (see S.K.R. Rao 1979). *Yoga-Vasista*, a mystical work written probably after Samkara, is an interesting blend of Advaita and Vijnanavada Buddhism. Vidyaranya of the 13th century wrote a treatise entitled *Jivan-Mukti-Veveka*. In this book, Vidyaranya refers to the authorities that espoused the *jivan-mukti* concept. He discusses the nature and the distribution of instinctive propensities (*vasnas*) and the control/negation of the mental functions (*vrittis*). He goes on to describes the ultimate goal of *jivan-mukti* and the characteristics of those who achieved that state (*jivan-muktas*). In this work, Vidyaranya draws from the views of Samkara as well as from those contained in *Yoga-Vasista* (Atreya 1954), attempting to reconcile them.

The route to transforming the conditioned person to the unconditioned state is the one of removing the cause of conditioning, which is none other than *karma*. The source of *karma* is ignorance (*avidya*). It is ignorance of the fundamental nature of being and the misleading conviction that the information processed by the mind via its sensory channels is true knowledge of the things themselves. Out of this conviction arise worldly desires, attachment, ego involvement, and pain and pleasure, which in turn lead to actions that have self-reference. These actions leave potent residues in the mind in the form of *karma*. *Karma* is the dormant source, the seed that sprouts in a series of subsequent actions and reactions. *Karma* is the deterministic source of the cause-effect continuum in human conduct, thought and action. In the Indian view, which asserts the continuity of life after death, *karma*, which does not sprout in a given lifetime, will be carried over to the next birth. In fact, it is believed that the mind-body complex with which one is born is determined by *karma* accumulated in previous lives. Such *karma* is called *prarabdha karma*. It is *karma* that has already begun to work itself out. It is likened to the potter's wheel, which, set in motion, will run its course before coming to a stop, and the arrow that left the bow, which will not stop until its momentum is exhausted. Two other kinds of *karma* are distinguished. *Sancita karma* is the residual *karma* from previous births, which is believed to determine one's tendencies to act and react in the present. *Agami Karma* is *karma* engendered by present conduct, which would effect future actions. It includes current tendencies to act and react in specific ways as well.

One may believe or not in reincarnation and the possibility of *karma* spilling over from one birth to another. We could,

however, hardly disagree that our beliefs and attitudes influence our actions and reactions, and that actions have their imprint on the mind, which in turn influences later actions. Again, our beliefs and motivations may be entirely unconscious. These are necessary postulates of psychological determinism. *Karma* in a secular sense is the underlying principle of determinism. Such determinism, in the Indian view, is neither fundamental nor absolute. The vortex of conditioned existence, caught in the cross currents of *karma*, can be overcome by disciplined practices to gain true knowledge, the realization of which dispels ignorance and releases the individual from the conditioned habits of action and reaction. In other words, the realization of truth in one's being that dispels ignorance born out of incomplete and biased knowledge revealed through and acted upon by the mind-body complex incapacitates and neutralizes the accumulated *karma* and eliminates the possibility of acquiring further *karma*. True knowledge dispels ignorance. When the cloud of ignorance disappears, the *karma* that influences our actions becomes visible. One is then in a position to burn it and be free from its influence. True knowledge, as we have seen, is partaking in consciousness-as-such. Thus, the state of *jivan-mukti* is a state of pure consciousness untainted by the fluctuations of the mind. In a state of pure consciousness one becomes an unconditioned person. Controlling and overcoming the *citta vrittis* (fluctuations of the mind) is a necessary condition for achieving a state of pure consciousness. Yoga is regarded as a time-tested means of achieving such control. Having reached a state of pure consciousness, one's endeavor is to stay in that state, which is described in Yoga and Advaita as *brahmakara-vritti*.

Vidyaranya asserts that *jivan-mukti* is the direct result of the cessation of instinctive propensities (*vasanas*), achieved by the negation of mental transformations (*mano-*

nasa) and consequent realization of a pure conscious state and true knowledge (*tattva jnana*). Yoga considers the *jivan-mukti* state as one in which all the roots of ignorance and *karma* are severed. The roots include normal cognitive activity as well as unconscious impressions and propensities (*vasanas*). *Jivan-mukta*, the realized person, the one who is a free being in the world, is not completely devoid of ordinary cognitive states. Rather, these states, with their roots in the mind severed, are passing shadows that produce no *karmic* impressions. They are like the snake whose poisonous fangs are pulled out. It might bite, but it could cause no harm.

Ignorance (*avidya*) in the Indian view is not merely absence of knowledge. More importantly, it implies the presence of wrong knowledge. It is believed that the knowledge born out of sense-mediated awareness is wrong knowledge. It is biased and incomplete. It binds the individual to a course of action that is detrimental to the goal of discovering one's essential being in pure consciousness. It sets the individual against others. Ignoring the underlying unity, ignorance promotes artificial distinctions such as "you" and "me," subject and object. In the process arise attachment and aversion, anxiety and distress, ego-involvement and greed, feelings of pleasure and pain and so on. With the dawn of wisdom engendered by pure conscious experience, however, the individual is transformed. The transformation not only results in the absence of negative feelings and emotions, aversions and attachments, but it also produces an integral state of oneness of being, a profound experience of truth, goodness and beauty. It is described as a state of peace and equanimity, freedom and spontaneity. The *Bhaggavad Gita* characterizes it as a state of steady enlightenment (*sthita-prajna*). Krishna describes it to Arjuna in considerable detail. So does Vasista to his pupil, Rama. Vidyaranya in his *Jivan-Mukti*

Viveka characterizes the *jivan-mukta* as one who protects his enlightened wisdom (*janaraksa*), experiences no discard (*visamvadabhava*) and stresses (*dukha*) and fills his life with joy (*sukha*).

In the second chapter of the *Bhagavad Gita* we find Krishna's description of the characteristics of the person who achieves a state of *sthita-prajna,* a state of steady realization and enlightenment. The *sthita-prajna* abandons the desires of the heart and finds satisfaction and happiness in realizing consciousness-as-such (II.55). His mind is not troubled by anxiety under afflictions; he is indifferent to pleasures and is free from passion, fear or anger (II.56). The one who has steady realization is completely unattached. He is neither excited with joy when encountering good things nor depressed with despair when bad things happen (II.57). The enlightened one withdraws his senses from the objects of perception like a tortoise pulls its limbs into its shell (II.58). The senses when excited seize the mind of even those who are wise. Therefore, restraining of the senses is of paramount importance. The *Bhagavadgita* states: "Paying attention to the objects of sense causes attachment to them. From attachment arises desire. Desire gives to anger. Anger leads to delusion. Delusion results in confused memory. Lack of correct memory destroys the discriminating ability. With the loss of discrimination (between right and wrong) one perishes" (II.62–63).

The ultimate freedom emphasized in the Eastern tradition, complete liberation in a disembodied state (*videha-mukti*), may be utopian ideal. The state of *jivan-mukti*, however, may be seen as an attainable goal even from a secular perspective. The *jivan-mukti* concept is developed from the self-certifying experiences recorded extensively in the Indian subcontinent. Even in modern India, people like Ramakrishna Paramahamsa and Ramana Maharishi are reported to have achieved a state of steady realization.

In fact it stands to reason to consider saints in the Catholic tradition and the Western mystics throughout the ages as possibly *jivan-muktas*. While *jivan-mukti* is an advanced state of a steady experience of pure consciousness, as the concept *sthita-prajna* implies, it is likely that sporadic manifestations of pure conscious experience may be more frequent and widespread than acknowledged. The so-called self-actualized persons Maslow speaks of may be the ones who experience pure consciousness. Inasmuch as pure conscious states have transformational consequences as mentioned earlier, achieving such states may have important ramifications for improving the human condition. Therefore, the next stage of evolution, the development of supermind, as Aurobindo among others has suggested, may indeed involve the mind's ability to partake in pure consciousness with greater ease and frequency than is apparent now. Even in the contemporary context of rare access to this domain, a greater understanding of the process and the practices believed to lead to pure conscious states may give rise not only to new therapeutic techniques but also to useful innovative strategies to promote creativity in people, and peace and harmony in the community and among nations.

Having thus emphasized the complementary aspects of the Eastern approach, we may not ignore some of its limitations. First and foremost, the Eastern approach is clearly focused on the "other-worldly" concerns rather than on being in the world. One may grant that there is life beyond death, that the empirical world is only an appearance of reality, and that what is ultimately true is realized in a state of pure consciousness. Yet we may not ignore the fact that in the human condition we are strongly tied to the world as experienced. Our knowledge in the present condition is representational and for the most part it seems to work pretty well. Therefore, being in the

world demands that we pay attention to the world around us, make the best of the knowledge resources available to us, and get to the truth as close as we can with the means that are readily available. In this endeavor, the Western approach with its focus on the external and its emphasis on physical aspects is clearly warranted. However, an open mind to the possibilities that may lie outside the physical paradigm is not unwarranted either. A healthy *sangamam* (confluence) of the two streams (Western and Eastern) may enable us to irrigate other areas of our being that we are currently unable to harvest. It may pave the way to a more enriched life now and prepare us for a better life after, if there is one.

Concluding Summary

Consciousness refers to awareness. Awareness is either explicit or implicit. Explicit awareness is experience. It is awareness of awareness. Experience has two components, information and sensitivity to that information. Sensitivity is the "what it is like" feel for accessible information. Information consists of phenomenal data, which include sensory and proprioceptive inputs as well as the contents of thoughts and beliefs. Sensitivity is the "feel" for the data. It consists of cognitive, affective and conative components, which mix in various proportions. They can be conceptually distinguished but not existentially isolated in experience. Thus there can be no "pure" thoughts or perceptions in experience without some element of emotion and volition. In the human condition, having information and being sensitive to it can be dissociated. Such dissociation may result in implicit awareness when one has information with no awareness of it. Or it may lead to a state of pure consciousness with no sensory content.

How we acquire information and

process it in the brain are accessible to third-person observation. However, the sensitivity aspect of experience, the subjective in consciousness, is accessible only from the first-person perspective. It has so far eluded all attempts to capture its essence from the perspective of the third-person. The epistemic asymmetry between the sensitivity and information aspects of consciousness leads to the problem of the explanatory gap. This problem in turn has the effect of either eliminating human subjectivity all together as a legitimate topic for inquiry altogether, or asserting that subjectivity is essentially beyond the reach of scientific scrutiny and understanding.

In the Western scholarly tradition, "consciousness" and "mind" are not adequately distinguished. For the most part, they are treated as synonymous and used interchangeably. If they are ever distinguished, consciousness is considered an adventitious quality of awareness or a species of awareness. In the former sense, consciousness becomes an epiphenomenon, not central to our understanding of mental phenomena. As a species of awareness, conscious awareness may be thought of as something reducible to brain states and functions. Alternatively, it may be assumed to be basic and fundamental in nature. Reductive exercises have met with little success, unable to capture the essence of subjectivity in any reductive analysis. If conscious awareness is indeed fundamental and irreducible, then it cannot be considered a species or a subcategory of awareness. The facts that sensitivity and information are dissociable, and the possibility that experiential sensitivity is a fundamental and irreducible phenomenon, suggest that consciousness in its subjective aspect, though associated with awareness, is not intrinsic to it. Consequently, it may well fall outside the conceptual space of the mind.

From the Western perspective, intentionality is the defining characteristic of consciousness/mind. A necessary corollary is the belief in a representational theory of knowledge, which entails a fundamental distinction between the knowing subject and the object known. Also, the possibility of pure conscious states that do not contain any phenomenal representations is ruled out a priori. The exercise of studying consciousness then becomes one of understanding the contents of consciousness and the processes that give rise to them. This strategy has worked well in some respects. Some very productive and promising programs of research have been undertaken. We now know a great deal about the brain states associated with various forms of awareness. Many mysteries surrounding mental states have either been unraveled or are on their way to be resolved. We appear to be on the right track. Nevertheless, this approach inspires little confidence in the possibility of finding a reasonable understanding of subjectivity in experience. There is also the negative implication of rejecting the possibility of pure conscious states on theoretical rather than on empirical grounds. Furthermore, several kinds of extraordinary experiences for which there is credible evidence have fallen outside the explanatory scope of the Western theories of the mind.

There is thus a felt need to revise and supplement the assumptive base of consciousness studies in the West. In this context, the classical ideas of some of the Eastern systems of thought may be useful. They may offer provocative alternatives or useful supplementary lines of thought. Relevant ideas gathered from a review of Samkhya-Yoga, Advaita Vedanta and Buddhist traditions provide a model, which may be broadly considered as the Eastern perspective, that has heuristic implications for a more comprehensive understanding of consciousness than is currently available.

The Eastern model, unlike its Western counterpart, makes a fundamental distinction between "consciousness" and "mind,," and a secondary distinction between "mind" and "brain." Reality is a composite of being and knowing. Consciousness is the knowledge side of the universe. It is the ground condition for all awareness. Consciousness is not a part or aspect of the mind, which, unlike consciousness, is physical. Consciousness does not interact with the mind or any other objects or processes of the physical universe. Nor does it have any causative role in our mental activity. Therefore, there is no problem of interaction between two fundamentally different entities and no violation of physical laws.

Mind in this view is the interfacing instrumentality that faces consciousness on one side and the brain and the physical world on the other side. The mind thus gives the impression of having two faces — the physical side in its relation to the brain and other physical systems, and the subjective side facing consciousness. From the physical side, the mind collects information by processing the inputs it receives. When this information is exposed to consciousness at the other end, when the light of consciousness is reflected on it, there is subjective awareness and conscious experience of the phenomenal data.

Though physical like the brain, the mind is different from it. The mind is closely connected to the different systems of the brain. It influences and is influenced by events in the brain. The mind comprises of subtler forms of matter than the brain. Consequently, it has different characteristics such as nonlocality. Its subtle character makes it possible to receive the light of consciousness to reflect its contents. In virtue of its implicit nonlocal nature, it is possible for the mind to act on systems beyond the body complex with which it is associated. Such a conception of mind leaves open the possibility that the mind may survive the destruction and cessation of the associated body.

Mind thus enjoys dual citizenship in the physical world as well as in the realm of consciousness. As a material form, the mind's citizenship in the material world is by birth as it were. Its naturalization in the domain of consciousness is a matter of choice and an outcome of significant effort. Its citizenship in the material realm bestows on it the right to process information through its sensory channels and neural connections. The mind also has involuntary and passive access to consciousness, in that the light of consciousness shines on it to illumine its critically poised contents, which become subjectively revealed. The mind also has within its reach the possibility of partaking in consciousness-as-such by disciplined practice so that it may have direct and unmediated knowledge. This possibility is generally remote because of mind's habitual involvement with the cortical processes.

In its dual roles, two distinct processes, the normal and the paranormal, aid the mind. The sensory-motor processes are those that come under the category of the normal. The paranormal process involves accessing consciousness-as-such and achieving pure conscious states. There is, however, an intermediary process, which may be called the anomalous process. When the mind moves itself away from the normal mode of processing information from the sensory and proprioceptive inputs it receives, it will be in a position to make direct contact with objects and events outside. Because of its nonlocal characteristic, the mind has the capacity to reach out to objects and events that may be remote in space and time. When the mind successfully exercises this capacity, it has anomalous awareness, which is very different from awareness in pure conscious states, such as those of the mystics. The common ground covered by the paranormal and anomalous processes is that withdrawing attention from normal sensory processes facilitates both. An anomalous event like an ESP experience or a PK influence is not a pure conscious state. Nor is it a sensory experience. Therefore, it may be appropriately called anomalous.

From the Western perspective, the main concern is with the normal processes of the mind. Therefore, the spotlight is on the brain and the sensory processes that give us information. Observational techniques from the third-person perspective are appropriately employed to study mental phenomena. Consciousness-as-such, which is not accessible to third-person observation, is ignored. The consequence is a physical paradigm of the mind functioning in a mechanical universe. Functions of the mind, it is assumed, are best understood by identifying the correlated brain states. Significant shortcomings of this approach include: (a) subjective aspects of mental phenomena are not accounted for; (b) paranormal phenomena and extraordinary experiences are either ignored or rejected; (c) higher states of consciousness are lost sight of and in a sense have fallen outside the scope of consciousness studies; and (d) the interest in studying consciousness is confined to the theoretical side, with little appreciation of its practical implications.

In contrast, the East is obsessed with the esoteric, the paranormal and the life beyond. The focus is on consciousness-as-such. Experiential techniques and first-person accounts have proliferated. The goal is practical. The quest is for the transformation of the individual and for achieving higher states of consciousness. As a consequence, there is in the East a rich harvest of profound phenomenological accounts, useful classification of a variety of conscious states and the development of valuable techniques for enhancing human potential and well being. Again, these developments have been lopsided. To a significant extent, normal processes are ignored and sometimes rejected as obstacles in the quest for pure conscious states. In its search for certainty and perfection, the Eastern perspective has failed

to come to terms with what is very pervasive and basic to human nature, i.e., the normal processes. It may well be that there are entities some where in this vast universe who are so evolved as to be able to access pure consciousness with the same ease as we process our sensory inputs. Also, it may not be unreasonable to assume that further evolution may enable Homo sapiens to acquire easier access to consciousness-as-such. However, to ignore the normal processes, considering the way humans are situated, may not be considered a normal act. Whatever may be the benefits of partaking in pure consciousness for those who may be able to achieve those states, the vast majority of us during most of our lives are consumed with involvement in sensory processes. This is a fact too obvious to ignore. Therefore, while the effort to understand higher states of awareness is commendable, the negation of normal processes to achieve the higher states is a significant negative.

The Eastern and Western streams are thus flowing in two different directions. However, the two together appear to contain most aspects of consciousness. Therefore, if there is a confluence of the two, we may be better positioned to understand consciousness in its multiple facets. William James and Frederic Myers in their own way attempted something of this sort.

On the contemporary scene, transpersonal psychologists have been pursuing this line of investigation with some vigor. Unfortunately, however, they appear to be content with drawing conceptual maps. Lacking the necessary methodological tools, they have made little progress in covering the empirical ground. One would think that parapsychologists with their feet on the ground with solid empirical data and armed with rigorous research tools might be the ones to take on the leadership role. Regrettably again, they are themselves caught in the vortex of crosscurrents. On the one hand, they are struggling unsuccessfully to shed the mindset of methodological behaviorism, a legacy of the Rhinean research paradigm. On the other hand, they are taunted with guilt by association. Parapsychology is often confused in the public mind with a host of things that the researchers in this area justifiably consider to be outside their field. There is good reason to be concerned when parapsychology is discussed along with tarot-card and tea-leaf reading, palmistry, past life regression therapies, astrology, and unidentified flying objects. Again, the widespread chicanery of the past in the dimly lit séance rooms of the entranced mediums, the mysterious ectoplasm, furniture flying, musical instruments playing by themselves, dead relatives talking and a host of similar questionable phenomena, mistakenly confused with scientific investigations in parapsychology, have made researchers in this area too defensive to pursue the implications of their research results to their logical conclusion. In any case, parapsychologists as a group have become an isolated bunch unable to connect with researchers in other related areas so that they could make a difference.

There are, however, some hopeful signs of East-West confluence in consciousness studies. There is among Western scholars studying consciousness an increasing recognition of the shallowness of their stream. There is now a greater appreciation of the significance of subjectivity and its irreducibility to brain states. There are academic psychologists like Max Velmans, though still too few to be heard, who are willing to stick their neck out in search of new models. There are other mainstream scientists like Francisco Varela who are not afraid of borrowing from the Eastern tradition to develop more workable methods for studying consciousness. Finally, there is the case of meditation research, which combines Eastern concepts and techniques with Western research tools and methods that have made significant strides in bringing the two streams together. There is thus reason to hope for an East-West *Sangamam*.

This has been a long journey exploring the cross-cultural contours of consciousness studies. Traveling West, we gained glimpses of what consciousness is about, its processes and functions. We noted, however, that the basic question of what it is like to be conscious is left little understood and the reality and role of extraordinary experiences is little appreciated. There is in the West a certain equivocation regarding the concepts "consciousness" and "mind," resulting in the "clouding" of consciousness, as it were. Consciousness, when recognized, is seen to be no more than a qualifying adjunct of mental phenomena, which holds no intrinsic interest over and above the phenomena themselves. Going East, we noted an overarching concern for controlling sensory phenomena, which usually "crowd" consciousness, to gain access to states of consciousness-as-such.

In the human condition, the mind functions in two modes. In the normal mode, it gives us awareness of the world, and consciousness bestows subjectivity on it. In the paranormal mode, the mind transcends the normal sensory processes, accesses consciousness-as-such, and has extraordinary experiences. It knows by being. Self-realization is an integrated state of cognition and conduct, where there is no possibility of dissociation between knowing and being. Knowing gives one understanding, and being involves realization. Understanding truth is the Western goal. Realizing truth is the Eastern ideal. The two are complementary in that knowing in the final analysis involves both understanding and realization. We not only want to know the truth but we also endeavor to live by it.

Bibliography

Adelson, J. (1982). Still vital after all these years. *Psychology Today*, 16, 4–6.

Akhilananda, S. (1946). *Hindu psychology: Its meaning to West*. London: George Allen & Unwin.

_____. (1952). *Mental health and Hindu psychology*. London: George Allen & Unwin.

Akishige, Y. (ed.) (1968). Psychological studies on Zen. Kyushu psychological studies. *Bulletin of the Faculty of Literature of Kyushu University*, No. 5. Fukuoka, Japan.

Akolkar, V.V. (1992). Search for Sharada: Report of a case and its investigation. *Journal of the American Society for Psychical Research*, 86, 209–247.

Alexander, C.N., Chandler, H.M., Newman, E.J., Newman, R., and Davies, J.L. (1989). Transcendental meditation, mindfulness, and longevity; An experimental study with the elderly. *Journal of Personality and Social Psychology*, 57, 950–964.

Alexander, C.N., Robinson, P., Orme-Johnson, D.W., Schneider, R.H., and Walton, K.G. (1994). The effects of transcendental meditation compared to other methods of relaxation and meditation in reducing risk factors, morbidity, and mortality. *Homeostasis*, 35 (4-5), 243–263.

Allers, R., and Teler, J. (1924). On the utilization of unnoticed impressions in associations (J. Wolff, D. Rapaport and A.H. Annin trans.). *Psychological Issues*, 2 (3, pt. 7), 121–150.

Allison, P.D. (1973). *Sociological aspects of innovations: The case of parapsychology*. Unpublished Master of Science dissertation, University of Wisconsin.

Allport, G.W. (1946). Introduction in S. Akhilananda, *Hindu psychology: Its meaning for the West*. New York: Harper.

Almond, P. (1990). Mysticism and its contexts. In R.K.C. Forman (ed.). *The problem of pure consciousness: Mysticism and philosophy* (pp. 211–219). New York: Oxford University Press.

Altom, K., and Braud, W.G. (1976). Clairvoyant and telepathic impressions of musical targets. *Research in Parapsychology 1975* (pp. 171–174). Metuchen, NJ: Scarecrow Press.

Anand, B.K., and Chhina, G.S. (1961). Investigations on yogis claiming to stop their heart beats. *Indian Journal of Medical Research*, 49, 90–94.

_____, _____ and Singh, B. (1961a). Some aspects of electroencephalographic studies in yogis. *Electroencephalography and Clinical Neurophysiology*, 13, 452–456.

_____, _____, and _____. (1961b). Studies of Shri Ramananda Yogi during his stay in our air-tight box. *Indian Journal of Medical Research*, 49, 82–89.

Anantaraman, R.N., and Kabir, R. (1984). A study of yoga. *Journal of Psychological Research*, 28, (2) 97–101.

Anderson, M.L., and White, R.A. (1956). Teacher-pupil attitudes and clairvoyance test results. *Journal of Parapsychology*, 20, 141–157.

Andresen, J. (2000). Meditation meets behavioral medicine. *Journal of Consciousness Studies*, 7 (11-12), 17–73.

Angell, J.R. (1908). *Psychology*. New York: Henry Holt & Co.

Armstrong, D.M. (1968). *A materialistic theory of the mind*. London: Routledge.

_____. (1980). *The nature of mind and other essays*. Ithaca, NY: Cornell University Press.

_____. (1988). Mind-body problem: Philosophical theories. In R.L. Gregory (ed.). *The Oxford com-*

panion to mind. (pp. 490–491). Oxford: Oxford University Press.

_____, and Malcolm, N. (1984). *Consciousness and causality: A debate on the nature of Mind.* Oxford: Basil Blackwell.

Aserinsky, E., and Klietman, N. (1953). Regularly occuring periods of eye motility and concomitant phenomena during sleep. *Science*, 118, 273–274.

Aspect, A., & Grangier, P. (1986). Experiments on Einstein-Podolsky-Rosentype correlations with pairs of visible photons. In J.A. Wheeler and W.H. Zurek (eds.). *Quantum theory and measurement.* Princeton, NJ: Princeton University Press.

Asthana, H.S. (1988). Personality. In J. Pandey (ed.), *Psychology in India. The State-of the-Art.* Vol. 1. (pp. 153–196). New Delhi: Sage Publications.

Astin, J.A. (1997). Stress reduction through mindfulness meditation: Effects on psychological symptomology, sense of control, and spiritual experiences. *Psychotherapy and Psychosomatics*, 66, 97–106.

Atreya, B.L. (1954). *The philosophy of Yogavasistha*, rev. ed. Banares: Indian Book Shop.

Aung, S.Z. (trans.) (1929). *Compendium of philosophy.* London: Oxford University Press.

Aurobindo, S. (1949). *The life divine.* New York: Sri Aurobindo Library.

Austin, J.A. (1998). *Zen and the brain: Toward an understanding of meditation and consciousness.* Cambridge, MA: MIT Press.

Avant, L.L. (1965). Vision in the ganzfeld. *Psychological Bulletin*, 64, 245–258.

Baars, B.J. (1988). *A cognitive theory of consciousness.* New York: Cambridge University Press.

_____. (1994). Roger Penrose and the quest for quantum soul. *Journal of Consciousness Studies*, 1, 261–263.

_____. (1996). *In the theatre of consciousness: The Workspace of the Mind.* New York: Oxford University Press.

_____. (1997a). Contrastive Phenomenology: A thoroughly empirical approach to consciousness. In N. Block, O. Flanagan and Guzeldere (eds.). *The Nature of Consciousness: Philosophical Debates.* (pp. 187–201). Cambridge, MA: MIT Press.

_____. (1997b). Reply to commentators. *Journal of Consciousness Studies*, Vol 4 (4): 329–331.

_____, and McGovern, K. (1994). Consciousness. In V.S. Ramachandran (ed.), *Human behavior* Vol. 1 (pp. 687–699). New York: Academic Press.

Badarayana (1979). *The Vedanta-sutras of Badarayana with commentary of Baladeva* (trans. Srisa Chandra Vasu). New Delhi: Oriental Books Reprint Corporation. (First published in 1912.)

Badawi, K., Wallace, R., Orme-Johnson, D. et al. (1984). Electrophysiologic characteristics of respiratory suspension periods occurring during the practice of the transcendental meditation program. *Psychosomatic Medicine.* 46, 267–276.

Bagchi, B.K., and Wenger, M.A. (1957). Electrophysiological correlates of some yogi exercises. *Electroencephalography and Clinical Neurophysiology*, Spplement No. 7, 132–149.

_____, and _____. (1958). Simultaneous EEG and other recordings during some yogic practices. *Electroencephalography and Clinical Neurophysiology*, 10, 193.

Banquet, J.P. (1972). EEG and meditation. *Electroencephalography and Clinical Neurophysiology*, 33, 449–458.

_____. (1973). Spectral analysis of the EEG in meditation. *Electroencephalography and Clinical Neurophysiology*, 35, 143–151.

Barber, T.X., DiCara, L., and Kamiya, J. (eds.). (1972). *Biofeedback and self-control.* Chicago: Aldine.

Bartlett, F.C. (1932). *Remembering.* Cambridge: Cambridge University Press.

Battista, J.R. (1978). The science of consciousness. In K.S. Pope and J.L. Singer (eds.). *The stream of consciousness: Scientific investigations into the flow of human experience* (pp. 55–87). New York: Plenum Press.

Bauer, R.M. (1984). Autonomic recognition of names and faces in prosopagnosia: A neuropsychological application of the guilty knowledge test. *Neuropsychologia*, 22, 457–469.

Beary, J.F., and Benson, H. (1974). A simple psychophysiologic technique which elicits the hypometabolic changes on the relaxation response. *Psychosomatic Medicine*, 36, 115–120.

Bechtel, W., and Abrahamsen, A. (1991). *Connectionism and the mind: An introduction to parallel processing in networks.* Oxford: Basil Blackwell.

Becker, D., and Shapiro, D. (1981). Physiological responses to clicks during Zen, Yoga, and TM. *Psychophysiology*, 18, 694–699.

Becker, R.O. (1992). Electromagnetism and psi phenomena. *Journal of the American Society for Psychical Research*, 86, 1–17.

Behanan, R.T. (1937). *Yoga: A scientific evaluation.* New York: Macmillan.

Beloff, J. (1962). *The existence of mind.* London: MacGibbon and Kee.

_____. (1974a). The Subliminal and the extrasensory. In A. Angoff & B. Shapin (eds.), *Parapsychology and the Sciences.* New York: Parapsychology Foundation.

_____. (1974b). ESP: The search for a physiological index. *Journal of the Society for Psychical Research*, 47, 403–420.

Belvedere, E., and Foulkes, D. (1971). Telepathy

and dreams: A failure to replicate. *Perceptual and Motor Skills,* 33, 783–789.

Bem, D.J., and Honorton, C. (1994). Does Psi exist? Replicable evidence for an anomalous process of information transfer. *Psychological Bulletin,* 115, 4–18.

_____, Palmer, J., and Broughton, R.S. (2001). Updating the ganzfeld database: A victim of its own success. *Journal of Parapsychology,* 65, 207–218.

Benson, H. (1975). *The relaxation response.* New York: William Morrow.

_____. (1977). "Systemic hypertension and the relaxation response," *New England Journal of Medicine,* 296, pp. 1152–6.

_____, Alexander, S., and Feldman, C.L. (1975). "Decreased premature ventricular contactions through the use of relaxation response in patients with stable ischemic heart disease," *Lancet* 2, pp. 380–2.

_____, Beary, J.F., and Carol, M.P. (1974). The relaxation response. *Psychiatry,* 37, 37–46.

_____, Malhotra, M.S., Goldman, R.F., Jacobs, G.D., and Hopkins, P.J. (1990). Three case reports of the metabolic and electroencephalographic changes during advanced buddhist meditation techniques. *Behavioral Medicine,* 16, 90–95.

_____, Marzetta, B.R., and Rosner, B.A. (1974). "Decreased blood pressure associated with regular elicitation of the relaxation response: A study of hypertensive subjects," in *Contemporary problems in cardiology, Volume 1: Stress and the Heart,* ed. R.S. Eliot (Mt. Kisco, NY: Futura).

_____, Rosner, B.A., Marzetta, B.R., and Klemchuk, H.M. (1974). "Decreased blood pressure in pharmacologically treated hypertensive patients who regularly elicited the relaxation response," *Lancet,* 1 (852), pp. 289–91.

_____, and Wallace, R.K. (1972). Decreased blood pressure in hypertension subjects who practice meditation. *Circulation,* 2 (45, supplement), p. 516.

Berger, R.E., and Persinger, M.A. (1991). Geophysical variables and behavior: LXVII. Quieter annual geomagnetic activity and larger effect size for experimental psi (ESP) studies over six decades. *Perceptual and Motor Skills,* 73, 1219–1223.

Bergson, H. (1911). *Creative evolution* (trans. A. Mitchell). New York: Henry Holt.

_____. (1912). *Time and free will: An essay on the immediate data of consciousness* (trans. F.L. Pogson). London: George Allen.

_____. (1913). *Matter and memory* (trans. N.M. Paul & W.S. Palmer). New York: MacMillan.

_____. (1921). *Mind-energy.* London: Macmillan

& Son (1921).

Berkeley, G. (1975). *Berkeley: Philosophical works.* Edited by M.R. Ayers. London: Dent and Sons.

Bermudez, J.L. (1998). *The paradox of self-consciousness.* Cambridge, MA: MIT Press.

Bernard, T. (1947). *Hindu philosophy.* Delhi: Motilal Banarasidass.

Berry, Dianne, and Dienes, Zoltan P. (1993). *Implicit learning: Theoretical and empirical issues.* Hillsdale, NJ: Erlbaum Associates.

Bhadra, B.J. (1966). The relationship of test scores to belief in ESP. *Journal of Parapsychology,* 30, 1–17.

Bhattacharya, K.C. (1909). *Studies in Vedantism.* Calcutta: Calcutta University Press.

_____. (1930). *The subject as freedom.* Amalner, India: Indian Institute of Philosophy.

Bhole, M.V., Karambelkar, P.V., and Vinekar, S.L. (1967a). Underground burial or *bhugrbha samadhi*–Part I. *Yoga Mimsa,* 10, (1), 1–8.

_____, _____, and _____. (1967b). Underground burial or *bhugrabha samadhi*–Part II. *Yoga Mimsa,* 10 (2), 2–16.

Bisaha, J., and Dunne, B.J. (1979). Multiple subject and long-distance precognitive remote viewing of geographical locations. In C.T. Tart, H.E. Puthoff, and R. Targ (eds.), *Mind at large* (pp. 107–124). New York: Praeger.

Bisiach, E., and Rusconi, M.L. (1990). Break-down of perceptual awareness in unilateral neglect. *Cortex,* 26, 643–649.

Block, N. (1991). "Troubles with functionalism." In D.M. Rosenthal (ed.). *The nature of mind.* New York: Oxford University Press, 211–228.

_____. (1995). On a confusion about a function of consciousness. *Brain and Behavioral Sciences,* 18, 227–247.

_____, Flanagan, O., & Guzeldere, G. (eds.) (1997). *The nature of consciousness: Philosophical debates.* Cambridge, MA: MIT Press.

Blumenthal, A.L. (1977). *The process of cognition.* Englewood Cliffs, NJ: Prentice-Hall.

Bogart, G. (1991). "Meditation in psychotherapy: A review of literature," *American Journal of Psychotherapy,* 45, pp. 383–412.

Bohm, D.J. (1973). Quantum theory as an indication of a new order in physics. Part B. Implicate and explicate order in physical law. *Foundations of physics,* 3(2), 139–168.

_____. (1980). *Wholeness and the implicate order.* Boston: Routledge & Kegan Paul.

_____. (1986). A new theory of the relationship of mind and matter. *Journal of the American Society for Psychical Research,* 80, 113–135.

Bohm, D., and Hiley, B.J. (1993). *The undivided universe: An ontological interpretation of quantum thoery.* London; New York: Routledge.

Bohr, N. (1934). *Atomic theory and the description*

of nature. Cambridge: Cambridge University Press.

Bornstein, R.F. (1989). Exposure and affect: Overview and meta-analysis of research, 1968–1987. *Psychological Bulletin,* 106, 265–289.

_____, and Pittman, T.S. (eds.) (1992). *Perception without awareness: Cognitive, clinical, and social perspectives.* New York: Guilford Press.

Bowes, P. (1971). *Consciousness and freedom.* London: Methuen.

_____. (1981). Differing views of consciousness in Western and Indian thought and their implications. *Journal of Indian Psychology,* 3, (2) 23–30.

Brady, J.P., and Lind, D.L. (1961). Experimental analysis of hysterical blindness. *Archives of General Psychiatry,* 4, 331–339.

Braud, L.W., & Braud, W.G. (1974). Further studies of relaxation as a psi-conductive state. *Journal of the American Society for Psychical Research,* 68, 229–245.

Braud, W.G. (1975). Psi-conducive states. *Journal of Communication,* 25, 142–152.

_____, and Braud, L.W. (1973). Preliminary explorations of psi-conducive states: Progressive muscular relaxation. *Journal of the American Society for Psychical Research,* 67, 26–46.

Braude, S.E. (1986). *The limits of influence: Psychokinesis and the philosophy of science.* New York: Routledge & Kegan Paul.

_____. (1992). Survival or super-psi? *Journal of Scientific Exploration,* 6, 127–144.

_____. (1995). *First person plural: Multiple prsonality and the philosophy of mind.* Lanham, MD: Rowman and Littlefield.

Brentano, F. (1973). *Psychology from an empirical standpoint.* (trans. A.C. Rancurello). New York: Humanities Press. (Original work published 1874.)

Broad, C.D. (1951). *Mind and its place in nature.* New York: Humanities Press. (Original work published 1925.)

_____. (1953). *Religion, philosophy and psychical research.* New York: Harcourt, Brace.

Broadbent, D.E. (1958). *Perception and communication.* New York: Pergamon.

Brosse, T. (1946). *Main currents in modern thought,* 4, 77–84.

Brown, B.B. (1970). Recognition of aspects of consciousness through association with EEG alpha activity represented by a light signal. *Psychophysiology,* 6, 442–452.

Brugman, H.J.F.W. (1922). Une communication sur des expériences télépathiques au laboratoire de psychologie a Groningue faites par M. Heymans, Docteur Weinberg et Docteur H.I.F.W. Brugmans, *Le Compte Renda Officiel du Premier Congrès International des Recherches Psy-*

chiques (pp. 396–408). (For a free translation from the French into English see G. Murphy [1961] *Challenge of psychical research,* New York: Harper.)

Bryant, R.A., and McConkey, K.M. (1990). Hypnotic blindness and the relevance of cognitive style. *Journal of Personality and Social Psychology,* 59, 756–761.

Buddhaghosa (1920). *Althasalini (The Expositor),* 2 Vols. (trans M. Tin). London: Oxford University Press.

_____ (1923). *Visuddhimagga* (The path of purity). 3 vols., trans. M.T. in London: Oxford University Press.

Burke, M.L. (1958). *Swami Vivekananda in America: New discoveries.* Calcutta: Advaita Ashram.

Burns, J.E. (1990). Contemporary models of consciousness: Part I. *Journal of Mind and Behavior,* 11, 153–172.

Butler, J. (1897). *Works of Bishop Butler.* Edited by W. E. Gladstone. Oxford: Oxford University Press. (Original work published in 1736.)

Calvin, A.D., and Dollenmayer, K.S. (1959). Subliminal Perception: Some negative findings. *Journal of Applied Psychology,* 43, 187–188.

Camp, B.H. (1937). Statement under "notes." *Journal of Parapsychology,* 1, 305.

Campbell, K. (1970). *Body and mind.* London: Macmillan.

Capra, F. (1983). *The Tao of physics.* Boulder, CO: Shambhala.

Carington, P. (1977). *Freedom in meditation.* Garden City, NY: Doubleday.

Carpenter, J.C. (1971). The differential effect and hidden target differences consisting of erotic and neutral stimuli. *Journal of the American Society for Psychical Research,* 65, 204–214.

_____. (1977). Intrasubject and subject-agent effects in ESP experiments. In B.B. Wolman (ed.), *Handbook of Parapsychology,* New York: Van Nostrand Reinhold.

Casler, L. (1962). The improvement of clairvoyance scores by means of hypnotic suggestion. *Journal of Parapsychology,* 26, 77–87.

_____. (1964). The effects of hypnosis on GESP. *Journal of Parapsychology,* 28, 126–134.

Chakrabarti, K.K. (1999). *Classical Indian philosophy of mind: The Nyaya dualist tradition.* New York: State University of New York.

Chakroborty, A. (1970). Yoga and psychoanalysis (letter). *British Journal of Psychiatry,* 117, 478.

Chalmers, D.J. (1996a). *The conscious mind: In search of a fundamental theory.* New York: Oxford University Press.

_____. (1996b). Facing up to the problem of consciousness. In S.R. Hameroff et al. (eds.). *Towards a science of consciousness* (pp. 5–28). Cambridge, MA: MIT Press.

_____. (1997). Availability: The cognitive basis of experience. In N. Block, O. Flanagan and G. Guzeldere (eds.). *The nature of consciousness: Philosophical debates* (pp. 421–424). Cambridge, MA: MIT Press.

Champion, J., Latto, R., and Smith, Y.M. (1983). Is blindsight an effect of scattered light, spared cortex, and near-threshold vision? *Behavioral and Brain Sciences*, 3, 423–447.

Channakesavan, S. (1991). *Concept of mind in Indian Philosophy* (2nd rev. ed.). Delhi: Motilal Banarsidass.

Chari, C.T.K. (1967). New light on an old doctrine. *International Journal of Parapsychology*, 9, 217–222.

Cheesman, J., and Merikle, P.M. (1984). Priming with and without awareness. *Perception and Pyschophysics*, 36, 387–395.

_____ and _____. (1985). Word recognition and consciousness. In D. Besner, T.G. Waller, and G.E. MacKinnon (eds.). *Reading Research: Advances in theory and practice* (Vol. 5. pp. 311–352). New York: Academic Press.

Child, I.L. (1985). Psychology and anomalous observations. The question of ESP in dreams. *American Psychologist*, 40, 1219–1230.

Churchland, P.M. (1988). *Matter and consciousness* (rev. ed.). Cambridge: MIT Press.

_____. (1989). *A neurocomputational perspective: The nature of mind and the structure of science.* Cambridge: MIT Press.

_____. (1995). *The engine of reason, the seat of the soul: A philosophical journey into the brain.* Cambridge: MIT Press.

_____. and Churchland, P.S. (1982). Functionalism, qualia, and intentionality. In J. Biro and R. Shahan (eds.). *Mind, brain, and function.* Norman, OK: University of Oklahoma Press, 121–145.

_____, and _____. (1999/1998) *On the contrary: Critical essays, 1987–1997.* Cambridge: MIT Press.

Churchland, P.S. (1986). *Neurophysiology.* Cambridge: MIT Press.

CIBA Foundation (1993). *Experimental and theoretical studies of consciousness.* CIBA Foundation Symposium 174. Chichester, UK: Wiley.

Combs, Allan (1997). Commentary on Bernard Baars' "In the theatre of consciousness." *Journal of Consciousness Studies*, Vol 4(4): 314–316.

Conze, E. (1969). *Buddhist meditation.* New York: Harper and Row.

Cooley, C.H. (1902). *Human nature and the social order.* New York: Scribner.

Coover, J.E. (1975). *Experiments in psychical research.* New York: Arno Press (first published in 1917).

Corby, J.C., et al. (1978). Psychophysiological correlates of the practice of tantric yoga meditation. *Archives of General Psychiatry*, 35, 571–577.

Corey, P.W. (1977). Airway conductance and oxygen consumption changes associated with practice of the transcendental meditation techniques. In D.W. Orme-Johnson and J.T. Farrow (eds.), *Scientific research on the transcendental meditation program: Collected papers.* Weggis, Switzerland: Maharishi European Research University Press.

Coster, G. (1972). *Yoga and Western psychology: A comparison.* Harper and Row.

Coward, H.G. (1979). Mysticism in the analytical psychology of Carl Jung and the Yoga psychology of Patanjali. *Philosophy East and West*, 29, 323–336.

_____. (1983). Psychology and karma. *Philosophy East and West*, 29, 323–336.

Crick, F.H.C. (1993). *The astonishing hypothesis.* New York: Basic Books.

_____, and Koch, C. (1990). Towards a neurobiological theory of consciousness. *Seminars in Neuroscience*, 2, 263–275.

Das, N.N., and Gastaut, H. (1955). Variations de l'activité électrique, du cerveau, du coeur et des muscles squelletique au cours de la méditation et de l'extase yogique. *Electroencephalography and Clinical Neurophysiology*, 6 (supplement), 211–219.

Dasgupta, S. (1924). *Yoga as philosophy and religion.* London: Kegan Paul.

_____. (1930). *Yoga Philosophy in Relation to Other Systems of Indian Thought.* Calcutta: University of Calcutta.

_____. (1988). *History of Indian philosophy* (5 Vols.). Delhi: Motilal Banarasidass (first published in 1922).

Datey, K.K., Deshmukh, S.N., Davi, C.L., and Vinekar, S.L. (1969). "Shavasan": A yogic exercise in the management of hypertension. *Angiology*, 20, 325–333.

Davids, C.A.F.R. (ed. and trans.) (1923). *A Buddhist manual of psychological ethics.* London: Royal Asiatic Society.

_____. (trans.) (1963). *Milinda Panha (The questions of King Milinda).* New York: Dover Publications.

Davidson, J. (1976). Physiology of meditation and mystic states of consciousness. *Perspectives in Biology and Medicine*, 19, 345–380.

Davidson, R.J., and Goleman, D.J. (1977). The role of attention in meditation and hypnosis: A psychological perspective on transformation of consciousness. *International Journal of Clinical and Experimental Hypnosis*, 25, 291–308.

_____, _____, and Schwartz, G.E. (1984). Attentional and affective concomitants of meditation. In D.H. Shapiro, and Walsh, R.N. (eds.)

(1984), *Meditation: Classic and contemporary perspectives.* Hawthorne, NY: Aldine Publishing Co.

Davies, J. (1977). The transcendental meditation program and progressive relaxation: Comparative effects on trait-anxiety and self-actualization. In D.W. Orme-Johnson and J.T. Forrow (eds.). *Scientific research on the transcendental meditation program: Collected papers.* Second edition. Weggis, Switzerland: Maharshi European Research University Press.

Davies, P. (1983). *God and new physics.* London: Penguin.

Davis, J.D., and Braud. W. (1980). Autonomic "recognition" of ESP targets. In W.G. Roll (ed.). *Research in Parapsychology.* 1979. Metuchen, NJ: Scarecrow Press.

Dean, E.D. (1962). The Plethysmograph as an indicator of ESP. *Journal of the Society for Psychical Research,* 41, 351–353.

_____, and Nash, C.B. (1967). Coincident plethysmograph results under controlled condition. *Journal of the Society for Psychical Research,* 44, 1–14.

Deepak, K.K., Manchanda, S.K., and Maheswari, M.C. (1994). Meditation improves clinicoelectroencephalographic measures in drug-resistant epileptics. *Biofeedback and Self-Regulation,* 19(1), 25–40.

de Haan, E.H.F., Young, A.W., and Newcombe, F. (1987). Face recognition without awareness. *Cognitive Neuropsychology,* 4, 385–415.

_____, Bauer, R.M. and Greve, K.W. (1992). Behavioral and physiological evidence for covert recognition in a prosopagnostic patient. *Cortex,* 28, 77–95.

Deikman, A.J. (1966). Deautomatization and the mystical experience. *Psychiatry,* 29, 324–338.

_____. (1969). Experimental meditation. In C.T. Tart (ed.). *Altered States of Consciousness.* New York: Wiley.

_____. (1973). Biomodal consciousness. In R.E. Ornstein (ed.), *The nature of consciousness: A book of readings* (pp. 67–86). San Francisco: W.H. Freeman.

Delmonte, M.M. (1986). Meditation as a clinical intervention strategy: A brief review. *International Journal of Psychosomatics,* 33, (3) 9–12.

Dennett, D.C. (1978). *Brainstorms.* Cambridge, MA: MIT Press.

_____. (1991). *Consciousness explained.* New York: Little Brown.

_____. (1997). Quining qualia. In N. Block, O. Flanagan, and G. Guzeldere (eds.). *The nature of consciousness: Philosophical debates.* Cambridge: MIT Press, 619–642.

_____, and Kinsbourne, M. (1997). Time and the observer: The where and when of consciousness in the brain. In N. Block, O. Flanagan and G. Guzeldere (eds.). *The nature of consciousness: Philosophical debates* (pp. 141–174). Cambridge, MA: MIT Press.

Descartes, R. (1952). *Meditations.* In R.M. Hutchins (ed.). *Great books of the Western world* (Vol. 31). Chicago: Encyclopaedia Britannica Inc.

_____. (1969). *The philosophical works of Descartes* (trans. E.S. Haldane and G.R.T. Ross). Cambridge: Cambridge University Press. (Original work published in 1911.)

_____. (1985). *The philosophical writings of René Descartes* (2 Vols.). Translated by J. Cottingham, R. Stoothoff, and D. Murdoch. Cambridge: Cambridge University Press.

_____. (n.d.) *Discourse on method and metaphysical meditations* (trans. G.B. Rawlings). London: Walter Scott.

De Silva, C. L. A. (1988). *A Treatise on Buddhistic Philosophy of Abhidhamma.* Delhi: Sri Satguru Publications.

Devereux, G. (ed.) (1953). *Psychoanalysis and the occult.* New York: International Universities Press.

Dewey, J. (1893). *Psychology* (3rd ed.). New York: Harper. (Original work published in 1886.)

Dhanaraj, H., and Singh, M. (1977). Reduction in metabolic rate during the practice of the TM technique. In D. Orme-Johnson and J. Farrow (eds.), *Scientific research on transcendental meditation programs: Collected papers,* Vol. 1. Weggis, Switzerland: Maharishi European Research University Press.

Dharmarajadhvarindra (1942). *Vedanta-Paribhasa* (trans. S.S. Sastry). Madras: Adayar Library.

Diaconis, P. (1978). Statistical problems in ESP research. *Science,* 201, 131–136.

Dillbeck, M.C., and Orme-Johnson, D.W. (1987). Physiological differences between transcendental meditation and rest. *American Psychologist,* 42, 879–881.

Dingwall, E.J. (ed.) (1967 and 1968). *Abnormal Hypnotic Phenomena* (4 Vols.). New York: Barnes & Noble.

Dixon, N.F. (1956). Symbolic associations following subliminal stimulation. *International Journal of Psychoanalysis,* 37, 159–170.

_____. (1958). The effect of subliminal stimulation upon autonomic and verbal behavior. *Journal of Abnormal and Social Psychology,* 57, 29–36.

_____. (1979a). Subliminal perception and parapsychology: Points of contact. *Parapsychology Review,* 10 (No. 3), 1–6.

_____. (1979b). *Subliminal perception: The nature of controversy.* London; McGraw-Hill.

Dobyns, Y., Dunne, B., Jahn, R., and Nelson, R. (1994). Reply to Hansen, Utts, and Markwick's "Statistical and methodological problems of the

PEAR remote viewing [*sic*] experiments." In E.W. Cook and D.L. Delanoy (eds.), *Research in Parapsychology 1991* (pp. 108–111). Metuchen, NJ: Scarecrow Press.

Don, N.S., McDonough, B.E., and Warren, C.A. (1998). Event-related brain potential (ERP) indicators of unconscious psi: A replication using subjects unselected for psi. *Journal of Parapsychology*, 62, 127–145.

Donchin, E., McCarthy, G., Kutas, M., and Ritter, W. (1983). Event-related brain potential in the study of consciousness. In R.J. Davidson, G.E. Schwartz and D. Shapiro (eds.), *Consciousness and self-regulation: Advances in research and theory*, Vol. 3. New York: Plenum Press.

Dorcas, A. (1997). Chinese *Qigong* research: An overview. In H.S.R. Kao and D. Sinha (eds.), *Asian perspectives on psychology* (pp. 309–332). New Delhi: Sage.

Dubey, B.L., and Kumar, H. (1986). Management of stress and mental health of executives. *Indian Journal of Clinical Psychology*, 13 (2), 155–160.

Dwivedi, C.B. (1987). On Yogadarsana's *asampramosa* doctrine of memory. *Journal of Indian Psychology*, 6 (172), 1–6.

Ebbinghaus, H. (1964). *Memory*. New York: Dover. (Originally published in 1885.)

Eccles, J.C. (1953). *The neurophysiological basis of mind: The principles of neurophysiology*. Oxford: Clarendon Press.

_____. (1965). *The brain and the unity of conscious experience*. Cambridge: Cambridge University Press.

_____. (1976). Brain and free will. In G.G. Globus, G. Maxwell, and I. Savodnik (eds.). *Consciousness and the brain: A scientific and philosophical inquiry* (pp. 101–121). New York: Plenum Press.

_____. (1977). The human person in its two-way relationship to the brain. In J.D. Morris, W.G. Roll and R.L. Morris (eds.), *Research in parapsychology* 1976 (pp. 251–262). Metuchen, NJ: Scarecrow.

_____. (1994). *How the self controls its brain*. Berlin; New York: Springer-Verlag.

Eddington, A. (1978). *The nature of the physical world*. Ann Arbor, MI: University of Michigan Press.

Ehrenwald, J. (1947). *Telepathy and medical psychology*. London: George Allen & Unwin.

_____. (1977). Psi phenomena and brain research. In B.B. Wolman (ed.), *Handbook of Parapsychology*. New York: Von Nostrand Reinhold.

_____. (1978). *The ESP experience: A psychiatric validation*. New York: Basic Books.

Eisenbud, J. (1970). *Psi and psychoanalysis*. New York: Grune & Stratton.

Eppley, K.R., Abrams, A.I., and Shear, J. (1989). Differential effects of relaxation techniques on trait anxiety: A meta-analysis. *Journal of Clinical Psychology*. 45, 957–974.

Epstein, S. (1973). The self-concept revisited: Or a theory of a theory. *American Psychologist.*

Erdelyi, M.H. (1985). *Psychoanalysis: Freud's cognitive psychology*. New York, NY: W.H. Freeman.

Estabrooks, G. (1961). A contribution to experimental telepathy. *Journal of Parapsychology*, 25, 190–213. (Originally published in 1927.)

Evans, C., and Richardson, P.H. (1988). Improved recovery and reduced postoperative stay after therapeutic suggestions during general anesthesia. *Lancet* (27 August) 491–493.

Eysenck, H.J. (1967). Personality and extra-sensory perception. *Journal of the Society for Psychical Research*, 44, 55–71.

Fahler, J. (1957). ESP card tests with and without hypnosis. *Journal of Parapsychology*, 21, 179–185.

_____, and Cadoret, R.J. (1958). ESP card tests of college students with and without hypnosis. *Journal of Parapsychology*, 22, 125–136.

Farah, M.J. (1997). Visual perception and visual awareness after brain damage: A tutorial overview. In N. Block, Flanagan, O. and G. Guzeldere (eds.), *The nature of consciousness: Philosophical debates* (pp. 203–236). Cambridge, MA: MIT Press.

Farrow, J.T., and Hebert, R. (1982). Breath suspension during transcendental meditation technique. *Psychosomatic Medicine*, 44, 133–153.

Farthing, G.W. (1992). *The psychology of consciousness*. Englewood cliffs, NJ: Prentice Hall.

Feather, S.R. (1967). A quantitative comparison of memory and psi. *Journal of Parapsychology*, 31, 93–98.

Feigl, H. (1967). *The "mental" and the "physical."* Minneapolis: University of Minnesota Press.

Fenwick, P. (1987). Meditation and the EEG. In *The psychology of meditation*. Ed. M.W. West. Oxford, Clarendon Press.

_____, et al. (1984). Metabolic and EEG changes during transcendental meditation: An explanation. In D.H. Shapiro and R.N. Walsh (eds.) (pp. 447–464), *Meditation: Classic and Contemporary Perspectives*. New York: Aldine.

Figar, S. (1959). The application of plethysmography to the objective study of so-called extrasensory perception. *Journal of the Society for Psychical Research*, 40, 162–172.

Flanagan, O. (1991). *The science of the mind*. Cambridge, MA: MIT Press.

_____. (1992). *Consciousness reconsidered*. Cambridge, MA: MIT Press.

_____. (1997). The robust phenomenology of consciousness. In N. Block, O. Flanagan and G. Guzeldere (eds.), *The nature of consciousness:*

Philosophical debates (pp. 89–94). Cambridge, MA: MIT Press.

_____. (1997). Conscious inessentialism and the epiphenomenologist suspicion. In N. Block, O. Flanagan and G. Guzeldere (eds.), *The nature of consciousness: Philosophical debates* (pp. 357–374). Cambridge, MA: MIT Press.

Forman, R.K.C. (1990). Introduction: Mysticism, constructivism and forgetting. In R.K.C. Forman (ed.), *The problem of pure consciousness: Mysticism and philosophy* (pp. 3–49). New York: Oxford University Press.

Forster, K.I. (1987). *Form-priming with masked primes: The best-match hypothesis.* In M. Coltheart (ed.), *Attention and performance* (Vol.12) (pp. 127–146). Hillsdale, NJ: Elbaum.

Foulkes, D. (1962). Dream reports from different stages of sleep. *Journal of Abnormal and Social Psychology*, 65, 14–25.

_____, and Vogel, G. (1965). Mental activity at sleep onset. *Journal of Abnormal Psychology*, 70, 231–43.

_____, Spear, P.S., and Symonds, J.D. (1966). Individual differences in mental activity at sleep onset. *Journal of Abnormal Psychology*, 71, 280–86.

Freeman, J.A., and Nielsen, W. (1964). Precognition score deviation as related to anxiety levels. *Journal of Parapsychology*, 28, 239–249.

_____. (1969). Decline of variance in school precognition tests. *Journal of Parapsychology*, 33, 72–73.

Freud, S. (1915). The unconscious. In J. Strachey (ed.), *Standard edition of the complete psychological works of Sigmund Freud* (Vol.14). London: Hogarth.

_____. (1933). *New introductory lectures on psychoanalysis.* New York: W.W. Norton.

_____. (1953). *The interpretation of dreams.* London: Hogarth Press (originally published in 1900).

_____. (1953). The occult significance of dreams. In G. Devereaux (ed.), *Psychoanalysis and the occult.* New York: International Universities Press. (Originally published in 1925.)

Frey-Rohn, L. (1990). *From Freud to Jung: Comparative study of the psychology of the unconscious.* Boston: Shambhala.

Fung, Yu-lan (1952). *A history of Chinese* (trans. Derk Bodde). London: George Allen & Unwin.

Fuster, J.M. (1958). Effects of stimulation of brain stem on tachistoscopic perception. *Science*, 127, 150.

Galin, D. (1996). The structure of subjective experience: Sharpen the concepts and terminology. In S.R. Hameroff et al. (eds.), *Toward a science of consciousness: The first Tucson discussions and debates* (pp. 121–140). Cambridge, MA: MIT Press.

Gaylord, C., Orme-Johnson, D.W., and Travis, F.

(1989). The effects of transcendental meditation techniques and progressive relaxation on EEG coherence, stress activity, and mental health in black adults. *International Journal of Neuroscience*, 46, 77–86.

Gazzaniga, M.S. (1988). Brain modularity: Towards a philosophy of consciousness. In A.J. Marcel and E. Bisiach (eds.), *Consciousness in contemporary science.* Oxford: Clarendon Press.

_____, and Le Doux, J.E. (1978). *The integrated mind.* New York: Plenum Press.

Gergen, K. (1971). *The concept of self.* New York: Holt, Rinehart & Winston.

Girodo, M. (1974). Yoga meditation and flooding in the treatment of anxiety neurosis. *Journal of Behavior Therapy and Experimental Psychiatry*, 5, 157–160.

Gleick, J. (1988). *Chaos.* London: Heinemann.

Globus, G.G., Maxwell, G., and Savodnik, I. (eds.) (1976). *Consciousness and the brain: A scientific and philosophical inquiry.* New York: Plenum Press.

Glueck, B.C., and Stroebel, C.F. (1975). Biofeedback and meditation in the treatment of psychiatric illness. *Comprehensive Psychiatry*, 16, 303–321.

Goldman, B.L., Domitor, P.J., and Murray, E.J. (1979). Effects of Zen meditation on anxiety reduction and perceptual functioning. *Journal of Consulting and Clinical Psychology*, 47, 551–556.

Goleman, D. (1971). Meditation as meta-therapy: Hypotheses towards a proposed fifth state of consciousness. *Journal of Transpersonal Psychology*, 3, 1–25.

_____. (1972a). The Buddha on meditation and states of consciousness, Part I: The teachings. *The Journal of Transpersonal Psychology*, 4, 1–43.

_____. (1972b). The Buddha on meditation and states of consciousness, Part II: A typology of meditation techniques. *The Jounal of Transpersonal Psychology*, 4, 151–210.

_____. (1978). *The varieties of the meditative experience.* New York: Irvington Publishers.

_____, and Schwartz, G. (1976). Meditation as an intervention in stress reactivity. *Journal of Consulting and Clinical Psychology*, 44, 456–466.

Goswami, A. (1989). The idealistic interpretation of quantum mechanics. *Physics essays, beyond biofeedback.* 2, 385–400. New York: Delacorte.

_____. (1990). Consciousness in quantum physics and the mind-body problem, *Journal of Mind and Behavior.* 11, 75–96.

_____, Reed, R.E., and Goswami, M. (1995/1993). *The self aware universe: How consciousness creates the material world.* New York: Putnam's Sons.

Govinda, L.A. (1961). *The psychological attitude of early Buddhist philosophy.* London: Rider & Co.

Greenwald, A.G. (1992). New Look 3: Unconscious cognition reclaimed. *American Psychologist*, 47, 766–779.

_____, Klinger, M.R., and Liu, T.J. (1989). Unconscious processing of dichoptically masked words. *Memory and Cognition*, 17, 35–47.

Grela, J.J. (1945). Effect on ESP scoring of hypnotically induced attitudes. *Journal of Parapsychology*, 9, 194–202.

Griffin, D.R. (1988). Of minds and molecules: Postmodern medicine in a psychosomatic university. In D.R. Griffin (ed.), *The reenchantment of science*, (pp. 141–163). Albany, NY: State University of New York Press.

_____. (1991). What is consciousness and why is it so problematic? In K.R. Rao (ed.), *Cultivating consciousness: Enhancing human potential and healing*. Westport, CT: Praeger.

Grinshphon, Y. (2002). *Silence unheard: Deathly otherness in Patanjala-Yoga*. Albany, NY: State University of New York Press.

Grosz, H.J., and Zimmerman, J.A. (1970). A second detailed case study of functional blindness: Further demonstration of the contribution of objective psychological laboratory data. *Behavior Therapy*, 1, 115–123.

Guenther, H.V. (1976). *Philosophy and psychology in Abhidharma*. Berkeley, CA: Shambala.

_____. (1976). *Philosophy and psychology in the Abhidharma*. Lucknow: Pioneer Press.

Gurney, E., Myers, F.W.H., and Podmore, F. (1886). *Phantasms of the living* (2 Vols.). London: Trubner.

Haber, R.N., and Erdelyi, M.H. (1967). Emergence and recovery of initially unavoidable perceptual material. *Journal of Verbal Hearing and Verbal Behavior*, 6, 618–628.

Hall, J.A. (1991). *Patterns of dreaming: Jungian techniques in theory and practice*. Boston: Shambhala.

Hameroff, S.R. (1994). Quantum coherence in microtubules: A neural basis for emergent consciousness. *Journal of Consciousness Studies*, 1, 91–118.

_____, Kaszniak, A.W., and Scott, A.C. (eds.) (1996). *Towards a science of consciousness*. Cambridge, MA: MIT Press.

Hamlyn, D.W. (1977). Self-knowledge. In T. Mischel (ed.), *The self: Psychological and philosophical issues* (pp. 170–200). Totowa, NJ: Rowman and Littlefield.

Hansel, C.E.M. (1966). *ESP: A scientific evaluation*. New York: Scribners.

_____. (1980). *ESP and parapsychology: A critical re-evaluation*. Buffalo, NY: Prometheus Books.

_____. (1989). *The search for psychic power: ESP & parapsychology revisited*. Buffalo, NY: Prometheus Books.

Hansen, G.P., Utts, J., and Markwick, B. (1994). Statistical and methodological problems of the PEAR remote viewing experiments. In E.W. Cook and D.L. Delanoy (eds.), *Research in Parapsychology 1991* (pp. 103–107). Metuchen, NJ: Scarecrow Press.

Haraldsson, E. (1978). ESP and the defense mechanism test (DMT): A further validation. *European Journal of Parapsychology*, 2, 104–114.

Hardy, A.C. (1965). *The living stream*. London: Collins.

Hebb, D.O. (1951). The role of neurological ideas in psychology. *Journal of Personality*, 20, 39–55.

_____. (1974). What psychology is about. *American Psychologist*, 29, 71–79.

Heidegger, M. (1962). *Being and time* (trans. J. Macquarrie and E.Robinson). New York: Harper.

_____. (1982). *The basic problems of phenomenology* (trans. A. Hofstadter). Bloomington, IN: Indiana University Press.

_____. (1984). *The metaphysical foundations of logic* (trans. M. Heim). Bloomington, IN: Indiana University Press.

Heil, J. (1988). *Philosophy of mind: A contemporary introduction*. London: Routledge.

Hiley, B.J. (1997). Commentary on Bernard Baars' "In the theatre of consciousness." *Journal of Consciousness Studies*, Vol 4 (4): 329–331.

Hilgard, E.R. (1962). What becomes of the input from the stimuli? In C.W. Eriksen (ed.), *Behavior and awareness: A symposium of research and interpretation*. Durham, NC: Duke University Press.

_____. (1977/1986). *Divided consciousness: Multiple controls in human thought and action* (rev.ed.). New York: Wiley-Interscience.

_____, and Hilgard, J.R. (1983). *Hypnosis in the relief of pain*. Los Altos, CA: W. Kaufman.

_____, and Marquis, D.G. (1940). *Conditioning and learning*. New York: Appleton-Century-Crofts.

Hodgson, D. (1991). *The mind matters*. New York: Oxford University Press.

_____. (1994). Why Searle has not rediscovered the mind. *Journal of Consciousness Studies*, 1, 264–274.

Hoeing, J. (1968). Medical research on yoga. *Confinia Psychiatrica*, 11, 68–89.

Holender, D. (1986). Semantic activation without conscious identification in dichotic listening, parafoveal vision, and visual masking: A survey and appraisal. *Behavioral and Brain Sciences*, 9, 1–66.

Holmes, D.S. (1984). Meditation and somatic arousal reduction: A review of the experimental evidence. *American Psychologist*, 39, (1) 1–10.

Honorton, C. (1965). The relationship between

ESP and manifest anxiety level. *Journal of Parapsychology*, 29, 291–292. (Abstract.)

_____. (1969). Relationship between EEG alpha activity and ESP card-guessing performance. *Journal of the American Society for Psychical Research*, 63, 365–374.

_____. (1976). Has science developed the competence to confront claims of the paranormal? In J.D. Morris, W.G. Roll, and R.L. Morris (eds.), *Research in Parapsychology, 1975*. Methuchen, NJ: Scarecrow Press.

_____. (1977). Psi and internal attention states. In B.B. Wolman (ed.) *Handbook of parapsychology*. New York: Van Nostrand Reinhold.

_____. (1985). Meta-analysis of ganzfeld research: A response to Hyman. *Journal of Parapsychology*, 49, 51–91.

_____, Davidson, R., and Bindler, P. (1971). Feedback-augmented EEG alpha, shifts in subjective state, and ESP card-guessing performance. *Journal of the American Society for Psychical Research*, 65, 308–323.

_____, Ferrari, D.C., and Bem, D.J. (1998). Extroversion and ESP performance: A meta-analysis and new confirmation. *Journal of Parapsychology*, 62, 255–276.

_____, and Harper, S. (1974). Psi-mediated imagery and ideation in an experimental procedure for regulating perceptual input. *Journal of the American Society for Psychical Research*, 68, 156–168.

_____, Krippner, S., and Ullman, M. (1971). Telepathic transmission of art prints under two conditions. *Proceedings of the 80th Annual Convention of the American Psychological Association*, 319–320.

_____, and Tremmel, L. (1979). Psi correlates of volition: A preliminary test of Eccles' "neurophysiological hypothesis" of mind-brain interaction. In W.G. Roll (ed.), *Research in Parapsychology* 1978 (pp. 36–38). Methuchen, NJ: Scarecrow Press.

Hopkins, B.C. (1993). *Intentionality in Husserl and Heidegger*. London: Kluwer Academic Publishers.

Hume, D. (1978). *A treatise on human nature* (Edited by L.A. Selby-Bigge, revised by P.H. Niddtich). Oxford: Oxford University Press.

Humphrey, B.M. (1946a). Success in ESP as related to form of response drawings. I. Clairvoyance experiments. *Journal of Parapsychology*, 10, 78–106.

_____. (1946b). Success in ESP as related to form of response drawings. II. GESP experiments. *Journal of Parapsychology*, 10, 181–196.

Husserl, E. (1931). *Ideas: General introduction to pure phenomenology* (trans. W.R. Boyce Gibson). London: George Allen & Unwin.

_____. (1960). *Cartesian meditations* (trans. D. Cairns). The Hague: Martinus Nijhoff.

_____. (1965). *Phenomenology and the crisis of philosophy* (trans. and ed. S. Lauer). New York: Harper.

_____. (1966). *The phenomenology of internal time consciousness* (trans. J.S. Churchill). Bloomington: Indiana University Press.

_____. (1971). Phenomenology (trans. R. Palmer). *Journal of the British Society for Phenomenology*, 2 (No.2), 77–90.

_____. (1982). *Logical investigations,* 2 vols. (trans. J.N. Findlay). New York: Humanities Press.

Hyman, R. (1985). The ganzfeld ESP experiment: A critical appraisal. *Journal of Parapsychology*, 49, 3–49.

_____. (1994). Anomaly or artifact? Comments on Bem and Honorton. *Psychological Bulletin*, 115, 19–24.

_____. (1996). Evaluation of a program on anomalous mental phenomena. *Journal of Scientific Exploration*, 10, 31–58.

_____, and Honorton, C. (1986). A joint communiqué: The psi ganzfeld controversy. *Journal of Parapsychology*, 50, 351–364.

Ikemi, A. (1988). Psychophysiological effects of self-regulation method: EEG frequency analysis and contingent negative variations. *Psychotherapy and Psychosomatics*, 49, (3 and 4), 230–239.

Inglis, B. (1977). *Natural and supernatural: A history of the paranormal from earliest times to 1914*. London: Hodder and Stoughton.

Irwin, H.J. (1979). *Psi and the mind: An information processing approach*. Metuchen, NJ: Scarecrow Press.

_____. (1999). *An introduction to parapsychology*. 3rd ed. Jefferson, NC: McFarland & Co.

Jackendoff, R. (1987). *Consciousness and the computational mind*. Cambridge, MA: MIT Press.

Jackson, C.W., and Pollard, J.C. (1962). Sensory deprivation and suggestion: A theoretical approach. *Behavioral Science*, 7, 332–342.

Jackson, F. (1982). Epiphenomenal qualia. *Philosophical Quarterly*, 32, 127–136.

Jacobson, E. (1938). *Progressive relaxation*, 2nd ed. Chicago: University of Chicago Press.

Jacoby, L.L., and Dallas, M. (1981). On the relationship between autobiographical memory and perceptual learning. *Journal of Experimental Psychology: General*, 3, 306–340.

Jahn, R.G. (1982). The persistent paradox of psychic phenomena: An engineering perspective. *Proceedings of the IEEE*, 70, 136–170.

_____, and Dunne, B.J. (1987). *Margins of reality: The role of consciousness in the physical world*. New York: Harcourt Brace Jovanovich.

_____, and _____. (1999). *Two decades of Pear: An*

anthology of selected publications. Princeton, NJ: Princeton Engineering Anomalies Research Laboratory, Princeton University.

Jaiswal, O.P. (1999). An evaluation of the nature of consciousness in Vjnanavada philosophy. In S. Singh (ed.), *Buddhism in comparative light*. Delhi: Indo-Asian Publishing House.

James, W. (1890). *The principles of psychology*. New York: Henry Holt & Co.

_____. (1900). *Psychology: Briefer course*. New York: Henry Holt & Co. (Original work published in 1892.)

_____. (1914). *The varieties of religious experience: A study in human nature*. New York: Longmans, Green & Co. (Original work published in 1902.)

_____. (1947). *Essays in radical empiricism*. New York: Longmans, Green & Co. (Original work published in 1912.)

_____. (1952). *The principles of psychology*. Chicago: Encyclopedia Britannica. (Original work published in 1890.)

Janet, P. (1907). A symposium on the subconscious. *Journal of Abnormal Psychology*. 2, 58–67.

_____. (1920). *The major symptoms of hysteria*. New York: Macmillan. (First published in 1907.)

Jaynes, J. (1976). *The origin of consciousness in the breakdown of the bicameral mind*. Boston, MA: Houghton Mifflin Co.

Jevning, R.A., and O'Halloran, J.P. (1984). Metabolic effects of transcendental meditation: Toward a new paradigm of neurobiology. In D.H. Shapiro and R.N. Walsh (eds.), *Meditation: Classic and contemporary perspectives* (pp. 465–472). New York: Aldine.

Jevning, R., Wallace, R.K., and Beidebach, M. (1992). The physiology of meditation: A review. A wakeful hypometabolic integrated response. *Neuroscience and Biobehavioral Reviews*, 16, 415–424.

Johansson, R.E.A. (1969). *The psychology of nirvana*. London: Allen & Unwin.

John, E.R. (1976). A model of consciousness. In G. Schwartz & D. Shapiro (eds.), *Consciousness and self-regulation* (Vol.1) (pp. 1–50). New York: Plenum Press.

Johnson, L.C. (1970). A psychophysiology for all states. *Psychophysiology*, 6, 501–516.

Johnson, M., and Haraldsson, E. (1984). Icelandic experiments IV and V with the defense mechanism test. *Journal of Parapsychology*, 48, 185–200.

Johnson, M., and Kanthamani, B.K. (1967). The defense mechanism test as a predictor of ESP scoring direction. *Journal of Parapsychology*, 31, 99–100.

Johnson-Laird, P. (1983). *Mental models*. Cambridge, MA: Harvard University Press.

Johnson-Laird, P.N. (1988). *The computer and the mind*. Cambridge, MA: Harvard University Press.

Josephson, B.D. (1988). *Foundations of Physics*, 18, 1195–1204.

_____. (1992). The elusivity of nature and the mind-matter problem. In B. Rubik (ed.), *The interrelationship between mind and matter* (pp. 219–222). Philadelphia, PA: Center for Frontier Sciences, Temple University.

Jung, C.G. (1954). On the nature of psyche. In H. Read et al. (eds.), *Collected works of C.G. Jung* (Vol.8) (trans. R.F.C. Hull). Princeton, NJ: Princeton University Press. (Original work published 1919.)

_____, and Pauli, W.(1955). *The interpretation of nature and the psyche: Synchronicity and the influence of archetypal ideas on the scientific theories of Kepler*. New York: Pantheon.

Kahn, S.D. (1976). "Myers' problem" revisited. In G.R. Schmeidler (ed.), *Parapsychology: Its relation to physics, biology, psychology and psychiatry*. Metuchen, NJ: Scarecrow Press.

Kahneman, D. (1973). *Attention and effort*. Englewood Cliffs, NJ: Prentice-Hall.

Kakar, S. (1981). *The inner world: A psychoanalytic study of childhood and society in India*. New Delhi: Oxford University Press.

_____. (1982). *Shamans, mystics and doctors: A psychological enquiry into India and its healing properties*. Bombay: Oxford University Press.

Kalupahana, D. (1978). *The principles of Buddhistic psychology*. Albany, NY: State University of New York Press.

Kamiya, J. (1969). Operant control of the EEG alpha rhythm and some of its reported effects on consciousness. In C.T. Tart (ed.), *Altered States of consciousness*. New York: Wiley.

Kant, I. (1929). *Critique of pure reason* (trans: N. Kemp Smith). London: Macmillan.

_____. (1948). *Ground work of the metaphysic of morals* (trans: H.J. Paton). London: Hutchinson.

_____. (1956). *Critique of practical reason* (trans: L.W. Beck). New York: Liberal Arts.

Kanthamani, B.K. (1965). A study of differential response in language ESP tests. *Journal of Parapsychology*, 29, 27–34.

_____, and Rao, H.H. (1974). A study of memory ESP relationships using linguistic forms. *Journal of Parapsychology*, 38, 286–300.

_____, and Rao, K.R. (1973a). Personality characteristics of ESP subjects: IV. Neuroticism and ESP. *Journal of Parapsychology*, 37, 37–50.

_____, and _____. (1973b). Personality characteristics of ESP subjects: V. Graphic expansiveness and ESP. *Journal of Parapsychology*, 37, 119–129.

Kao, S.R., and Sinha, D. (eds.) (1997). *Asian perspectives on psychology*. New Delhi: Sage Publications.

Kasamatsu, A., and Hirai, T. (1966). An electroencephalographic study of the Zen meditation (zazen). *Psychologia*, 12, 205–225.

Katz, S.T. (1978). Language, epistemology, and mysticism. In S.T. Katz (ed.), *Mysticism and philosophical analysis* (pp. 22–74). New York: Oxford University Press.

Kelly, E.F. (1979). Converging lines of evidence on mind/brain relations. In B. Shapin and L. Coly (eds.), *Brain/mind and parapsychology* (pp. 1–31). New York: Parapsychology Foundation.

_____, Kanthamani, H., Child, I., and Young, F.W. (1975). On the relationship between visual and ESP confusion structures in an exceptional ESP subject. *Journal of the American Society for Psychical Research*, 69, 1–31.

Kentridge, R.W., and Heywood, C.A. (1999). The status of blindsight: Near threshold vision, islands of cortex and the Riddoch phenomenon. *Journal of Consciousness Studies*, 6, 3–11.

_____, _____, and Weiskrantz, L. (1999). Effects of temporal cueing on residual visual descrimination in blindsight. *Neuropsychologia*, 37, 479–485.

Kihlstrom, J.F. (1979). Hypnosis and psychopathology: Retrospect and prospect. *Journal of Abnormal Psychology*, 88, 459–473.

_____. (1980). Posthypnotic amnesia for recently learned material: Interactions with "episodic" and "semantic" memory. *Cognitive Psychology*, 12, 227–251.

_____. (1984). Conscious, subconscious, unconscious: A cognitive perspective. In K.S. Bowers and D. Deichenbaum (eds.), *The unconscious reconsidered* (pp. 149–211). New York: Wiley.

_____. (1990). Anesthesia, amnesia, and the cognitive unconscious. In *Memory and awareness in anesthesia*, (eds.), B. Bonke, W. Fitch and K. Millar. Amsterdam: Swets-Leiglinger.

_____, Barnhardt, T.M., and Tataryn, D. J. (1992). Implicit perception. In R.F. Bornstein and T.S. Pittman (eds.), *Perception without awareness*. (pp. 17–54). New York: Guilford Press.

Kim, J. (1985). Psychophysical laws. In E. Lepone and B. McLaughlin (eds.), *Action and events* (pp. 369–386). Oxford: Blackwell.

King, C.D. (1932). *The psychology of consciousness.* New York: Harcourt Brace.

Kinsbourne, M. (1988). Integrated field theory of consciousness. In A.J. Marcel and Bisiach (eds.), *Consciousness in contemporary science*, Oxford: Clarendon Press.

Klein, D.B. (1984). *The concept of consciousness: A survey.* Lincoln, NE: University of Nebraska Press.

Klein, G.S. (1959). Consciousness in psychoanalytic theory: Some implications for current research in perception. *Journal of the American Psychoanalytic Association, 7, 5–34.*

_____, and Holt, R.R. (1960). Problems and issues in current studies of subliminal activation. In J.G. Peatman and E.L. Hartley (eds.), *Festschrift for Gardner Murphy.* New York: Harper Brothers.

Klemm, O. (1914). *A history of psychology* (trans. E.C. Wilm and R. Pinter). New York: Charles Scribner's Sons.

Knight, M. (1950). *William James.* Harmondsworth: Penguin Books.

Kocher, H.C. (1972). Yoga practice as a variable in neuroticism, anxiety and hostility. *Yoga Mimamsa*, 15 (2), 37–46.

_____. (1976a). Anxiety, general hostility and its direction as a result of yogic practice. *Yoga Mimamsa*, 17 (3 and 4), 73–82.

_____. (1976b). Research note: Effect of yogic practices on immediate memory. *Yoga Mimamsa*, 18 (3 and 4), 57–62.

_____, and Pratap, V. (1971). Neurotic trend and yogic practices. *Yoga Mimamsa*, 14 (1 and 2), 34–40.

_____, and _____. (1972). Anxiety level and yogic practices. *Yoga Mimamsa*, 15 (1), 11–15.

Kogan, I.M. (1966). Is telepathy possible? *Telecommunications and Radio Engineering*, 21 (No.1, Part 2), 75–81.

Kolsawalla, M.B. (1978). An experimental investigation into the effectiveness of yogic variables as a mechanism of change in the value-attitude system. *Journal of Indian Psychology*, 1 (1), 59–68.

Kragh, U., and Smith, G. (1970). *Percept-genetic analysis.* Lund: Gleerups.

Kramer, J.K., and Terry, R.L. (1973). GESP and personality factors: A search for correlates. *Journal of Parapsychology*, 37, 74–75. (Abstract.)

Kreitler, H., and Kreitler, S. (1973). Subliminal perception and extrasensory perception. *Journal of Parapsychology*, 37,163–188.

Kripke, D.F., and Sonnenschein, D. (1978). A biologic rhythm in waking fantasy. In K.S. Pope and J.L. Singer (eds.), *The stream of consciousness: Scientific investigations into the flow of human experience.* New York: Plenum.

Krippner, S., Honorton, C., and Ullman, M. (1972). A second precognitive dream study with Malcolm Bessent. *Journal of the American Society for Psychical Research*, 66, 269–279.

_____, _____, and _____. (1973). A long-distance ESP dream study with "Grateful Dead." *Journal of the American Society for Psychosomatic Dentistry and Medicine*, 20, 9–17.

_____, _____, _____, Masters, R., and Houston, J. (1971). A long distance "sensory bombardment" study of ESP in dreams. *Journal of the American Society for Psychical Research*, 65, 468–475.

Krishna, S.R., and Rao, K.R. (1991). Effect of ESP feedback on subjects' responses to a personality questionnaire. *Journal of Parapsychology*, 55, 147–158.

Krishnamurti, J. (1979). *Meditation*. Ojai, CA: Krishnamurti Foundation.

Krishnan, V. (1985). Near-death experiences: Evidence for survival? *Anabiosis: The Journal of Near-Death Studies*, 5 (1), 21–38.

_____. (1988). OBEs in the blind. [Letter to the editor.] *The Journal of Near Death Studies*, 7, 139.

_____. (1993). The physical basis of out-of-body vision. [Letter to the editor.] *Journal of Near-Death Studies*, 11, 257–260.

Kübler-Ross, E. (1969). *On death and dying*. New York: Macmillan.

Kulkarni, T.R. (1948). *Experimental studies in Asanas and Pranayama*. Unpublished master's dissertation. Calcutta: Calcutta University.

_____. (1972). *Upanishads and Yoga: An empirical approach to their understanding*. Bombay: Bharatiya Vidya Bhavan.

_____. (1978). Psychology: The Indian point of view. *Journal of Indian Psychology*, 1 (1), 22–39.

Kunst-Wilson, W.R., and Zajonc, R.B. (1980). Affective discrimination of stimuli that cannot be recognized. *Science*, 207, 557–558.

Ladd, G. (1909). *Psychology: Descriptive and explanatory*. New York: Scribner's Sons.

Lancaster, B. (1991). *Mind, brain and human potential*. Rockport, MA: Element.

Lantz, N.D., Luke, W.L., and May, E.C. (1994). Target and sender dependencies in anomalous cognition experiments. *Journal of Parapsychology*, 58, 285–302.

Latha, and Kaliappan, K.V. (1992). Efficacy of yoga therapy in the management of headaches. *Journal of Indian Psychology*, 10 (1 & 2), 33–36.

Lawrence, T. (1993). Gathering in the sheep and goats: A meta-analysis of forced-choice sheep-goat ESP studies, 1947–1993. *Proceedings of the Parapsychological Association 36th Annual Convention* (pp. 75–86).

Lazar, S.W., Bush, G., Fricchione, G., Gollub, R.L., Khalsa, G., and Benson, H. (1999). Functional brain mapping of the relaxation response using 3T fMRI. *Society for Neuroscience Abstracts*, 11, 1581–1585.

Lazar, S.W., Farwell, L., and Farrow, J.T. (1977). Effects of transcendental meditation program on anxiety, drug abuse, cigarette smoking and alcohol consumption. In D.W. Orme-Johnson and J.T. Farrow (eds). *Scientific research on the transcendental meditation program: Collected papers*. Second edition. Weggis, Switzerland: Maharshi European Research University Press.

Lazarus, R.S., and McCleary, R.A. (1951). Autonomic discrimination without awareness: A study of subception. *Psychological Review*, 58, 113–122.

LeDoux, J.E. (1985). Brain, mind and language. In D.A. Oakley (ed.), *Mind and brain* (pp. 197–216). New York: Methuen.

Leggett, A.J. (1987). Reflection on the quantum measurement paradox. In B.J. Hiley, and D.F. Peat (eds.), *Quantum implications: Essays in honour of David Bohm* (pp. 85–104). London: Routledge and Kegan Paul.

Lehmann, D., Beeler, G., and Fender, D. (1967). EEG responses during the observation of stablized and normal retinal images. *Electroencephalography and Clinical Neurophysiology*, 1967, 22, 136–142.

LeShan, L. (1976). *Alternate realities*. New York: M. Evans & Co.

Levinson, B.W. (1965). States of awareness under general anaesthesia. *British Journal of Anaesthesia*, 37, 544–546.

Libet, B. (1993). The neural time factor in consciousness and unconscious events. In Ciba foundation symposium. *Experimental and theoretical studies of consciousness*. New York: John Wiley and Sons.

_____. (1994). A testable field theory of mind-brain interaction. *Journal of Consciousness Studies*, 1, 119–126.

_____, Alberts, W.W., Wright, E.W., and Feinstein, B. (1967). Responses of human somatosensory cortex to stimuli below threshold for conscious sensation. *Science*, 158, 1597–1600.

Linden, W. (1971). Practicing meditation by school children and their levels of field dependence-independence, test anxiety, and reading achievement. *Journal of Consulting and Clinical Psychology*, 41, 139–143.

Locke, John (1975). *An essay concerning human understanding*, edited by P.H. Nidditch. Oxford: Oxford University Press. (First published in 1689.)

Lockwood, M. (1989). *Mind, brain, and the quantum*. Oxford: Basil Blackwell.

Lovitts, B. (1981). The sheep-goat effect turned upside down. *Journal of Parapsychology*, 45, 293–310.

Luria, A.R. (1978). The human brain and conscious activity. In G.E. Schwartz, and D. Shapiro (eds.), *Consciousness and self-regulation: Advances in research and theory* (Vol. 2). New York: Plenum.

Lycan, W.G. (1987). *Consciousness*. Cambridge, MA: MIT Press.

_____. (1996). *Consciousness and experience*. Cambridge, MA: MIT Press.

MacGregor, G. (1989). *Dictionary of religion and philosophy*. New York: Paragon House.

Mackay, D.G. (1973). Aspects of a theory of comprehension, memory, and attention. *Quarterly Journal of Experimental Psychology*, 25, 22–40.

Mackenzie, B. (1977). Three stages in the history of parapsychology. Paper presented at the Quadrennial Congress on History of Science, Edinburgh, Scotland.

Mahesh Yogi (1963a). *The science of being and the art of living*. London: George Allen & Unwin.

_____ (1963b). *Transcendental meditation*. New York: New American Library.

Malhotra, J.C. (1963). Yoga and psychiatry: A review. *Journal of Neuropsychiatry*, 4, 375–385.

Mandler, G. (1975). *Mind and emotion*. New York: Wiley.

Mann, R.D. (1991). *The light of consciousness: Explorations in transpersonal psychology*. Delhi: Sri Satguru Publications (first published in 1984 by State University of New York).

Marcel, A.J. (1983). Conscious and unconscious perception: Experiments on visual masking and word recognition. *Cognitive Psychology*, 15, 197–237.

_____. (1986). Consciousness and processing: Choosing and testing a null hypothesis. *Behavioral and Brain Sciences*, 9, 40–41.

_____, and Bisiach, E. (eds.) (1988). *Consciousness in contemporary science*. Oxford: Oxford University Press.

Marcel, Y. (1985). *Cognitive psychology: An essay in cognitive science*. New York: Erlbaum.

Margenau, I.T. (1984). *The miracle of existence*. Woodbridge, CT: Ox Bow Press.

Maritain, J. (1953). *Creative intuition in art and poetry*. Princeton, NJ: Princeton University Press.

Marks, D.F. (1986). Remote viewing revisited. In K. Frazier (ed.), *Science confronts the paranormal* (pp. 110–121). Buffalo, NY: Prometheus Books.

_____, and Kammann, R. (1978). Information transmission in remote viewing experiments. *Nature*, 274, 680–681.

_____, and _____. (1980). *The psychology of the psychic*. Buffalo, NY: Prometheus Books.

_____, and Scott, C. (1986). Remote viewing exposed. *Nature*, 319, 444.

Marshall, J.C., and Halligan, P.W. (1988). Blindsight and insight in visuospatial neglect. *Nature*, 336, 766–767.

Marzi, C.A., Tassinari, C., Aglioti, S., and Lutzemberger, L. (1986). Spatial summation across the vertical meridian in hemianopics: A test of blindsight. *Neuropsychologia*, 24, 749–758.

Maslow, A.H. (1973). *Dominance, self-esteem, self-actualization: Germinal papers of A.H. Maslow* (edited by Richard J. Lowry). Monerey, CA: Brooks/Cole Publishing Co.

Mason, L.I., Alexander, C.N., Travis, F.T., March, G., Orme-Johnson, D.W., Gackenbacki, J.,

Mason, D.C., Rainforth, M., and Walton, K.G. (1997). Electrophysiological correlates of higher states of consciousness during sleep in long-term practitioners of transcendental meditation program. *Sleep*, 2000(2), 102–110.

Matas, F., and Pantas, L. (1971). A PK experiment comparing meditating versus non-meditating subjects. *Proceedings of the Parapsychological Association*, 7, 12–13.

Matlock, J.G. (1990). Past life memory case studies. In S. Krippner (ed.), *Advances in Parapsychological Research*, Vol. 6 (pp. 184–267). Jefferson, NC: McFarland.

Mauskopf, S.H., and McVaugh, M.R. (1980). *The elusive science: Origins of experimental psychical research*. Baltimore: Johns Hopkins University Press.

May, E.C. (1998). Response to "Experiment one of the SAIC remote viewing program: A critical reevaluation." *Journal of Parapsychology*, 62, 309–318.

McClenon, J. (1982). A survey of elite scientists: Their attitudes towards ESP and parapsychology. *Journal of Parapsychology*, 46, 127–152.

McConnell, R.A., Snowden, R.J., and Powell, K.F. (1955). Wishing with dice. *Journal of Experimental Psychology*, 50, 269–275.

McGinn, C. (1991). *The problem of consciousness*. Oxford: Blackwell.

McMahan, E. (1946). Success in ESP as related to form of response drawings. II. GESP experiments. *Journal of Parapsychology*, 10, 169–180.

McVaugh, M.R., and Mauskopf, S.H. (1976). J.B. Rhine's extra-sensory perception and its background in psychical research. *Isis*, 67, 161–189.

Mead, G.H. (1934). *Mind, self and society*, Chicago: University of Chicago Press.

Meehl, P. (1966). The complete autocerebroscopist: A thought experiment on Professor Feigl's mind/body identity thesis. In *Mind, matter, and method* (ed. P.K. Feyerabend and G. Maxwell). Minneapolis: University of Minnesota Press.

Merikle, P.M., and Reingold, E.M. (1990). Recognition and lexical decision without detection: Unconscious perception. *Journal of Experimental Psychology, Human perception and performance*, 16, 574–583.

Merrell-Wolff, F. (1973). *The philosophy of consciousness without an object: Reflections on the nature of transcendental consciousness*. New York: Julian Press.

Metzinger, T. (ed.) (1995). *Conscious experience*. Paderborn: Ferdinand Schoningh.

Miller, G.A. (1987). *Psychology: The science of mental life*. New York: Penguine.

Miller, J.G. (1939). Discrimination without awareness. *American Journal of Psychology*. 52, 562–578.

_____. (1940). The role of motivation in learning without awareness. *American Journal of Psychology*, 53, 229–239.

Miller, J.J., Fletcher, K., and Linn, J. (1995). Three year follow-up and clinical implications of a mindfulness meditation-based stress reduction intervention in the treatment of anxiety disorders. *General Hospital Psychiatry*, 17, 192–200.

Miller, N.E., Barber, T.X., Dicara, L.V., Kamiya, J., Shapiro, D., and Stoyva, J. (eds.). (1974). *Biofeedback and self-control 1973: An Aldine annual on the regulation of bodily processes and consciousness*. Chicago: Aldine.

Mills, G.K., and Campbell, K. (1974). A critique of Gellhorn and Kiely's mystical states of consciousness: Neurophysiological and clinical aspects. *Journal of Nervous and Mental Disease*, 159, 191–195.

Milton, J., and Wiseman, R. (1999). Does psi exist? Lack of replication of an anomalous process of information transfer. *Psychological Bulletin*, 125, 387–391.

Mohanty, J.N. (1972). *The concept of intentionality*. St. Louis: W.H. Green.

_____. (1993). *Essays on Indian philosophy: Traditional and modern*. Edited by P. Bilimoria. Delhi: Oxford University Press.

Monro, R., Ghosh, A.K., and Kalish, D. (1989). *Yoga research bibliography*. Cambridge, UK: Yoga Biomedical Trust.

Monroe, R.A. (1971). *Journeys out of the body*. New York: Doubleday.

Moody, R.A. (1975). *Life after life*. Covington, GA: Mocking Bird Books.

Moore, G.E. (1922). *Philosophical studies*. London: Harcourt, Brace.

Moray, N. (1959). Attention in dichotic listening: Affective cues and the influence of instructions. *Quarterly Journal of Experimental Psychology*, 9, 56–60.

_____. (1969). *Attention: Selective processes in vision and hearing*. London: Hutchinson.

Morris, R.L., Roll, W.G., Klein, J., and Wheeler, G. (1972). EEG patterns and ESP results in forced-choice experiments with Lalsingh Harribance. *Journal of the American Society for Psychical Research*, 66, 253–268.

Moss, S., and Butler, D.C. (1978). The scientific credibility of ESP. *Perceptual and motor skills*, 46, 1063–1079.

Murphy, G., and Ballou, R.O. (eds.) (1960). *William James on psychical research*. New York: Viking Press.

Murphy, G., and Murphy, L.B. (1968). *Asian Psychology*. New York: Basic Books.

Murphy, M., and Donovan, S. (1997). *The physical and psychological effects of meditation: A review of contemporary research with a comprehensive bibliography, 1931–1996*. Sausolito, CA: Institute of Noetic Sciences.

Murti, T.V.R. (1983). *Studies in Indian Thought*. (Collected papers of T.R.V. Murti.) Harold G. Coward (ed.). Columbia, MO: South Asia Books.

Myers, F.W.H. (1915). *Human personality and its survival of death* (2 vols.). New York: Longmans, Green & Co. (Original work published 1903.)

Nagendra, H.R., and Nagaratna, R. (1986). An integrated approach of yoga therapy for bronchial asthma: A 3–54 month perspective study. *Journal of Asthma*, 23, 123–137.

Nagaratna, R., and Nagendra, H.R. (1985). Yoga for bronchial asthma: A controlled study. *British Medical Journal*, 291, 1077–1079.

Nagel, T. (1974). What is it like to be a bat? *Philosophical Review*, 83, 435–450.

_____. (1986). *The view from no where*. New York: Oxford University Press.

Nandy, A. (1974). The non-paradigmatic crisis in psychology: Reflections on a recipient culture. *Indian Journal of Psychology*, 49, 1–20.

Naranjo, C., and Ornstein, R.E. (1971). *On the psychology of meditation*. New York: Viking Press.

Natsoulas, T. (1978). Consciousness. *American Psychologist*, 33, 906–914.

_____. (1983). Addendum to "consciousness." *American Psychologist*, 38, 121–122.

_____. (1983). Concept of consciousness. *Journal of Mind and Behavior*, 4 (1), 13–59.

Neisser, U. (1967). *Cognitive psychology*. New York: Appleton-Century-Crofts.

_____. (1976). *Cognition and reality*. San Francisco, CA: Freeman & Co.

Nelkin, N. (1996). *Consciousness and the origins of thought*. Oxford: Oxford University Press.

Nelson, R.D., and Radin, D.I. (1989). Statistically robust anomalous effects: Replication in random event generator experiments. In L.A. Henkel and R.E. Berger (eds.), *Research in Parapsychology 1988*. Metuchen, NJ: Scarecrow Press.

_____, Dunne, B.J., and Jahn, R.G. (1984). *An REG experiment with large data base capability. 3: Operator related anomalies*. (Technical Note PEAR 83002.) School of Engineering/ Applied Science, Princeton University.

Nelson, T. (1978). Detecting small amounts of information in memory: Savings for nonrecognized items. *Journal of Experimental Psychology: Human learning & Memory*, 4, 453–468.

Newman, J. (1997 a). Putting the puzzle together: Part I. *Journal of Consciousness Studies*, 4, 47–66.

_____. (1997 b). Putting the puzzle together: Part II. Towards a general theory of the neural correlates of consciousness. *Journal of Consciousness Studies*, 100–121.

Nielsen, W. (1956). Mental states associated with

success in precognition. *Journal of Parapsychology*, 20, 96–109.

Novak, P. Lepicovaka, V., Dostalek, C., and Hajek, P. (1990). Influence of rhythmic nasal air insufflation upon EEG mapping: Modelling of *Kapalabhati. Yoga Mimamsa*, 29 (2), 13–26.

Nunn, C.M.H., Clarke, C.J.S., and Blott, B.H. (1994). Collapse of a quantum field may affect brain function. *Journal of Consciousness Studies*, 1, 127–139.

Oak, J.P., and Bhole, M.V. (1982). ASR and NSR studies in asthmatics undergoing yogic treatment. *Yoga Mimamsa*, 20 (4), 17–24.

O'Keefe, J. (1985). Is consciousness the gateway to the hippocampal cognitive map? A speculative essay on the neural basis of the mind. In D.A. Oakley (ed.), *Mind and brain* (pp. 59–98). New York: Methuen.

Oliver, L. (1987). *Meditation and the creative imperative*. Dryad Press.

Orme-Johnson, D.W. (1977). EEG coherence during transcendental consciousness. *Electroencephalography and Clinical Neurophysiology*, 43 (4), 581.

_____. (1987). Transcendental meditation and reduced health care utilization. *Psychosomatic Medicine*, 49, 493–507.

_____, and Farrow, J.T. (eds.) (1977). *Scientific research on the transcendental meditation program*. Vol. 1, 2nd edition. Los Angeles: Maharishi European Research University Press.

Ornstein, R.E. (1977). *The psychology of consciousness* (2nd ed.). New York: Harcourt Brace Jovanovich. (Original work published 1972.)

_____ (ed.) (1973). *The nature of consciousness: A book of readings*. San Francisco: W.H. Freeman.

Osis, K. (1961). *Deathbed observations by physicians and nurses*. New York: Parapsychology Foundation.

_____. (1978). Out-of-the-body research at the American Society for Psychical Research. In D.S. Rogo (ed.), *Mind beyond body* (pp. 162–169). New York: Penguin Books.

_____, and Bokert, E. (1971). ESP and changed states of consciousness induced by meditation. *Journal of the American Society for Psychical Research*, 65, 17–65.

_____, and Haraldsson, E. (1977). *At the hour of death*. New York: Avon Books.

Otani, S. (1965). Some relations of ESP scores to change in skin resistance. *In Parapsychology: From Duke to FRNM*. Durham, NC: Parapsychology Press.

Pagano, R.R. (1981). Recent research in the physiology of meditation. In G. Adam, I. Meszaros and E. Banyai (eds.). *Advances in physiological sciences*, Vol. 17, Budapest: Pergamon.

_____, and Frumpkin, I.R. (1977). Effects of tran-

scendental meditation on right hemispheric functioning. *Biofeedback and Self Regulation*, 2, 407–415.

_____, Rose, R.M., Stivers, R.M., and Warrenburg, S. (1976). Sleep during transcendental meditation. *Science*, 191, 308–309.

_____, and Warrenburg, S. (1983). Meditation in search of a unique effect. In R.J. Davidson et al. (eds.), *Consciousness and self-regulation*. New York: Plenum Press.

Palmer, J. (1971). Scoring in ESP tests as a function of belief in ESP. Part I: The sheep-goal effect. *Journal of the American Society for Psychical Research*, 65, 373–408.

_____. (1972). Scoring in ESP tests as a function of belief in ESP. Part II. The Sheep-goat effect. *Journal of the American Society for Psychical Research*, 66, 1–26.

_____. (1978). Extrasensory perception: Research findings. In S. Krippner (ed.), *Advances in parapsychological research II: Extrasensory perception*. New York: Plenum Press.

_____, and Carpenter, J.C. (1998). Comments on the extroversion-ESP meta-analysis by Honorton, Ferrari and Bem. *Journal of Parapsychology*, 62, 277–282.

Pandey, J. (ed.) (1988). *Psychology in India: State of the art*, 3 vols. New Delhi: Sage Publications.

Paranjpe, A.C. (1981). Indian psychology in the cross-cultural setting. *Journal of Indian Psychology*, 3 (2), 10–15.

_____. (1984). *Theoretical Psychology: The meeting of East and West*. New York: Plenum Press.

_____. (1988). A personality theory according to Vedanta. In A.C. Paranjpe, D.Y.F. Ho and R.W. Rieber (eds.), *Asian contributions to psychology* (pp. 215–231). New York: Praeger.

_____, and Hanson, R.K. (1988). On dealing with the stream of consciousness: A comparison of Husserl and Yoga, in *Asian contributions to psychology*, ed. A.C. Paranjpe, D.Y.F. Ho, and R.W. Rieber. New York: Praeger.

Pasricha, S.K. (1990). *Claims of reincarnation: An empirical study of cases in India*. New Delhi: Harman Publishing House.

Patel, C. (1973). Yoga and biofeedback in the management of hypertension. *Lancet*, 2, 1053–1055.

Patel, C.H. (1975). Twelve-month follow up of yoga and biofeedback in the management of hypertension. *Lancet*, 1, 62–65.

_____. (1977). Biofeedback-aided relaxation and meditation in the management of hypertension. *Biofeedback and Self-Regulation*, 2, 1–41.

_____. (1993). Yoga-based therapy. In P.M. Lehrer and R.L. Woolfolk (eds.). *Principles and practice of stress management*. 2nd edition (pp. 89–138). New York: Guilford Press.

Pekala, R.J., Kumar, V.K., and Marcano, G.

(1995). Anomalous/paranormal experiences, hypnotic susceptibility, and dissociation. *Journal of the American Society for Psychical Research*, 89, 313–332.

Pelletier, K.R. (1984). Influence of transcendental meditation upon autokinetic perception. In D.H. Shapiro and R.N. Walsh (eds.), *Meditation: Classic and contemporary perspectives* (pp. 223–226). New York: Aldine.

Penfield, W. (1958). *The excitable cortex in conscious man.* Liverpool: Liverpool University Press.

_____. (1975). *The mystery of the mind.* Princeton, NJ: Princeton University Press.

Penrose, R. (1989). *The emperor's new mind: Concerning computers, minds, and the laws of physics.* Oxford: Oxford University Press.

_____. (1994a). *Shadows of the mind. A search for the missing science of consciousness.* New York: Oxford University Press.

_____. (1994b). "Shadows of the mind," a preview of his new book. *Journal of Consciousness Studies,* 1, 17–24.

_____. (1994c). Mechanisms, microtubules and the mind. *Journal of Consciousness Studies,* 1, 241–249.

Peo (1978). *Medical and psychological scientific research on yoga and meditation.* Copenhagen: Bindu.

Perry, R.B. (1904). Conceptions and misconceptions of consciousness. *Psychological Review*, 11, 282–296.

Persinger, M.A. (1985). Subjective telepathic experiences, geomagnetic activity and the ELF hypothesis: Part II. Stimulus features and neural detection. *Psi Research*, 4(2), 4–23.

_____. (1989). Psi phenomena and temporal lobe activity: The geomagnetic factor. In L.A. Henkel and R.E. Berger (eds.), *Research in parapsychology 1988* (pp. 121–156). Metuchen, NJ: Scarecrow Press.

_____, and Krippner, S. (1989). Dream ESP experiments and geomagnetic activity. *Journal of the American Society for Psychical Research*, 83, 101–116.

Peters, R.S. (ed.). (1962). *Brett's history of psychology.* New York: Macmillan Co.

Picton, T.W., and Hillyard, S.A. (1974). Human auditory evoked potentials, II: Effects of attention. *Electroencephalography and Clinical Neurophysiology*, 36, 191–200.

Pierce, C.S., and Jastrow, J. (1884). On small differences in sensation. *Memoirs of the National Academy of Science*, 3, 75–83.

Pillsbury, W.B. (1908). *Attention.* New York: Macmillan.

Podmore, F. (1894). *Apparitions and thought-transference.* London: Scott.

Poetzl, O. (1917). The relationship between experimentally induced dream images and indirect vision. *Psychological Issues*, 2, 41–120.

Polanyi, M. (1958). *Personal knowledge.* Chicago: University of Chicago Press.

Popper, K.R., and Eccles, J.C. (1977). *The self and its brain: An argument for interactionism.* Berlin: Springer-Verlag.

Posner, M. (1975). Psychobiology of attention. In M. Gazzaniga and C. Blakemore (eds.), *Handbook of psychobiology.* New York: Academic Press.

Posner, M.J., and Snyder, C.R.R. (1975). Facilitation and inhibition in the processing of signals. In P.M.A. Rabbit and S. Dornick (eds.), *Attention and performance* V. New York: Academic Press.

Pratap, V. (1971). Scientific studies on yoga: A review. *Yoga Mimamsa*, 13 (4), 1–18.

Pratt, J.G., Rhine, J.B., Smith, B.M., and Stuart, C.E. (1940). *Extra-sensory perception after sixty years.* New York: Henry Holt (reprinted, Boston: Bruce Humphries, 1966).

Pribram, K.H. (1971). *Languages of the brain: Experimental paradoxes and principles in neuropsychology.* Englewood Cliffs, NJ: Prentice-Hall.

_____. (1976a). Problems concerning the structure of consciousness. In G.G. Globus, G. Maxwell, and I. Savodnik (eds.), *Consciousness and the brain* (pp. 297–313). New York: Plenum Press.

_____. (1976b). Self-consciousness and intentionality: A model based on an experimental analysis of the brain mechanisms involved in the Jamesian theory of motivation and evolution. In G.E. Schwartz and D. Shapiro (eds.), *Consciousness and self-regulation* (Vol.1) (pp. 51–100). New York: Plenum Press.

_____. (1978). Consciousness: A scientific study. *Journal of Indian Psychology*, 1, 95–118.

_____. (1984). Mind, brain and consciousness, the organization and conduct. In M. Cazenare (ed.), *Science and consciousness: Two views of the universe* (pp. 327–341). New York: Pergamon Press.

Price, H.H. (1940). Some philosophical questions about telepathy and clairvoyance. *Philosophy*, 15, 363–374.

_____. (1948). Psychical research and human personality. *Hibbert Journal*, 47, 105–113.

Puligandla, R. (1970). Phenomenological reduction and yogic meditation. *Philosophy East and West*, 20, pp. 19–33.

Puryear, H., and Cayce, C. (1976). Anxiety reduction associated with meditation: Home study. *Perceptual & Motor Skills*, 43, 527–531.

Puthoff, H.E., and Targ, R. (1976). A perceptual channel for information transfer over kilometer distances: Historical perspective and recent research. *Proceedings of the IEEE*, 64(3), 329–354.

Putnam, F.W. (1989). *Diagnosis and treatment of multiple personality disorders.* New York: Guilford.

Putnam, H. (1991). The nature of mental states. In D.M. Resenthal (ed.), *The nature of mind* (pp. 197–203). New York: Oxford University Press.

Quine, W.V.O. (1960). *Word and object:* Cambridge, MA: Harvard University Press.

Radhakrishnan, S. (1989). *Indian Philosophy* (centenary edition), 2 Vols. Delhi: Oxford University Press.

Radin, D.I., May, E.C., and Thomas, M.J. (1985). Psi experiments with random number generators: Meta-analysis, Part-I. In D.H. Weiner and D.I Radin (eds.), *Research in parapsychology 1985* (pp. 14–17), Methuchen, NJ: Scarecrow Press.

Radin, D.I., and Nelson, R.D. (1989). Evidence for consciousness-related anomalies in random physical systems. *Foundations of physics,* 19, 1499–1514.

Raja, C.K. (1963). *The Samkhya karika of Isvarakrishna: A Philsopher's exposition.* Hoshiyapur, India: V.V. Research Institute.

Raju, P.T. (1992). *Introduction to comarative philosophy.* Delhi: Motilal Banarasidass.

Ramachandran, V.S. (1980). Twins, split brains and personality identity. In B.D. Josephson and V.S. Ramachandran (eds.), *Consciousness and the physical world* (pp. 139–163). New York: Pergaman Press.

Ramana Maharshi (1968). *The Collected Works.* Tiruvanamalai: Sri Ramanasram.

Rani, N.J., and Rao, P.V.K. (1990). Self-ideal disparity and yoga training. *Journal of Indian Psychology,* 10 (172), 35–40.

Rao, K.R. (1962). The preferential effect in ESP. *Journal of Parapsychology,* 26, 252–259.

_____. (1963a). Studies in the preferential effect I: Target preference with types of targets unknown. *Journal of Parapsychology,* 27, 23–32.

_____. (1963b). Studies in the preferential effect II: A language ESP test involving precognition and "intervention." *Journal of Parapsychology,* 27, 147–160.

_____. (1963c). Studies in the preferential effect III: The reversal effect in psi preference. *Journal of Parapsychology,* 27, 242–251.

_____. (1964). The differential response in three new situations. *Journal of Parapsychology,* 28, 82–92.

_____. (1965a). ESP and the Manifest Anxiety Scale. *Journal of Parapsychology,* 29, 12–18.

_____. (1965b). The bidirectionality of psi. *Journal of Parapsychology,* 29, 230–250.

_____. (1965c). ESP and the manifest anxiety scale. *Journal of Parapsychology,* 29, 12–18.

_____. (1966). *Experimental parapsychology: A Review and interpretation.* Springfield, IL: Charles C Thomas.

_____. (1977). On the nature of psi: An examina-tion of some attempts to explain ESP and PK. *Journal of Parapsychology,* 41, 294–351.

_____. (1978). Theories of psi. In S. Krippner (ed.), *Advances of parapsychological research, Vol.2: Extrasensory perception* (pp. 245–295). New York: Plenum Press.

_____. (1978). Psi: Its place in nature. *Journal of Parapsychology,* 42, 276–303.

_____. (1979). "The scientific credibility of ESP." *Perceptual and motor skills,* 49, 415–429.

_____. (1981). Correspondence. *Journal of the Society for Psychical Research,* 51, 191–194.

_____. (1982). J.B. Rhine and his critics. In K.R. Rao (ed.), *J.B. Rhine: On the frontiers of science.* Jefferson, NC: McFarland & Co.

_____. (1988). Psychology of transcendence: A study in early Buddhistic psychology, in *Asian Contributions to Psychology,* A.C. Paranjpe, D.Y.F. Ho, and R.W. Rieber (eds.). New York: Praeger.

_____. (1989). Meditation: Secular and sacred: Review and assessment of some recent research. *Journal of the Indian Academy of Applied Psychology,* 15, 51–74.

_____. (1991a). Consciousness research and psi. *Journal of Parapsychology,* 55, 1–43.

_____. (ed.) (1991b). *Cultivating Consciousness: Enhancing human potential wellness, and healing.* Westport, CT: Praeger.

_____. (1992). On the other hand: The two sides of the psi debate. *Contemporary Psychology,* 37, 1106–1108.

_____. (1998). Two faces of consciousness: A look at eastern and western perspectives. *Journal of Consciousness Studies,* 5, 309–327.

_____, Dukhan, H., and Rao, P.V.K. (1978). Yogic meditation and psi scoring in forced-choice and free-response tests. *Journal of Indian Psychology,* 1, 160–175.

_____, and Feola, J. (1979). Electrical activity of the brain and ESP: An exploratory study of alpha rhythm and ESP scoring. *Journal of Indian Psychology,* 1979, 2, 118–133.

_____, Morrison, M., and Davis, J.W. (1977). Paired-associates recall and ESP: A study of memory and psi-missing. *Journal of Parapsychology,* 41, 165–189.

_____, _____, _____, and Freeman, J. (1977). The role of association in memory-recall and ESP. *Journal of Parapsychology,* 41, 190–197.

_____, and Palmer, J. (1987). The anomaly called Psi: Recent research and criticism. *Behavioral and Brain Sciences,* 10, 539–555.

_____, and Puri, I. (1978). Subsensory perception (SSP), extrasensory perception (ESP) and transcendental meditation, *Journal of Indian Psychology,* 1, 69–74.

Rao, P.V.K., and Rao, K.R. (1982). Two studies of

ESP and subliminal perception. *Journal of Parapsychology*, 46, 185–207.

Rao, S.K.R. (1962). *Development of psychological thought in India*. Mysore: Kavyalaya Publishers.

_____. (1979). *Jivanmukti in Advaita*. Bangalore: IBH Prakashana.

Reid, T. (1941). *Essay on the intellectual powers of man* (ed. A.D.Woozley). London: Macmillan. (Original work published in 1785.)

Rhine, J.B. (1936). Some selected experiments in extrasensory perception. *Journal of Abnormal and Social Psychology*, 31, 216–228.

_____. (1938). Experiments bearing on the precognition hypothesis. *Journal of Parapsychology*, 2, 38–54.

_____. (1950). The shifting scene in parapsychology. *Journal of Parapsychology*, 14, 161–167.

_____. (1952). The problem of psi-missing. *Journal of Parapsychology*, 16, 90–129.

_____. (1969). Psi-missing re-examined. *Journal of Parapsychology*, 33, 1–38.

_____. (1973/1934). *Extra-sensory perception*. Brookline Village, Mass.: Branden Press. (Originally published in 1934.)

_____. (1977). Extra-sensory perception. In B.B. Wolman (ed.), *Handbook of Parapsychology*. New York: Van Nostrand Reinhold.

_____, and Pratt, J.G. (1954). A review of the Pearce-Pratt distance series of ESP tests. *Journal of Parapsychology*, 18, 165–177.

_____, and _____. (1961). A reply to the Hansel critique of the Pearce-Pratt series. *Journal of Parapsychology*, 25, 92–98.

Rhine, L.E. (1961). *Hidden channels of the mind*. New York: Willam Sloane Associates.

_____. (1962a). Psychological processing in ESP experiences I. Waking experiences. *Journal of Parapsychology*, 26, 88–111.

_____. (1962b). Psychological processing in ESP experiences. Part II. Dreams. *Journal of Parapsychology*, 26, 172–199.

_____. (1965). Toward understanding psi-missing. *Journal of Parapsychology*, 29, 259–274.

_____. (1967). *ESP in life and lab: Tracing hidden channels*. New York: Macmillan.

Ribot, T. (1898). *The psychology of attention* (4th ed.). Chicago: Open Court Publishers.

Ring, K. (1980). *Life at death: A scientific investigation of near-death experience*. New York: McCann & Geoghegan.

Rogers, L.J. (1976). *Human EEG response to certain rhythmic patterned auditory stimuli, with possible relations to EEG lateral asymmetry measures and EEG correlates of chanting*. Unpublished Ph.D. dissertation. Los Angeles, CA: University of California.

Rogo, D.S. (1978). *Mind beyond the body: The mystery of ESP projection*: New York: Penguin Books.

Roll, W.G. (1966). ESP and memory. *International Journal of Neuropsychiatry*, 2, 505–521.

_____. (1976). *The poltergeist*. Metuchen, NJ: Scarecrow Press.

_____. (1987). Memory and the long body. *Theta*, 15, 10–29.

Romijin, H. (2002). Are virtual photons the elementary carriers of consciousness? *Journal of Consciousness Studies*, 9, 61–81.

Rosenthal, R. (1966). *Experimenter effects in behavioral research*. New York: Appleton- Century-Crofts.

_____, and Rubin, D.B. (1978). Interpersonal expectancy effects: The first 345 studies. *The Behavioral and Brain Sciences*, 3, 377–386.

Ross, C.A. (1989). *Multiple personality disorder: Diagnosis, clinical features and treatment*. New York: Wiley.

Rozemond, M. (1998). *Descartes's dualism*. Cambridge, MA: Harvard University Press.

Russell, B. (1981). *History of western philosophy* (trans.). New York: Chadlidze Publications.

Ryle, G. (1949). *The concept of mind*. New York: Harper Collins.

Ryzl, M., and Ryzlova, J. (1962). A case of high-scoring ESP performance in the hypnotic state. *Journal of Parapsychology*, 26, 153–171.

Sailaja, P., and Rao, K.R. (1973). *Experimental studies of the differential effect in life setting*. Parapsychological Monographs (No.13). New York: Parapsychology Foundation.

Samkara (1980). *Vedanta-Sutras with Samkara's commentary* (trs. Thibaut). Oxford: Clarendon Press.

Sanders, M.S. (1962). A comparison of verbal and written responses in a precognition experiment. *Journal of Parapsychology*, 26, 23–24.

Sargent, C.L. (1981). Extraversion and performance in "extra-sensory perception" tasks. *Personality and Individual Differences*, 2, 137–143.

Sartre, J.P. (1948). *The psychology of imagination* (trans. Bernard Frechtman). New York: Philosophical Library.

_____. (1956). *Being and nothingness* (trans. Hazel E. Barnes). New York: Philosophical Library.

_____. (1957). *The transcendence of the ego, an existentialist theory of consciousness* (trans. F. Williams and R. Kirkpatrick). New York: Noonday.

Sastri, S.S. (ed. and trans.) (1935). *The Samkhyakarika of Isvara Krishna*. Madras: University of Madras.

Savage, C.W. (1976). An old ghost in a new body. In G.G. Globus, G. Maxwell and I. Savodnik (eds.), *Consciousness and the brain* (pp. 125–153). New York: Plenum Press.

Schacter, D.L. (1985). Priming of old and new

knowledge in amnesic patients and normal subjects. *Annals of New York Academy of Sciences*, 444, 41–53.

_____. (1989). On the relation between memory and consciousness: Dissociable interaction and conscious experience. In H.L. Roediger, and F.I.M. Craik (eds.), *Varieties of memory and consciousness: Essays in honor of Endel Tulving*. Hillside, NJ: Erlbaum.

Schechter, E.I. (1984). Hypnotic induction vs. control conditions. Illustrating an approach to the evaluation of replicability in parapsychological data. *Journal of the American Society for Psychical Research*, 78, 1–27.

Schlitz, M., and Gruber, E. (1980). Transcontinental remote viewing. *Journal of Parapsychology*, 44, 305–317.

Schmeidler, G.R. (1970). High ESP scores after a swami's brief instruction in meditation and breathing. *Journal of the Society for Psychical Research*, 64, 100–103.

_____. (1971). Respice, adspice, prospice. *Proceedings of the Parapsychological Association*, 8, 117–143.

_____, and McConnell, R.A. (1958). *ESP and personality patterns*. New Haven, CT: Yale University Press.

_____, and Murphy, R. (1991). Perceptual processing of psi: A model. *Journal of the American Society for Psychical Research*, 85, 217–236.

Schmidt, H. (1969a). Precognition of a quantum process. *Journal of Parapsychology*, 33, 99–108.

_____. (1969b). Clairvoyance tests with a machine. *Journal of Parapsychology*, 33, 300–306.

_____. (1971). Mental influence on random events. *New Scientist and Science Journal*, 24, 757–758.

_____. (1973). PK tests with a high-speed random number generator. *Journal of Parapsychology*, 37, 105–118.

_____, and Pantas, L. (1972). Psi tests with internally different machines. *Journal of Parapsychology*, 36, 222, 232.

Schneider, R.H., Staggers, F., Alexander, C.N., Sheppard, W., Rainforth, M., Kondwani, K., Smith, S., and King, C.G. (1996). A randomized controlled trial of stress reduction for hypertension in older African Americans. *Hypertension*, 26, 820–827.

Schultz, J.H., and Luth, W. (1959). *Autogenic training*. New York: Grune and Stratton.

Schuman, M. (1980). The psychophysiological model of meditation and altered states of consciousness: A critical review. In J.M. Davidson and R.J. Davidson (eds.), *The psychobiology of consciousness* (pp. 333–378). New York: Lenum Press.

Schwartz, G.E., Davidson, R.J., and Goleman, D.J.

(1978). Patterning of cognitive and somatic processes in the self-regulation of anxiety: Effects of meditation versus exercise. *Psychosomatic Medicine*, 40, 321–328.

Scott, A. (1995). *Stairway to the mind: The controversial new science of consciousness*. New York: Springer.

Scriven, M. (1962). The frontiers of psychology: Psychoanalysis and parapsychology. In R.G. Colodny (ed.), *Frontiers of science and philosophy* (pp. 9–129). Pittsburgh, PA: University of Pittsburgh Press.

Searle, J.R. (1983). *Intentionality: An essay in the philosophy of mind*. New York: Cambridge University Press.

_____. (1992). *The rediscovery of the mind*. Cambridge, MA: MIT Press.

_____. (2000). Consciousness, free action and the brain. *Journal of Consciousness Studies*, 7 (10), 3–22.

Sellars, W. (1963). *Science, perception, and reality*. London: Routledge & Kegan Paul.

Selvamurty, W. Nayar, H.S. Joseph, N.T., and Joseph, S. (1983). Physiological effects of yogic practice. *Nimhans Journal*, 1 (1), 71–80.

Settiwar, R.M., Singh, H.C., Singh, R.K., and Udupa, K.N. (1983). Metabolites of biogenic amines in management of essential hypertension by yoga. *Yoga Mimamsa*, 22 (3 and 4), 87–93.

Shallice, T. (1988a). *From neuropsychology to mental structure*. Cambridge: Cambridge University Press.

_____. (1988b). Information-processing models of consciousness: Possibilities and problems. In A.J. Marcel and E. Bisiach (eds.), *Consciousness in contemporary science*. Oxford: Oxford University Press.

Shalom, A. (1985). *The body/mind conceptual framework and the problem of personal identity*. Atlantic Highlands, NJ: Humanities Press International.

Shapiro, D.H., and Giber, D. (1978). Meditation and psychotherapeutic effects. *Archives of General Psychiatry*, 35, 294–302.

Shapiro, D.H.,, and Walsh, R.N. (eds.) (1984). *Meditation: Classic and contemporary perspectives*. New York: Aldine.

Sharma, M.P., Kumaraiah, V., Mishra, H., and Balodhi, J.P. (1990). *Journal of Personality and Clinical Studies*, 6 (2), 201–206.

Shear, J. (2001). Experimental studies of meditation and consciousness. In W. Parsons and D. Jonte-Pace (eds.), *Mapping religion and psychology*. London: Routeledge.

_____, and Jeving, R. (1999). Pure consciousness: Scientific exploration of meditation technique. *Journal of Consciousness Studies*, 6, 189–209.

Sheldrake, R. (1994). *Seven experiments that could change the world*. London: Fourth Estate.

Shevrin. H. (1973). Brain wave correlates of subliminal stimulation, unconscious attention, primary and secondary-process thinking, and repressiveness. *Psychological Issues*, 8, 56–87.

Shoemaker, S. (1991). India and consciousness. *Mind*, 100, 507–524.

_____, and Swinburne, R. (1984). *Personal identity*. Oxford: Blackwell.

Sidgwick, H., Sidgwick, E.M., and Smith, G.A. (1989). Experiments in thought transference. *Proceedings of the Society for Psychical Research*, 6, 128–170.

Silverman, L.H., and Weinberger, J. (1985). Mommy and I are one: Implications for psychotherapy. *American Psychologist*, 40, 1296–1308.

Sim, M.K., and Tsoi, W.F. (1992). The effects of centrally acting drugs on the EEG correlates of meditation. *Biofeedback and Self-Regulation*, 17(3), 215–20.

Sinari, R. (1965). The method of phenomenological reduction and yoga. *Philosophy East and West*, 21, pp. 255–264.

Sinclair, U. (1930). *Mental Radio*. Monrovia, CA: Sinclair.

Singer, J.L. (1975). Navigating the stream of consciousness: Research in daydreaming and related inner experience. *American Psychologist*, 30, 727–738.

Sinha, D. (1981). Non-Western perspectives in psychology; Why, what and whither? *Journal of Indian Psychology*, 3 (2), 1–9.

_____. (1994). Origin and development of psychology in India: Outgrowing the alien framework. *International Journal of Psychology*, 29, 695–706.

_____, and Kao, S.R. (1997). The journey to the East: An introduction. In D. Sinha and S.R. Kao (eds.), *Asian Perspectives on psychology* (pp. 9–22). New York: Sage Publications.

_____, and Sinha, M. (1997). Orientations to psychology: Asian and Western. In H.S.R. Kao and D. Sinha (eds.). *Asian perspectives on psychology* (pp. 25–39). New Delhi: Sage Publications.

Sinha, J. (1958, 1961). *Indian Psychology*, 2 Vols. Calcutta: Sinha Publishing House.

Sinha, J.B.P. (1993). The bulk and front of psychology in India. *Psychology and Developing Societies*, 5 (2), 135–150.

Sinha, S. (1963). Fifty years of science in India: Progress of psychology. Calcutta: Indian Science Congress Association.

Skinner, B.F. (1971). *Beyond freedom and dignity*. New York: A.A. Knopf.

_____. (1974). *About behaviorism*. New York: A.A. Knopf.

Smart, N. (1965). Interpretation and mystical experience. *Religious Studies* 1, 75–87.

_____. (1983). The purification of consciousness and the negative path. In S.T. Katz (ed.), *Mysticism and religious traditions* (pp. 117–129). Oxford: Oxford University Press.

Smith, H. (1966). Parapsychology in the Indian tradition. *International Journal of Parapsychology*, 8 (2), 248–263.

Smith, J.C. (1975). Meditation and psychotherapy: A review of the literature. *Psychological Bulletin*, 82, 558–564.

_____. (1976). Psychotherapeutic effects of TM with controls for expectations of relief and daily siting. *Journal of Consulting and Clinical Psychology*, 44, 630–637.

_____. (1986). *Meditatation: A sensible guide to timeless discipline*. Champaign, IL: Research Press.

Smythies, J.P., and Beloff, J. (eds.) (1989). *The case for dualism*. Charlottesville, VA: University Press of Virginia.

Spanos, N.P., Jones, B., and Malfara, A. (1982). Hypnotic deafness: Now you hear it—Now you still hear it. *Journal of Abnormal Psychology*, 90, 75–77.

Spence, D.P., and Holland, B. (1962). The restricting effects of awareness: A paradox and an explanation. *Journal of Abnormal and Social Psychology*, 64, 163–174.

Spencer-Brown, G. (1953). *Probability and scientific inference*. New York: Longmans, Green.

Sperry, R.W. (1969). A modified concept of consciousness. *Psychological Review*, 76, 532–536.

_____. (1976). Mental phenomena as causal determinants in brain function. In G.G. Globus, G. Maxwell and I. Savodnik (eds.), *Consciousness and the brain* (pp. 163–177). New York: Plenum Press.

_____. (1983). *Science and moral priority: Merging mind, brain, and human values*. New York: Columbia University Press.

_____. (1984). Consciousnes, personal identity and the divided brain. *Neuropsychologia*, 22, 661–673.

_____. (1988). Psychology's mentalist paradigm and the religion/science tension. *American Psychologist*, 43, 607–613.

_____, Zaidel, E., and Zaidel, O. (1979). Self-recognition and social awareness in the disconnected minor hemisphere. *Neuropsychologia*, 17, 153–166.

Spiegel, D., Cutcomb, S., Ren, C., and Pribram, K. (1985). Hypnotic hallucination alters evoked potentials. *Journal of Abnormal Psychology*, 94, 249–255.

Squires, E.J. (1990). *Conscious mind in the physical world*. New York: Adam Holger.

_____. (1994). Quantum theory and the need for consciousness. *Journal of Consciousness Studies,* 1, 201–204.

Sridhara. (1985). *Nyayakandali.* Benares: Vizayanagaram Sanskrit Series.

Stace, W.J. (1960). *The teachings of the mystics.* New York: Mentor Books.

Stanford, R.G. (1970). Extrasensory effects upon "memory." *Journal of the American Society for Psychical Research,* 64, 161–186.

_____. (1971). EEG alpha activity and ESP performance: A replicative study. *Journal of the American Society for Psychical Research,* 65, 144–154.

_____. (1973). Extrasensory effects upon associative processes in a directed free-response task. *Journal of the American Society for Psychical Research,* 67, 147–190.

_____. (1974). An experimentally testable model for spontaneous psi events. I. Extrasensory events. *Journal of the American Society for Psychical Research,* 68, 34–57.

_____. (1977). Experimental psychokinesis: A review from diverse perspectives. In B.B. Wolman (ed.), *Handbook of parapsychology* (pp. 324–381). New York: Van Nostrand Reinhold.

_____, and Mayer, B. (1974). Relaxation as a psiconducive state: A replication and exploration of parameters. *Journal of the American Society for Psychical Research,* 68, 182–191.

_____, and Palmer, J. (1973). Meditation prior to the ESP task: An EEG study with an outstanding ESP subject. In W.G. Roll, R.L. Morris, and J.D. Morris (eds.), *Research in Parapsychology 1972,* Methuchen, NJ: Scarecrow Press.

_____, and Stanford, B.E. (1969). Shifts in EEG alpha rhythm as related to calling patterns and ESP run-score variance. *Journal of Parapsychology,* 33, 39–47.

_____, and Stein, A.G. (1994). A meta-analysis of ESP studies contrasting hypnosis and a comparison condition. *Journal of Parapsychology,* 58, 235–269.

_____, and Stevenson, I. (1972). EEG correlates of free-response GESP in an individual subject. *Journal of the American Society for Psychical Research,* 66, 357–368.

Stanovich, K.E. (1991). Damn! There goes that ghost again! *Behavioral and Brain Sciences,* 7, 696–698.

Stapp, H.P. (1982). Mind, matter, and quantum mechanics. *Foundations of Physics,* 12, 363–398.

_____. (1990). *A quantum theory of the mind-brain interface.* Lawrence Berkeley Laboratory Report LBL–28574.

_____. (1992). *A quantum theory of consciousness.* In B. Rubik (ed.), *The interrelationship between mind and matter,* 207–217. Philadelphia, PA:

Center for Frontier Sciences, Temple University.

_____. (1993). *Mind, matter and quantum mechanics.* Berlin: Springer-Verlag.

_____. (1999). Attention, intention, and will in quantum physics. *Journal of Consciousness Studies,* 6, 143–164.

Steinkamp, F., Milton, J., and Morris, R.L. (1998). A meta-analysis of forced-choice experiments comparing clairvoyance and precognition. *Journal of Parpsychology,* 62, 193–218.

Stevenson, I. (1960). Criteria for the ideal case bearing on reincarnation. *Indian Journal of Parapsychology,* 2, 149–155.

_____. (1967). An antagonist's view of parapsychology. A review of Professor Hansel's "ESP: A scientific evaluation." *Journal of the American Society for Psychical Research,* 61, 254–267.

_____. (1974). *Twenty cases suggestive of reincarnation* (2nd edition). Charlottesville, VA: University Press of Virginia.

_____. (1975). *Cases of the reincarnation type: Vol. 1. Ten cases in India.* Charlottesville, VA: University Press of Virginia.

_____. (1992). Survival or super-psi: A reply. *Journal of Scientific Exploration,* 6, 145–150.

Stokes, D.M. (1997). *The nature of mind: Parapsychology and the role of consciousness in the physical world.* Jefferson, NC: McFarland & Co.

_____. (1998). Book Review: K. Frazier (ed.). *Encounters with the paranormal: Science, knowledge and belief. Journal of Parapsychology,* 62, 158–170.

Stout, G.F. (1899). *A manual of psychology,* New York: Hinds, Noble, and Eldredge.

Suedfeld, P. (1969). Theoretical formulations: II. In J. Zebek (ed.), *Sensory Deprivation: Fifteen Years of Research.* New York: Appleton-Century-Crofts.

Sutherland, S. (1989). *The international dictionary of psychology.* New York: Continuum.

Swatmarama, Y. (1933). *Hatha yoga pradipika.* Madras: Theosophical Publishing House.

Taddonio, J.L. (1976). The relationship of experimenter expectancy to performance on ESP tasks. *Journal of Parapsychology,* 40, 107–115.

Talbot, M. (1981). *Mysticism and the new physics.* New York: Bantam Books.

Targ, R., and Puthoff, H.E. (1977). *Mind research.* New York: Delacorte Press/Eleanor Friede.

Tart, C.T. (1963). Possible physiological correlates of Psi cognition. *International Journal of Parapsychology,* 5, 375–386.

_____. (1968). A psychophysiological study of out-of-body experiences in a selected subject. *Journal of the American Society for Psychical Research,* 62, 3–27.

_____. (ed.). (1969). *Altered States of Consciousness: A Book of Readings.* New York: Wiley.

_____. (1972). States of consciousness and state-specific sciences. *Science*, 176, 1203–1210.

_____. (1975). *States of consciousness.* New York: Dutton.

_____. (1975). The physical universe, the spiritual universe, and the paranormal. In C.T. Tart (ed.), *Transpersonal psychologies.* New York: Harper & Row.

_____, Puthoff, H.E., and Targ, R. (1980). Information transmission in remote viewing experiments. *Nature*, 204, 191.

Taylor, E.I. (1996). *William James on consciousness beyond the margin.* Princeton, NJ: Princeton University Press.

Tenny, K. (1962). Physiological responses during an ESP test. Abstract. *Journal of Parapsychology*, 13, 138.

Thatcher, R.W., and John, (1977). *Foundations of cognitive processes.* Hillsdale, NJ: Erlbaum.

Thorndike, E.L. (1907). *The elements of psychology* (2nd ed.). New York: Seiler.

Thouless, R.H., and Weisner, B.P. (1948). The psi process in normal and paranormal psychology. *Proceedings of the Society for Psychical Research*, 48, 177–196.

Titchener, E.B. (1908). *Lectures on the elementary psychology of feeling and attention.* New York.

_____. (1909). *A test-book of psychology.* New York: Macmillan & Co.

_____. (1915). *A beginner's psychology.* New York: Macmillan & Co.

Tolman, E.C. (1927). A behaviorist's definition of consciousness. *Psychological Review*, 34, 433–439.

Torgerson, W.S. (1962). *Theory and Methods of Scaling.* New York: Wiley.

Torjussen, T. (1978). Visual processing in cortically blind hemifields. *Neuropsychologia*, 16, 15–21.

Tranel, D., and Damasio, A.R. (1985). Knowledge without awareness: An autonomic index of facial recognition by prosopagnosics. *Science*, 228, 1453–1454.

_____, _____, and Damasio, H. (1988). Intact recognition of facial expression, gender, and age in patients with impaired recognition of face identity. *Neurology*, 38, 690–696.

Travis, F.T., and Pearson, C. (2000). Pure consciousness: Distinct phenomenological and physiological correlates of "consciousness itself." *International Journal of Neuroscience*. 100, 77–89.

Travis, F.T., and Wallace, R.K. (1997). Autonomic patterns during respiratory suspensions: Possible markers of transcendental consciousness. *Psychophysiology*, 34, 39–46.

_____, and _____. (1999). Autonomic and EEG patterns during eyes-closed rest and transcen-dental meditation practice: The basis for a neural model of TM practice. *Consciousness and Cognition*, 8, 302–318.

Triesman, A.M. (1960). Contextual cues in selective listening. *Quarterly Journal of Experimental Psychology*, 12, 242–248.

_____. (1969). Strategies and models of selective attention. *Psychological Review*, 76, 282–299.

Tulving, E., Schacter, D.L., and Stark, H.A. (1982). Priming effects in word-fragment completion are independent of recognition memory. *Journal of Experimental Psychology: Learning, Memory and Cognition*, 8, 336–342.

Turing, A.M. (1950). Computing machinery and intelligence. *Mind*, 59, 433–460.

Tye, M. (1995). *Ten problems of consciousness: A representational theory of the phenomenal mind.* Cambridge, MA: MIT Press.

Tyrrell, G.N.M. (1947). The modus operandi of paranormal cognition. *Proceedings of the Society for Psychical Research*, 48, 65–120.

Udupa, K.N., and Singh, R.H. (1972). The scientific basis of yoga. [Letter.] *Journal of the American Medical Association*, 220, 1365.

_____, _____, and Settiwar, R.M. (1975a). Neurohumaral changes following meditation. *Journal of Research in Indian Medicine*, 10:2, 64–66.

_____, _____, and _____. (1975b). Physiological and biochemical studies on the effect of yogic and certain other exercises. *Indian Journal of Medical Research*, 63, 620–624.

_____, _____, and _____. (1975c). Studies on the effect of some yogic breathing exercises (*pranayams*) in normal persons. *Indian Journal of Medical Research*, 63, 1066–1071.

Ullman, M. (1977). Psychopathology and psi phenomena. In B.B. Wolman (ed.), *Handbook of parapsychology* (pp. 557–574). New York: Van Nostrand Reinhold.

_____, and Krippner, S. (1970). *Dream studies and telepathy.* (Parapsychological Monographs No. 12.) New York: Parapsychology Foundation.

_____, and _____, with Vaughan, A. *Dream telepathy.* New York: Macmillan.

_____, _____, and Feldstein, S. (1966). Experimentally induced telepathic dreams: Two studies using EEG-REM monitoring techniques. *International Journal of Neuropsychiatry*, 2, 420–437.

Underwood, B. (1969). Attributes of memory. *Psychological Review*, 76, 559–573.

Underwood, G. (1979). Memory systems and conscious process. In G. Underwood and R. Stevens (eds.), *Aspects of consciousness: Psychological issues.* New York: Academic Press.

_____. (1982). Attention and awareness in cognitive and motor skills. In G. Underwood (ed.),

Aspects of consciousness: Awareness and self aware-ness. New York: Academic Press.

Vacaspatimisra. (1969). *Samkhyatatvakaumudi.* Bombay: Samvat.

Vahia, N.S., Vineker, S.I., and Doongaji, D.R. (1966). Some ancient Indian concepts in the treatment of psychiatric disorders. *British Journal of Psychiatry*, 112, 1089–1096.

_____, et al. (1973). Psychophysiologic therapy based on the concepts of Patanjali: A new approach to the treatment of neurotic and psychosomatic disorders. *American Journal of Psychotherapy*, 112, 557–565.

Vakil, R.J. (1950). Remarkable feat of endurance of a yogi priest. *Lancet*, 259 (2), 871.

Van Busschback, J.G. (1953). An investigation of extrasensory perception in school children. *Journal of Parapsychology*, 17, 210–214.

_____. (1955). A further report on an investigation of ESP in school children. *Journal of Parapsychology*, 19, 73–81.

_____. (1956). An investigation of ESP between teacher and pupils in American Schools. *Journal of Parapsychology*, 20, 71–80.

_____. (1959). An investigation of ESP in first and second grades of Dutch schools. *Journal of Parapsychology*, 23, 227–237.

_____. (1961). An investigation of ESP in first and second graders in American schools. *Journal of Parapsychology*, 25, 161–174.

Van de Castle, R. (1977). Sleep and dreams. In B.B. Wolman (ed.), *Handbook of parapsychology* (pp. 473–499). New York: Van Nostrand Reinhold.

Van Gulick, R. (1989). What difference does consciousness make? *Philosophical Topics*, 17, 211–230.

_____. (1993). Understanding the phenomenal mind: Are we all just armadillos? In M. Davies and G. Humphreys, *Consciousness*. Oxford: Blackwell.

Varela, F.J., and Shear, J. (1999). First-person methodologies: What, why, how? *Journal of Consciousness Studies*, 6, (2–3), 1–14.

Varela, F.J., Thompson, E., and Rosch, E. (1993). *The embodied mind: Cognitive science and human experience*. Cambridge, MA: MIT Press.

Vasiliev, L.L. (1963). *Experiments in mental suggestion*. Church Crookham: Institute for the Study of Mental Images.

_____. (1976). *Experiments in distant influence*. New York: Dutton. (Original work published 1963.)

Velmans, M. (1991). Is human information processing conscious? *Behavioral and Brain Sciences*, 7, 131–178.

_____. (1993). A reflexive science of consciousness. In *Experimental and theoretical studies of consciousness* (Ciba Foundation symposium). New York: John Wiley & Sons.

_____. (ed.) (1996). *The science of consciousness: Psychological neurological, and clinical reviews*. London: Routledge.

_____. (1999). Intersubjective science. *Journal of Consciousness Studies*, 6 (2–3), 299–306.

_____. (2000). *Understanding consciousness*. London: Routledge.

Vermersch, P. (1999). Introspection as practice. *Journal of Consciousness Studies*, 6 (2–3), 17–42.

Vijnanabhiksu. (1909). *Samkhyapravaacanadhasya*. Benares: Vizayanagaram Sanskrit Series.

Vinod, S.D., Vinod, R.S., and Khire, V. (1991). Evaluation of the effect of yoga on anxiety in youth in relation to anxiety inducing areas of life. *Yoga Mimamsa*, 30 (2 and 3), 25–30.

Volpe, B.J., LeDoux, J.E., and Gozzaniga, M.S. (1979). Information processing of visual stimuli in an "extinguished" field. *Nature*, 282, 722–724.

Von Bekesy, G. (1967). *Sensory inhibition*. Princeton, NJ: Princeton University Press.

Walker, E.H. (1970). The nature of consciousness. *Mathematical Biosciences*, 7, 131–178.

_____. (1975). Foundations of paraphysical and parapsychological phenomena. In L. Oteri (ed.), *Quantum physics and parapsychology*. New York: Parapsychology Foundation.

_____. (2000). *The physics of consciousness*. Cambridge, MA: Perseus Books.

Wallace, R.K. (1970a). Physiological effects of transcendental meditation. *Science*, 167, 1751–1754.

_____. (1970b). *The physiological effects of transcendental meditation, a proposed fourth major state of consciousness*. (Ph.D. dissertation, University of California, Los Angeles, 1970.) Ann Arbor, MI: University Microfilms.

_____, and Benson, H. (1972). The physiology of meditation. *Scientific American*, 226, 84–90.

_____, _____, and Wilson, A.F. (1971). A wakeful hypometabolic physiologic state. *American Journal of Physiology*, 221, 795–799.

Warner, R., and Szubka, T. (eds.) (1994). *The mind-body problem: A guide to the current debate*. Oxford: Blackwell.

Warren, C.A., McDonough, B.E., and Don, N.S. (1992a). Event-related brain potential changes in a psi task. *Journal of Parapsychology*, 56, 1–30.

_____, _____, and _____. (1992b). Partial replication of single subject event-related potential effects in a psi task. *Proceedings of the Parapsychological Association 35th Annual Convention*, 169–181.

Warshal, D. (1980). Effects of the transcendental meditation technique on normal and jendrassik reflex time. *Perceptual and Motor Skills*, 50, 1103–1106.

Watson, J.B. (1928). The unconscious of the behaviorist. In C.M. Child, Kurt Koffka, and John E. Anderson (eds.), *The unconscious: A symposium* (pp. 91–113). New York: A.A. Knopf.

Waxman, W. (1994). *Hume's theory of consciousness.* Cambridge: Cambridge University Press.

Wehr, G. (1987). *Jung: A biography* (D.M. Weeks, trans.). Boston, MA: Shambhala Publications.

Weinberger, J., Kelner, S. and McClelland, D.C. (1990). *The effects of subliminal symbiotic stimulation on free-response and self-report mood.* Unpublished manuscript, Derner Institute, Adelphi University, Garden City, New York.

Weiskrantz, L. (1986). *Blindsight: A case study and implications.* Oxford: Oxford University Press.

_____. (1988). Some contributions of neuropsychology of vision and memory to the problem of consciousness. In A.J. Marcel and Bisiach, E. (eds.), *Consciousness in contemporary science.* Oxford: Oxford University Press.

Wenger, M., and Bagchi, B. (1961). Studies of autonomic functions in practitioners of Yoga in India. *Behavioral Science,* 6, 312–323.

_____, _____, and Anand, B. (1961). Experiments in India on "voluntary" control of the heart and pulse. *Circulation,* 24, 1319–1325.

Weserman, H.M. (1819). Versuche willkürlicher träumbilung. *Archiv,* f.d. Tierischen Magnnetismus, 6, 135–142.

West, M.A. (1980a). Meditation and EEG. *Psychological Medicine,* 10, 369–375.

_____. (1980b). Meditation, personality and arousal. *Personality and individual differences,* 1, 135–142.

_____. (ed.). (1987). *The psychology of meditation,* Oxford: Clarendon Press.

_____. (1987). Traditional and psychological perspectives on meditation. In M.A. West (ed.). *The psychology of meditation.* Oxford: Clarendon Press.

White, R.A. (1964). A comparison of old and new methods of response to targets in ESP experi-

ments. *Journal of the American Society for Psychical Research,* 58, 21–56.

Whyte, L. (1960). *The unconscious before Freud.* New York: Basic Books.

Whyte, L.L. (1962). *The unconscious before Freud.* New York: Doubleday.

Wigner, E.P. (1972). The place of consciousness in modern physics. In C. Muses and A.M. Young (eds.), *Consciousness and reality: The human pivot point.* New York: Avon Books.

Wilber, K. (1993). *The spectrum of consciousness.* Wheaton, IL: Quest.

_____. (1997). An integral theory of consciousness. *Journal of consciousness studies,* 4 (1), 71–92.

_____. (2000). Waves, streams, states and self: Further considerations for an integral theory of consciousness. *Journal of consciousness studies,* 7 (11–12), 145–176.

Wiseman, R., and Milton, J. (1998). Experiment one of the SAIC remote viewing program: A critical re-evaluation. *Journal of Parapsychology,* 62, 297–308.

Wittgenstein, L. (1953/1968). *Philosophical investigation* (trans. G.E.M. Anscombe). Oxford: Basil Blackwell.

Woods, J.H. (1927). *The yoga system of patanjali.* Cambridge, MA: Harvard University Press.

Wulff, D.M. (1992). *Psychology of religion: Classic and contemporary views.* New York, NY: John Wiley & Sons.

Wundt, W. (1896). *Outlines of psychology* (trans. C.H. Judd). Leipzig: Engelmann.

Zaidel, E. (1976). Auditory vocabulary in the right hemisphere following brain bisection and hemidecortication. *Cortex,* 12, 191–211.

Zorab, G. (1963). Yoga and parapsychology. *Research Journal of Philosophy and Social Sciences,* 1, 78–83.

Zukav, G. (1979). *The dancing Wu Li masters: An overview of the new physics.* New York: Rider.

Index